Lorenzo Carcaterra

SLEEPERS

APACHES

This edition published in 2000 by Cresset Editions,
an imprint of The Random House Group Ltd,
20 Vauxhall Bridge Road, London SW1V 2SA

Copyright © Lorenzo Carcaterra 2000
Sleepers first published in 1995 by Century
Apaches first published in 1997 by Century

Printed and bound in Germany

ISBN 0 09187 159 X

Sleepers

For Sleepers everywhere

ACKNOWLEDGEMENTS

This book would not have been possible without the support of the silent citizens of Hell's Kitchen. I will honor their requests to remain anonymous voices and never forget their contributions.

Through the years, I've been fortunate to have worked with many editors who have helped me in various stages of my career. None has had more confidence in my abilities than Peter Gethers. With this book, he made a leap of faith few editors are willing to risk. Then, he guided the work and shaped it and edited it as few can. He also supplied an endless stream of jokes that helped ease me through the rough spots. No writer could have a better partner.

Any writer would love to have a great agent. I have three. Loretta Fidel was *always* there, *always* listened, and *always* cared. Amy Schiffman and Adam Berkowitz believed in me as much as they did in the book. Together, they kept the wolves from the door and the book on everyone's front burner.

Clare Ferraro found a place in her heart and on her Ballantine shelf for my first book. Then, over a terrific lunch, she fell in love with my second. Then, she waited and she waited and she waited. Through it all, she supplied patience, friendship, and encouragement. I would also like to thank Steve Golin and the people at Propaganda Films for their passionate belief in *Sleepers*.

I need to thank my doctors, who helped me fight off a

variety of illnesses during the writing of this book – Dr. Paul Chrzanowski, Dr. Nancy Nealon, and my main man David at the Rusk Institute.

Then there are the cops – Steve Collura for the kind words; Joe Lisi for the laughter and concern; and, above all, Sonny Grosso, for everything he has meant to me throughout a friendship that now numbers in the decades.

To my phone buddies – Hank Gallo, Carlo Cutolo, Mr. G., Marc Lichter, Leah Rozen, and Keith Johnson – for being there and for listening. To Liz Wagner for the laughs. And to Bill Diehl for the wisdom and the care.

To my wife, Susan Toepfer, I owe everything. She has always had my respect, will always have my love, and will always be my friend.

To my son, Nick, thank you for the smiles and the chance to forget my work for a period of time. To my daughter, Kate, thank you for showing me what a warm heart can beat beneath such a pretty face.

And thanks to my crew of suspects – the Fat Man, Bobby C., Bam-Bam, Carmine, Doc, Big D., Mike Seven, and Sammy Weights. You were always where you were supposed to be. I never expected any less.

Sleeper (colloq.): 1. Out-of-town hit man who spends the night after a local contract is completed. 2. A juvenile sentenced to serve any period longer than nine months in a state-managed facility.

Prologue

'Let's go say a prayer for a boy who couldn't run as fast as I could.'
– Pat O'Brien to the Dead End Kids in *Angels With Dirty Faces*.

Winter 1993

I sat across the table from the man who had battered and tortured and brutalized me nearly thirty years ago. I had imagined him to be in his sixties – he had seemed so old to me back then – but, in fact, he was in his late forties, less than a decade older than me. His thinning hair was combed straight back, and his right hand, trembling and ash white, held a filtered cigarette. His left clutched a glass of ice water. He looked at me from behind a pair of black-rimmed glasses, his brown eyes moist, his nose running, the skin at its base red and flaky.

'I don't know what you want me to say,' he said in a voice devoid of the power it once held. 'I don't know where to start.'

In my memory, he was tall and muscular, arrogant and quick-tempered, eager to lash out at those under his command at the juvenile home where I spent nine months when I was thirteen years old. In reality, sitting now before me, he was frail and timid, thin beads of cold sweat forming at the top of his forehead.

'I need to keep my job,' he said, his voice a whining plea. 'I can't lose this one. If any of my bosses find out, if *anybody* finds out, I'm finished.'

I wanted to stand up and grab him, reach past the coffee and the smoke and beat him until he bled. Instead, I sat there and remembered all that I had tried so hard, over so many years, to forget. Painful screams piercing silent nights. A leather belt against soft skin. Foul breath on the back of a neck. Loud laughter mixed with muffled tears.

I had waited so long for this meeting, spent so much time and money searching for the man who held the answers to so many of my questions. But now that he was here, I had nothing to say, nothing to ask. I half-listened as he talked about two failed marriages and a bankrupt business, about how the evil he committed haunts him to this very day. The words seemed cowardly and empty and I felt no urge to address them.

He and the group he was a part of had stained the future of four boys, damaged them beyond repair. Once, the sound of this man's very walk caused all our movement to stop. His laugh, low and eerie, had signaled an onslaught of torment. Now, sitting across from him, watching his mouth move and his hands flutter, I wished I had not been as afraid of him back then, that I'd somehow had the nerve and the courage to fight back. So many lives might have turned out so differently if I had.

'I didn't mean all those things,' he whispered, leaning closer toward me. 'None of us did.'

'I don't need you to be sorry,' I said. 'It doesn't do me any good.'

'I'm beggin' you,' he said, his voice breaking. 'Try to forgive me. Please. Try.'

'Learn to live with it,' I told him, getting up from the table.

'I can't,' he said. 'Not anymore.'

'Then die with it,' I said, looking at him hard. 'Just like the rest of us.'

The pained look of surrender in his eyes made my throat tighter, easing the darkness of decades.

If only my friends had been there to see it.

This is a true story about friendships that run deeper than blood. In its telling, I have changed many of the names and altered most of the dates, locations and identifying characteristics of people and institutions to protect the

6

identities of those involved. For example, I have changed the location of the murder trial, which did not take place in Manhattan. I've also changed where people live and work – and made many of them a lot better looking than they really are. It is a story that has taken two years to write and parts of two decades to research, forcing awake in all the principals memories we would have preferred to forget. I have been helped in the re-creation of the events of this story by many friends and a few enemies, all of whom requested nothing more in return than anonymity. So while their deeds have been accurately documented, their names – heroes and villains – will remain unknown.

However hidden their identities, this is still my story and that of the only three friends in my life who have truly mattered.

Two of them were killers who never made it past the age of thirty-five. The other is a non-practicing attorney living within the pain of his past, too afraid to let it go, finding reassurance instead in confronting its horror.

I am the only one who can speak for them, and for the children we were.

BOOK ONE

'This much I do know – there's
no such thing in the world as
a bad boy.'
– Spencer Tracy as Father
Eddie Flanagan in *Boys Town*.

Summer 1963

ONE

Labor Day weekend always signaled the annual go-cart race across the streets of Hell's Kitchen, the mid-Manhattan neighborhood where I was born in 1954 and lived until 1969.

Preparations for the race began during the last two weeks of August, when my three best friends and I would hide away inside our basement clubhouse, in a far corner of a run-down 49th Street tenement, constructing, painting and naming our racer, which we put together from lifted lumber and stolen parts. A dozen carts and their teams were scheduled to assemble early on Labor Day morning at the corner of 50th Street and 10th Avenue, each looking to collect the fifteen dollars first prize money that would be presented to the winner by a local loan shark.

In keeping with Hell's Kitchen traditions, the race was run without rules.

It never lasted more than twenty minutes and covered four side streets and two avenues, coming to a finish on the 12th Avenue end of the West Side Highway. Each go-cart had a four-man team attached, one inside and three out. The three pushed for as long and as hard as they could, fighting off the hand swipes and blade swings of the opponents who came close. The pushing stopped at the top of the 50th Street hill, leaving the rest of the race to the driver. Winners and losers crossed the finish clothesline scraped and bloody, go-carts often in pieces, driver's hands burned by ropes. Few of us wore gloves or helmets and there was never money for knee or elbow pads. We kept full plastic water bottles tied to the sides of our carts, the fastest way to cool off hot feet and burning wheels.

The runt of the litter among my team, I always drove.

John Reilly and Tommy Marcano were spreading black paint onto thick slabs of dirty wood with color-by-number brushes.

John was eleven years old, a dark-haired, dark-eyed charmer with an Irishman's knack for the verbal hit and run. His clear baby face was marred by a six-inch scar above his right eye and a smaller, half-moon scar below the chin line, both the results of playground falls and home-made stitches. John always seemed to be on the verge of a smile and was the first among my friends to bring in the latest joke off the street. He was a poor student but an avid reader, a mediocre athlete with a penchant for remembering the batting and fielding statistics of even the most obscure ballplayers. He loved Marx Brothers and Abbott & Costello movies and went to any Western that played the neighborhood circuit. If the mood hit him the right way, John would prowl the streets of Hell's Kitchen talking and walking as if he were Ralph Kramden from *The Honeymooners*, proclaiming 'Hiya, pal,' to all the neighborhood vendors. Sometimes, in return for his performance, we would each be given free pieces of fruit. He was born with a small hole in his heart which required regular doses of a medication his mother often could not afford to buy. The illness, coupled with a frail frame, left him with a palpable air of vulnerability.

Tommy Marcano, also eleven, was John's physical opposite. He had his Irish mother's carrot-colored hair and his father's ruddy, Southern Italian complexion. Short and flabby around the waist and thighs, Tommy loved sports, action movies, Marvel Comics and adventure novels. Above all else, Tommy loved to eat – meatball

14

heros, buttered rolls, hard-cherry candy barrels. He collected and traded baseball cards, storing each year's set in team order inside a half-dozen Kinney shoe boxes sealed with rubber bands. He had a natural aptitude for math and built model ships and planes out of raw wood with skill and patience. He had a sensitive nature and a feel for the underdog, always cheering on teams and athletes that were destined to lose. He was quick to laugh and needed prodding to lose the grip on his temper. A botched surgical procedure when he was an infant forced him occasionally to wear a pad and brace around his right leg. On those days, Tommy chose to wear a black eye patch and tie a red handkerchief around his head.

Michael Sullivan, at twelve the oldest of my friends, was quietly hammering nails into a sawed-down Dr. Brown's soda crate.

The best student among us, Michael was a smooth blend of book smart and street savvy. His black Irish eyes bore holes through their targets, but his manner was softened by a wide, expansive smile. He kept his thick, dark hair short on the sides and long on top. He was never without a piece of gum in his mouth and read all the tabloids of the day, the only one among us to move beyond the sports pages to the front page. He was also never without a book, usually a rumpled paperback shoved inside the rear pocket of his jeans. Where we still favored the tales of Alexandre Dumas, Jack London and Robert Louis Stevenson, Michael had graduated to the darker domain of Edgar Allan Poe and the chivalry and romance of Sir Walter Scott. He initiated most of our pranks and had a cutting sense of humor that was doused with a wise man's instinct for fair play. He was our unofficial leader, a position he valued but never flaunted and one that required him to care and maintain our collection of Classics Illustrated comics.

I was busily applying biker's grease onto two stroller wheels taken off a baby carriage I'd found abandoned on 12th Avenue.

15

'We need a better name this year,' I said. 'Somethin' that sticks in people's heads.'

'What was it last year?' Tommy asked. 'I forget.'

'*The Sea Hawk*,' I reminded him. 'Like the movie.'

'Sea*weed* woulda been more like it,' Michael said. That was his subtle way of reminding us that we hadn't done so well in the previous race, finishing next to last.

'Let's name it after *The Count of Monte Cristo*,' John said.

'Nanh,' I said, shaking my head. 'Let's name it after one of the Musketeers.'

'Which one?' Tommy asked.

'D'Artagnan,' I said immediately.

'To start with, he's not a *made* Musketeer,' Michael said. 'He jus hangs with them.'

'And he's only cool 'cause he's got three other guys with him all the time,' Tommy said to me. 'Just like you. Alone, we're talkin' dead man. Just like you. Besides, we'll be the only ones with a French guy's name on the side of our cart.'

'That oughta be good enough to get our ass kicked by somebody,' Michael observed.

'Go with The Count,' John said. 'He's my hero.'

'Wolf Larson's *my* hero,' Tommy said. 'You don't see me bustin' balls about gettin' *his* name on the cart.'

'Wolf Larson from *The Sea Wolf*?' I asked. 'That's your *hero*?'

'Yeah,' Tommy said. 'I think he's a real stand-up guy.'

'The guy's a total scumbag.' Michael was incredulous. 'He treats people like shit.'

'Come onnn, he ain't got a choice,' Tommy insisted. 'Look at who he deals with.'

'Scumbag or not,' Michael said. 'Wolf's name *would look* better on the cart.'

'They'll think we named the friggin' cart after our dog,' John muttered.

'We don't *got* a dog,' Tommy said.

16

'Okay, it's settled,' I told everybody. 'We name the cart *Wolf*. I think it'll bring us luck.'

'We're gonna need more than luck to beat Russell's crew,' John said.

'We may lose this race,' Michael announced. 'But we ain't gonna lose it to Russell.'

'He's always there at the end, Mikey,' I said.

'We always look to block him at the end,' Michael said. 'That's our mistake.'

'He stays away till then,' Tommy said. 'He's no dope. He knows what to do.'

'Maybe,' Michael said. 'But this time, we go and get him outta the race early. With him out, nobody comes near beatin' us.'

'How early?' I asked.

'Right after Tony Lungs drops the flag,' Michael said. 'Near the hill.'

'How?'

'Don't worry,' Michael said. 'I got a plan.'

'I *always* worry when you say that,' I said.

'Relax,' Tommy said, putting the final paint strokes on the wood. 'What could happen?'

A dozen go-carts were ready to go, four to a row. I was behind the unsteady wheels of *Wolf*, on the front line, next to Russell Topaz's cart, *Devil's Pain*. The crowd of onlookers, drawn out by the heavy September heat, was larger than most years, standing two deep behind rows of illegally parked cars. Thick-armed men in white T-shirts held kids atop their shoulders, wives and girlfriends at their sides, red coolers filled with beer and soda by their feet. Tenement windows were opened wide, old women leaning out, stubby arms resting on folded bath towels, small electric fans blowing warm air behind them.

I looked over at Russell, nodded my head and smiled – as friendly a way as I could manage.

'Hey, Russell,' I said.

'Eat shit, greaseball,' he said back.

Little was known about Russell or the three other boys who were always with him, each as sullen as their leader. We knew he went to St. Agnes on West 46th Street, which meant he wore knickers. That alone was enough permanently to ruin his mood. He lived with foster parents on West 52nd Street, in a building guarded by a German Shepherd. There were two other foster children in the family, a younger boy and an older girl, and he was as mean to them as he was to everybody else.

He liked to read. Many times I would see him in the back room of the Public Library on West 50th Street, his head buried in a thick book about pirates loose on the high seas. He played basketball on the playgrounds for pocket money and was never without a lit cigarette. He had no girlfriend, always wore a brown leather vest and hated baseball.

I couldn't help but stare at Russell's cart. It was made of fresh wood and was unpainted, except for the name stenciled on both sides. The rear wheels were thick and new and the brakes were molded from real rubber, not the blackboard erasers we used on ours. His crate seat was padded and the sides were smooth. He had on black gloves and a Chicago Bears helmet. His three teammates were in sweatpants and sneakers, had handkerchiefs tied around their heads and also wore gloves.

'You a Bears fan?' I asked him, waiting for the starting flag to drop.

'No, asswipe,' Russell said. 'I'm not.'

Russell was chubby with a round face, soft, pudgy hands and a practiced sneer. A small scar decorated his right brow and he never smiled, even in victory.

'They got a great coach,' I said. 'My dad says he's the best football coach ever.'

'Who gives a shit?' was Russell's always pleasant response.

'What's goin' on?' Michael asked, leaning next to me.

'We were just wishing each other luck,' I explained.

18

'Never mind that,' Michael told me, lowering his voice. 'You all straight on what you have to do?'

'No,' I said.

'Just remember, at the hill, don't swing away,' Michael said. 'Go right at him. It'll knock him off balance.'

'What if it doesn't?'

'Then you're on your own,' Michael said.

Tony Lungs, our local loan shark and the benefactor of this yearly event, stepped forward, facing the carts, wiping his brow with the starter's flag. Below his checkerboard shorts were black loafers, no socks, and he also wore no shirt. The folds of his belly hung over the beltless loops of the garish pants. He ran a hand over his bald head, scanning the crowd: 'What say we get this thing started?'

Tony lifted his right arm, holding the starter's flag high enough for all to see. The crowd began to chant and applaud, eager for action. I moved the go-cart a couple of inches forward, leaving only elbow room between Russell and myself.

'Remember,' Michael whispered. 'At the hill, make your cut. The rest is pure race.'

Tony Lungs moved his head from left to right, checking to make sure the carts were in proper position.

'Get ready!' he shouted. 'Get set! And remember, any fuck runs over my toes gets their ass kicked. Now, go!'

I ran over the starter's flag as Tommy, Michael and John pushed our cart up the street.

'How are the pedals workin'?' Tommy asked, his face red from the effort.

'Good,' I said.

'Watch yourself,' John said, looking at the other carts. 'I seen three zip guns already and you *know* Russell's got something in his cart.'

'Don't worry,' Michael said. 'Just get to the hill.'

The crowd noise grew louder as the carts made their way past Fat Mancho's Candy Store, where all the betting action took place. The people of Hell's Kitchen would lay bets on anything and go-cart racing was no exception. To the working poor of the neighborhood, gambling was as time-honored a tradition as church on Sunday morning, boxing matches on Friday nights and virgin weddings all year round.

Devil's Pain was listed on the large blackboard outside Fat Mancho's store as the 3–1 odds-on choice. *Wolf*, our cart, was down as second favorite at 5–1. John Radman's cart, *Eagle's Anger*, was the longshot in the field, going off at 35–1. That was primarily because in the three years Radman had bothered to enter the race he always quit half-way through, abandoning his vehicle and walking away. 'You gonna waste a whole lotta time bettin' on Radman,' Fat Mancho said. 'Might as well set fire to your money.'

We were coming up to the edge of the hill, Tommy, Michael and John sweaty and breathless from the hard pushing. We were in the middle of the pack, Russell still on our left, a Puerto Rican crew from Chelsea, driving a purple cart, on our right.

'More speed,' I told the guys. 'We're not getting there fast enough.'

'Relax,' Michael said. 'We're right where we're supposed to be.'

'If I go any faster, I'll have a heart attack,' John muttered between wheezes.

The brake pads by my feet flapped against the sides of the cart and one of the front wheels started to wobble.

'I don't know if these brakes are gonna hold,' I said.

'Don't think brakes,' Michael hissed. 'Think speed.'

'How do I stop?' I asked with a hint of panic.

'You'll hit somethin',' Michael said. 'Don't worry.'

'That's what I love, Mikey,' I told him. 'You just think of everything.'

At the top of the hill I was on my own, two feet from

Russell's cart. We quickly glanced at one another, the sneer still on his face. I locked my cart against his, the spin of my wheels chipping at his wood, trying to move him over to the hard side of the curb.

'Don't, man,' Russell shouted. 'You're gonna lose a wheel.'

A cart driven by a pock-faced redhead in goggles was up behind me, pushing me even closer into Russell. My hands were raw and my legs stiff. We came down fast, the carts bunched together, my hopes of knocking Russell from the race diminishing with each wobbly spin of my front wheel.

At the south end of 11th Avenue, a few feet from a Mobil Gas Station crowded with on-lookers, the front wheel finally gave way and snapped off. The cart tilted down, breaking pace with Russell, small sparks shooting from the pavement.

'You're lookin' at a wheelchair,' Russell yelled at me as he zoomed past, snarl locked in place, not even the slightest hint of pity in his voice.

I was heading straight for a street divider, the eraser brakes my feet were pumping now as useless to me as the rest of the cart. The remaining carts had gone straight down the street, toward 12th Avenue. The skin on my hands was split and streams of blood ran through my fingers. Holding the ropes as tight as I could, I used my weight to steer away from the divider.

The cart was starting to lose some speed, but still moved with enough force to do damage. My arms were tired and I couldn't hold the ropes any longer: the nylon ridges were cutting in too deep. I let go and braced myself against the sides of the Dr. Brown case. The cart veered wildly left and right, bounced across 11th Avenue, past a double-parked station wagon, jumped the curb and slammed against the side of a corner mail box.

I got out, kicked it angrily over onto its side and sat down on the fender of a parked Chevy. I put my face up to the sun and my elbows on the trunk and waited for

Michael, Thomas and John to make their way down the hill toward me.

'You okay?' John wanted to know, pointing to my hands, which were bleeding badly.

'What happened?' Michael asked. 'We saw you locked in with Russell, then we lost you in the crowd.'

'Woulda taken a bulldozer to knock over Russell's cart,' I said.

'Next year we gotta steal better wood,' Tommy said. 'And maybe get better sets of wheels.'

'I'm sorry,' I said. 'I thought we'd do better.'

'That's okay,' Michael said. 'Not your fault. You just suck as a driver.'

'Mikey's right,' John said. 'You ain't exactly Andretti behind the wheel.'

'I ain't got a wheel, first of all,' I said. 'And Andretti's got brakes.'

'Little things,' Michael said sadly. 'You let little things get to you.'

'I hate you guys,' I said.

'Next year we'll get you a parachute.' John patted me on the back. 'Make your bailout a lot easier.'

'And gloves too,' Tommy said. 'Black ones. Like the real race drivers wear.'

'I *really* hate you guys.'

We walked together back to 10th Avenue and Fat Mancho's Candy Store to get some ice and clean rags for my bloody hands.

TWO

My three friends and I were inseparable, happy and content to live within the closed world of Hell's Kitchen. The West Side streets of Manhattan were our private playground, a cement kingdom where we felt ourselves to be nothing less than absolute rulers. There were no curfews to contend with, no curbs placed on where we could go, no restrictions on what we could do. As long as we stayed within the confines of the neighborhood.

Hell's Kitchen was a place where everyone knew everything about everybody and everybody could be counted on. Secrets lived and died on the streets that began on West 35th and ended on West 56th, bordered on one side by the Hudson River and on the other by the Broadway theater district. It was an area populated by an uneasy blend of Irish, Italian, Puerto Rican and Eastern European laborers, hard men living hard lives, often by their own design.

We lived in railroad apartments inside red-brick tenements. The average rent for the typical six rooms was thirty-eight dollars a month, gas and utilities not included, payment due in cash. Few mothers worked and all had trouble with the men they married. Domestic violence was a cottage industry in Hell's Kitchen. Yet there was no divorce and few separations, for Hell's Kitchen was a place where the will of the Church was as forceful as the demands of a husband. For a marriage to end, someone usually had to die.

We had no control over the daily violence that took place behind our apartment doors.

We watched our mothers being beaten and could do little more than tend to their wounds. We saw our fathers romance other women, sometimes dragging us along to serve as alibis. When their anger turned to us, our fathers were just as brutal. Many were the mornings when my friends and I would compare bruises, welts and stitches, boasting of the beatings we had taken the previous night.

A lot of the men drank, stomachs full of liquor fueling their violent urges. Many of them gambled heavily, large portions of their union paychecks making their way into the pockets of bookies. This lack of table money also contributed to the charged atmosphere of our private lives.

Yet despite the harshness of the life, Hell's Kitchen offered the children growing up on its streets a safety net enjoyed by few other neighborhoods. Our daily escapades included an endless series of adventures and games, limited only by imagination and physical strength. There were no boundaries to what we could attempt, no barricades placed on the quest for fun and laughter. While many were the horrors we witnessed, our lives were also filled with joy. Enough joy to fend off the madness around us.

In the summer months, my friends and I played games that ran the gamut of inner city past-times in the early 1960s: Sewer-to-sewer stickball, with sawed-down broom handles substituting for bats and parked cars used as foul lines; eighteen-box bottlecap tournaments, where a cap filled with melted candle wax was hit by hand into numbered chalk squares; Johnny-on-the-Pony; stoop ball and dodge ball; knock hockey and corner pennies. In the evenings, wearing cut-off T-shirts and shorts, we washed off the day's heat with the cold spray of an open fire hydrant.

In the fall, roller hockey and ash-can football took over the streets, while in the winter we would fashion sleds from cardboard boxes and wooden crates and ride them down the icy slopes of 11th and 12th Avenues.

Throughout the year, we collected and hoarded baseball cards and comic books and, on Monday and Friday nights, walked the two long blocks to the old Madison Square Garden on Eighth Avenue to watch as many boxing and wrestling matches we could sneak our way into, innocently believing both sports to be on the same professional level: To us, Bruno Sammartino was Sonny Liston's peer.

We raced pigeons across rooftops and dove off the 12th Avenue piers into the waters of the Hudson River, using the rusty iron moorings as diving boards. We listened to Sam Cooke, Bobby Darin and Frankie Valli and The Four Seasons on portable radios and imitated their sounds on street corners late into the night. We started to think and talk about girls, hormones fueled by the cheap skin magazines handed down to us by older boys. We went to the movies once a week and saw the second acts of any Wednesday Broadway matinee that caught our fancy, allowed in by the ticket matrons who worked the theaters and were our neighbors. Inside those ornate and darkened halls, standing in the back or sitting on the top steps of the balcony, we laughed at the early comedies of Neil Simon, were moved by the truth of *A View from the Bridge* and admired the pure showmanship of *My Fair Lady.* The only show we avoided was *West Side Story*, insulted by its inaccurate depiction of what we thought of as our way of life.

There was also an active competition among the four of us to see who could come up with the best and boldest prank.

Tommy had his best moment when he set loose a small shopping bag filled with mice during a Saturday afternoon mass honoring a retiring nun. The sight of the mice sent the nearly two dozen nuns in attendance running for the front doors of Sacred Heart Church.

Michael scored a bullseye when he got a number of older kids to help him switch the living room furniture in the apartments of two men who had a decade-long feud raging between them.

25

On one hot summer afternoon, John climbed three floors of fire escapes to reach the crammed clothesline of the meanest woman in the neighborhood, Mrs. Evelyn McWilliams. Hanging upside down and shirtless, his legs wrapped around thin iron bars, he took her laundry off the line, folded the clothes neatly as he could, put them in an empty wine box and donated them to the Sisters of Sacred Heart Convent, to be distributed to the needy.

For the longest time, my pranks never measured up to those my friends managed with such apparent ease. Then, two weeks into the 1963 school year, I found a nun's clacker in a school hallway and was ready for the big leagues.

The girls sat on the left hand side of the church, the boys on the right, all of us listening to another in a series of inane lectures on the sacrament of confirmation. Three nuns, in white habit and cloth, sat behind the four rows of girls. One priest, Father Robert Carillo, sat behind the boys. It was early afternoon and the lights of the large church were still dark, votive candles casting shadows over the wall sculptures depicting Christ's final walk.

I was in the last row of boys, left arm resting on the edge of the pew, right hand in my jacket pocket, fingers wrapped around the found clacker. To a nun, a clacker was the equivalent of a starter's pistol or a police whistle. In church, it was used to alert the girls as to when they should stand, sit, kneel and genuflect, all based on the number of times the clacker was pressed. In the hands of a nun, a clacker was a tool of discipline. In my pocket, it was cause for havoc.

I waited until the priest at the altar, white-haired and stooped-shouldered, folded his hands and bowed his head in silent prayer. I squeezed the clacker twice, the signal for the girls to stand. Sister Timothy Morris, an overweight nun with tar-stained fingers and a crooked smile, shot up in her seat as if hit by a bolt. She quickly clacked once, returning the confused girls to their seats. I clacked four times, getting them to genuflect. Sister Timothy clacked the girls back into position, shooting a pair of hateful eyes across the rows of pews filled with boys.

I gave the clacker three quick hits and watched the girls stand at attention. The priest at the altar cut short his prayer, casually watching the commotion before him, listening as the echoes of the dueling clackers bounced off the walls of the church. The boys kept their eyes rooted to the altar, holding their smiles and silencing their snickers. Sister Timothy clacked the girls back to their seats, her cheeks visibly red, her lips pursed.

Father Carillo slid into my row, one hand holding onto my left elbow.

'Let me have the clacker,' he said without turning his head.

'What clacker?' I asked, doing the same.

'*Now*,' Father Carillo said.

I took my hand out of my jacket pocket, moved the clacker across my knees and palmed it over to Father Carillo. He took it from me without much body movement, each of us glancing over toward Sister Timothy, hoping she had not noticed the quick pass-off.

The priest spread his arms outward and asked all in attendance to rise. Sister Timothy snapped her clacker three times and watched as the girls rose in unison, nodding her head in approval at the two nuns to her left.

'Let us pray,' said the priest.

Father Carillo, his back straight, his eyes focused on the altar, his face free of emotion, gave the clacker in his hand one soft squeeze.

The girls all sat back down. Sister Timothy fell into her pew. The priest at the altar lowered his eyes and shook his head. I looked over at Father Bobby, my mouth open, my eyes unable to hide their surprise.

'Nuns are such easy targets,' Father Bobby whispered with a wink and a smile.

Hell's Kitchen was a neighborhood with a structured code

of behavior and an unwritten set of rules that could be physically enforced. There was a hierarchy that trickled down from the local members of both the Irish and Italian mobs to a loose-knit affiliation of Puerto Rican numbers brokers and loan sharks to small groups of organized gangs recruited to do a variety of jobs, from collections to picking up stolen goods. My friends and I were the last rung on the neighborhood ladder, free to roam its streets and play our games, required only to follow the rules. On occasion, we would be recruited for the simplest tasks, most of them involving money drop-offs or pick-ups.

Crimes against the people of the neighborhood were not permitted and, on the rare occasions when they did occur, the punishments doled out were severe and, in some cases, final. The elderly were to be helped not hurt. The neighborhood was to be supported not stripped. Gangs were not allowed to recruit anyone who did not wish to join. Drug use was frowned upon and addicts were ostracized, pointed out as 'on the nod' losers to be avoided.

Despite the often violent ways of its inhabitants, Hell's Kitchen was one of New York's safest neighborhoods. Outsiders walked its streets without fear, young couples strolled the West Side piers without apprehension, old men took grandchildren for walks in De Witt Clinton Park, never once looking over their shoulders.

It was a place of innocence ruled by corruption. There were no drive-by shootings or murders without reason. The men who carried guns in Hell's Kitchen were all too aware of their power. Crack cocaine had yet to hit and there wasn't enough money around to support a cocaine habit. The drug of choice when I was a child was heroin and the hard-core addicts numbered a handful, most of them young and docile, feeding their needs with cash hand-outs and petty thievery. They bought their drugs outside the neighborhood since dealers were not welcome in Hell's Kitchen. Those who ignored the verbal warnings, wrote them off as the ramblings of pudgy old men, paid with their lives.

One of the most graphic images I can recall from my childhood is of standing under a street light on a rainy night, holding my father's hand and looking up at the face of a dead man, hanging from a rope, his face swollen, his hands bound. He was a drug dealer from an uptown neighborhood who had moved heroin in Hell's Kitchen. A packet of it had killed the twelve-year-old son of a Puerto Rican numbers runner.

It was the last packet the dealer ever sold.

Friendships were as important as neighborhood loyalty. Your friends gave you an identity and a sense of belonging. They afforded you a group you could trust that extended beyond the bounds of family. The home lives of most of the children in Hell's Kitchen were unruly and filled with struggle. There was little time for bonding, little attention given to nurturing and few moments set aside for childish pleasures. Those had to be found elsewhere, usually out on the street in the company of friends. With them, you could laugh, tell stupid jokes, trade insults and books and talk about sports and movies. You could even share your secrets and sins, dare tell another person what you thought about important childhood issues such as holding a girl's hand.

Life in Hell's Kitchen was hard. Life without friends was harder. Most kids were lucky enough to find one friend they could count on. I found three. All of them older, probably wiser and no doubt smarter. There is no memory of my early years that does not include them. They were a part of every happy moment I enjoyed.

I wasn't tough enough to be part of a gang nor did I care for the gang members' penchant for constant confrontation. I was too talkative and out-going to be a loner. I lived and survived in a grown-up world, but my concerns were that of a growing boy – I knew more about the Three Stooges, even Shemp, than I did about street gangs.

I cared more about a trade the Yankees were about to make than about a shooting that happened three buildings down. I wondered why James Cagney had stopped making movies and if there was a better cop in the country than Jack Webb on *Dragnet*. In a neighborhood where there was no Little League, I worked on throwing a curve ball like Whitey Ford. Surrounded by apartments devoid of books, I pored through the works of every adventure writer the local library stocked. Like most boys my age, I molded a world of my own and stocked it with the people I came across through books, sports, movies and television, making it a place where fictional characters were as real to me as those I saw every day. It was a world with room for those who felt as I did, who hated Disney but loved Red Skelton, who would take a Good Humor bar over a Mister Softy cone, who went to the Ringling Brothers circus hoping that the annoying kid shot out of the cannon would *miss* the net and who wondered why the cops in our neighborhood couldn't be more like Lee Marvin from *M Squad*.

It was a world made for my three friends.

We became friends over a lunch.

Word spread one afternoon that three pro wrestlers – Klondike Bill, Bo Bo Brazil and Haystacks Calhoun – were eating at a Holiday Inn on 51st Street. I rushed there and found Michael, John and Thomas standing outside, looking through the glass window that fronted the restaurant, watching the large men devour thick sandwiches and slabs of pie. I knew the guys from the school yard and the neighborhood, but had been too intimidated to approach them. The sight of the wrestlers eliminated such concerns.

'They don't even stop to chew,' John said in wonder.

'Guys that big don't have to chew,' Tommy told him.

'Haystacks eats four steaks a night at dinner,' I said, nudging my way past Michael for a closer look. '*Every* night.'

'Tell us somethin' we don't know,' Michael muttered, eyes on the wrestlers.

'I'm gonna go and sit with them,' I said casually. 'You can come if you want.'

'You know them?' John asked.

'Not yet,' I said.

The four of us walked through the restaurant doors and approached the wrestlers' table. The wrestlers were deep in conversation, empty plates and glasses the only remnants of their meal. They turned their heads when they saw us.

'You boys lost?' Haystacks Calhoun asked. His hair and beard were shaggy and long and he was wearing bib overalls large enough to cover a banquet table. The wrestling magazine stories I had read about him put his weight at 620 pounds and I was amazed that anyone that big could slide into a booth.

'No,' I said.

'Then what do you want?' Klondike Bill asked. His hair and beard were darker and thicker than Calhoun's and he was half his weight, which made him the second biggest man I'd ever seen.

'I've watched you guys wrestle a lot,' I said. I pointed a finger to the three behind me. 'We all have.'

'You root for us to win?' Bo Bo Brazil asked. He was more muscular than his cohorts, and looked like sculpted stone leaning against the window, his shaved black head gleaming, his eyes clear and bright. Bo Bo's one noted move, the head-crushing co-co butt, was said to be a weapon harsh enough to leave an opponent paralyzed.

'No,' I said.

'Why not?' Calhoun demanded.

'You usually fight the good guys,' I said, my palms starting to sweat.

Haystacks Calhoun lifted one large hand from the table and placed it on my shoulder and around my neck. Its weight alone made my legs quiver. He was breathing through his mouth, air coming out in thick gulps. 'Your friends feel the same way?'

'Yes,' I said, not giving them a chance to respond. 'We all root against you.'

Haystacks Calhoun let out a loud laugh, the fat of his body shaking in spasms, his free hand slapping at the table top. Klondike Bill and Bo Bo Brazil were quick to join in.

'Get some chairs, boys,' Calhoun said, grabbing a glass of water to wash down his laugh. 'Sit with us.'

We spent more than an hour in their company, crowded around the booth, treated to four pieces of cherry pie, four chocolate shakes and tales of the wrestling world. We didn't get the impression that they made a lot of money and, judging by their scarred faces and cauliflowered ears, we knew it wasn't an easy life. But the stories they told were filled with exuberance and the thrill of working the circuit in arenas around the country, where people paid money to jeer and cheer every night. To our young ears, being a wrestler sounded far better than running away to join the circus.

'You boys got tickets for tonight?' Haystacks asked, signaling to a waitress.

'No, sir,' John said, scraping up the last crumbs of his pie.

'Get yourself over to the box office at seven,' Calhoun said, slowly squeezing out of his side of the booth. 'You'll be sittin' ringside by seven-thirty.'

We shook hands, each of ours disappearing into the expanse of theirs and thanked them, looking up in awe as they smiled and rubbed the top of our heads.

'Don't disappoint us now,' Klondike Bill warned on his way out. 'We wanna hear you boo loud and clear tonight.'

'We won't let you down,' Tommy said.

'We'll throw things if you want,' John said.

We stood by the booth and watched as they walked out of the Inn and onto 10th Avenue, three large men taking small steps, heading toward Madison Square Garden and the white lights of a packed arena.

I was the youngest of my friends by three years, and yet they treated me as an equal. We had so much else in common that once I was accepted, my age never became an issue. A sure sign of their acceptance was when, less than a week after we met, they gave me a nickname. They called me Shakespeare, because I was never without a book.

We were each the only child of a troubled marriage.

My father, Mario, worked as a butcher, a trade he learned in prison while serving six years of a five-to-fifteen-year sentence for second degree manslaughter. The victim was his first wife. The battles my father fought with my mother, Raffaela, a silent, angry woman who hid herself in prayer, were neighborhood legend. My father was a con man who gambled what little he earned and managed to spend what he never had. Yet he always had time and money to buy me and my friends ice cream cones or sodas whenever he saw us on the street. He was a man who seemed more comfortable in the company of children than in a world of adults. Growing up, for reasons I could never put into words, I was always afraid my father would disappear. That one day, he would leave and not return. It was a fear fed by his separations from my mother, when I would not hear from him for weeks.

Michael, twelve, was the eldest of my friends. His father, construction worker Devlin Sullivan, had fought in Korea and, for his trouble, earned a steel plate in his head. Always angry, Mr. Sullivan had a foul mouth and great thirst. Tall and strapping, muscular from the work, he kept his wife at a distance, living for weeks with an assortment of mistresses, who soaked his money and then sent him packing. Michael's mother, Anna, always took him back and forgave him all trespasses. Michael never spoke about his father, not in the way I always did about mine, and seemed uncomfortable the rare times I saw them together.

33

His parents' marriage fed in Michael a distrust about the strong neighborhood traditions of marriage, family and religion. He was the realist among us, suspicious of others' intentions, never trusting the words of those he didn't know. It was Michael who kept us grounded.

His stern exterior, though, was balanced by a strong sense of honor. He would never do anything that would embarrass us and demanded the same in return. He never played practical jokes on those he perceived as weaker and he always rose to defend anyone he believed unable to defend himself. That rigid code was reflected in the books he read and the shows he watched. The only time I ever saw him on the verge of tears was near the end of a Broadway production of *Camelot*, affected by Lancelot's betrayal. His favorite of the Three Musketeers was the more troubled Aramis and when we played games based on TV shows or movies, Michael always sought out the role of leader, whether it was Vic Morrow's character on *Combat* or Eliot Ness in *The Untouchables*.

It was harder to make Michael laugh than the others. He was big brother and as such had to maintain a degree of maturity. He was the first among us to have a steady girlfriend, Carol Martinez, a half-Irish, half-Puerto Rican girl from 49th Street, and the last in our crew to learn to ride a bike. He was called Spots when he was younger, because of the dozens of freckles that dotted his face and hands, but not often since he hated the name and the freckles had begun to fade the closer he got to puberty.

It was Michael who kept the older, explosive boys of the neighborhood at bay, often with nothing more than a look or movement. That ability reinforced his position as our leader, a title he accepted but never acknowledged. It was simply his role, his place.

In the years we spent together as children, Tommy Marcano's father was away in Attica in upstate New York, serving a seven-year sentence for an armed robbery conviction. Billy Marcano was a career criminal who kept his wife Marie out of his business affairs. Like most of the neighborhood mothers, Marie was devoutly religious, spending her free time helping the parish priests and nuns. During the years her husband was in prison, she remained a devoted wife, working a steady job as a telephone receptionist for an illegal betting parlor.

Tommy missed his father, writing him a letter every night before he went to bed. He carried a crumpled picture of the two of them together in his back pocket and looked at it several times a day. If Michael was the brains behind the group, Tommy was its soul. His was a gentle goodness, and would share anything he had, never jealous of another's gift or good fortune. His street name was Butter, because he spread it across everything he ate and he seemed happiest when he had a fresh roll in one hand and a hot cup of chocolate in the other. He was shy and shunned any chance for attention, yet he played the dozens, a street game where the key is to out-insult your opponent.

I can never think of Tommy without a smile on his face, his eyes eager to share in the laugh, even if it came at his expense. The only time I saw a hint of sadness to him was when I was with my father, so I made an effort to include him in whatever we were planning to do together. My father, who liked to eat as much as Tommy did, usually obliged. When that happened, the smile was quick to return.

While Michael seemed older than his years, Tommy seemed far younger than eleven. He had a little boy's affability and eagerness to please. He had a fast tongue, was swift with a comeback and never forgot a joke. His pranks were tinged with innocence. Tommy would never want to be leader of the group, never would have been comfortable with the burden. It was more in keeping with his personality to go along, to watch, to listen and always, to laugh.

He also had a natural ability to build things, working away on a discarded piece of wood or an old length of pipe from which would emerge a wooden train or a make-shift flute. He never kept his creations and never took money for his work. Many of the pieces he made were mailed to his father in prison. He was never told if his father received them and he never asked.

John Reilly was raised by his mother, an attractive woman with little time to devote to anything other than church, her work as a Broadway theater usher and her boyfriends. John's father was a petty hood shot and killed in a foiled armored truck heist in New Jersey less than a week after his son was born. John knew nothing of the man. 'There were no photos,' he once told me. 'No wedding picture, no shots of him in the Navy. Nobody talked about him or mentioned his name. It was as if he never existed.'

John earned his discipline from the hands of his mother's various suitors, an endless stream of men who knew only one way to handle a boy. He seldom spoke about the beatings, but we all knew they took place.

Even though he was only four months younger than Michael, John was the smallest of the group and was nicknamed the Count, due to his fascination with *The Count of Monte Cristo*, which was also my favorite book. John was brash and had the sharpest sense of humor of any of us. He loved comedy and would spend hours debating whether the Three Stooges were gifted comedians or just jerks who beat each other up.

He was our heart, an innocent surrounded by a violence he could not prevent. He was the most handsome among us and often used a smile and a wink to extricate himself from trouble. He loved to draw, etching sketches of sailboats and cruise ships onto thin strips of fine paper with a dark pencil. He would spend afternoons down by the piers feeding pigeons, watching waves lap against the dock and drawing colorful pictures of the ocean liners in port, filling their decks with the familiar faces of the neighborhood.

He was a born mimic, ordering slices of pizza as John

Wayne, asking for a library book like James Cagney and talking to a girl in the schoolyard sounding like Humphrey Bogart. Each situation brought about its intended smile, allowing John to walk away content, his mission accomplished. He concealed the ugliness of his home life behind a shield of jokes. He never set out to hurt, there was too much of that in his own everyday moments. John, more than any one of us, was always in need of someone else's smile.

Together, the four of us found in each other the solace and security we could not find anywhere else. We trusted each other and knew there would never be an act of betrayal among us. We had nothing else – no money, no bikes, no summer camps, no vacations. Nothing, except one another.

To us, that was all that mattered.

THREE

The Catholic church played a large part in our lives. Sacred Heart was the center of the neighborhood, serving as a neutral meeting ground, a peaceful sanctuary where problems could be discussed and emotions calmed. The priests and nuns of the area were a visible presence and commanded our attention, if not always our respect.

My friends and I attended Sacred Heart Grammar School on West 50th Street, a large, red brick building directly across from PS 111. Our parents paid a two dollar a month tuition fee and sent us out each morning dressed in the mandatory uniform of maroon pants for boys and skirt for girls, white shirts and clip-on red ties.

The school was rife with problems, lack of supplies being the least of them. Most of us were products of violent homes, and therefore prone to violence ourselves, making playground fights daily occurrences. The fights were often in response to a perceived slight or a violation of an unwritten code of conduct. All students were divided into cliques, most based on ethnic backgrounds, which only added tension to an already tight situation.

In addition to the volatile ethnic groupings, teachers were faced with the barriers of language and the difficulties of overcrowded classrooms. After third grade, students were divided by sex, with the nuns teaching the girls and priests and brothers working with the boys. Each teacher faced an average class size of thirty-two students, more than half of whom spoke no English at home. To help support their families, many of the children worked jobs after school, reducing the hours they were free to concentrate on homework.

Few of the teachers cared enough to work beyond the three o'clock bell. There were a handful, however, as there are in all schools, who did care and who took the time to tutor a student, to feed an interest, to set a goal beyond neighborhood boundaries.

Brother Nick Kappas spent hours after school patiently helping me learn the basic English I had not been taught at home, where both my parents spoke Italian. Another, Father Jerry Martin, a black priest from the Deep South, opened my eyes to the hate and prejudice that existed beyond Hell's Kitchen. Still another, Father Andrew Nealon, an elderly priest with a thick Boston accent, fueled my interest in American history. Then there was Father Robert Carillo, my cohort in the clacker escapade, and the only member of the clergy who had been born and raised in Hell's Kitchen.

Father Bobby, as the neighborhood kids called him, was in his mid-thirties, tall and muscular, with thick, dark, curly hair, an unlined face and an athlete's body. He played the organ at Sunday mass, was in charge of the altar boys, taught fifth grade and played basketball for two hours every day in the school playground. Most priests liked to preach from a pulpit; Father Bobby liked to talk during the bump and shove of a game of one-on-one. He was the one priest in the neighborhood who challenged us to do better, and who was always ready to help when a problem arose.

Father Bobby introduced me and my friends to such authors as Sir Arthur Conan Doyle, Victor Hugo and Stephen Crane, further instilling in us a passion for written words. He chose stories and novels by authors he felt we could identify with, and who could, for a brief time, help us escape the wars waged nightly inside our apartments.

It was through him that we learned of such books as *Les Miserables*, *A Tree Grows in Brooklyn* and *A Bell for*

Adano and how they could provide a night-light to keep away the family terror. It was easy for him to do so, because he had been raised in the same manner, under the same circumstances. He knew what it meant to find sleep under the cover of fear.

Sacred Heart Church was quiet, its overhead lights shining down across long rows of wooden pews. Seven women and three men sat in the rear, hands folded in prayer, waiting to talk to a priest.

My friends and I spent a lot of time inside that small, compact church with the large marble altar at its center. We each served as altar boys, working a regular schedule of Sunday and occasional weekday masses. We were also expected to handle funerals, spreading dark clouds of incense above the coffins of the neighborhood dead. Everyone wanted to work funeral masses, since the service included a three dollar fee and a chance to pocket more if you looked sufficiently somber.

In addition, we went to mass once a week and sometimes more, especially if Father Bobby needed someone to escort the elderly of the parish to weeknight services. Other times, I would just stop inside the church and sit for hours, alone or with one of my friends. I liked the feel and smell of the empty church, surrounded by statues of saints and stained glass windows. I didn't go so much to pray, but to relax and pull away from outside events. John and I went more than the others. We were the only two of the group to give any thought to entering the priesthood, an idea we found appealing because of its guaranteed ticket out of the neighborhood. A Catholic version of the lottery. We were much too young to dissect the issue of celibacy and spent most of our time fretting over how we would look wearing a Roman collar.

John and I were intrigued by the powers a priest was given. The ability to serve mass, say last rites, baptize babies, perform weddings and, best of all, sit in a dark booth and listen to others confess their sins. To us, the

40

sacrament of confession was like being allowed inside a secret world of betrayal and deceit, where people openly admitted dark misdeeds and vile indiscretions. All of it covered by an umbrella of piety and privacy. Confession was better than any book we could get our hands on or any movie we could see because the sins were real, committed by people we actually *knew*. The temptation to be a part of that was too great to resist.

There were two confessional booths on both sides of Sacred Heart lining the walls closest to the back pews, each shrouded with heavy purple curtains. The thick wood door at the center of the confessional locked from the inside. Two small mesh screens, covered by sliding wood panels, allowed the priest, if he could stay awake, to sit and listen to the sins of his parish. Every Saturday afternoon, from three to five p.m., a handful of parishioners would head into those booths. There, every affair, every curse, every transgression they made during the week would be revealed. On those days, there was no better place to be in Hell's Kitchen.

John and I sat in that church every Saturday afternoon. We knew Father Tim McAndrew, old, weary and with a hearing disorder, always worked the first hour in one of the booths closest to the altar. Father McAndrew had a penchant for handing out stiff penalties for the slightest trespass, whether he heard it confessed or only thought he did. He was especially rough on children and married women. Self-abuse was worth a dozen Hail Marys and a half-dozen Our Fathers.

On a few occasions and always at my urging, John and I would sneak into the booth alongside McAndrew's, shut the door and hear the sins we had only read about. We couldn't imagine what the penalty would be for getting caught, but whatever it was it couldn't possibly surpass the joy of hearing about a neighbor's fall from grace.

I was inside the second booth, squeezed onto the small

41

wooden bench, my back against the cool wall. The Count, John Reilly, sat next to me.

'Man, if we get caught, they'll burn us,' he whispered.

'What if our mothers are out there?' I asked. 'What if we end up hearing *their* confessions?'

'What if we hear somethin' worse?' John said.

'Like what?' I couldn't imagine anything worse.

'Like a murder,' John said. 'What if somebody cops to a murder?'

'Relax,' I said, as convincingly as I could. 'All we gotta do is sit back, listen and remember not to laugh.'

At ten minutes past three, two women from the back pew stood and headed for the first confessional, ready to tell their sins to a man who couldn't hear them. They moved one to each side, parted the curtains, knelt down and waited for the small wood doors to slide open.

Seconds later, the sides of our booth came to life.

'Here we go,' I said. 'Get ready.'

'God help us,' John said, making the Sign of The Cross. 'God help us.'

We heard a man's low cough on our right, as he shuffled his way to a kneeling position and leaned his elbow on the small ledge facing him. He chewed gum and sniffed in deep breaths as he waited for the door to open.

'We know him?' John asked.

'Quiet!'

There was a woman's sneeze from the other side of the booth as she searched through an open purse for a tissue. She blew her nose, straightened her dress and waited.

'Which one?' John asked.

'The guy,' I said and moved the small door to my right. The man's thick lips, nose and stubble faced us, separated only by the mesh screen, his heavy breath warming our side of the booth.

'Bless me Father, for I have sinned,' he said, his hands folded in prayer. 'It has been two years since my last confession.'

42

John grabbed onto my shoulder and I tried to keep my legs from shaking. Neither of us spoke.

'I done bad things, Father,' the man said. 'And I'm sorry for all of them. I gamble, lose all my rent money to the horses. Lie to my wife, hit her sometimes, the kids too. It's bad, Father. Gotta get myself outta this hole. What can I do?'

'Pray,' I said in my deepest voice.

'I *been* prayin',' the man said. 'Ain't helped. I owe money to loan sharks. A lot of it. Father, you gotta help me. This the place you go for help, right? I got nowhere else to go. This is it.'

John and I held our breath and stayed silent.

'Father, you there?' the man said.

'Yes,' I said.

'So,' the man said. 'What's it gonna be?'

'Three Hail Marys,' I said. 'One Our Father. And may the Lord bless you.'

'Three Hail Marys!' the man said. 'What the hell's that gonna do?'

'It's for your soul,' I said.

'Fuck my soul!' the man said in a loud voice. 'And fuck you too, you freeloadin' bastard.'

The man stood up, pulled aside the purple drapes hanging to his right and stormed out of the booth, his outburst catching the attention of those who waited their turn.

'That went well,' I said to John, who finally loosened his grip on my shoulder.

'Don't do the woman,' John said. 'I'm beggin' you. Let's just get outta here.'

'How?' I asked.

'Don't take anymore,' John said. 'Let 'em all go over to the other booth. Have 'em think no one's in here.'

'Let's do one more,' I said.

'No,' John said. 'I'm too scared.'

'Just one more,' I pleaded.

'No.'

'Only one more.'

43

'One,' John said. 'Then we're outta here.'

'You got it,' I agreed.

'Swear on it?'

'You can't swear in church,' I said.

The woman's voice was soft and low, barely above a whisper. The edge of a veil hung across her face, her hands curled against the darkness of the booth, the tips of her fingernails scraping the base of the wood.

'Bless me Father,' she began. 'It has been six weeks since my last confession.'

We both knew who she was, had seen her more than once walking the streets of Hell's Kitchen, arm in arm with the latest man to catch her fancy. She was a woman our fathers smiled about and our mothers told us to ignore.

'I'm not happy about my life, Father,' she said. 'It's like I don't want to wake up in the morning anymore.'

'Why?' I asked, my voice muffled by the back of John's shirt.

'It's wrong,' she said. 'Everything I do is wrong and I don't know how to stop.'

'You must pray,' I said.

'I do, Father,' she said. 'Believe me, I do. Every day. It's not doing any good.'

'It will,' I said.

'I sleep with married men,' the woman said. 'Men with families. In the morning I tell myself it's the last time. And it never is.'

'One day it will be,' I said, watching her hands curve around a set of rosary beads.

'It's gonna have to be soon,' the woman said, holding back a rush of tears. 'I'm pregnant.'

John looked at me, both hands locked over his mouth.

'The father?' I asked.

'Take a number,' the woman said. The sarcasm could not hide the sadness in her voice.

'What are you going to do?'

'I know what *you* want me to do,' the woman said. 'And I know what I *should* do. I just don't know what I'm gonna do.'

'There's time,' I said, sweat running down my neck.

'I got lotsa things,' the woman said. 'Time just isn't one of 'em.'

The woman blessed herself, rolled up the rosary beads and put them in the front pocket of her dress. She brushed her hair away from her eyes and picked up the purse resting by her knees.

'I gotta go,' she said, and then, much to our shock, she added, 'Thanks for listening, fellas. I appreciate it and I know you'll keep it to yourselves.'

She knocked at the screen with two fingers, waved and left the booth.

'She knew,' John said.

'Yeah,' I said. 'She knew.'

'Why she tell us all that?'

'I guess she had to tell somebody.'

John stood up and brushed against the wall, accidentally sliding open the small door to the confessional. A man knelt on the other side, obscured by the screen.

'Bless me Father for I have sinned,' the man said, his voice baritone deep.

'So?' John said. 'What's that make you? Special?'

John opened the main door and we both walked out of the booth, our heads bowed, our hands folded in prayer.

Summer 1964

FOUR

We were well-schooled in revenge.

Hell's Kitchen offered graduate workshops in correcting wrongs. Any form of betrayal had to be confronted and settled. Our standing in the neighborhood depended on how quickly and in what manner the reprisals occurred. If there was no response, then the injured party earned a coward's label, its weight as great as that of any scarlet letter. Men, boys, women, girls were shot, stabbed, even killed for a variety of motives, all having to do with the simple act of getting even.

When my friends and I were young, Hell's Kitchen was run by a man named King Benny.

In his youth, King Benny had been a hit man for Charles 'Lucky' Luciano and was said to have been one of the shooters who machine-gunned 'Mad Dog' Coll on West 23rd Street on the night of February 8, 1932. King Benny ran bootleg with 'Dutch' Schultz, owned a couple of clubs with 'Tough Tony' Anastasia and owned a string of tenements on West 49th Street, all listed in his mother's name. He was tall, well over six feet, with thick dark hair and eyes that never seemed to move. He was married to a woman who lived outside the neighborhood and had no children of his own.

'He was fourteen when I first met him,' my father told me one night. 'Wasn't much of anything back then. Always getting the shit kicked out of him in street fights. Then, one day, for who knows what reason, an Irish guy, about twenty-five years old, takes him and throws him down a flight of stairs. King Benny breaks all his front teeth in the fall. He waits eight years to get that Irish guy. Walks in on him in a public bath house, guy soaking in a tub. King Benny looks in a mirror, takes out his front teeth, lays them on a sink. Looks down at the guy in the tub and says, "When I look in a mirror, I see your face." King Benny pulls out gun and shoots the guy twice in each leg. Then says to him, "Now when you take a bath, you see mine." Nobody ever fucked with King Benny after that.'

His decisions were never rash and were always final. His words were, in Hell's Kitchen, respected as the law. It was the only law never broken.

King Benny used diplomacy when called for, force when necessary. He earned his money from old fashioned mob enterprises – policy running, loan sharking, truck hijacking, swag sales and prostitution. These crimes were quietly condoned by a police department warmed by weekly pay-offs and supported by a neighborhood addicted to illegal action. King Benny ruled with a tight fist and lashed out with deadly purpose against any threat to his domain. A lot of people tried taking over his business during his reign and a lot of people ended up dead.

He would do favors for those he liked and ignored the financial requests of those he considered liabilities. He would listen to people with problems and offer opinions on how those problems could be solved. He was a Father confessor without a conscience.

The large room was wrapped in darkness. Three men in black jackets and black sports shirts sat at a table by an open window, playing sette bello and smoking unfiltered cigarettes. Above them, a dim bulb dangled from a knotted cord. Behind them, a jukebox played Italian love songs. None of the men spoke.

At the far end of the room, a tall, thin man stood behind a half-moon bar, scanning the daily racing sheet.

A large white cup filled with espresso was on his left, a Kenmore alarm clock ticked away on his right. He was dressed in black shirt, sweater, shoes and slacks, with a large oval-shaped ring on the fourth finger of his left hand. His hair was slicked back and his face was clean shaven. He chewed a small piece of gum and had a thick, wood toothpick in the corner of his mouth.

I turned the knob on the old wood door that led into the room and swung it open, thin shafts of afternoon sunlight creeping in behind me. No one looked up as I walked toward King Benny, the heels of my shoes scraping against the wood floor.

'Can I talk to you for a minute?' I asked, standing across from him, on the far side of the bar, my back to the three men playing cards.

King Benny looked up from his racing sheet and nodded. He reached out for his coffee, raised it to his lips and took a slow sip, eyes still on me.

'I would like to work for you,' I said. 'Help you out, do whatever you need.'

King Benny put the cup back on the bar and wiped his lower lip with two fingers. His eyes didn't move.

'I can be a lot of help to you,' I said. 'You can count on that.'

One of the men playing cards slid his chair back, stood up and walked toward me.

'You the butcher's kid, am I right?' he asked, his three-day-old beard growing in gray, the bottoms of his teeth brown and caked.

'Yeah,' I said.

'Well, what kind of work you lookin' for?' he asked, leaning his head toward King Benny.

'Whatever,' I said. 'It doesn't matter.'

'I don't think we got anything, kid,' he said. 'Somebody musta steered you some wrong info.'

'Nobody steered me wrong,' I said. 'Everybody says this is the place to come to for jobs.'

'Who's everybody?' the man said.

51

'People from the neighborhood,' I said.

'Oh,' the man said. 'Them. Well, let me ask ya', what the fuck do they know?'

'They know you guys got jobs,' I said, moving my eyes from the old man and back to King Benny.

'Smart ass,' the old man said, turning away, heading back to his chair and his game.

King Benny and I looked at each other, the coffee by his side growing cold.

'Sorry I wasted your time,' I told him, looking away and heading toward the door.

I pulled the knob and opened it, letting in some gusts of air, letting out wisps of smoke.

'Hold it a minute,' King Benny finally said.

'Yeah?' I said, turning my head to face him.

'Come back tomorrow,' King Benny said. 'If you wanna work.'

'What time tomorrow?'

'Anytime,' King Benny said, his eyes back on the racing sheet, his hand reaching for the cold cup of coffee.

My first job for King Benny paid twenty-five dollars a week and ate up only forty minutes of my time. Twice a week, on Monday mornings before school and Friday afternoons after dismissal, I went to the large room on 12th Avenue where King Benny conducted his business. There, one of the three men would hand me a crumpled paper bag and direct me to one of the two nearby police precincts for its delivery.

It was a perfect way to handle payouts. Even if we got caught with the drop money, there wasn't anything the law could do about it. Nobody was going to jail for simply handing somebody a paper bag. Especially a kid.

Not long after I began work for King Benny, I was walking across 10th Avenue, a paper bag filled with money nestled under my right arm. The spring afternoon was warm and cloudless; a mild threat of rain had disappeared with the lunchtime traffic. I stopped at the corner of 48th

Street, waiting while two trucks drove past, leaving dust and fumes in their noisy wake.

I didn't notice the two men standing behind me.

The shorter of the two, dressed in tan slacks and a brown windbreaker, leaned across and grabbed my elbow, pulling me closer to him. The second man, taller and stronger, locked one of his arms into mine.

'Keep walkin',' he said. 'Make a sound, you die.'

'Where are we going?' I asked, trying to disguise my panic.

'Shut up,' the shorter man said.

We had shifted direction and were moving toward the waterfront, walking down 47th Street, past a car wash and an all-night gas station. The shorter man tightened his grip on my arm as we walked, his foul breath warm on my neck.

'Here we are,' he said. 'Get in there. C'mon. Stop stallin'.'

'You guys gotta be nuts,' I said. 'You know who you're takin' off?'

'Yeah, we know,' the tall man said. 'And we're scared shitless.'

The tall man ripped the paper bag from under my arm and pushed me crashing through the front of a tenement doorway. The inside hallway was dark and narrow, blood red walls cold to the touch. A forty-watt bulb cast the stairs and cement floor in shadow. Three garbage cans, lids on tight, were lined up alongside the super's first-floor apartment. Down the far end of the hall a wood door, leading to a cluttered back yard, creaked open.

I was on my knees, watching the two men count the money from the paper bag. They stopped when they saw me staring.

'This is a lot of money for a kid,' the tall man said, smiling. 'Don't know if I would trust a kid like you with this much money. What if you lose it?'

'It's only money,' I said, looking behind me, at the door which led out the back way.

'Whatta ya' get outta this?' the short man asked me. 'What's your cut?'

'Don't get a cut,' I said.

'Then you ain't nowhere as smart as you think,' the short man said.

'Lots of people tell me that,' I said, getting to my feet, rubbing my hands against my pants legs.

The tall man rolled the money back up, rubber bands holding the two bundles in place, and put them in the paper bag. He crumpled the bag again and shoved it inside the front pocket of his jacket. The short man had turned his back to me, checking out the street traffic through the open doorway.

Then the super's door clicked open.

The super, an old man in a sleeveless T-shirt and brown corduroy pants, stood in his doorway staring at the three strangers in his building.

'What you do?' he said in a husky Italian accent. 'Answer me. What you do here?'

'Relax,' the tall man said, his words tight, controlled. 'We were just leavin'. Okay with you?'

'What you do to the boy?' the old man asked, stepping out of the doorway, his arms by his side, walking closer to me.

'They took my money,' I said to the old man. 'They followed me and took my money.'

'You take money?' the old man asked, his voice an angry challenge.

'Kid's talkin' trouble,' the tall man said. 'Don't listen to him.'

'It's in the bag,' I said. 'The money they took is in the bag.'

The super's eyes moved to the paper bag, stuffed inside the tall man's jacket.

'Lemme see the bag,' the old man said.

'Fuck you,' the tall man said.

The old man brought a hand to the small of his back, his manner calm, his eyes steady. The hand came back holding a cocked .38 caliber pistol, its shiny silver cylinder pointed at the tall man's chest.

'Lemme see the bag,' the old man said again.

The tall man took the bag from his jacket pocket and handed it to the old man, careful not to make a sudden move. The old man tossed the bag to me.

'Get out,' he said. 'Use the back door.'

'What about them?' I asked.

'You care?'

'No,' I said.

'Then go.'

I turned around, shoved the bag under my arm, and ran out the building. I jumped the short back fence, cut through a small alleyway and came out on 11th Avenue.

I never looked back, not even when I heard the four shots that were fired.

'I need somebody with me,' I said to King Benny. 'What if that old guy hadn't showed?'

'But he did,' a man to King Benny's left said. 'And he took care of it.'

'Maybe next time we don't walk into the wrong building,' I said, sweat lining my face.

'There ain't no next time,' the man said, lighting a cigar.

'Maybe you just ain't up for the work,' another of King Benny's men said. 'Ain't as easy as you was thinkin'.'

'I'm up to it,' I insisted.

'Then there's no problem,' the man behind me said.

King Benny brushed a stream of cigar smoke away from his eyes. His look was cold and steady, his black jacket and slacks sleek and tailored, a large-faced Mickey Mouse watch strapped to his left wrist.

'Whatta ya need?' he asked me, his lips barely moving as he spoke.

'My friends,' I said.

'Your friends?' the man behind me asked, a laugh to the question. 'What do you think this is, *camp*?'

'It won't cost you extra,' I said. 'You can take the money out of my end.'

'Who are these friends?' King Benny asked.

'From the neighborhood.' I looked directly at him. 'You know their families, just like you know mine.'

The guy behind me threw his hands up in the air. 'We can't trust no kids.'

'These kids you can trust,' I said.

King Benny brushed aside a fresh stream of cigar smoke, pushed his chair back and stood.

'Get your friends,' he said, then turned and walked toward the rear of the room. 'And Tony,' King Benny continued, without looking back, his shoulders straight, his walk slow, his damaged right leg sliding across the floor.

'Yeah, King?' the man with the cigar in his mouth asked.

'Never smoke in here again,' King Benny said.

FIVE

Fat Mancho was the meanest man in Hell's Kitchen and we loved him for it. He owned a candy store sandwiched between two tenements in the middle of 50th Street. His wife, a dour woman with a thin scar across her right cheek, lived on the second floor of one building. His mistress, who looked to be older than his wife, lived on the third floor of the other. Each woman collected monthly social security checks based on false disability claims. Both checks were signed over to Fat Mancho.

In the back room of the candy store, Fat Mancho ran a numbers operation, keeping for himself a quarter off every dollar that was bet. The store was owned, on paper, by Fat Mancho's mother, who allegedly lived in Puerto Rico and was never seen by anyone in Hell's Kitchen. Fat Mancho, who collected monthly welfare checks, also owned a piece of an open-air parking lot on West 54th Street, near the theater district. Fat Mancho was only in his mid-thirties, but because of his large bulk and unshaven face looked at least ten years older. He cursed at anyone he saw, had trust in only a handful, and made it his business to know everything that went on in the streets around him. Fat Mancho lived the American dream, without ever having to do a day's work.

In Hell's Kitchen, the fast way was the preferred way.

We were standing in front of Fat Mancho's Candy Store waiting to turn on the johnny pump. I had the heavy wrench hidden halfway down the back of my pants; my T-shirt hung out, covering what the jeans could not. John was next to me, an empty can of Chock Full O'Nuts coffee in his hand, both ends cut out. Behind us, two Puerto Rican rummies were giving Fat Mancho heat over the price of a can of Colt .45 Malt Liquor.

While it could safely be said that Fat Mancho hated most everyone he met, for some reason he tolerated us. To him, we were harmless street rats, out for nothing more than a good time. He liked to joke with us, poke fun at everything we did and insult us whenever he felt the urge. We had known him all our lives and felt that he trusted us. We would never steal from him or try to deceive him in any way. We never asked for money and never caused trouble in front of his store. He liked our company, liked it when we gave back as good as we got from him, his eyes gleaming on the rare occasions we bested his taunts. We always felt that Fat Mancho had a good heart and that he liked kids. He just never wanted anybody to know that.

'What is that shit, anyway?' John wanted to know, pointing to the Colt .45s.

'Beer mixed with piss,' Tommy told him, one foot resting on the fire hydrant in front of the store.

'Then the drunks are right,' John said. 'Mancho *is* chargin' them too much.'

'When you gonna open up the pump?' Tommy asked.

'Cops are due for one more pass around,' Michael said, standing behind him. 'After that.'

'Hey, Mancho,' John yelled into the back of the store.

'What?' the Fat Man said.

'Can I use your bathroom?' John asked.

'Fuck you, punk,' Fat Mancho said, laughing. This was his idea of major fun. 'Wet your pants.'

'That a no?' John asked me.

'I think so,' I shrugged.

'Hey, Mancho,' Tommy said. 'Give the guy a break. He's really got to go.'

'Blow me,' Fat Mancho said, having a great time.

'That's it,' Tommy said. 'We're never gonna buy from your store again.'

'Kill yourself,' Fat Mancho said.

'C'mon,' I said to John. 'You can go at my place. I gotta pick something up anyway.'

'You sure?'

'It's either there or the back of Fat Mancho's car,' I said.

'Where's he parked?' John said.

Apartment doors in Hell's Kitchen were never locked during the day and ours was no exception. John and I took the two flights at full throttle, chasing Mrs. Aletti's black alley cat up the stairs ahead of us. We scooted past the large potted plant outside Mrs. Blake's and rushed to my door. I turned the handle and walked into the kitchen, John right behind me. The bathroom was on the left, next to the kitchen table, a Padre Pio calendar tacked to the wooden door which, for reasons known only to the previous tenant, locked from the outside. I could hear my mother whistling an Italian pop song from one of the back rooms. A fresh pot of espresso was on the stove and two cups and a sugar bowl were on the table.

'Didn't think I was gonna make it,' John said, reaching for the bathroom door.

'Hurry,' I said. 'Before you pee on the floor.'

The door swung open and both John and I stood as still as ice sculptures.

There, on the bowl, in full white habit, sat Sister Carolyn Saunders, my second grade teacher and one of my mother's best friends. She stared back, as motionless as we were.

She had a wad of toilet paper bunched up in one hand.

'Holy shit!' John said.

'Oh my God!' said Sister Carolyn.

We were back on the street in seconds, John nearly tripping down the final steps in his rush to get out of the building. Michael and Tommy were pitching pennies against a brick wall.

'That was quick,' Michael said. 'What'd you do, start in the hallway?'

'I'm dead,' I said. 'Dead and buried.'

Tommy looked confused. 'Because John took a piss in your house?'

'We saw a nun.' John was bent over, hands to knees, trying to catch his breath.

'Where?' Michael asked. 'In the hall?'

'On the bowl!' John said. 'She was sittin' on Shakes' toilet! Takin' a piss!'

'No shit,' Tommy said. 'You never think of nuns doin' stuff like that.'

'Which nun?' Michael asked.

'Sister Carolyn,' I said, still shaking from the memory.

'Good choice,' Tommy said. 'She's really cute.'

'Did you see her snatch?' Michael asked.

'A nun's snatch!' John said. 'We're gonna burn like twigs for this, Shakes!'

'Relax,' Michael said. 'Nothin's gonna happen.'

'What makes you so sure?' I asked.

'She's a nun, right? So she's not gonna tell. If people find out, it's more trouble for her than it is for you.'

'Maybe,' John wailed. 'But we still shouldn't've seen what we saw.'

'Are you kidding me?' Tommy said. 'It don't get better than nun snatch.'

'I only saw skin,' John said. 'I swear it. White clothes and white skin. Nothin' else.'

'She say anything?' Tommy asked.

'Ask her yourself,' Michael said, looking over John's shoulder. 'She's coming this way.'

'My heart just stopped,' John said, his face pale, his voice cracking.

'She's coming for us,' I said, turning my head in Sister Carolyn's direction, watching her walk down the steps of my apartment building, check for traffic and make her way to where we were standing.

'What the fuck's that nun want?' Fat Mancho said, slurping a Yoo-Hoo and scratching at his three-day growth.

'Stay quiet, Fat Man,' Michael said.

'Eat my pole,' Fat Mancho said, walking back behind the bodega counter.

'Hello, boys,' Sister Carolyn said, her manner calm, her voice soft.

She was young, her face clear and unlined. She was Boston big-city bred and had spent three years in Latin America working with the poor before a transfer brought her to Sacred Heart. Sister Carolyn was popular with her students and respected by their parents and, unlike some of the other nuns of the parish, seemed at ease among the people of Hell's Kitchen. Though she spoke no Italian and my mother hardly a word of English, they had formed a solid friendship, with Sister Carolyn visiting her an average of three times a week. She knew the type of marriage my mother was in and was always quick to check in on her after my father had administered yet another beating.

'Hey, Sister,' Michael said casually. 'What's goin' on?'

Sister Carolyn smiled and put one hand on top of John's shoulder. Nothing but fear was keeping John in his place.

'The bathroom's free now if you still need to use it,' she said to him softly.

'Thank you,' John mumbled.

'We're very sorry,' I said.

'I know,' she said. 'Forget it happened. I already have.'

'Thank you, Sister,' I said.

'I'll see all you boys in church,' she said, turning to leave.

'Bet on it,' Tommy said.

'What a peach,' John said, watching her as she walked up the street back to the Convent on 51st, her long white skirt swaying at her feet.

61

'And not a bad lookin' ass, either,' Michael said, winking at me.

'Fuck do any o' you know about ass,' Fat Mancho said from behind his counter.

'I'm gonna go pee,' John said, running back across the street. 'Can't hold it in anymore.'

'Watch now,' Tommy said to me. 'This time he walks in on your mother coppin' a squat.'

'That happens,' Michael said. 'He might as well just throw himself out a window.'

'He should throw himself out a window anyway,' Fat Mancho said. 'Useless fuck.'

'Go wash your mouth out with shit, Fat Man,' Tommy said.

'Set yourself on fire,' Fat Mancho said. 'All of you. Burn till you die.'

We all looked over at Fat Mancho and laughed, walking away from his store, toward the fire hydrant and a dose of wet relief from the heat of the day.

SIX

Father Robert Carillo was a longshoreman's son who was as comfortable sitting on a bar stool in a back alley saloon as he was standing at the altar during high mass. Raised in Hell's Kitchen, he toyed with a life of petty crime before finding his religious calling. Carillo left for a midwestern seminary three weeks before his sixteenth birthday. When he returned ten years later, he asked to be assigned to the Sacred Heart parish.

As far as we were concerned, he wasn't like a priest at all. He would spring for pizza after an afternoon pick-up game or twist a few neighborhood arms and raise money for new sports equipment for the gym. He was a friend. A friend who just happened to be a priest.

Like us, Father Bobby had an extensive comic book and baseball card collection, was an avid boxing fan and favored James Cagney over any other actor. He had a small office near the back of the church, lined with books and old blues albums. At its center was a huge framed picture of Jack London standing on a snowbank. If I was ever tempted to steal something from Father Bobby's office, it was that picture.

Despite the criminal bent of the neighborhood, the church exerted considerable influence and its leaders were visible members of the community. Priests openly recruited boys for the priesthood, presenting the clerical life as a way out of Hell's Kitchen. Nuns often took girls aside to talk to them in frank terms about sex and violence.

The priests, nuns and brothers of the neighborhood knew they served a violent clientele and they were there to tend to our physical and psychological wounds. They listened to battered wives who came to them for solace and gave words of comfort to frightened children. They helped when and where they could, careful not to stray outside the established framework of the neighborhood and always aware that there were a number of situations over which they held no control.

The clergy knew the rules of Hell's Kitchen. They knew some people had to break the law in order to feed their families. They knew the clothes many of us wore were bootlegged and the meat most of us ate came from stolen trucks. And they knew not to butt heads with someone like King Benny. But in the ways they could, they helped us. If nothing else, they offered a quiet room, some hot coffee and a place to talk when you needed it. Few people in the neighborhood would have asked more from any religion.

Father Bobby cared for us in a significant way and as much as we were capable of loving an outsider, we loved him for that care.

He knew the problems my mother and father were having, of the beatings she was handed and the debts he incurred. He tried to balance that by talking to me about books and baseball and verbally guiding me away from the fast money and easy times offered by King Benny and his crew.

He understood Michael's instinctive resistance to any outsider, even one from the neighborhood. He saw in Michael a boy who was given very little reason to trust. He sensed the loneliness behind his tough talk and the fear hidden by his swagger. Father Bobby knew that Michael was a boy who merely longed for a father who did more than lash out at his only son. He gave Michael distance, leaving a book he would like at his desk rather than handing it to him after school. He fed his streak of independence instead of fighting it.

He joked with John, keying in on a sense of humor built around insults and fast comebacks. He traded comic books with him, giving up valued *Flash* editions for mediocre *Fantastic Four* exploits, ignoring the sucker snickers after the deals were completed. On John's tenth birthday, he gave him a Classics Illustrated edition of *The Count of Monte Cristo*, a gift that moved John to tears.

He encouraged John's quiet desires to be an artist, sneaking him an endless supply of pencils and paper. In return, John would give Father Bobby original illustrations from a comic book series he was working on. John was also his favorite altar boy and Father Bobby made it a point to work as many masses with him as possible, even if it meant pulling him out of an early class.

'John would have made a good priest,' Father Bobby told me years later. 'He was filled with goodness. He cared about people. But he had a knack, like all you boys did, of being in the wrong place at the worst possible time. A lot of people have that knack and seem to survive. John couldn't.'

But of all of us, Father Bobby was closest to Tommy.

Butter never adjusted to having a father away in prison and, while he never talked about it, we knew it gnawed at his otherwise happy nature. Father Bobby tried to fill the paternal void, playing one-on-one basketball with him on spring evenings, taking him to James Bond movies on winter nights, helping him manage the pigeon coop Tommy kept on the roof of his building. He made sure Tommy was never alone on Father's Day.

Father Bobby had the soul of a priest, but the instincts of a first grade detective. He was a vigilant neighborhood presence, the first to take our class on outings and the first to question our outside involvements. He knew my friends and I did work for King Benny and was not pleased by that fact. But he understood the need for table money. In his time, Father Bobby had helped augment his own family's income by running errands for 'Lucky' Jack and the Anastasia family.

He wasn't worried about the pocket money. He worried about the next step. The one where they ask you to pick up a gun. He didn't want that to happen to us. He wanted to get to the damage before it got started. Before we saw too many things we shouldn't be seeing. Unfortunately, there were things even Father Bobby couldn't prevent.

The school auditorium was filled to overflow with balloons, poker tables topped with pitchers of beer and bowls of pretzels. Paper banners wishing the bride and groom luck lined the walls. A bald disc jockey in a wrinkled tux stood on a small stage, focused on a large stereo, four speakers and three piles of records.

It was a neighborhood wedding reception, open to all.

The bride, a tall, dark-haired girl from 52nd Street, was five months pregnant and spent most of her time locked inside a bathroom off the main stairwell. The groom, a Mobil mechanic with bad teeth and a black beard, drank boilermakers and munched peanuts from a paper bag, well aware of the talk that said the child his wife carried belonged to someone else.

Outside, the night was rainy. Inside, large corner fans did nothing to still the heat.

'You know either one of 'em?' Tommy asked, chafing at the starched collar and tight tie around his neck.

'The guy,' I said, drinking from a bottle of Pepsi. 'You know him too. From the gas station. Lets us drink from his water hose.'

'You're not used to seeing him without grease on his face,' Michael said, filling the pockets of his blue blazer with salt pretzels.

'You think it's his kid?' Tommy asked.

'Could be anybody's kid,' Michael said. 'She's not exactly shy.'

'Why's he marrying her?' I said. 'I mean, if *you* know all about her, how come he doesn't?'

'Maybe it *is* his kid,' Tommy said. 'Maybe she told him it was. You don't know.'

'That's right, Tommy,' Carol Martinez said. 'You *don't* know.'

Carol Martinez, twelve, was as much our friend as she was Michael's steady. Carol was a Hell's Kitchen half-breed. She inherited her temper and dark good looks from her Puerto Rican father, while her sarcastic wit and sharp tongue came courtesy of a strong-willed Irish mother who died in childbirth. Carol read books, worked after school in a bakery and, by and large, stayed to herself.

She ignored the pleas of the girl gangs to join their ranks, never carried a weapon, loved Westerns as well as sappy love stories and went to church only when the nuns forced her to go. Except for her father, Carol wasn't close to any members of her family and always appeared saddest around the holidays. The mothers of the neighborhood were fond of her, the fathers looked out for her and the boys kept their distance.

Except for us. She was always comfortable in our company. She stood up to Michael's quiet authority, was conscious of my youth and Tommy's sensitivity and fretted like a nurse over John's various illnesses. John had asthma and was quick to panic when caught in closed quarters or in any place he felt at a disadvantage, such as swimming far from shore. He also had a digestive defect and could not eat dairy products. He would get severe headaches, strong enough at times to make him drowsy. While John never complained about his health problems, including his minor heart condition, we were very much aware of them and considered them whenever we planned a prank or an outing.

That night she was wearing a blue ruffled dress with a small white flower pinned at the waist. She had on ankle socks and her Buster Browns were shiny and new. Her hair was in a pony tail.

'Everybody's here,' John said when he saw her.

'I'm a friend of Janet's,' Carol said.

67

'Who's Janet?' John said.

'The bride, asswipe,' Michael said, and led Carol by the arm off to dance.

The three men came in just as the bride and groom started slicing the three-tiered wedding cake. They stood off to the side, their backs to the front door, their hands nursing long-necked bottles of Budweiser: one of them had a lit cigarette hanging from the corner of his mouth.

We were standing in the shadows next to the disc jockey, Michael and Carol holding hands, Tommy and John sneaking beers. I held a Sam Cooke 45, 'Twistin' the Night Away', which was next on the play list.

'You know 'em?' Michael asked, putting his arm around Carol's shoulders.

'The one with the cigarette,' I said. 'I've seen him in King Benny's place a few times.'

'What's he do for him?'

'He always passed himself off as a shooter,' I said. 'I don't know. Could be nothing more than talk.'

'Why's he here?' Tommy asked.

'Maybe he likes weddings,' John said.

The three men walked toward the center of the room, their eyes on the groom, who was eating cake and sipping champagne from the back of his wife's spike-heeled shoe. They stopped directly across the table from the couple and rested their beers on a stack of paper plates.

'What do you want?' the groom asked, wiping his lips with the back of his hand.

'We come to offer our best,' the man in the middle said. 'To you and to the girl.'

'You just done that,' the groom said. 'Now maybe you should leave.'

'No cake?' the man in the middle said.

The crowd around the table had grown silent.

'C'mon, guys,' a middle-aged man said, his speech slurred, the front of his white shirt wet from beer. 'A wedding's no place for problems.'

The man stared him back into silence.

'Maybe your friend's right,' the man said. 'Maybe a wedding's no place for what we have to do. Let's take it outside.'

'I don't wanna go outside,' the groom said.

'You got the money?'

'No,' the groom said. 'I ain't got that kind of money. I told you that already. It's gonna take a while.'

'If you don't have the money,' the man said, nodding toward the bride, 'you know the deal.'

She had not moved since the men approached, paper plate full of cake in one hand, empty champagne glass in the other, heavily-made up face flushed red.

'I ain't gonna give her up,' the groom said in a firm voice. 'I ain't ever gonna give her up.'

The man in the middle was quiet for a moment. Then he nodded and said, 'Enjoy the rest of your night.'

The three men turned away from the bride and groom and disappeared into the crowd, making their way toward the back door and the dark street.

We sat braced against the thin bars of the first floor fire escape, staring at the alley below. Four garbage cans and an empty refrigerator carton stood against one wall; the shadows of a forty-watt bulb filtered across the auditorium's back door. The rain had picked up, a steady Hudson River breeze blowing newly laundered sheets across the dirt and empty cans of the alley.

Michael had positioned us there. He was positive something was going to happen and he'd picked the most strategic place to observe the action.

We watched as the bride and groom stood in the narrow doorway, arms wrapped around each other, both drunk, kissing and hugging. The harsh light from the auditorium forced us to move back toward the window ledge.

The groom took his wife by the hand and stepped into

69

the alley, moving toward 51st Street, holding a half-empty bottle of Piels in his free hand. They stopped to wave at a handful of friends crowding across a doorway, the men drunk, the women shivering in the face of the rain.

'Don't leave any beer behind,' the groom shouted. 'It's paid for.'

'Count on that,' one of the drunks shouted back.

'Goodbye,' the bride said, still waving. 'Thank you for everything.'

'Let's go,' the groom now said to his new wife. 'It's our wedding night.' With that, a grin stretched across his face.

The first bullet came out of the darkness and hit the groom just above his brown belt buckle, sinking him to his knees, a stunned look on his face. The bride gave out a loud scream, hands held across her chest, eyes wide, her husband bleeding just inches away.

The group by the door stood motionless, frozen.

The second shot, coming from the rear of the alley, hit the groom in the throat, dropping him face first onto the pavement.

'Help!' the bride screamed. 'Jesus, God, please help! He's gonna die! Please help, *please*!'

No one moved. No one spoke. The faces in the doorway had inched deeper into the shadows, more concerned with avoiding the shooter's scope than with rushing to the side of a fallen friend.

Sirens blared in the distance.

The bride was on her knees, blood staining the front of her gown, crying over the body of her dying husband. A priest ran into the alley, toward the couple. An elderly woman came out of the auditorium holding a large white towel packed with ice, water flowing down the sides of her dress. Two young men, sobered by the shooting, moved out of the doorway to stare down at the puddles of blood.

'Let's get outta here,' John said quietly.

'So much for getting married,' I said, just as quietly.

Michael, Tommy and Carol said nothing. But I knew what they were thinking. It was what we were all thinking. The street had won. The street would always win.

Fall 1965

SEVEN

My friends and I were united in trust.

There was never a question about our loyalty. We fed off each other, talked our way into and out of problems and served as buffers against the violence we encountered daily. Our friendship was a tactic of survival.

We each wanted a better life, but were unsure how to get it. We knew enough, though, to anchor our hopes in simple goals. In our idle moments, we never imagined running large companies or finding cures for diseases or holding elected office. Those dreams belonged to other places, other boys.

Our fantasies were shaped by the books we read and reread and the movies we watched over and over until even the dullest dialogue was committed to memory. Stories of romance and adventure, of great escapes and greater tastes of freedom. Stories that brought victory and cheers to the poor, allowing them to bask in the afterglow of revenge.

We never needed to leave the cocoon of Hell's Kitchen to glimpse those dreams.

We lived inside every book we read, every movie we saw. We were Cagney in *Angels With Dirty Faces* and Gable in *The Call of the Wild*. We were *Ivanhoe* on our own city streets and the Knights of the Round Table in our clubhouse.

It was during those uninhibited moments of pretend play that we were allowed the luxury of childhood. Faced by outsiders, we had to be tough, acting older than our years. In our homes we had to be wary, never knowing when the next violent moment would come. But when we were alone we could be who we really were – kids.

We never pictured ourselves, as adults, living far from Hell's Kitchen. Our lives were plotted out at birth. We would try to finish high school, fall in love with a local girl, get a working man's job and move into a railroad apartment at a reasonable rent. We didn't see it as confining, but rather as a dramatic step in the right direction. Our fathers were men with sinful pasts and criminal records. We would not be.

I loved my parents. I respected King Benny. But my friends meant more to me than any adult. They were my lifeblood and my strength. Our simple dreams nourished by a common soil.

We thought we would know each other forever.

'It's simple,' Michael said.

'You always say it's simple,' Tommy said. 'Then we get there and it ain't so simple.'

'It's a new store,' Michael explained. 'Nobody knows us. We walk in, take what we need and walk out.'

'What do they have?' John demanded to know.

'At least fifty different titles,' Michael said. 'Flash, Green Lantern, Aquaman, you name it. Just waiting for us.'

'How many work the store?' I asked.

'Two, usually,' Michael said. 'Never more than three.'

'When?'

'Afternoon's the best time.'

'You sure?'

'Follow the plan,' Michael said, looking at us. 'It'll work if we just follow the plan.'

My friends and I were thieves who stole more for fun than profit. We took what we felt we needed but could not afford to buy. We never went to our parents for money, never borrowed from anyone and never walked into a situation armed.

We hit candy stores for their comic books, toy stores

76

for games, supermarkets for gum. And we were good at it. The few times we were caught, we either talked, fought or cried our way out of trouble. We knew that *nobody* was going to send a kid to jail for rounding out a Classics Illustrated collection.

We kept our escapades from our parents. Though most of them were involved in small-time scams of their own, none would have been pleased to know their children were chasing fast on their heels. Still, *Thou Shalt Not Steal* carried little weight in Hell's Kitchen. The neighborhood was a training ground for young criminals and had been throughout most of its history.

Time spent in the company of made men, their allegiance sworn to a life of crime, led to a desire to flex our own criminal muscles. Where once we were content to walk out of a store with a handful of Green Hornets, we now felt the need to empty entire racks, from Sgt. Rock to The Fantastic Four.

In the neighborhood, the gaze on us intensified with each small job we pulled. The old-line hoods would glance our way, an acknowledged nod toward a new generation, as active in their recruiting methods as any Ivy League head hunter. We were the promise, the raw rookies who could one day hold the neighborhood together, score the deals and keep the illegal traffic moving.

There were many roads a young man could travel on the streets of Hell's Kitchen. None promised great rewards. The majority turned into dead ends.

Career criminal was simply one such option.

Michael was the first one in the candy store.

I followed soon after. John and Tommy – Butter and the Count – waited outside, close to the front door. The entry was curved and narrow, a hardwood candy stand running down the length of the counter. Two men worked the place, both middle-aged, both smoking. A small electric fan, pennant strips attached to the rim, whirred in a side corner.

Michael walked to the comic book racks, reached for a Batman and handed it to me.

'Read that one yet?' he asked.

'No,' I said, looking over my shoulder at the two men cutting open candy cartons. 'It's new.'

'Want it?'

'Not today,' I said.

'What is it, Shakes?' Michael asked, racking back the Batman.

'Let's not do this,' I said, lowering my voice to a whisper.

'Why not?'

'It just doesn't feel right.'

'We're here *now*,' Michael said.

'And we can leave *now*.'

'Don't crap on me now, Shakes. We can do this. You and me.'

'It feels different this time,' I said.

'It feels different every time,' Michael said.

'You sure?' I asked.

'I'm sure,' Michael said.

I hesitated, then I nodded my compliance. 'Make your move,' I said.

Michael pulled three comic books from a top rack, well aware that the two men were staring in his direction. I took four Sgt. Rock comics from a lower shelf, put them under my right arm and followed Michael further down the aisle. Behind me, one of the men lifted the counter top and began to walk toward us. He was tall and thin, thick dark hair sitting in clumps on the sides of his head and a large, circular scar resting below his left eye. He had a small iron pipe in one hand.

Tommy and John came into the store, pushing and shoving as per the plan. The man behind the counter stared at them between puffs on a fresh cigarette.

'No trouble. No trouble in here,' he said, his voice thick with a Middle Eastern accent, his cigarette filter clenched between stained teeth.

'I don't want trouble,' John said to him, pushing Tommy against the newspaper trays. 'I want candy.'

'That's the last time you push me,' Tommy said, picking up a paper and throwing it at John.

'Stop it!' the man behind the counter shouted. 'Outside. You like a fight? Go outside.'

The thin man facing us turned and walked away, moving toward Tommy and John and the front of the store. He walked slowly, slapping the base of the pipe against the palm of his hand.

'Get out, punks,' the man said, giving John's shoulder a shove. 'Get out!'

John turned and faced the store owner. Angrily, he put both hands on the man's shirt front and pushed him back.

'Don't touch me,' he said, watching the man tumble backwards, the pipe falling on top of discarded editions of the *New York Post*.

Things immediately got out of hand. The man jumped to his feet, his face red with embarrassment, and rushed John, catching him around the chest and dropping him to the ground. He straddled John's upper body and gripped his face with one hand, while the other formed a fist.

Tommy ran up from behind. He threw one arm around the man's throat and shoved a knee into the base of his spine.

Michael and I made our way to the front of the store, the sides of our jackets filled with dozens of comic books. We kept our eyes on the man behind the counter, watching for him to make a move. He never looked our way, frozen by the sight of his partner in a scrap with two boys.

John now freed one arm and landed two short blows to the man's stomach. Tommy scored with a steady torrent on the side of the man's head, causing his ear and temple to flush. The man fell to one side, tumbling off John, the bulk of his weight resting against the candy counter. One arm was dangling, free, inches from the iron pipe he had moments earlier dropped.

'We ain't *ever* comin' here again,' John said, back on his feet, shouting at the man behind the counter. He reached over, picked up a copy of the *Daily News* and threw it down on the head of his fallen enemy.

Michael and I moved past Tommy, John and the two men and walked out of the store, our stolen gains snug in their place.

John turned and followed us out. That left Tommy alone with the two men.

And before any of us knew what was happening, the man on the ground grabbed the iron pipe and came to his feet swinging, mouth twisted in rage.

'I kill you, punk!' he shouted. 'I kill you!'

The blows landed in rapid succession.

The first blow glanced off Tommy's shoulder. The second found a spot above his right eye, drawing blood. The third landed on the hard edge of Tommy's left wrist, the bone immediately giving way.

Tommy, his knees buckling from the pain, inched his way out of the store. A fourth shot caught him on the back of the neck, sending him crashing against the door and out to the street. Tommy fell to the cement, his eyes lifeless, his body limp.

John was the first to reach his side. 'I think he killed him,' he said, staring up at me and Michael.

'Then he's gonna have to kill us too,' Michael said.

'I no fight you,' the man with the pipe said, his anger receding, his arms by his side. 'No problem with you. No problem!'

'Yeah you do,' Michael said as he nudged his way forward. 'Your *only* problem is with me.'

Michael opened the front of his blue denim jacket and reached a hand into one of the inside sleeves. He pulled out four folded, stolen comic books and dropped them to the ground. Then he yanked four more books from his other sleeve. Then he reached both hands into the back of his jeans and took out three more, dropping them all at his feet. The man moved toward him, stepping over Tommy's body.

'I kill all of you,' he said with teeth clenched.

'You're gonna have to,' Michael said, balling his hands into fists, an arm's length from the pipe.

'This is bad,' I remember saying. 'This is so bad.'

The man left his feet and swung the pipe, missing Michael's head by inches.

My eye caught John, his arms around Tommy, sweat streaking down his forehead, concern etched on his face. As a crowd collected, I looked at the faces surrounding me, the men focused on the action, most of them smoking, a few offering Michael free advice.

No one ever broke up a fight on the streets of Hell's Kitchen, no matter who the combatants were, regardless of the weapons used. A street fight was a respected ritual and no one dared step in.

Fights took place for any number of reasons, from unpaid debts to three-way love affairs gone sour, but the overwhelming majority occurred because they were the fastest and easiest way to settle a dispute.

Great street fights were talked about in the same nostalgic manner in which old boxers were recalled. The more street fights somebody had, the higher the esteem in which he was held.

Short of murder, nothing proved manhood more.

Michael swung a sharp right and missed, grunting loudly as the punch sailed over the man's head. A fast follow-up left also failed. Large sweat circles formed on the back of his jacket and under both arms. As the crowd drew closer, the man moved to narrow the gap between the two. He took three steps forward, flashing the pipe, holding it low, squinting against the overhead sun, staring at Michael's face.

He swung the pipe, short, fast and hard, landing one across Michael's hip. A second blow caught him on the side of the face. Another quick swing, this one grazing

Michael's jaw, sent him backwards, hands reaching for the ground, his head just missing the side of a fire hydrant.

The man walked to where Michael lay and raised the pipe over his head.

'You no steal from me again,' he said in a voice meant for everyone to hear. '*Nobody* steal from me again.'

Michael's arms hugged the hydrant, his eyes cloudy, thin streams of blood streaking down his lips. John stood next to Tommy, his face emptied of all emotion other than fear. Butter still had his back to the candy store wall. There were tears running down his face.

I couldn't move. I stood there, shivering in the afternoon sun, my legs heavy and numb, my stomach queasy, looking down at the beaten body of my best friend.

The crowd sensed a finish and closed the circle even tighter, breaking off any chance of a quick escape.

The street wanted someone to die.

'Drop the pipe!'

The voice came out of the shadows.

It was confident and webbed with the threat of violence. The man with the iron pipe took two steps back when he heard it, panic invading his macho veneer. I turned my head and saw King Benny standing there, a cup of espresso in one hand, a copy of *Il Progresso* in the other. He was flanked by two men, dressed in black, arms at their sides.

'Didn't hear me?' King Benny asked.

'Yes,' the man said, his voice breaking. 'I hear.'

'Then do it,' King Benny said.

The pipe fell to the ground, loud enough to echo.

'You wanna finish this?' King Benny asked, looking down at Michael.

'Yeah,' Michael said, pulling himself up against the side of the hydrant. 'I do.'

'Then hurry,' King Benny said. 'It's gettin' late.'

Michael was up on shaky legs. He turned and faced his opponent.

'Fight me,' Michael said to him.

'No,' the man said, his eyes on King Benny.

Michael charged the man, both of them falling to the ground, arms and legs in full swing. He landed two hard punches against the side of the man's head and then threw a crushing elbow to the base of his nose.

The man swung once and missed, a steamless punch thrown more in frustration than anger. Michael answered with two more closed blows to the face, the second drawing blood. The men in the crowd whistled and applauded each landed punch.

'Kid's got him now,' a fat man in an oil-stained work shirt said. 'Couple more, the bastard'll be done for good.'

'Too bad he ain't got a knife,' a short man lighting a pipe said. 'He could cut him for sure.'

Michael landed three more punches, all flush to the man's face. He jumped to his knees, slamming an ankle against the man's throat. Two more punches to the neck and a quick kick to the chest brought it to an end.

Michael stepped over the man, ignored the pleas of the crowd to finish his foe, and walked to the comic books strewn on the ground. He bent down, picked each up and went back to where he had left the man. He stood over him, staring for a minute and then dropped the comic books across his face and chest.

'You can keep your comic books,' Michael said. 'I don't want 'em anymore.'

EIGHT

As we grew older, the violence around us intensified. The moment a boy's age hit double digits, he was no longer a mere nuisance to the older neighborhood kids; he was a potential threat. The most minor infractions could easily escalate into major street brawls.

We had now also reached an age where we were targeted by outsiders looking for quick scores.

Puerto Ricans coming down from San Juan Hill in upper Manhattan would jump a kid, lift his money and head back home. Blacks from Inwood, near the Heights, would cross the designated racial divide of Ninth Avenue. Traveling in packs of a half dozen or more, they would swarm, attack and leave before any retaliation could be mounted.

A number of the local street gangs attempted to recruit us, without success. The idea of being a gang member never held much appeal and neither did the idea that we had to kick back portions of earnings to the leader of the pack we joined.

We also weren't keen on the initiation process most gangs required: rubbing hot pieces of iron on your arm until all the skin came off; scarring you with strange, permanent tattoos; forcing you to pick a fight with the toughest guy from a rival gang, and *if* you beat him you were in. If you lost, you were a forgotten man. It wasn't for us. We stayed with who we trusted and we covered each other's backs. Just like in the western movies we admired.

The worst beating I ever got in Hell's Kitchen came not from my father or any other man or boy. It was at the hands of Janet Rivera, street leader of the Tornadoes.

Girl gangs had, throughout Hell's Kitchen history, been in many ways the most vicious. Unlike their male counterparts, the girls often attacked without warning or reason. They were also the more aggressive criminals, wantonly stalking passersby for street muggings and casing buildings for doorway robberies. They did not belong to any organized crime faction, but worked as independent operators, hired out for the best price.

In the sixties, these gangs could already trace their lineage back to the Lady Gophers, who terrorized the Manhattan waterfront at the turn of the century. The Lady Gophers had a special calling card: They left the amputated hands and fingers of their victims behind. A few years later, Sadie the Cat and her crew beat and mugged at will. Gallus Meg was a match for any man she came across, boasting till death of never having lost a fist fight. Hell Cat Maggie was said to have once beaten four of the toughest members of the Pug Uglies Gang into submission on a 10th Avenue street corner, then taken a fifth one home to her boarding house bed.

A number of the female gang leaders who lived long enough to survive their street battles opened saloons in their later years. Not surprisingly, many served as bouncers in their own watering holes.

'They *demanded* respect, those women,' one of King Benny's back room men once told me. 'They didn't take any shit, they were always ready for a fight. Knew how to run a business, too, turned a profit on most things they touched. They were tough and mean and everything they did, they made sure they did better than a man. They fought dirty, drank till they were drunk and slept with

85

whoever they wanted. For a time there, they ran the Kitchen and they ran it well.'

The prevailing image of the mid-twentieth-century Hell's Kitchen street gang comes from the musical *West Side Story*. While Leonard Bernstein's masterpiece contains traces of truth – the racial tensions, a sense of place, the fear of falling in love on forbidden turf, the inability to move beyond social labels – such elements weren't enough for neighborhood cynics.

West Side Story was the most hated film in Hell's Kitchen.

'That movie sucked,' Fat Mancho complained. 'Guys dancin' around like jerks, girls hangin' on to their boys for life, cops dumb as flies. All bullshit. Made the gangs look soft. Made *everybody* look soft. In real life, soft didn't last long. They *buried* soft in Hell's Kitchen.'

Janet Rivera stood in front of the monument at the entrance to De Witt Clinton Park and popped the lid of a can of Reingold. She was with three friends, all members of her street gang. One of them, Vickie Gonzalez, had a straight razor in the back pocket of her Levis. Janet swigged the beer and watched me walk into the park with John, both of us bouncing spauldeens against the ground.

'Hey!' she yelled. 'Get your asses over where I can see them.'

'Now what,' John muttered.

'They're just breakin' balls,' I said. 'We got no beef with them.'

'We got no time for this,' John said.

'Let's see what they want,' I said.

'C'mon,' Rivera said. 'Don't be draggin' ass on me.'

'She is one ugly girl,' John said as we made our way toward the monument. 'Her family must take ugly pills.'

'You pricks walk through the park like you own it,' Rivera said, pointing at us with the hand holding the beer. 'Where the fuck you think you're goin'?'

'We're gonna play some ball,' I said. 'I don't think there's a problem with that.'

'You're wrong,' Rivera said. 'There is a major fuckin' problem.'

'Fill us in, gorgeous,' John said.

We knew what the problem was. Two weeks earlier, Michael, rushing to Tommy's defense, got into a street brawl with a Puerto Rican kid named Hector from the West 60s. He won the fight and forced Hector to walk out of Hell's Kitchen buck naked. Unfortunately, Hector was Janet Rivera's cousin, and she was looking to us for a payback.

Vickie Gonzalez put a hand in the pocket that held the razor. The other two girls wrapped sets of brass knuckles around their hands. Janet Rivera tossed her beer can into a clump of grass behind her. None of them looked happy. What *would* make them happy would be to leave me and John the way Michael had left Rivera's cousin – beaten, bruised and naked. Neither of us was eager to see that happen and it left us with only one choice, one that any tough, street-savvy, Hell's Kitchen hard-case would have made. We decided to run.

'Through the fence!' I yelled to John as we started. 'Head for the candy store.'

'They catch us, we're dead,' John said. 'That ugly one wants to kill me. I can tell.'

'They're *all* ugly,' I said, looking over my shoulder. 'And what's worse is they're *all* fast.'

We ran through a circular hole in a fence on the 11th Avenue side of the fields, across the red clay pitcher's mound and out the other side, past the Parkies' way station and the sprinkler pool. We were crisscrossing around the black pool bars when I slipped on a sandhill and landed on my side against a cement edge.

John stopped when he saw me fall.

'Get up, Shakes,' he urged. 'They're right on us.'

'I can't,' I said.

'You better,' John said.

The pain in my side was intense, jolts sharp and sudden.

'You keep running,' I said. 'Go for Butter and Mikey. Get them here.'

'I can't leave you,' John said.

'You'll be back in five minutes,' I said a lot more bravely than I felt. 'What can they do to me in five minutes?'

I stayed on the ground, clutching my side, watching John run down the hills of De Witt Clinton Park.

It was not the fear of getting a beating that held me. It was the fear of catching that beating from a girl gang. As I lay there, watching Rivera and her crew close in, I imagined the taunts and ridicule that would come, from friends and strangers alike. A lot of boys in Hell's Kitchen took home cuts and bruises handed out by Rivera and her Tornadoes. Not one of them ever admitted to it, at least publicly, and I was not about to be the first.

Janet Rivera stood over me and smiled, exposing a thin row of cracked teeth. 'I knew a little fucker like you couldn't outrun us.'

'You didn't outrun me,' I said. 'I took a break and waited for you to catch up.'

Rivera walked over toward Gonzalez, putting one hand around her shoulder.

'I *hate* clowns,' she said. 'They're not funny, you know? They only *think* they're funny.'

'What they did to Hector, that ain't funny, neither,' Gonzalez said, brushing the heel of her sneaker against my leg. 'But I bet they laughed.'

'Gimme your belt,' Rivera said. 'We're gonna teach this clown to be serious.'

The park was empty, except for an old rummy sleeping under a pile of newspapers on a bench. My face and arms were glazed with sweat and my right leg twitched from tensions. One of my shoelaces had come undone and I couldn't breathe free of pain.

Gonzalez stood over me and opened her straight razor. She leaned down and grabbed the top of my white shirt and cut it in half, stopping just above my pants.

'This is for Hector,' Rivera said, swinging the belt above her shoulder.

'Hurt him,' Gonzalez said. 'Make him hurt.'

Rivera's lashes landed across my face and neck, the pain causing my eyes to well with tears. She then lowered the gate of her swing, my chest and stomach now taking the force of the blows. My chest was soon red, the sting as hard as anything I'd felt, a steady torrent of belt against flesh.

Rivera landed one last blow and stopped.

'You wanna piece?' she said to Gonzalez.

'He ain't man enough for me to whip,' Gonzalez said, looking at me with a smile.

'Thank you,' I mumbled.

The first rock landed next to Rivera's feet. The second hit her above the thigh. Gonzalez turned her head and caught one on the arm. The two girls who were holding me down let go and moved away.

'We're goin',' one of them said. 'No more of this.'

I looked past Gonzalez, at the fence behind the sprinklers and saw Michael and John climbing over. Tommy stood facing the fence, tossing rocks over the side.

Gonzalez looked down at me, her eyes filled with hate. She took a deep breath, bent closer to me and spit her bubble gum above my right eye. She took two steps back and let out two kicks to my groin, the hard rubber of her sneakers finding a mark both times.

'So long, fucker,' she said. 'Be seein' you again.'

When they got to me, Michael and John lifted me up, hands wrapped under my shoulders.

I was slow stepping my way out of the park, toward the bar on 52nd Street. The inside of my chest felt as seared as the outside. But more than anything, I was humiliated.

'I don't want anybody to know,' I said.

'Might be in the papers tomorrow,' John smirked. 'Not every day one of King Benny's boys gets his ass bopped by some girls.'

'It would've been better if they killed me,' I said.

'You're right,' Tommy said. 'Much easier to explain.'

'This only proves what we always knew,' Michael said.

'What?'

'You can't fight for shit.'

'I hear they make guys have sex with 'em,' John said. 'You know, force 'em.'

'Now I'm sorry we came along,' Michael said. 'You might have finally gotten laid.'

'I think I'm gonna faint,' I said.

'Ugly sex is better than no sex,' John said.

'Anybody asks, tell 'em a gang from Inwood came down and kicked my ass,' I said.

'Which gang?' Tommy asked.

'The Cougars,' I said. 'They're pretty tough.'

'How about the gang from the School for the Blind?' John said. 'You could say they bumped into you on the street. You had no choice. You hadda fight 'em.'

'There was eight of them and only one of you,' Tommy said. 'The deck was stacked.'

'And they had dogs too,' John said. 'You didn't have a chance.'

'All I know is the Count of Monte Cristo never got his ass kicked by a girl,' Michael said.

'He was lucky,' I sighed. 'He didn't know Janet Rivera.'

Summer 1966

NINE

King Benny shuffled the cards, large espresso cup to his left, drawn window blind shielding his face from the sun. I sat across from him, chest near the edge of a small round table, hands folded, 7-Up bottle at my side, waiting for the game to begin. I was eleven years old.

'Sure you wanna play me?' King Benny asked.

'Why not?'

'I cheat.'

'Me too,' I said.

'Good,' he said and opened the deal.

The game was sette bello, Italian black jack, and the stakes were low, a penny a win, nickel on a two-card hit. We were in the middle of King Benny's club, three empty tables around us, the door behind us locked. White dust particles, heavy enough to hold, curled their way up toward the hanging overhead lights. A jukebox played Sinatra and 'High Hopes'.

'Hungry?' King Benny asked, tossing me two cards.

'No,' I said. 'Thanks.'

'Sure?'

'I'm sure,' I said.

'What's it gonna be?' he said, nodding toward my cards.

'Give a hit.'

King Benny flipped a card from the top of the deck, his eyes on me.

'You're over,' he said. 'You're into me for a penny.'

'Double or nothing,' I told him.

'A sucker bet,' he said, dealing out a fresh set of cards and sipping from his coffee.

I lost the first ten hands we played, King Benny picking up the pennies and piling them next to his cup. He kept the deck of cards in his right hand, dealing with one finger, his eyes always on me, never on the table. He shuffled the cards every other deal and ignored the phone when it rang.

'You always end up with a six,' I said. 'How is that?'

'Lucky,' he said.

'Got any pretzels?' I asked.

'Behind the bar,' he said. 'Help yourself.'

'Want anything?'

'What time is it?' he asked.

'Quarter to five,' I said, looking at my Timex watch, a swag present he had given me.

'Too early,' he said.

King Benny never ate before seven and only slept for two hours a night. He always carried a thousand dollars in twenties and singles in his pants pocket, never wore a gun and was said to have a brother in jail, doing natural life on a double murder charge.

I sat back down, picking at a bag of salt pretzels. He sipped his coffee, shuffled the cards and leaned back in his chair.

'I hear you got trouble at home,' he said, putting the cup back by his side.

'It's nothing.'

'If it was nothing,' he said, 'I wouldn't have heard about it.'

'My father owes money,' I admitted.

'Who this time?'

'The Greek,' I said. 'He's six months late on the payments.'

'How much?'

'Three thousand,' I said. 'As of yesterday. Goes up every day.'

'Yeah,' King Benny said. 'It does.'

'The Greek sent a coupla guys over late last night,' I said. 'Scare him a little.'

'It work?'

'Scared or not,' I said, 'he doesn't have the money and can't get it from anybody else.'

'No,' King Benny said. 'He can't.'

'He's hiding out,' I said. 'Until it blows over or he makes a big score.'

'Guys like your father never make big scores,' King Benny said. 'They just keep guys like me in business.'

'Will they kill him?'

'No,' he said. 'He'll just wish they did.'

'I got sixty bucks put aside,' I told him. 'My mother can come up with another forty. That should be good for something.'

'Forget it,' King Benny said.

'I can't forget it,' I said. 'He's my father.'

King Benny shook his head. 'The loan's been squared.'

'Who squared it?'

'You did. This morning. The Greek picked up an envelope with three grand and a note from you. Him and your father are even.'

I didn't show any real emotion. That wasn't allowed. All I said was, 'I can't pay you back right away.'

'You don't have to pay me back at at all,' I was told.

'Why'd you do it?' I wanted to know. 'You never liked my father.'

'Still don't,' King Benny said. 'He lives or dies, don't mean a thing to me.'

I took a drink of the 7-Up.

'Thanks,' I said. 'Thanks a lot.'

'Always watch out for men like your father,' King Benny said. 'They go down bad streets. And they never go down alone.'

'He tries,' I said. 'He just gets caught up.'

'There are other ways,' he said. 'Better ways. You should walk away from the table knowing that.'

'He wants to make money,' I said. 'Same as everybody around here.'

'Looking for easy money,' King Benny said. 'Every one of them. And guess what?'

'What?'

'Ain't no such thing,' he said.

'Does my father know?' I asked. 'About the payment.'

'Not yet.'

'Can I tell him?'

'Soon as you see him,' he said.

The room was turning dark, the sun's shadows giving way to early evening. King Benny's coffee cup was empty and my soda was warm. The jukebox had abandoned Sinatra and settled now on 'Don't Be That Way' by Benny Goodman. In a corner, an old steam radiator sizzled, despite the outside heat.

'He's down in a basement apartment on 47th Street,' King Benny said. 'Near Ninth Avenue.'

'I know.'

'He's not alone,' he said.

'I know that too,' I said.

'You want some dinner before you go?' he asked.

'What's it gonna be?'

'Pasta and snails,' King Benny said.

'Maybe not,' I said.

'It's good for you,' King Benny said.

'I should go.'

'One thing,' King Benny said. 'Before you go.'

'What?'

'The business with the Greek,' King Benny said. 'It stays between you and me.'

'He's gonna ask where I got the money.'

'Lie,' King Benny said.

'Can't,' I said.

'He lies to *you*.' King Benny pushed his chair back and stood up, cup clasped in both hands. 'All the time.'

'That's different.'

96

'How?' Now King Benny walked to the bar, his face free of emotion.

'He's my father,' I said.

'Think he cares?'

'Doesn't matter,' I said. '*I* care.'

King Benny nodded and turned, walking behind the bar, his right leg dragging across the floor.

'See you tomorrow,' he said, his voice even.

'Only if I get to deal,' I said.

'We'll cut for it,' he said, washing his cup in the sink under the counter.

'You'll win the cut,' I said. 'You always do.'

'Can't trust a thief,' he said, drying off his hands. 'Or a liar.'

'Which are you?'

'Both,' King Benny said.

He folded a hand towel in half and laid it on the bar. Then he walked over to the small wooden door at the end of the hall, turned the knob and went into the kitchen, closing it softly behind him.

Winter 1966

TEN

The pizzeria was empty except for the four of us at a back table and Joey Retard at the counter, shaking black pepper on a hot slice. Mimi was working the ovens and the register, his white shirt and work pants stained red with sauce.

'I'm gettin' another slice,' I said, wiping my mouth with a napkin.

'Me too,' John said.

'Get me a soda,' Tommy said. 'Orange. Lots of ice.'

'You lose your legs in the war?' I said.

'I got no money, either,' Tommy said.

'Want anything?' I asked Michael.

'Half of Tommy's soda,' he said.

John and I walked to the counter and stood next to Joey Retard. Joey was fourteen, with an honest face and a ready smile. He was always well-dressed and was friendly with everyone in the neighborhood. He spoke slowly, stuttering his way through difficult phrases, his manner gentle, his eyes dark as olive pits.

Joey was adopted, taken out of a West Side orphanage by a childless Irish couple. He went to a special school on Ninth Avenue and earned pocket money washing cars for King Benny. He was shy around girls, loved pizza with extra cheese, cheap horror movies and sewer-to-sewer stickball. Every Halloween he walked the streets dressed as Stooge Villa from *Dick Tracy*.

'What's doin', Joe?' John asked him.

'Good,' Joey said. 'I'm good.'

'You want anything?' I asked. 'John's buyin'.'

'Where'd you hear that?' John said.

'No,' Joey said. 'Thanks.'

John ordered and I asked Joey how school was.

'I like it,' Joey said.

'Am I really payin' for this?' John asked me, watching Mimi take the pizza out of the oven.

'You got money?'

'I'll take the Fifth,' John said.

'I'll buy tomorrow,' I said, grabbing a paper plate with a slice.

'Swear,' John said, reaching a hand into his jean pocket and pulling out two crumpled bills.

'Swear,' I said, taking my pizza and soda back to the table.

'Grab the change for me,' John said, patting Joey on the shoulder, reaching for the second slice.

'Can I keep it?' Joey asked.

'Knock yourself out,' John said.

Joey was on his second slice when the burly man walked through the door.

He stood at the counter, hands in his pockets, ordered a large Coke and watched Joey dust his pizza with black pepper.

'That's not too smart,' the man said, taking a sip from his soda. 'It's gonna taste like shit.'

'I like pepper,' Joey said, shaking some more on the crust. 'I like pepper a lot.'

'There's enough on it,' the man said, reaching for the pepper shaker.

'No!' Joey said, pulling back, still holding the pepper in his hand. 'My pizza.'

'Lemme have the pepper, you fuckin' retard,' the man said, grabbing Joey's hand until the shaker came loose.

'My pizza!' Joey said, his voice breaking from the strain, his eyes blinking like shutters. 'My pizza!'

'There's your fuckin' pizza,' the man said, pointing to the counter. 'Nobody touched it.'

'I want pepper!' Joey said, his words coming in short bursts, his hands by his side. 'I want pepper!'

The burly man smiled.

He looked over at Mimi, frozen in place behind the counter, and winked. He unscrewed the top off the pepper shaker.

'You want pepper, retard?' the man said.

Joey stared at the burly man, his body quivering, his eyes filled with tears.

'Here,' the man said, pouring the bottle of pepper out over Joey's pizza. 'Here's your fuckin' pepper.'

Joey started to cry, full sobs rising from his chest, his hands slapping his sides.

'What's your problem now, retard?' the man asked.

Joey didn't answer. Tears ran down his cheeks and over his lips, snot ran out of his nose.

'Go on,' the burly man said. 'You fuckin' retards turn my stomach.'

Joey didn't move.

'Go,' the man said. 'Before I slap the shit outta ya' and really make you cry.'

Michael walked past Joey and stepped to the counter, next to the burly man. He reached for the salt shaker, loosened the top and poured the contents into the man's soda.

'You can leave now,' Michael said to him, stirring the drink with his finger. 'You and Joe are even.'

'A tough little punk,' the man said. 'Is that what I'm lookin' at?'

'A dick with lips,' Michael said. 'Is that what I'm lookin' at?'

Tommy put an arm around Joey and moved him from the counter. John stood behind the burly man, hands in his pockets. I was across from the burly man, arms folded, waiting for his move.

'Four tough little punks,' the burly man said. 'And a cryin' retard.'

'That's us,' Michael said.

The burly man lifted a hand and slapped Michael across the face. The blow left red finger marks on Michael's cheek and an echo loud enough to chill.

Michael stared at the man and smiled.

'The first shot should always be your best,' Michael said. 'And your best sucks.'

'I'll show you my best, punk,' the burly man said, moving off his feet and taking a full swing at Michael. 'Your fuckin' teeth are gonna be all over the floor.'

Michael ducked the punch, throwing his body against the burly man's stomach. Tommy and John jumped on the man from behind, pulling at his hair and neck. I grabbed the pizza slice with all the pepper on it and rubbed it into his eyes.

'Take it outside!' Mimi screamed.

John chewed on the man's ear, his bite hard enough to draw blood. Tommy started pounding at his kidneys. I took a red pepper shaker and rammed it against his face.

'My eyes!' the burly man said, trying to shake us off. 'My fuckin' eyes.'

Michael picked up a counter stool and started ramming it against the front of his legs. John had grabbed his thick hair and was knocking his head on the edge of the front door. I kept hitting him with the red pepper shaker until it broke above the bridge of his nose. Shards of glass mixed with blood down the front of his face.

The pain brought the man to his knees, one hand reaching for the counter.

'Never come in here again,' Michael said, kicking at his crumpled body. 'Hear me? *Never.*'

Mimi ran from behind the counter and grabbed Michael around the waist, pulling him away.

'You no wanna kill him,' he said.

'Don't be too sure,' Michael said.

*

Our lives were about protecting ourselves and our turf. The insulated circle that was life in Hell's Kitchen closed tighter as we grew older. Strangers, never welcome, were now viewed as outsiders bent on trouble. My friends and I could no longer afford to let others do the fighting.

It was our turn to step up, and we were led, as always, by Michael.

Outside events meant little. In a society changing radically by the hour, we focused on the constants in our own small, controlled space.

It was the sixties, and we watched the images scattered nightly across TV screens with skepticism, never trusting the players, always suspecting a scam. It was the way we were taught to look at the world. Life, we had been told, was about looking out for number one and number one didn't waste time outside the neighborhood.

On television, the young protesters we saw spoke about how they were going to change our lives and fix the world. But we knew they didn't care about people like us. While they shouted their slogans, my friends and I went to funeral services for the young men of Hell's Kitchen who came back from Vietnam in body bags. That war never touched those angry young faces we saw on TV, faces protected by money and upper-middle-class standing. They were on the outside yelling about a war they would never fight. To me and my friends, they were working the oldest con in the world and they worked it to perfection.

Civil rights had become the battle of the day, but on our streets, it was a meaningless issue. There, gangs of different ethnic backgrounds and skin colors still waged weekly skirmishes. A growing army of feminists marched across the country, demanding equality, yet our mothers still cooked and cared for men who abused them mentally and physically.

Students would be killed on the campus of Kent State University in Ohio. Martin Luther King, Jr. and Senator Robert F. Kennedy would be shot dead. Governor George Wallace would take one in the spine.

Whole sections of American cities were about to burn to the ground.

The summer of love was set to bloom.

Drugs would go beyond the junkie.

The country was on a fast-ticking timer, ready to explode.

For me and for my friends, these developments carried no weight. They might as well have occurred in another country, in another century. The mating call of a new generation, one whose foundation was to be built on peace, love and harmony, simply floated past us.

Our attention was elsewhere.

The summer Senator Kennedy was killed, I found out my father was a convicted murderer, a wife killer who had served nearly seven years in upstate prisons for a crime of passion.

The week the students at Kent State were shot down, Tommy's father was stabbed in the chest in Attica prison and was put on a respirator for three months.

Michael's mother died of cancer during that summer and Carol Martinez had an uncle who was shot dead in front of an 11th Avenue bar.

While thousands of angry war protestors filtered into Washington, D.C., we sat with Father Bobby in a third floor hospital ward, praying for John to recover from a punctured lung, a gift from one of his mother's overzealous boyfriends. The man had had too much to drink and John said more than he should have about it and was given a severe beating as a result. He also suffered an asthma attack and was lucky to escape the night with his life.

One of the earliest lessons learned in Hell's Kitchen was that death was the only thing in life that came easy.

Summer 1967

ELEVEN

The temperature topped out at ninety-eight degrees on the day our lives were forever altered. It was the middle of a summer when the country's mood plunged into darkness. Race riots had already rocked 127 cities across the United States, killing seventy-seven people and putting more than 4,000 others in area hospitals, and neither side seemed ready to give up the battle.

Along with the turmoil came change.

Thurgood Marshall was appointed to the Supreme Court by President Lyndon Johnson after Justice Thomas C. Clark resigned. In return, Ramsey Clark, the son of the retired Justice, was named to the Attorney General's post.

The Six-Day War was fought in the Middle East.

The New York World-Journal & Tribune folded and *Rolling Stone* published its first issue. *Bonnie and Clyde* brought crowds to theaters and *Rosemary's Baby* kept readers up all night. The Beatles sang 'All You Need is Love', while 'Ode to Billy Joe' suggested otherwise, playing and playing on the radio. Mickey Mantle, limping toward the end of his baseball days, hit his 500th home run, and Muhammad Ali, at the height of his boxing achievements, was stripped of the heavyweight crown for refusing to fight in Vietnam.

We had spent our morning in the cool shadows of a second-floor pool room on West 53rd Street, watching a craggy-faced lug in a T-shirt and torn jeans rack up a dozen games against four different opponents. As he played, he smoked his way through two packs of Camels and finished off a pint of Four Roses.

'Bet this guy could even beat Ralph Kramden,' Tommy said, watching the man side-pocket the six ball.

'Ralph Kramden doesn't play pool,' I said. 'He drives a bus.'

'Not on *The Honeymooners*,' Tommy said. 'In that movie.'

'*The Hustler*,' Michael said. 'That the one you mean?'

'The one where they break Fast Eddie's thumbs,' John said.

'You need directions to figure out the way you think,' I said to Tommy.

'It wasn't Kramden?' Tommy asked.

'Let's get outta here,' Michael said, looking around the smoke-filled room. 'We're startin' to smell as bad as this place.'

We made a right out of the pool room, late morning sun warming our shoulders, our attention jointly fixed on lunch. We ran a red light crossing 11th Avenue, dodged a school bus and two cabs, then eased back into a fast walk in front of old man Pippilo's barber shop. At 51st Street and 10th Avenue we turned left, side by side on the silent streets.

Between us, we had less than two dollars in our pockets.

'Let's go get some pizza,' John said. 'We can tell Mimi we'll pay him down the road.'

'Mimi charges for *water*,' Tommy said. 'He ain't gonna go for any IOUs.'

'We can grab something at home,' I said. 'Leftovers.'

'The only leftovers in my house are dirty dishes,' John said.

'And week-old bread,' Tommy said.

'Why not hot dogs?' Michael asked. 'We haven't hit the cart in a couple of weeks.'

'I don't know, Mikey,' Tommy said. 'That cart guy ain't

like the others. He gets pretty crazy when you take him off.'

'Tommy's right,' I said. 'Last week, he chased Ramos and two of his friends all the way to the piers. Almost cut one of 'em.'

'A hot dog ain't worth bleedin' over,' John said.

'We can eat hot dogs or we can eat air,' Michael said. 'You guys choose.'

'Air's probably safer,' Tommy said.

'May even taste better,' John said.

'Whose turn is it?' I asked.

'Yours,' Michael said.

'You think he'll recognize me?' I asked.

'I hope so,' Tommy said. 'I'm really hungry.'

The scam was simple. We'd done it dozens of times before, with almost as many vendors. We picked it up from an Irish crew on 48th Street who used it every summer to score free Puerto Rican ices.

I was to walk up to the hot dog cart and order what I wanted. The vendor would then hand me my hot dog and watch as I ran off without paying. This left the vendor with two choices, neither very appealing. He could stand his ground and swallow his loss. Or he could give chase. This second choice forced him to abandon the cart, where my friends could feast in his absence.

The hot dog vendor at this corner was tall and slender and in his mid-twenties, with thick, dark hair and a round, bulbous nose. A recent addition to Hell's Kitchen, his English was as poor as his clothes, ragged blue shirts and jeans, front pockets frayed at the edges. He owned a Yankee warm-up jacket and soiled cap and wore them on colder days.

The vendor worked the far corner of 51st Street and 10th Avenue, standing under the partial shade of a red and yellow Sabrett umbrella, selling cold sodas, hot dogs and sausages to an array of passing customers – local merchants, longshoremen and truckers, school children.

Seven days a week, late morning to early evening, he was there, plying a trade that was all too easy for us to ridicule.

We never saw the vendor as a man, not the way we saw the other men of the neighborhood, and didn't care enough about him to grant him any respect. We gave little notice to how hard he worked for the few dollars he earned. We didn't know about the young wife and two kids he left in Greece and how he hoped to build for them a new foundation in a new country. We didn't pay attention to the tedious twelve-hour days he endured, slicing buns and sifting through chunks of ice through cold spells and heat waves. All the time stamping his feet on hard ground, to keep the blood flowing.

We never saw the tiny, airless fourth-floor room he lived in, a forty-minute walk from his station, its only comfort a tattered collection of pictures from home, crudely taped to the wall nearest the worn mattress of his bed. We never saw the hot stove, topped by empty cans of Campbell's Pork and Beans. Or the crumpled packs of Greek cigarettes, tossed in a corner trash bin, gifts from his wife, his only stateside pleasure.

We didn't see any of that.

We only saw a free lunch.

'Mustard and onions,' I said, avoiding the vendor's suspicious look. 'No soda.'

He nodded, wary, his eyes over my shoulders, looking for hidden shadows.

'I know you,' he said, accusation more than question.

I shrugged and smiled.

'Can I have two napkins?' I asked, reaching my hand out for the hot dog. 'Onions get messy.'

The vendor pulled a second napkin from its cannister and wrapped it under the bun. He hesitated for an instant, his hand out toward mine, our eyes fixed. We both sensed a wrong about to happen, though we were ignorant of its eventual weight. He shifted his feet and handed over the hot dog. I took it from him and ran.

I scooted past Tommy Mug's dry cleaners and

Armond's shoe repair. The vendor, the anger behind his months of frustration broken beyond any reasonable point, gave chase, a wood-handled, prong fork in one hand.

As I ran, slivers of red onions flew off the top of the hot dog, dotting my cheek and the front of my white T-shirt. I cut past the P.A.L. entrance and turned the corner at 50th Street.

He was close on me, arms and legs moving in their own furied rhythm, the fork still gripped in one hand, his breath coming in measured spurts.

'Pay my money, thief!' he shouted after me. 'Pay my money *now*!'

Michael, John and Tommy were on their second hot dogs, leaning casually against the side of the cart, faces turned to the sun.

'How long you think he'll be?' John asked, wiping brown mustard from his lower lip.

'Shakes or the hot dog guy?' Michael asked.

'You got one, you got the other,' Tommy said. 'That guy looked pissed enough to kill.'

'Gotta catch him to kill him,' John said. 'Don't worry.'

'These things are heavier than they look,' Michael said, standing now, hands gripping the cart's wooden handles.

'The heavy shit's underneath,' Tommy said. 'Where nobody can see it.'

'What heavy shit?' John asked.

'The gas tanks,' Tommy said. 'The stuff that keeps the food hot. Or maybe you thought the sun made the water boil.'

'Think we can push it?' Michael asked. 'The three of us?'

'Push it where?' John asked.

'Couple of blocks away,' Michael said. 'Be a nice surprise for the guy when he gets back from chasing Shakes not to find his cart.'

'What if somebody takes it?' Tommy said.

'You gotta be pretty dumb to steal a hot dog cart,' Michael said.

'Ain't we doin' that?' John asked.

'We're just *moving* it,' Michael said. 'Making sure nobody *else* steals it.'

'So, we're helpin' the guy out,' Tommy said.

'Now you're listening,' Michael said.

The vendor tired at 52nd Street and 12th Avenue.

He was bent over, hands on his knees, the fork long since discarded, face flushed, his mouth open and hungry for breath. I was on the other side of the street, against a tenement doorway, hair and body washed in sweat. My hands were still greasy from the hot dog I held for most of the run.

I looked over at the vendor and found him staring back at me, anger still visible, his hands now balled up and punching at his sides. He was beat but not beaten. He could go ten minutes more just on hate alone. I decided against a run toward the piers, choosing instead to double back and head for neighborhood safety. By now, I figured, the guys should have downed enough hot dogs and sodas to satisfy Babe Ruth's appetite.

I took three deep breaths and started running toward 51st Street, traffic moving behind me. I turned my head and looked back at the vendor, his body in the same position as it was a block earlier. I slowed when I reached the corner and allowed myself a smile, content that the chase, while not over, had drifted to my favor.

If I got to the cart fast enough I might even have time for a hot dog.

Michael, John and Tommy were standing at the corner of 50th Street and Ninth Avenue, tired from having pushed the cart up the one long block. They stopped in front of a florist, a short woman, her hair in a bun, clipping stems from a handful of roses, watching them with curiosity.

'Let's have a soda,' John said, sliding open the aluminum door and plunging a hand into dark, icy water. 'A Dr. Brown sounds about right.'

'I'll take a cream,' Tommy said.

John handed Tommy a sweaty can of soda. 'How about you, Mikey?'

'I don't want anything,' Michael said, looking down the street, arms across his chest.

'What's wrong?' Tommy asked, taking a slurp from his soda.

'Shakes is taking too long,' Michael said. 'He should've been back by now.'

I stopped at the light at 51st Street and 10th Avenue and looked for my friends and the hot dog cart.

The vendor was one avenue down, running again at a full pace, his stride seemingly stronger than ever. I bent over to tie my laces and caught a glimpse of him.

'Give it up,' I whispered. 'Let it go.'

I stood and continued to run, this time toward Ninth Avenue. My sides hurt and my legs were starting to cramp. I was light-headed, my throat dry and my lungs heavy. I ran past Printing High School, the yard empty except for two rummies drinking coffee and smoking cigarettes, thinking of ways to score their first drink of the day. I dodged past a heavy-set woman tugging a shopping wagon piled with groceries and jumped two garbage can lids tossed to the side by a passing sanitation crew.

Then, halfway up the block, the vendor still on my trail, I saw the hot dog cart being pushed toward Eighth Avenue by my friends. They were hunched low and moving easy, walking within the shadows of the arches of the old Madison Square Garden, as calm and steady as if they were out walking a dog.

The vendor saw them too.

'Stop them!' he shouted, not breaking stride. 'Stop them! Stop the thieves!'

In a neighborhood where silence in the face of crime is a virtue and blindness a necessity, no one moved.

I ran as fast as burnt lungs and tired legs would permit and reached my three friends as they went past a poster announcing the much-heralded rematch between World Wrestling Federation champion Bruno Sammartino and challenger Gorilla Moonsoon.

'You're only supposed to take the hot dogs,' I said when I got to them, my hands holding a side of the cart. 'Not the wagon.'

'Now you tell us,' John said.

'Just leave it here,' I panted. 'You guys are lookin' to push somethin', push me. I can't take another step.'

'No, not here,' Michael said, pointing to our right. 'Up there. Over by the subway station.'

'The guy's comin' fast, Mikey,' John said. 'I don't think we got time to make it to the subway.'

'I got a plan,' Michael said.

I turned around and saw the vendor gaining on us by the second. 'I'm sure he's got one too,' I said, helping to lift the cart onto the sidewalk, toward the top step of the IRT subway station.

'I don't even *like* hot dogs,' John said.

The plan, as it turned out, was as simple and as dumb as anything we had ever done. We were to hold the cart on the top edge of the stairwell, leaning it downward, and wait for the vendor. We were to let go the second he grabbed the handles and leave the scene as he struggled to ease the cart back onto the sidewalk.

To this day, I don't know why we did it. But we would all pay a price. Everyone. All it took was a minute, but in that minute everything changed.

People who've been shot always recall the incident as if it happened to them in slow motion and that's how I'll always remember those final seconds with the hot dog cart. The action around me moved at quarter speed and the background was nothing but haze – quick hands, fleeing legs, scattered bodies, all shaped in dark, nasty blurs.

116

That moment arrived for me and my friends on a day and time when Mickey Mantle was crossing the plate with a home run we would have all been proud to witness.

Michael held the cart the longest, his arms bulging at the strength needed to keep it from falling down the steps. John had slipped on his side, his back against the station's wooden bannister, both hands sliced by the wooden handles. Tommy fell to his knees, desperately grabbing at one of the wheels, his knees scraping concrete. I held both my hands to the base of the umbrella stand, grip tight, splashes of hot water showering my arms and face.

The vendor was a few feet behind us, on his knees, his hands spread out across his face, his eyes visible.

'It's not gonna hold!' Tommy said, the wheel slipping from his grip.

'Let it go,' Michael said.

'Don't stop now!' I said. 'We can't stop now!'

'Let it go, Shakes,' Michael urged, his voice a surrender to the inevitable. 'Let it go.'

Watching the cart tumble down the stairs was as painful as trying to keep it from going down. The noise was loud, numbing and eerie, two cars colliding on an empty street. Hot dogs, onions, sodas, ice, napkins and sauerkraut jumped out in unison, splattering against the sides of the stairwell, bouncing and smacking the front of a Florida vacation poster. One of the rear wheels flew off halfway down the landing. The umbrella stand split against the base of the stair wall.

Then came the loudest noise, one that rocked the entire subway station. It was a sound no one expected to hear.

A crunching sound of wood against bone.

It is a sound I have heard every day of my life since.

James Caldwell was a sixty-seven-year-old retired printer. He had been married to the same woman for thirty-six years, had three grown children, all daughters, and four grandchildren, three of them boys. He had spent his

117

morning in lower Manhattan, visiting with one of those daughters, Alice, newlywed to a junior executive working for a midtown accounting firm. He had stopped in a bakery in Little Italy to buy his wife a box of her favorite pastries, which he carried in his left hand. On doctor's orders, Caldwell had turned his back on a two-pack-a-day cigarette habit less than a week earlier. He refused to give up his scotch, however, a drink he liked straight up, ice water on the side, a bowl of pretzels at the ready.

He was chewing two pieces of Juicy Fruit gum and was digging into his front pants pocket for enough loose change to buy the late edition of the *Daily News* when the cart landed on him, barreling in at chest level. His hands reached out to grab the sides of the wagon in a futile attempt to ward off its runaway power.

The cart was a destructive missile, taking with it all in its wake. That wake now included the body of James Caldwell, who had no bigger plans for the rest of his day than reading the sports pages.

Together, both cart and man came to rest as one, slamming against a white tile subway wall. The cart crumpled, wheels rolling off in opposite directions, handles splintered, boiling water and pieces of ice crashing on top of Caldwell's bloody head, looking no bigger than a hairless tan ball, lodged against the sharpest edge of the wagon.

The silence after the crash was as numbing as the noise during it.

We held our positions, feet cemented in place. No one spoke and three of us choked back tears. We heard the wail of sirens and prayed they were headed our way. I looked down at the wreckage and saw the lower half of Caldwell's legs twitching under the weight. Thin lines of blood mixed with dirty hot dog water to form a puddle in one corner.

The smell of excrement filtered through the air.

Michael turned to me and, for the first time since I'd known him, I saw fear on his face.

John and Tommy didn't move, their bodies trembling,

faces ashen, both unnerved enough to pass out. The four of us felt much older than we had less than an hour earlier, the ticking of our personal clocks accelerating with the speed of the unfolding incident.

To our left, a thin, middle-aged woman, in a checkered house dress and white apron, strands of long, dark hair hiding the anger fanning her eyes, crossed the street in a run and stood at the top stair of the subway station. Hands on her hips, shoulders hunched in a tight pattern, she stared down at the scene.

'My sweet Jesus,' she shouted, turning her gaze toward us, her voice a sharp, loud, high pitch. 'What have you boys done? What in God's good name have you boys done? Tell me, now, what have you done?'

'I think we just killed a man,' Michael said.

TWELVE

That afternoon, the police issued an *order of immediate custody*, a juvenile arrest warrant, against the four of us. We were charged with a series of crimes: reckless endangerment; assault in the first; possession of a dangerous instrument; assault with intent; misdemeanor assault; petty theft. We were each assigned PINS status, branding us persons in need of supervision. We were also tagged as youthful offenders, Y.O. on the streets. The label came with the luxury of keeping our records sealed and the knowledge that Y.O.'s were seldom dealt adult-length sentences, even by the harshest family court judge.

While James Caldwell lay in critical condition in the intensive care unit of St. Clare's Hospital, clinging to life on a respirator, we were remanded into our parents' custody. The shock of the day still had not worn away as we moved with great speed and little care through the system of arrest and booking, our eyes and ears closed to the sobs and screams surrounding us. We were in another world. Above the action. Our parents cried and cursed, the cops were stone-faced, Caldwell's family wanted us dead and the whole neighborhood, it seemed, was waiting for us outside the station house. We'd always been on the other side looking in at the guys gettting busted. Now it was us. We were the ones they pointed at. The ones they talked about. We were the guilty ones now.

My father had just slapped me, hard, across my face. I

stared at him; he was slumped on a chair next to the kitchen table, wearing only briefs and a T-shirt. His face was red, his hands were twitching, his eyes welled with tears. My mother was in a back room, face down on her bed, crying.

My parents had always granted me free reign, confident in my ability to steer clear of street jams, believing I was not the type to bring trouble knocking at the front door. This freedom also served to keep me out of view of their daily physical and verbal battles.

I lost that freedom the instant the hot dog cart crashed against the body of James Caldwell.

'I'm sorry, Dad,' was all I could manage to say.

'Sorry ain't gonna do you much good now, kid,' my father said, softening. 'You gotta face up to what you did. The four of you.'

'What's going to happen to us?' I asked, my voice breaking, tears falling down my cheeks.

'The old man lives, you might catch a break,' my father said. 'Do a few months in a juvenile home.'

I could barely ask the question. 'And if he doesn't?'

My father couldn't answer. He reached out his arms and held me, both of us crying, both of us afraid.

Over the next several days, Hell's Kichen, which, in the past, never failed to embrace its criminals, seemed a neighborhood in shock. It wasn't the crime that had hands raised to the sky, but the fact that Michael, John, Tommy and I had committed it.

'You guys were different,' Fat Mancho told me years later. 'Yeah, sure, you fooled around, busted balls, got into fights, shit like that. But, you never went outta your way to hurt anybody. You were never punks. Until you did the job with the cart. That was an upstate number and that's something nobody figured on.'

By the day, two weeks later, when we stood before a family court Judge, we knew that James Caldwell was going to make it out of the hospital alive. The news had been relayed to us by Father Bobby, who counseled all the families involved.

During the time between our arrest and scheduled judgment, I was not allowed to associate with my friends, be seen in their company or talk to them by phone. We were each kept under close family scrutiny, spending the bulk of our days buried inside our apartments. Father Bobby visited each of us daily, bringing with him a handful of comics and a few words of encouragement. He always left a little sadder than when he arrived.

Our crime had not been terrible enough to make any of the papers, so our notoriety did not move further than the neighborhood. Still, we couldn't help but feel like public enemies. There were whispers behind my mother's back whenever she went for groceries or headed off to church. John's mother missed so many days of work she was close to losing her job. When Michael was sent out on a fast errand, a beer bottle was tossed his way. Tommy was denied entry to a local movie theater.

'Your kind ain't welcome,' he was told. 'Not here. Not in my place.'

'I didn't do anything to you,' Tommy said.

'You got a problem with what I done?' the theater manager asked. 'Call the cops.'

During those two long, frightening and tedious weeks, I left my apartment on just three occasions.

The first two, I went to church with my mother.

The third, I went to see King Benny.

I poured myself an espresso from a two-cup pot, King Benny staring across the table. It was late Sunday afternoon of the Labor Day Weekend, and a transistor radio resting against the window behind me was tuned in low to a Yankee game. Two men, wearing dark slacks and sleeveless T-shirts, sat outside the club on wooden chairs.

I drank my coffee and listened to Phil Rizzuto call the game, taking it into the bottom half of the eighth inning,

122

Yanks down by three runs. King Benny's hands were spread flat on the table, his face a clean-shaven mask.

'They suck this year,' he said, lifting a finger in the direction of the radio.

'They sucked last year,' I said.

'Gets to be habit,' he said. 'A bad habit. Like going to jail.'

I nodded and lowered my head, averting his gaze.

'We didn't mean to hurt anybody,' I said.

'You didn't mean it don't make it not happen.'

'We didn't go out looking to hurt is what I meant,' I said.

'Few do,' King Benny said.

'How long do you think we'll get?'

'A year,' King Benny told me and it made my knees go weak. 'Maybe more. Depends on the mood the judge is in.'

'I hear the one we got is tough,' I said. 'Likes to set examples.'

'They're all tough,' King Benny said.

I drank some more coffee and scanned the room, framing it in my mind, not wanting to forget its look, its stench, its feeling of safety. King Benny's foul-smelling club was a second home to me and, like the library, had become a place to escape the harshness of the life I knew.

It was an escape to the quiet company of the single most dangerous man in Hell's Kitchen.

'Your father tell you what to expect?' King Benny asked. 'Tell you how to handle yourself?'

'He hasn't talked much,' I said. 'He's pretty upset. Most of the time, he and my mom just sit and cry. Or they fight. One or the other.'

'I can't help you up there,' King Benny said, leaning closer to me, his eyes tight on my face. 'Or your friends. You're gonna be on your own in that place. It won't be easy, Shakes. It's gonna be hard. The hardest thing you and your friends are ever gonna have to do.'

123

'My father thinks that too,' I said. 'That's why he's crying.'

'Your father *knows* that,' King Benny said. 'Only he don't think you're ready for it. Don't think you can take it.'

'Do you believe that?'

'No,' King Benny said. 'I don't. There's a part of you that's a lot like me. A small part. That should be enough to bring you back alive.'

'I better go,' I said, pushing the cup to one side. 'I'm not allowed to stay out alone too long.'

'When do you leave?'

'I see the judge on Thursday,' I said, looking at the man I had grown to love as much as my own father. 'That's when we find out where we go and for how long.'

'Your parents be with you?'

'My father,' I said. 'I don't think my mother can handle it. You know how she gets.'

'It's better that way,' King Benny said. 'She shouldn't see you in a courtroom.'

'Will you still be here when I get back?' I asked, my voice choked, my eyes focusing on the two men outside, trying not to let King Benny see me cry.

'I'll *always* be here,' he said. 'Doing what I always do.'

'What *do* you do here?' I asked, a smile at the center of my tears.

King Benny pointed to the empty espresso pot.

'I make coffee,' he said.

THIRTEEN

My friends and I stood behind a scarred oak table in the middle of a high-ceilinged, airless room, hands at our sides, staring straight ahead. We were dressed in the only good clothes we owned, our communion suits, the dark jackets, dark slacks, white shirts and sky grey ties standing out against the cream-colored courtroom walls of New York State's Division of Family Justice.

John and I were on the right side of the table, next to our lawyer, a short, doe-eyed man who had trouble breathing through his nose. His hair was slicked down with gel and the tail of his white shirt was popping out the back of his brown pants.

Michael and Tommy stood to his left.

None of us looked at him and none bothered to listen to a word he uttered.

Our families were behind us, held apart by a wooden barrier and two court officers. My father sat in the first row of benches, directly behind me, his sad, angry presence like hot air on my neck. We had talked very little on the subway ride downtown. He assured me all would go well, that no one beyond the neighborhood would know where I was and that, maybe, just maybe, all this was for the good, that it was a lesson waiting to be learned.

'Be like goin' to camp,' my father said as the train careened toward Chambers Street. 'Plenty of fresh air, lots of runnin' around, decent food. And they'll keep you in line. Maybe teach you and your friends some discipline. Do what I couldn't do.'

'I'm gonna miss you, Dad,' I said.

'Save that shit,' my father said. 'You can't think like that. You gotta be like a stone. Can't think about anybody. Can't worry about anybody. Except yourself. It's the only way, kid. Believe me, I know what I'm talkin' about here.'

We rode the rest of the way in silence, wrapped in the noisy company of the rattling car.

I was two months shy of my thirteenth birthday and about to leave home for the first time in my life.

'Have the defendants been made aware of the charges against them?' the Judge asked.

'Yes they have, your Honor,' our lawyer responded, sounding as low-rent as he looked.

'Do they understand those charges?'

'Yes they do, your Honor.'

In truth we didn't understand. We were told the night before our appearance that the charges against us would be lumped together under the umbrella tag of assault one, which constituted reckless endangerment. The petty theft charge would be dropped in everyone's case but mine, since my action was what precipitated all that followed.

'It's the best I could do,' our lawyer told us, sitting behind a cluttered desk in his one-room office. 'You have to admit, it's better than getting hit with attempted murder. Which is what the other side wanted.'

'You're a regular Perry Mason,' John told him, seconds before his mother cuffed the side of his face.

'What does it *mean* for the boys?' Father Bobby asked, ignoring the slap and the comment.

'They'll do a year,' the lawyer said. 'Minimum. Lorenzo may get a few months more tacked on since he initiated the action. But then, he may get less time since he was last on the scene. That's the only open question.'

'It wasn't his idea,' Michael said. 'It was mine.'

'The idea doesn't matter as much as the act,' the lawyer

126

said. 'Anyway, I should be able to convince the Judge not to tack on any extra time given how young Lorenzo is.'

'They're *all* young,' Father Bobby said.

'And they're *all* guilty,' the lawyer said, closing a yellow folder on his desk and reaching for a pack of cigarettes.

'Where?' Father Bobby asked.

'Where what?' the lawyer said, a menthol cigarette in his mouth, his hands coiled around a lit match.

'Where will they be sent?' Father Bobby asked, his face red, his hands gripping his knees. 'Which home? Which prison? Which hole are you going to drop them in? That clear enough for you?'

'Wilkinson's,' the lawyer said. 'It's a home for boys in upstate New York.'

'I know where it is,' Father Bobby said.

'Then you know what it's like,' the lawyer said.

'Yes,' Father Bobby said, the color drained from his face. 'I know what it's like.'

I looked over my shoulder, to the left, for a quick glance at the members of the Caldwell family, sitting in a group in the first two rows behind the prosecutor's table. Old man Caldwell was home, recuperating from his numerous wounds. According to a medical statement filed with the court, he would never again gain full use of his left leg and would suffer from dizziness and numbness in his other limbs for the rest of his life. His hearing and vision had also been affected.

Each of us had written him a note, delivered by Father Bobby, telling Mr. Caldwell and his family how sorry we were.

Each note went unanswered.

'Do any of you wish to say anything before sentence is passed?' the Judge asked, moving aside a sweaty glass of ice water.

'No, sir,' each of us said in turn.

The Judge nodded, looking at his notes one last time. He was in his late fifties, a short, stout man with a head full of thick white hair and brown eyes that revealed little. He lived in a Manhattan housing complex with his second wife and two dogs. He had no children, was an avid poker player and spent his summer vacations fishing off the dock of his Cape Cod home.

He cleared his throat, sipped some water and closed the folder before him.

'I'm sure by now, you boys have been made aware of the severity of the crime you committed,' the Judge began. 'It was a crime which combined a careless disregard for one man's place of business, in this case a hot dog stand, with a criminal attitude toward another man's safety and well-being. The end result left one man ruined and another nearly dead. All for the price of a hot dog.'

It was hot in the room and I was sweating through my shirt and jacket. I kept my hands clasped in front of me while staring straight ahead. I heard the mumblings of those behind me, the people on my right fearful of the Judge's words, the people on the left anticipating the punishment to come. John's mother, sitting next to my father, whispered the prayers of the rosary, her fingers moving slowly down the row of beads.

'Mr. Kratrous has been forced to give up his business and his dream of building a home here. He returns to his native Greece, his belief in our way of life torn apart by the wanton and remorseless act of four boys intent on thievery. Mr. Caldwell is an even more tragic case. Left for dead by a prank gone asunder, his life will never be what it was prior to that fateful day. He will suffer each and every single moment he has left on this earth, drugged with medications to numb the pain, walking with the aid of a cane, fearful of leaving his house. And all this for what? So four boys could sit back and share a laugh, enjoy a joke caused by the pain of others. Well, the joke backfired didn't it?'

It was nine-forty in the morning when the Judge pushed back the sleeves of his robe, took another drink of water and sent us to what he called a home for boys and what everyone else called a prison.

He took us on one at a time, starting with the Count.

'John Reilly,' the Judge said. 'The court hereby sentences you to be remanded for a period of no more than eighteen months and no less than one year to the Wilkinson Home for Boys. In prior agreement with the attorneys for both parties, the term is to begin effective September 1 of this year.'

Behind me, John's mother let out a low scream.

'Thomas Marcano,' the Judge said, shifting his attention to Butter. 'The court hereby sentences you to be remanded for a period of no more than eighteen months and no less than one year to the Wilkinson Home for Boys. In terms agreed upon by counsel, your sentence is to begin on September 1 of this year.'

'Michael Sullivan,' the Judge said, his tone turning harsher, convinced he was addressing the group ringleader. 'The court hereby sentences you to no more than eighteen months and no less than one year to the Wilkinson Home for Boys. In terms agreed upon by counsel, your sentence is to begin on September 1 of this year. I might add, were it not for the intervention of Father Robert Carillo of your local parish, who spoke in glowing terms on your behalf, I would have sentenced you to a much stiffer punishment. I still have my doubts as to your inherent goodness. Only time will serve to prove me wrong.'

I wiped at my upper lip and forehead, waiting for my name to be called. I turned around and saw my father sitting with his eyes closed, his arms folded, the top of his bald head wet with sweat.

'Lorenzo Carcaterra,' the Judge said, the contempt in his voice no less than it had been for my friends. 'In your case, the court will take into account the fact that you are the youngest of the four and arrived on the scene after the theft of the cart had already occurred. With that in mind, the court hereby sentences you to serve no more than

129

one year and no less than six months at the Wilkinson Home for Boys. In terms agreed upon by counsel, you will begin your sentence on September 1 of this year.'

The Judge rested his head on his high-backed chair and stared out at us in silence. He tapped the edge of a case folder with the fingers of his right hand, his face an empty canyon, a small, nondescript man made large by the weight of judicial power.

'I hope,' he said in conclusion, 'you make good use of your time at Wilkinson. Learn a trade, perhaps, or further your education. If not, if you turn the other way and ignore the possibilities available to you, then I can guarantee you will stand before me again, guilty of another violent act. And I assure you, next time I won't be as kind as I was today.'

'Thank you, your Honor,' our lawyer said, sweat lines streaking the sides of his face.

'Look at the scumbag,' my father said to Father Bobby, sitting in the row behind him, his voice loud enough to reach the bench, watching the Judge head back to his chambers. 'Look at him smile. Puts four kids away for a year and he smiles. I oughta break his fuckin' jaw.'

Father Bobby leaned over and put a hand on my father's shoulder.

'Easy, Mario,' Father Bobby said. 'This isn't the place and now's not the time.'

'It's never the place,' my father said. 'And it sure as shit ain't *never* the time.'

Our lawyer reached over the barrier and put out a hand toward Father Bobby, his low voice barely audible over the din coming from the Caldwell family side of the courtroom.

'It went as well as could be expected,' the lawyer said.

'For you, maybe,' Father Bobby said.

'They could have gotten a lot more time,' the lawyer said. 'For what they did, a lot more time.'

Father Bobby stood and leaned on the barrier, his Roman collar off his neck and in his right hand.

'This isn't a game,' Father Bobby said. 'It's not about deals or less time or more time. It's about four boys. Four boys whose names you didn't even bother to learn. So don't be so quick to pat yourself on the back.'

'I did my job,' the lawyer said.

'The sworn oath of the mediocre,' Father Bobby said.

'You could have done better with them yourself, Father,' the lawyer said. 'Then you wouldn't have needed the services of a shit like me.'

Father Bobby sat back down, his eyes catching mine, his face ashen and pained.

'It won't be so bad,' the lawyer told him. 'After all, it's not like everybody who spends time at Wilkinson ends up a criminal.'

The lawyer turned away and cleared off the top of the defense table, shoving a handful of manilla folders inside his tattered brown bag and snapping it closed.

'Some of them even find God and become priests,' the lawyer said, turning again to face Father Bobby. 'Don't they?'

'Go to hell,' Father Bobby said.

Outside, a light summer rain began to fall.

BOOK TWO

'*Live then, beloved children of my heart, and never forget that, until the day God deigns to reveal the future to man, the sum of all human wisdom will be contained in these two words: Wait and hope.*'
– The Count of Monte Cristo

ONE

I had been in my cell for less than an hour when the panic set in. To fight it, I closed my eyes and thought of home, of the neighborhood, of the streets where I played and of the people I knew. I imagined a hydrant spreading its cold spray over my face, felt the stitches of a baseball in my hand, heard soft music floating off a rooftop. I wasn't yet thirteen years old and I wanted to be in those places, back where I belonged. I wanted everything to be the way it was before the hot dog cart. I wanted to be in Hell's Kitchen and not in a place with cold walls and a tiny cot. A place where I was too afraid to move.

It was dark and I was hungry, the dank air heavy with the smell of cleaning fluids. I didn't like tight places or dark rooms and my cell was both. Its walls were cracked and peeling, a torn photo of James Dean taped to one. I hated to be alone, to be without books to read or baseball cards to sort through, forced to stare at a thick iron door that was locked from the outside. The steady rumbling sounds that came out of the other cells were difficult to ignore, making me long for those peaceful hours when I would sit in Sacred Heart church and find solace in its silence.

It doesn't take very long to know how tough a person you are or how strong you can be. I knew from my first day at Wilkinson that I was neither tough nor strong. It only takes a moment for the fear to find its way, to seep through the carefully constructed armor. Once it does, it finds a permanent place. It is as true for a hardened criminal as it is for a young boy.

The first guard I met inside Wilkinson was Sean Nokes, who was then twenty-five years old. He stood inside my cell, his legs pressed close together, a black baton cupped in bo·h hands. He had a thick ruddy face and close-cropped blond hair and he wore sharply-creased brown slacks, thick-soled black shoes and a starched white button-down shirt with a black name tag clipped to the front pocket. His eyes were cold, his voice deep.

'Toss your old clothes to the floor,' were the first words he said to me.

'Here?'

'If you're expecting a dressing room, forget it. We don't have any. So lose the clothes.'

'In front of you?' I asked.

A smile cracked the side of Nokes's face. 'For the time you're here, day or night, you do *everything* in front of *someone*. Piss, shit, shower, brush your teeth, play with yourself, write letters home. Whatever. Somebody's gonna be looking. Most times, that somebody's gonna be *me*.'

I tossed my shirt to the floor, unzipped my pants and let them drop past my knees. I stepped out of the pants, kicked them aside and, wearing only my white cotton briefs, white socks with holes in both heels and a laceless pair of Keds, looked back up at Nokes.

'*Everything*,' Nokes said, still standing in stiff military posture. 'Here on, the only clothes you wear are state issued.'

'You want me to stand here naked?' I asked.

'Now you're catching on. I knew you Hell's Kitchen boys couldn't be as dumb as people say.'

I took off my underwear, kicked off my sneakers and balled up the white socks, dropping them all on the pile beside me. I stood there naked and embarrassed.

'Now what?'

'Get dressed,' Nokes said, nodding his head toward the

136

clothes that had been left on my cot. 'Assembly's in fifteen minutes. That's when you'll meet the other boys.'

'Are my friends on this floor?' I asked, taking two steps toward the cot and reaching for a folded green T-shirt.

'Friends?' Nokes said turning away. 'You got a lot to learn, little boy. Nobody's got friends in this place. That's something you best not forget.'

The bus ride up to the Wilkinson Home for Boys had taken more than three hours, including two stops for gas and a short bathroom break. Lunch was eaten on board: soggy butter sandwiches on white bread, lukewarm containers of apple juice and Oh! Henry candy bars. Outside the temperature topped ninety degrees. Inside, it was even hotter. The old air conditioner hissed warm air and half the windows were sealed shut, dust lines smearing their chipped panes.

The bus was old, narrow and dirty, painted slate gray inside and out. Half the thirty-six seats were taken up by boys younger than I was; none was older than sixteen. There were three guards along for the ride, one in the front next to the driver and two in the back sharing a pack of smokes and a skin magazine. Each guard had a long black nightstick and a can of mace looped inside his belt. The guard up front had a small handgun shoved inside the front band of his pants.

Four of the boys were black, two looked to be Hispanic and the rest were white. We sat alone, occupying every other seat, our feet chained to a thin, iron bar that stretched the length of the bus. Our hands were free and we were allowed to speak, but most seemed content to stare out at the passing countryside. For many, it was their first trip beyond New York City borders.

Michael sat two rows ahead of me and John and Tommy were close behind to my left.

'This is like the bus Doug McClure drove in *The Longest Hundred Miles*,' John said to a pock-marked teen across the aisle. 'Don't you think?'

137

'Who the fuck is Doug McClure?' the kid said.

'Not important,' John said, turning his attention back to the sloping hills of upstate New York.

Earlier that morning, we had said our goodbyes to relatives and friends outside the courtroom across from Foley Square. My father hugged and held me until one of the guards told him it was time for us to go.

'Treat him right,' my father told the guard.

'Don't worry,' he answered. 'He'll be okay. Now, please, step away.'

I walked from my father and into a line forming near the bus. The crowd around us drew closer, older hands reaching out for a final touch, mothers crying softly, fathers bowing their heads in angry silence. I saw John's mother lay a strand of rosary beads over his head, her knees buckling from emotion. Michael and Tommy stood behind me on the line, their eyes staring at empty spaces; there was no one there to see them off.

I looked to my left and saw Father Bobby standing next to an open-air parking lot, his back pressing a light pole. I nodded in his direction and tried but couldn't bring myself to smile. I watched as he flicked his cigarette to the sidewalk and walked toward the bus.

I wished he wasn't there. I wished none of them were there. I didn't want *anyone*, let alone people I cared about, to see me get on a bus that was going to take me to a place I could only think of as a jail. Father Bobby especially. I felt I had let him down, betrayed his trust in me. He tried to help us as much as he could – sent a stream of letters to the Judge, hoping to get the charges dropped or reduced; argued to have us assigned to another institution; begged to have us placed in his custody. None of it worked and now he was left with only prayer.

He stood across from me, his eyes saddened, his strong body sagging.

'Will you write to me?' he asked.

I wanted so much to cry, to put my arms around him

and hold him as close as I had held my father. I fought back the tears and tried to swallow, my mouth dirt dry.

'Don't worry,' I managed to say. 'You'll hear from me.'

'It'll mean a lot,' Father Bobby said, his voice as choked and cracked as mine.

He stared at me with wet eyes. Years later I would realize what that look contained, the warnings he wished he could utter. But, he couldn't tell me. He didn't dare risk making me even more frightened. It took all the strength he had not to grab me, to grab all of us, and run from the steps of that bus. Run as far and as fast as we could. Run until we were all free.

'Would you do me a favor?' I asked him.

'Name it.'

'Check on my mother and father,' I said. 'These last few weeks, they look ready to kill each other.'

'I will,' Father Bobby said.

'And no matter what you hear, tell 'em I'm doin' okay,' I said.

'You want me to lie?' Father Bobby said, a smile breaking through the sadness, one hand on my shoulder.

'It's a good lie, Father,' I said. 'You can do it.'

Father Bobby moved from the bus and watched as I boarded, his eyes scanning the faces of the other boys already in their seats. He pulled another cigarette from his shirt pocket and lit it, inhaling deeply. He then went over to my father and stood by his side until the bus closed its doors and pulled away from the curb. Then the two men – one a priest, the other an ex-con – walked with heads down and hands inside their pockets toward a nearby subway station for the ride back to the only place either one ever trusted.

TWO

The Wilkinson Home for Boys held 375 youthful offenders, housed in five separate units spread across seven well-tended acres. It had two large gyms, a football field, a quarter-mile oval track and one chapel suitable for all religions.

From the outside, the facility resembled what those who ran it most wanted it to resemble – a secluded private school. One hundred guards were on hand to monitor the inmates. The majority were local recruits only a few years older than their oldest charges. For them, this was a way-stop on a path to other jobs in law enforcement or government. A two-year tour of duty at Wilkinson, which was the average stay for most guards, always looked good on a resume.

The teachers, groundskeepers, handymen, cooks and maintenance crews were also local hires. This served the dual function of keeping labor costs low and secrecy high. No one was going to do damage to one of the largest employers in the area, regardless of what they might see or hear.

The facility was run by a warden and his two assistants.

The warden, a disinterested and overweight man in his late forties, was more concerned with appearances than the reality of life inside Wilkinson. He lived with his wife and two children in a large house less than a five-minute drive from the main gate. He left his office every afternoon at four and was never at his desk any earlier than ten. His

140

young assistants, who both hoped one day to run facilities of their own, kept similar schedules.

The guards were in charge of the day-to-day operations. They ran the drills, which started with a six a.m. wake-up and a twenty-minute breakfast and ended with a nine-thirty lights out. Each day was a series of whistles directing us to our next station – classroom, gym, showers, meals, clinic, library and field work.

Michael, Tommy, John and I were assigned to the second tier of Group C in the third and smallest of the buildings dotting the property. We were each placed in a private twelve-foot cell that came equipped with a cot and a spring mattress, a toilet with no lid and a sink with only a cold water faucet. The iron door leading into the room had three bars across the center and a slide panel at its base. Above the sink was a small window, its glass intwined with wire, which offered a view of what seemed to me to be an always colorless sky.

We were allowed a shower every three days and were given clean clothes every Friday morning; the dirty laundry was thrown into a hamper wheeled by a white-haired man with a limp. To avoid confusion, our green shirts, white pants, white socks and dark blue sneakers were stenciled with the first two letters of our last name. Those old enough to shave did so under a guard's supervision. Beards and moustaches were not permitted. Neither were portable radios or any type of recording device. There was only one television per building and that was usually watched by the guards.

Once a month, a movie was shown in the main hall and all 375 inmates were required to attend.

There were four guards assigned to each floor, with one, in our case Nokes, designated group leader. The three men working with Nokes were named Ferguson, Styler and Addison. We were never told their first names nor were we encouraged to ask. None was older than his mid-twenties, and they seemed to be close friends.

Ferguson was tall and angular, with feminine hands and

141

a thin face that quickly betrayed his thoughts. He was the only son of a slain New York State trooper and was on the waiting list for both the New York City and Suffolk County police departments. He had just completed his first year at Wilkinson and was both distrusted and disliked by the juveniles. He had a flash temper and a brute strength that went against his physical appearance. 'You could see it in him from the first day, from the first time you laid eyes on the guy,' John said. 'He had the kind of temper that was either going to kill or going to get him killed. Or both.'

Styler was using his job at Wilkinson's to finance his way through law school. He was short but muscular and made as much use of the gym as any of the inmates. On his evening breaks, he would do chin-ups on the railing bars, his body dangling over the second-level of the tiers, openly daring any juvenile to make a move. Styler was always in a foul mood, brought on by the dual demands of work and school and the frustration of spending time at a job he viewed with contempt. He was a poor kid who looked down on other poor kids. They only reminded him of where he came from and how far he had to go to get away.

Addison was a graduate of a local high school who wanted nothing more than a steady job that paid well, offered good benefits and a twenty-year pension. He took every civil service test he found out about and was on the waiting list for eight police and fire departments throughout the area. He was the youngest of the guards assigned to us and also the loudest, eager to flex verbal muscles by barking out orders. We had seen many men like him in Hell's Kitchen. He had little else in life but his mundane job. Off the job, he took a lot of shit; on the job, he shit on everyone.

At first look, there were no surprises to Addison. There were no surprises to any of them. But that was a first look, and for once, we had no idea what to look for.

*

I was sitting next to John, our backs up against the gym wall, our knees stretched out, shirts drenched with sweat, watching six black inmates play an intense game of three-on-three basketball. We were only in the middle of our third day at Wilkinson. It already felt like three months.

I watched a muscular teen in full sweats hit a corner jumper, my eyes looking beyond him at the cement walls that kept us prisoners. Nothing that had happened during my first days at the Home had helped ease my anxiety. The food was tasteless, the sleeping conditions horrid and the atmosphere in the yards and classrooms charged. There was always a sense of impending danger and I just couldn't envision living a full year of my life in such a way.

As bad as it was for me, it was worse for John. The tight quarters gave weight to his claustrophobia and worsened his asthma attacks. He wasn't eating and couldn't drink the milk that was served at every meal, reducing his liquid intake to the tepid water he sipped from playground fountains. His skin was pale, his nose always seemed to be runny, and he looked as frightened as I felt.

'Is this how you Hell's Kitchen boys spend your days?' It was Nokes. He was standing above us, facing the game, a black baton in his hand. 'Watching niggers shoot baskets?'

'We're takin' a break,' John said. 'That's all.'

'I *decide* when you get a break,' Nokes said, a smirk on his face.

It didn't take long for Sean Nokes to make his presence among us felt. He was one of those men who enjoyed the power he held and who looked to cause trouble at every turn. He was in the middle of his second year at Wilkinson and had been married less than six months. He lived in a two-bedroom, third-floor apartment less than a five mile drive from the Home. He sent a small portion of his paycheck to his widowed mother in nearby Rochester and was captain of the guards' bowling team. He smoked heavily and his breath often smelled of bourbon.

143

Nokes talked and acted tough, especially around the inmates, but I always got the feeling that on his own, without the back-up guards and the power of his position, he wouldn't amount to much. In a fair fight, on a Hell's Kitchen street corner, any one of us could probably take him. I *knew* Michael would bring him down, maybe even Janet Rivera. But for now, we were locked in his house, forced to play according to his rules.

'Get back out there,' Nokes said, pointing an end of the baton toward the crowded courts. '*Now.*'

I shrugged, turned to John and said, 'One more game won't kill us.' Then, I got up and, as I did, brushed one of my shoulders against the side of Nokes' uniform.

Nokes, inches behind me, lifted his baton and swung it down hard, against my lower back. The pain was sharp, intense and numbing. The force brought me to one knee.

Nokes' second shot landed against the center of my back and was quickly followed by a third, a swing that was hard enough to crack bone. I was down on both knees now, gasping for breath, staring into the eyes of a black teen with a gel Afro. He looked back, still and silent, except for the basketball bouncing at his side.

I heard John scream from behind me. 'What are you doing? He didn't do anything to you!'

'He touched my uniform,' Nokes said calmly. 'That's against institute rules.'

'He didn't touch you,' John said, his entire body trembling. 'And if he did, he didn't mean it.'

'Stay outta this,' Nokes told him.

'You didn't have to hit him,' John said, a touch of Hell's Kitchen to his tone. 'Don't hit him again.'

'Okay.' Nokes' voice softened, but his eyes stayed hard. 'Help him up. Take him back to his cell.' When John hesitated, Nokes said, 'Go ahead, pick him up. Don't be afraid.'

'I'm not afraid,' John told him.

Nokes just smiled.

*

144

Back in the cell, John helped ease me down on my bunk and covered my legs with a folded blanket.

'I can't believe he hit you like that,' John said.

'He's hit before,' I told him.

'How do you know?'

'While I was down, I looked over at the others. None of them seemed surprised.'

And now I wasn't either. I understood what Father Bobby had wanted to tell me but couldn't. I realized the weight of my father's words. I figured out what was behind all of King Benny's veiled warnings. They had tried to prepare me, prepare us all. But none of them, not even King Benny, could have envisioned the full extent of the horror we would face.

We felt their presence before we heard them. John had lingered, making sure I was all right, delaying his return to the harsher world outside the cell. Somehow, when it was just us, we could make believe that things were fine. But things weren't fine and would never be again.

Nokes stood in the cell doorway, his arms folded across his chest, a crooked smile on his face. Behind him stood Ferguson, Styler and Addison, black batons at their sides. Nokes led them into my cell. Addison closed the door behind him. They didn't say anything except when John, as fearlessly as he could muster, asked them what they wanted.

'You see?' Nokes said with a laugh. 'See how tough this Irish punk is?'

Ferguson and Styler moved past Nokes and each grabbed one of John's arms. Addison instantly went up behind him and wrapped a thick cloth around John's mouth, knotting it from the back. Nokes stood over me, one of his knees pressed against my chest. I looked away from him, my eyes toward John, both our faces betraying our terror.

'Undo his pants,' Nokes said.

145

John's pants slipped down around his ankles, white legs shining under the glare of the outside light.

'Hold him tight,' Addison said to Ferguson and Styler. 'I wouldn't want him to slip and hit his head.'

'We got him,' Ferguson said. 'Don't worry.'

'Okay, Irish,' Nokes said. 'Let's see how tough you really are.'

Addison beat against John's back, rear and legs with his baton, the blows causing the skin to swell immediately and my friend's eyes to well with tears. His back turned beet-red and the thin muscles of his legs bent under the pounding. Each blow brought a low moan from John's mouth, until the fifth blow caused him to lose consciousness. Still, Addison didn't stop. He lifted his baton higher and brought it down with even more force, his face gleaming with sweat, his eyes filled with pleasure at the pain he was inflicting. He finally stopped after a dozen shots had found their mark, pausing to wipe rows of sweat from his brow with the sleeve of his shirt. Ferguson and Styler still held John's arms, all that was keeping him from dropping to the floor.

'Think he's had enough?' Nokes asked me.

'Yes,' I said, staring up at him.

'Yes what, you guinea fuck?'

'Yes, sir,' I said. 'I think he's had enough.'

Nokes and I watched in silence as the trio pulled John's pants up and undid the gag around his mouth. Then John was dragged out of my cell, back to his.

Nokes walked around my cell, hands behind his back, head down.

'See things my way,' he said to me. '*Do* things my way. Don't fight us. And there'll never be another problem like there was today. If not, you Hell's Kitchen boys may never get outta here alive. It's something to think about, isn't it?'

It was the end of our third day at the Wilkinson Home for Boys.

146

THREE

It was not a group of innocent young boys at Wilkinson. Most, if not all, of the inmates belonged there.

Our population was composed of the toughest kids from the poorest and most dangerous areas of the state, a number of them riding out their second and third convictions. All were violent offenders. Few seemed sorry about what he had done or appeared on the brink of any rehabilitation.

A few of the inmates enjoyed their stay, viewing it as a break from the pressured street world they inhabited. Others, ourselves included, marked off the days on the walls against our bunks, scratching lines against concrete, much like we had seen actors do in many a prison film.

Most of the convicted were there on assault charges, more than half of them drug-related. Cocaine had just begun to sink its sinister fangs into poor neighborhoods, quickly replacing the more tranquil heroin as the drug of choice among the wayward.

Blacks and Hispanics were the first among the poor to taste the drug's power, to feel its need and, as a result, their crimes, previously bordering on the petty, had taken a more vicious direction. Unlike their suburban compatriots, they had no parents with crammed wallets who could be counted on when the urge for the powder grew strong. And so, they turned to the defenseless to support their habits and desires.

The Italian and Irish poor, in 1967, still found their

troubles through drink and bravado. Street fights were quick to turn into vendettas when the cork was out of the bottle. A sizeable portion of the white inmates were serving time on assault charges, almost all fueled by booze and revenge. The others were nabbed for foiled attempts at robbery, committed either while drunk or in the company of older men.

My friends and I fell uncomfortably in the middle. We were there on assault charges, caused neither by drunkenness nor anger.

We were there because of pure stupidity.

There were few solid friendships at Wilkinson. A handful of alliances existed, all of them uneasy. Blacks and whites, as in any penal institution, separated themselves by color. Ethnic groups paired off, neighborhood factions looked to stay together, friends on the streets tried to cover for each other.

It was the guards' function to break through the allegiances, to cause dissent, to eliminate any barriers to their own power. Up against a lone individual, the guards easily maintained control. Up against a united group, it would not be so easy.

My friends and I were one of many groups who tried to stick together. That was one reason we were singled out by the guards in our block. Nokes and Styler in particular. They also knew we were an easier problem to solve than other groups, many of which numbered far more than four members. It might be hard, even dangerous for Nokes and his crew to do battle with the tougher, more seasoned inmates. Keeping those groups in line was merely a part of their job. Recreation came in the form of me and my friends.

We were regarded, from the beginning, as a group that could be toyed with, partly because of our ages, partly because of the simple nature of our crime and partly because we didn't belong to an already existing gang. With other inmates, other groups, the guards drew a line and waited for that line to be crossed before they attacked.

148

With us, there never was a line. With us, Nokes and his crew could go on the attack at any moment, for any reason.

For us, there were never any rules.

Fall 1967

It was the morning of my thirteenth birthday.

Our first month at Wilkinson had passed without further incident. Except for Butter – Tommy – my friends and I had lost a few pounds, due to the quality of the food and our inability to sleep through the night. My father had warned me that the noise inside a prison was, initially, the hardest adjustment, and he was right. The moans and groans, the constant coughs, the occasional screams, the flushing toilets, the music from hidden radios – none of it ceased until sun-up.

I was walking in the middle of a line of eight, coming out of a morning math session taught by a sleepy-eyed former drug addict named Greg Simpson. The classes at Wilkinson were, at best, mediocre. Most were over-crowded, often numbering close to forty students, the majority of them as openly bored as the teachers. English and history were still my favorite classes and, while neither of the teachers could hold a torch to Father Bobby, they at least attempted to get some points across. My friends and I welcomed the homework assignments since they gave us something to do in our cells besides stare at the walls or listen to the constant cries.

We were on the first tier, Michael in front of me, John bringing up the rear, all heading for the Tomaine Tavern, as the inmates had nicknamed the mess hall.

'Hold the line,' Nokes barked out from my left.

153

'Carcaterra, Sullivan, Reilly step out. The rest of you, mouths shut and eyes forward.'

We had, ever since the beatings John and I had taken, kept our distance from Nokes and his cohorts. We had withstood their steady barrage of verbal abuse, ignored their nudges, slaps and taunts. It was certainly our safest play and, as we saw it, probably our only play.

We stood at attention, arms brushing the sides of the iron rail, eyes straight ahead.

Nokes eased his body in alongside mine and, with a broad smile on his face, ordered the three of us back to our cells. He knew it was my birthday and began to tease me about it. He told me his was coming up later in the week and Styler's was soon after that. I tried to avoid his gaze, his breath coming on me heavy and strong. He looked drunk, his footing unsteady, his face red, eyes slightly glazed. Whatever was going to happen, I knew it wasn't going to be good.

Nokes stepped away from me and moved toward Michael. He stared at him for a few seconds and then tapped him lightly on the shoulder with the end of his baton, the smile still on his face. He told us he had planned a birthday party, a special celebration we would all enjoy. While Nokes talked, his speech slurred by the booze, a few of the other inmates on line began to giggle.

John and I were too scared to move and had to be pushed along by Nokes. John turned to look at me, his face pale with apprehension. Michael walked with his head down, hands at his side, powerless to help the friends he had always been there to protect.

We didn't know what Nokes had in store for us, but we knew enough not to expect a cake, balloons and party hats. The four of us had been locked inside the walls of Wilkinson long enough to expect nothing but the unimaginable.

I walked into my cell, Michael still in front of me, and found Styler, Ferguson and Addison sitting on my bunk, two of them smoking cigarettes. In the corner, wedged in between the bowl and sink, Tommy stood at attention.

Ferguson had his shirt off and kept his back against the wall. He patted Addison on the shoulder and winked, eager for the fun to begin. Ferguson seldom initiated any of the acts against us, but once they began he joined in with a viciousness that belied his size and demeanor. He fancied himself a comic and was known to slap and kick inmates until they laughed aloud at one of his stories.

I looked around the room, heard the door behind me slam shut and watched Addison, Styler and Nokes undo their shirts. My body was wet with sweat and I felt weak enough to faint. I saw Michael open and close his fists and Tommy shut his eyes to all movement. I heard John start to wheeze, his breath coming in small bursts.

Nokes pulled a cigarette from his shirt pocket and asked me if I liked surprises. When I answered no, they all shared a long, loud laugh. Ferguson came off the cot and rubbed the palm of his hand across my face as he asked how old I now was.

'Thirteen,' I said.

Addison pointed a finger in Tommy's direction and ordered him to turn and face the wall. Tommy, moving slowly, did as he was told.

Ferguson moved away from me and ordered both John and Michael to do the same. They walked to the wall furthest from the bunk and turned their faces to it.

Nokes, cigarette dangling from his mouth, tossed one arm casually over my shoulders. Addison put out his cigarette and checked his watch, moving back, closer to my bunk, leaving Nokes with all the free room he wanted.

My eyelids moved like shutters, trying to block out the droplets of sweat falling into them. My voice cracked from fear and nerves. 'What do you want?' I managed to ask.

'A blow job,' Nokes said.

I don't remember much more about that day. I remember being forced down to my knees, closing my eyes, my consciousness, to all but the laughter and jeers. I remember Nokes' sweaty hands holding the back of my head. I remember feeling numb and wishing they would kill me before the night was over.

I never spoke to my friends about it, nor did they ever mention it to me. We tried as best we could to annihilate those moments – which occurred with dulling regularity after that birthday morning – as deep inside ourselves as possible. To this day, no clear picture of the sexual abuse we endured at the Wilkinson Home for Boys has surfaced in my mind. I have buried it as deep as it can possibly go. But it is there and it will always be there, no matter how hard I work at blocking it out. It occasionally surfaces, not during my most violent nightmares, of which there have been many, but in softer moments. It will show itself across more innocent images – a glimpse of a uniform, the sounds of a man's laugh, a darkened room, the clanging of a fence. It lasts for the briefest of seconds. Just long enough to once more send a chill.

The details of those forced sexual encounters have been relegated to a series of stop-action blurs.

I see hands slap bare skin. I see pants torn and shirts ripped apart. I feel hot breath against my neck and strong legs wrapped around mine. I hear groans and frenzied laughter, my back and neck wet from another man's sweat and spit. I smell cigarette smoke and hear mute talk once it's over, the jokes, the comments, the promises to return.

In those blurry visions I am always alone and crying out against the pain, the shame and the empty feeling the abuse of a body leaves in the tracks of the mind. I am held in place by men I hate, helpless to fight back, held by fear and the dark end of a guard's baton.

What I remember most clearly from that chilly October day was that it was my thirteenth birthday and the end of my childhood.

FOUR

I was walking next to Michael in the outfield of Wilkinson Park, facing empty wooden stands. It was nearing Thanksgiving and the weather was taking a cold turn. We wore thin pea-green jackets above our prison issues, hands shoved inside the pockets of our pants.

We had been inside Wilkinson for two months. Ten months of our sentences remained. In that short span of time, the guards at Wilkinson had beaten our bodies and had weakened our minds. All that was left was the strength of our spirit and I knew it wouldn't take much longer for that last part to go.

I began to think I might never make it out of Wilkinson, that my life would end within its walls. There were plenty of rumors floating around about inmates found dead in their bunks or in the shower stalls. I didn't know how many of those rumors were true and I didn't care to know. All that mattered to me was that I was being broken down by a system built to break people like me. I slept less than two hours a night and ate no more of the food than I needed. I had lost interest in most things and went through the routine of my day with shuttered eyes, closed to as much around me as possible.

It seemed even worse for my friends. I looked over at Michael, his face tired and worn, his movements slow and tentative, humbled by the beatings and the surroundings. His passion seemed dissolved, his strength sheared. All that was left beneath the sunken eyes and beat-up body was his pride and his concern for our collective safety. I hoped it would be enough to get him through.

John's condition was even worse. He was sickly to begin with and the constant beatings and rapes combined with the lack of food he could eat had reduced his body to a withered state. He spent more time in the infirmary than he did in class or in the exercise yard. He spoke in a low, raspy voice and was losing that sharp edge of humor that had always sustained him.

Butter looked the same on the outside, his body weight holding steady, his manner seemingly unaffected. But his eyes were lifeless, stripped of any vibrancy, emptied of their spark. He was cold and distant now, his emotions locked, his responses monosyllabic. It was a survival method, the only way he could think of to make it through one more day.

Each of the guards had chosen one of us as a regular target, tagged us as his own personal pet. In my case, it was Addison. He would call on me to run his errands and even had me wash his car once a week. His hatred of me knew no barriers, his abuse no gates. He would spend hours telling me how easy my life was compared to his, how I was lucky to have a father who cared about me and a mother who didn't sleep around. He told me I should appreciate having grown up in New York City and been able to see all the things he could never afford to see. He told me I was lucky to have a friend like him in a place like Wilkinson.

Ferguson had it in for John, whose very presence would set off the guard's explosive temper. He would kick John as he walked by or hit him on the back of the head with his baton. Often the abuse would be rougher, its ugly results visible the next morning when John walked the yard with swollen eyes or puffy lips. Ferguson had a villain's heart and enjoyed whipping the weakest member of our pack. I always felt it was because he was weak himself, constantly ridiculed by Nokes and Styler. He couldn't lash out at them, so he sought an easier target. He found that target in John Reilly.

Styler claimed Tommy as his personal property. He forced him to carry his free weights around the yard and left a pair of shoes outside his cell every night to be shined by morning. He slapped and verbally abused him at will, a muscular man lording his advantage over a chubby boy. Tommy's presence set off in Styler too many reminders of his own impoverished childhood. He thought himself better than Tommy, constantly berating him over the most minor of infractions. He never let a day pass without attacking him in some form.

While Nokes abused us all, he took his greatest pleasure from beating Michael. He saw it as a match between two group leaders and always made sure that the rest of us were aware of his numerous assaults. He relished the cruelty he showered on Michael, forcing him to wipe up puddles of urine and wash the soiled clothes of other inmates. He ordered him to run laps around the playground track late into the night and then would wake him before the morning bell. He would slap and kick him randomly and trip him from behind while he walked the lunch line. It was all meant to make Michael beg him to stop, beg Nokes to leave him alone. But through it all, Michael Sullivan never spoke a word.

All four of the guards used sex as one more vicious tool in their arsenal. The repeated rapes were not only the ultimate form of humiliation, but the strongest method of control the guards could wield. The very *threat* of a rape kept us frightened of them all the time, never knowing when the door to the cell would swing open, always wondering when we would be pulled from a line.

We weren't the first group that Nokes and his crew treated with such levels of inhumanity and they weren't the only guards to abuse inmates. All across Wilkinson, young boys were left to the control of out-of-control guards. And the cruelty was all in the open, done without fear of reprisals. No one spoke out against the abuse and no one reported it. The guards who did nothing other than maintain order in Wilkinson could ill afford to bring attention to the situation; to do so might cost them their own jobs. The support personnel were in similar positions. The warden and his assistants were blind to what went on, at ease with the pretense that they fulfilled a necessary function by keeping kids like us off the streets. In truth, they were probably right in their thinking. After all, not many in town would waste time worrying about the well-being of juvenile offenders.

The town that surrounded Wilkinson was small and weathered. Most of the houses had been built around the turn of the century. There was nothing in the way of industry other than a few parcels of farmland, two dairies and a large plastics factory that employed nearly half of the 4,000 population. The townsfolk were friendly, the police department was small and honest and the high school football team was said to be one of the best in the county. There wasn't much money, but there wasn't much to spend it on, either. Church bells rang loud and clear on Sunday mornings and pork picnics were summer weekend staples. The citizens voted Republican every November and kept to themselves year-round. They would seem to have little time or patience for the concerns of boys sent to their town to live behind locked doors.

I stopped walking and stood looking around the fields, a group of inmates to my left playing football, a smaller group to my right huddled in a circle, talking in whispers and hand signals. The wind was blowing cold, the over-head sky dark with thick clouds that buried the autumn sun in shadow.

There were fifteen more minutes to go on our break. I left Michael to finish his walk and headed toward the library. We all needed to find a place of solace and I found mine in the pages of John's favorite book, *The Count of Monte Cristo*. I read and reread the novel, sifting through the dark moments of Edmond Dantes' unjust imprisonment, smiling when he eventually made his escape and walked from the prison where he had been condemned to live out his life. Then, I would put down the book and say a prayer, looking toward the day when I could walk out of Wilkinson.

FIVE

Visitors were allowed into Wilkinson on rotating weekend mornings, for a maximum of one hour. Only one visitor per inmate was permitted.

Early into my stay, I had written and asked my father not to come, explaining how it would make it harder for me to do time seeing him or my mother. I couldn't look at my father and have him see on my face all that had happened to me. It would have been too much for either one of us. Michael had done the same with the interested members of his family. Tommy's mother could never get it together to visit, satisfied with the occasional letter he sent telling her all was well. John's mother came up once a month, her eyes always brimming with tears, too distraught to notice her son's skeletal condition.

No one could stop Father Bobby from visiting.

News of his Saturday arrival was always presented with a stern warning, delivered by Nokes, to keep the conversation on a happy note. He warned us not to tell Father Bobby anything and that if we did, reprisals would be severe. He assured us that we belonged to him now and that no one, especially some priest from a poor parish, could be of any help to us.

Father Bobby was sitting on a fold-out chair in the center of the large visitors' room. He had placed his black jacket over the back of the chair and kept his hands on his lap. He was wearing a short-sleeved black shirt with Roman

162

collar, black pants and a shiny pair of black loafers. His face was tense and his eyes looked straight at me as I walked toward him, not able to hide their shock at what he saw.

'You lost some pounds,' he said, a trace of anger in his voice.

'It's not exactly home cooking,' I said, sitting down across from him, at the long table.

Father Bobby nodded and reached out his hands to touch mine. He told me I looked tired and wondered if I was getting the sleep I needed. He asked about my friends and told me he was scheduled to see each of them later in the day.

I didn't speak much. I wanted to tell him so many things, but I knew I couldn't. I was afraid of what Nokes and his crew would do if they found out. I was also ashamed. I didn't *want* him to know what was being done to me. I didn't want *anybody* to know. I loved Father Bobby, but right now, I couldn't stand to look at him. I was afraid that he would be able to see right through me, see past the fear and the shame, right through to the truth.

'Shakes, is there anything you want to tell me?' Father Bobby asked, moving his chair closer to the table. 'Anything at all?'

'You shouldn't come here anymore. I appreciate it. But it's not a good thing for you to do.'

I looked at him and was reminded of everything I missed, everything I couldn't have anymore. I needed to keep those thoughts out of my mind if I expected to survive. I couldn't fight through those feelings with every visit. If I was going to come out of Wilkinson, I was going to have to come out of it alone.

Father Bobby sat back in his chair, then pulled out a Marlboro and lit it with a butane. He blew a line of smoke toward the chipped ceiling, gazing over my right shoulder at a guard standing at rest. 'I stopped over at Attica on

163

my way up here,' he told me. 'To see an old friend of mine.'

'You have any friends *not* in jail?' I asked.

'Not as many as I'd like,' he answered, smiling, cigarette still in his mouth.

'What's he in for?' I asked.

'Triple murder,' Father Bobby said. 'He killed three men in cold blood fifteen years ago.'

'He a *good* friend?'

'He's my *best* friend,' Father Bobby said. 'We grew up together. We were close. Like you and the guys.'

Father Bobby took a deep drag on his cigarette and exhaled slowly. I knew he had been a troubled teenager, a street brawler with a bad temper who was always being dragged in by the cops. I felt that was part of the reason he went to bat for us. But it wasn't until this moment that I knew he had served time in Wilkinson.

'We were both sent up here,' Father Bobby said, his voice lower, his eyes centered on me. 'It wasn't easy, just like it's not easy for you and the guys. This place killed my friend. It killed him on the inside. It made him hard. Made him not care.'

I stared away from him, fighting off the urge to cry, grateful that there was one person who cared about me, cared about us, who knew what we were going through and who understood and would respect our need for silence. It was not surprising to me that the person would turn out to be Father Bobby.

It was also a comfort to know it hadn't killed or weakened him, but that somehow, in some way, Father Bobby found the courage to take what happened and place it behind him. I knew now that if I could get out of Wilkinson in one piece I had a chance to live with what happened. Maybe I would never be able to forget it, just like I was sure Father Bobby had visions of his own hell every day. But I might be able to live my life in step with those painful memories. Maybe my friends could too. All we needed was to find the same strength that Father Bobby found.

'Don't let this place kill you, Shakes,' he told me, the bottom of his hands squeezing the tops of mine. 'Don't let it make you think you're tougher than you are.'

'Why?' I asked. 'So I can come out and be a priest?'

'God, no,' Father Bobby said with a laugh. 'The church doesn't need another priest who lifts from the poor box.'

'Then why?' I asked.

His voice softened. 'The road only leads back to this place. And it's a road that will kill you. From the inside out. Just like it did my friend.'

Father Bobby stood up from his chair, reached his arms out and gave me a long, slow hug. I didn't want to let him go. I never felt as close to anyone as I felt to him at that moment. I was so thankful for what he had told me, relieved that my burden and that of my friends could be placed, if we needed to, on his sturdy shoulders.

I finally let go and took three steps back, watching him put on his jacket and button it, a Yankee cap folded in his right hand.

'I'll see you in the Kitchen,' I said.

'I'm counting on it, Shakes,' Father Bobby said before turning away and nodding for the guard to open the iron door leading out.

SIX

Once a year, in the weeks between Thanksgiving and Christmas, the Wilkinson Home for Boys sponsored a touch football game. Local residents were invited to huddle in the bleachers surrounding the football field, at a price of two dollars a ticket, with the money going back to the town. Children under ten were allowed in free.

But it was never about football. It was about the process of breaking down an inmate. First, the body was taken, ripped apart as if it were a tackle dummy, toyed with as if it were a stage prop. Next a young man's mind was molested, hounded until all he saw was a guard's face, all he heard was a prison whistle, all he feared was to break an unknown rule. Then, to complete the process, the guards would parade their creations onto a football field in front of the good people of a small town and play a game against them. A game they were too sick, too beaten up, too mentally ruined to compete in. All this to show off the perfect picture of a perfect institution.

The breakdown didn't work with all the inmates. But it worked with enough of them to keep the portait intact.

The guards assembled their team much in advance, practiced as often as four times a week and had full use of the fields. The inmates' team was chosen the Monday before the game, eleven reluctant players selected randomly from the various ethnic groups, placed together and told to play as a unit. They were allowed one two-hour practice, held under strict supervision. It wasn't meant, in

166

any way, to be a fair or equal match. It was just another chance for the guards to beat up on the inmates, this time in front of a paying crowd. And the way those games were played, you didn't need a ref; you needed a doctor.

Nokes was captain of the guards' team during my months at Wilkinson. Addison, Ferguson and Styler were players. My friends and I knew, without having to wait for a roster sheet, that we would be chosen for the inmates' team. Even Tommy, who had a badly swollen left ankle, the result of a recent battering he received from Styler. The guards were on our case for days, talking football, asking if we played it in Hell's Kitchen, asking who our favorite players were. It was just their way of telling us to get ready for another beating.

We were twenty minutes into practice, surrounded by guards on the four corners of the field, when I was tackled from behind by a black kid with braces and wine-barrel arms. My face was pushed into the dirt, grass covering my nose and chin. I turned my head and stared at him.

'It's *touch* football,' I muttered.

'I touch hard,' he said.

'Save it for the guards,' I told him. 'I'm on your side.'

'Don't need nobody on my side,' he mumbled, moving back to the huddle.

'It's not bad enough that the guards are gonna hand us our ass,' I said, walking with Michael. 'We've got these losers thinking they're the Green Bay Packers.'

'What's the point of even *having* a practice?' John said, coming up behind us.

'For them.' I nodded toward a group of guards at mid-field, arms folded, laughing and nudging one another.

'We're like a coming attraction,' Tommy said, walking slowly, trying not to put weight on his damaged ankle.

'Maybe,' Michael said, looking at the inmates on the other side of the field. 'Shakes, who's the toughest guy out here?'

'How do you mean tough?' I said.

'Who can talk and have everybody listen?' Michael said.

'Rizzo,' I told him. 'Tall black guy with the shaved head. The one holding the ball.'

'A black Italian?' John said.

'I don't know what he is. I just know his name's Rizzo. He's the main guy down in B block.'

'What's he here for?' Tommy asked.

'Manslaughter,' I told him. 'Involuntary.'

'What's that mean?'

'There was a fight,' I explained. 'He walked away and the other guy was *carried* away.'

'There's gonna be another one if we don't get back and play,' Tommy said. 'Let's not get Rizzo angry *before* the game.'

'They say he's got his own crew on the outside,' I said. 'He's up from Harlem or Bed-Stuy. I forget which. And the guy he killed?'

'What about him?' Michael said.

'His mother's boyfriend. Got a little too friendly with Rizzo's kid sister.'

'That's our guy then,' Michael said.

'Our guy for what?' I said.

'I'll tell you after practice,' Michael said.

Rizzo sat by himself in the library, at a wooden table in the center of the room, turning the pages of a football magazine, the top of his shaved head enveloped in a halo from the glare of the fluorescent lights overhead. I stood to his left, browsing through the library's collection of adventure books, most of them paperback, many missing pages and covers, a few littered with pornographic sketches.

Michael, a copy of *Tom Sawyer* under his arm, walked to the table, pulled back a chair and sat across from Rizzo.

'Okay with you if I use this chair?' he asked.

'Okay with me if you set yourself on fire,' Rizzo said,

his voice and body more man than boy. 'Okay with me if you die. I don't give a fuck.'

'Thanks,' Michael said, and sat down.

They read in silence for a few minutes, Michael turning his head once to look back in my direction, his face a blend of concern and confidence.

'Rizzo,' Michael said in a whisper. 'I need to talk to you. It won't take long.'

'How the fuck you know my name?' Rizzo snarled.

'I'd have to be stupid not to know,' Michael said. 'You the guy everybody points to and stays away from.'

'That *was* true,' Rizzo said. 'Till today.'

'We're wasting time,' Michael said. 'You interested or not?'

Rizzo took a deep breath and stared at Michael, his jaw set, his hands flat on the surface of the table, his eyes the color of lit cigars.

'Tell your friend over there to pull a chair next to you,' Rizzo said. 'He ain't smart enough to look cool.'

Michael smiled at Rizzo and without turning his head called for me to join them.

I walked down the aisle and eased my way toward the table, looking around the library, empty except for a guard standing by the entrance. I nodded at Rizzo as I sat down, a copy of *Scaramouche* in my hand.

'You been in here longer than a year?' Michael asked him.

'Closer to three,' Rizzo said. 'Should be out come the spring.'

'How many of these football games you play in?' Michael asked.

'This one be my second,' Rizzo said. 'Why?'

'The guards win the first?'

'The guards ain't ever lost one,' Rizzo said.

'What if they did?'

'Look, white boy,' Rizzo said, sitting straight up in his chair, a tint of anger seeping through the icy veneer. 'Don't know what your play was on the street. Don't care.

169

But, in here, the guards call the play and the play calls for them to win the game.'

'Why?'

'You think they fuck with you now,' Rizzo said. 'Beat them Saturday and see what happens. Won't be just you. Be all, in every cell block. Now, you tell me, white boy, we all supposed to get our ass split open just so you can look good in a football game?'

'They don't fuck with you,' I said, inching closer to the conversation.

'No,' Rizzo said. 'They don't. But they'll find them a nigger that ain't me and make him eat it double.'

'I'm not saying we gotta win,' Michael said. 'I just don't want to take a beating.'

'You do every day,' Rizzo said. 'Why's Saturday special?'

'On Saturday, we can hit back,' Michael said.

'You don't need me to hit them back,' Rizzo said.

'It won't work unless we're all in it,' Michael said. 'The only one who can make that happen is you.'

'Guards steer clear of me,' Rizzo said. 'They stay back and let me do my time. I play the game, put a hurt on one of them, it might change my cushion.'

'You're still nothin' but a nigger to them,' Michael said.

'Easy, white boy,' Rizzo told him. 'Just 'cause we talkin' don't mean we on the same side.'

'They don't hit you or fuck with you like they do us,' Michael said, excited now. 'They fuck with you another way. They treat you like an animal. A street animal. One they talk about when his back's turned.'

'I don't give a fuck what they say about me,' Rizzo said.

'Yeah, you do,' Michael said. 'You give a fuck. Else you wouldn't be the man back where you are.'

'And puttin' a hurt on the guards is gonna change that?' Rizzo sneered. 'That what you think?'

'It won't change a thing,' Michael said.

That stopped Rizzo cold. Now he was interested. 'Then

170

why, white boy?' he asked. He bolted up and shoved his chair behind him. 'If it ain't gonna change nothin'?'

Michael stood up and looked briefly past Rizzo's shoulders at the guard to his right. He then leaned across the table, his eyes tilted up toward Rizzo.

'To make them feel what we feel,' Michael said. 'Just for a couple of hours.'

Rizzo said nothing for the longest time. Then his lips curled up in what I can only assume was a smile.

'Hope you play as good as you talk,' Rizzo said, turning to leave.

'I hope so too,' Michael said.

It was the first Saturday in December.

The afternoon sun did little to contain the cold winds whipping around the grounds. The stands were filled with bodies buried under the weight of wool coats, flap-down hats, furry hoods, leather gloves, wrap-around scarves and thick quilts. The crowd's collective breath broke through the protective barriers of their clothing, sending waves of warm air snaking toward the slate gray sky.

Vendors sold peanuts, hot chocolate and coffee from their stations at the base of the stands. Armed guards circled the perimeters of the field, eyeing the crowd. Another group of guards stood in a straight-line formation behind our bench, watching with smirks as, shivering in our thin pants and sweatshirts, we laced our sneakers tight.

I turned to stare at the crowd, wondering who they would root for and how far they had come just to see a touch football game between a group of guards and a collection of teenage inmates. I also stared at them with a fair amount of envy, knowing that once the game was over, they were free to leave, to return to their safe homes, dinner waiting, our game reduced to nothing more than table conversation.

The guards came out wearing shoulder and elbow pads, the spikes on their cleats shiny and new. A handful were dressed in jeans and the rest wore sweat pants. All of them had on thick cotton sweaters, a few of them with hoods. We were left to play in our prison issues, from sweats to sneakers.

The two captains, Nokes for the guards and Rizzo for the inmates, met in the center of the field for the coin toss, a guard posing as a referee standing between them. Rizzo had insisted on being named captain, feeling it would send the guards an early signal that this was not going to be just another football game. Neither one attempted a handshake, but Nokes offered to skip the toss and let us have the ball first.

Rizzo turned down the request and called for heads. Nokes didn't want any part of Rizzo, well aware of his reputation. But he couldn't back up, not with the other guards watching and not with the warden sitting in the front row of the stands. He offered Rizzo a deal. He would go easy on him and the other three members of his crew who were on the team if he laid down and stayed out of the game. If not, Nokes warned, they would be as rough on them as they planned to be on the rest of the inmates. Rizzo listened to the offer without any show of emotion, his eyes never moving from Nokes'. face. He took several deep breaths and then, once again, asked for the coin to be tossed.

The coin came down heads.

Michael was in the center of the huddle, down on one knee, staring at the faces around him. He needed to see how rough the guards were going to be. He called a running play with me getting the ball. If I was touched as the rules called for, then we would be playing fair. But if I was tackled, as we all anticipated I would be, then we were in for a long and probably bloody afternoon. As Michael broke the huddle, Rizzo warned me not to fumble, regardless of how hard I was hit.

I stood behind Michael and next to Juanito, a fifteen-year-old in a T-shirt and torn pants. Tommy and John were on the line alongside Rizzo and a chubby black kid. Four inmates were spread at wideout, two on each side.

The guards played four men up front, three in the middle and four in the backfield.

Nokes and Addison were in the center of the line, both looking straight at me, their breath coming out in clouds, arms swinging at their sides, their bodies tense. Ferguson and Styler were playing deep, in a crouch, the front end of their cleats digging into hard ground.

'Watch out for the pass,' Nokes shouted to the guards positioned around him. 'Those wideout niggers can really run. Don't let 'em get in front of you.'

Michael grabbed the snap, took three steps back and flipped me the ball. I clutched it to my side, holding it with both hands, and followed Juanito into the line. The guards came off the ball with a grunt-filled fury, Nokes leading the charge. I turned a sharp left, darting from the center of the crowd, looking for an open space.

Three yards in, I was hit on the side by Addison, his arms around my waist, his weight dragging me down. From the corner of my eye, I saw Nokes, bearing down fast and hard, primed to pin me to the ground.

The elbow came out straight and hard, a black blur that was felt before it was seen. It caught Nokes flush on the side of the face and sent him sprawling to the dirt, Rizzo hovering above him, a smile on his face.

'The nigger on the line can really hit,' Rizzo said to him. 'Don't let him get in front of you.'

'All right!' Juanito said, helping me up. 'We got ourselves a game now, motherfuckers. We got ourselves a game.'

'That's right,' Michael said, giving Rizzo a wink. 'We got ourselves a game.'

For ninety minutes, spread across four quarters and a half-time break, we played the guards in the toughest and bloodiest game of touch football ever seen on the playing fields of the Wilkinson Home for Boys. For those ninety minutes, we took the game out of that prison, moved it miles beyond the locked gates and the sloping hills of the

173

surrounding countryside and brought it back down to the streets of the neighborhoods we had come from.

For those ninety minutes, we were once again free.

We were down by a touchdown mid-way through the fourth quarter, our energy sapped by the cold and brutal tactics employed by the guards in their all-out effort to emerge with a victory.

Michael stood in the center of the huddle, the sleeve of his left arm drenched in blood, courtesy of a cleat stomping he received from Addison and Styler on a long run shortly before the end of the half. Two thin streaks of blood flowed down the right side of his face. Tommy was breathing heavily, his ankle thick and purple. Johnny was barely able to stand, having been sandwiched a number of times by Nokes and Ferguson out in the middle of an open field.

I sat on my knees, spitting blood from a split lip, my breath coming in spurts, the pain from my rib cage too strong to ignore. I looked around at the others, all of them bleeding and raw. Rizzo's right hand was broken, twisted in a pile-on four plays earlier.

Behind us, the crowd, so clearly rooting for the guards early in the game, sat stunned into eerie silence, stilled by the sight of a field filled with red-tinged grass. The spectators were left with little else to do but watch the drama play itself out.

We had come so far, our energy level as high as the pain we felt in our bodies. We were all tired from the long game and weak from the blows we had taken. A tall kid, standing next to me in the huddle, had blood running down both his legs.

We needed one more play. A big play, one the guards wouldn't expect us to be able to carry out. It would have to be a street play. The kind that ends in a touchdown and a knockout. All the inmates had played in games that ended in blood. But for the guards this was a new experience and they didn't much care for it.

Rizzo called the play. Michael would fake pump a pass

to a wide-out named R.J. and then turn and throw deep, about forty yards downfield, right to the edge of the goal line. Rizzo would be there, step by step with Styler, both of them reaching for the ball. Rizzo's broken right hand was now hanging softly against his waist. It was Styler who had crushed the knuckles and bones and it would have to be Styler who was paid back, which now meant that the play required more than a touchdown to be successful. We came out of the huddle looking at six points for our team and a broken jaw for Styler. It didn't matter which came first.

Michael called for a quick snap and dropped back as far as he could, one arm useless at his side. I stayed next to Juanito, looking to block anyone who crossed our path. The two front lines banged at each other hard, blood, saliva and tiny pieces of flesh flying through the air. Nokes, bloody and bruised, came in from the left side of the field, leaping over one inmate and reaching both arms out for Michael. I jumped from my feet and met him square on, both of us falling within inches of Michael's legs, just as the ball left his one good hand to head downfield on a spiral.

'You fucker!' Nokes shouted, slapping and punching at me with both hands. 'I'm gonna fuckin' kill you!'

'Get off him!' Juanito screamed, pulling at Nokes' hair, grabbing one of his arms. 'Get the fuck off him!'

Michael and another guard were pushing at each other. Two of the inmates were squared off against two other guards. Punches and kicks were being tossed up and down the field. Bodies were crumpled on all sides. Shrill alert whistles were going off in every direction. Guards, in uniform, armed with mace cans and swinging batons, were running onto the playing area. The warden and his assistants were being driven down the sidelines, in a car with siren blaring, coming in from the goalposts to our backs.

Then the crowd, long silenced, erupted.

They stomped their feet against the base of the wooden

175

stands, clapped their gloved hands in a wild frenzy, and screamed out in a uniformed chorus of cheers.

Michael fell to his knees and pumped a fist in the air. Downfield, his arms raised to the sky, Rizzo basked in the applause, waiting for the guards to come take him away. He held the football in his good hand, a smile as open and as free as the emotion he felt spread across his face.

Styler's body lay inches from Rizzo. He was face-up, his legs spread, his head at an angle, motionless.

From inside the prison we heard shouts and yells.

The other inmates, forced to watch the game from their cells or outside open gym windows, celebrated the moment, many screaming out Rizzo's name. A number of the players rushed toward Rizzo, hoping to get to him before the guards, to lay a hand on the hero of the yard.

Nokes stood up on one knee, staring at me and Michael, the blood from his nose running into his mouth.

'You're dead,' he said. 'You are gonna pay for this in ways you never dreamed of. All of you. You're all gonna pay.'

'You ain't worth shit, Nokes,' Juanito said to him. '*We* always knew it. After today, *everybody* knows it.'

'Outta my way, you fuckin' spic,' Nokes said, standing on both legs, limping away to join the rest of the guards.

Michael walked up to him, waiting until he was inches away. 'Hey, Nokes?'

'What?' Nokes said, turning, the hate in his eyes enough to chill the blood oozing out of our bodies.

'Good game,' Michael said.

SEVEN

It was my second day in the isolation ward, my back against a damp wall, my knees tight against my chest, sitting alone in darkness. I was brought down to the place the inmates called 'the hole' immediately after the game, dragged down by Ferguson and a heavy-set guard with a red beard. They threw me face forward to the cold cement floor and watched as I crawled about, looking for a way to lift myself up.

They laughed at me and mocked my movements as I tried to make my way around the room. Then they slammed the door behind them, bolting it from the outside, their heavy footsteps soon an empty and distant echo. There was no bed in the hole. There was no toilet. There was no noise. There was no food. There was no water and there was no fresh air. There was only darkness and large hungry rats.

In the hole there was only madness.

I inched my way toward a corner of the room, trying to ignore the dust, the blood that still flowed from my football wounds and, most of all, the soft squeaks of the rats moving somewhere in the black of the cell.

I spent my first day in the hole sleepless, moving my legs from side to side, hoping to keep the rats away from my cuts, knowing that sooner or later, I would have to give in and close my eyes and they would make their move.

My hours were filled with terror. Any noise, even the

slight whine of a floor board, sent fear through my body. My clothes were drenched with sweat, my face was wet to the touch, my hair matted against my forehead. I took deep, shivering breaths, my eyes open wide, looking out into the stillness that surrounded me, my hands and feet numb from the cold.

I could not distinguish morning from night, dawn from dusk, each passing moment awash in a darkness that promised no rescue. The guards had not brought in any food or water, and the stench of dried urine and feces was overwhelming.

I was not alone in the hole.

I knew that my friends were somewhere down in the depths with me, each in his own cell, each in his own pain, suffering his own demons. Rizzo was there too, brought down by the guards, his other hand broken on his way in. There was no use shouting out to them; the walls and the cell door were much too thick for sounds to slip past.

I knew enough about the hole to know it was the place where the guards put inmates who had trouble adapting to their system. It was where they earned their control. The usual length of time spent in isolation was a week, never more than two. No one came out of it the same.

I had been there only a matter of hours when I began to think about death. It was what I most wished for, the only thing worth praying for to any God willing to listen.

I do not know how long I had been there when I heard the click of the lock, the bolt being pushed back, the handle as it snapped down. The sharp light that filtered in sent the rats scurrying into corners and forced me to shield my eyes. I heard footsteps approach as a large shadow hovered near.

'Thought you might be hungry, football star,' a voice said. It was Nokes, standing above me, a large bowl in his hand. 'I brought you some oatmeal.'

He placed the bowl down by his feet, in the center of

178

the room, sliding it closer to me with the edge of his shoe.

'Looks a little dry though,' he said. 'Nobody likes dry oatmeal. Tastes like shit.'

I heard a zipper slide down, watched him spread his legs and listened as he peed into the bowl of food.

'There,' he said, when he had finished. 'That's better. That should help it go down easier.'

He walked out of the room, a set of keys rattling in his hand.

'Enjoy your meal, football star,' Nokes said, closing me back into my dark world.

The minute I heard the lock turn and the bolt shut down I rushed for the bowl and ate my first meal in the hole.

I stared at the rat, inches from my face, watching him nibble on the skin of my stretched out fingers. I was resting flat against the hard surface of the cell floor, my clothes soiled, my body empty of feeling. I had lost any sense of time, any grasp of place, my mind wandering back and forth on the cloudy road between delusion and nightmare. Rats crawled up and down my back and legs, feasting on my cuts and scabs, nestling in the holes in my clothes.

One of my eyes wouldn't open, feeling sticky and swollen to the touch. One of my hands was balled into a tight fist, the fingers locked in place. My lips were swollen and dry and there was steady pain from my neck to the base of my spine. I couldn't compose a complete thought, and when I tried to call up memories, I could see only fragments of faces. I heard the voices of friends and enemies, the thick tones of my father and King Benny, the empty sounds of Nokes and his crew, the gutter accents of Fat Mancho and Father Bobby, floating in and out, words and faces mixing as one.

I felt the open hydrants of Hell's Kitchen on my body, the cool spray of water stripping away summer heat. I tasted Sno-Kones and hot pepper sandwiches and listened to Frankie Valli hit a high note and Dinah Washington ache with the blues. I tossed pennies against the side of a warehouse wall, dropped water balloons on the head of a passing stranger, ran into the winds of De Witt Clinton Park and fished off the piers of 12th Avenue. Left for dead in that hole of despair, I sought refuge in the safest spot my mind could wander – the streets of Hell's Kitchen.

Only then, during those rare cloudless moments, could I escape my dark surroundings, clear away the dirt and the pain, the rats and the pools of urine.

Only then could I move away from the wails of the walking dead and feel, for a fragment of time, that I was still alive.

I was released from the hole after two weeks and sent to the prison infirmary, where my wounds were cleaned, my clothes thrown away and my meals served on plastic trays. I was carried into the twenty-two-bed ward fifteen pounds lighter than the day of the football game, my body wracked with a high fever and a series of infections.

The medical staff at Wilkinson was a small one, led by an elderly doctor with a chronic cough and three nurses years past their prime. For each, it was a last stop in an otherwise undistinguished career. While they all must have been aware of what went on, they lacked the desire or conviction to question it, let alone bring the abuse to the eyes of a higher authority. They had more to lose than to gain by such confrontation and would be out-manned, out-maneuvered and out-smarted if they dared.

'You're lucky,' I heard the prison doctor say to me. 'Another day in there and we wouldn't be any help.'

'I wasn't alone,' I said, my voice barely above a whisper, my mind still circling around empty spaces.

'They took everyone out,' the doctor said.

'Were we all lucky?' I asked.

'No,' the doctor said. 'Not all.'

*

Rays of sunlight came down through an open window, warming my face, my left eye still sealed shut. The bed and the sheets felt soft against my bare skin, white bandages covering whole sections of my chest, arms, legs and feet. An IV bag dripped fluid into one of my arms and·two plastic tubes were in my nose, feeding me air from an oxygen cannister off the side of the bed. Somewhere in the distance, a radio played a song I hadn't heard before.

I turned my head to the right and saw Michael in the bed next to mine. His left arm and right leg were in soft casts, his face was puffy and bruised, the rest of his body bandaged as heavily as mine.

'I thought you'd never wake up,' Michael said, looking over.

'I never thought I'd want to,' I croaked.

'John and Butter are at the other end of the hall,' Michael said.

'How are they?'

'Alive.'

'Who isn't?'

'Rizzo,' Michael said.

'They *killed* him?'

Michael nodded. 'They took turns beating him until there wasn't anything left to beat.'

Rizzo was dead because of us. We made him think that going up against the guards in a meaningless football game had some value, would somehow make us better than them. That it would give us a reason to go on. And, once again, we were wrong. We had made another mistake. While it is normal in the course of growing up to have lapses in judgments, our errors always seemed to carry a deadly price. We were *wrong* to take the hot dog cart and that mistake nearly ruined a man and landed us in a juvenile home. We were *wrong* to go to Rizzo and talk him into taking part in our silly plan. That conversation cost him his life.

The mistakes we were making could never be repaired. I could never give James Caldwell back the feeling in his

181

arm or take away his pain. I could never give the hot dog vendor back his business or his dreams. I could never bring smiles back to John and Tommy, return the sweetness that was at the core of their personalities. I could never take the hardness out of Michael and the hurt out of me. And I could never bring Rizzo back to life. A young man was dead because he went deep against the guards and reached for a ball he shouldn't have caught. Who went deep because we asked him to.

I looked over at Michael and he stared back at me and I knew we both had the same thoughts raging through our brains. I turned away and laid my head against the pillow, staring at the white ceiling with my one good eye, listening to a voice on the radio talk about threats of snow and holiday sales. I looked down at my hands, the tips of my fingers wrapped in gauze, scratches like veins marking their way across my flesh. My eye felt heavy and tired, the antibiotics and painkillers making me as foggy as a street junkie.

I shut my eye and gave in to sleep.

It was two days later when I heard the footsteps, familiar in their weight.

'Hello, boys,' Nokes said, standing between our two beds, a smile on his face. 'How we feelin' today?'

Michael and I just stared back, watching him swagger up and down, checking our charts, eyeballing our bandages and wounds.

'You should be outta here in no time,' Nokes snarled. 'It's gonna be good havin' you back. We missed you and your friends. Especially at night.'

Michael turned his head, looking down the corridor, checking the faces of the other sick inmates. Juanito was two beds down, his face a mask of cuts, welts and stitches.

'It's been nice visitin' with you,' Nokes said, standing close enough for us to touch. 'But I gotta go. I'm on shift. I'll see you soon, though. You can count on that.'

Michael motioned for Nokes to stop. 'Kill me now,' Michael whispered.

'What?' Nokes moved to Michael's side of the bed. 'What did you say?'

'Kill me now.' It wasn't a whisper this time. It was in a normal tone of voice, calm and clear. 'Kill us all now.'

'You're fuckin' crazy,' Nokes said.

'You *have* to kill us,' Michael said. 'You *can't* let us out alive.'

Nokes was still startled, but he shook it off and replaced his uneasiness with his usual smirk. 'Yeah?' he said. 'And why's that, tough guy?'

'You can't run the risk,' Michael told him.

'What risk you talkin' about?'

'The risk of meeting up,' Michael said. 'In a place that ain't here.'

'That supposed to scare me? That street shit of yours supposed to scare me?' Nokes laughed. 'Your friend Rizzo was tough too. Now he's buried tough.'

'Kill us all,' Michael said. 'Or sign yourself up for life in here. That's the choice.'

'I've been right all along,' Nokes said. 'You *are* crazy. You Hell's Kitchen motherfuckers are really crazy.'

'Think about it,' Michael said to our tormentor. 'Think about it hard. It's the only way out for you. Don't take a chance. You can't afford it. You kill us and you kill us now.'

183

Winter 1968

I squeezed the mop through a wooden ringer, dirty brown water filtering back into the wash pail. I was on the third tier of C block, washing the floors outside the cells. It was my first week out of the infirmary and my wounds, bound by tight strips of gauze bandages against my ribs and thighs, still ached. After a few strokes with the mop, I rested against the iron railings, my legs weak from days in the hole. It was early morning and the cell block was quiet, inmates either attending classes or exercising in the gym.

I looked around the block, gray, shiny and still, winter light from outside merging with the glare of overhead fluorescents that were kept on twenty-four hours a day. In its silence, Wilkinson looked serene, cell doors open, floors glistening, steam from large central radiators keeping out the cold winds of winter.

The peace was not meant to hold. Wilkinson was a prison on the brim of a riot. Rizzo had been right. The guards did not take kindly to our playing them even. The day after the game, all inmate privileges were cancelled. The late-night beatings and abuse accelerated to the point where no inmate felt safe. The most minor infraction, ignored in the past, was now cause for the most severe punishment.

For their part, the inmates were stirred by Rizzo's death and the conditions in which the rest of the team were released from the isolation ward. Makeshift weapons – zip

187

guns, sharpened spoons stuck into wooden bases, mattress coils twisted into brass knuckles – now appeared in every cell block. The inmates still obeyed every order, but their faces were now masked by defiance.

I was half-way down the corridor when I saw Wilson on the circular staircase, making his way to the third tier. Wilson was the only black guard in our cell block and the only guard who shunned the physical attacks enjoyed by his coworkers. He was a big man, a one-time semi-pro football player with a scarred knee and a waistline that stretched the limits of his uniform. He smoked non-stop, and always had an open pack of Smith Brothers cherry cough drops in his back pocket. He had a wide smile, stained yellow by the smoke, and big hands, topped by thick, almost-blue fingers. The inmates called him Marlboro.

Marlboro was older than the other guards by a good ten years and had two younger brothers who held similar jobs at other state homes. In summer months, he was known to smuggle in an occasional six-pack to some of the older inmates.

He was also Rizzo's connection to the outside.

'Seem to be doin' a good job,' he said when he reached my end of the hall, his breath coming in short spurts, a long stream of smoke flowing out his nose. 'You take to the mop real good.'

'Some people do,' I said. 'Some people teach.'

'Got that right,' he said, laughing, a rumble of a cough starting in his chest.

'How many of those you go through a day?' I said, pointing to the lit cigarette in his hand.

'Three,' he said. 'Maybe four.'

'Packs?'

'We all got habits, son,' Marlboro said. 'Some that are good. Some that are bad.'

I went back to mopping the floor, moving the wet

strands from side to side, careful not to let water droplets slip over the edge of the tier.

'How much more time you got?' Marlboro said from behind me. 'Before they let you out.'

'Seven months if they keep me to term,' I said. 'Less if they don't.'

'You be out by spring,' Marlboro said. 'Only the baddest apples do full runs.'

'Or end up dead,' I said.

Marlboro lit a fresh cigarette with the back end of a smolder between his fingers, tossed the old one over the side and swallowed a mouth of smoke.

'Rizzo was my friend,' Marlboro said. 'I didn't have a piece of what went down.'

'Didn't break your ass to stop it,' I said.

'Look around, son,' Marlboro said, cigarette clenched between his teeth, veins thick on his bulky arms. 'You see a lot of other nigger guards around here?'

'*Guards* is all I see around here,' I said.

'I got me a good job,' Marlboro said. 'Work is steady. Pension, if I make it, a good one. Vacation and holidays are paid and every other weekend belongs to me and my lady.'

'And it keeps you in cigarettes,' I said.

'I *hate* what they do to you and the other boys,' Marlboro said, cigarette out of his mouth, sadness etched across the stark contours of his face. '*Hate* what they did to Rizzo. That boy was blood to me. But there ain't nothin' I can do. Nothin' I can say gonna change this place.'

I put the mop back into the pail and ran it through the ringer, hands on the top end of the handle, eyes on Marlboro.

'You ever hit a kid?' I asked.

'Never,' Marlboro said. 'Never will. Don't get me wrong. There's some mean sons of bitches in here could take a beatin'.' But it ain't what I do. Ain't part of the job. Least not the job I took.'

189

'How do the other guards feel about you?'

'I'm a nigger to them,' Marlboro said. 'They probably think I'm no better than any of you. Maybe worse.'

'They always been like this?'

'Since I been here,' Marlboro said. 'Goin' on three years come this June.'

'How about you and Nokes?' I asked.

'I do my work and keep my distance,' Marlboro said. 'He does the same.'

'What's the deal?' I said.

'Same as the others,' Marlboro said. 'They don't like who they are. They don't like where they are.'

'There's lots of people like that,' I said. 'Where I live, every man I know feels that way. But they don't go around doing the shit Nokes and his crew pull.'

'Maybe they different kind of men,' Marlboro said. 'Nokes and his boys, they ain't seen much of life and what they seen they don't like. You grow up like that, most times, you grow up feelin' empty. And that's what they are. Empty. Nothin' inside. Nothin' out.'

'What about the warden?' I asked, leaning the mop handle against the rail. 'The people on his staff. They've *got* to know what goes on.'

'But they *act* like they don't,' Marlboro said, taking still another drag. 'Same as the town folk. *Nobody* wants to know. What happens to you don't touch them.'

'So they dummy up,' I said.

'That's the jump,' Marlboro said. 'And don't forget, from where those folks stand, *you* the bad guys. Nokes and his boys, they ain't gonna break into people's homes. Ain't gonna hold 'em up at gun point. You the guys pull that shit. That's why you here to begin with. So, don't expect no tears. To them that's free, you *belong* inside.'

'You've got all the answers,' I said to Marlboro, pushing the water pail further down the center of the floor.

'If I did I wouldn't need a state check every two weeks,' he said. 'I just know what I know.'

190

'I've got to finish up,' I said, pointing down to the rest of the corridor.

'And I gotta get me some more cigarettes,' Marlboro said. 'That give us both somethin' to do.'

He moved away with a wave, a snap to his walk, his baton slapping against the railing bars. A small pattern of crushed cigarette butts lay in the spot where he had stood.

'You know there's no smoking on the tiers?' I shouted after him.

'What they gonna do?' Marlboro turned to face me, a grin spread across his face. 'Arrest me?'

EIGHT

My hands were folded behind my head, resting against my pillow, a thin sheet raised to my chin. It was late on a Saturday night, one week after Valentine's Day. Outside, heavy snow fell, white flakes pounding the thick glass. I was fighting a cold, my nose stuffed, my eyes watery, a wad of toilet paper bunched in my right hand. My throat was raw and it hurt to swallow.

I thought about my mother, wishing I had a cup of her *ricotta* to take away the aches and chills. She would fill a large pot with water and set it to boil, throw in three sliced apples and lemons, two tea bags, two spoonfuls of honey and a half glass of Italian whiskey. She boiled everything down until the contents were just enough to fill a large coffee cup.

'Put this on,' she would say, handing me the heaviest sweater we owned. 'And drink this down. Now. While it's hot.'

'Sweat everything right outta you,' my father would say, standing behind her. 'Better than penicillin. Cheaper too.'

I tried to sleep, closing my eyes to the noises coming from outside my cell. I willed myself back to my Hell's Kitchen apartment, sipping my mother's witches' brew, watching her smile when I handed her back an empty cup. But I was too tense and too sick to find rest.

A number of the inmates, as tough as they acted during

192

the day, would often cry themselves to sleep at night, their wails creeping through the cell walls like ghostly pleas.

There were other cries too.

These differed from those filled with fear and loneliness. They were lower and muffled, the sounds of pained anguish, raw cries that begged for escape, for a freedom that never came.

Those cries can be heard through the thickest walls. They can cut through concrete and skin and reach deep into the dark parts of a lost boy's soul. They are cries that change the course of a life, that trample innocence and snuff out goodness.

They are cries that once heard can never be erased from memory.

On this winter night, those cries belonged to my friend John.

The darkness of my cell covered me like a mask, my eyes searching the night, waiting for the shouts to die down, praying for morning sun. I sat up in my cot, curled in a corner, wiped sweat from my upper lip and cleaned my nose with the toilet paper. I shut my eyes and capped both hands over my ears, rocking back and forth, my back slapping against the cold wall behind me.

The door to my cell swung open, thick light filtering in, outside noise coming in on a wave. Ferguson stood in the doorway, beer bottle in one hand, baton in the other. He had a two day growth of beard on his face and his thin head of hair looked oily and in need of a wash. His heavy eyelids always gave him a sleepy appearance and the skin around his thin lips was chapped, a small row of pimples forming at the edges.

'I just fucked your little friend,' he said, his speech slurred, his body swaying.

He took three steps into the cell.

I rolled off the cot and stood across from him, my eyes on his, toilet paper still in my hand.

'Take your clothes off,' Ferguson said, moving the beer

bottle to his lips. 'Then get back in bed. I wanna play with you for awhile.'

'No,' I said.

'What was that?' Ferguson asked, taking the bottle away from his face, smiling, his head at half-tilt. 'What did you say to me?'

'No,' I said. 'I'm not taking my clothes off and I'm not gettin' into bed.'

Ferguson moved closer, his feet sliding across the hard floor.

'You know what you need?' he said, smile still on his face. 'You need a drink. Loosen you up a little. So, have your drink. Then, we'll play.'

He lifted the beer bottle above my head and emptied it. Streams of cold beer ran down my face and shirt, my mouth and eyes closed to the flow, puddles forming around my feet. Ferguson wiped the beer from my face with the fingers of his hand.

He put his fingers in his mouth and licked them dry.

'There's all kinds of ways to drink beer,' he said, throwing the bottle on my cot. 'And there's all kind of ways to fuck.'

Ferguson threw his baton on the cot and watched it land inches from the bottle. He turned back to me and undid the buckle on his belt and lowered the zipper of his pants with one hand.

He ran the other hand across my face and chest.

'You're right,' Ferguson said in a whisper. 'You don't have to take off your clothes, if you don't·want to. And you don't have to get back in your bed.'

'Please, Ferguson,' I said, my voice barely audible. 'Don't do this.'

'Don't do what, sweet thing?' Ferguson asked, his eyes glassy, rubbing my chest harder, bringing his hand lower.

'Don't do what you're doin',' I said.

'But I thought you liked it,' Ferguson said. 'I thought all you boys liked it.'

'We don't,' I said. 'We don't.'

194

'That's too bad,' Ferguson said, his face close to mine, his breath a foul mix of beer and smoke. ''Cause I like it. I like it a lot.'

Ferguson ran his hand past my chest and up to my face and along my neck, resting it against the back of my head. He moved even closer to me, placing his face on my shoulder.

'Take my dick out,' Ferguson said.

I didn't move, my eyes closed, my feet still, Ferguson's weight heavy against my body, his breath warm on the sides of my face.

'C'mon sweet thing,' Ferguson whispered. 'Take it out. I'll do the rest.'

I opened my eyes and saw John standing in the doorway.

He had a makeshift knife in his hand.

John moved out of the light and into the darkness of the cell. He was naked expect for a pair of briefs, stained red with blood, and one sock drooping down the sides of his ankle. He was breathing through his mouth and kept the knife, held to his hand by a rubber guard, flat by his leg.

'Don't be afraid, sweet thing,' Ferguson whispered in my ear. 'Take it out. It's ready for you.'

'I'm not afraid,' I said.

'Then do it,' Ferguson said.

'Move out of the light,' I said. 'It hurts my eyes.'

Ferguson lifted his head and grabbed both of my cheeks in his hand, a wild, maniacal smile on his face.

'You. *supposed* to keep your eyes *closed*,' he said, moving backwards, closer to John, dragging me with him. 'Didn't you know that?'

We were inches from my cot, my hand close enough to reach the empty beer bottle and the baton. John was by the side of the bed, the knife still against his leg. Ferguson let go of my face, undid his pants and took two more steps back.

'All right,' he said. 'Let's stop fuckin' around, sweet thing. It's time for fun.'

I eased down to my knees, my head up, looking into Ferguson's eyes, my hand reaching for the baton to my right.

'That's it, sweet thing,' Ferguson said. 'And remember, I like it slow. Nice and slow.'

Ferguson felt the edge of the knife before he heard John's voice.

'That's how I'm gonna let you die, dip shit,' John said. 'Nice and slow.'

'You little punk,' Ferguson said, more with surprise than fright. 'What the hell you tryin' to do?'

'It's time for me to have a little fun,' John said.

'I can have you killed for this,' Ferguson said.

'Then I've got nothin' to lose.'

I grabbed the baton, jumped to my feet and held it with both hands. I looked past Ferguson at John, saw something in his eyes that had never been there before.

'You can't cut him, Johnny,' I said.

'Watch me, Shakes,' John said. 'Sit down on your cot and watch me.'

'Go back to your cell,' I said. 'Leave him to me.'

'He's not gonna get away with it,' John said. 'He's not gonna walk away from what he did to me. What he's been doin' to all of us.'

'He *has* to get away with it,' I said.

'Who says?' John asked. 'Who the fuck says?'

'We're gonna get out of here in a few months,' I whispered slowly. 'If you stick him, we aren't going anywhere.'

'Listen to your friend, Irish,' Ferguson said. 'He's talkin' sense here.'

I braced my legs and shoved the fat end of the baton into the center of Ferguson's stomach. I watched him flinch from the blow, his lungs hurting for air.

'Stay outta this, scumbag,' I said. 'Or I'll kill you myself.'

John moved the knife away from Ferguson's neck, step-

196

ping back, holding the sharp edge of the blade in the palm of his hand. His face was a portrait of hard hate, emptied of its sweet-eyed charm, a resting place for all the torment and abuse he had endured.

In so many ways, he was no longer the John I had known, the John I had grown up with. Wilkinson had done more than beat and abuse him. It had taken him beyond mere humiliation. It had broken him down and pulled him apart. It had ripped into the most gentle heart I had known and emptied it of all feeling. The John Reilly who would turn our clubhouse into a safe haven for lost kittens was gone. The John Reilly who stole fruits and vegetables off supermarket trucks and left them at the apartment door of Mrs. Angela DeSalvo, an elderly invalid with no money and no family, was dead and buried. Replaced by the John Reilly who stood before me now, ready to kill a man and not give it another thought.

'Let it go, John,' I said. 'He's a piece of shit and he's not worth it.'

'Glad to see you got smart,' Ferguson said, getting his wind back, looking up at me. 'I'll go easy on you in my report.'

'There won't be a report,' I said.

'Fuck you mean, there won't be a report?' Ferguson said, the drunken slur of his words replaced by a steadfast anger. 'You two assaulted a guard. There's *gotta* be a report.'

'Just go, Ferguson,' I said, handing him back his baton. 'Fix your pants and get the fuck outta here.'

'I ain't leavin' before Irish over there hands me the knife,' Ferguson said.

'There isn't any knife,' I said.

I walked over to where John was standing, the steel look still on his face, his eyes honed in on Ferguson. I rested my hand against the one holding the knife, knuckles tight around the edge of the blade.

'It's okay, Johnny,' I said. 'You can let go now. It's okay.'

197

'He's not gonna touch me again,' John said, the voice no longer that of the boy who cried at the end of sad movies. 'You hear me, Shakes? He's not gonna touch me again.'

'I hear you,' I said, taking the knife from my friend's hand.

I nudged past Ferguson and walked over to my cot. I lifted the thin mattress and put the knife on top of the springs.

'Like I said Ferguson,' I said, turning to face him. 'There's no knife.'

'I ain't gonna forget you did this,' Ferguson said, pointing a shaking finger at both me and John. 'You two hear me? I ain't gonna forget this.'

'It's a devil's deal, then,' I said.

'What the fuck's that mean?' Ferguson said.

John explained it to him. 'First one to forget dies,' he said.

NINE

The English teacher, Fred Carlson, stood before the class, his tie open at the collar, his glasses resting on top of his head, a thick piece of gum lodged in the corner of his mouth. He had his back to the blackboard, hands resting on its edge. He was young, not much past thirty, in his first semester at Wilkinson, paid to pass on the finer points of reading and writing to a class of disinterested inmates.

'I was expecting to read thirty book reports over the weekend,' Carlson said in a voice that echoed his country home. 'There were only six for me to read. Which means I'm missing how many?'

'This here's English class,' a kid in the back shouted. 'Math's down the hall.'

A few inmates laughed out loud, the rest just smirked or continued to stare out the classroom windows at the snow-filled fields below.

'I'm doing my best,' Carlson said, his manner controlled, his frustration apparent. 'I want to help you. You may not believe that or you may not care, but it's the truth. But I can't force you to read and I can't make you write the reports. That's something only you can do.'

'Must be easy to read where you live,' an inmate in a thin-cropped Afro said. 'Easy to write. It ain't that easy to do in here.'

'I'm sure it's not,' Carlson said. 'But you have to find

a way. If you expect to get anywhere once you get out of here, you have to find a way.'

'I gotta try stayin' alive,' the inmate said. 'You got a book that's gonna teach me that?'

'No,' Carlson said, stepping away from the blackboard. 'I don't. No one does.'

'There you go,' the inmate said.

'Then I'm just wasting your time,' Carlson said. 'Is that what you're saying to me?'

'You wastin' *everybody's* time,' the inmate said, hand slapping a muscular teenager to his right. 'Give it up and keep it home. Ain't no place for what you got here.'

Fred Carlson pulled a metal chair from behind the center of the desk and sat down, both hands on his legs, his body rigid, his eyes on the inmate.

He stayed that way until the whistles sounded the end of the period.

'See you Friday, teach,' the inmate said on his way out the classroom door. '*If* you still here.'

'I'll see you then,' Carlson said. '*If* you're still alive.'

I was walking down a row behind four other inmates, a black-edged notebook in my hand, a dull pencil hanging in my ear flap.

'You got a second?' Carlson asked as I passed by his desk.

'I do something wrong?' I asked.

'No,' he said, shaking his head and smiling. 'I just want to talk to you.'

I stood my ground, waiting for the classroom to empty, hands in my pants pockets.

'You did a great job on your book report,' Carlson said.

I mumbled a thank you.

'How come you were able to find the time to do the work?' Carlson asked, with a slight hint of sarcasm. 'Aren't you worried about staying alive?'

'I worry about it all the time.' I said. 'That's why I read and write. It keeps my mind off it awhile.'

'You really seemed to like the book,' Carlson said. My report had been on *The Count of Monte Cristo*.

'It's my favorite,' I explained. 'I like it even more since I been in here.'

'Why's that?'

'I told you why in the report,' I said.

'Tell me again.'

'He wouldn't let anybody beat him,' I said. 'The Count took what he had to take, beatings, insults, whatever, and learned from it. Then, when the time came for him to do something, he made his move.'

'You admire that?' Carlson asked, reaching across the desk for a brown leather bag stuffed with books and loose papers.

'I *respect* that,' I said.

'Do you have a copy of the book at home?'

'No,' I said. 'I've only got the Classics Illustrated comic. That's how I first found out about it.'

'It's not the same thing,' Carlson said.

'There's a librarian in my neighborhood, she knows how much I like the story,' I said. 'She makes sure the book's always around for me. It's not that big a deal. Not many people look to take it out.'

Carlson had his head down, rummaging with both hands through his bag.

'I gotta get goin', Mr. Carlson,' I said. 'Can't miss morning roll.'

'One more minute,' Carlson said. 'I've got something for you.'

'What is it?' I asked.

'This,' Carlson said, a hardbound copy of *The Count of Monte Cristo* in his hand. 'I thought you might like to have it.'

'To keep?'

'Yes,' Carlson said.

'Are you serious?' I asked.

'Very serious,' Carlson said. 'You love a book that much, you should have a copy of your own.'

201

'I can't pay you,' I told him.

'It's a gift,' Carlson said. 'You've received gifts before haven't you?'

'It's been a while,' I said, opening the book, flipping through its familiar pages.

'This one's from me to you,' Carlson said. 'My way of saying thanks.'

'Thanks for what?' I asked.

'For not making me think I'm just spinning my wheels in here,' Carlson said. 'That *somebody*, even if it is only one student, listens.'

'You're a good teacher, Mr. Carlson,' I said. 'You're just stuck with a bad bunch.'

'I can't imagine being locked in here,' Carlson said. 'For one night, let alone months.'

'I can't imagine it either,' I said.

'It's not what I thought it would be like,' Carlson said, with a slow shake of his head.

'I don't think it's what *anybody* thought it would be,' I said.

'No, I suppose not,' Carlson said.

'Listen, I've got to run,' I said. 'Thank you again for the book. It means a lot.'

'Will the guards let you keep it?' Carlson asked.

'They won't know I've got it,' I told him.

'We can discuss the book in class on Friday,' Carlson said. 'That's if you think *The Count* can hold their attention.'

'He's got a shot,' I smiled.

'Any special section I should read from?' Carlson asked, snapping his leather bag shut.

'That's easy,' I said, moving toward the door, book in my hand. 'The part when he escapes from prison.'

TEN

It was my first time inside the guards' quarters, a series of lockers, couches, bunks, shower stalls, soda machines and coffee makers spread through four large rooms at the back end of C block. The rooms smelled of old clothes and damp tile and the floors were dusty and stained, cigarette butts scattered in the corners. Floor lamps, covers torn and smeared, cast small circles of light, keeping the quarters in a state of semidarkness. Dirty clothes were tossed on the floor and on the furniture. A large framed photo of the Wilkinson Home for Boys, taken during a snowbound winter many years earlier, hung in the main room.

Nokes sat behind a desk, its top cluttered with memos, open binders, a tape recorder, two phones, a handful of magazines and open packs of cigarettes. A thick toaster-size cardboard box, its center slit open, rested in the middle.

'You asked to see me?' I said, standing in front of him.

'Hang on a second, soldier,' Nokes said. 'I wanna get the other guys for this.'

Nokes lifted the phone off its cradle and pressed a yellow intercom button.

'Get off your asses,' he shouted into the speaker. 'He's here.'

Addison, Styler and Ferguson walked in from a side room, each in various stages of undress. Ferguson had shaving cream along his face and neck, a straight razor in his hands. Styler, naked except for a pair of white briefs, was smoking a cigar with a plastic tip. Addison held a folded paper in one hand and a slice of pepperoni pizza in the other.

They stood behind Nokes, their attention more on the box than on me.

'You know the rules about mail?' Nokes asked, looking up at me, an unlit cigarette clenched between his teeth. 'About what you can get and what you can't?'

'Yeah,' I said. 'I know them.'

'You can't know 'em too fuckin' well,' Nokes said, a finger pointing to the open box. 'Havin' your mother send all this shit.'

'That box's from my mother?' I asked.

'I mean, look at this shit,' Nokes said to the three guards surrounding him, ignoring my question. 'Where the fuck she think her son is at, the army?'

'What the fuck is this?' Styler asked, his hand pulling out a small jar filled with roasted peppers in olive oil.

'The warden is supposed to clear the mail,' I said. 'Not the guards.'

'Well, the warden ain't around,' Nokes said. 'And when he ain't around, we clear it.'

'None of the shit I see would get past the warden,' Styler said. 'Ain't none of it on the approved list.'

'I'm sure your mama got a copy of that list,' Addison said. 'It gets sent to all the parents.'

'My mother doesn't read English,' I said.

'Don't blame us for her being stupid,' Nokes said, tossing a jar of artichoke hearts to Styler.

'Those are things she made,' I said. 'Things she knows I like. She didn't look to do anything wrong.'

'Other than have a jackoff for a son,' Styler said, opening the jar and putting it to his nose.

'Can I have the box?' I asked. 'Please?'

'Sure,' Nokes said. 'The box is yours. What's in it is ours. That seem fair?'

'Is there anything in there other than food?' I asked, my hands bunched in fists by my side.

'Just this.' Nokes held up a brown set of rosary beads. 'Mean anything to you?'

'More than they would mean to you,' I said.

'Suppose you'd like to have them then?' Styler said, his mouth filled with artichoke hearts.

'They belong to me,' I told him.

'What do you do with these things?' Nokes asked, fingering the rosary beads in his hand.

'You pray,' I said.

'Fuckin' losers like you ain't got a prayer,' Styler said.

'Take the food, Nokes,' I said. 'All of it. Just let me have the beads.'

Styler walked around the desk and came up alongside me, one of his arms around my shoulders.

'You gonna let us hear you pray?' he asked me.

'I like to do it alone,' I said, my eyes still on Nokes. 'It works better that way.'

'Like jerkin' off,' Addison said.

'Just this once,' Styler said, smiling and winking at the other three. 'Let us hear you.'

'Maybe he needs something to pray about,' Nokes said, reaching a hand under the desk, coming up with a black baton.

He gave the baton to Styler who took it with his free hand, pushing me closer to his side.

'Put your hands on the desk,' Styler said to me. 'Lay them down flat.'

'And start thinkin' up some prayers,' Addison said.

My hands were inches from the box my mother had sent. Styler spread my legs apart and pushed down my pants, tearin' off the top button with the force of his effort. Nokes laid the brown rosary beads across both sets of my knuckles. I felt Styler's hands rub against the base of my back, his skin coarse, his manner rough.

'Remember, fucker,' Nokes said, eating my mother's peppers with his hands. 'We want to hear you pray. Loud!'

205

Styler put an arm around my stomach and slid the front end of the baton inside me. The pain came in a rush, leg muscles cramping, chest heaving, stomach tied in a knife-like nerve of knots.

'We can't hear no prayers,' Nokes said.

'You better start,' Ferguson had a terrible smile on his face. 'Before Styler there loses his baton up your ass.'

'Our Father,' I said, my lips barely moving, my breath short, my lungs on fire. 'Who art in heaven.'

'Nice and loud,' Styler said from behind me. 'Pray nice and loud.'

'Hallowed be thy name,' I said, tears falling down the sides of my face. 'Thy kingdom come. Thy will be done.'

'Don't say come in front of Styler,' Nokes said with a loud laugh. 'You don't wanna get him excited.'

'On earth as it is in heaven,' I said, my legs starting to buckle, my body damp with cold sweat. 'And forgive us our trespasses. . . .'

'That part must be about us,' Addison said, his eyes wide, his tongue licking at his lips.

'As we forgive those,' I said, my hands starting to slide off the desk, knuckles still gripping the rosary beads. 'Who trespass against us.'

'Louder, fucker!' Nokes said, standing now, holding my face with two hands. 'Make like you're in a fuckin' church.'

'And lead us not into temptation,' I said, the room around me a shifting blur, my arms and legs empty of feeling. 'But deliver us from evil.'

'Too fuckin' late for that now, loser,' Styler said, as he released me and let my body crumple to the floor. 'Too fuckin' late.'

I woke up in my cell, on my cot, my pants still wrapped around my knees. I was shivering, sheet and blanket under me, my body numb to movement. The rosary beads were still in my hand, the cross wedged into my palm. I brought the beads to my lips, slowly, and kissed them.

I opened my eyes, looked out into the darkness and cried till the sun came up.

Spring 1968

Michael hit the handball against the cement wall, watching it one-bounce its way toward John, who waited for it near the middle of the white divider line. I played off the back line, alongside Tommy, my mind more on the weather than on the game.

It was early afternoon and warm for a mid-April day. The sun was still strong, scattered rays bouncing off the hardened tar floor and onto our arms, legs and faces. The air was dry, humidity low, soft breeze blowing at our backs.

The handball court was seldom free: the black inmates had co-opted the area as part of their domain. But, for now, they were out of the picture, joined together in organized protest, a reflection of their outrage over the murder earlier in the month of Martin Luther King, Jr. They stayed in their cells and refused to engage in any prison activity, insisting that even meals be brought to them. Initially, the guards reacted as expected, with intimidation and force, but the inmates held firm, anger and pride keeping the rules of the prison at bay. The warden, fearing outside attention, ordered the guards to back off and allow the protest to flame itself out.

The ball came in a dark blur toward Tommy, who took two quick steps back, balanced his weight, swung his hand and missed. He turned around, picked up the ball and tossed it back to Michael.

211

'I don't get this game,' Tommy said. 'I don't understand it at all.'

'That makes me *really* glad you're on my team,' I said.

'What's the point?' Tommy asked.

'We don't *have* any points,' I said. 'Michael and John, they have all the points. Go ask them.'

'It's six to nothing,' Michael said, walking toward me, bouncing the ball against the tar, his right hand wrapped in heavy black adhesive tape. 'You wanna switch sides?'

'How about we take a break?' I said. 'I'm not used to getting this much sun.'

'There ain't much shade around here,' Michael said.

'Let's go near the trees,' I said. 'The guards can still see us from there and it's gotta be cooler.'

We walked past the wall, wiping sweat from our faces and arms, toward a small chestnut tree with drooping limbs, the duty guard following us with his eyes.

We sat around the tree, our arms spread behind us, legs rubbing against grass, staring out at the square-shaped brick facade of C block, our home these past seven months.

'Nice view,' John said.

'Just looks like any other place from here,' Tommy said. 'It don't look like what it is.'

'I'll never forget what it looks like,' I said. 'Or what it is.'

'You might,' Michael said. 'If you're lucky.'

'They give you your release date yet?' Tommy asked me.

'Nokes had the letter from the warden,' I said. 'He waved it in front of me. Then he tore it up.'

'When do you figure?' Michael asked.

'End of June,' I said. 'Maybe early July. Something like that.'

'I wish we were goin' with you,' John said, his voice crammed with sadness. 'Woulda been nice for us to all walk out together.'

'I wish you were, too,' I said, smiling over at him.

212

'No use thinking about it,' Michael said. 'We're gonna do a full year. Not an hour less.'

'I could talk to Father Bobby after I get out,' I said. 'Maybe he could make some calls, shave a month or two off.'

'There's nothing to talk about,' John said.

'There's *lots* to talk about, Johnny,' I said. 'Maybe if people knew what goes on in here, they'd make a move.'

'I don't *want* anybody to know, Shakes,' John said, the center of his eyes filling with tears. 'Not Father Bobby or King Benny or Fat Mancho. Not my mother. Not anybody.'

'I don't either,' Tommy said. 'I wouldn't know what to say to anybody that *did* know.'

'What about you?' I asked, turning my head toward Michael. 'You gonna stay quiet?'

'I can't think of anybody who needs to hear about it,' Michael said. 'Guys did time in this place or places like it, they know what went on. Those who didn't won't believe it or won't give a shit. Either way, it's nothin' but a waste of time.'

'I don't even think *we* should talk about it,' John said. 'Once it's over.'

'I want it buried, too, Shakes,' Tommy said. 'I want it buried as deep as it can go.'

'We've got to live with it,' Michael said. 'And talking makes living it harder.'

'People might ask,' I said.

'Let 'em,' Michael said, standing up, brushing loose grass off the back of his sweats. 'Let 'em ask, let 'em think. But the truth stays with us.'

'Just be glad you're going home, Shakes,' John said. 'Forget everything else.'

'And try to stay out of trouble till we get back,' Michael said.

'That should be easy,' I said. 'Without you guys around.'

213

'What's the first thing you're gonna do when you get back?' John asked.

'Go to the library,' I said. 'Sit there for as long as I want. Look through any book I want. Not have to get up when somebody blows a whistle. Just sit there and listen to the quiet.'

'Know what I miss the most?' Tommy asked in a sad tone, his face up to the sun, his eyes closed.

'What?' John said.

'Running under an open johnny pump late at night,' Tommy said. 'Water cold as winter. Stoops filled with people eatin' pretzels and drinkin' beers outta paper bags. Music coming out of open windows and parked cars. Girls smilin' at us from inside their doorways. Shit, it was like heaven.'

'Two slices of hot pizza and an Italian ice at Mimi's is heaven,' I said.

'Walkin' with Carol down by the piers,' Michael said. 'Holdin' her hand. Kissing her on a corner. That's hard to beat.'

'What about you, John?' I asked.

'I don't want to be afraid of the dark again,' John said in a voice coated with despair. 'Or hear an open door in the middle of the night. And I don't wanna be touched, don't wanna feel anybody's hands on me. Wanna be able to sleep, not worry about what's gonna happen or who's comin' in. If I can get that, I'd be happy. I'd be in heaven. Or close to it.'

'Some day, John,' Michael said. 'I promise that.'

'We *all* promise that,' I said.

In the short distance behind us, a guard's whistle blew. Overhead, rain clouds gathered, darkening the skies, hiding the sun in their mist.

ELEVEN

The prison cafeteria was crowded, long rows of wooden tables filled with tin trays and inmates elbowing their way through a macaroni and cheese dinner. Each inmate had twenty minutes to eat a meal, which included time spent on the serving line, finding a seat and dropping an empty tray on the assembly wheel in the back of the large room. Talking was not permitted during meal time and we were never allowed to question either what we were given to eat or the amount doled out.

The food was usually at the low end of the frozen food chain, heavy on processed meat, eggs, cheese and potatoes, weak on vegetables and fruit. Each table sat sixteen inmates, eight to a bench. One guard was assigned to every three tables.

As with every other social situation at Wilkinson, the dining area offered limited opportunities to make friends. The guards were always wary of cliques forming or expanding and moved quickly to split up any such attempts. This left the inmates with no choice but to stick to their original alliances. Living in an atmosphere that stressed survival above all else, random friendships posed too great a risk, for they required a level of trust that no one was willing to concede. It was safer to stay within your own group.

I was fourth on the serving line, standing a few feet behind Michael, empty trays held in our hands. A blank-faced counterman dropped an empty plate on each of our

215

trays, his head rocking up and down, rolling to its own private rhythm. Further down the line, I grabbed for two spoons and an empty tin cup.

'Can you see what we're having?' I asked Michael.

'Whatever it is, it's covered with brown gravy.'

'*All* our meals are covered with brown gravy.'

'They must think we like it,' Michael said. Then he turned off the line and moved to his left, his tray filled with dark meat, gray potatoes, a small, hard roll and a cup of water, looking for a place for us to sit. He headed for the back of the room, where there were two spots. I followed, right behind him.

The spaces between the tables were narrow, wide enough for only one person at a time to make his way through. The guards stood to the sides, their eyes focused on the tables assigned them. They controlled who left his seat and who sat in his place, all accomplished with hand gestures, nods and shoulder taps. It was a system that functioned through precision and obedience, guards and inmates merged in an assembly line of human movement. There was no room for error, no space for accidents, no place for a mental lapse.

No time to bring the assembly line to a halt.

Michael was halfway down the row of tables, his eyes focused on two seats in the rear of the room. I was directly behind him, followed by a short teenager with a limp. None of us saw the inmate on Michael's left stand and begin to move out of his row.

Michael moved three steps forward, the edge of his tray barely grazing the arm of the inmate walking toward him on his left. The inmate shot his arm against the tray and sent it skyward, out of Michael's hands and crashing to the floor in full view of a guard.

Michael whirled to face the inmate who called himself K.C. and who was now standing with a smile on his face and his hands balled into fists. 'What the fuck you do that for?'

'You brushed me,' K.C. said.

'So?'

'*Nobody* touches me,' K.C. said. 'I ain't like you and the rest of your fag friends.'

Michael swung a hard right at K.C., landing it flush against the much taller boy's jaw. The blow, one of the hardest I'd seen Michael land, barely caused a flinch. Michael looked at me in disbelief and, for a moment, it was almost funny, like something out of a James Bond movie. But K.C. wasn't in on the joke and, as we knew all too well, this was no movie.

K.C. looked to be about three years older than Michael, perhaps eighteen, with broad shoulders, bulked arms and a crew cut so close it showed little more than scalp. In the few months that he had been inside Wilkinson's, K.C. had already razor-slashed another inmate, done time in the hole for his part in a gang rape and spent a week in a strait-jacket after he took a bite out of a guard's neck.

He rushed Michael and they both fell to the floor, shirts and skin sliding against spilled food. K.C. threw two sharp right hands, both landing against Michael's face, one flush to the eye. A circle of inmates formed around them, quietly watching the action, a few holding trays and eating the remains of their lunch. The guard, less than a month on the job, stood off to the side, his face a blank screen.

I held my ground and scanned the circle for other members of K.C.'s crew, watching to see if any weapons were passed over, waiting for one of them to make a move and join their friend against Michael.

K.C. was rubbing a fist full of meat against Michael's face, grinding it into his eyes. Michael shot a hard knee into K.C.'s groin and followed it with a short left to his kidney.

'Your fuckin' life's over,' K.C. said, putting his hands around Michael's throat and tightening his grip. 'You gonna die here today, punk. Right on this floor.'

I tossed my tray aside and jumped on K.C.'s back, punching at his neck and head, trying to loosen his hold. K.C. let one hand go and turned it to me, swinging his punches upward, brushing my shoulder and side. The reduced pressure allowed Michael to take in some fresh breath. K.C. swung his body at an angle, his open hand against my chin, trying to push me off his back. He rolled over with me still clinging to him, his strength taking Michael around with us. I landed on top of the spilled tray, my shirt wet and sticky from the gravy, meat and potatoes spread across the floor. K.C. was now all flailing arms and legs, kicking and punching at us both with a wild, animallike intensity. I covered my face with my hands and kept my elbows slapped against my sides, blocking as many of K.C's kicks and punches as I could.

Michael did the same.

The crowd inched in closer, sensing that what they wanted to see was about to take place – a bloody finish to the battle.

A sharp kick to the throat stripped me of wind and a wild punch to my jaw forced blood out of my nose. Voices in the crowd, fueled by the rush for the kill, cheered K.C. on.

'Finish him!' someone from behind me shouted.

'Kick him dead!' another said.

'One and two belong to you!' still another screamed. 'Step back and just watch 'em die.'

The shrill sound of a police whistle brought the shouts to an end.

The crowd parted to let Nokes walk past, each inmate staring at him in silence. Nokes held a can of mace in one hand and the thick end of his baton in the other. He was chewing a piece of gum and had a cigarette tucked behind one ear. The back of his shirt was streaked with sweat. His eyes moved from me to Michael to K.C. The three of us stood facing him, our bodies washed head to knee in food and blood.

Nokes stood in front of me and took the cigarette from behind his ear, put it to his mouth and lit it with a closed matchbook. He took in a lung full of smoke and let it out slow, through his nose, his closed jaw still moving to the gum.

'All these months here, they haven't taught you shit,' Nokes said. 'You're still the same fuckin' clowns you were when you walked in.'

Nokes turned from us and faced the inmates behind him. He scanned their faces, running a hand through his hair, cigarette still hanging from his lower lip.

'Back to your seats and finish your lunch,' Nokes said to them. 'There's nothin' more to see.'

'That go for me too?' K.C. said, rubbing his hands against the sides of his pants.

'No,' Nokes said, turning back to him. 'No, it don't go for you. I want you back in your cell. You're done with lunch.'

'Me and you finish this some other time,' K.C. said, looking over at Michael. 'Some time real soon.'

'Maybe at dinner,' Michael said, watching K.C. walk out of the lunch room.

'You two get any lunch?' Nokes asked, stubbing out the cigarette with the front end of his boot.

'I got to smell it,' Michael said. 'That's better than eating it.'

'How about you finish it now?' Nokes said.

'I'm not hungry,' Michael said.

'I don't give a fuck you hungry or not,' Nokes said. 'You eat 'cause I'm tellin' you to eat.'

I started to walk past Nokes, back toward the lunch counter to get a new tray. Nokes put a hand against my chest and held it there.

'Where you think you're goin'?' he asked, his voice louder, playing it up for the inmates watching.

'You said to get lunch,' I said, confused.

'You boys don't need to go back on line for food. There's plenty to eat right where you standing.'

I stared at Nokes and tried to imagine what had been done to him to make him this cruel, had driven him to the point that his only pleasure came from the humiliation of others. I more than just hated him. I had passed that state months ago. I was digusted by him, his very presence symbolizing the ugliness and horror I felt each day at Wilkinson. I thought there wasn't much more he could do to me, do to any of us, but I was wrong. There was no limit to Nokes' evil, no end to his torment. And now, we were about to take one more plunge into the hellish world he had forced on us.

Michael and I didn't move.

The inmates were pointing and whispering among themselves. A few of them giggled. The guard in the center of the aisle held his position.

'Let's go boys,' Nokes said, smiling now, his anger having found an outlet. 'There ain't much more time in the lunch period.'

'I'm still not hungry,' Michael said.

Nokes immediately brought the back end of the baton down against the side of Michael's head. He quickly followed it with a level blast across his face. The force of the shot sent blood from Michael's nose and mouth spraying onto Nokes' uniform shirt.

'I tell you when you're hungry!' Nokes shouted, swinging the baton again, this time landing a sharp blow to Michael's neck. 'And *I* tell you when you're not! Now, get on your fuckin' knees and eat.'

Michael dropped to one knee, a shaky hand reaching for a fork, his eyes glassy, the front of his face dripping with blood. He picked up the fork and jabbed at a piece of meat near his leg, slowly bringing it to his mouth.

'What the fuck are *you* waitin' for?' Nokes asked me. 'Get down on your knees and finish your goddamn lunch.'

I looked beyond Nokes at the faces of the inmates staring back at me, their eyes a strange mixture of relief and pleasure. They had all been at the edge of Nokes' baton, had all felt his fury, but none would ever move against him for the sake of two prisoners they barely knew. Nokes could have killed us on the floor of that lunch room and no one would have said a word.

I went down on my knees, picked up a spoon, scooped up a potato slice and put it in my mouth.

I looked up at Nokes, his shirt drenched and tinged red, his face splattered with Michael's blood.

'Eat faster,' Nokes said, swinging his baton against the base of my spine. 'Don't think you got all fuckin' day.'

Nokes walked between us as we ate, smiling and winking at the other inmates, stepping on the pieces of food we were about to put in our mouths.

'Let's go,' he said, pulling the top of Michael's hair and slapping his face. 'Nobody leaves here until you clowns are finished with your meal.'

Nokes walked to the edge of one of the tables and rubbed his boot on top of a crushed slice of bread. He took a cigarette out of an open pack in the front of his shirt and put it in his mouth. He lit it and sat on the side of the table.

'There's some bread over here,' Nokes said, blowing two smoke rings toward the ceiling. 'Can't have a good lunch without a slice of bread.'

Nokes spread his legs, looked down at the bread, took in a deep breath and spit on it. He took another drag of the cigarette and wiped at the sweat and blood on his face with the sleeve of his shirt.

'Now, how about you boys crawl over here and get yourself some?' Nokes said.

We were on our knees, chewing our food, our bodies trembling more out of shame than fear. Each humiliation plotted by Nokes and his crew was meant to be a breaking point, to make us crack and finally give in to Wilkinson. We were too young to know that the break line had been passed the minute we entered the prison walls and we were much too stubborn to understand that nothing we did or didn't do would allow us to defeat Nokes while we were still behind those walls.

'I don't see either of you scumbags crawlin',' Nokes said, finishing the cigarette and dropping it down on top

221

of the bread. 'Don't make me come drag you on over here.'

We went down on our elbows, rubbing against the gravy that was spread across the ground, our faces inches from the food and dirt. Michael's nose was still bleeding and the swelling on his face had forced one eye to shut.

'That's it, now you're startin' to listen,' Nokes said. 'Show the boys here how to do a good crawl. Show them you know how to follow my rules.'

'It's one o'clock, Nokes,' Marlboro said, standing behind us, his voice filled with smoke. 'Your lunch shift is over.'

'I'm not through here yet,' Nokes said. 'Got a few more things that need cleanin' up before I can leave.'

'It's my tour now,' Marlboro said calmly, walking past us and moving closer to Nokes. 'I'll clean what needs cleanin'.'

'Stay outta this one,' Nokes said. 'This ain't got nothin' to do with you.'

'I stayed outta too many as it is,' Marlboro said, putting a cigarette to his mouth and lighting it. 'This one I'm gonna stay in.'

Nokes jumped down from the table, his face as red with rage as his shirt was with blood. He walked up to Marlboro, standing no less than five inches from the taller man's face.

'Don't fuck with me, boy,' Nokes said. 'I'm *warnin'* you.'

'Fuck with me, Nokes,' Marlboro said in a calm voice. 'I'm *askin'* you.'

Nokes continued the stare-down, his eyes locked in on Marlboro. None of the inmates moved, their attention focused on the first visible break in the wall of guard unity. Michael had stopped chewing his food, tossing his fork to the ground, too humiliated to care who would win the battle shaping before him. I held a spoon in my hand, rolling its head against my thigh, my eyes on the floor, wrapped in the silence around me.

222

Nokes took a deep breath, letting air out through his mouth, and shifted the weight on his feet. He slapped the baton against his open palm, measuring Marlboro, the crease of a smile inching its way to the sides of his face. Marlboro stood his ground without a change in expression, content to let the pressure of the situation percolate at its own pace.

Nokes was the one to back down. His smile faded and he let his head drop, so his eyes didn't meet Marlboro's.

'You eatin' into my shift,' Marlboro said.

'I'll get out of your way,' Nokes said. 'For now.'

'I take what I can get,' the black guard said, walking away from Nokes and over toward us. 'Just like you.'

Marlboro helped Michael to his feet and looked over at me, the soles of his shoes sliding on the slippery turf smeared with food, spit and hardened gravy. He nudged his head toward the guard standing in the aisle.

'If you through standin',' Marlboro said to him, 'I could use some help.'

'What do you need?' the guard said, his eyes darting, checking to see if Nokes was clear out of the room.

'Get the boys on their way,' Marlboro said, pointing to the inmates at the tables. 'They've seen enough to last till supper time. I'll take care of these two and what needs cleanin' up.'

The guard nodded and began to clear out the lunch room, one table row at a time. The inmates moved with a quiet precision, eager to leave now that the threat of violence was at an apparent end.

I stood next to Michael and Marlboro, watching the inmates exiting the hall, the three of us knowing there would be a price to pay for all that had happened on this day. Sean Nokes was not the kind of man to let a slight go by or leave an act of torment unfinished. He would go after Marlboro through the system, use whatever clout he could muster to make life difficult for the good man with the bad smoking habit. But he would save his true wrath for me and Michael. We both knew that. What it would

223

be, what it *could* be after all the horrors that he had already initiated, was something neither one of us could envision. All we knew was that it would happen soon and, as with everything Nokes planned, it would be something we would never be able to erase from our minds.

Summer 1968

July 24, 1968 was my last full day at Wilkinson.

Two weeks earlier, a five-member panel of The New York State Juvenile Hearing Board had determined that a period of ten months and twenty-four days was enough penance for my crime. A written request had been forwarded to the warden, with all necessary release forms attached. Also included in the package was the name of my designated control officer, the four days in August I was scheduled to report to him, and a psychological profile written by someone I had never met.

The thick manilla envelope, sealed with strips of tape, sat on the warden's desk for three days before he opened and signed it.

'The cook makin' anything special for your last day?' Tommy asked, walking alongside me in the yard during the middle of our morning break.

'If he *really* cared, he'd take the day off,' I said. 'The food in here has been killin' my insides.'

'Two cups of King Benny's coffee will set you straight,' Tommy said. 'No time flat.'

'It can't happen soon enough,' I said.

'Don't forget us in here,' Tommy said, his voice a tender plea.

I stopped and looked over at him. He still had the baby weight and face, but had changed in so many other ways. His eyes were clouded by a veil of anger and, in place of a swagger, there was now a nervous twitch to his walk.

227

His neck and arms were a road map of cuts and bruises and his left knee cap had been shattered twice, both above and below the main joint.

It was the body of a boy who had done a man's prison time.

'I won't *ever* forget you,' I said, watching the anger briefly melt from his eyes. 'In *or* out of here.'

'Thanks, Shakes,' he said, picking up the walk. 'Might help knowin' that one body outta here gives a shit.'

'More than one body, Butter,' I said. 'You'd be surprised.'

'It's gonna be a bitch,' Tommy said. 'These last coupla months.'

'It'll be over soon,' I said, passing a grunting trio of weightlifters. 'By the time the Yankees drop out of the pennant race, you'll be home.'

'Nokes say anything yet about you leavin'?' Tommy asked.

'There isn't much more he can do,' I said. 'Time's on my side now.'

'Until you're out of those gates,' Tommy said, 'there ain't nothin' on your side.'

TWELVE

I sat in my cell, quiet and alone, in my last hours as an inmate at the Wilkinson Home for Boys. I looked around the small room, the walls barren, the sink and toilet cleaned to a shine, the window giving off only hints of nighttime sky. I had folded the white sheet covering, wedged it under the mattress and laid against it, my legs stretched out, feet dangling off the end of the cot. I was wearing white underwear and a green T-shirt in the stifling heat.

All my prison issues, except for a toothbrush, had been taken away by the guards earlier that afternoon. In the morning, they would be replaced by the clothes I wore on the day I first arrived at Wilkinson. A sealed white envelope containing four copies of my release form rested against one of my thighs. One was to be handed to the guard at the end of the cell block. A second was to be given to the guard stationed at the main gate. A third was for the driver of the bus that would take me back to lower Manhattan.

The last copy was to be mine, the final reminder of my time behind the bars of Wilkinson.

I reached over, picked up the envelope, opened it and fingered the four copies of the form. I stared at them, my mind filled with the images of pain and punishment, humiliation and degradation it took to get these forms in hand.

To get back my freedom and send me on my way.

I had walked into Wilkinson a boy. Now, I wasn't at all sure who or what I was. The months there had changed me, that was for certain. I just didn't know how or in what way the changes would manifest themselves. On the surface, I wasn't as physically ruined as John, nor as beaten down as Tommy. I wasn't the lit fuse Michael had become.

My anger was more controlled, mixed as it was with a deep fear. In my months there, I never could mount the courage that was needed to keep the guards at bay, but at the same time I maintained a level of dignity that would allow me to walk out of Wilkinson.

I don't know what kind of man I would have grown to be had I not served time at The Wilkinson Home for Boys. I don't know how those months and the events that occurred there shaped the person I became, how much they colored my motives or my actions. I don't know if they made me any braver or any weaker. I don't know if the illnesses I've suffered as an adult have been the result of those ruinous months. I'll never know if my distrust of most people and my unease when placed in group situations are byproducts of those days or simply the result of a shy personality.

I *do* know the dreams and nightmares I've had all these years are born of the nights spent in that cell at Wilkinson. That the scars I carry, both mental and physical, are gifts of a system that treated children as prey. The images that screen across my mind in the lonely hours are mine to bear alone, shared only by the silent community of sufferers who once lived as I did, in a world that was deaf to our screams.

I couldn't sleep, anxious for morning to arrive. It was still dark, the early hours offering little more than thin blades of light filtering into my cell from the outside hall.

I wondered what it would be like to sleep once again in a bed not surrounded by bars, to walk in a room not monitored by alternating sets of eyes. I was anxious to eat a meal of my choosing without fear that the food had been toyed with or tainted.

I thought about the first things I would do once I was back out on the familiar streets of Hell's Kitchen. I would buy a newspaper and check the box scores and standings, see how my favorite players had fared while I was away. I would walk up to the Beacon on West 74th Street and see whatever movie was playing, just to sit once more in those plush seats and breathe air ripe with the smell of burning popcorn. I would go to Mimi's and order two hot slices with extra cheese, stand at the counter and look out at the passing traffic. I would go to the library next to my apartment building, find an empty table and surround myself with all the books I loved, running my hands across their pages, holding their torn binders; reading the fine old print.

It was my way of life and I wanted to get back to it.

I never heard the key turn in the latch. Never heard the snap of the bolt. I only saw the door swing open, a crowd of shadows washing across the floor of my cell.

'You should be asleep,' Nokes said, his words slurred. He was the first to enter, his uniform shirt off, an empty pint of bourbon in his right hand. 'Need all your rest for the big trip back home.'

'Told you he'd be up,' Addison said, walking in behind Nokes, just as drunk, face, neck and arms wet with sweat. 'These fuckers are like rats. They never sleep.'

'What do you want?' I asked as calmly as I could manage.

'I just want to say good-bye,' Nokes said. 'We all do. Let you know how much we gonna miss havin' you around here.'

'We're friends, right?' Styler said, entering the cell, sober and in full uniform, holding John and Tommy by his side. 'All of us.'

John looked at me with dead eyes, as if he knew what was going to happen and was trying to shut it out of his mind. Tommy was crying, full tears running down the sides of his face, afraid more for me than for himself.

'Must be hard to leave your friends,' Ferguson said,

231

walking in with Michael and locking the cell door behind him. 'We've been together for so long.'

'Can't leave your friends without a party,' Nokes said. 'It just wouldn't be right.'

Michael, as always, stayed silent, his face, his eyes, his entire body, coiled into one large mask of hate. John and Tommy may have lost their heart, but Michael was in danger of losing his humanity. Everything that was done to him, everything that was said, only served to fuel his hate. By now, he had enough fuel to last a lifetime.

'It's over, Nokes,' I said, standing up in the crowded room, the heat strong, the air rancid. 'Please let it go.'

'It ain't over till morning,' Nokes said. 'It ain't over till the party's over.'

'I don't want a party,' I said.

'That's too bad,' Styler said. 'I even went out and got you a gift.'

'A special gift,' Nokes said. 'One you ain't ever gonna forget.'

Ferguson and Addison stood next to me and held my arms while Styler reached into his pocket and pulled out a few feet of nylon cord. He tied the cord around my arms, knotting it secure at the back. Styler shoved a wad of tissues into my mouth and held my face as Addison ran thick yellow tape across my lips. Nokes walked over, a wide black belt dangling in one hand.

'Tie his feet too,' Nokes said, handing the belt to Styler. 'I don't want him to move.'

My three friends stood before me, as still as the air, only their eyes betraying their terror. John's lips were trembling and Tommy kept his head tilted to the ceiling, his mouth mumbling a secret prayer. Michael was a silent statue, his rage at rest.

'We got a full house tonight,' Nokes said, leaning over and whispering in my ear, his breath bourbon-coated. 'First we take care of your friends. And then we take care of you.'

I watched Styler walk over to John and lock a handcuff

around one of his wrists. The other half of the cuff was put on Tommy's wrist. Addison did the same to Michael and Tommy, locking the three together.

'Move them up closer,' Nokes said, sitting on the cot, one arm hanging over my shoulder. 'We wanna get a good look.'

Styler pushed the three forward with one hand, lighting a cigarette with the other. Ferguson wiped sweat from his face and forehead with the sleeve of his shirt. Addison stood with his back against the door and giggled.

'Best seats in the house,' Nokes said to me. 'You won't miss a thing from here.'

There was no place for us to go, nowhere for us to run. Our screams would go unheeded. Shouts for the warden would be ignored. No one would listen. No one would care. Fear ruled the night and fear controlled this place.

My friends were face down on the floor, their pants stripped off and tossed to the side, the three guards on their knees behind them, laughing, sweating, hands rubbing flesh, glazed, watery eyes looking at Nokes, waiting for the nod of his head.

'Everybody's ready,' Nokes said to me, squeezing me closer to his side. 'Time to drop the ball.'

Nokes pushed my head onto his shoulder and wiped his mouth with the back of his hand, sweat pouring out of both of us like a light, steady rain.

Styler was slapping John's back, playful taps that echoed off the walls of the small room.

Addison hovered over Tommy, fondling himself and staring at me.

'I'm gonna fuck your friend,' he said in a shaky voice. 'Every night. Every night you ain't here, I'm gonna fuck your friend.'

Ferguson rested his body on top of Michael's, his eyes wide with anticipation.

'Let's go, Nokes,' he said. 'Stop wastin' time. Let's give 'em what they want.'

233

Nokes pushed us both back against the wall, one of his hands holding my face to the scene before me.

'Go to it,' Nokes said, his eyes, his breath, his body on me. 'Make it party time.'

They tore at my friends, attacked them as if they were animals freed from a cage. The cries, the screams, the shrieks were all a valued part of their beastly game. I sat there, sweat running down my body and onto the sheet beneath me, and watched three boys be ripped apart, living playthings lost in a garden filled with evil intent.

'You gonna think about this when you're gone,' Nokes said, rubbing his arms over my body. 'Ain't ya', you little fuck? Ain't ya'?'

Nokes leaned over and pushed me face down on my cot. His hands tore at the few clothes I was wearing, stripping me naked, my arms still bound by the nylon cord. He undid the belt around my legs, folded it and began to lash at my back and rear with it.

'You're gonna remember this little party, all right,' Nokes said, as he continued to hit at me with the thick edges of the belt. 'You gonna remember but good. I'm gonna see to that. Don't worry, fucker. I'm gonna see to that.'

Nokes tossed the belt to the floor and lowered his pants, his breath coming in heavy waves, sweat slicing down off his body. His mouth rested against my ear, his teeth chewing on the lobe.

'This is so you don't forget me,' he said again, the weight of his body now on top of mine. 'Can't let you do that, sweet thing. You gotta remember me like you gotta remember this night. Forever.'

I heard John cry, pitiful moans coming from a well deep inside his soul. I saw Tommy's head bounce like a rubber ball against the cement floor, blood flowing from dual streams above his forehead, his eyes blank, the corners of his mouth washed in foam. I saw Michael's left arm bend across the side of his back until the bones in the joint snapped, the pain strong enough to strip the life from his body.

I felt Nokes pulling at me, hitting me with two closed fists, his mouth biting my shoulders and neck, drawing blood. The front of his head butted against the back of mine with every painful thrust, my nose and cheeks scraping the sharp edges of my cot. One of his knees, the pointy end of his belt now wrapped around it, was wedged against the fleshy part of my thigh, stabbing into it, blood coming out in spurts.

A part of all of us was left in that room that night. A night now far removed by the passage of time. A night that will never be removed from my mind.

The night of July 24, 1968.

The summer of love.

My last night at the Wilkinson Home for Boys.

BOOK THREE

Lazzaro erased with his hand anything Billy Pilgrim might be about to say. 'Just forget about it, kid,' he said. 'Enjoy life while you can. Nothing's gonna happen for maybe five, ten, fifteen, twenty years. But lemme give you a piece of advice: Whenever the doorbell rings, have somebody else answer the door.'
– Kurt Vonnegut
Slaughterhouse-Five.

BOOK THREE

Fall 1979

ONE

Hell's Kitchen had changed. The streets were no longer swept daily and graffiti marred many of the buildings. A scattering of low-income high-rises had replaced stretches of run-down tenements, and storefronts now needed riot gates to guard against the night. Many of the Irish and Italians tenants had left the area, heading for the safer havens of Queens and Long Island, and the Eastern Europeans had deserted the neighborhood altogether, moving to Brooklyn and New Jersey. Replacing them were a larger number of Hispanics and a mixture of uptown blacks and recent island immigrants. In addition to these groups, young middle-class couples, flush with money arrived, buying and renovating a string of tenements. The young and rich even set about changing the neighborhood's name. Now, they called it Clinton.

The old order was in turmoil, guns and drugs replacing gambling and stolen goods as the criminals' best route to a fast dollar. Cocaine use was rampant and dealers dotted the area, openly selling on corners and out of parked cars. Residents fell alseep most nights to the sounds of police sirens. There were many gangs, but the deadliest was Irish and numbered close to forty sworn members.

They called themselves the West Side Boys and they controlled the Hell's Kitchen drug trade. The deadliest gang to invade the neighborhood since the Pug Uglies, the West Side Boys would do anything for money, both within and the area beyond. They hired themselves out to the Italian mob as assassins; they hijacked trucks and fenced the stolen goods; they shook down shopkeepers for protection money; they swapped cocaine and heroin with uptown dealers for cash and then returned to shoot the dealers dead and reclaim their money. Heavily fueled by drugs and drink, the West Side Boys considered no crime beyond their scope.

They even had their own style of dress – black leather jackets, black shirts and jeans. In winter, they wore black woolen gloves with the tips cut off. They also left their signature on every body they discarded: bullets through the head, heart, hands and legs. Those they didn't want found were hacked up and scattered throughout the five boroughs of New York City.

Hell's Kitchen was not alone in the changes affecting its streets. Similar sounds of violence and decay were being heard in cities and neighborhoods throughout the country. In Atlanta, a serial killer was still on the loose, preying on young black children. Eleven people were crushed to death at a Who concert in Cincinnati. Sony introduced the Walkman. The first test-tube baby, Louise Brown, was born in a British hospital. The Camp David peace accord was signed and England's Lord Mountbatten was killed by IRA terrorists. Chrysler was saved from bankruptcy by an act of Congress and John Wayne died of cancer.

During all these changes, a few familiar faces remained. King Benny still ran a piece of Hell's Kitchen, working out of the same dark room where I first met him. He openly ignored the drug and gun trade, content with his profits from less violent, if equally illegal, enterprises. He was older, a little wiser, and still as dangerous as ever. Even the West Side Boys conceded him his turf.

Time had not mellowed Fat Mancho, either. He still stood in front of his bodega, snarling and screaming at all who passed. But time had also brought him another wife, a new Social Security number, one more apartment and another monthly disability check.

Bars and restaurants still dotted the neighborhood, though many were new, designed to draw an uptown clientele. But the best establishments were old and frayed, and among them, the Shamrock Pub on West 48th Street, with the sweetest Irish soda bread in town, was the finest place to eat in Hell's Kitchen. It was a joint that kept true to the past, where a local could run a tab, place a bet and even spend the night on a cot in the back. It was also a place where a secret could still be kept.

The Shamrock Pub was unusually crowded for a late Thursday night. Two men in outdated suits, ties undone, sat at the center of a wooden bar that ran the length of the restaurant, each clutching a sweaty Rob Roy, arguing about the economic policies of President Jimmy Carter. An old, raw-faced Irishman in a heavy wool coat sat at the far end of the bar, nursing his third beer, pointedly ignoring their conversation.

Five leather booths faced the bar, each positioned next to a window and lit by lanterns hanging overhead. Four circular tables, draped with white tablecloths, lined the rear wall. Framed photos of champion racehorses hung above them, along with tranquil Irish settings and a color portrait of the restaurant's original owner, a sour-looking Dubliner named Dusty McTweed.

The Shamrock Pub was a neighborhood institution, known to all who lived or worked on the West Side. It catered to an odd assortment of locals, publishing types with a taste for ale, beat cops with a thirst, tourists and, in recent years, to the volatile members of the West Side Boys.

A young couple sat at one of the tables, their backs to the bar, holding hands, a half-empty bottle of white wine between them. Another couple, older, more friends than lovers, sat in a front booth, their attention fixed on their

243

well-done lamb chops and second basket of Irish soda bread.

Two waitresses in their early twenties, wearing short black skirts and white blouses, stood against a side wall, smoking and talking in whispers. They were actresses and roommates, earning enough in tips to pay the rent on a third-floor Chelsea walk-up. One was divorced, the other had a relationship with a long-haul trucker with a drinking problem.

There was one other customer in the restaurant.

A chunky man in his late thirties sat in the last booth. He smoked a cigarette and drank a glass of beer while the meal in front of him cooled. He had ordered the day's special – meat loaf and brown gravy, mashed potatoes and steamed spinach. He had asked for a side order of pasta, which was served with canned tomato sauce. On top of the sauce, he had placed two pats of butter, turning the overcooked strands until the butter melted.

The man had long, thick blond hair that covered his ears and touched the collar of his frayed blue work shirt. His face was sharp and unlined, his eyes blue and distant. The shirt of his uniform was partly hidden by a blue zippered jacket with Randall Security patches on both arms. A .357 magnum revolver was shoved into his gun belt. A small pinky ring decorated his right hand.

Putting out the cigarette in an ashtray lodged between the glass salt shaker and a tin sugar cannister, he picked up his fork, cut into his meat loaf and stared at the television screen above the bar. The New York Knicks and the Boston Celtics were playing their way through a dreary second quarter on the soundless screen.

Outside, a crisp fall wind rattled the windows. The overhead sky threathened rain.

It was eight-fifteen in the evening, less than a week before the Presidential election.

At eight twenty-five p.m., two young men walked through the glass and wood doors. They were both dressed in black leather jackets, black crew shirts and black jeans. One was bone-thin, with dark curly hair framing his wide, handsome face. He wore black gloves, the fingers on each cut to the knuckle, and a pork-pie hat with the brim curved up. He had a half-pint of bourbon stuffed in one back pocket of his jeans and three grams of coke in a cigarette case in the other. He was smoking a Vantage and was the first one through the door.

The second young man was heftier, his black jeans tight around his waist, the open black leather jacket revealing the bulk of his neck and shoulders. His mouth was hard at work on a wad of chewing tobacco. He wore a long-shoreman's watch cap atop his light brown hair. His calf-length black boots had a fresh spit shine and he walked into the tavern favoring his right leg, damaged in childhood.

The bartender nodded in their direction. He knew their faces as well as most of the neighborhood knew their names. They were two of the founding members of the West Side Boys. They were also its deadliest. The thinner man had been in and out of jail since he was a teenager. He robbed and killed at will or on command and was currently a suspect in four unsolved homicides. He was an alcoholic and a cocaine abuser with a fast temper and a faster trigger. He once shot a mechanic dead for moving ahead of him on a movie line.

The second man was equally deadly and had committed his first murder at the age of seventeen. In return, he was paid fifty dollars. He drank and did drugs and had a wife he never saw living somewhere in Queens.

They walked past the old man and the couple in the first booth and nodded at the waitresses, who eagerly smiled back. They sat down three stools from the business-men and tapped the wood bar with their knuckles. The bartender, Jerry, an affable middle-aged man with a wife, two kids and his first steady job in six years, poured them each a large shot of Wild Turkey with beer chasers and left the bottle.

The thinner man downed the shot and lit a fresh

cigarette. He nodded toward the bartender and asked what the two men in suits were discussing. He didn't change expression when he was told of the Carter debate. He leaned closer to the bar, his eyes on the young couple at the table in the rear of the pub and poured himself and his friend another double shot. He told the bartender to bring the two men in suits a drink and to run it on his tab. He also told Jerry to tell them that Republicans were not welcome in Hell's Kitchen and that either a political conversion or a change in conversation was in order.

The chubby man checked his watch and nudged his friend in the ribs. They were running late for an appointment. A dealer named Raoul Reynoso was holed up at the Holiday Inn three blocks away, expecting to complete a drug deal with them no later than nine p.m. Reynoso was looking to buy two kilos of cocaine and was ready to hand off $25,000 as payment. The two men had other plans. They were going to take his money, put four bullets in his heart, cut off Reynoso's head and leave it in an ice bucket next to the television set in his room.

The thin man reached over the bar, grabbed a menu, looked at his friend and shrugged his shoulders. He hated to kill *anybody* on an empty stomach. He gave the menu to his friend and asked him to order for them both. He needed to use the bathroom. The chubby man took the menu and smiled. He had known the thin man all his life, they had grown up together, gone to the same schools, served time in the same prisons, slept with the same women and put bullets in the same bodies. In all those years, the thin man, without fail, *always* had to use a bathroom before a meal.

The thin man stood up from his stool and finished off his beer. He then turned and walked down the narrow strip of floor separating booths from bar stools, his hands at his sides, his face turned to the street outside. At the end of the bar, across from the rear booth, his eyes moved from the passing traffic and met those of the man eating the meat loaf special. Both men held the look for a number

246

of seconds, one set of eyes registering recognition, the other filled with annoyance.

'I help you with somethin', chief?' the man in the booth said, his mouth crammed with mashed potatoes.

'Not right now,' the thin man said, heading to the back. He smiled down at the man in the booth and told him to enjoy the rest of his meal.

He stumbled into the men's room and ran the cold water in the sink, looking at himself in the mirror. He looked much older than his twenty-six years, the drugs and drink taking a toll on an Irish face still handsome enough to coax a smile from a reluctant woman. He took off his gloves and checked his hands, calm and steady, the skin raw, the scars across both sets of knuckles white and clear. He put the gloves back on and stepped over to the urinal.

'Reynoso, you're one lucky fucker,' he thought to himself. 'This piss saved your life.'

He walked out of the men's room and past the man in the back booth. He took his seat next to his friend, put a cigarette in his mouth and poured himself a refill.

'I ordered brisket on a roll,' his friend said. 'With fries. And two baskets of soda bread. I know you like that shit. That okay by you?'

The thin man's eyes were on the small mirror above the bar, riveted on the man in the uniform finishing his meat loaf dinner.

'C'mon,' his friend said, tapping him on the shoulder. 'Let's take the booth behind us. We can spread out all we want.'

The thin man turned to face his friend. He asked him to take a look at the last booth in the pub. To take a good look and study the face of the man sitting in it.

His friend turned in his stool and stared at the man in the zippered jacket. His face stayed blank for the few moments it took to link the man to memory, but his eyes betrayed his swirling emotions.

'You sure it's him?' he asked, his voice harsh, his upper lip twitching. 'You sure it's really him?'

'You know me,' the thin man said. 'I never forget a friend.'

They stayed at the bar long enough to release the safeties on the guns hidden beneath their jackets. They stood up together and walked toward the booth at the back of the pub, the thin man leading the way.

'Hello,' the thin man said, pulling up a chair. 'It's been a long time.'

'Who the fuck are you guys?' the man in the booth demanded. He didn't seem particularly afraid, merely annoyed at the intrusion. 'And who the fuck asked you to sit down?'

'I thought you'd be happy to see us,' the chubby man said. 'Guess I was wrong.'

'I always thought you would do better,' the thin man said, looking at the patches on the sleeves of the jacket. 'All that training, all that time you put in, just to guard somebody else's money. Seems like a waste.'

'I'm askin' you for the last time,' the man said, his temper as hot as his coffee. 'What the fuck do you want?'

The thin man took off his gloves and put them in the front pocket of his leather jacket. He laid his hands flat on the table, the tips of his fingers nudging the sides of the security guard's empty beer glass.

'See the scars?' he asked. 'Look at them. Take your time. It'll come to you.'

The guard stared at the thin man's hands, his upper lip wet with sweat, his body tense, sensing danger, feeling cornered.

Then, he knew.

The knowledge fell across his face like a cold cloth. He sat back, his head resting against the top of the leather booth. He tried to speak but couldn't. His mouth went dry as his hands gripped the edge of the table.

'I can see how you would forget us,' the thin man said

248

softly. 'We were just somethin' for you and your friends to play with.'

'It's a little harder for us to forget,' the chubby one said. 'You gave us so much more to remember.'

'That was a long time ago,' the security guard said, the words coming out in a struggle. 'We were just kids.'

'We're not kids now,' the thin man said.

'Whatta ya' want me to say?' the security guard asked, anger returning to his voice. 'That I'm sorry? Is that what you want? An apology?'

'No,' the thin man said, moving his hands off the table and onto his lap. 'I *know* you're not sorry and hearin' you say it won't change a fuckin' thing.'

'Then *what*?' the security guard asked, leaning over his empty platter. 'What do you want?'

'What I've *always* wanted, Nokes,' the thin man said. 'To watch you die.'

The thin man, John Reilly, and his chubby friend, Tommy 'Butter' Marcano, were on their feet, a gun in each hand. All movement in the pub ceased. The young woman at the back table took her hand off her boyfriend and clasped it over her mouth.

The bartender clicked off the Knicks game.

The two waitresses slipped into the kitchen.

Sean Nokes, thirty-seven, was a security guard with a gambling problem. He was two months behind on his rent and his wife was threatening to leave him and take their daughter home to her mother. He had not fared well since his years at Wilkinson, moving from job to job, small town to small town. He was hoping he had finally turned the corner, working a Manhattan job that paid decent money. He had come to Hell's Kitchen to pay off a debt and stopped into the pub for dinner before heading home to his wife, hopeful of landing one more chance at a reconciliation. He never planned on a Wilkinson reunion.

'Too bad you ordered the meat loaf,' Tommy said. 'The brisket's real good here. Only you'll never know it.'

'You were scared little pricks,' Nokes said. 'Both of you.

249

All of you. Scared shitless. I tried to make you tough, make you hard. But it was a waste of time.'

'I had you all wrong, then,' Tommy said. 'All this time, I just figured you liked fuckin' and beatin' up little boys.'

'You are gonna burn in hell!' Sean Nokes said. 'You hear me! You two motherfuckers! You are gonna burn in hell!'

'After you,' John said.

The first bullet came out the back of Nokes' head, the second went through his right eye and the third creased his temple. Nokes rested with his head back and his hands spread, mouth twisted into an almost comical grimace. Tommy stepped out of the booth and walked over to Nokes' side. He put a bullet into each of his legs and one into each hand. John stood his ground and pumped three slugs into Nokes' chest, waiting for the body jerks to stop each time before pulling the trigger again.

The bartender closed his eyes until the gunfire stopped.

The young couple fell to the ground, hovering for cover under their table.

The couple in the first booth sat frozen with fear, staring at one another, still holding their knives and forks.

The two businessmen never turned their heads. One of them, the pretzels in his hand crushed to crumbs, had wet his pants.

The two waitresses stayed in the kitchen, shivering near the grill, the cook by their side.

The old man in the corner had his head on the bar and slept through the shooting.

John and Tommy put the guns back in their holsters, took one final look at Sean Nokes and turned to leave the pub.

'Hey, Jerry,' Tommy called over. 'Be a pal, would ya'?'

'Name it,' the bartender said, his eyes now open, trying not to look over at the fresh body in the back booth.

'Make those brisket sandwiches to go,' Tommy said.

TWO

It had been eleven years since my friends and I had been released from the Wilkinson Home for Boys.

In all those years, we had never once spoken to each other about our time there. We remained caring friends, but the friendship had altered as we traveled down our separate paths. Still, we were friends. By the time of Nokes' murder, the friendship had become less intimate, but no less intense.

Michael Sullivan, twenty-eight, had moved out of Hell's Kitchen shortly after being released from Wilkinson. Never again would he have a problem with the law. Father Bobby called in a handful of chits to get Michael accepted at a solid Catholic high school in Queens, where Michael was sent to live with his mother's sister and her accountant husband. He continued to date Carol Martinez, twenty-seven, until the middle of his sophomore year, when the distance and their evolving personalities finally conspired to cool their longing. But he continued to see his Hell's Kitchen cohorts as often as he could, unwilling to give up the friendship, needing to be with us as much as we needed to be with him.

Michael graduated with honors from high school and moved on to a local university. Then, after a hot and fruitless summer working as a waiter at a Catskills resort, he decided to enroll in a Manhattan law school.

At the time of Nokes' shooting, Michael was rounding

251

out his first six months as a New York City assistant district attorney.

We tried to share a meal once a week, the bond between us difficult to sever. When we were together, often joined by Carol, Michael still held sway over the group. He was always our leader and still the toughest of the group. Only now, his strength was of a different part, not physical and violent like that of John and Tommy, but carried quietly within. The months at Wilkinson had changed Michael in many ways, but they could not strip him of his drive. If anything, the horrors he endured gave a focus to his life, a target toward which he could aim.

He worked out at a gym, two hours every morning, a strenuous mix of aerobics and weights. He didn't smoke and he drank only with dinner. His fellow students and coworkers considered him to be a loner, a reticent man with a sharp humor but a gentle manner. He had grown tall and good-looking, his boyhood freckles giving way to the clear face of a confident man. He had a deep, soulful voice and a twelve-inch scar running across his shoulders.

Michael kept his world private.

He had an apartment in Queens that few were permitted to see. He dated frequently, but never seriously. His loves were kept to a minimum – the Yankees, foreign movies, Louis L'Amour westerns, the silent halls of museums. In a loud city, Michael Sullivan was a quiet stranger, a man with secrets he had no desire to share.

He walked the streets of Hell's Kitchen only occasionally, and then only to visit Father Bobby, who by now had risen to principal of our former grammar school. He loved his work and buried himself in studying ways the law could be maneuvered.

'There are a thousand different crimes that someone can commit,' he said to me shortly before the shooting. 'And there are more than a thousand ways to get him out of any one of them.'

John and Tommy had both stayed in Hell's Kitchen, finished grammar school then attended a technical junior high, close to the neighborhood, for less than the required two years. In that time, they continued to do odd jobs for King Benny, took in some numbers action for an Inwood bookie and occasionally strong-armed players late on loan shark payments. They also began carrying guns.

They never recovered from the abuse of Wilkinson. In our time there, Michael and I realized that we weren't anywhere near as tough as we had thought. John and Tommy, however, came away with an entirely diffferent frame of mind. They would let no one touch them again, let no one near enough to cause them any harm. They would achieve their goal in the most effective way they knew – through fear. It was a lesson they learned at the Wilkinson Home for Boys.

By the mid-seventies, John and Tommy had helped found the West Side Boys, farming the initial five-member group out as enforcers, thugs for hire. As the gang grew, they progressed to more lethal and lucrative action, including moving counterfeit cash and buying and selling large amounts of cocaine. They also took on contract murders. Their specialty – dismembering their victims' bodies and disposing the pieces throughout the area – evoked fear in even their closest associates.

When they killed, they got rid of everything except for the hands.

Those they kept in freezers in a select number of Hell's Kitchen refrigerators, preserved to provide finger prints on the guns used by the gang. It was a tactic that made it virtually impossible for the police to pin the crew to any one murder. When prints were checked, the patterns led back to men who were already dead.

Along the way, both John and Tommy got hooked on cocaine and began to drink heavily. They remained best friends and lived in the same West 47th Street tenement, two floors apart. They were respectful toward King Benny, who, recognizing the changing times, gave their operation the space it needed to thrive and survive.

They still joked with Fat Mancho, played stickball in

front of his candy store and helped his bookie operation rake in thousands a week, their powerful support insuring that no one dared back down from a phone-in bet.

I saw them as often as I could and when we got together, it was easy for me to forget what they had become and only remember who they were. We went to ball games together, took long Sunday morning walks down by the piers and helped Father Bobby with the basket collections at mass. I seldom asked them about their business and they always teased me about mine.

Like Michael, I moved out of Hell's Kitchen soon after my release from Wilkinson. Father Bobby also pulled some strings for me: I was admitted to a first-rate Catholic high school for boys in the Bronx. By my late teens, I was taking night courses at St. John's University in Queens, working a nowhere day job in a Wall Street bank and wrestling with a fresh set of demons – the discovery that my father was a convicted murderer who had served nearly seven years for killing his first wife. I divided my time between a bed in my parents' Bronx apartment and a two-room basement sublet in Babylon, Long Island.

One summer afternoon in 1973, I was reading an early edition of the *New York Post* on my lunch hour, sitting on a bench in front of a noisy and crowded outdoor fountain, half a ham sandwich by my side. There, under the heat of a New York sun, I read a Pete Hamill column about former Vice-President Spiro T. Agnew. By the time I got to the last paragraph, I knew I wanted to work on a newspaper.

It would take three years before I would land a job as a copy boy for the *New York Daily News*, working the midnight-to-eight shift, sharpening pencils, making coffee runs and driving drunken editors home after a night on the prowl. By the time of Nokes' death, I had worked my way up to the clerical department, typing movie schedules for the next day's editions.

It was easy work, leaving me with plenty of free time and most of it was spent in Hell's Kitchen. I still liked the feel of the neighborhood, no matter how much it had changed. I still felt safe there.

I had coffee twice a week with King Benny, once again seeking refuge in the stillness of his club, as much a home to me as any place. Benny's espresso was as bitter as ever, his mood as dark and he still cheated at every hand of cards we played. The years had made him older, his black hair touched by lines of white, but no one in the neighborhood dared question his strength.

I bought sodas from Fat Mancho every time I passed his store. He ran enough businesses from that front to fill a mall and was easily spotted in his loud shirts, sprayed with colorful birds and palm trees, which his older sister sent over from Puerto Rico. Every time he saw me he cursed. We had known each other for more than twenty years and I remained one of the few people he fully trusted.

On weekends, I would drive down and endure two-hour one-on-one basketball games against Father Bobby more than twenty years older than me and still two steps faster. We all were aging, but Father Bobby always looked young, his body trim, his face relaxed. Whatever problems he had, he handled beneath the silent cover of prayer.

On occasion, I would have dinner with Carol, who still lived in the neighborhood and worked as a social worker in the South Bronx. She had moved with ease from awkward teenager to a young woman of striking grace and beauty. Her hair was long and dark, her face unlined, covered by only the softest makeup. She had long legs and spend-the-night eyes that lit up when she laughed. Her concern for us was undiminished by the passing years.

Carol was passionate about her work and quiet about her life, living alone in a third-floor walk-up not far from where we had gone to school. She dated infrequently and never anyone from outside the neighborhood. Though I never asked, I knew she still held strong feelings for Michael. I also knew that when that relationship ended she had been with John during his more sober periods.

She always had a special affection for John, could always see the boy he once had been. Whenever we went out as a group, Carol would walk between Michael and John, grasping their arms, at ease and in step between the lawyer and the killer.

These were my friends.

We accepted each other for what we were, few questions asked, no demands made. We had been through too much to try to force change on one another. We had been through enough to know that the path taken is not always the ideal road. It is simply the one that seems right at the moment.

Wilkinson had touched us all.

It had turned Tommy and John into hardened criminals, determined not to let anyone have power over them again. It had made me and Michael realize that while an honest life may not offer much excitement, it pays its dividends in freedom.

It cost Father Bobby countless hours in prayer, searching for answers to questions he feared asking.

It made Fat Mancho a harder man, watching young boys come out stone killers, stripped of their feelings, robbed of all that was sweet.

Wilkinson even touched King Benny, piercing the protective nerve he had developed when it came to the four laughing boys who turned his private club into their own. It awakened the demons of his own horrid childhood, spent in places worse than Wilkinson's, where he was handled by men more fearsome than those who tortured us. It made the hate he carried all the heavier.

None of us could let go of the others. We all drifted together, always wondering when the moment would arrive that would force us to deal with the past. Maybe that moment would never come. Maybe we could keep it all buried. But then John and Tommy and luck walked in on Sean Nokes half way through a meat loaf dinner. And for the first time in years, we all felt alive. The moment was out there now, waiting for us to grab it. Michael was

256

the first to realize it. To figure it out. But the rest of us caught on fast. It was that we had been living for, what we had waited years for. Revenge. Sweet lasting revenge. And now it was time for all of us to get a taste.

THREE

Michael sat across from me, quietly mixing sour cream into his baked potato. We were at a corner table at the Old Homestead, a steak house across from the meat market in downtown Manhattan. It was late on a Thursday, two weeks after Nokes was killed in the Shamrock Pub.

The second I read about the shooting, I knew who had pulled the triggers. I was as afraid for Tommy and John as I was proud of them. They had done what I would never have had the courage to do. They had faced the evil of our past and eliminated it from sight. Though Nokes' death did nothing to relieve our anguish, I was still glad he was dead. I was even happier when I learned that Nokes not only knew why he died, but at whose hands.

John and Tommy did not remain fugitives for long.

They were arrested within seventy-two hours of the shooting, finger-printed, booked and charged with second-degree murder. Police had four eyewitnesses willing to testify – the older couple in the first booth and the two businessmen sitting at the bar. All four were outsiders; strangers to Hell's Kitchen. The restaurant's other patrons, as well as its workers, stayed true to the code of the neighborhood: they saw nothing and they said nothing.

John and Tommy were held without bail.

The two hired a West Side attorney named Danny O'Connor, known more for his boisterous talk than for his ability to win. They pleaded not guilty and admitted

258

to nothing, not even to their lawyer. There seemed to be no connection between the deceased and the accused, and both the press and police shrugged the murder off as yet another drug-related homicide.

'Have you gone to visit them yet?' Michael asked, cutting into his steak. It was the first time either of us had talked about the shooting since dinner began.

'The day after the arrest,' I said, jabbing a fork into a cut of grilled salmon. 'For a few minutes.'

'What did they have to say?' Michael asked.

'The usual small talk,' I said. 'Nothing with any weight. They know enough not to say anything in a visitor's room.'

'What about Nokes?' Michael said. 'They talk about him?'

'John did,' I said. 'But not by name.'

'What'd he say?'

'All he said was, "One down, Shakes." Then he tapped the glass with his finger and handed me that shit-eatin' grin of his.'

'How do they look?' Michael asked.

'Pretty relaxed,' I told him. 'Especially for two guys facing twenty-five-to-life.'

'I hear they hired Danny O'Connor to defend them,' Michael said. 'That right?'

'That's temporary,' I said. 'King Benny's gonna move in one of his lawyers when the trial starts.'

'No,' Michael said. 'O'Connor's who we want. He's perfect.'

'*Perfect?*' I said. 'The guy's a fall-down drunk. Probably hasn't won a case since LaGuardia was mayor. Maybe not even then.'

'I know,' Michael said. 'That's why he's perfect.'

'What are you talking about?'

'You covering this story for the paper?' Michael asked, lifting his beer mug and ignoring my question.

'I'm a timetable clerk, Mikey,' I said. 'I'm lucky they let me in the building.'

'Anybody at work know you're friends with John and Butter?'

'No,' I said. 'Why would they?'

'You didn't finish your fish,' Michael said. 'You usually eat everything *but* the plate.'

'I'm still used to my old hours,' I said. 'Eating dinner at five in the morning and breakfast at eleven at night.'

'You should have had eggs.'

'I *will* have a cup of coffee.'

'Order it to go,' Michael said, waving to a waiter for the check. 'We've got to take a walk.'

'It's pouring out,' I said.

'We'll find a spot where it's not. Down by the piers.'

'There are rats down by the piers,' I pointed out.

'There are rats everywhere.'

The rain was falling in soft drops, loud blasts of thunder echoing in the distance. We were standing in an empty lot along the gates of Pier sixty-two, West Side Highway traffic rushing by behind us. Michael had thrown his raincoat on over his suit. His hands were stuffed inside the side pockets and his briefcase was wedged between his ankles.

'I'm going in to see my boss in the morning,' Michael said, the words rushing out. 'I'm going to ask him to give me the case against John and Tommy.'

'What?' I looked at his eyes, searching for signs that this was nothing more than the beginning of a cruel joke. 'What are you going to do?'

'I'm going to prosecute John and Tommy in open court.' His voice was filled with confidence, his eyes looked square at me.

'Are you fuckin' nuts?' I shouted, grabbing his arms. 'They're your friends! Your *friends*, you heartless fuck!'

A smile curled the sides of Michael's lips. 'Before you take a swing, Shakes, hear me out.'

'I should shoot you just for talking about shit like this,' I said, easing my grip, taking in deep gulps of air. 'And if anybody else hears it, I'll have to open a freezer door to shake your hand.'

'You decide who else knows,' Michael said. 'Just you. You'll know who to tell.'

'You take this case, *everybody's* gonna know!' I shouted again. 'And *everybody's* gonna be pissed.'

'You'll take care of all that,' Michael said. 'That'll be part of your end.'

'Do something smart,' I said. 'Call in sick tomorrow. It might save your life.'

'I'm not taking the case to win,' Michael said. 'I'm taking it to lose.'

I didn't say anything. I *couldn't* say anything.

'I've got a plan,' Michael said. 'But I can't do it without you. I can only work the legal end. I need you to do the rest.'

I took two steps forward and held my friend's face in my hands.

'Are you serious?' I asked. 'You crazy bastard, are you really serious?'

'It's payback time, Shakes,' Michael said, water streaming down his face and mixing with tears. 'We can get back at them now. John and Tommy started it. You and I can finish it.'

I let go of Michael's face and put my hands in my pockets.

'Let's walk for awhile,' I said. 'We stand here much longer; we'll get arrested for soliciting.'

'Where to?'

'The neighborhood,' I said. 'Where it's safe.'

We huddled in the doorway of my old apartment building, rain now lashing across 10th Avenue. Down the street, two old rummies argued over a pint of raspberry brandy.

Michael's plan was as simple as it was bold. At nine in the morning, he would walk into the office of the

261

Manhattan District Attorney and ask for the murder case against John Reilly and Thomas Marcano. He would explain that he was from the same neighborhood as the two shooters and that he understood the mentality of the area better than anyone else in the office. He would tell the D.A. he knew how to keep the witnesses from running away scared, hold the case together and win it. Other than that, Michael would admit to no connection to either John or Tommy and was counting on me to quell any neighborhood talk about their friendship.

There was also no need to worry about the link with Wilkinson. Like all juvenile records in the state, ours had been destroyed after seven years. In addition, he would have someone alter the Sacred Heart School records to eliminate the evidence of our one-year absence. Besides, for the D.A., it was a can't-miss proposition. There were four eyewitnesses and two shooters with murderous reputations. The perfect case to hand an ambitious young attorney like Michael Sullivan.

Michael took a deep breath and wiped the water from his face. There was more to this, a lot more. I knew Michael well enough to know that Nokes wasn't it for him and that freeing John and Tommy wouldn't do. He needed to go after the other guards. He needed to go after Wilkinson. I felt nervous watching him, waiting for him to continue, fearful that we would all be caught and once again be brought to such a place.

He crouched down and laid his briefcase across his knees. Inside were four thick yellow folders, each double-wrapped with rubber bands. He handed all four to me. I looked at them and read the names of the guards who tormented us all those months at the Wilkinson Home for Boys stenciled across the fronts. The first folder belonged to Tommy's chief abuser, Adam Styler, now thirty-four, who had scotched his dreams of being a lawyer and, instead, worked as a plainclothes cop.

Styler was assigned to a narcotics unit in a Queens precinct. It didn't surprise me to learn that he was also dirty, shaking down dealers for dope and cash. He had a major coke problem that was supported by $3000 a month in bribe money. The rest of the folder contained personal information – daily routines; women he dated; food he liked; bars he frequented. There were lists of trusted friends and hated enemies. A man's life bound inside a yellow folder.

The second bundle belonged to my tormentor, Henry Addison, thirty-two. I felt nauseous as I read that Addison now worked for the Mayor of the City of New York as a community outreach director in Brooklyn. He was good at his job, honest and diligent. But, his sexual habits hadn't changed much since our time at Wilkinson. Addison still liked sex with young boys. The younger they were, the more he was willing to pay. Addison belonged to a group of well-heeled pedophiles who would party together three times a month, paying out big dollars for all-nighters with the boys they bought. The parties were usually taped, the kids and the equipment supplied by an East Side pimp with the street name of Radio.

The third folder belonged to Ralph Ferguson, thirty-three, the man who helped give John Reilly a killer's heart. He wasn't a cop, though I'd expected him to be. He was a clerk, working for a social service agency on Long Island. Ferguson was married and had one child. His wife taught preschool during the week and they both taught Catholic Sunday school. He sounded as clean as he was boring. Which is exactly how Michael wanted him to be. Ralph Ferguson was going to be called as a character witness, to talk about his best friend, Sean Nokes. Once he was on the stand, Michael could finally open the door to the Wilkinson Home for Boys.

I moved further into the hall, trying to keep the folders dry, trying to absorb all that Michael was telling me. He had waited twelve years for this moment, planned for it, somehow *knowing* it would happen and, when it did, he would be prepared.

He insisted that John and Tommy be told nothing of

263

our plan, that it would play better in court if they didn't know. There was to be no jury tampering. The 'not guilty' we sought had to be a verdict that no one would dare question. Danny O'Connor was to remain as the defendants' attorney. We needed to keep him sober and alert and, since he was going to be as deeply involved as we were, too scared to tell anybody what we were up to.

Michael would relay the information I needed through a system of messengers and drop boxes. I would pass information back to him in a similar manner. He pulled three keys out of his coat pocket and handed them to me. They belonged to lockers at the Port Authority, the 23rd Street YMCA and a Jack LaLanne Health Club on West 45th Street. Once I had the packets in hand I would pass them on to O'Connor. I would make sure we weren't seen.

For the plan to succeed, we needed total secrecy and the involvement of only people we completely trusted. My first step was to get to King Benny. He would be our weight, our muscle and could get us through doors we didn't even know existed. He would put enough fear into Danny O'Connor's heart to gently seal his lips. King Benny would also call off the West Side Boys, who were sure to be gunning for Michael the minute they knew he had taken the case against John and Tommy.

I also needed Fat Mancho to turn over some rocks and Carol Martinez to open some more files.

After this night, Michael would not be available to any of us. The only time we would see him would be in court.

It was a foolproof plan in one respect. If it worked, we would avenge our past and, in the process, bring down the Wilkinson Home for Boys. If it didn't work, if we were caught, people would want to know why we did what we did. Either way, information would get out.

Michael's way, however, insured that John and Tommy would walk with us and share in the victory.

'Is that it?' I asked, gazing down at the folders in my arms. 'Is that all you need?'

'Just one more thing,' Michael said.

'What?'

He sighed, leaving the best for last. 'We've got four witnesses who say they saw the shooting and are willing to testify. We need to knock that number down.'

'I'll work on it,' I said. 'But if you lose more than two, it might get some people nervous.'

'I'll take two,' Michael said. 'If you can get us one for our side.'

'One what?' I asked.

'One witness. A witness who'll put John and Tommy somewhere else the night of the murder. *Anywhere* else. A witness they can't touch. Strong enough to knock out whatever anybody else says.'

'Don't they have a name for that?' I asked.

'A judge would call it perjury,' Michael said.

'And what are we calling it?'

'A favor,' Michael said.

FOUR

King Benny stood behind the bar of his club, drinking from a large white mug of hot coffee, reading the three-page letter I had written and left for him in a sealed envelope on the counter. When he had finished, he laid the letter down and walked to the edge of the bar. He looked out at the streets of Hell's Kitchen, the mug cradled in both hands.

'Tony,' King Benny said to one of four men sitting around a card table, sorting early morning betting slips.

Tony dropped the slips from his hands, pulled back his chair and walked over.

'Bring Danny O'Connor to see me,' King Benny said, his eyes never leaving the window.

'Danny O'Connor the lawyer?' Tony asked.

'You know more than one Danny O'Connor?' King Benny said.

'No, King,' Tony said.

'Then bring me the one you know,' King Benny said.

King Benny turned from the window and moved further down the bar, stopping at the empty sink next to the beer taps. He put down his coffee mug and grabbed a book of matches from the top of the bar. He took one final look at my letter and then dropped it into the sink. He lit a match and put it to the letter and stood there, in silence, watching as it burned.

Then, for the first time in many years, King Benny laughed out loud.

FIVE

'You got time for me, Fat Man?' I said, standing in the middle of Fat Mancho's bodega, watching him as he bent over to open a carton of Wise potato chips.

'I'm a busy man, fucker,' Fat Mancho said, standing up, hugging his bulky pants above his waist, a smile on his face. 'I got a business. Ain't like you paper boys, with time on my fuckin' hands.'

'This won't take long,' I said, grabbing a pack of Wrigley's Juicy Fruit gum from one of the racks. 'I'll wait for you outside.'

'You gonna pay me for that, you little prick?' Fat Mancho asked.

'I never did before,' I said, putting two pieces in my mouth and walking out into the cool of the day. 'Why ruin a good habit now?'

Fat Mancho came out carrying two wood crates for us to sit on and a cold, sweaty Yoo-Hoo for him to drink. I sat down next to him, leaned my back against his storefront window and stretched my legs. I pointed to the fire hydrant in front of us.

'Kids still use that in the summer?' I asked.

'It still gets hot, don't it?' Fat Mancho said. 'That pump's the only beach they know. Just like you fuckers. You all cut the same.'

'I need your help, Fat Man,' I said, turning to look at him. 'A big favor. It would be easier for you to say no. A lot smarter too. And there's no problem if you do.'

Fat Mancho downed his Yoo-Hoo in two long gulps and wiped his mouth with the rolled-up sleeve of a green shirt dotted with orange flamingos.

'I bet you *would* like me to say no,' Fat Mancho said, laying the bottle by his feet. 'Then you can tell your buddies that the Fat Man don't stand up. Don't back his friends.'

'Are you callin' me your friend?' I said with a smile. 'I'm touched, Fat Man.'

'I ain't callin' you shit,' Fat Mancho said. 'I'm just tellin' you I'm here. You fuckers can't pull off anything alone. You ain't got the brass and you ain't got the brains. There's two of you in jail right now. Ain't lookin' to make it four.'

'I guess King Benny's been around to see you,' I said.

'Some fuckin' team we puttin' together,' Fat Mancho said. 'A drunk lawyer on one side, fuckin' kid lawyer on another. A paper boy makin' like Dick Tracy. Four eyeballs swear they saw the whole thing. And the two on trial killed more people than cancer. That motherfucker Custer had a better shot at a walk.'

'Nobody's expecting it,' I said. 'That's the biggest card in our favor.'

'This ain't no fuckin' book, kid,' Fat Mancho said. 'You best remember that. And this goes bad, it ain't a fuckin' year upstate in a kid jail. This is *real*. You get caught on this, you lookin' straight at serious.'

'There's no choice,' I said. 'Not for us.'

'They were good boys,' Fat Mancho said. 'That little fucker Johnny give you his shirt he thought you need it. That other prick, Butter, always chewin' on a mouthful of somethin', his lips covered with chocolate.'

He turned to look at me. 'But they ain't good boys anymore. They killers now, cold as stone.'

'I know,' I said. 'I know what they were and I know what they are. It's not about that.'

'Ain't worth throwin' away a life just to get even,' Fat Mancho said. 'You and the lawyer got a shot. You can make it out the right way. You ready to flip that aside? Just to get even with three fuckin' guards?'

'I think about what they did every day,' I said, looking away from Fat Mancho, my eyes on the street in front of us. 'It's a part of me, like skin. When I look in a mirror, I see it in my eyes. Sometimes, I see it in other people's faces. It's a nasty feeling. It's a feeling that makes you think a piece of you is already dead. And there's no way to bring it back.'

'Gettin' away with this gonna make you feel all better?' Fat Mancho asked. 'Gonna make you forget every fuckin' thing that happened?'

'No,' I said, turning back to face him. 'It'll just give me something a little sweeter to remember. Somethin' nicer to think about.'

'I read that shitty paper you workin' on now,' Fat Mancho said, standing and picking up his soda crate. 'Read it every day. Still ain't seen your fuckin' name anywhere.'

'Be patient,' I said. 'Some day you will. Just keep on buyin' it.'

'I don't buy shit,' Fat Mancho said, walking back into his bodega. 'I never put any of my money in a stranger's pockets.'

'You still married to two women?' I asked him, standing and dusting the back of my pants.

'Two wives and a lady friend,' Fat Mancho said. 'They can't get enough of what I got.'

'Must be good,' I said.

'They like it,' Fat Mancho said. 'That's what counts.'

'Thanks, Fat Man,' I said, leaning against his doorway. 'I owe you. I owe you big time.'

'Bet your ass you owe me, fucker,' Fat Mancho said. 'And you ain't leavin' this spot till you pay me for that fuckin' pack of gum.'

SIX

I was sitting on the hallway steps, my back inches from the apartment door, a bag holding a six-pack of beer by my side, when Carol Martinez lifted her head and saw me.

'Mug me or marry me, Shakes,' Carol said, searching through her open purse for her keys. 'I'm too tired for anything else.'

'Will you settle for a couple of beers?' I asked, tapping the paper bag.

'If that's your best offer,' she said.

'I'll throw in a hug and a kiss,' I said.

'Sold,' she said.

I stood up and put my arms around her waist and held her close to me, feeling her soft curves, even under the layers of thick jacket and sweater. She looked as pretty as I'd ever seen her.

'You need something, don't you, Shakes?' Carol asked, warm hands rubbing the back of my head and neck.

'I could use a glass,' I said. 'I hate drinking out of a can.'

Her apartment was clean and orderly, filled with books and framed posters of old movies. The kitchen had a small table in its center and a large cutout of Humphrey Bogart in a trench coat smoking a cigarette was taped to the fridge.

'You pour the beer,' Carol said, taking off her jacket. 'I'll put on some music.'

'You got any Frankie Valli?' I asked.

'You're so old-fashioned, Shakes,' Carol said with a laugh. 'Valli was gone before the pill.'

'At least he's alive,' I said. 'Which is more than I can say for your pal Bogart.'

'Bogie's always gonna be cool,' she said. 'I can't say the same about the Four Seasons.'

'Well, don't throw away their albums just yet,' I said, handing her a glass of beer, watching as she put a Bob Seger record on the turntable.

'I don't *have* any to throw away,' she said, sitting down next to me on the small, pull-out couch in the center of the living room.

We sat there quietly, listening to Seger frog his way through 'Tryin' to Live My Life Without You', sipping our beer, my head resting against a thick, hand-quilted throw pillow.

'You look tired,' Carol said, placing a hand on my knee. 'They don't give you time for sleep on this new job of yours?'

'How much do you know?' I asked, turning my eyes toward hers.

'Just what the neighborhood says,' Carol said.

'And what does the neighborhood say?'

'That they're going to put John and Tommy away,' she said, sadness touching her eyes and voice. 'And that their best friend is going to be the one to do it.'

'You believe that?'

'It's hard not to, Shakes,' Carol said. 'I mean, unless we all have it wrong, he did take the fucking case.'

'Yeah, he did take the case,' I said.

'Then what else is there to say?' she asked, drinking the rest of her beer and trying not to cry.

I sat up and moved closer to her, our hands touching, our eyes on one another.

271

'You know Michael very well,' I said. 'Maybe even better than I do.'

'I thought I did,' Carol said. 'I really thought I did. Now, I don't know.'

'You *do* know, Carol,' I said. 'You know he loves you. And you know he'd *never* do anything to hurt you or me or Johnny or Butter. Never.'

'Then why take the case?' Carol said. 'For God's sake, he even went in and asked for it. What the hell kind of friend is that?'

'The best kind,' I said. 'The kind who will throw whatever he has away, just to help his friends. The kind who never forgets who he is and what he is. The kind who's crazy enough to think he can get away with what he's trying to do.'

'What are you telling me, Shakes?' Carol asked.

'You've lived in this neighborhood a long time, Carol. Long enough to know that everything is a shakedown or a scam. Why should this be any different?'

'I'll go get us another beer,' Carol said, walking back into the kitchen. By now, Bob Seger was singing 'Against the Wind'. 'You want a sandwich with it?'

'You got any fresh mozzarella and basil?' I asked.

'How about a couple of slices of old ham on stale bread?'

'With mustard?'

'Mayo,' Carol said.

'You got me,' I said.

We ate our sandwiches, drank our beer and listened to music, the two of us relaxed in each other's company and lost in the valleys of our own thoughts. After many moments had passed, I asked her why she had stopped dating Michael.

'It just happened,' Carol said. 'He was living in Queens, working and going to school. I was here and doing the same. We'd go weeks without seeing each other. After a while, it was easier to let it go.'

'You still love him?'

'I don't think about it, Shakes,' Carol said. 'If I did, I'd say yes. But Michael needed to get away from Hell's Kitchen. Get away from the people in it. I was one of those people.'

'And you're with John now,' I said.

'As much as anybody can be with John,' Carol said. 'The man I know is not the boy you remember. But there's something special about John. You just have to look harder to see it.'

'You visit him?'

'Once a week,' Carol said. 'For about an hour.'

'Good,' I said. 'Keep that up. Just don't tell him you see me. In fact, don't tell him anything. The more it looks hopeless to him the better this might work.'

'Why not tell him?' Carol said. 'Might make things easier.'

'He'll put on a tougher act in court if he thinks he's cornered,' I said. 'I want that little baby face of his looking straight at the jury and I don't want it to look happy.'

'Why didn't *you* ever ask me out?' Carol said, a thin hand running through her thick hair.

'You were Mikey's girl,' I said. 'He got to you first.'

'And after Mikey?' she said, her face shiny and clear.

'I never thought you'd say yes,' I said.

'Well, you were wrong, Shakes,' Carol said.

'Will you say yes to me now?' I said, holding her hand in mine. 'No matter what I ask?'

Carol leaned over and put both arms around me and rested her head against my neck.

'Yes,' she whispered. 'What do you want me to do?'

'Break the law,' I said.

SEVEN

Michael's plan relied heavily on Hell's Kitchen to deliver information and to keep silent. Both were skills the neighborhood had in abundance.

The plan also depended on keeping Michael alive, which meant that word had to get to John and Tommy's killing crew that he was not an open target. Within days of Michael taking the case, the West Side Boys got a visit from King Benny. The King requested that the verbal abuse directed toward Michael continue, but that there never be a death move against him. The hit on Michael Sullivan, if there were to be one, could only come from King Benny.

While the neighborhood, led by King Benny, Fat Mancho and Carol, worked their end, I received and relayed the information I got from Michael back down the line. In turn, I fed Michael all that he needed to know.

We had set up a simple method of communication.

If Michael was sending, messages were left at work for me to call my nonexistent girlfriend, Gloria. Once I received the signal, I would send one of King Benny's men to pick up an envelope no later than noon of the next day at one of three designated drop spots.

If I needed to get word to Michael, I would have someone from the neighborhood pick up an early edition of the *New York Times*, script the word Edmund on the upper-right-hand corner of the Metro section and drop it in front of his apartment door. Later that day, Michael would pick up his envelope at an upper East Side P.O. box.

We spent our early weeks going beyond Michael's files, digging up information that could be used either in a courtroom or on the street against the three remaining guards. We also were working the witnesses, gathering their backgrounds, finding their weak spots. A full folder was also being developed on the Wilkinson Home for Boys, finding former guards, employees and inmates willing to speak out, hunting down wardens and assistants, locating the names of juveniles who died during their stay there and checking on the given cause of death.

Michael supplied us with a list of questions for O'Connor to ask in court. He also gave us the questions he intended to ask and the answers he expected to receive. Any additional information on the guards or on Wilkinson that he came across was also passed along.

All written messages, once delivered, were destroyed. Phone conversations were permitted only through the use of coded numbers on clear third party lines. There was never any personal contact between the main participants.

Our margin of error was zero.

Hell's Kitchen, a neighborhood that came to the aid of its allies as quickly as it rushed to bury its enemies, thrived under Michael's plan. The verbal shots at Michael continued, cries of traitor and gutter rat heard up and down the avenue, but those were bellowed for the sole benefit of strangers. The underground word, the only one that mattered, had spread through the streets with the speed of a late-night bullet – King Benny's 'sleepers' were making their play. 'Sleepers' was a street name for anyone who spent time in a juvenile facility. It was also a mob phrase attached to a hit man who stayed overnight after finishing a job. There were many 'sleepers' in Hell's Kitchen, but my friends and I were the only four King Benny considered his crew.

'You want a Rolls Royce, you go to England or wherever the fuck they make it,' Fat Mancho said. 'You want champagne, you go see the French. You want money, find a Jew. But you want dirt, scum buried under a rock, a secret nobody wants anybody to know, you want that and you want that fast, there's only one place to go – Hell's Kitchen. It's the lost and found of shit. They lose it and we find it.'

EIGHT

King Benny sat on a park bench in De Witt Clinton feeding pumpkin seeds to a circle of pigeons, the late fall sun scanning his back. It was one week past Thanksgiving and three weeks into our work. The weather had begun its turn to New York cold.

He wore the same black outfit he usually wore in his club, ignoring the frigid air much as he ignored everything else. He had a coffee cup resting next to his right leg along with a small bottle of Sambuca Romana.

'I didn't know you liked pigeons,' I said, sitting down next to him.

'I like anything that don't talk,' King Benny said.

'I heard from Mikey today,' I said. 'The case goes to trial first Monday in the new year. It'll be a small story in the papers tomorrow.'

'You only got two witnesses who are gonna testify,' King Benny said. 'Two others changed their minds. That won't be in the papers tomorrow.'

'Which two?'

'The suits at the bar,' King Benny said. 'They said they had too many drinks to know for sure who they saw walk in.'

'That leaves the couple in the booth,' I said.

'For now,' King Benny said.

'Everything else is falling into place?' I asked, blowing breath into my hands.

'Except for your witness,' King Benny said. 'That pocket's still empty.'

'I've got somebody in mind,' I said. 'I'll talk to him when the time's right.'

'He good?'

'He will be,' I said. 'If he does it.'

'Make sure then,' King Benny said, tossing more seeds at the pigeons, 'that he does it.'

'None of this would work without you,' I said.

'You'd find a way,' King Benny said. 'With me or without.'

'Maybe,' I said. 'But I'm glad you're with us on this.'

'I don't know if I coulda been any help to you back in that place,' King Benny said. 'But I shoulda tried.' It was the only time he ever alluded to the fact that he knew what had gone on when we were at Wilkinson.

'Things happen when they're supposed to,' I said. 'It's what you always said to me.'

'Good things and bad,' King Benny said. 'Goin' in, you never know which one you're gonna find. Always be prepared for both.'

'And most of the time,' I said, 'bet on the bad.'

'You better go now,' King Benny said. 'You don't wanna be late for your appointment.'

'What appointment?'

'With Danny O'Connor,' King Benny said. 'He's waitin' for you in Red Applegate's bar. Should be on his second scotch by now. Get to him before he has a third.'

'Is he ready to go along?' I asked.

'He'll go,' King Benny said. 'He's too young to have his friends drive their cars with their lights on.'

Winter 1980

The court officers led John Reilly and Thomas Marcano into the crowded court room, both defendants walking with their heads down and their hands at their sides. They were wearing blue blazers, blue polo shirts, gray slacks and brown loafers. They nodded at their attorney, Danny O'Connor, and sat down in the two wooden chairs by his side.

The court stenographer, a curly-haired blonde in a short black skirt, sat across from them, directly in front of the Judge's bench, her face vacant.

The chairs of the jury box were filled by the twelve chosen for the trial.

Michael Sullivan sat at the prosecutor's table, his open briefcase, two yellow legal folders and three sharp pencils laid out before him, his eyes on the stenographer's legs. He was in a dark wool suit, his dark tie crisply knotted over his white shirt.

I sat in the middle of the third row. Two young men, both of whom I knew to be part of the West Side Boys, sat to my left. Carol Martinez, eyes staring straight ahead, was to my right. She held my hand.

Judge Eliot Weisman took his place behind the bench. He was a tall, middle-aged man with a square face topped by a cleanly shaved head. He appeared trim and fit, muscular beneath his dark robes. He was known to run a stern courtroom and allowed scant time for theatrics and stall tactics. Criminal attorneys claimed his scale of justice

281

almost always tipped toward the prosecutor. The assistant district attorneys themselves called him fair, but by no means an easy touch.

Michael knew that Judge Weisman's inital take on John and Tommy would be one of disdain, a response that would be further fueled by the facts of the case. Michael also knew that the evidence against the two defendants would be so heavy that, combined with their history of violence, it would prod Weisman to try to avoid a trial. He expected Weisman to pressure both sides to work out a plea-bargain agreement.

Three times the Judge privately asked both counsels for such an agreement and three times they refused. John and Tommy stuck to their not-guilty plea and the Judge stuck to holding them without bail. Michael insisted that the people, as represented by his office, would want these men prosecuted to the fullest extent of the law. As the case entered the jury selection phase, Judge Weisman did not appear pleased.

At no time during those early weeks in that uncomfortable courtroom did Michael give any indication of what he planned to do. He interviewed and selected his jury carefully, as well as any young assistant district attorney would, asking all pertinent questions, attempting to weed out, as honestly as possible, any juror he felt would not or could not deliver a fair verdict. Both counsels settled on a jury of eight men and four women. One of the women was Hispanic as were two of the men. Two other men were black. Three jurors, two men and a woman, were Irish.

When mentioning the defendants, Michael always referred to them by their names to establish their identities and so move them beyond a pair of anonymous faces. He insisted that prospective jurors gaze at the two men on trial while he catalogued their reputations and asked anyone fearful of those reputations not to feel compelled to serve. John and Tommy always made a point of looking at Michael, but he carefully averted their gaze, not willing to take the chance that some spectator would notice even a hint of their relationship.

Michael's vision on where he wanted this case to go was very clear.

He was aiming for a guilty.

A charge of guilty against the Wilkinson Home for Boys; a charge of guilty against Sean Nokes, Adam Styler, Henry Addison and Ralph Ferguson.

Michael sat impassively through Danny O'Connor's unemotional opening statement, listening to the grizzly voiced attorney refer to John and Tommy as two innocent pawns, quickly arrested and just as quickly prosecuted on the slightest threads of evidence. O'Connor would prove, he insisted, beyond any reasonable doubt, that John Reilly and Thomas Marcano did not kill Sean Nokes on the night in question. That, in fact, they were nowhere near the Shamrock Pub at the time of the shooting.

No one was impressed by O'Connor's performance, least of all Judge Weisman who fidgeted throughout the fifteen minutes it took for his statement. The few reporters covering the case, scattered through the front rows, stopped taking notes after O'Connor's inital remarks. Veteran spectators, accustomed to more volatile defense attorneys, shook their heads in boredom.

'He's not exactly Perry Mason,' Carol whispered.

'He got their names right,' I said. 'For him, that's a great start. Besides, if he wins this case, he'll be bigger than Perry Mason.'

Michael stood up, unbuttoned his suit jacket and walked in front of his table, toward the jury box. He had his hands in his pockets and a friendly smile on his face.

'Good morning,' he said to the jurors. 'My name is Michael Sullivan and I am an assistant district attorney for the county of Manhattan. My job, like most jobs I suppose, seems, on the surface, an easy one. I have to prove to you and only to you that the two men who stand accused killed a man named Sean Nokes in cold blood, without any apparent motive. I will present to you evidence and offer into account testimony to prove that. I will place them at the scene of the crime. I will bring witnesses to the stand who will confirm that they were there on that deadly night. I will present to you enough facts that you can then go into the jury room and come out with a clear decision that's beyond a reasonable doubt. Now, I know you all know what that means since you probably watch as much TV as I do.'

Three of the women on the jury smiled and one of the men, a postal employee from the Upper West Side, laughed out loud. 'I hear that,' he said, pointing a finger at Michael.

'Let me remind one and all that this is a *court*room,' Judge Weisman said in a somber tone. 'Not a *living* room. With that in mind, will the jurors please refrain from making any further comments.'

'My fault, your Honor,' Michael said, turning to face the judge. 'I gave the impression that a response was required. It won't happen again.'

'I'm sure it won't, counselor,' the Judge said, relaxing his tone. 'Proceed.'

'Look at their faces,' I said to Carol, nudging her attention toward the jury box. 'Their eyes. They're falling in love with him.'

'That's not a hard thing to do,' Carol said.

'The past history of these two young men is not important and not an issue in this case,' Michael said, turning back to the jury, his hands on the wood barrier, his eyes moving from face to face. 'Violent or peaceful, criminal or honest, saints or sinners. None of it matters. What *does* matter is what happened on the night of the murder. If I can prove to you that these two men were the men who walked in, had two drinks and shot Sean Nokes dead, then I expect no less than a guilty verdict. If I can't do that, if I can't put them there, put the guns in their hands, put the body before them and make you firmly believe that they pulled the triggers, then the weight of guilt is cleanly off your shoulders and on mine. If that happens,

284

I will have failed to do my job. But I will do my best not to fail you and not to fail to find the truth. I will do my best to seek justice. And I know you will too.'

NINE

I was twenty minutes late. I had told Carol to meet me in front of the church at six, but had lost track of time kneeling in prayer in one of the back pews in Sacred Heart. I walked out of the church and saw her sitting on the steps, the collar of her leather jacket lifted against the strong winds whipping up from the river.

'Sorry I'm late,' I said. 'I was lighting candles.'

'Now you've got St. Jude in on this too,' Carol said. 'Anybody else?'

'Just one more,' I said.

'We supposed to meet up with him here?' Carol asked.

'No. He's waitin' for us at his place.'

'Which is where?'

'Which is there,' I said, pointing a finger at the red brick building next to the church. 'The rectory.'

'Oh, my God!' Carol said, her eyes opened wide. 'Oh, my God!'

'Not quite,' I said. 'But it's as close as I could come on short notice.'

Father Bobby sat in a recliner in his small, book-lined first floor room, his back to a slightly opened window. He lit a cigarette and took a deep drag, letting the smoke out his nose. He held a bottle of Pepsi in his right hand. Carol sat across from him, her legs crossed, elbow on her knee, chin in the palm of her hand.

I sat on a window sill in the corner of the room that

looked down on the school yard, hands in my pockets, my back brushing white lace curtains.

'How was court today?' Father Bobby asked, his voice tired.

'Like the first round of a fight,' I said. 'Everybody just feeling each other out.'

'How do the boys look?'

'Like they wished they were someplace else,' Carol said. 'I think that's how we all felt.'

'I've been in this parish nearly twenty years,' Father Bobby said, flicking cigarette ash into his empty bottle of soda. 'Seen a lot of boys grow into men. And I've seen too many die or end up in jail for most of their lives. I've cried over all of them. But this one, this one's been the hardest. This one's cost me every prayer I know.'

Father Bobby knew that it wasn't the streets that had chilled John Reilly and Thomas Marcano. And it wasn't the allure of drugs or gangs that led them to stray. You couldn't blame their fall on the harsh truth of Hell's Kitchen. There was only one place to blame.

'You did what you could, Father,' I said. 'Helped me. Michael too. We'd all be on trial today, wasn't for you.'

'It's the sheep that strays that you most want back,' Father Bobby said.

'It's not too late, Father,' I said, moving away from the window and closer to his side. 'We still have a chance to bring in a couple of stray sheep. One last chance.'

'Is that one chance legal?' Father Bobby asked.

'Last chances never are,' I said.

'Is King Benny behind this?'

'He's in it,' I said. 'But he's not calling the shots.'

'Who is?'

'Michael,' I said.

Father Bobby took a deep breath and leaned forward in his chair.

'There's a bottle of Dewer's in the middle drawer of my desk,' Father Bobby said. 'I think we're going to need some.'

I told Father Bobby everything. If he was going to be involved, he deserved to know what he was getting into. If he wasn't going to help, I still trusted him enough to know that the truth would move no further than his room.

'I should've smelled it,' Father Bobby said. 'The minute Michael went for the case, I should have figured something was up.'

'It's a good plan,' I said. 'Mikey's got it all covered. Every base you look at, he's got it covered.'

'Not every base, Shakes,' Father Bobby said. 'You're still short something or else you wouldn't be here.'

'Don't shit a shitter,' I said with a smile.

'That's right. So, spill it. Where do you come up short?'

'A witness,' I said. 'Somebody to take the stand and say they were with John and Tommy the night of the murder.'

'And you figured a priest would be perfect?' Father Bobby said.

'Not just any priest,' I said.

'You're asking me to lie,' Father Bobby said. 'Asking me to swear to God and then to lie.'

'I'm asking you to help two of your boys,' I said. 'Help them stay out of jail for the rest of their lives.'

'Did they kill Nokes?' Father Bobby asked. 'Did they walk into the pub and kill him like they say?'

'Yes,' I said. 'They killed him. Exactly like they say.'

Father Bobby stood up and paced about the small room, his hands rubbing against the sides of his legs. He was still dressed in the black street garments of a priest, short-sleeve shirt under his jacket, keys rattling in a side pocket.

'This is some favor you're asking me,' Father Bobby said, stopping in the center of the room, staring at me and Carol.

'We know, Father,' Carol said.

'No,' Father Bobby said. 'I don't think you do.'

'You always said if there was ever anything I needed to come and ask you,' I said.

'I was thinking more along the lines of Yankee tickets,' Father Bobby said.

'I don't need Yankee tickets, Father,' I said. 'I need a witness.'

Father Bobby undid the top button of his shirt and peeled out the Roman collar beneath it. He held the collar in both hands.

'This is my *life*,' Father Bobby said, holding up the collar. 'It's all I've got. I've given everything to it. *Everything*. Now, you two come walking in here with some plan that asks me to throw it away. To throw it away so two murderers can walk free. To kill again. And you ask me that as a favor.'

'Two lives should be worth more than a Roman collar,' I said.

'What about the life that was taken, Shakes?' Father Bobby asked, standing inches from my face. 'What's that worth?'

'To me, nothing,' I said.

'Why not, Shakes?' Father Bobby asked. 'Tell me.'

I sat in the chair next to the desk, Father Bobby and Carol on the other end of the room. I stared at the shelves crammed with the books I had read as a child and the many more I wanted to read. I held an empty glass in my hand, struggling to recall the faces and images that had, for so long, been safely buried.

Faces and images I never wanted to believe were real.

I sat in that chair and told Father Bobby what was in my heart. It was the first and only time I've ever told anyone – until now – exactly what the life of Sean Nokes was worth.

I spoke for more than an hour, my words weighed with anger and urgency, letting Father Bobby and Carol know the things I never thought I would be telling anyone. To Father Bobby, it was a shock, a jolt of pain straight to his heart. Carol had been close enough to Michael and John to suspect, but the specifics stunned her, made her sit bolt upright and took her breath away.

I told them about the Wilkinson Home for Boys.

I told them about the torture, the beatings, the humiliation.

I told them about the rapes.

I told them about four frightened boys who cried themselves to sleep and who prayed to Father Bobby's God for help that never came. I told them about endless nights spent staring into darkness, rats owning the corners, keys rattling jail cell locks, nightsticks swinging high in the air, a guard's grip, a boy's scream.

I told them everything.

And when I was done, Carol said, quietly, in almost a whisper, 'Now you tell me, Father. What would a good priest do?'

Father Bobby stared straight ahead, as he had for the past hour, only his eyes registering any change. He blew out a mouthful of breath and then looked toward the ceiling, his hands resting on the soft edges of his chair.

'It's getting late,' he finally said. 'You should go. You both look tired.'

He stood up and placed a hand on my arm.

'I've got a decision to make,' Father Bobby said. 'All I can do is pray that it's the right one.'

'It will be, Father,' I said. 'Whichever way you go.'

'The boys were on target about you,' Father Bobby said, reaching out for Carol and holding her in his arms.

'About what?' Carol asked, lifting her head.

'They always said you had balls,' Father Bobby said. 'And they were right.'

'I'll take that as a compliment,' Carol said. 'Especially coming from a priest.'

TEN

Michael smiled at the witness, a dark-haired, handsome woman from New Jersey. She had her legs crossed under the chair, her skirt pleated, her white blouse buttoned to the throat. Her hands were folded on her lap.

'Mrs. Salinas how often have you had dinner at the Shamrock Pub?' he asked.

'Just that one night,' she answered, her voice assured, speaking in the manner of a woman with nothing to hide.

'What night would that be?' Michael asked.

'The night of the murder,' she said.

'What time did you get there?'

'Near seven-thirty,' Mrs. Salinas said. 'I met a friend for dinner.'

'What's the name of your friend?'

'David,' she said. 'David Carson.'

'Who was the first to arrive?'

'I was,' she said. 'But only by a couple of minutes.'

'You waited for Mr. Carson outside?'

'No,' she said. 'By the coat rack. As I said, it wasn't much of a wait.'

'Okay,' Michael said. 'You and Mr. Carson go in, sit down, order a drink, start catching up on your day. That right?'

'Pretty much,' Mrs. Salinas said. 'We hadn't seen each other for a few weeks. David had been away on a business trip.'

'Who decided to eat at the Shamrock Pub?'

'I did.'

'Why?'

'I read about it in a magazine,' she said. 'They said it was colorful.'

'And was it?'

'Up until the shooting,' Mrs. Salinas said.

I looked over at the defense table and caught a smirk from John and a smile from Tommy. Their lawyer, head down, was furiously scrawling notes on a legal pad.

'What's he taking notes for?' Carol whispered. 'He knows the questions he's supposed to ask.'

'Maybe he forgot them,' I said. 'Left them on a bar stool.'

'She's good,' Carol said, indicating Mrs. Salinas.

'We want her to be,' I said.

'Had Mr. Carson ever been there before?' Michael asked now. 'With or without you?'

'No,' she said. 'It was the first time for both of us.'

'Where were you seated, Mrs. Salinas?'

'In a booth,' she said. 'The one closest to the door.'

'Was that by choice?'

'Yes,' she said. 'All but one of the booths was free, so we could have sat anywhere. But David likes fresh air and I don't mind it either.'

'Do you remember what you ordered?'

'I asked for the lamb chops,' she said. 'It was one of the specialties mentioned in the magazine. David had his usual.'

'For those of us not familiar with Mr. Carson's eating habits, could you tell us what his usual consists of?' Michael asked, throwing Mrs. Salinas a wide smile.

'Steak,' she said. 'David *always* orders steak, baked potato and a tossed salad.'

'Did you have anything to drink?'

'We ordered a bottle of red wine,' Mrs. Salinas said. 'A chianti I believe.'

'That's all?'

'Yes,' she said. 'That's all.'

'Did you notice the number of people in the pub?'

'There were only a few scattered about,' she said. 'It was quiet. A good place to meet someone and talk.'

'Did you notice the victim, Sean Nokes?'

'No,' she said. 'I did not.'

'You didn't even see him when you walked in?' Michael asked.

'No,' she said. 'Our table was right near the coat check and I didn't bother looking around.'

'Your attentions were focused on Mr. Carson,' Michael said.

'Yes, they were,' Mrs. Salinas said. 'As I said, I hadn't seen him for a while.'

'Which way were you facing?' Michael asked. 'Which side of the booth were you sitting on?'

'The one facing the rear of the pub,' she said.

'The side facing down the row of booths?'

'Yes.'

'The side facing Mr. Nokes' booth,' Michael said.

'I believe so,' Mrs. Salinas said. 'Yes.'

'But you couldn't see him from where you were sitting?'

'I wasn't looking to see him,' she said. 'I knew there was someone sitting in the rear booth. I just didn't notice.'

'Did you notice the two men who walked in shortly after you sat down for dinner?'

'I heard them come in,' she said. 'You couldn't help but hear them.'

'Why's that?'

'They were loud,' she said. 'They caused a commotion. I'm sure everyone noticed.'

'Did you see their faces when they came in?'

'No,' she said. 'Not when they came in.'

'Why not?'

'I was talking to David,' she said. 'When I finally looked up, they had moved past me.'

'Did you notice their faces when they went to the bar?'

'From the side,' she said. 'I could see them in profile.'

293

'Both of them?'

'Yes,' Mrs. Salinas said, the confidence in her voice never wavering. 'Both of them.'

'Did you see them approach the booth where Mr. Nokes was sitting?' Michael asked.

'I noticed it,' she said. 'Yes.'

'Did you hear what was said between them?'

'No,' she said. 'I didn't.'

'Did you see them pull out their guns?'

'No,' she said.

'Did you hear the shots?'

'Yes,' Mrs. Salinas said. 'I heard the shots.'

'What did they do after the shooting?' Michael asked.

'They walked out of the pub,' she said. 'As if nothing had happened.'

'Did you see their faces then?'

'Yes,' she said. 'I looked up as they walked by.'

'Are you positive of that, Mrs. Salinas?'

'Yes,' she said. 'Very positive.'

'And are the two men you saw in the Shamrock Pub in this room today?'

'Yes,' Mrs. Salinas said. 'They are.'

'Can you point them out to me, please?'

'They're sitting right over there,' Mrs. Salinas said, aiming a finger at John and Tommy.

'Your Honor, will the record reflect that Mrs. Salinas identified defendants John Reilly and Thomas Marcano as the two men in question.'

'Noted,' Judge Weisman said.

'I have no further questions,' Michael said.

'Counselor?' Judge Weisman said, lifting an eyebrow in Danny O'Connor's direction. 'Are you ready to proceed?'

'Yes, your Honor,' Danny O'Connor said. 'The defense is ready.'

'It better be,' Carol whispered.

Danny O'Connor was wearing a charcoal-gray suit that needed cleaning and a white shirt tight around his neck.

His shoes were scuffed and his blue tie stopped at an Oliver Hardy length.

'He's got that *Columbo* look down,' I muttered. 'All he's missing is the cigar.'

'It's probably in his pocket,' Carol said. 'Still lit.'

'Good morning,' Danny O'Connor said to Mrs. Salinas.

'Good morning,' she said.

'I just have a few questions,' he said. 'I won't take up too much more of your time.'

'Thank you,' she said.

'You said you only had wine to drink with dinner,' O'Connor said, looking away from Mrs. Salinas and making eye contact with the jury. 'Is that correct?'

'Yes,' she said. 'That's correct.'

'Are you sure about that?' O'Connor asked. 'Are you sure that was all you ordered, one bottle of wine?'

'Yes,' she said. 'A bottle of red wine.'

'Had you had anything to drink prior to that?'

'What do you mean prior?' Mrs. Salinas asked.

'At lunch, maybe,' O'Connor said. 'Did you have anything to drink at lunch?'

'Yes, I did,' she said. 'But that was hours earlier.'

'What did you have, Mrs. Salinas?'

'I went shopping and stopped for lunch at a place on Madison Avenue,' she said.

'I didn't ask where you went,' O'Connor said. 'I asked what you had to drink at lunch?'

'A martini,' she said.

'And what else?'

'And some wine,' she said.

'How much wine?'

'One glass,' she said. 'Maybe two.'

'Closer to two?' O'Connor asked.

'Yes,' Mrs. Salinas said, her cheeks turning a light shade of red. 'Probably two.'

'What time did you have lunch, Mrs. Salinas?'

'Objection, your Honor,' Michael said, without standing. 'What Mrs. Salinas did on the day of the murder has nothing to do with what she saw the night of the murder.'

'How much she had to drink does, your Honor,' O'Connor said.

'Overruled,' Judge Weisman said.

'What time, Mrs. Salinas,' O'Connor said, 'did you have lunch?'

'About one-thirty,' she said.

'And what did you have for lunch?'

'A salad,' she said.

'A martini, two glasses of wine and a salad,' O'Connor said. 'Is that correct?'

'Yes,' Mrs. Salinas said, her eyes looking to Michael for help. 'Yes, that's correct.'

He gave her none.

'And then you had wine at dinner,' O'Connor said. 'About six hours later. Is that right?'

'Yes, that's right,' she said.

'How much wine did you have to drink by the time my clients allegedly walked into the Shamrock Pub?'

'Two glasses,' she said, anger now undercutting the confident tone.

'Do you drink this much every day, Mrs. Salinas?'

'No,' she said. 'I do not.'

'So would you say four glasses of wine and a martini in a six-hour period is a lot for you to drink?' O'Connor asked.

'Yes it is,' Mrs. Salinas said.

'Are you married, Mrs. Salinas?' O'Connor asked.

'Yes, I am,' she said.

'Happily?'

'As happy as anyone married for fifteen years can expect to be.'

'I've been divorced twice, Mrs. Salinas,' O'Connor said, smiling at the jury. 'Fifteen years sounds like a lifetime to me. How happy would that be?'

'I'm still in love with my husband,' Mrs. Salinas said.

'Objection,' Michael said. 'This line of questioning is out of order.'

'I'll allow it,' Judge Weisman said, looking at O'Connor. 'But get to your point.'

'Yes, your Honor,' O'Connor said. 'Thank you.'

The defense attorney now walked alongside the jury, one hand inside the pocket of his wrinkled pants, his thin brown hair combed straight back.

'What is your relationship with Mr. Carson?'

'I've already said.'

'Tell me again,' O'Connor said. 'Please.'

'We're friends,' she said. 'Very old and dear friends.'

'Is Mr. Carson a friend of your husband's as well?' O'Connor asked.

Mrs. Salinas paused and pursed her lips before she answered.

'No,' she said. 'He isn't.'

'Mrs. Salinas, what were you talking about at dinner?'

'The usual,' she said. 'Catching up on things.'

'What things?'

'His family,' she said. 'Mine. Things like that.'

'And did you and Mr. Carson have any plans beyond dinner?' O'Connor asked.

'What do you mean?' Mrs. Salinas asked.

'I mean, was your evening going to end with just a dinner?' O'Connor asked.

'No,' she said, her eyes cast down. 'It wasn't.'

'Sounds romantic,' O'Connor said.

'Objection,' Michael said. 'The twice-divorced counsel seems to have an overactive imagination.'

'Sustained,' Judge Weisman said. 'Let's get on with it, Mr. O'Connor.'

'Had you ever heard a gun fired, Mrs. Salinas?' O'Connor asked, shifting his questioning and walking closer to the witness stand. 'Prior to the night in question, that is.'

'No, I hadn't,' she said.

'How would you describe the sound?'

'Loud,' she said. 'Like firecrackers.'

297

'Did the sound frighten you?'

'Yes, very much,' she said.

'Did you close your eyes?'

'At first,' she said. 'Until the shooting stopped.'

'Did you think the men who did the shooting were going to kill everyone in the pub?'

'I didn't know what to think,' she said. 'All I knew was that a man had been shot.'

'Did you think *you* might be shot?' O'Connor asked. 'Shot dead by two cold-blooded killers?'

'Yes,' Mrs. Salinas said, nodding her head firmly. 'Yes I did.'

'Yet, despite that fear,' O'Connor said, 'despite the risk to your life, you looked at their faces as they left the pub. Is that right?'

'Yes,' she said. 'Yes, that's right.'

'*Is it*?' O'Connor said, his voice rising. 'Did you really look at their faces?'

'Yes.'

'Did you, Mrs. Salinas, really *look* at their faces?' O'Connor asked, now standing inches from her.

'I glanced at them as they walked by,' she said. 'But I *did* see them.'

'You *glanced*,' O'Connor said, his voice hitting a higher pitch. 'You didn't *look*?'

'I *saw* them,' Mrs. Salinas said.

'You *glanced* at them, Mrs. Salinas,' O'Connor said. 'You *glanced* at them through the eyes of a frightened woman who may have had too much to drink.'

'Objection, your Honor,' Michael said, his hands spread out in front of him, still sitting in his chair.

'No need, your Honor,' O'Connor said, clearly relishing his first dance in the spotlight. 'I have no further questions.'

'Thank you, Mrs. Salinas,' Judge Weisman said to the now shaken woman. 'You may step down.'

'Looks like *Columbo* did his homework,' Carol said.

'Today anyway,' I said, my eyes on John and Tommy, watching them wink their approval at O'Connor.

'Have you got time for lunch?' Carol asked.

'I'll make the time,' I said.

'Where would you like to go?'

'How about the Shamrock Pub,' I said. 'I hear it's colorful.'

ELEVEN

The detective in the front seat kept the engine running, his hands on the steering wheel, a container of coffee by his side, the lid still on. I sat in the back, opposite the driver's side, a heavy manilla envelope on my lap. Another detective sat to my left, looking out the window, watching the wind whip shreds of garbage down Little West 12th Street. The defogger was on and all four windows of the late-model sedan were open a crack, letting in thin streams of January air.

It was six-fifteen on a Sunday morning and the downtown streets were empty.

'So, you gonna show me?' the detective to my left asked, pointing down at the envelope. 'Or you just gonna ride the suspense?'

His name was Nick Davenport. He was twenty-eight years old and a sergeant in the Internal Affairs Division of the New York City Police Department. It is the unit responsible for dealing with corrupt cops.

'You've got to agree to a couple of things first,' I said. 'Then we deal.'

'Frankie, what is this shit?'

'Hear the kid out, Nick,' the detective in the front seat said. 'It'll be worth your time. Believe me.'

The detective in the front seat, Frank Magcicco, worked out of a Homicide unit housed in a Brooklyn precinct. He grew up in Hell's Kitchen and remained friendly with many of the people who lived there. He was a first grade detective with an honest name and a solid reputation. He was thirty-three years old, owned a two-family house in Queens, had two preschool children and was married to a woman who worked part-time as a legal secretary.

He was also King Benny's nephew.

'Okay,' Nick Davenport said. 'What's it gonna cost?'

He had a blue-eyed, boyish face hidden by a three-day stubble and an older man's voice. He'd been on the force seven years, two as a patrolman in Harlem and two working plainclothes in Brooklyn, before making the move to I.A.D. He was cold to the fact that most cops hated anyone associated with Internal Affairs and ambitious enough to want to make captain before he hit forty. He knew the fastest way up that track was to reel in the maximum number of dirty cops in a minimum amount of time.

'I don't want any deals cut,' I said.

'How so?' Davenport asked, shifting his body.

'You don't offer him *anything*,' I said. 'You don't use him to finger other cops. You bring him in and you bring him down.'

'That ain't up to me,' Nick said. 'Once a case starts, a lot of other people get involved. I can't shut 'em all out.'

'I heard you can,' I said, toward Frank in the front seat. 'But, maybe I heard wrong. Maybe I should take this to somebody else.'

'Where'd you find this fuck?' Nick asked Frank, chuckling as he pulled a cigarette from his shirt pocket.

'I were you, I'd do what the kid says,' Frank said, staring out through the windshield, sipping his coffee. 'You make this one, you're gonna be havin' breakfast once a month with the Commissioner.'

'Okay, Eliot Ness,' Nick said to me. 'You got it. He won't be offered any deals. No matter how much he talks, no matter who he fingers. No deals. Anything else?'

'Two more things,' I said.

'Let me hear 'em,' Nick said.

'He gets convicted, he gets state time,' I said. 'I don't

want him sent to one of those cop country clubs. He's gotta do prison time.'

'You got a real hardon for this guy,' Nick said. 'What's your beef with him?'

'There's one more thing,' I said. 'You wanna hear it or not?'

'I can't wait,' Nick said.

'It's simple,' I said. 'Nobody knows who fed you the information. How you got it. How you found it. And I mean *nobody*.'

'How *did* you get it?'

'It fell into my lap,' I said. 'Just like it's falling into yours.'

'That it?' Davenport asked, tossing his cigarette out through the crack in the window. 'That's all you want?'

'That's all I want,' I said.

Davenport stared at me for a few long moments and then turned to look back outside. One hand rubbed the stubble on his face, one foot shook nervously back and forth.

'You okay with this, Frank?' he asked the detective in the front seat.

'I'm here ain't I?' Frank said, watching him in the rear view mirror.

'Okay, Mr. Ness,' Davenport said, putting out his hand. 'You and me got ourselves a deal.'

I handed him the thick envelope. Inside was the file that Michael had given me on former Wilkinson guard Adam Styler, plus additional information dug up in the past three months by King Benny and Fat Mancho.

'Christ Almighty!' Davenport said, sorting through the material. 'You got everything in here but a confession.'

'I thought I'd leave that to you,' I said. 'And my preference is that you beat it out of him.'

'Dates, times, phone numbers,' Davenport said, his eyes wide, a smile spread across his face. 'Get a load of this, Frankie, there's even surveillance photos. This piece of

302

shit's pulling in about five grand a month. Rippin' off pushers. Has been for about three years.'

'More like four,' I said.

'He ain't gonna see five,' Davenport said. 'I'll tell you that right now.'

'Do you have enough to get a conviction?' I asked.

'That ain't up to me, kid,' Davenport said. 'That's up to a jury.'

'Then show the jury this,' I said.

I reached into my jacket pocket and pulled out a plastic bag. In it was a snub nose. 44 revolver and three spent shells.

'Whatta ya' got there, Ness?' Davenport asked, taking the bag.

'Three weeks ago the body of a drug dealer named Indian Red Lopez was found in an alley in Jackson Heights,' I said. 'There were three bullets in his head and nothing in his pockets.'

'I'm with you so far,' Davenport said.

'That's the gun that killed him,' I said. 'Those are the shells.'

'And what's behind door number three?' Davenport asked.

'The prints on the gun belong to Adam Styler,' I said.

'Do me a favor, would ya', Ness?' Davenport said, putting the gun in his pocket.

'What?'

'I ever make it onto your shit list, give me a call,' he said. 'Give me a chance to apologize.'

'You'll find a woman's name and phone number in the folder,' I said. 'Pay her a visit. Her English isn't too good. But it's good enough to tell you she saw Adam Styler put the gun to Lopez's head and pull the trigger.'

Davenport lit a fresh cigarette, folding the spent match in his hand. He put Styler's folder back together and slid it into the envelope.

'I'll take it from here, Ness,' Davenport said, putting out his hand. 'You did your part.'

'You need anything else, Frank knows how to reach me,' I said, shaking hands.

'Want us to drop you off anywhere?' Frank asked, turning to face me.

'No, it's okay,' I said. 'I'll get out here.'

'Say hello for me,' Frank said.

'I will,' I said, opening the car door. 'And thanks, Frank. Thanks for all your help.'

'Take care of yourself, kid,' Frank said, winking at me as I got out of the car. 'Water gets choppy out your way.'

'I'll do what I can,' I said, leaving the car and closing the door behind me.

'Hey, Ness,' Davenport said, sliding over to where I had been sitting and rolling down the window.

'What?' I said, standing by the curb.

'You ever think of becoming a cop?' he asked, smiling.

'And leave the good guys?' I said with a laugh. 'Never happen.'

TWELVE

By the end of the first week of the trial, Michael had done all that could be expected of an assistant district attorney seeking a conviction in the murder case of People vs. Reilly and Marcano. He had presented a detailed drawing of the interior of the Shamrock Pub, giving the jury a picture to go along with the verbal scenario. He had a replica made to scale, with little wax figures sitting in place of the patrons and employees. He then showed the jury how it was possible for two wax figures to walk into the pub, sit at a bar, have a few drinks, move to the rear booth, shoot dead another wax figure and leave the pub without a problem.

He just never put faces on the two wax figures.

He had the crime scene photos blown up, with Nokes' riddled corpse surrounded by two plates of jelled food and a cold cup of coffee, then displayed them for the jury. He had a forensics expert detail the make and caliber of the gun that killed Nokes and encouraged the coroner to drone on about the bloody manner of his death.

He just never had a weapon, the murder weapon, to show them.

The officers at the scene all testified as to what they found when they first arrived at the Shamrock Pub on the night of the shooting. They ran through the statements presented to them by those present. Michael then brought on the detectives assigned to the case, two veteran cops who combined those statements with other information they gathered to bring in John Reilly and Thomas Marcano.

He just never gave the jury a motive for the murder.

Michael kept to the plan, a plan that called for the action to stay simple.

He had left doubt in the minds of the jury. He had given them dozens of facts, but no weapon, no motive and, more importantly, no prints that would put John and Tommy at the scene that night. The gloves they wore helped some. Jerry the bartender quietly took care of the rest. Michael had brought two eyewitnesses to the stand, but both were shaky and one, David Carson, had his back to the shooting and saw nothing but leather jackets and blurred faces come in and out of the Shamrock Pub.

Danny O'Connor did his part as well, asking the questions he was told to ask and occasionally throwing in pertinent queries of his own. His sloppy attire and lack of finesse played well with the working-class jury Michael had helped to select. He came off as a seasoned pro, a ruffled man of the people who had seen his share of victories and defeats. He talked to them and never lectured, but always made time, when the moment called for it, for a touch of Irish drama.

Michael had been right. Danny O'Connor was perfect.

At two-thirty p.m., a half hour before the close of the Friday session, Michael Sullivan prepared to announce the final witness in his prosecution of case docket number 778462. Judge Weisman asked him to hold the witness until Monday morning, as Michael knew he would. He agreed and wished both the Judge and jury a pleasant weekend, then sat down, the first part of his job nearly finished.

He looked about five years older than he did when he and I met on that rainy night nearly four months earlier. The tension of his task, the hours we were all keeping, the uncertainty about the outcome all weighed heavy. If the plan worked it would be everyone's success. If it failed, the fault would fall to Michael.

We still didn't know if we had Father Bobby locked in as a witness and wouldn't know up until he walked into that courtroom. We decided it would be best for him to deal directly with O'Connor and not risk being seen talking to either me or Carol. If Father Bobby were to take the stand, we wanted it to be as late into the trial as possible, allowing the impact of his testimony to stay with the jury as they headed into the deliberation room.

Father Bobby Carillo, a priest with the best outside jump shot on the West Side, remained the key to a plan that called for all involved to get away with murder.

THIRTEEN

King Benny stood in front of his club, hands folded at his back, eyes staring straight ahead. Three of his men huddled close by, stamping their feet against the cold. The door to the club remained open, the lilting sound of Doris Day singing 'Que Sera, Sera' easing its way onto the street.

It was King Benny's favorite song.

'I see you've still got a thing for Doris Day,' I said, coming up next to him.

'She's a good woman,' King Benny said.

'You like her movies?' I asked.

'I don't go to movies,' King Benny said. 'C'mon, let's take a walk.'

We crossed 11th Avenue and walked down 52nd Street. I kept my head down and my collar up, the wind blowing hard, the air now cutting sharp as ice. King Benny was, as usual, dressed in black shirt, slacks and jacket. His hair was slicked back and his bum leg dragged, but he walked with a slight jaunt and seemed not to notice the weather.

'This guy Addison,' King Benny said. 'The one works for the Mayor.'

'I know him,' I said.

King Benny went after Henry Addison with a vengeance. It went beyond mere business. King Benny took Henry Addison and made it personal. He knew that he was part of a young, well-to-do crowd that paid lots of money for sex parties with little boys. It didn't take King Benny long to find out who supplied those boys and how much their bodies were worth. The East Side pimp with the street name of Radio gave up everything – names, dates, videotapes and photos. Enough material to cost Henry Addison a cushy city job that was handed to him by a friend in the Mayor's office.

It took King Benny even less time to find out ·that, unlike his other friends, Henry Addison didn't have much money. So, he was forced to borrow for his pleasure. This put him in debt to the kind of people who charged interest in return for their loans.

'He's gonna quit his job in two weeks,' King Benny said.

'Why's that?'

'He don't want nobody to know the kind of guy he is,' King Benny said. 'Don't want nobody to see pictures of him they shouldn't see.'

'He knows this?'

'He will,' King Benny said.

'That it?' I said.

'The boys he buys for parties are expensive,' King Benny said, taking a handkerchief from his back pocket and wiping the edge of his nose. 'Addison makes good money. He don't make real money.'

'What's he owe?'

'Eight grand,' King Benny said. 'With a heavy vig.'

'To who?'

'Three small-timers downtown,' King Benny said. 'They were letting him pay it off for a piece a week. Until this morning.'

'What happened this morning?'

'They were paid off,' King Benny said. 'In full.'

'Who paid 'em?'

'Henry Addison's chits belong to me now,' King Benny said.

'You hate debts,' I said.

'I hate Henry Addison,' King Benny said.

We stopped at the corner of 52nd Street and 12th Avenue. I looked over at King Benny and saw in his dark eyes the dangerous void that he usually hid so carefully. It was an emptiness his enemies had good reason to fear.

It was an emptiness about to be filled with Henry Addison.

His black sedan was across the street, one of his men behind the wheel, the windows up, the engine running. We walked slowly toward the car.

'We going for a ride?' I asked him.

'I am,' he said. 'You're going home. To sleep, in case anybody ever asks.'

'Where are you going?'

'Pick up my money,' King Benny said.

'Take me with you,' I said. 'I want to be in on this.'

'Go home,' King Benny said. 'We're in the dirty end of the field now. That's where I play. And I like to play alone.'

King Benny watched as his driver opened the back door of the sedan. He looked over at me and nodded.

'You're a good kid,' King Benny said. 'You always were. Don't let this change it.'

The living room was dark, the only light coming from two bare windows and the glimmer of a floor lamp. All the furniture was new, two black leather couches taking up one end, a white shag pull-out sofa shoved against the opposite wall. In the center of the room was a long butcher-block table surrounded by four black leather chairs on rollers. There was a framed wall poster of Dr. J hanging on one wall and a cardboard cutout of Earl 'The Pearl' Monroe leaning against a door that led to the small kitchen. The room smelled of fresh paint and incense.

A tall, reed-thin black man sat in one of the black leather chairs, his feet flat on the floor, his hands folded and resting on the butcher-block table. He was wearing a black turtleneck and black leather slacks. He had a Rolex on his left wrist and a diamond pinky ring on his right hand. He wore black Gucci loafers and no socks.

His mother named him Edward Goldenberg Robinson,

310

after her favorite actor. To continue the Hollywood connection, Eddie Robinson took the street name Little Caesar as he made his way up the ranks of the lucrative drug trade. He was Brooklyn's number one mover among black dealers and was rivaled only by the remains of the infamous Nicky Barnes' crew for power over the entire city. He earned close to $50,000 a day on cocaine, raked in another $25,000 on heroin and skimmed a ten percent fee off any marijuana that sold on his streets.

Eddie Robinson was thirty-six years old and had already fathered six kids with three different women. His oldest child, a son, was twelve years old and attended a private school in upstate New York, where he lived with his mother. Little Caesar named his son Rizzo after his youngest brother, who died while in the custody of the Wilkinson Home for Boys.

'You alone?' Eddie Robinson asked King Benny, who was sitting on the other side of the butcher-block table.

'Got a guy downstairs,' King Benny said. 'In the car. Your guy shoulda told you before you let me in.'

Eddie Robinson smiled and turned toward a thick-muscled black man in a sweatsuit standing in a corner by the window.

'Bip can't talk,' Eddie Robinson said.

'Smart move,' King Benny said.

'I'm not looking for partners,' Eddie said, thick moustache highlighting his thin face. 'If that's your reason for the meet.'

'I don't want a partner,' King Benny said.

'Then what?' Eddie Robinson said.

'I want you to give me some money,' King Benny said.

'How much money?'

'Eight thousand dollars,' King Benny said.

'I'll play along,' Eddie Robinson said with a smile. 'Say I give you the eight grand. How long before you pay it back?'

'I'm not paying it back,' King Benny said, reaching a

311

hand into his jacket pocket and taking out a folded piece of paper. 'Somebody else is.'

'This somebody somebody I know?' Eddie Robinson said, taking the paper from King Benny and placing it in his own pocket.

'Your little brother knew him,' King Benny said.

'Rizzo?' Eddie Robinson asked, a sudden deadness to his voice. 'How did he know Rizzo?'

'The man was a guard at an upstate home,' King Benny said. 'Was there the same time as Rizzo. Before and after he died.'

'Bip,' Eddie Robinson said, not moving his eyes from King Benny. 'Count out eight thousand and put it in an envelope.'

King Benny and Eddie Robinson stared at one another in silence, waiting for Bip to walk into the kitchen and come back out with a white envelope. Bip handed the envelope to Eddie Robinson.

'You go back a long time, old man,' Eddie Robinson said as he passed it on to King Benny.

'Old men always do,' King Benny said.

'Ran with the guineas back when the guineas were tough,' Eddie Robinson said.

'Ran when I could run,' King Benny said.

'Maybe you and me can do some business,' Eddie Robinson said. 'Close us a deal.'

'We just did,' King Benny said, putting the envelope in the side pocket of his jacket and turning to leave the room.

'I'll look up our friend soon,' Eddie Robinson said as King Benny walked away. 'And collect the money he owes me.'

'He owes you somethin' more than money,' King Benny said, standing in the entryway, his face in the shadows. 'Something worth more.'

Eddie Robinson stood up from his chair, hands spread out before him. 'Ain't nothin' worth more than the green.'

312

'This is,' King Benny said.

'What, old man?' Eddie Robinson said. 'What's this guy owe means more to me than dollars?'

'He owes you Rizzo,' King Benny said. 'He's the man that killed your brother.'

King Benny walked past the light, opened the apartment door and disappeared.

FOURTEEN

'You have a witness for us, counselor?' Judge Weisman asked Michael.

'Yes, your Honor,' Michael said.

'Let's get to it then,' Judge Weisman said.

'Your Honor,' Michael said. 'The prosecution would like to call Ralph Ferguson to the stand.'

I took a deep breath and turned to my right, looking at Ferguson as he walked down the center aisle of the court room. Twelve years had passed, but I still recognized the sound of his walk and the slight, feminine manner in which he moved his shoulders. He had gained some weight and lost some hair and appeared uncomfortable in his baggy blue blazer.

The last time I saw Ralph Ferguson I was tied up in my cell, my mouth taped shut, Sean Nokes holding me down, watching him rape and beat one of my friends. It was a night of terror that Ferguson probably dismissed soon after it happened. It is a night that, for me, has never ended.

Michael kept his head down as Ferguson walked past, heading for the stand to be sworn in by the bailiff. Michael and Ferguson had not yet met. He had another attorney in his office handle Ferguson's deposition and the initial Q & A, not wanting to tip his hand before he and O'Connor were to question the former guard in open court.

Ralph Ferguson and Sean Nokes had remained friends

beyond their years at Wilkinson. They spent vacations together hunting deer in upstate woods and long weekends in a rented cabin by a lake fishing for bass. They drank beer and whiskey, talked about old times and made plans for the future. They hoped one day to go in as partners on a bait and tackle shop in central New Hampshire.

The unhappily married Nokes often visited the happily married Ferguson and his wife, Sally, staying in the spare room in the small tract house they owned in the Long Island town of Freeport. Ferguson had been best man at Nokes' first wedding, a union that had lasted less than a year. Nokes was godfather to Ferguson's only child, his four-year-old daughter, Shelley Marie.

On the surface, Ralph Ferguson was a model citizen. Pee-Wee soccer coach. A dedicated employee who never missed a day and helped organize company parties. He even handled the Sunday collections at his church.

A perfect character witness.

Ferguson fidgeted on the stand, too nervous to focus his attention on Michael, gazing instead at the faces of the jury and the spectators.

John and Tommy sat quietly, staring at him with open contempt.

'Doesn't look so tough up there, does he?' I whispered to Carol.

'Nobody does,' she said.

'He looks like anybody,' I said. 'No one would ever know he did the things he did.'

'Sit tight, sweetheart,' Carol said, slowly rubbing my arm. 'They're gonna know today. Everybody's gonna know. Saint Ferguson is about to fall on his ass.'

'Good morning, Mr. Ferguson,' Michael said, buttoning his jacket and standing on the far side of the witness stand. 'I'd like to thank you for coming. I realize it's a long trip for you.'

'I'm sorry I had to do it,' Ferguson said. 'I'm sorry it had to be for something like this.'

'I understand,' Michael said, his voice coated with sympathy. 'You and the victim, Sean Nokes, were good friends. Is that right?'

'We were *great* friends, yeah,' Ferguson said. 'The best. You'd have to look hard to find a better friend.'

'How long did you two know each other?'

'About fourteen years,' Ferguson said.

'How often did you see each other?'

'We got together as much as we could,' Ferguson said. 'I'd say about ten, maybe twelve times a year. On weekends, holidays, vacations. Things like that.'

'Would you say you were his best friend?'

'His closest, that's for sure,' Ferguson said. 'We could talk to each other, you know. Talk about things that only good friends talk about.'

'What sort of things?' Michael asked, walking past the defense table, his head down.

'Normal stuff,' Ferguson said, shrugging. 'Women sometimes, sports during football season, our jobs all the time. Nothin' you would call deep. Just talk. Plain talk between friends.'

'What kind of man was Sean Nokes?' Michael asked.

'He was a good man,' Ferguson said. 'Too good to be shot dead by a couple of street punks.'

'Objection, your Honor,' O'Connor said, standing. 'Statement is one of opinion, not fact.'

'He was *asked* his opinion,' Michael said.

'Overruled,' Judge Weisman said. 'Please continue.'

'When you say Sean Nokes was a good man, how do you mean that?' Michael asked, moving closer to the witness stand. 'Did he give money to charities, adopt stray pets, shelter the homeless? Tell us, please, Mr. Ferguson, how Sean Nokes was a good man.'

'Nothing like that,' Ferguson said, a smile creasing his nervous exterior. 'Sean just cared about you. If you were his friend, there's nothing he wouldn't do for you. I really mean that. There was nothing.'

'Did he have any enemies you were aware of?'

316

'You mean, other than the two who killed him?' Ferguson asked.

'Yes,' Michael said with a smile. 'Any enemies other than the two who killed him?'

'No,' Ralph Ferguson said. 'Sean Nokes had. no enemies.'

'Thank you, Mr. Ferguson,' Michael said, turning his back to the stand. 'I have no further questions, your Honor.'

'Mr. O'Connor,' Judge Weisman said. 'He's your witness.'

'Can you tell us how you and Sean Nokes first met, Mr. Ferguson?' O'Connor asked, sitting in his chair, elbows on the defense table.

'We worked on a job together upstate,' Ferguson said.

'As what?'

'We were guards at the Wilkinson Home for Boys,' Ferguson said.

'What is that?' O'Connor asked. 'A prison?'

'No,' Ferguson said. 'It's a juvenile facility for young boys.'

'Young boys who have broken the law,' O'Connor said. 'Is that correct?'

'Yes, that's correct,' Ferguson said.

'And your function was what?'

'Standard stuff,' Ferguson said. 'Keep the boys in line, see they got to their classes on time, keep an eye out for trouble, put them down for the night. Nothing exciting.'

'As guards, were you and Mr. Nokes allowed to use force to, as you say, keep the boys in line?' O'Connor asked, pushing his chair back and standing by the side of his desk.

'What do you mean, force?' Ferguson asked, looking over at Michael.

'I mean, were you allowed to hit them?'

'No, of course not,' Ferguson said.

'Were any of the boys hit by any of the guards?'

317

O'Connor asked, walking around his desk, arms folded at his chest. 'At any time?'

'I'm sure something like that may have happened,' Ferguson said, sweat starting to form around his neck. 'It was a big place. But it wasn't a common practice.'

'Let's narrow the place down, then,' O'Connor said. 'Did you or Mr. Nokes ever hit any of the boys under your care at the Wilkinson Home?'

Both Judge Weisman and Ferguson stared at Michael, waiting for the obvious objection to the question.

Michael sat at his desk and kept his eyes on Ferguson, not moving.

John and Tommy turned and gave Michael a quick glance, one filled with curiosity and confusion.

'Would you like me to repeat the question, Mr. Ferguson?' O'Connor asked, walking toward the witness stand.

'No,' Ferguson said.

'Then answer it,' O'Connor said. 'And remember you're under oath.'

'Yes,' Ferguson said. 'A few of the boys we considered to be discipline problems were hit. On occasion.'

'And these discipline problems, how were they hit?' O'Connor asked.

'What do you mean how?' Ferguson asked.

'Fist, open hand, a kick,' O'Connor said. 'A baton, maybe. What was the best way, Mr. Ferguson, to calm a discipline problem?'

'It depended on what the situation called for,' Ferguson said.

'And who determined that?'

'The guard on the scene,' Ferguson said.

'So you and Sean Nokes would decide in what way a discipline problem would be dealt with,' O'Connor said. 'Is that correct?'

'Yes,' Ferguson said. 'That's correct.'

'That's a lot of power to have over a boy,' O'Connor said. 'Isn't it?'

'It came with the job,' Ferguson said.

'Did torture come with the job?' O'Connor asked.

'No, it did not,' Ferguson said.

'But boys were tortured weren't they?' O'Connor said, his face turning a shade of red. '*Weren't* they, Mr. Ferguson?'

The spectators all leaned forward, waiting for Ferguson's answer. Judge Weisman poured himself a glass of water and rolled his chair back, his angry eyes focused on Michael.

'On occasion,' Ferguson said, looking as if he were about to faint.

'Who tortured them?' O'Connor asked.

'The guards,' Ferguson said.

'*Which* guards?' O'Connor asked.

'I can't remember all of them,' Ferguson said.

'Remember one,' O'Connor said.

Ferguson wiped at his lips with the back of his hand. He looked over at Michael who sat in his chair, hands folded before him. He looked at John and Tommy, who stared back impassively. He put his head back and took a deep breath.

'Sean Nokes,' Ferguson said.

O'Connor waited for the court room murmurs to quiet. He watched as Judge Weisman lifted his gavel and then placed it back down, as troubled as everyone else by the testimony he was hearing.

I looked over at Carol and saw tears streaming down her face. I put my arm around her and moved her closer.

'Let me ask you, Mr. Ferguson,' O'Connor said, standing next to him, one hand in his pocket. 'Was there any sexual abuse at the Wilkinson Home for Boys?'

'Counselor,' Judge Weisman said to O'Connor. 'This line of questioning better lead someplace having to do with this case.'

'It will, your Honor,' O'Connor said, keeping his eyes on Ferguson.

'For your sake,' Judge Weisman said.

'Answer the question, Mr. Ferguson,' O'Connor said.

'Was there any sexual abuse at the Wilkinson Home for Boys?'

'Yes,' Ferguson said. 'I heard that there was.'

'I'm not asking if you *heard*,' O'Connor said. 'I'm asking if you *saw*.'

'Yes, I saw,' Ferguson said in a low voice.

'Did you and Sean Nokes ever force yourselves on any of the boys?' O'Connor asked, taking two steps back, his voice hitting full range. 'Did you and Sean Nokes *rape* any of the boys at the Wilkinson Home? And again, I remind you that you are under oath.'

The courtroom held the silence of the moment, no moving, no coughing, no crumbling of paper. All eyes were on the witness stand. The twelve heads of the jury were turned at an angle. John and Tommy sat at attention. Carol gripped my hand as Michael looked above the bench at the painting of blind justice gripping her sword.

'Counselors,' Judge Weisman said, breaking the silence. 'Approach the bench. *Now*.'

Michael and O'Connor moved to the sidebar, on the end furthest from the witness stand.

'What the *hell* is going on here?' Judge Weisman asked Michael, temper flashing above his calm demeanor.

'Well, your Honor,' Michael said, glancing over at Ferguson, 'it looks like I called the wrong character witness.'

'And what are you going to do about it?' Judge Weisman asked.

'Nothing, your Honor,' Michael said. 'There's nothing I can do.'

'Or maybe, counselor,' Judge Weisman said, 'you've already done enough.'

The lawyers returned to their positions.

'Please answer the question, Mr. Ferguson,' Judge Weisman ordered.

'Yes,' Ferguson said in a choked voice, tears lining his face.

'Yes *what*?' O'Connor asked.

'Yes, boys were raped,' Ferguson said.

320

'By you and Sean Nokes?' O'Connor said.

'Not just by us,' Ferguson said.

'By *you* and *Sean Nokes*?' O'Connor said, repeating the question, raising his voice even louder.

'Yes,' Ferguson said.

'On more than one occasion?' O'Connor asked.

'Yes,' Ferguson said.

'With more than one boy?'

'Yes,' Ferguson said.

'Now, do you still think Sean Nokes was a good man, Mr. Ferguson?' O'Connor asked.

'He was my *friend*,' Ferguson said.

'A friend who raped and abused boys he was paid to watch over,' O'Connor said. 'Boys who could maybe grow up and become an *enemy* of such a *good* man.'

'Are you finished?' Ferguson asked, his eyes red, his hands shaking.

'Not just yet,' O'Connor said.

'I want it to be over,' Ferguson said. 'Please, your Honor, I want it to be over.'

'Mr. O'Connor?' the Judge asked.

'This won't take long, your Honor,' O'Connor said.

'Proceed,' Judge Weisman said.

'Sean Nokes spent a lot of time at your home, is that right?' O'Connor asked.

'Yes,' Ferguson said.

'As much as a week at a time, is that also correct?'

'Yes,' Ferguson said.

'And you have a child, is that correct?'

'Yes,' Ferguson said. 'A daughter.'

'In all the time your *good* friend Sean Nokes spent in your home, all the days, all the hours, did either you or your wife ever allow him to be alone with your daughter?' O'Connor asked. 'At *any* time? For *any* reason?'

Ferguson stared at O'Connor, his fear evident, his body leaning toward the Judge's bench for support.

'No,' he finally said. 'No, we never did.'

'Why was that, Mr. Ferguson?' O'Connor asked. 'If he was such a *good* man.'

'Objection, your Honor,' Michael said for the first time, looking at Ferguson. 'Question doesn't call for an answer.'

'Counselor's right, your Honor,' O'Connor said. 'I withdraw the question.'

'Witness is excused,' Judge Weisman said.

'Thank you, your Honor,' Ferguson said, stepping down from the stand.

'Mr. Ferguson, if I were you, I wouldn't stray too far from home,' Judge Weisman said. 'People will need to talk to you. Do you understand?'

'Yes, your Honor,' Ferguson said meekly, his eyes darting from John to Tommy and then to Michael, slowly, finally recoiling in recognition. 'I understand.'

Michael waited until Ferguson walked out of the courtroom and then stood up.

'The prosecution rests its case, your Honor,' he said. 'We have no further witnesses.'

'Thank God for that,' Judge Weisman said.

FIFTEEN

Fat Mancho bounced a spauldeen against the ground, his eyes fixed on the brick wall in front of him. He was wearing a long-sleeve wool shirt, a Baltimore Orioles baseball cap, scruffy blue jeans and high-top PF Flyers.

I stood five feet to his left, wearing a leather jacket, two black wool gloves and a pull cap. My jeans felt stiff in the windy cold and my sneakers and thin white socks weren't enough to prevent the late Sunday afternoon chill from seeping through.

Carol stood with her back to the chain fence separating the open lot from the sidewalk. She was on her third cup of coffee and had two thick winter scarves wrapped around her neck.

'Most people play handball in the summer,' I said to Fat Mancho, rubbing my hands together. 'It's easier to see the ball without tears in your eyes.'

'I give a fuck about most people,' Fat Mancho said.

'What do you have planned for after the game?' I asked. 'A swim?'

'Your balls all twisted up 'cause you gonna lose the game,' Fat Mancho said. 'And you one of them fuckers that can't live with losin'.'

'Freezing, Fat Man,' I said. 'I'm one of those fuckers who can't live with freezing.'

Fat Mancho slapped the ball against the wall, a hard shot, aimed low, with a heavy spin to it. I took three steps back and returned the hit. Fat Mancho was ready for the

323

return, crouched down, hands on his knees, not wearing gloves, his eyes on the ball, looking like an overweight third baseman who forgot his Old-Timer's Day uniform.

His right hand whipped at the ball, sending it higher than the serve, faster, forcing me to move back, the soles of my sneakers slipping on a thin slab of ice. I watched as the ball bounced over my head.

'That's six for me, loser,' Fat Mancho said. 'Two for you.'

'You never *play* this game,' I said, my breath coming heavy. 'How can you be good?'

'You never *seen* me play, fool,' Fat Mancho said. 'I was your age, I was all-spic. Played the best. Beat the best.'

I looked over his shoulder and saw Carol walking toward us, a cup of coffee in one hand and a cold beer in the other.

'Good news,' I said. 'It's halftime.'

We sat against the handball wall, sitting on top of three copies of the Sunday *Daily News*, Carol and I sharing the coffee, Fat Mancho slurping gulps of Rheingold.

'How's Irish holdin' up?' Fat Mancho asked about Michael.

'I only know what I see in court,' I said. 'That end seems good. His side of the table's finished.'

'He did good,' Fat Mancho said. 'I seen lawyers *weren't* tossin' the case look more fucked up. You *didn't* know, you *won't* know. That kid's colder than a hit man.'

'John and Tommy are starting to smell something,' I said. 'They just don't know what.'

'A spic be livin' in the White House time it reaches their fuckin' brain,' Fat Mancho said.

'O'Connor's come through big,' Carol said. 'He looks like F. Lee Bailey's twin brother out there.'

'He *was* a good one,' Fat Mancho said. 'Then he lost a few and he found the bottle. Been chasin' nothin' but skid cases since.'

'He sobered up for this,' I said. 'He's got a shot at a win. Even without a witness.'

324

'He's a drunk, but he ain't a fool,' Fat Mancho said, putting the can of beer on the ground next to him. 'He wins this, every killer both sides of the river have his card in their pocket.'

'Is that true?' Carol asked, lifting one of the scarves up to where it covered everything but eyes.

'Is what true?' I said.

'Can we win the case without a witness?'

'You already won,' Fat Mancho said. 'You got the taste. Now, you're just lookin' to get away with it.'

'They've got to walk, Fat Man,' I said. 'We only win when John and Tommy walk.'

'Then you gotta get 'em outta the shootin' hole,' Fat Mancho said. 'Put 'em someplace else. Only your witness does that. And he's doin' a Claude Rains so far. Nobody's seen the fucker.'

'What if he doesn't show?' Carol said. 'What if we go in the way we are?'

'You *got* street justice,' Fat Mancho said. 'That's the real. You come up with empty hands on court justice, that's the bullshit.'

'They both take your life away, Fat Man,' I said. 'The street just does it faster.'

'Street's only one matters,' Fat Mancho said. 'Court's for uptown, people with suits, money, lawyers with three names. You got cash, you can *buy* court justice. On the street, justice got no price. She's blind where the judge sits. But she ain't blind out here. Out here, the bitch got eyes.'

'We need both,' I said.

'Then you *need* a witness,' Fat Mancho said, standing up, taking the black rubber ball out of his pants pocket. 'And I *need* to finish beatin' your ass. Let's go, loser. You down to me by four.'

'Can we finish this later?' I asked, too numb from the cold to stand.

'When later?' Fat Mancho asked, looking down at me.

'The middle of July,' I said.

SIXTEEN

Danny O'Connor pieced together a credible defense for the jury to ponder during the course of his first three days on the attack. He called to the stand a limited range of John and Tommy's friends and family, most of them middle-aged to elderly men and women with sweet eyes and trusting faces. All of them testifying that while both boys were sometimes wild, they were not killers.

None of them had ever seen John Reilly or Tommy Marcano hold a gun.

The two waitresses on duty the night of the shooting testified that they knew both defendants and found them to be pleasant whenever they entered the pub. Neither remembered seeing John Reilly or Tommy Marcano the night Sean Nokes was killed. The women said they were in the kitchen at the time of the shooting and did not come out until the police arrived.

'Were the two shooters in the pub when the police got there?' O'Connor asked one of the waitresses.

'No,' she said. 'I guess they already left.'

'Why do you guess that?'

'Killers don't wait for cops,' she said. 'In the neighborhood, *nobody* waits for cops.'

'You're from the neighborhood,' O'Connor said. 'And you waited.'

'I was getting *paid* to wait,' she said.

Jerry the bartender testified he served the defendants two drinks and two beers on the afternoon of Nokes' death. They sat quietly and were gone in less than an hour. They paid tab and tip with a twenty left on the bar. He was in the back picking up his dinner when the shooting occurred and therefore did not see anyone pump shots into Sean Nokes. Jerry also phoned the police as soon as the gunfire died down.

Through it all, Michael kept his cross-examinations simple, never venturing beyond where the witnesses wanted to go, never calling into dispute any parts of their accounts. He was always polite, cordial and relaxed, easily buying into the professed innocence of those called to the stand.

O'Connor's intent was to continue to mine the doubts planted in the jury's mind, doubts that had first taken root with the testimony of the prosecutor's key eyewitness, Helen Salinas.

To that end, Dr. George Paltrone, a Bronx general practitioner who also ran a detox clinic, was called to the stand as an expert witness. In Dr. Paltrone's opinion, if Mrs. Salinas drank as much alcohol as she claimed in the amount of time that she stated, her testimony had to be deemed less than credible.

'Are you saying Mrs. Salinas was drunk?' O'Connor asked Dr. Paltrone.

'Not quite drunk,' Dr. Paltrone said. 'But she had more than enough drink in her to impair judgment.'

'Wouldn't witnessing a shooting sober her up?'

'Not necessarily,' Dr. Paltrone said. 'The fear she felt may have made a rational judgment even more difficult.'

'In other words, doctor, drink and fear don't always lead to truth?'

'That's right,' Dr. Paltrone said. 'More often than not they don't.'

I sat through the three days of O'Connor's defense, in my usual third row seat, barely listening, unable to focus on the action before me. My mind was on Father Bobby and what he had decided to do. I knew without him that our best chance was a hung jury, which meant nothing more than another trial and an almost certain conviction.

I had not seen Father Bobby since the night I asked him to take the stand. I thought it too risky to approach O'Connor and find out what he knew, and Michael was beyond my reach. Everyone in the neighborhood seemed aware that we had a witness stashed.

But no one, not even King Benny, had the word on who the witness was and when he would show.

'If he's not here tomorrow, then forget it,' I said to Carol as the third day ground to an end. 'It's over.'

'We could try to find somebody else,' Carol said. 'We still have some time.'

'Who?' I said. 'The Pope's in Rome and I don't know any rabbis.'

'We can go and talk to him again,' Carol said. 'Or maybe have somebody else talk to him.'

'He's not afraid of King Benny,' I said, walking with Carol down the courthouse corridors. 'And Fat Mancho won't even go *near* a priest.'

'Then we can force him to do it,' Carol said with a shrug and a half-smile. 'Put a gun on him.'

'You want your witness to have one hand raised in court,' I said. 'Not two.'

We stopped by the elevator bank and waited, Carol pushed closer to me by the surrounding cluster of court officers, reporters, lawyers, defendants and their families. The down arrow rang and lit and the double doors to the elevator creaked open. We squeezed in with the pack, pushed to the back of the car. We both managed to turn and face forward, my eyes looking at the scarred neck of a husky Hispanic wearing an imitation leather jacket with a fake fur hood. He was breathing through his open mouth and his dank breath further fouled the musty air.

As we rode down the nine floors, the elevator stopping at each one, I looked over to my far left and saw Danny O'Connor standing there. He had his back against the elevator buttons, a tudor hat on top of his head and his eyes on me. He was chewing a thick piece of gum and had an unlit cigarette in his mouth.

If he knew anything, his face wasn't showing it.

The doors finally opened onto the main floor and the passengers stormed out of the car. I grabbed Carol by the arm and made my way closer to O'Connor, who was content to let the rush of people pass him by before he stepped off. The three of us came out of the elevator at the same time, my elbow brushing against O'Connor's side.

'I'm sorry,' I said.

'Not a problem,' he said, looking at me and Carol. 'Riding these elevators is like riding the IRT. Only not as safe.'

'Lucky it's cold,' I said. 'I'd hate to see what it's like in there during a heat wave.'

'It was nice bumping into you,' O'Connor said with a smile, moving toward the revolving exit doors.

'Why the rush?' I asked, watching him leave.

'Gotta go,' he said over his shoulder. 'I'm late.'

'Late for what?'

'Mass,' O'Connor said.

SEVENTEEN

'Call your next witness,' Judge Weisman said to Danny O'Connor.

'Your Honor, the defense calls to the stand Father Robert Carillo.'

Father Bobby walked through the courtroom with the confidence of a fighter heading into a main event. His thick hair was brushed back, his eyes were clear and his care-worn face shone under the glare of the overhead lights.

'Raise your right hand,' the baliff said. 'And place your left hand on the Bible.'

'Do you swear that what you say shall be the truth, the whole truth and nothing but the truth?'

'I do,' Father Bobby said.

'Take the stand,' the bailiff said.

'Father Carillo, to which parish do you belong?' Danny O'Connor asked.

'The Sacred Heart of Jesus on West 50th Street.'

'And how long have you been there?'

'It will be twenty years this spring.'

'And what is your position there?'

'I'm a priest,' Father Carillo said, smiling.

O'Connor, the spectators and the jury all joined in the laugh; even Judge Weisman cracked a smile, but John and Tommy sat in stone silence, hands cupped to their faces, while Michael chewed on the end of a blue Bic pen.

'I'm sorry, Father,' O'Connor said. 'I meant, what do you *do* there?'

'I'm the school principal,' Father Bobby said. 'I teach seventh grade and coach most of the sports teams. I'm also acting Monsignor, serve mass daily, listen to confessions and try to repair whatever needs fixing.'

'They keep you busy,' O'Connor said.

'It's a poor parish,' Father Bobby said. 'Low on funds and short on staff.'

'Do you know most of the people in your parish?'

'No,' Father Bobby said. 'I know *all* the people in my parish.'

'Do you know the two defendants, John Reilly and Thomas Marcano?'

'Yes I do,' Father Bobby said.

'How long have you known them?'

'Since they were boys,' Father Bobby said. 'They were students of mine.'

'How would you describe your relationship with them today?'

'We try to stay in touch,' Father Bobby said. 'I try to do that with all my boys.'

'And how do you do that?'

'Through sports, mostly,' Father Bobby said. 'We either organize a game or go to one. It's a common ground. Makes it easier to get together.'

'Father, do you recall where you were on the night of November first of this past year?'

'Yes I do,' Father Bobby said.

'And where was that?'

'I was at a basketball game,' Father Bobby said. 'At the Garden. The Knicks against the Celtics.'

'What time does a Knick game begin?'

'They usually start at about 7:30,' Father Bobby said.

'And at what time do they end?'

'Between nine-thirty and ten,' Father Bobby said. 'Providing there's no overtime.'

'Was there any that night?'

'No, there wasn't,' Father Bobby said.

'And who won the game, Father?'

'Sad to say, it was the Celtics,' Father Bobby said. 'Kevin McHale and Robert Parish were a little too much for our guys that night.'

'Were you at the game alone?'

'No,' Father Bobby said. 'I went there with two friends.'

'And who were those two friends, Father?'

'John Reilly and Thomas Marcano,' Father Reilly said.

'The two defendants?'

'Yes,' Father Bobby said, gesturing toward John and Tommy. 'The two defendants.'

The spectators sitting behind the wooden barrier gave a collective cry. Carol put her head down, her hands covering her mouth, her shoulders shaking. Michael took a deep breath and looked toward the ceiling.

John and Tommy turned around, scanning the spectators, their bodies relaxing. As they turned to face the bench, they looked over at me. I smiled as they looked down at the cover of the book in my hands.

John had tears in his eyes.

I was holding a copy of *The Count of Monte Cristo*.

'What time did you meet with Mr. Reilly and Mr. Marcano?' O'Connor asked, soon after Judge Weisman hammered a call to order.

'They picked me up outside the school playground,' Father Bobby said. 'It must have been about six-thirty or thereabouts.'

'How did you get to the Garden, Father?'

'We walked,' Father Bobby said. 'It's less than twenty blocks.'

'And Mr. Reilly and Mr. Marcano walked with you the whole time?'

'Yes,' Father Bobby said. 'We walked together.'

'And at eight twenty-five p.m., the time police say the victim, Sean Nokes, was murdered, were you still with Mr. Reilly and Mr. Marcano at the basketball game?'

'Yes I was,' Father Bobby said. 'If they were out of my sight at all during the game, it was either to go to the bathroom or to get something to drink.'

'What did you three do after the game?'

'We walked back to the parish,' Father Bobby said.

'Was it a cold night?'

'Windy as I recall,' Father Bobby said.

'Did you stop anywhere?'

'At a newsstand on Eighth Avenue,' Father Bobby said. 'I bought an early edition of *The Daily News*.'

'And at what time did you, Mr. Reilly and Mr. Marcano part company?'

'About ten-thirty, maybe a few minutes later,' Father Bobby said. 'They left me in front of the rectory, near where they picked me up.'

'Did the two defendants tell you where they were going after they left you?'

'No,' Father Bobby said. 'But I would imagine after a night spent with a priest, they went looking for the first open bar they could find.'

O'Connor waited for the snickers to subside.

'So then, Father, if the two defendants were with you on the night of the murder, they couldn't have shot and killed Sean Nokes, as the prosecution claims. Isn't that correct?'

'Unless they shot him from the blue seats at the Garden,' Father Bobby said.

'No, Father,' O'Connor said with a smile. 'He wasn't shot from there.'

'Then he wasn't shot by those boys,' Father Bobby said.

'I have no further questions,' O'Connor said. 'Thank you, Father.'

'It was my pleasure,' Father Bobby said.

'Your witness, Mr. Sullivan,' Judge Weisman said.

'Thank you, your Honor,' Michael said, standing up and walking over to Father Bobby.

'Did you buy the tickets for the game, Father?' Michael asked. 'Or were they given to you?'

333

'No, I bought them,' Father Bobby said.

'On the day of the game?'

'No,' Father Bobby said. 'I went to the box office about a week before.'

'How did you pay for the tickets?'

'With cash,' Father Bobby said. 'I pay for everything with cash.'

'Did you get a receipt?'

'No,' Father Bobby said. 'I didn't.'

'Did anyone know you were going to the game?' Michael asked, 'Other than the two defendants?'

'I don't think so,' Father Bobby said.

'When did you ask the defendants to go to the game with you?'

'The Sunday before,' Father Bobby said.

'Was anyone else present?'

'No,' Father Bobby said.

'So, no one saw you buy the tickets,' Michael said. 'There's no record of any purchase. And no one else knew you were going with the defendants. Is that right?'

'That's right,' Father Bobby said.

'So how do we know you were there?' Michael asked. 'How do we *really* know you and the two defendants were at the game on the night of the murder?'

'I'm telling you both as a witness *and* as a priest,' Father Bobby said. 'We *were* at that game.'

'And a priest wouldn't lie,' Michael said. 'Isn't that right?'

'A priest with ticket stubs wouldn't *need* to lie,' Father Bobby said, putting a hand into his jacket pocket and pulling out three torn tickets. 'And I always keep the stubs.'

'Why's that, Father?' Michael asked, standing next to him. 'Why do you keep them?'

'Because you never know,' Father Bobby said, looking straight at Michael, 'when someone will want more than your word.'

'Has anyone questioned your word before today?'

'No,' Father Bobby said. 'No one *ever* has. But there's a first time for most things in this world.'

'Yes, Father,' Michael Sullivan said. 'I guess there is.'

Michael turned from Father Bobby and looked up at Judge Weisman.

'I have no further questions at this time,' Michael said. 'Witness is free to go.'

The spectators applauded as Father Robert Carillo, a Catholic priest from Hell's Kitchen, stepped down from the stand.

EIGHTEEN

I put one foot on a rusty mooring, my hands in my pockets as I looked out at the Hudson River. The skies were overcast and the winter air felt heavy with impending snow. Carol had her back to me, staring past the iron legs of the West Side Highway toward the streets of Hell's Kitchen. It was early evening, six hours removed from Father Bobby's testimony.

I still hadn't recovered from seeing him take the stand and lie for us. He didn't just testify for John and Tommy, he testified against Wilkinson and the evil that had lived there for too long. Still, I was sorry he had to do it, to tell the lie that I know must have cost him dearly, just to help us get our ounce of revenge.

I was sorry any of us had to go through this trial. I wondered about Carol, and how these days would affect her. She was smart and attractive, and should have been spending her time meeting men who did more than simply combat the ghosts of their pasts. I prayed that the trial would free Michael of his demons and allow him to go on with his life. As for John and Tommy, I hoped the best for them, but feared only the worst.

It just seemed that no matter how hard we tried, no matter how many of them we got, we could never rid ourselves of the Wilkinson Home for Boys. My friends and I *had* to live with it. Now, Carol and Father Bobby had to live with it as well.

Carol turned toward me and, sensing my unease, leaned over and hugged me.

'That place is a part of me and a part of Father Bobby too,' Carol said. 'In different ways, maybe. But it's in our lives. And it's going to stay in our lives. No matter what we do now.'

'None of it helps make it even,' I said. 'We've got a long way to go till we get to even.'

'But you've got to admit,' Carol said, 'you're off to a helluva nice start.'

'I was real proud of him up there,' I said, wiping at tears I couldn't control.

'We were all proud of him,' Carol said. 'And Father Bobby did it not because we asked him to. But because it was the *only* thing he *could* do. He had no choice either, Shakes.'

'He looked like Cagney up there,' I said. 'Looked everybody square in the eye. Didn't back off for a second.'

'More like Bogart, you mean,' Carol said, smiling, putting an arm around my waist.

'I'll never understand how you could have grown up around here and still think Bogart's better than Cagney,' I said.

'I suppose you think the Three Stooges are better than the Marx Brothers, too.'

'Hands down, porcupine head.'

'And you probably like John Wayne westerns too,' she said.

'There's where you're wrong,' I said. 'I *love* John Wayne westerns.'

'You're hopeless.' And then Carol Martinez laughed out loud. It was the first time I'd heard real laughter in a very long time.

'We're all hopeless,' I said, walking with her alongside the dock, up toward Pier eighty-two, her arm under my elbow. 'That's why we're still together.'

'But I swear, if you tell me you still think Soupy Sales

337

is funnier than Woody Allen, it's gonna be all over,' Carol said. 'I mean it.'

'Can Woody Allen do *White Fang*?' I asked her.

'Probably not,' she said.

'That's right,' I said. '*Nobody* does what Soupy does, because *nobody* can.'

'No, Shakes,' Carol said. 'It's because nobody *wants* to.'

The sound of our laughter echoed off the empty steel piers and out into the rough waters of the Hudson.

338

NINETEEN

At nine-ten a.m., on a rainy Thursday morning in January of 1980, Michael Sullivan stood in the well of a courtroom and addressed a jury for the last time in his career.

That morning, he had carefully chosen his dark grey suit, blue tie and black loafers. Two thin specks of dried blood clung to his right cheek, thanks to a close shave with an old razor. He had a Superman wrist watch on his left hand, an egg-shaped college graduation ring on his right and a cherry Life Saver in his mouth.

'Is counsel ready?' Judge Weisman asked.

'Yes, your Honor,' Michael said. 'I'm ready.'

'Please proceed,' Judge Weisman said.

Michael pushed his chair back and walked toward the jury box, twelve faces studying his every move. He put one hand in his pants pocket, caught the eye of the eldest member of the panel and smiled.

'You have to admit, it's been an interesting couple of weeks,' Michael began, his free hand rubbing the rail of the jury bench. 'And it sure beats deciding a civil court case.'

He waited with his head down for the scattered laughter to fade.

'But now, you have a decision to make. A very difficult decision. A decision whose weight will determine the fate of two young men.

'You've heard the arguments from both sides. My side

tells you the defendants, John Reilly and Thomas Marcano, shot and killed the victim, Sean Nokes. The other side tells you they didn't. In fact, if you *really* want to know the truth, they weren't even *there* to kill him.

'So, who to believe? *That's* what you must now decide.'

Michael moved slowly down the jury box, taking care to look at every member of the panel, looking beyond their faces, beyond their eyes.

'So how do you reach a decision? You start by going over what you know based on the evidence that was presented. You *know* that Sean Nokes was murdered on November 6, 1979 at eight twenty-five in the evening. You *know* he was shot to death while sitting in the back booth of the Shamrock Pub. And you *know* he was gunned down by two men in black jackets. But which two men? That's where things start getting a little fuzzy.'

Michael had both hands in his pockets now as he walked past the court stenographer, his head raised, his back to the jury. The spectators in the crowded courtroom were, with a handful of exceptions, all from Hell's Kitchen.

'You heard testimony that painted the two defendants as less than ideal citizens. *Does that make them killers*? Then you heard testimony that described Sean Nokes as a man with an ugly past. *Does that make it less than a crime to kill him*? You heard from an eyewitness who saw the two defendants walk out of the Shamrock Pub moments after shooting Sean Nokes dead. Then you heard from a priest who said the two defendants were with *him* at a Knicks game, eating hot dogs and drinking beer at the same time Sean Nokes was sitting up dead in a back booth. So, who do you believe? Who's lying? Who's telling the truth?'

Michael ambled past the defense table, inches away from John and Tommy, hands still in his pockets, his eyes back on the jury.

'It's not going to be easy for you to decide,' Michael said. 'It's not supposed to be. Decisions where people's lives are at stake *should* be hard. They should take time.

They should take a great deal of search and thought. You have to look at the facts, and then beyond them. You have to listen to the testimony, and then read through it. You have to weigh the witnesses and then go past their words and search out *their motives*. You have to go beyond the one victim and the two defendants. You must look to the lines that connect them.'

Michael stopped at his desk and sipped from a cup of cold coffee. He put the cup down, unbuttoned his jacket and moved back toward the jury box.

'With this case, I'm asking you to do what few juries are asked to do,' Michael said. 'I'm asking you to look at the facts and *then* look at the reasons for those facts. I'm asking you to find the truth in what you've heard, in what you've seen and in what you *believe*. It might be the only way for you to come up with a decision you can live with. A decision that will not cause you doubt. A decision that you will *know* is the right one.'

Michael had both hands spread across the jury rail, his body leaning against it, his eyes focused on the men and women before him.

'You have to make your decision based on the guilt of two men and the innocence of one, and you have to *believe* it. You have to go *beyond* a reasonable doubt; you have to go to where there is *no* doubt. You take everything you know to be true and then take all the time you need to move past the truth and past the doubt and come out with a decision we can all live with. A decision that many may question, but *you* know to be the *right* one. Because now, *you* are the only judges. In your hands will rest the evidence and the testimony. In your hands will rest the facts. In your hands will rest the fate of two men and the memory of a third. In your hands will rest the truth.

'I have confidence in those hands. I *believe* in those hands. And I believe those hands will find a verdict that will be filled with truth. And filled with justice. An honest truth and an honorable justice.'

Michael Sullivan then thanked a jury for the last time, walked back to his seat and put his legal pads into his black briefcase.

'Do you have anything to add, counselor?' Judge Weisman asked.

'No, your Honor,' Michael Sullivan said. 'There's nothing else. I've said it all.'

TWENTY

'Let me have a hot dog with mustard, sauerkraut and onions,' Michael told a chubby vendor in a leather flap cap, standing on the sidewalk outside the courthouse. 'And let me have a Coke, too.'

'No ketchup?' I asked.

'I'm on a diet,' he said without turning around.

It was a snowy, windy Monday afternoon and the jury had been in deliberation since the previous Thursday night. The courthouse rumor mill was working on overdrive, with most of the gossip predicting a verdict of guilty.

'You got a place to eat that?' I asked Michael, pointing to his hot dog.

'Behind you,' Michael said, lifting the bun toward a park bench over my shoulder.

'Okay if I join you?'

'What can they do?' Michael asked. 'Arrest us?'

'You did good in there, counselor,' I said to Michael, sitting on the bench, taking a bite out of a pretzel.

'How I did won't matter until they come back in and hand me a win,' Michael said.

'Will you settle for a loss?' I asked, smiling over at him.

'I can live with it,' Michael said, finishing his hot dog and snapping open his soda can.

'What happens to you now?' I asked. 'After this ends?'

'I walk away,' Michael said. 'Wait a few weeks and then

hand in my notice. After the way I handled this case, there won't be a rush to keep me from the door.'

'You can switch to the other side,' I said. 'Work as a defense lawyer. More money in it, probably, and you'll never be short on clients. There are always going to be more bad guys than good. The work from John and Tommy's crew alone will get you a house with a pool.'

'Not for me,' Michael said. 'I've seen all the law I want to see. It's time for something else.'

'Like what?'

'I'll let you know when I know,' Michael said.

'You're too old to play for the Yankees,' I said. 'And you're too young to take up golf.'

'You're shooting holes all through my plans,' Michael said, smiling. 'I'm starting to panic.'

'You'll work thing out,' I said, finishing the last of my soda. 'You always have.'

'It's time for quiet, Shakes,' Michael said, staring down at the ground. 'That I do know. Give things a rest. Find a spot where I can shut my eyes and not have to see the places I've been. Maybe I'll even get lucky and forget I was ever there.'

'It took pieces out of us, where we were,' I said. 'What we had to do to get out. Big pieces we didn't even know we had. Pieces we gotta learn to do without or find again. All that takes time. Lots of time.'

'I can wait,' Michael said.

'You always seemed to know how,' I said. 'The rest of us didn't have the patience.'

'I've got to get back in there,' Michael said, standing up and moving toward the courthouse building. 'The jury may be coming in.'

'Don't disappear on me, counselor,' I said, my eyes meeting his. 'I may need a good lawyer someday.'

'You can't afford a good lawyer,' Michael said. 'Not on your salary.'

'I may need a good friend,' I said.

'I'll find you when you do,' Michael said. 'Count on it.'

'I always have,' I said, watching Michael walk through the revolving doors of the courthouse to the elevators and up nine floors to face a jury's verdict.

TWENTY-ONE

The area outside Part forty-seven was crowded with the familiar faces of Hell's Kitchen. They stood against stained walls, smoking cigarettes and drinking coffee, or sat on long wooden benches, reading the *Daily News* and *Post*. Others jammed the phone banks, calling in their bets and checking in on either an angry parole officer or an impatient loan shark.

They were waiting for the verdict.

Walking past them, I shook a few hands and nodded to a few faces before finding an empty spot in a corner near the black double doors.

After fifteen minutes, the doors swung open. A court officer, tall and muscular, his gun buckle hanging at an angle, held the knob in one hand, his body halfway in the hall.

'They're coming in,' he said in a listless voice. 'In about five minutes. You wanna hear, better come in now.'

I stood to the side and watched as the crowd slowly trooped in. Then I moved away, and walked over to a bench and sat down. I leaned over, my head in my hands, eyes closed, sweating, shaking, praying that we could finish this the way we planned. I went over everything we did and tried to think of things we should have done. The plan had only one flaw. Its success or failure hinged on the whims of twelve strangers.

'You're not going in?' Carol asked, standing above me.

'I don't want to go in alone,' I said, taking my hands from my face.

'You're not alone,' she said.

'I don't want to lose, either,' I said.

'You're not going to lose.'

'It sounds like you've got all the answers,' I said, standing up and taking her by the arm.

'Maybe I do,' Carol said. 'Maybe I do.'

'Has the jury reached its verdict?' Judge Weisman asked, sitting impassively behind his bench.

'We have, your Honor,' answered the jury foreman, a stocky, bald man in a plaid shirt.

The bailiff took the folded piece of paper from the foreman and walked it over to Judge Weisman. The Judge opened the paper and looked down, his face betraying nothing.

I looked past the wall of heads and shoulders surrounding me and glanced over at John and Tommy, sitting up close to their table, their hands bunched in fists. Danny O'Connor sat next to them, rubbing a hand against the back of his neck, beneath the frayed collar of his shirt. Across from them, Michael sat and stared at the empty witness box. He was taking deep breaths, his fingers twirling a felt tip pen over his knuckles.

Judge Weisman nodded to the foreman, who stood in front of his seat.

'On the count of murder in the second degree, how do you find the defendant, John Reilly?' Judge Weisman asked.

The foreman bit his lips and looked around the courtroom with nervous eyes.

'Not guilty,' the foreman said.

'On the count of murder in the second degree, how do you find the defendant, Thomas Marcano?'

'Not guilty,' the foreman said.

The courtroom erupted in a thunder of applause,

screams, shouts and whistles, few hearing the Judge's call to order and dismissal of charges against the defendants.

I stood up and hugged Carol.

'You did it, Shakes,' she whispered in my ear.

'*We* did it,' I said, holding her tight. 'We *all* did it.'

I looked over and saw Michael pick up his briefcase, shake hands with Danny O'Connor and walk into the crowd, where he was swallowed up by the mass of bodies. I saw John and Tommy smiling and laughing, reaching out for as many hands as they could, cries of not guilty filling the air around us. I saw Judge Weisman walk down from his place behind the bench.

Flashbulbs popped.

A pair of women in the middle of the room began to cry hysterically.

Four young men in the back, heading out of the room, sang the words to 'Danny Boy'.

An old lady behind me stayed seated and fingered the beads of her rosary, her lips moving to a series of silent prayers.

The jury members filed out of the box, some with their heads bowed, a few waving to people in the crowd.

Danny O'Connor, all smiles and sweat, walked out of the courtroom to a chorus of men and women chanting his name.

John and Tommy stood by their places, arms in the air, basking in the glory of their moment.

Michael Sullivan was already in the elevator, heading down to the lobby, his mission completed, his career over.

I took Carol by the hand and led her out of the courtroom, the loud, happy sound of the crowd following us down the corridor.

It was the sound of justice.

Spring 1980

The long table and chairs ran nearly the length of the restaurant's back room, just off the main dining hall. Pitchers of beer and bottles of Dewar's and Johnny Walker Red dotted the cloth, along with candles flickering inside hurricane shells. Two large floral arrangements, resting in the middle of a pair of wicker baskets with half-moon handles, anchored the ends.

A full month had passed since the acquittal. In those few weeks, our lives had reverted back to what they had been prior to the murder of Sean Nokes.

Carol returned to her stack of social service files, helping troubled teens and single mothers fight a system that had neither time enough nor funds enough to care.

John and Tommy went back to the streets, running the West Side Boys, drinking heavily and once again breaking laws with abandon. No one had expected them to change. It was too late.

King Benny went back to his club and Fat Mancho returned to his bodega.

I was promoted from clerk to reporter trainee, covering the entertainment beat. It meant I got to go to the movies for free, just like I used to do when I was a kid. Except now I didn't have to sneak my way in.

Michael was the only one of us who had made any significant change in his life. As he had promised, he had resigned from his job, three weeks after working the losing end of a can't-miss case.

*
351

I was the first to arrive and chose a seat at the center of the table, my back to the wall. A young waiter in white shirt and black bow tie came into the room and asked if I wanted anything. I looked at the line of beer and whiskey and smiled.

'This is an Irish table,' I said. 'And I'm Italian.'

'What's missing?' the waiter asked.

'Wine.'

'Red or white?'

'Both,' I said.

The waiter bumped into John and Tommy on his way out of the room. I stood up and we stared at each other for a few minutes. Then they both came around the table and squeezed me in a long, silent hug.

'I don't even know *how* to fuckin' thank you,' Johnny said, holding me even tighter.

'I can't believe what you did,' Tommy said. 'And I can't believe you got away with it.'

'What do you mean?' I said. 'Don't tell me you *really* killed him?'

They both laughed, and loosening their hold, pulled back chairs on both sides of me.

'Besides, I had nothin' to do with it,' I said, sitting down as well. 'It was all Mikey. It was his plan.'

'I gotta tell you,' John said, pouring himself a glass of beer, 'when I first heard he took the case I was gonna have him burned.'

'What stopped you?'

'He was a friend,' John said. 'And if you're gonna go away on a murder rap, who better to send you?'

'Then, the way he was handlin' his end of the case, I thought he just sucked as a lawyer,' Tommy said. 'I started feelin' sorry for the bastard.'

'Never feel sorry for a lawyer,' Michael said, standing in front of us, a wide smile on his face.

'Get over here, counselor,' John said, grabbing Michael's arm and dragging him around the table.

Tommy rushed in from the other side and squeezed me

against them as they hugged. We were nothing more than a small circle of arms and crunched faces.

'You're the real Count!' John shouted. 'Alive and well and working in downtown New York City!'

'Not after this week,' Michael said. 'This Count's on the dole now.'

'What'd you do with all that buried treasure?' Tommy asked. 'Gamble it away?'

'How do you think we paid off King Benny?' Michael said.

Carol stood in the entryway, her arms folded, laughing and shaking her head.

'What is this?' she asked. 'A gay bar?'

We turned when we heard her voice. Her hair was freshly cut and styled, and she wore a short, tight black dress, a black purse hanging off her shoulder on a long strap.

'It *was*,' John said. 'Till you walked in.'

'You want us to hug you too?' Tommy asked.

'How about just a hello,' Carol said.

'How about a kiss to go with the hello?' John asked.

'Deal,' Carol said, coming around to our end.

'Hurry up,' I said. 'Before the waiter comes in.'

'Yeah,' Tommy said. 'Then we're gonna have to kiss him too.'

'I saw him on my way in,' Carol said. 'He's cute. I'd throw him a kiss.'

'That's funny,' John said. 'That's what Shakes said.'

We sat around the table, ordered our dinners, poured our drinks and talked until night turned to morning.

We talked about everything we could think of, five friends with so many shared moments, afraid to let our time together come to an end. We talked about everything but the trial. And the months we had sworn never to resurrect with speech.

Carol let loose her frustration with city bureaucracy and the battles she lost each day.

John and Tommy talked about their lives of crime. They

knew it was a fast lane that could only end with a bullet or iron bars. But it was the only way they knew to feel control, to push away the demons that gnawed at them during their rare sober moments.

Michael was at peace with his decision and curious about where it would take him. He had saved enough money to live for a year without working and had already invested in a one-way ticket on a plane leaving for London the following weekend. He had made no plans beyond that.

I half joked that my career choices were narrowed down to two. I was either going to be a reporter or an usher at one of the theaters whose running times I knew so well.

Eventually, the beer, wine and liquor took hold and we switched gears, laughing over simpler times, in the years before Wilkinson starved us of laughter. Over and over we recalled our many pranks, relishing the freedom and foolishness a Hell's Kitchen childhood allowed.

'You guys remember when you formed that stupid singing group?' Carol asked, pouring water into a glass.

'The Four Gladiators,' Michael said, smiling. 'Best quartet to ever hold a Hell's Kitchen corner.'

'Remember what Shakes wanted to call the group?' Johnny said, lighting a cigarette.

'The Count and His Cristos,' Tommy said. 'Man, that woulda sent albums flyin' outta the stores.'

'We weren't *that* bad,' I said. 'Some people *wanted* to hear us sing.'

'That group from the deaf school don't count,' John said.

'Why not?' I said. 'They applauded.'

'You guys were *awful*,' Carol said, laughing. 'Kids cried when they heard you sing.'

'They were sad songs,' I said.

'Fat Mancho was gonna be our manager,' Tommy said. 'And King Benny was gonna be the bankroll. You know, get us suits and travel money, shit like that.'

'What happened to *that* plan?' Carol asked.

354

'They heard us sing,' I said.

'Fat Mancho said he'd eat flesh before he put his name next to ours,' John said.

'What'd King Benny say?' Carol asked.

'He didn't say anything,' I said. 'He walked back into his club and closed the door.'

'We stole from everybody we liked,' Tommy said, finishing a mug of beer.

'So what's changed?' Carol asked, watching me pour her a fresh glass of wine.

'We had enough cuts to make an album,' I said. 'We ripped off Frankie Valli, Dion, Bobby Darin.'

'The cream,' Carol said.

'Only with us it was sour cream,' Tommy said.

'Let's do a song from our album,' Michael said, leaning across the table, smiling. 'For Carol.'

'Don't you guys have to go out and shoot somebody?' Carol said, hiding her face in her hands.

'We *always* got time for a song,' John said, standing and leaning against the wall.

'You pick it, Mikey,' Tommy said, standing next to Johnny. 'Nothin' too slow. We wanna keep Carol on her toes.'

'Let's do "Walk Like a Man",' Michael said. 'Shakes does a good Valli on that one.'

'Back us up,' I said to Carol, handing her two soup spoons. 'Hit these against some glasses when I point.'

'Not too loud,' Carol said, looking through the doorway behind her. 'Some people might be eating.'

'We sing better in men's rooms,' Tommy said. 'The walls there hold the sound.'

'There's one downstairs,' Carol said. 'I'll wait here.'

'This is like The Beatles getting together again,' I said. Carol just snorted.

The four of us huddled in a corner of the room, me in front. Michael, Tommy and John each kept one hand on my shoulder, snapping their fingers to an imaginary beat.

Carol sat back in her chair, looked at the four of us, and smiled.

She clapped her hands as we started to sing.

'*Walk like a man, fast as you can, walk like a man my son.*' We began in our best Frankie Valli and The Four Seasons voices. '*Go tell the world, forget about the girl and walk like a man, my son.*'

Then we all cupped a hand to an ear, fingers still snapping, and hit all the right acapella notes.

Carol stood on her chair and slapped the spoons against the side of her leg, mixing in with the beat.

Three waiters stood in the doorway and joined in.

Two diners standing behind them whistled their approval.

The bartender drummed his hands against the counter and handed out free drinks to all.

An elderly couple, in for a late-night espresso, wrapped their arms around each other and danced.

It was our special night and we held it for as long as we could. It was something that belonged to us. A night that would be added to our long list of memories.

It was our happy ending.

And it was the last time we would ever be together again.

TWENTY-TWO

Early on the morning of March 16, 1984, John Reilly's bloated body was found face up in the hallway of a tenement on West 46th Street. His right hand held the neck of the bottle of lethal boiler room gin that killed him. He had six dollars in the front pocket of his black leather coat and a ten-dollar bill in the flap of his hunter's shirt. A .44 caliber bulldog nestled at the base of his spine and a stiletto switchblade was jammed inside his jeans.

At the time of his death, he was a suspect in five unsolved homicides.

He was two weeks past his thirty-second birthday.

Thomas 'Butter' Marcano died on July 26, 1985. His body was found in an empty cabin in upstate New York, five bullets shot into his head at close range. The body lay undiscovered for more than a week, the heat of summer and the gnashing of animals rushing its decay. There was little in the cabin beyond a dozen empty beer cans, two bottles of Dewar's and three fully loaded semi-automatics. There was a crucifix and a picture of St. Jude in the pocket of Butter's crewneck shirt.

Thomas Marcano was thirty-three years old.

Michael Sullivan lives in a small town in the English countryside, where he works part-time as a carpenter. On his infrequent visits to New York he has never returned to Hell's Kitchen. He no longer practices law and has never married. He lives quietly and alone.

He is forty-four years old.

Carol Martinez still works for a social service agency and still lives in Hell's Kitchen. She too has never married, but is a single mother supporting a growing twelve-year-old son. The boy, John Thomas Michael Martinez, loves to read and is called Shakes by his mother.

Neighbors all say he has his mother's smile and her dark olive eyes.

The rest of his features come from his father, John Reilly.

Carol Martinez is forty-three years old.

Father Robert Carillo is the Monsignor of an upstate New York parish where he still plays basketball every day. He keeps in touch with all his boys and is always there when needed.

He prays every day for the boys he lost.

Father Bobby is sixty years old.

King Benny lives in a home for the elderly in Westchester County, miles from his Hell's Kitchen kingdom. He still drinks strong coffee, hiding his stash from the duty nurses charged to his care. He still hates to talk and suffers from Italian Alzheimer's. 'I forget everything these days,' he says. 'Everything except my enemies.'

King Benny is seventy-eight years old.

Fat Mancho suffered a mild stroke in the middle of August, 1992. It left his right hand numb and blinded him in his right eye. He passed the bodega on to a nephew, but still takes half the profits. He divides his time between his three Hell's Kitchen apartments and a new house in Queens.

He still bets on stickball games.

Fat Mancho is seventy-two years old.

358

Sean Nokes was shot to death in a back booth in the Shamrock Pub on November 6, 1979. His killers have yet to be apprehended.

Sean Nokes was thirty-seven years old at the time of his death.

Adam Styler was fired from the New York Police Department on February 22, 1982, brought up on corruption and murder charges. He pleaded guilty and was sentenced to a twelve-year prison term as part of a plea-bargain agreement. He served eight of those years in a maximum security prison. He was transfered to a minimum security facility only after a fourth attempt on his life left him paralyzed from the waist down. He was paroled in the spring of 1991 and now lives in a New Jersey suburb in a home for the disabled.

Adam Styler is fifty years old.

Henry Addison resigned from his job as community outreach director working for the Mayor of the City of New York in the spring of 1981. He found work in a downtown investment banking firm. After six months of impressive earnings, he was in line for a promotion. On New Year's Day, 1982, his body was found in a marsh off a LaGuardia Airport runway. Autopsy reports indicated he was beaten and tortured to death.

His killer or killers have never been found.

Henry Addison was thirty-six years old.

Ralph Ferguson's wife filed for divorce soon after he testified at John and Tommy's trial, gaining custody of their only child. He quit his job and fled the state, fearful of being brought up on multiple charges of child endangerment and rape. He eventually settled in California and, under another name, opened a hardware business. A second marriage ended when his wife was informed of her husband's true identity and hidden past. The business closed after a fire gutted it in 1989. He now works as a shoe salesman in the San Francisco area. He lives alone, is heavily in debt and has trouble sleeping at night.

He was the man brought to me by King Benny in 1993 to beg my forgiveness. I lived for nearly a year afraid of his every move. He will live the rest of his days equally afraid of mine.

Ralph Ferguson is forty-nine years old.

In the fall of 1982, a board of inquiry impaneled by the New York State Department of Juvenile Justice looked into allegations of abuse at the Wilkinson Home for Boys. They were confronted by a list of forty-seven witnesses, including the parents of three boys who died under the care of the institution and a dozen guards who were witness to a variety of assaults. In a report condemning all past and present directors of the Wilkinson Home for Boys, the board of inquiry called for a complete and total overhaul of the system and method of operations at the juvenile facility. A new warden was appointed and video cameras were installed on every block. Inmate privileges were extended and the hole was eliminated. Even the cells were freshly painted.

Edward Goldenberg 'Little Caesar' Robinson is serving a life sentence in a maximum security prison in upstate New York, convicted on charges of drug trafficking and murder in 1990. He will be eligible for parole in twenty-one years. He was never questioned in the murder of Henry Addison.

Edward Goldenberg 'Little Caesar' Robinson is fifty-one years old.

Gregory 'Marlboro' Wilson retired on a full pension and lives on a Pennsylvania farm. He spends his days reading books, writing letters to his children and playing cards with friends. Every Christmas he gets two cartons of Marlboro cigarettes from a Sleeper who remembers.

Gregory 'Marlboro' Wilson is sixty-three years old.

360

I am now forty years old, with a wife and two children. I love my wife and adore my son and daughter. My family has helped me escape from many of the pains of my past. But the haunting memories of childhood are always close at hand. My body is older than its years and my mind is filled more with horror than with the pleasures of life. The dreams I have are still vivid, the nightmares painful, the fears steady. The nighttime hours always carry a sense of dread.

I sometimes feel that the lucky Sleepers are the ones who died.

They no longer have to live with the memories.

They are free of the dreams.

Epilogue

Many's the road I have walked upon
Many's the hour between dusk and dawn
Many's the time
Many's the mile
I see it all now
Through the eyes of a child

Take It Where You Find it – *Van Morrison*

Summer 1966

Rueben, a Puerto Rican kid with dark curly hair and tight gray slacks, the crease sharp enough to cut skin, was the favorite to win the contest and the fifty dollars first prize. He stood in a corner of the gym, his back to the three-piece band, chewing gum, sneaking puffs on a Viceroy, waiting for the disc jockey on stage to signal a start to the school-sponsored Chubby Checker King Twister competition.

'He looks good,' I said, staring over at Rueben. 'He looks ready to win.'

'He looks like he seen *West Side Story* a couple of times too many,' Johnny said.

'He won't figure you to be any good, Shakes,' Michael said. 'Since he don't know you.'

'I don't figure you to be any good neither,' Tommy said, putting an arm around my shoulder. 'And I know you.'

'He's got you beat on the shoes,' John said. 'He's wearing those roach stompers. They're good twist shoes. They got a light look, but good soles.'

'Who are you, Tom McCann?' I asked. 'The shoes I got are okay.'

'Who else is in this?' Michael asked. 'Outside of him.'

'Three Irish guys from 46th Street,' Tommy said.

'They any good?' I asked.

'I hear they're pretty stupid,' Tommy said.

367

'Now you need to go to college to do the twist?' Michael asked.

'They just signed on as a goof,' Tommy said. 'Make each other laugh. These guys couldn't get laid in a women's prison.'

'There's that goofy kid from the pizza place,' I said. 'I hear he signed up.'

'I know him,' John said. 'He's got all those zits and that black shit on his teeth. I make sure he *never* touches any of my slices.'

'Anybody else?' Michael asked.

'That black kid who spits when he talks,' Tommy said. 'The one whose father just got shot.'

'They might give it to him just for that,' I said. 'Start feelin' sorry for him.'

'Don't worry, Shakes,' Michael said. 'We see the vote goin' that way, we'll have somebody stab you.'

'Not too deep,' I said. 'I need this shirt for school.'

'Just deep enough to win,' Michael said.

The gym's overhead lights were turned off, the spotlights shining on the center of the floor. Eighty or more kids surrounded the circle, many of the boys and girls holding hands, some sneaking soft kisses in the dark.

'Will the twist contestants please enter the circle,' the disc jockey ordered from the stage, his jacket tight around his shoulders, his pants cuffed, white socks sagging below the ankles.

'Go get 'em, Shakes,' Tommy said, patting me on the back

'Anybody gets close to us, we push,' John said 'Knock 'em off balance.'

'We'll be here waitin' for you, Shakes,' Michael said. 'Win or lose.'

'We can't let you go out there without a good luck kiss,' Carol Martinez said, easing her way through the crowd to join our group. She was wearing a white dress

368

with black shoes and white lace stockings. Her long dark hair was done up in a pony tail.

'You give it to him,' Michael said. 'We already kissed him once today.'

Carol put her arms around my neck and kissed me firmly on the lips.

'Kiss or no kiss,' Tommy said, 'we ain't cuttin' her in on the prize money.'

'You're nothin' but heart,' John said.

Each contestant was placed under one of the six spotlights, the circle large enough to give us all room to dance. I was sandwiched between the kid from the pizza parlor and one of the Irish guys from 46th, still in his St. Agnes school uniform. Rueben was across from me, a relaxed look on his face, a toothpick hanging from the side of his mouth. The tall black kid, the best-dressed of the group, was the only one who looked nervous.

'C'mon, everybody!' the disc jockey shouted in a poor Chubby Checker imitation. 'Clap your hands, we're gonna do the twist and it goes like this.'

Chubby Checker's joyful voice boomed out of the faulty sound system and we began to twist, cheered on by the screams and cries of our friends in the crowd. We all kept it simple at the start, except for the three Irish guys, who tossed in spins and whirls to impress the audience.

It was an easy contest to lose. If you fell, missed your motion or stopped twisting, you were automatically bounced. Barring that, the disc jockey, the designated twist judge, walked among the dancers and tapped out those he felt were not up to the demands of the dance.

It would take less than twenty minutes to declare a winner. The Irish kid in the St. Agnes uniform was the first out, losing his balance on a one-knee twist. One of his friends followed soon after, trying to do a foot and hand move that backfired.

'They're Irish,' Tommy said, laughing and nudging Michael. 'Just like you.'

'They're stupid, too,' Michael said. 'Just like you.'

By the third go-around I was getting winded, sweat coming off my face and back, the heat of the spotlights and the constant movement causing the faces around me to blur. Rueben kept his pace steady, his eyes on me, every so often flashing a smile to show he was in the game and breathing easy.

By the end of 'Twistin'' U.S.A.' the kid from the pizza parlor grabbed his side, stopped dancing and walked out of the circle. A short girl reached toward him, put her arms around his waist and kissed his cheek.

'You see that?' John asked with a look of disgust. 'She kissed him on the zits.'

'A connect-the-dot face has a girlfriend and I go to movies alone,' Tommy said, shaking his head. 'Is that fair?'

'Yes,' Michael said.

Rueben was moving faster now, shaking down lower, twisting his body till his knees seemed to be waxing the floor. The toothpick was still in his mouth and a sneer had replaced the smile, his confidence building with every beat.

The black kid was all sweat and little style, his legs starting to cramp, the overhead lights bothering him more with each move. He was favoring his right knee, wincing whenever he went down on it.

The disc jockey, hands folded behind his back, walked over and whispered something in his ear. The black kid looked at him and nodded. He stopped dancing and limped off the floor.

'Poor guy,' Carol said. 'His knee must be really bad.'

'His father takin' a bullet meant nothin',' Tommy said.

'You gotta have somebody *die* to catch a break in this contest,' John said.

It was now down to three dancers.

I figured I had enough left in me for five more good minutes. Any more, and they could use the fifty dollars

370

to bury me. Rueben looked like he could twist all night, with or without the music.

'Let's hear it for these guys that are left,' the disc jockey shouted. 'The twisting kings of New York City.'

The Irish kid stopped dancing to applaud along with the crowd and was forced to leave the contest.

'That guy's dumber than a plant,' Johnny said.

'The DJ?' Tommy asked. 'Or the Irish kid?'

'Both,' Michael said.

'All right, boys, let's see what you got,' the disc jockey said to me and Rueben. 'You're the only ones left.'

I was soaked through with sweat, my shirt sticking to my chest and back, my hair matted to my face. My jeans were loose and the sweat around my waist made them looser. Even my shoes were starting to slip on the gym floor.

I had a few moves left and started to use them, twisting down on one knee, leaving the free leg up. Through the darkness, my end of the crowd reacted with applause and whistles.

I moved as low to the ground as I could, still twisting, then planted my hands between my legs, did a split and brought them back up to twist position.

'That's it,' Tommy said. 'That's what you gotta show 'em. They eat that Fred Astaire shit up.'

'The Puerto Rican has to make his move now,' Michael said. 'Or take the loss.'

'What happens if he swallows that toothpick?' John asked.

'We win,' Michael said.

Rueben made his move, but it was the wrong one.

With his end of the crowd clapping and cheering behind him, Rueben went down to a low position, laid his hands flat on the ground and tried a head-over flip. He made the flip, an impressive head past shoulder acrobatic move, but the soles of his shoes slipped when he landed back on his feet. He slid to the ground and fell onto his rear, toothpick still in his mouth.

I stopped dancing, walked over to Rueben, reached out my hand and helped him to his feet.

'Great move,' I said.

'I'll get you next summer,' he said.

'You almost got me *this* summer,' I said, shaking his hand.

The crowd closed in on us, applauding, whistling and shouting. Their screams and chants grew even louder when the disc jockey slapped a fifty-dollar bill in my palm and raised my hand in victory.

'We're rich!' Tommy shouted, rushing toward me with John, Michael and Carol fast behind. 'We're rich!'

'We can live for a month,' John said. 'Pizza. Comic books. Italian ices. The town's ours.'

'You were lucky,' Michael said to me with a smile. 'It's always better to be lucky.'

'Don't expect another kiss,' Carol said.

'I'm too tired to kiss anybody,' I said. 'I'm too tired to even walk.'

'You don't have to walk,' Tommy said. 'You're the champ. We'll drive you.'

He grabbed one of my legs and John and Michael grabbed the other, hoisting me on their shoulders, the crowd behind me still chanting their support.

They carried me through the gym, carefully lowering me past the black exit doors and out onto the street.

'Where we goin'?' I asked, tilting my head back, letting the warm evening breeze cool my face.

'Anyplace,' Michael said. 'Do anything we want.'

'We got the time,' John said. 'And we finally got the money.'

'We can go anywhere,' Tommy said. 'There's nothin' can stop us.'

We were under a street light on the corner of West 50th Street and 10th Avenue. John, Tommy and Michael holding me on their shoulders. Carol next to them, a smile on her face, slowly dancing around a garbage can.

*

The night and the streets were ours and the future lay sparkling ahead.

And we thought we would know each other forever.

APACHES

Lorenzo Carcaterra

For the fallen

Acknowledgements

None of what follows would have happened without the help and guidance of many. Here are a few:

Peter Gethers, who proved once again to be a great editor and, as I learned with the writing of this book, a patient one. The jokes aren't bad either. No writer could hope to have a better publisher or friend than Clare Ferraro. A tip of the hat to the rest of my Ballantine gang: Linda Grey, Alberto Vitale, Sally Marvin (no more Big Macs), and Nate Penn.

Loretta Fidel has always had my respect and, this time around, she earned her stripes; Amy Schiffman, Rob Carlson, and Carol Yumkas are great agents and good friends. A big thank-you also to Arnold Rifkin. Thanks to Jake Bloom and Robert Offer for taking me along for the ride. And to Barry Kingham for being there.

A warm thanks to Jerry Bruckheimer, Susan Lyne, Jordi Ros, Donald De Line, and Joe Roth for their passion. And to Christy Callahan and Christian McLaughlin for their help.

To John Manniel for all he did for my family. A heartfelt thank-you to Steve Collura. I'll see you at Toscana's. And to Sonny Grosso, the best cop ever to pin on an NYPD badge and a friend for life. The next Fernet's on me.

To my phone circle: Liz Wagner, Leah Rozen, William Diehl, Stan Pottinger, Mr. G., Brother Anthony, Hank Gallo, and Joe Lisi. Thanks for listening.

To Vincent, Ida, and Anthony – for the great meals and the happy nights.

To Susan, who makes what I write read better than it should. In return, I can only give my heart. And to my two best accomplishments: Kate, who lets me steal her great plot ideas without complaints, and Nick, who keeps me laughing.

They have taught me how to love.

Prologue

My mother groan'd, my father wept,
Into the dangerous world I leapt;
Helpless, naked, piping loud,
Like a fiend hid in a cloud.

– William Blake, 'Infant Sorrow'

February 18, 1982

Carlo and Anne Santori wanted nothing more than to be alone.

They had planned this weekend getaway for six months, their first one in fifteen years. No kids, no phones, no work, nothing but music, dance, and a little bit of romance at the Jersey shore.

They left behind their fifteen-year-old son, Anthony, to care for the house and his twelve-year-old sister, Jennifer. They felt that both children were old enough to be trusted, allowing them to enjoy a short respite from the daily grind of parental responsibility. Carlo handed Anthony the house keys and three simple instructions – don't stray from the neighborhood, set the burglar alarm and lock the house, and never let Jennifer out of your sight. The boy stared at his father and swore to obey all three.

Anthony, however, had his own plans for the weekend.

His parents were no less than ten minutes out of the driveway when Anthony woke Jennifer from a sound sleep, yelling for her to get ready. They had two hours to catch a bus for a ride into Manhattan, to spend a Saturday in the city his parents had always told him was not to be trusted.

Anthony needed to get away almost as much as Carlo and Anne. He was a teenager eager for the taste of a day without parents, without rules, and with pockets jammed with allowance money. All of it out there waiting less than an hour's ride from the safety of a New Jersey colonial. His only obstacle had been to convince Jennifer.

She balked when she first heard the plan, and it was all he could do to keep her from spilling the secret. Jennifer was afraid something would go wrong, believing all the horror stories she had heard. But she stayed silent, her arms always wrapped around a Kermit the Frog doll, confident Anthony would protect her and allow nothing bad to happen.

Confident that he would be the one to keep her safe.

Jennifer was a frail girl, with a thin, freckled face, eager to cross the bridge from pre-teen to young adult. She wore a long-sleeved Gap denim shirt over a white pocket T. The jeans were tight and bleached, bottoms scraping a pair of red hightops. Black bangs brushed the corners of her eyes.

'Should we really do this?'

'Stay home if you're scared,' Anthony said, walking from her room.

'I'm not scared,' Jennifer said right back.

'Then get ready,' Anthony told her. 'And don't forget to bring your own money.'

They walked down a sloping hill, ice, dirt, and moldy leaves brushing against their shoes. Jennifer kept her hands inside her coat pockets. On her shoulders was a backpack filled with a change purse, Kermit, and a hairbrush. Anthony kept his face away from the arctic blasts of wind bouncing past trees and houses. They moved in silence, each excited at the prospect of doing something forbidden.

Anthony held the door to the 7-Eleven across the two-lane street from the bus shelter. He checked his watch as his sister walked past.

'Ten minutes,' he said. 'Get what you want and meet me by the stop.'

They boarded the 11:04.

Anthony paid for the one-way tickets with exact change. They walked down the center aisle toward the back of the

4

bus, taking two empty seats four rows from an old couple bundled into down coats. Anthony unzipped his black leather jacket and leaned back, thick black curls resting against the torn edge of the seat. He closed his eyes as the bus swung past a series of mini-mart shops, fast-food outlets, and used-car dealerships, heading for the speed lane of a congested thruway and the streets of New York City.

'I can't wait to see the stores,' Jenny said, her Styrofoam cup of tea now cold in her hand.

'We'll walk around a bit,' Anthony said, eyes still closed. 'Get a feel for the place.'

'Will it be crowded?'

'It's New York.' Anthony turned his head toward the window. 'It's *always* crowded.'

'We gonna be home before dark?'

Anthony didn't answer, rocked to sleep by the motion of the bus.

'I hope we're home before dark,' Jennifer Santori whispered to herself.

The bus pulled into the top level of New York's Port Authority terminal at 11:56 A.M., three minutes past its projected arrival. Jennifer put a hand on her brother's shoulder and woke him.

'What will we do first?' Jennifer asked, zipping her parka.

'Find a bathroom,' Anthony said.

They walked among thick crowds, Anthony holding Jennifer's hand. He repeated his warnings not to leave him. To wait where he left her.

To speak to no one.

To look at no one.

Anthony pushed open the men's room door, the one directly across from the Papaya King. He left Jennifer against the wall next to the door, pointed a finger in her face, and again told her not to move.

She answered with a nod.

5

He was out in less than five minutes.

He looked to his left and swallowed hard, feeling the sweat and the chill. Anthony Santori stood there and did the only thing he could think to do. He shouted his sister's name. Again and again and again and again. He shouted it as loud and as strong and as often as he could.

But there never was a response.

His ears were filled with the din of passing conversations. People stopped to stare at him now, curious about the panicked boy shouting out a girl's name. But he didn't care. Not about them. Not about what they thought. Not about what they were saying.

There was only one truth that mattered.

Jennifer had disappeared.

His only sister was gone.

Swallowed by a city not her own.

BOOK ONE

No hero without a wound.

– Bulgarian proverb

1
Boomer

Giovanni 'Boomer' Frontieri never wanted to be a cop. He was a three-letter athlete during his school years at St. Bernard's Academy, a private high school in downtown Manhattan his parents insisted he attend. He would leave their cold-water railroad apartment each morning before sunup and return each evening after dark, eating dinner and doing homework at the kitchen table facing the fire escape. He was a model student, never complained about his packed schedule, and kept the friends he trusted to a minimum.

He had two younger sisters, Angela and Maria, whom he would either dote on or ignore, depending on his mood. His older brother, Carmine, had already dropped out of school and followed their father, John, into the heavy-lifting, well-paying labor of the meat market. Their relationship was reserved, at best.

John Frontieri was a stern man who commanded respect and demanded his family's full attention. His upper body, conditioned by years of lugging 250-pound hindquarters off the backs of refrigerated trucks, was a weight-lifter's dream. He was quick to give a slap of the hand to one of the children if he felt they were out of line, but never hit or screamed at his wife, Theresa, a homely, chunky woman whose face displayed a weariness far greater than her years.

On spring and summer Sunday mornings, after the nine o'clock mass, Johnny Frontieri would change quickly out of his blue dress suit and into work pants, construction shoes, and a sweatshirt. He and little Giovanni would then take their fishing poles and tackle down from the living room closet and rush out of the apartment for a twenty-minute subway ride downtown. There, after a brisk walk, the two would spend the day, feet brushing the sand on the edges of the East River, their backs to the Manhattan Bridge, fishing for whatever could survive the currents.

It was their time together.

'If I catch a shark, can I stay home from school tomorrow?' Giovanni, then nine, asked his father.

'You catch a shark,' John said, 'and you can stay home from school for a *month*.'

'What about if I catch an eel?'

'You reel an eel and I'll make you go to school on weekends,' John said.

The two looked at one another and laughed, the morning sun creeping past the expanse of the bridge and onto their faces.

'You're always lookin' to get outta school, Giovanni,' his father said. 'Why is that?'

'I *hate* it,' Giovanni said.

'Then quit.' His father shrugged. 'Quit right now. Today.'

'You mean it?' Giovanni asked, his face beaming.

'You should always walk from somethin' you hate doin',' his father said. 'Turn your eye to somethin' else.'

'Like what?'

'You can come work with me if you want. Put in your ten, twelve hours a day, help bring some table money home. Or maybe go down to the docks to work with your cousins. Do a full four-day shift with them and get locked into the union. How's that feel to you?'

'I don't know, Dad,' Giovanni said, swaying his fishing line to the right of a swirl, pulling on the reel. 'None of it sounds like fun.'

'If you're gonna forget about school, then you can forget about fun,' John said, sitting down on wet sand, gripping his fishing rod with both hands.

Giovanni stared down at his father and then back across at the water, concentrating on a nibble. '*You* have fun,' he said after a long stretch of silence. 'And you didn't go to any school.'

'Working man's fun,' John said. 'It's not the same.'

'Mama thinks I should become a dentist,' Giovanni said. 'I don't know why.'

'I think she's got a thing for Dr. Tovaldi,' John said, lifting his face to the sun. 'She always dresses up nice when she goes to him and gets her teeth cleaned.'

'What do you want me to be?' Giovanni asked. 'You never say, one way or another.'

'What you end up becomin' is up to you,' John said. 'I can't lead you down any road. But whatever it is you do, don't go into it half-assed. You'll only wind up hatin' yourself. Give it everything, the full shot. This way, at the end of the day, when the sun's down and you *know* you put in a hundred percent, you'll feel good about yourself. Maybe even feel proud.'

'You proud of me now?' Giovanni asked.

'You goin' back to school tomorrow?' his father asked, standing up, dusting off the back of his pants.

'Yeah,' Giovanni said.

'Then I'm proud of you,' Johnny Frontieri said. 'And if you end up catchin' a fish we can all eat, I'll be even prouder.'

As he got older, Giovanni would often dream of a career designing great structures in cities around the world. His would be a life far removed from one confined to tenements and churches, a life in which a hard day's labor was rewarded only by a solid meal. As a young man, he looked with disdain upon the fabric of his neighborhood – the old women longing for dead men, street hoods living off the gambling habits of the working poor, the church offering solace and peace to the faithful, demanding silent suffering in return. As an adult, he would pine for that lost world, but in his early years in the New York City of 1955, Giovanni Frontieri was intent on hitting the fast lane out of his East Harlem ghetto.

The murder of his father brought those plans to a halt.

It rained the day Giovanni's father died. His legs crossed, John was leaning back in a two-seater in the third car of a near-empty IRT train, on his way to work. It was nearly three in the morning when they passed the Twenty-third Street station. The passengers were either heading to a working man's job or coming back from an uptown night of drink and dance. Three of the latter, two loud men and one giggling woman, sat in the middle of the car, to the left of John Frontieri. The men were drunk and unsteady, the taller of the two drinking from a pint of Jack Daniel's, free hand resting on the woman's knee. The train was stifling, heat hissing from open vents under the seats.

John Frontieri shook his head as he read his Italian newspaper. He was more concerned about Naples losing a title game to Florence than about the hard looks exchanged by the two men across the aisle. He didn't see one of the men stand and reach for an overhead strap handle. John was reading about an open goal conceded by an inept Naples defense when the man standing pulled a gun and aimed it at the other man, who, five hours earlier, had been his best friend.

In a hard city, a man's life is often decided by the actions of a simple moment. For Johnny Frontieri that moment arrived in the form of a train engineer who hit the brakes too hard coming into the Fourteenth Street subway stop. The squealing halt turned the man with the gun away from his friend and toward Johnny.

Frontieri was forty-one years old and had never missed a day's work in his life. In the spark of an instant, he knew he was about to die: the images of his wife and children meshed into one warm thought.

The bullet from the cocked gun hit John Frontieri in the forehead. The back of his skull spread across a subway map behind him as his newspaper fell to the floor.

The doors to the train opened.

The woman stared up at the standing man and the thin line of smoke from the fired gun in his hand. She then turned to look at the man in the corner of the train, slumped in his seat, blood thick as mud dripping down his chest. She shook her head, tears frozen to her eyes, and screamed.

Giovanni was driven downtown with his older brother to identify their father's body. He looked with impassive eyes as the white sheet was lifted to reveal the dead man whom he loved more than any other. There had been few words between the two, fewer smiles, no middle-American fantasies of touch football games in the yard, camping trips in the summer, or boisterous talks around a dinner table. There was just a love and respect built around a solid wall of silence, a silence only broken on those Sunday morning fishing trips.

Giovanni Frontieri reached down, grabbed his father's cold hand, and kissed it. He then turned away and never looked back. He never cried for the man on the icy slab, not then, not at the well-attended funeral, not at the cemetery. Giovanni would shed his tears in another way, one which his father would appreciate.

He would get even.

That night, riding in the back of a quiet squad car, heading home to a crying mother and two hysterical sisters, his slow breathing clouding the sides of the window, Giovanni Frontieri decided to become a cop. He was sixteen years old.

He raced from high school to the army to the Police Academy with a boxer's fury. On the streets, he hated the uniform but liked the taste left in his mouth from being a cop. He stayed clear of neighborhood tags, choosing instead to go for the big arrests. He never wrote up a parking violation, hassled a bookie, or shook down a numbers runner. He saw the working poor not as the enemy, but as important allies to be used against the larger

13

fish that floated in the nearby swamps of drugs, murder, and shakedowns.

In November 1964, the same week Lyndon B. Johnson won a landslide presidential election, Giovanni Frontieri was moved out of uniform and into plainclothes. He was assigned to buy-and-bust operations in Harlem, a neighborhood he had watched change all too quickly from a haven of hardworking families living in well-kept apartments to the central headquarters for desperate men hungry for heroin. He ignored skin color, age, sex, and language. If you moved drugs on his streets, regardless of who you were or who you knew, Giovanni Frontieri made it a point to move you.

Three weeks into plainclothes duty, Frontieri scored his first major case. He brought down three members of Little Nicky Matthews's drug crew, costing the gang $250,000 in cash profit and eventually earning them double-decade stretches behind bars. The junkies on the streets were hungry for their score, and the dealers were sour over the lost money. It didn't help anybody's image that the bust was orchestrated by a street cop who was as green as a dollar.

Four days after the bust went down, one dealer, Sammy 'Dwarf' Rodgers, decided it was time to teach the young cop a lesson. He offered $25,000, a same-day cash payout, to anyone who would bring him one of Giovanni Frontieri's eyes.

'Ain't nothin' personal against the boy,' Rodgers said to members of his Black Satin gang. 'I just need me a new key chain. Besides, I like the color of his eyes. They match my car.'

Sammy Rodgers was tall, well over six feet, with a big stomach, wide chest, and full Afro. The street called him Dwarf because he employed half a dozen dwarfs as drug couriers, sending them from house to house, door to door, pockets crammed with nickel bags of junk and rubber band rolls of cash.

'I love watching the fuckers walk,' he once said. 'Move down my streets like fuckin' robots. Time you see 'em, they already past you. Cops hate bustin' 'em too. Makes 'em feel cheap.'

Dwarf was standing in front of his bar, La Grande, on the corner of 123rd Street and Amsterdam, when Giovanni Frontieri pulled his car up to the corner. Giovanni had grown solid, muscular like his father, his hair thick and black, his face sharp, handsome, and unmarked except for a thin scar above his right eye. He spoke in a strong but low voice, never shouted, not even during the heat of a bust. His first partner called him 'Boomer' because of it, and the name stuck.

He stepped out of the car and walked over to the dealer, stopping when he was only inches from the man's face.

'Hey, Dwarf,' Boomer said. 'I hear you're looking for me.'

Dwarf looked around at his men and then back at Boomer. He had to keep his street-cool façade or lose face. Any sign of a backdown to a young cop could easily give the gunmen behind him ideas, any one of which could end with Dwarf packed in ice.

'What I need with you?' Dwarf said. 'I ain't lonely.'

'Twenty-five large,' Boomer said. 'That's a lot to pay out for one eye.'

'Got me a business,' Dwarf said, 'and you startin' to cost me.'

Boomer reached a hand into the side pocket of his leather jacket, his eyes on Dwarf. The hand came out holding a black switchblade. Boomer clicked it open with his thumb and tossed it to Dwarf, who caught it awkwardly with both hands.

'You take it,' Boomer said.

'Take what?'

'My eye,' Boomer said. 'You got the knife, so, take it. Right here. Right in front of your crew.'

'You crazy,' Dwarf said, inching two steps back. 'Pull a move on me like this, you got to be fuckin' crazy.'

15

'Take the eye now,' Boomer said, pulling a cigarette from his shirt pocket, his voice steady and controlled. ''Cause it's your only chance.'

'And if I don't?'

'Then your business is shut.' Boomer lit his cigarette with his father's silver clip. 'I don't care where you go or what part of town you move your shit to. But if I see you on this corner ever again, I drop you and leave you dead.'

Dwarf held his ground, not a move, not a sound.

Boomer smiled and nodded, as if they'd just been exchanging pleasantries about the weather, then put both hands in his pockets and turned. He walked to the driver's side of his jet black Plymouth and took another look at Dwarf.

'Keep the blade,' he said, smiling, cigarette still in his mouth. 'And enjoy what's left of your life.'

Boomer Frontieri got behind the wheel of the Plymouth, kicked over the .427-liter engine, shifted into first, and pulled out into the Harlem street traffic, radio tuned to Sam Cooke singing 'It's All Right'.

He spent eighteen years on the force, rising to the highest rank he sought, gold-shield detective, faster than anyone in the history of the department. In his career, working with a variety of partners, Boomer Frontieri was credited with more felony arrests and convictions than any other New York City cop. The job consumed him; he lived it and loved it. He never married and had no desire for a family. A bullet had killed his father, had left his mother alone at night, crying herself to sleep. He was a cop and he knew his bullet could arrive at any moment. He didn't want to leave anyone behind.

Boomer kept his pleasures to a minimum. He worked out regularly, running as many as twelve miles each morning, long before it became fashionable. He would allow nothing to get in the way of the run. During all-day stakeouts, Boomer would, at some point, jump into

16

the back seat, change into sweats, bolt from the car, and hit the pavement.

'What do I do if they come out while you're gone?' a stunned new partner once asked.

'That's why they gave you a badge and a gun too,' Boomer told him.

'They're gonna know you're a cop,' his partner whined. 'The minute you step outta the car, they're gonna know.'

'They already know I'm a cop,' Boomer said. 'I've been sitting in front of their house all day.'

'I ain't takin' 'em down alone.'

'I'll be back if you need me,' Boomer said, starting his run.

'How you gonna know if I need you?' his partner asked. 'You'll be miles away.'

'I'll hear you scream,' Boomer said, turning a corner, eager to break a sweat.

The dark weight Boomer Frontieri carried into his work grew heavier through the years. He felt surrounded by the face and smell of death. It had touched many of those around him, from partners to family members to street friends, but had merely toyed with him, hanging him from the brink before returning him to the safety net of a dangerous life.

When his mother died from a stroke in a New York hospital bed, Boomer was asleep on his stomach in a crosstown hospital as a nervous intern sewed thirty-six stitches down his back, closing up a razor slash courtesy of a pimp riding a cocaine high. His baby sister Maria, a month shy of her thirtieth birthday, was killed crossing a Jackson Heights street; the hit from a drunk driver's front end sent her through the window of a shuttered bar. Boomer had to go to her funeral on crutches, his ankles shattered from a two-storey fall off a fire escape. His brother, Carmine, suffered a severe heart attack when he was thirty-one years old and sat home in Bellmore, Long Island, living hand-to-mouth on a small disability pension.

17

Boomer would spend time with him, the emptiness of his brother's life further fueling his own thirst for action.

Three of Boomer's seven partners died in the line of duty, each working by his side.

The majority of cops go through their entire careers never pulling gun from holster. Boomer was not one of those. He viewed his job under a bright, unmistakable moral light. To him, it was all a battle for turf. The dealers were foreign invaders. The more of them who went down, the safer it would be for a man heading to work, looking to keep a family fed and warm.

The truth be known, he enjoyed his dance with death. And that made him the deadliest type of cop to have on the street, the kind who never thinks he will live long enough to see a pension. In his years on the force, plain-clothes and detective, Boomer had been involved in fourteen serious shootouts, half a dozen knifings, and hundreds of street fights. Once, his car was machine-gunned to pieces while he sat in his favorite Italian restaurant, eating a plate of pasta with red clam sauce.

'You just going to sit there and let them do that to your car?' asked his date, Andrea, a dark-haired detective working out of a Brooklyn fingerprint unit.

'It *was* my car,' Boomer said, wiping his pasta plate with a chunk of Italian bread. 'Sold it to Pete Lucas over in Vice a couple of days ago.'

'What are you going to tell him?'

Boomer sipped from a glass of red wine and looked through the window at the shell of what had started the evening as a shiny Impala.

'To keep up his insurance payments,' Boomer said.

Boomer lived in a well-kept two-bedroom apartment on the second floor of a four-storey brownstone on West Eighty-fourth Street, between Columbus and Amsterdam. The living room furnishings were simple, boiled down to one frayed blue couch, two dusty-gold wing chairs, and a marble coffee table. He kept his twenty-one-inch Zenith

18

in the bedroom and had small stereo speakers in every room. His extensive record collection, jazz, blues, and Sam Cooke mostly, filled the left side of the living room. A framed photo of Rocky Marciano landing the knockout blow to Jersey Joe Walcott's chin in their 1952 heavyweight title bout hung over the mantel of the shuttered fireplace. A small statue of the Blessed Mother rested on a bureau in the hall, left to him by his mother.

The kitchen was well stocked, although Boomer was hardly ever home long enough to make himself a meal. He picked up fresh fruit and vegetables from the nearby Fairway market. But for fish he traveled all the way down to the Fulton market and for meat to Murray's on Fourteenth Street. There, old man Hirsch himself would cut up the rib steaks and chops, wrapping them tight in butcher paper. Murray Hirsch had been his father's employer and closest friend. Two immigrants from two different cultures, trying to make a go of it in a new country. Whenever Boomer saw Murray, he always came away with the feeling that Hirsch missed his father as much as he did.

Boomer dated an assortment of women, staying with them long enough for companionship but never long enough to fall in love. Some were cops, a couple worked in bars he scouted, one was an ex-hooker now earning a living as a meter maid. There was even a college professor he helped clear on a marijuana bust. Of them all, the only woman Boomer Frontieri ever gave any thought of marrying was Theresa.

They met at a cookout at his sister's home in Queens. She was tall and thin, had red hair flowing long down her back, and hazel eyes that twinkled mischievously from an unlined face. She worked in the check reconcilement department of a Wall Street branch of the Chase Manhattan Bank while taking night courses at St. John's, crawling her way toward a business degree. They both spoke Italian, drank coffee with their pizza, and loved music but hated to dance.

19

She never asked about his work, or complained when he disappeared for days or canceled long-standing dates with last-minute calls. From the go, she understood the nature of his job. Boomer could relax around Theresa, put down his guard as easily as he would slide his gun inside a desk drawer. He felt safe, instinctively knowing she would never betray him and would always be honest with him, tell him what was in her heart whether he wanted to hear it or not. He knew life for a cop's wife was, at best, difficult and lonely. But he trusted Theresa could handle that part. It was the other end of the table that troubled him, the steady gaze of death that hovered above him, the chill of a late-night ringing phone or doorbell. It was there that his doubts rested.

'It looks bad,' Theresa said to him, sitting on a plastic chair across from his hospital bed. Boomer looked back at her and smiled. His hands were bandaged, his chest wrapped tight, and his face marked with bruises, welts, and stitches, the results of a drug raid gone sour.

'Feels worse,' he said.

'Who'd you piss off?'

'My aunt Gracie,' Boomer said, still smiling. 'You ever meet her? She's got some kind of a temper.'

'She's got a knife too,' Theresa said, sadness touching her voice.

'It's nothing,' Boomer reassured her. 'Doctor says I can be out of here in two, maybe three days.'

'They arrest the guy who did it?'

Boomer stared at her through blurry eyes.

'They didn't have to,' he said.

She nodded and didn't talk about it anymore. But Boomer saw the look and knew that it was over. It lasted less than a second, and most men wouldn't have noticed, but Boomer stayed alive reading faces, and he knew what this one reflected.

Theresa could handle the parts of the job that most women couldn't, even his dying. But she could not get used to the fact that he would have to kill in order to stay alive. That would haunt her, keep her awake when he wasn't there, make her shudder in her sleep on empty nights.

'It's late,' he said to her. 'You should get home. One of us has to get up early in the morning, and I know it's not me.'

'Will it hurt if I kiss you?' she asked, standing. The force of her beauty now struck him as she stared down at him, less than a foot away. He knew he would never be this close to love again.

'It'll hurt more if you don't,' Boomer said.

She leaned down and they kissed for the last time.

In 1978, a small but effective group of radical black extremists bent on overthrowing the government declared war on the cops of New York City. In a span of four weeks, six officers were chosen at random, then shot and killed in cold blood. It was open season on anyone in a blue uniform. Boomer Frontieri, taken off narcotics and assigned to a special unit of the NYPD set up to go after the radicals, quickly and quietly declared his own war.

Boomer squeezed his street informants. He spread out photos of the suspects to all the hookers who trusted him, the ones he kept off the paddy wagon in return for a tip. He had coffee with organized crime members, mutual respect spread across the table, both sides calling a temporary halt to their separate struggles. He went to see the ministers of the black churches in the neighborhoods he worked, banking on their friendship for answers to a horror that plagued all.

He hit the streets and banged around dealers and pimps, roughed up the chicken hawks and seedy flesh peddlers, tossed Miranda out a nearby window, and let fists and fear take him to where he needed to go.

It was his search for the black extremists that, in 1980, led Boomer to a Brooklyn tenement, where his back was to the wall, gun drawn, flak vest under his black leather jacket. He had a .38 caliber cocked in one hand and a .44 semiautomatic in the other. He tilted his head toward a red wooden door only inches away. Across from him was another detective, Davis 'Dead-Eye' Winthrop. Boomer nodded at his partner and smiled. Winthrop smiled back. Boomer didn't know much about the man other than that Winthrop was twenty-seven, black, had lost a partner two years earlier in a botched buy-and-bust, had won the NYPD marksmanship award three years running, and was always eager to go through the door first. In Boomer's book, that gave Winthrop points for guts and incentive, but shooting at wooden targets on a grassy field wasn't the same as a shoot-out in a one-bedroom apartment, lights blown out, seven gunmen with nothing to lose on the other side.

A normal cop would have been on the talkie asking for backup. Boomer hated backup. He felt it lessened the odds in his favor. Cops are usually the worst shooters around, most of them lucky enough to get off a couple of rounds in the general direction of the perp. More likely to kill those with badges than the guys without. If Winthrop was as good a shot as they said, he would be all that Boomer needed.

Behind the locked red door, Skeeter Jackson sat at a poker table filled with cash. The apartment was well furnished, with two of Skeeter's men sleeping on a soft leather couch, guns resting across their chests. Three others were in the kitchen off the main room, one smoking dope, two munching on cold heros and drinking from bottles of Bud. Another was currently in the bathroom. Guns were spread across the table next to the cold cuts.

Skeeter was a dope courier working for Jimmy Hash's gang in Bed-Stuy. His take alone was $15,000 a day. Seven days a week. Skeeter hadn't even hit his twenty-first birthday and was already looking at a million-dollar haul.

In his free time, Skeeter Jackson shot young cops in the back, charging $500 for each bullet that pierced flesh. Boomer had known his name and reputation for a long time. A hooker on Nostrand Avenue had given him what he didn't have – an address.

Boomer lowered himself to the floor and crawled over to Dead-Eye.

'You want to put in a call for help, I understand,' Boomer whispered.

'How many in there?'

'They tell me seven, all heavy,' Boomer said. 'Probably got more bullets in their pockets than we've got in our guns.'

'So, what's the problem?' Dead-Eye asked with a smile.

'Talk to you after the dance,' Boomer said.

He crawled back to his position against the wall, checked his watch, and signaled over to Dead-Eye.

They went in with their guns drawn. Boomer came in high, his shoulder against the door, running right toward Skeeter, who stared back at him, stunned. In his hand was a wad of cash. Dead-Eye came in low, took a short roll into the foyer, and popped up on both legs, guns aimed at the two men on the couch. The three in the kitchen came out running, bites of sandwiches still crammed in their mouths. Their semis were pointed straight at the two cops.

Everyone held his place for what seemed like hours but measured no more than ten seconds. Skeeter was the first to speak.

'Hope you got money on you,' he said in a high-pitched voice that bordered on feminine. ''Cause I'm takin' it after you're dead. Pay for the fuckin' door you just busted up.'

'Take my watch,' Boomer said. 'I'd want you to have it anyway.'

'You here for the cash?' Skeeter pointed to the money spread across his table. 'If you ain't, then you gonna be dead for the dumbest of fuckin' reasons.'

'You really seem serious about us dyin',' Boomer said.

'All I gots to do is nod my head.'

'Your head'll be off before you finish the shake,' Boomer

23

said. 'Which makes it easy for me to die happy. And you see my partner behind me?'

'Spook with a badge.' Skeeter's voice quivered with contempt. 'What tree you shake him off of?'

'He takes two of yours before he dies,' Boomer said. 'That means only three walk out. We can save ourselves all that shit and make it easy for you and me.'

'I got ears,' Skeeter said.

'You let us lead you out of the building,' Boomer said. 'The manpower walks. It's only you we want.'

'Don't think so, white,' Skeeter said. 'I was born in this fuckin' building. Just as soon die in it.'

'Well, you can't shoot a guy for trying,' Boomer said.

Boomer heard the click of the semi before he saw the flash. He jumped to his right, landed on one knee, and fired four quick rounds toward the men by the kitchen door. Behind him, Dead-Eye laid out the two on the couch, fast-pumped them from head to heart without so much as a twitch. It all happened so quickly, Skeeter remained frozen in place, still holding the handful of bills.

Dead-Eye flipped over a coffee table, landed on his feet, and fired three shots into one of the men near the kitchen. He aimed his other gun at a crouched man coming out of the bathroom, had him in his sights, when Skeeter threw the money in the air and came up shooting. His first shot split the wall. His second got Dead-Eye in the shoulder.

Skeeter jumped over the table and made a run for the door, slipping over the thousands of dollars that were now raining on the faces of dead men.

Boomer followed him out.

Boomer caught Skeeter in the middle of the third-floor landing. He threw him against the wall and swung a hard left that found the thin man's stomach. Skeeter gave out a grunt loud enough to echo through the halls. He came back with a right hand of his own, grazing the side of Boomer's temple. Then he went for the throat, both hands

24

wrapped tight around Boomer, pushing him hard against a shaky railing. Boomer's hands went up against Skeeter's jaw, pushing the dope dealer's head back, causing his eyes to flutter toward the ceiling.

'You gonna die, you fucker,' Skeeter said, tightening his grip. 'Gonna die right here. In front of me.'

Boomer pulled one hand away from Skeeter's chin, moving it down his chest, trying to reach the .22 Special he kept in a crotch holster. As his hand found his pants, he heard the wood of the railing behind him start to give way. Skeeter's eyes were bulging now, spittle coming down the sides of his mouth, the strength of his hands cutting the air from Boomer's throat, forcing him to take short breaths through his nose.

Boomer had his hand around the gun when the railing gave way.

The two of them fell together down through the next railing, linked like dancers, wood and rusty iron flying through the air, one shard slashing the right side of Boomer's face. The muzzle of Boomer's gun was flush against Skeeter's stomach.

Boomer felt a sharp pain in his right side the instant his gun went off. He looked at Skeeter's face and knew the man was dead. If it wasn't the bullet that did him, it had to be the iron rail lodged through his throat. Boomer turned his head and saw half a rail hanging through the right side of his own chest, blood flowing out of the hole in his jacket.

He and Skeeter had fallen down three stories, taking every railing with them. There had been a fifteen-second firefight only minutes earlier. He could still hear Dead-Eye and the kitchen help exchanging shots. Sirens wailed in the distance. Yet despite that, not one apartment door had opened.

Boomer sat there, unmoving, blood oozing from his wound, Skeeter's dead body stretched across his chest. He closed his eyes, willing himself to another place.

The growl of a dog shook him from his dream.

Boomer turned his head to his left and saw a dark gray pit bull coming down the stairs. Boomer hated dogs, big or small. But he especially hated pit bulls.

'Let me take a wild guess,' he said, pointing to the body on top of him. 'This guy belongs to you.'

The dog stared and continued to growl and sniff for a minute or two, then turned and walked out of the building.

'Doesn't say much about you, does it, Skeeter?' Boomer said to the dead man. 'When your own dog doesn't give a shit whether you live or die.'

Boomer stared at the retirement papers in his hands, thick triplicate forms filled with numbers and statistics. They were all one big blur, none of the information making any sense. All that was clear to him was the reality of a fall down a set of tenement banisters and half a lung now missing from his chest. That one rusty iron rail had landed him what the beat cops liked to call 'the policeman's lotto'. A nifty three-quarter, tax-free disability pension doled out for the rest of his life.

Based on his 1980 earnings, complete with overtime and vacation days due him, Boomer's yearly take averaged out to a clean $38,500 a year. Plus full health coverage. Boomer Frontieri was only thirty-eight years old, and there should have been a smile as wide as a canyon on his face. Instead, on that drab early December morning in 1980, all Boomer wanted to do was find someplace quiet and cry.

Boomer had survived dozens of other wounds, healed up and returned to wear the shield once again. Not this time. Not with half a lung slowing his breath and a right leg that couldn't give him more than a quarter of a mile's run without crumbling in pain. Not even Boomer Frontieri could make it on the streets spotting the shooters those handicaps.

He could never be a cop again.

He took three weeks off and traveled to Italy, visiting

26

his father's hometown of Reggio di Calabria, talking to the old men and women who remembered the young John Frontieri. He spent his afternoons walking through the nearby hills as the towns below him slept through the heat. He briefly toyed with the notion of moving there full-time, but let the thought escape, knowing it was not truly the place where he belonged.

His first six months of retirement were spent fitfully and without much sleep. He went to movies, plays, museums, read books, even caught an opera at the Met, something he hadn't done since his father was killed. None of it seemed to shake him from his mental slumber. None of what he saw, read, or heard brought him peace. He still jumped with anticipation whenever he heard a police siren off in the distance. His instincts still told him which of the faces he passed on crowded streets were dirty, which were looking for the easy score. He still carried a gun, his old police revolver, which he bought from the department, and he carried a replica of his detective's badge in his back pocket. He even kept his cuffs, tossed in a desk drawer in his apartment. He often looked at them in the sad way a middle-aged man looks upon a photo of an old girlfriend.

He stayed away from other cops. They would only serve as a reminder of what he so desperately missed. He avoided the bars they drank in and the restaurants he knew they frequented. He limited his nights of eating and drinking to one place, Nunzio's, a small, out-of-the-way Italian restaurant on West Ninety-sixth Street, near the entrance to the Henry Hudson Parkway. The food was excellent, the drink plentiful, and the company just what he wanted it to be – quiet and distant.

Most of the regulars at Nunzio's were made mob guys near the end of their criminal careers. They had taken all the money they could, killed most of their enemies, and done their time. Now they were left alone to watch ball games, argue over old scores and cold feuds. They knew who Boomer was, and there was a time when they would

27

have shunned him. Yet now, in a strange way, the cop was one of them, cast adrift, not a threat to anyone. On occasion they would even send a drink to his table.

The restaurant was owned and managed by an old family friend, Nunzio Goldman. Boomer's father first worked in the meat market for Nunzio's Jewish father, Al, the Fourteenth Street boss who split his proceeds with the uptown Italian mob. On the streets, Al was known as the Rabbi, a man who would kill if he caught a dirty look. At home he was Anna Pasqualini's husband, a quiet, reserved businessman who doted on his family. When the kids were older and Anna got restless, he opened Nunzio's and put her in charge. After she died, their oldest son took over. Now Nunzio himself had grown old.

'How come you're the only one in the family who's got an Italian name?' Boomer once asked Nunzio, whose two brothers were named Daniel and Jacob.

'Spite,' Nunzio said. 'My father took one look down at me and said I had too much Italian blood to be Jewish. It was bad enough he fell in love with an Italian woman. Now this. So he let my mother name me. My other brothers, they got lucky. They were given names that fit. But I came out ahead of the game. They don't have a restaurant. They gotta eat the slop their wives cook. You're better off at Frank E. Campbell's than at their dinner table.'

Nunzio could always bring a smile to Boomer's face. Make him forget the emptiness that gnawed at his insides. The old man made sure Boomer didn't get too fond of the drink or spend too much time alone. He cared about his friend and didn't want him to fall into the bars-and-cars cycle he'd seen other cops pursue. A man doesn't have to die to end a life. Nunzio knew that.

Boomer Frontieri was retired for two years before he was able to shake the ghosts that haunted his soul. For most retired cops, the wake-up call never comes. But Boomer Frontieri wasn't just any cop. He was one of the best

28

detectives the city of New York had ever seen. In his eighteen years on the job, he had made a lot of enemies. Many of them were in jail. Many others were dead. Many more walked the streets. Boomer was well aware of who they were and, more important, where they were.

But, in the course of those eighteen years, Boomer Frontieri had also made a lot of friends. The helpless victims of those he dragged away in cuffs, the anonymous faces of their neighborhoods. Old or young, they all remembered a cop named Boomer Frontieri.

It was a phone call from one who remembered that changed Boomer's life. A call from a man he hadn't talked to in years. About a little girl he had never met.

Though he didn't know it then, from the moment Boomer's hand took the receiver from Nunzio, his course was set.

2
Dead-Eye

His mother cried when she heard the news. His father didn't speak to him for three months. His two older brothers and younger sister avoided any contact. His friends in the Brooklyn neighborhood where he was born and raised couldn't put together the words to ask him why. His girlfriend turned her back on him and his favorite high school teacher told him he was throwing the promise of a young life into a corner of a room.

All this because Davis Winthrop decided to become a cop.

On the streets he called home, a man walking by in a blue uniform or driving past in an unmarked sedan was seen not as friend but as foe. The skin behind that uniform or that wheel was more often than not pasty white. The eyes behind the badges were filled with anger, hate, or, worse, indifference. On the streets of Brownsville, Brooklyn, a policeman was anything but a friend.

But Davis Winthrop didn't feel that way. Never. He saw everything the others had seen. He had a number of friends who died mysteriously after being taken into custody for a minor offense. He heard the verbal abuse heaped on those around him from those protected by the law. He was aware of the looks of scorn, the snide comments mumbled under warm coffee breath, all meant to deride and keep the listener locked in place.

To many people, those sights and sounds built up a well of hate. In Davis Winthrop, it fueled an eagerness to

30

change. Unlike many in his neighborhood, Davis Winthrop wasn't blinded by the abuse of power. He saw the other side as well – the street dealers turning the promise of childhood into the emptiness of a junkie's life; the young men slain by stray bullets in the dark. He saw the abandoned mothers, many wasted by the ravages of white powder, their men nowhere to be found, dragging their children down the streets, too burnt to know that it was more than their own lives they were tossing into the garbage heap.

It wasn't lost on Davis Winthrop that the source of such sadness shared his skin color. That while white might be the enemy, it would often be black that betrayed the trust.

He vowed to do all he could to change that.

And he would do it in the place he knew best – the hard-edged streets of Brownsville.

Davis Winthrop went from uniform to undercover in less than a year. He was put on the street, posing as a gun runner for a South American outfit. He didn't go into the job blind. He made sure no one knew more about guns, from make and caliber to crate price and street value. He studied the weapons most in demand and learned the habits of the big-time buyers. He also realized that if he was going to be selling guns to people in the killing game, he needed to be an expert in handling them. He took classes to improve his marksmanship, working not only on accuracy but on speed, control, and range. He read all he could about the guns he sold, and was soon able to tear apart and put together any make or model in a matter of minutes.

Soon enough, to both cops and criminals, Davis Winthrop became the man to see. He was a walking edition of *Guns and Ammo*, his knowledge so detailed, even the feds called him in for advice. His shooting was so proficient, it earned him the well-deserved nickname 'Dead-Eye'. Put a scope on a rifle and he could split a cantaloupe from 150 yards out. In the dark. Give him a .44 caliber and he could put six through a man's chest as he slid across a bare floor. With a .22 in hand, Dead-Eye could land a clean head shot in the quiet of a darkened room.

Dead-Eye Winthrop was himself a weapon, coiled and let loose. And he loved working the danger zones most other cops avoided. It was where he felt most in control.

Dead-Eye stood in the center of the bar, lit a cigarette, and looked over at the man with the thick mustache and yellow teeth. Dead-Eye was tall, standing close to six feet three inches, and he towered over the man whose Porkpie was tilted up.

'You know what it is I want,' the man said, his accent cartoon-thick. 'Correct?'

'I look like fuckin' Carnac to you?' Dead-Eye said, his eyes making mental notes. 'No, I don't know what you want. I don't even know who you are.'

'Magoo tell you I'm good for the money?'

'Only reason why I'm here,' Dead-Eye said.

Two men were behind him at a table, playing cards, semis tucked tight against their rib cages. A guy too young to be as fat as he was polished glasses over by the cash register, his hands no doubt within easy reach of a weapon. Dead-Eye heard Spanish voices coming from the kitchen, all male, all loaded.

The man poured vodka into an open can of Coke, then took a long sip. He smiled over at Dead-Eye.

'You drink?' he asked.

'With friends,' Dead-Eye said. 'Now, why don't you take this where it's going.'

'I need magnums,' the man said. 'At least fifty.'

'Bulldogs do you right?' Dead-Eye asked.

'If those are the best,' the man said.

'Best I can get.'

'How soon?' the man asked.

'You skipped a spot,' Dead-Eye said. 'You're supposed to say how much.'

'The guns are important,' the man said. 'Not the price.'

32

'Just so you know, it's five hundred a gun, more if you want ammo,' Dead-Eye said. 'You give half now. I take the other half when you open the crate.'

'What guarantees do my people get?'

Dead-Eye put his cigarette out on the floor, twisting it with the tip of his work boot.

'Delivery of the guns,' Dead-Eye said. 'They'll be here on the date and time I say.'

'That's it?'

'You want more, shop at Sears. I just hand you guns. Straight up for cash. They don't work, don't mean shit to me. Trigger falls off in a shoot-out, bullet goes backward 'stead of forward, barrel melts before your eyes, any of that happens, don't call me. Complain to the Better Business Bureau. Write your congressman. I don't give a fuck what you do. Just don't call me.'

'I hope these guns work as well as your mouth,' the man said, eyes moving off Dead-Eye to the two behind him.

'And I hope it's true you got the kind of money Magoo says you do,' Dead-Eye said. 'You don't, I'm a walker.'

'Magoo told me something about you,' the man said, his voice armed with an edge. 'Something I hope is not true.'

Dead-Eye felt the tension in the room notch up a few degrees. The fat guy behind the bar had his hands flat across the wood surface. The two behind him let their cards drop to the table. The voices in the kitchen were stilled.

'I'm gonna hate it if you make me guess,' Dead-Eye said.

'Magoo thinks you're a cop,' the man said with a smile. 'He thinks that's a problem. And he wants that problem to go away. That's why he gave me this.'

The man reached into his jacket pocket and pulled out a thick wad of cash, $25,000 easy, cut green and fresh, white wrapper still around it. The man dropped it on the table and looked up at Dead-Eye.

33

'He must be pretty serious about this problem,' the man said. 'Put up money like this for one man. What do you think?'

'I'm touched,' Dead-Eye said.

'I get more later,' the man said. 'When I bring him your heart.'

'Magoo always was a romantic son of a bitch,' Dead-Eye said. 'Too soft for this kind of work.'

'Tell me, before you die, my friend,' the man said. 'Are you what Magoo says? Are you a cop?'

Dead-Eye looked around the room, kept the faces in their places, and turned back to the man.

'Yes,' Dead-Eye said.

The first gun was in Dead-Eye's right hand, aimed at the man's chest. The second gun, his favorite .38 Special, took out the fat guy behind the bar. The two at the table hadn't even had a chance to move.

'They can live if you let them,' Dead-Eye said to the man, nodding his head toward the two behind him. He saw three men stop at the kitchen entrance, guns drawn.

'I'm not armed,' the man said.

'That could be a problem,' Dead-Eye said. 'For you.'

Dead-Eye was impressed. The man kept his cool, unfazed by the gun aimed several inches from his heart.

'I know your country,' the man said. 'Your ways. The police don't kill unarmed people. You are too civilized. It's a shame, but it's true.'

'I bet your fat friend behind the bar believed that too,' Dead-Eye said.

'He was stupid,' the man said. 'You won't be.'

'That's right, compadre,' Dead-Eye said. 'I won't be. I just drop you and then take my chances with the rest of your buddies. If I live – and, believe me, the odds are in my favor – then I put a drop gun in your hand and walk away clean. Nobody's gonna give a shit.'

The man nodded, his eyes finally glancing down to the gun.

'May I light a cigarette?' he asked.

'It won't kill you,' Dead-Eye said.

The man took a cigarette from a pack on the table, put one in his mouth, and lit it. He took a deep drag, let out the smoke through his nose, and smiled.

'It would be an insult to offer you money,' the man said. 'Cop like you don't care about such things.'

'I like money,' Dead-Eye said. 'Just not your money.'

'But you want something,' the man said. 'And I don't think killing a room full of runners is what you want.'

'I wouldn't throw myself over your coffins either,' Dead-Eye said.

'We can settle this,' the man said. 'Just tell me what it is you want.'

'Magoo,' Dead-Eye said. 'I want you to set him up. Deliver him to me.'

'That could get me killed faster than the gun in your hand.'

'Your kind of work doesn't come with a pension plan,' Dead-Eye said. 'Die now, die later, it all works out the same to me.'

'And if I give you that?' the man asked. 'If I give you Magoo?'

'Then it won't be my bullet that kills you,' Dead-Eye told him. 'Least not today.'

The man stared into Dead-Eye's face, looking for signs of weakness.

He came away empty.

'I will give you Magoo,' the man said after a few minutes, sending his men back to their places with a quick brush of his hand. 'On one condition.'

'Let's hear it.'

'Have a drink with me,' the man said. 'Now that we're friends.'

Eddie Winthrop was a bigger man than his son, the onslaught of age having shaved only half an inch from his powerful six-foot-five frame. He walked with a slight limp, the arthritis having settled in his left knee, the payback for twenty-five years spent working for Con Ed, days and nights in darkness and dampness under the city streets.

An El Producto cigar was jammed into the corner of his mouth as he sat on the third step of the stoop leading to the four-story Brownsville brownstone he had bought with a G.I. loan and a $2,000 inheritance from his grandmother. He put thirty years into the house, paying off one mortgage and picking up another as soon as a son or daughter was old enough to head for college. He spent his happiest days there, tending his backyard garden, enjoying quiet Sunday afternoons with his wife, Elma.

His saddest days were spent there too.

It was on the second floor, in the back bedroom, where Elma died on a warm June day in 1977, three years ago this month, the heart attack stripping her of the smile he loved, taking away the best friend he would ever have.

A year later, Eddie was in his finished basement, shooting a quiet game of pool. Count Basie was on the turntable, and a cool drink was in his hand, when he got the call about his youngest son, Albert, shot dead on a tree-lined street in a Westchester town whose name he had never heard before.

Now he sat there, his days winding down, the cancer in his stomach spreading, content that he had done the best he could to raise his family. He looked across at his son Davis and wondered if Davis would someday feel the same. Eddie Winthrop had made his peace with the fact that his son had become a cop. He had never warmed to the idea, but he did like the way the neighborhood kids looked up to his boy.

'You want to go sit inside?' Dead-Eye asked his father, buttoning his baseball jacket.

'No,' Eddie said. 'I always liked the cold. You know that. It was your mother couldn't take it. Thirty years, every winter, had to hear her scream about how we would all be better off in North Carolina. Like it don't get cold there.'

Dead-Eye reached into a paper bag by his left leg and pulled out two containers of hot chocolate. He handed one to his father.

'There any sugar in this?' Eddie asked.

'Ain't supposed to be.'

'Says who?'

'Your doctor,' Dead-Eye said.

'What's he know?' Eddie said.

'Your blood count, your sugar and cholesterol levels,' Dead-Eye said. 'Want me to go on?'

'Only if you want to bore me to sleep,' Eddie said, sipping his hot chocolate. 'Only doctor I know puts a dyin' man on a diet.'

The two sat silently together, eyes on the passing traffic, ears numbed by heavy blasts of music coming off car radios.

'Still like your job?' Eddie asked his son, eyes focused straight ahead.

'It fits me, Pop,' Dead-Eye said. 'Don't really know why. But it always has.'

'I know,' Eddie said. 'I was the one wastin' breath tryin' to talk you out of doing it.'

'Sorry you didn't?'

'Sometimes,' Eddie said. 'Whenever I hear about a white cop shooting another black kid. Everybody rushin' in, from mayor to priest, lookin' to clear the shooter's name. Then they all go on the TV and talk about how killing a black teenager who might have had a gun was justified.'

'It's not always murder,' Dead-Eye said.

'Most times it is,' Eddie said, turning to face his son. 'You think about it at all?'

'About what?' Dead-Eye asked. 'Getting shot?'

'They put you in these places alone,' Eddie said. 'Then, if there's any trouble, they supposed to be there for you. Back you up. Make sure you don't die. Am I right so far?'

'Pretty much,' Dead-Eye said.

'You ever wonder what if they don't show?' Eddie

37

said. 'What if they don't want to risk their own white ass for some young black cop.'

Dead-Eye sipped his hot chocolate and stayed quiet.

'It's a white man's badge,' Eddie said. 'Just because they let you have one don't change that.'

'Times change, Pop,' Dead-Eye said. 'Old men like you forget that.'

'But people never change, Davis,' Eddie said, standing up and putting the spent cigar back in his mouth. 'And that's something a young man like you should never forget. Not if you want to stay alive.'

The offer from the Spanish man in the funny hat made Magoo smile.

Magoo was only twenty-six years old, but he already had control of all the illegal gun shipments moving in and out of New York City. In six years, starting as a street runner in a Queens housing project, Magoo had worked his way up the criminal ladder with bullet speed, killing anyone in his way, often with the very guns he sold them. He had a street force of more than four hundred men and women, each reporting to district subs who, in turn, handed over orders and proceeds to borough commanders.

They then handed everything over to Magoo.

Magoo had been raised in a series of foster homes, where he learned to trust no one. He especially hated cops and openly bragged about the three he himself had brought down, one of them a young undercover he made crawl on his knees and sing the theme from *Shaft* before putting three bullets in the back of his head.

He knew very little about guns other than that they were in great demand and the right people on the wrong side of the law would pay any amount to get them. He hired only blacks and put a permanent price on loyalty. He stayed clear of drugs and drink, figuring his line of income was risky enough without supervising it through hazy eyes. He banked his cash past a laundering system that was run out of Toronto, flowed into Europe, and eased back into his private Manhattan account. Money meant everything to Magoo, and he made it his business to remove any threat to the cash flow.

Davis 'Dead-Eye' Winthrop was such a threat.

Dead-Eye was a different man at home, caring for his wife, doting on his son.

On many evenings before he hit the streets, Dead-Eye would make it a point to rock and cradle the four-month-old baby to sleep, then lay him in his crib, belly side down.

He watched him sleep, the baby's eyes twitching to a dream, his lips pursed, hands balled into fists. The boy, Eddie, had his mother's pleasant smile and his grand-mother's sweet nature. Dead-Eye looked around the room, the stuffed toys bunched up on a corner window seat, soft dolls strewn around the floor. A warm room in a warm house. The house his father bought and paid for with hard work and now shared with his son and his family, keeping his own apartment two storeys below.

It was well into the middle of the night.

Dead-Eye's wife, Grace, was sound asleep in the bedroom next door. Dead-Eye moved away from his son's crib and sat on the floor, legs folded, taking in the creaks and moans of the quiet house. All that he loved took breath between its walls. Memories, pleasant and sad, lived within the curves, nooks, and cracks of a house built five years before the start of the First World War. There was no violence in this house, only love.

In there, the price of a gun had no history and a life had meaning and respect. If death did arrive, it came by way of disease or destiny, not in the form of late-night bullets. If only Dead-Eye could seal the contents of this house and keep everyone inside it safe and warm.

But he knew that was a dream.

Reality was waiting for Dead-Eye on the streets of Brooklyn. He had a meeting with Magoo in less than two hours. He had no reason to trust the Spanish man. He knew the odds were stacked against him. But Magoo had to be stopped, whatever the risks. Tonight, one of them would die.

Dead-Eye looked over at his son, asleep in this safe house of peace, and prayed that his guns would not betray him on this night.

Dead-Eye knew it was a setup the minute he stepped out of his car.

Four men stood around Magoo, each wearing a long leather coat, standard designer wear for the heavily armed.

The Spanish man was behind Magoo, nodding his head as Dead-Eye approached.

'Hello, my friend,' he said. 'You are here.'

'I'm here,' Dead-Eye answered, looking over at Magoo.

'Now we can do business,' the man told Dead-Eye. 'Enough of this silly talk between us. We have to trust each other. You can't do business without trust. And I trust you. It's what I told Magoo. If you are a cop, then I am a cop. Then we are all cops.'

'Chatty motherfucker, ain't he?' Magoo said, smiling over at Dead-Eye.

'Too chatty to be a cop,' Dead-Eye said.

'It's cold out here,' Magoo said. 'Let's take it upstairs. I think better when my teeth ain't chatterin'.'

They walked around the corner in a group, past graffiti-strewn walls, Magoo holding the middle, the Spanish man next to him, four leather coats filling out the huddle. Dead-Eye stayed in step behind Magoo.

'Lips here tells me you pretty good with a gun,' Magoo said, looking over his shoulder. 'Took out one of his boys before he could even blink. That true?'

'Pays to advertise,' Dead-Eye said.

Magoo stopped, bringing the entire caravan to a halt. He turned to face Dead-Eye.

'I ain't too bad myself,' Magoo said. 'In case you was wonderin'.'

'I wasn't,' Dead-Eye said.

40

They stood before the entrance to a large housing complex. The benches around them were filled with sleeping homeless and users eyeing their next score. The few patches of grass at their feet were littered with bottles, used condoms, and split needles.

'What sort of piece you carryin'?' Magoo asked Dead-Eye.

'Askin' to buy?' Dead-Eye answered with a smile. 'If you are, it's gonna cost you.'

'I ain't askin',' Magoo said.

Dead-Eye heard one of the leather coats to his left click a chamber into a semi. He looked over at the Spanish man, who smiled back at him and shrugged his shoulders.

Dead-Eye unzipped his pea-green army surplus and reached into a side pocket. Magoo put a hand on top of his arm.

'Do it slow,' Magoo said.

Dead-Eye nodded and pulled out a .44 semiautomatic, showing it to Magoo.

'Release the clip,' Magoo said, looking at Dead-Eye and not the gun.

'You ever do anything for yourself?' Dead-Eye asked, staring back, letting the silver cylinder slide from the gun to his cupped palm.

'Only what I need to,' Magoo said, turning away.

They moved as one, past a flurry of curious eyes. One of the leather coats held the heavy green door to unit number six open with one hand. The other stayed in his pocket, cradling a cocked gun.

Dead-Eye walked with his head bowed, mind racing. He had just made the biggest mistake an undercover could make – he had trusted a marked man. He had bet his life that the Spanish man feared him more than he did Magoo. Moving down the urine-stenched hallway of the project, Dead-Eye knew he had wagered wrong. Worse, he had told no one about his meeting, stubborn in his belief that he could bring Magoo down alone.

Now he had less than five minutes to figure out a way to save his life.

'You ever seen my place?' Magoo asked, the group stopping in front of the double doors of the elevator.

'Don't think so,' Dead-Eye said, scanning the faces of the men he was up against.

Except for the Spanish man, they were heavily armed and, considering the odds, confident enough to take him out at close range. Dead-Eye was down to one gun, a .9-millimeter Hauser, jammed in the back of his jeans. It might be good enough to drop two, maybe three. But in a large space, like Magoo's apartment, Dead-Eye had no chance. Too open, too vulnerable. It left him with only one choice, one place to make his move.

The elevator doors creaked open. The group got in and turned forward, one of the leather coats pressing the button for the fourth floor. Squeezed into the twenty-by-twenty space, they watched the doors close, then trained their eyes on the numbers above. The only light was a forty-watt bulb wrapped inside an iron basket.

Dead-Eye had inched his right arm out of his coat pocket and moved it to where his hand could feel the handle of the Hauser. He closed his eyes, took a deep breath, swallowed hard, and was ready.

'These things are so fuckin' slow,' the Spanish man said, watching the number move from one to two. 'Be faster if we walked it.'

'Healthier too,' Dead-Eye said, a smile on his face now.

'What's the rush?' Magoo said, looking over at the Spanish man and giving him a wink. 'We got ourselves all night.'

The elevator eased its way slowly from two to three.

'I can't stay that long,' Dead-Eye said. 'I made some plans.'

'Such as?' Magoo asked, still looking up at the numbers.

Dead-Eye came out with his Hauser, coat slipping off his shoulder, and put one into the back of Magoo's head. He then aimed up and shot out the forty-watt bulb,

42

plunging the elevator into pitch darkness. Within a fraction of a second, all guns were drawn and fired, sparks setting off steady flashes of light. The noise was deafening, screams and shouts as loud as the steady fusilage.

It lasted less than ten seconds.

More than sixty rounds were exchanged.

The door to the fourth floor slowly slid open. An old woman pulling a shopping cart stood by the entrance. A look of horror crossed her face as the light from the hallway entered the elevator with a sudden jolt. Blood dripped down the sides of the walls. Magoo's body slumped forward and fell onto the hallway floor. Two of the leather coats were piled on top of one another in a corner of the elevator. The other two lay wounded on the ground.

The Spanish man had taken three in the chest, yet stood with his back against the elevator buttons, a sly smile still on his face.

Dead-Eye was against the far wall of the elevator, facing the old woman. He was shot in the leg, chest, and both arms. His empty gun was still in his hand, blood pouring down his fingers. His face was splattered with other men's blood, thick enough to blur his vision. The pain was so intense, he could barely speak. He knew he couldn't move.

'My God!' the old woman said, shaking where she stood.

'Maybe you should wait for the next one,' Dead-Eye said to her, trying to manage a smile.

'I'll call the police,' she said through quivering lips.

'Doctor be better,' Dead-Eye whispered.

Dead-Eye fell to his knees and tossed the empty gun to the side, watching it land in a large circle of thick blood. He rested his head against the wall and closed his eyes, waiting for whatever help would arrive.

Dead-Eye wasn't in any rush. Not anymore.

It was March 8, 1981.

His last day as a cop.

3
Mrs. Columbo

Mary Silvestri was thirty-six years old and for a dozen of those years had been a member of the New York Police Department. As a rookie, she'd started working out of the Ozone Park section of Queens, moved to Brooklyn and plainclothes, and from there to her true calling, a homicide unit in the Wakefield section of the Bronx.

She had an affinity for the death detail and, each year, her conviction rate placed her in the top tier of detectives across the five boroughs. She never tossed a folder into the unsolved pile. The fewer the clues, the less the logic behind each murder, the more fascinated Mary Silvestri became.

She exploited her talents.

Silvestri studied forensics at the John Jay College for Criminal Justice and then spent three months working alongside the chief medical examiner, trying to understand what he looked for at a crime scene, what crucial information could be picked up from a cold body. She took courses in abnormal psychology at Queens College, wanting to know as much about the killer as she would end up knowing about the deceased. In her free time, Mary Silvestri read mystery novels and true crime accounts of sensational cases. She made ample use of all the available technology and was one of the few NYPD detectives familiar with the Violent Criminal Apprehension Program, then in its infancy. VICAP, when effective, searched for patterns among at-large serial killers and would then draw up psychological profiles. Most street cops scoffed at such notions. Mary Silvestri used one profile to capture a car salesman on Tremont Avenue who had razor-slashed to death four teenage prostitutes.

Mary was an attractive woman but paid little attention to keeping up her appearance. She was tall, close to five-ten on the few occasions she wore pumps, and svelte despite a steady cop diet of pizza, deli, and coffee. Her long red hair was often unruly and hastily brushed, held in place most mornings with clips. She dressed in a nondescript mix of L. L. Bean outdoor and S. Klein's indoor, favoring short skirts and sneakers, blouses open at the collar. She seldom carried her gun and always had a pack of saltines in her purse.

The homicide cops in her detail, all of them male, took delight in her flakiness. But when Mary worked a case, she was so focused, so zeroed in on the most minute aspects of the murder, she would forget everything and everyone around her. The more disheveled she grew, the more foglike she walked around the office, the closer, they knew, she was to cracking the case.

Homicide detectives see themselves as elite members of the department. They carry themselves with confidence and arrogance. Many wear their motto on a T-shirt under their shirts and sweaters. The shirt has a chalk outline of a dead body. Above the sketch are the words OUR DAY BEGINS WHEN YOURS ENDS. HOMICIDE.

Among such a group, Silvestri was considered the best, and her skill earned her the street name 'Mrs. Columbo', the female version of the rumpled TV detective.

Mary was the badge others turned to when the case seemed beyond solving. She was also the one that other detectives trusted the most in the interrogation room. She could crack a suspect in less time than it took to play a regulation hockey game. Once again, she used everything at her disposal – from sex appeal to physical force – to break down the man in the bare-back chair. She never came out of that cold room without a tired look and a signed confession.

The only thing Mary Silvestri wasn't good at was marriage.

She hated housework and cooking and had little patience for family gatherings. She had no siblings and both her parents were dead. Her husband was a mechanic who owned two Bronx Mobil gas stations and from day one groused about not having a stay-at-home wife. It was a lament encouraged by her in-laws, none of whom ever resigned themselves to having a cop in the family – let alone a female cop.

Mary loved her son and would sometimes take him out of school and bring him on the job with her, sitting surveillance in unmarked sedans. It was her version of bonding, and Frank ate up every minute.

'You want me to be a cop?' Frank asked one day as her police car sat in a Taco Bell lot.

'Not unless you want to be,' Mary said between bites.

'Then why bring me along?' Frank asked.

Mary looked out the window, took a sip of coffee, then turned to her son. 'So you understand what I do,' she said. 'And maybe why I am the way I am.'

'When are you and Dad gonna get a divorce?'

Mary was surprised at the question. 'Who says we are?'

'Somehow I don't think I have to worry about throwin' a surprise fiftieth anniversary party,' Frank said, finishing off a chicken burrito.

'We were kids when we married,' Mary said. 'Too stupid to know better. I finished high school and he pumped gas. I went to the Academy and he pumped gas. I was pregnant with you and there he was, still pumping gas.'

'And this is better?' Frank asked. 'Sitting in cold cars, waiting for some guy to make a mistake?'

'For me it is,' Mary said. 'Putting cuffs on a guy that iced somebody who should still be alive beats a ten-dollar fill-up in my book.'

'Dad likes what he does,' Frank said. 'He's good at it.'

'I like what I do,' Mary said. 'And *I'm* good at it.'

'You still love him?'

'In my own way,' Mary said, 'I do. It's just that my own way may not be good enough for him anymore. If it ever was.'

'Would you be happier married to a cop?' Frank asked.

'I don't think so.' Mary smiled at her son. 'They're good to have around at work, but a waste of time otherwise. Just like me. Given a choice, I'd stick with the guy pumping gas.'

'That's good, Mom,' Frank said, smiling back.

'And speaking of gas,' Mary said, holding her stomach. 'Why the hell do you always make me eat these damn tacos?'

'Don't forget,' Frank said. 'You're the one went in there once and asked for their recipe.'

'Had to flash my badge to get it too,' Mary said with a full laugh.

The body of the thirty-two-year-old bookkeeper had been hanging from a closet door for three days. The skin on his face was ash white, his limbs were stiff, eyes open and bulging. His feet had been cut off at the ankles and tossed on top of a nearby bed. There were puncture wounds, large and small, up and down the front and back of the semi-nude corpse. His hands were tied behind his back, held together by black leather straps, and his throat was slashed. Maggots were starting to fester.

'Did a knife do that to the throat, Doc?' Silvestri asked the ME on the scene.

'Worse,' the medical examiner said in a weary voice. He was short, bald, and looked older than his forty-eight years. Three years on a job that averaged close to two thousand homicides a year, and he was already looking for the fastest way out.

'What's worse, Jerry?' Mary asked.

'Corkscrew,' the doctor said. 'Same one that was used to open the bottle of wine over on the bureau.'

'How long's something like that take?' Tony Russo, Mary's partner on the case, asked.

'As long as the killer wants it to,' the doctor said with a shrug, walking with head bowed away from the crime scene.

'You wanna get some coffee?' Russo asked Mary. He watched as the forensic team went about their business of taking photos, dusting for prints, bagging evidence, sealing up the cramped one-bedroom second-floor apartment that overlooked the Bronx River Parkway.

'You have to really enjoy killing to end a life like that,' Mary said, eyes focused on the young man hanging from the closet door. 'How else do you explain it?'

'You can't,' Russo said. 'Not until we have ourselves a cup of coffee. And maybe a sweet roll.'

The bookkeeper, Jamie Sinclair, was single and unemployed. He had held one job over the last two years, working freelance on and off for a Manhattan firm specializing in TV commercials. He ran three miles a day, and, when he did work, attended an aerobics class four nights a week. He had a brother who lived in Jackson Heights and worked for the city in the marriage license bureau. His mother died in 1980 after a long battle with a brain disorder, and his father shared a two-bedroom Co-op City apartment with a twice-divorced mother of two. In a life that had spanned thirty-two years, there wasn't much else for Silvestri and Russo to go on. There were no known girlfriends or boyfriends. There were few friends of any kind. All indications were that Jamie Sinclair preferred to spend his time alone.

Except on the night he died.

'Uniform on the scene saw no sign of a break-in,' Russo said, taking a huge bite from an apple turnover. 'Whoever sliced and diced him was let in.'

'Or was already there when Sinclair came home,' Mary said, hands wrapped around a container of black coffee.

'Either way, the victim knew the perp,' Russo said.

The detectives looked down the street, neat row houses mingling with three-storey apartment buildings. Two blocks up, the el rumbled over White Plains Road. A squad car blocked off traffic access, and yellow crime-scene tape was spread across the front of the murder building. Onlookers stared from stoops and the tops of parked cars.

'Where you wanna start?' Russo asked her, finishing off the turnover.

'Let uniform do the first pass around the neighborhood,' Mary said. 'We'll follow up later. Let them look for the usual. Make sure they ask about anyone not from the area hanging around. Especially these past couple of days and especially if it's a woman.'

'You kiddin' me?' Russo put one hand on Mary's elbow. 'You know somethin' already? You were up there only, what, ten minutes.'

'Relax, Sweet Tooth,' Mary said, pulling her arm away. 'When I know, you'll know.'

'Tell you one thing, Mrs. Columbo,' Russo said. 'I hang around you, I'll be a captain before I lose my hair.'

Mary looked at Russo's thin strands of dark hair rising in the mild spring wind. 'Then we better work fast,' she said.

By the time Jamie Sinclair's body was toe-tagged and put in a freezer drawer, BCCI, the fingerprint unit of the department, had found three sets of prints in the apartment not belonging to him. One set belonged to his brother, who had a key and said he'd let himself in to leave some family documents for Sinclair to sign. Another belonged to the building's landlord, who also had a key and would occasionally let himself in to drop off books and other packages. The third set belonged to Alison Walker, a fifty-eight-year-old woman with a bad heart, hefty trust fund, and Upper West Side brownstone in her name.

Her name shot its way to the top of Silvestri and Russo's interview list.

'Why's a rich Manhattan chick hangin' with a loser from

49

the Bronx?' Russo wondered, dodging Manhattan traffic as he drove crosstown on Park Drive.

'She's fifty-eight years old,' Mary said, trying to read her notes. 'She passed the chick stage when Kennedy beat Nixon.'

'Think she's the one who murdered him?'

'*And* cut his feet off? I doubt it.'

'What, women don't kill?'

'Women don't kill brutal. A gun maybe. A knife if they're really determined. But no, not like that. Not vicious.'

Mary put her notebook in her purse and opened a paper bag resting against her hip. She took out a container of coffee, popped the lid, and poured in three packs of sugar.

'You had to ice somebody,' Russo said, swerving past a yellow cab. 'A guy. Husband. Boyfriend. Whoever. We're just talkin' now. What would you use, gun or knife?'

'Neither,' Mary said, stirring the sugar in the coffee.

'What then, a bomb?' Russo said. 'Put a timer in and crack his car?'

'Strychnine,' Mary said. 'Five drops in a clear drink and the muscles hit adenosine triphosphate stage. Guy'd be dead in a few minutes. It's also hard to trace, unless you hit the scene within three hours, because rigor sets in as soon as the body's dead, not when the temp is down.'

'You've given this some fuckin' thought, I see,' Russo said, looking away from the traffic and at his partner.

'Here's your coffee,' Mary said, handing Russo the cup and smiling. 'Fixed it the way you liked it.'

'You drink it,' Russo said. 'I ain't thirsty.'

'I was hoping that's what you'd say,' Mary said, taking a long sip.

Alison Walker led the two detectives into the living room and offered them cups of tea and a platter filled with an assortment of fresh-baked cookies. Alison was short, wiry, and, despite the skin lifted tight around her jaw and neck, quite attractive. She had on a peach-colored blouse, tan

50

skirt cut at the knee, and brown pumps. A double string of white pearls was wrapped around her collar, and a set of earrings matching her blouse hung under golden-brown hair that was brushed and curled.

Mary Silvestri sat on a thick cream-colored couch that from feel and texture cost double any piece of furniture in her own home. The room was large and immaculately kept, the many antiques chosen with a sharp sense of style and concern for detail. The window behind the pale gray silk curtains was open, letting in a soft spring breeze.

Silvestri looked at the older woman and smiled.

'It's a beautiful home you have here,' Mary said. 'Really. I wouldn't even know how to begin to keep up with a place like this.'

'It takes a great deal of time and work,' Alison Walker said in an accent so bland and flat, one would never know she was the only child of a New Jersey fisherman.

'And money too, right?' Mary said.

'That goes without saying,' Walker said, her manner finishing-school calm, her clear blue eyes devoid of emotion. 'There isn't much one *can* do without money.'

'Mind if I light one up?' Russo asked from the other end of the couch, trying hard not to polish off the entire tray of cookies.

'Yes,' Walker said, eyes never moving from Mary. 'I do mind.'

'Thanks for nothin', then,' Russo muttered, tucking his smokes into a shirt pocket.

'Did you know a man named Jamie Sinclair?' Mary asked.

'What do you mean, did?' Walker asked.

'He's dead,' Russo said. 'Someone used him as a coat hanger a couple of days ago. Other than the cookies, that's why we're here.'

A hand went over Walker's mouth and her eyes did a slow, calculated twitch.

Mary glared at Russo. 'I'm sorry,' she said, turning to Walker. 'Did you know him?' she asked again.

51

Alison Walker stood from her chair and walked toward the front door of her brownstone. She kept her head up as the sounds of her heels echoed on the polished wood floors.

'You must both leave,' Walker said without turning, the door now open to outside sunlight. 'Immediately.'

'We'll only have to come back again,' Russo said, tossing two cookies into his jacket pocket. 'Or have somebody bring you down to us.'

Mary took a napkin off a pile next to the teapot, filled it with cookies, and folded it. She handed the napkin to Russo.

'Wait for me in the car, Sweet Tooth,' Mary said to him. 'I'll be there before you polish these off.'

'You sure?'

'What, you want milk too?' Mary said. 'Now, go.' She turned back to the older woman.

'You knew him,' Mary said, now sitting next to Alison on the couch. 'You didn't kill him, but you did know him.'

The woman nodded her head slowly and took in a deep breath. 'Yes,' Walker said, avoiding eye contact, staring instead at a crystal vase in the center of the coffee table, a fresh rose dangling off its edge. 'We were friends.'

'And you knew he was dead,' Mary said, her voice soft and warm, two women talking about the demise of a mutual friend and not a cold-blooded murder. 'Even before we knocked on your door.'

'How do you know that?' Walker asked, moist eyes now looking over at Mary.

'Most people are surprised when two cops show up at their door,' Mary said. 'They go against normal behavior. You almost seemed happy to see us. You let us in without even asking what we wanted.'

'Next time I'll know better,' Walker said, trying to manage a smile.

'Were you and Sinclair lovers?' Mary asked, leaning closer.

'No,' Walker said. 'Jamie wasn't interested in the physical. At least he wasn't with me.'

'Sounds like any other husband,' Mary said with a smile.

'I wouldn't know,' Walker said. 'I've never married. Jamie was my last chance for that. At my age and in my position, most men are interested in only one thing. And it isn't sex.'

'How much money were you giving him?'

'I gave what I wanted to give,' Walker said, a hint of defiance to her words.

'And how much was that?' Mary asked, pressing the issue.

'Two, sometimes three thousand dollars,' Walker said.

'A week?'

'He earned it,' Walker said.

'Doing what?' Mary asked, looking around the room. 'You've got a housekeeper, you do all the cooking, and the place doesn't look like it needs a paint job.'

'Jamie was very good with numbers,' Walker said. 'He helped me with my investments, paid my bills, arranged my taxes. I trusted him. And he never gave me reason to think I shouldn't.'

'How long was he helping you?'

'Almost three years.'

'And you were paying him that kind of money all that time?' Mary asked. 'Three thousand a week?'

'Yes.'

'How did you pay him?' Mary asked. 'Check or cash?'

'Cash,' Walker said. 'As organized as Jamie may have been for me, that's how disorganized he was with his own life. He didn't even have a checking account.'

'Where'd he keep the money?'

'I never asked,' Walker said. 'I just know he never spent much of it, if any. Jamie didn't seem at all interested in money.'

'Interested enough to charge a few thousand a week to cook your books,' Mary said, standing and folding her notepad.

'Will I have to answer any more questions?' Walker asked, tilting her head toward the detective.

'Just one more for now,' Mary said.

'What?'

'Who else knew about you and Jamie?' Mary asked.

'I never told any of my friends,' Walker said. 'People gossip about me as it is. They always have. And I wanted to keep what Jamie and I had special and private.'

'What about him?' Mary asked. 'Did he tell anybody?'

'Just his brother,' Walker said. 'They were very close.'

'Did he tell his brother about the money too?' Mary asked.

'No,' Walker said. 'I don't think so. It's not the sort of thing Jamie would talk about. With anyone.'

'How'd you find out he was dead?' Mary asked. 'It barely got a mention in the tabloids. And they don't seem your kind of reading anyway.'

'His brother, Albert, told me,' Walker said. 'He called and told me when and how Jamie died.'

'Did Albert tell you anything else?' Mary asked.

'Not to talk to anyone,' Walker said, head bowed.

'You take care of yourself,' Mary said, heading for the front door. 'I'll be in touch.'

When Walker looked up again, she found herself staring at a closed door.

The bar was crowded despite the hour and the heavy rain pelting the streets and causing the windows to steam. They sat at a circular table in the back, away from the jukebox. The table was crammed with beer bottles, shot glasses, crumpled napkins, and bowls of salt pretzels. The place was dark, like most cop bars, scattered overhead lights giving off more shadow than glow. The four men and one woman around the table, members of the North Bronx Homicide Unit, were in a festive mood, their work for this day brought to a successful end.

Mrs. Columbo had solved another homicide.

'He cracked in the car,' Mary said, sipping from a scotch straight. 'Cried all the way to the station.'

'You gotta really hate your brother to slice him like that,' Captain Jo Jo Haynes, precinct commander, said. 'Corkscrew the throat and *then* cut his feet off. Christ! And I thought my family was fucked up.'

'If I got a fuckin' nickel, I'm not lettin' my brother know about it,' Russo said. 'And I *like* the guy.'

'It wasn't just the money,' Mary said.

'What else?' Rodriguez, a new badge, asked.

'The brother, Albert, has some sort of muscular disease,' Mary said. 'And his insurance doesn't pick up all the costs. So he's always behind the financial eight-ball.'

'He know this Jamie's pullin' in a few thou a week?' Johnson asked.

'No,' Mary said. 'Thinks the guy's on the balls of his ass. In fact, Albert lends him money. Feels sorry for him.'

'What a prick,' Jo Jo Haynes said.

'Albert's over at the apartment,' Mary said, finishing her scotch. 'Sees a bottle of wine and looks for a corkscrew.'

'He finds it,' Russo said. 'In a cabinet drawer next to a folded-up paper bag. Albie, curious as well as thirsty, pops open the bag.'

'And finds the money,' Johnson said.

'He sat on the bed for three hours,' Mary said. 'Holding the corkscrew and staring at all that cash.'

'Jamie walks in,' Russo said. 'Sees poor little Albie sittin' next to his stash and starts yellin' at the guy.'

'Albert snaps,' Mary said. 'All those years being suckered by Jamie melt down into a couple of bloody minutes.'

'He sliced and diced the fucker,' Russo said. 'Left him hangin', took the money, and walked out.'

'And he never got to drink the wine,' Johnson said.

'That's the sad part,' Rodriguez said. 'Guy comes in thirsty. Goes out the same way.'

'Except this time with a murder rap,' Russo said. 'And Mrs. Columbo here smellin' his ass out in no time flat.'

'What happens to the old lady?' Haynes asked. 'What's her name? Walker?'

'Who gives a fuck, Cap,' Russo said. 'She still got her feet and can swallow anything she chews.'

'She'll die alone,' Mary said in a low voice, 'Jamie was her only real friend. After this, she'll never let herself get close to anyone. She'll be warm in the winter and cool in the summer. And she'll die alone.'

'Think Albert cops an insanity?' Johnson said.

'Wouldn't you?' Russo said. 'He comes up Mr. Clean on the sheets. Not even a parking ticket. One of those jaboes goes through life nobody notices.'

'Two lives ruined and one ended,' Mary said. 'All for a glass of wine.'

'Let this be a lesson,' Russo said, holding up a bottle of Bud. 'Drink beer. You don't need a fuckin' weapon to open a bottle, and anybody who drinks it sure as shit don't have a paper bag filled with cash.'

'I guess this means you're not buying,' Mary said.

'Not unless one of you got a corkscrew in your pocket,' Russo said, standing up from the table.

'Hey, Cap,' Johnson said with a smile. 'Whatta we get if we each put a bullet into Russo right here and now?'

'A raise,' Jo Jo Haynes said.

Mrs. Columbo and the detectives ended their night of victory over death on a loud laugh.

Mary parked her car four blocks from her Whitestone row house. The rain had stopped and the air was cool and clean, early morning smells wafting down from the trees. Overhead lights cast broken shadows across cars and patches of lawn. It was closing in on three A.M. and the streets were empty as she walked with a slow step, head down, her purse hanging from a strap off her shoulder. Sated with drink, she let her mind ease past the events of the day.

She was nearly home: a small house with a leaky roof, bad plumbing, and two bedroom windows long painted shut. But Mary knew, as she walked down the cracked sidewalk of Thirty-seventh Avenue, that she had Alison Walker's life beat by a record mile. She had what the other woman would give everything to attain – a husband in her bed and a son in the next room.

Maybe her marriage wasn't such an uneasy fallback after all, and watching Frankie grow had given her plenty of reasons to smile. It was far better than sitting in a room alone, staring at an antique vase filled with a single red rose, knowing no phone would ever ring to a voice that cared and no door would ever open to let in a warm hug.

Mary Silvestri crossed against a flashing red light and picked up the speed of her pace, suddenly eager to get home. She never saw the man with the knife hunkered down in the alley, alongside the shuttered gates of Sergio's Deli. He stood perched on the balls of his feet, watching as she approached, waiting to time his leap and score the purse dangling against her hip.

When she was directly in front of him, he jumped.

The man, wiry and muscular, wrapped his right arm around Mary's throat and wedged the blade of a six-inch knife between her shoulders, hard against the soft wool of her camel's hair J. C. Penney blazer.

'You breathe, you die,' the man said. His breath against her neck reeked of alcohol.

He tightened his grip around Mary's throat and gave the edge of the knife a rough twist. He took backward steps, dragging Mary with him, pulling her away from the light and into the blind darkness of the alley.

Mary relaxed her body and let the man's strength do all the work. She kept her hands free, loose, waiting to make her move. The arm around her throat was wrapped in bandages, blood flowing through the white gauze as his fingers gripped thick clumps of her hair. She shifted her face away from him, brushing against the rough skin of his cheek as she moved.

They were in the alley now.

'What you got for me?' the man asked, leaning her face forward against the red brick wall. 'How much?'

'Take it all,' Mary said, forcing the words out. 'In the purse. Take it.'

He yanked her head back with a forceful grip of her hair and slammed her face against the wall.

'Don't tell me what to take, bitch. I take what I want. Understand me?'

'Yes,' Mary said, tasting the blood dripping down from her forehead.

He moved his arm from her throat and ripped the purse off her shoulder. He leaned her hard against the wall, the blade of the knife keeping her in place. Mary closed her eyes, took in a few deep breaths, and tried to think with a clear head. She knew she didn't have much time and was angry at herself for leaving her gun in the office, something she always did when she went out drinking with the squad.

She heard the man rifle through the purse and knew exactly what he would find – sixty dollars in cash, Visa and MasterCards, one overdue and the other at its limit, a few coins, her father's pocket watch, and an NYPD gold-shield detective's badge.

The man took the cash, missed the badge, and tossed the purse into a corner of the alley. He shoved the money into a front pocket of a pair of soiled jeans and leaned closer to Mary. He rested his head on her shoulder and put his lips to her ear, the knife still in its place.

'Like the way you smell,' he said, his tongue stroking the edges of her ear.

'You got what you wanted,' Mary said, fighting to keep her voice calm. 'You got enough to get a fix and make it through the night.'

She heard the man slide his zipper down and push himself closer.

'You gonna be my fix,' he said. 'You and me, we gonna make it through the night.'

The man was rubbing himself against her leg, free hand

58

pawing at her skirt and panties, trying to reach flesh. Mary struggled to free herself from his grip, using the wall as a brace, balancing her feet for leverage.

'That's it, baby,' the man said. 'Fight me. C'mon, trim, fight me.'

Mary turned her face from the wall, moving the man's arm away from her thigh. She looked in his eyes, brown, glazed, and empty, and saw in them what she had seen in the faces of so many killers over so many years. It was in that fragment of a second that she knew what awaited her. It wasn't just sex he wanted. Or drugs he needed.

It was blood.

Her blood.

She didn't feel the first stab or the second, but the man was laughing as he stood and watched her blood flow past his legs like melted Jell-O, moving down the cracked path of a dark alley on an empty street in Queens. Laughing and staring into Mary's eyes, watching as the life ebbed out of them.

It was the rush of the killer.

No one understood that feeling better than Mary Silvestri.

She woke up three days later in the intensive care unit of Mission Hospital. Doctors had removed a portion of her lung, sliced beyond use by the man's knife. Her stomach had also been slashed, requiring forty-seven stitches to close. There were welts and bruises up and down her body, and her right arm and left foot were broken and in casts. One eye was closed shut, and the side of her right cheek was bandaged.

Mary looked around the room, pale blue walls floating like waves, shards of sunlight warming the left side of her face. She saw an IV hanging off to the side, fluid slow-dripping into her arm. The inside of her mouth felt crusted, and there were two small plastic oxygen tubes in her nose. A set of rosary beads was wrapped around the fingers of her left hand.

She turned to her left, past the glare of the sun, and saw her son, Frank, sitting in a chair, wearing a New York Yankees jacket and cap, hands folded in his lap, staring back at her. She gazed at him for several seconds, read the concern etched on his youthful face, saw the tense way he leaned his body forward, and studied the eyes of a teenage boy terrified that his mother would die.

'Shouldn't you be in school?' she said, each word weighed down with a pain that reached into her chest.

'It's Sunday,' Frank said, surprised to hear her speak.

'Church, then,' Mary said, managing a slight smile. 'I could use a couple of prayers thrown my way.'

'Went this morning,' Frank said. 'With Dad.'

'Here alone?'

'No,' Frank said. 'Dad went down to the cafeteria. To get some coffee.'

'How's he doin'?'

'Scared,' Frank said. 'Stays here all day. Sleeps in the bed next to you at night. Leaves just to check on work and pick me up from school.'

'How about you?' Mary asked, wishing she could sit up, lean over, and, for the first time in many years, take her son in her arms.

'I'm not as scared,' Frank said.

'Why's that?'

'Dad forgets how tough you are,' Frank said. 'I don't.'

'I'm not as tough as the guy I ran into,' Mary said. 'Otherwise, we'd be sending him flowers.'

'They caught him,' Frank said.

'Who made the collar?' Mary asked.

'Not sure,' Frank said. 'Russo and some of the other guys started chasin' him down while you were in surgery. By the time you were in recovery, they had him.'

'I can't wait to see him in court,' Mary said. Her throat was dry and raw, and her jaw ached whenever she spoke.

'He won't be in court,' Frank said.

She didn't have to say anything. She just looked at him, first curiously, then knowingly.

60

'Russo told me and Dad the guy put up a fight.' Frank went on in a matter-of-fact tone that would have made any seasoned cop proud. 'Came at them with the same knife he used on you. Russo and Johnson stopped him.'

Mary nodded and turned from her son. She lifted her head slowly, eyes scanning the flowers and baskets that filled the room.

'I'm glad you're alive, Mom,' Frank said, standing up and moving closer to the bed.

'I am too, sweetie,' Mary said.

'Dad says now things are gonna be different,' Frank said. 'Better, you know, than they used to be.'

'Because I can't be a cop any more?' Mary asked. The sound of the words hurt more than saying them. A tear formed at the side of her good eye.

'You'll always be a cop, Mom,' Frank said, touching her hand.

When she was finally alone, she leaned her head back against the pillow, closed her eyes, and, for the first time since she was a child, began to cry. Her tears went beyond pain and past anger. They were filled with a sense of loss and a knowledge that something besides blood had been left back in that narrow alley.

4
Geronimo

Delgaldo Lopez sat under the altar of the church, staring at twelve sticks of dynamite. They were taped to a marble slab and set to a one-hour timer that was wound around a blasting cap. All about him, members of the Brooklyn Bomb Squad raced through the church, laying down heavy detainable mats and moving aside statues and votive lights. The front and back doors to the church had been sealed minutes before, and a dozen uniformed cops in heavy vests and pith helmets stood guard.

Lopez ran his index finger along the dynamite sticks, checking their moisture level, careful as hell not to nudge the array of red, green, and blue wires wound around the hardware store timer.

'How much time?' Gerry Dumane, the Bomb Squad commander, asked as he knelt down next to Lopez.

'Not enough,' Lopez said, eyes never moving from the device. 'Closing down to twelve minutes.'

'How strong?'

'Could take out half a block. Maybe more. Depends how fresh the dyno is and what else he packed in there.'

'Jesus,' Dumane said.

Lopez turned away from the bomb and looked over at his commander.

'Don't have to look too far,' Lopez said, pointing to a large crucifix hanging above the altar. 'He's right behind you.'

At age thirty, Delgaldo Lopez had already put in six years of service on the Bomb Squad. He joined the PD after an eighteen-month tour of army duty, where he earned his Special Forces stripes as a munitions expert. Delgaldo had always been fascinated by explosives, from his earliest years.

When he was ten, Delgaldo built his first explosive device out of rubber bands, baking soda, the face of his father's old Timex, powder from two boxes of firecrackers, and blue strands of wool from his mother's knitting basket.

In his teens, Delgaldo gave some thought to going on to college and studying to be a chemist. But a laboratory was too tame a place to spend a life. It wouldn't be enough for him just to know all there was about bombs and devices. Delgaldo was not meant to be a bystander.

He also needed to see the bombs in action. He wanted to be there when the last few seconds were ticking away, where one slip of a cutter would mean victory for the bomber and destruction for everyone else. It made Delgaldo Lopez, a tall, muscular young man with thick black hair and eyes so dark that staring into them was like looking at a blank screen, the perfect candidate for the Bomb Squad. He was the one who took the danger calls, who didn't sweat the risks, who never flinched as the final ticks of a timer echoed through an empty room. They called him Geronimo, because he was half-Cherokee on his mother's side. Like his distant ancestors, he was indeed a warrior.

'How you wanna play it?' Dumane asked, rubbing the back of his neck, looking around the boarded-up church.

'It's a simple mech,' Geronimo said, still studying the bomb. 'Won't take more than two minutes, three at the outside, to shut down.'

'So what's the problem?' Dumane said. 'Do it and let's get the hell outta here.'

'It's too easy,' Geronimo said. 'Guy goes to all the trouble of putting one in a church. Even calls us in, lets us know where it is and how much time is left. Then he leaves this, something a kid with a scope and scissors could take down?'

'Whatta ya sayin', G?' Dumane asked. 'Maybe he's just not that good.'

'Or maybe he's better than we think.'

Geronimo was on his feet now, scanning the empty church, searching for the shape of a bomb, the scent of the powder, his mind no longer that of a cop, but of a lone man bent on destruction.

'The crew peel through the church?' Geronimo asked, eyes looking up at a silver organ in the balcony.

'They stopped when they found the device,' Dumane said. 'Why?'

'I'll take this one down,' Geronimo said. 'But have them check everything else while I do.'

'You make me so fuckin' nervous when I hear you talk like this,' Dumane said. 'Whatta ya tellin' me?'

'He laid in two, Commander,' Geronimo said, looking at Dumane. 'The other one's the blaster. This one's just here to keep us busy.'

'You sure about this?'

'We could take a vote,' Geronimo said. 'If you think we got the time.'

'Dummy this one,' Dumane said, running from the altar. 'I'll send for you if we find another.'

'If I'm not here, I'll be up there,' Geronimo said, pointing to the balcony. 'Up by the organ.'

'Why there?' Dumane shouted over his shoulder.

'I like organs,' Geronimo said with a smile.

As he worked, he touched the medallion under his shirt. His mother had given it to him as a keepsake the first day he was a cop. It was in the shape of a horse hung from a thin gold chain. She had made him promise never to take it off.

*

The second bomb was packed in solid, wedged between a foot pedal and the base of the organ. Thick strips of retainer tape were wrapped around its center, insulated rows of coiled wiring folded over the sides. At its base were thirty-six pieces of heavy dynamite, the flex timer at the center surrounded by a six-pack of nitro vials. Six different-colored wires were all meshed together, each inserted into the silver lid toppings of the nitro.

Geronimo was on his back, under the organ, staring at the device. He followed the paths of the wires, each embedded in a batch of dynamite sticks, each alone holding enough power to destroy several city blocks. He admired the sheer simplicity of its design and wondered about the caliber of man he was dealing with, someone whose only pleasure came from turning loose such a force on the innocent.

He closed his eyes, both hands feeling for the medallion hidden under his bomb-resistant vest. He heard Commander Dumane squeeze in alongside him, stripped down to a T-shirt and bomb gear.

'Whatta ya need, G?' Dumane said. 'I'm here.'

Geronimo opened his eyes and looked at the timer.

He had seven minutes to defuse the bomb.

'I need a miracle,' Geronimo said. 'Got any handy?'

'What's the main contact – the nitro or the dynamite?' Dumane asked.

'Both,' Geronimo said. 'One feeds into the other.'

'You could clip the wires at the center. Defuse both at once.'

Geronimo shook his head. 'Timer's connected only to one. And there's too many wires to tell which.'

'Shit. I ain't seen a job like this in all the years I been snappin' bombs.'

'It's a copycat,' Geronimo said. 'Been used before.'

'Where?'

'German terrorist outfit, Baader-Meinhoff gang, used to plant them,' Geronimo said. 'Back in the early seventies.'

'How'd they take them down?' Dumane asked.

'Best I know, no one ever capped their bombs,' Geronimo said. 'German police just killed all the gang members.'

'Why don't we ever think of shit like that?' Dumane said.

Geronimo looked at the timer, now down to six minutes, and pulled a small pair of pliers from his kit. He wiped thick beads of sweat from his upper lip and forehead and took in a long, deep breath.

'How much of the neighborhood is clear?' Geronimo wanted to know, holding the pliers in his right hand.

'Three blocks up and down both sides,' Dumane said. 'Every building and store's emptied out.'

'This'd be a good time for you to split too,' Geronimo said, giving him a meaningful look. 'In case I fuck up.'

'You selfish bastard,' Dumane said, smiling. 'All you care about is glory. Well, Chief, I got bad news. This bomb you're gonna have to share.'

'I'm gonna click the blue wires first,' Geronimo said.

'Why blue?'

'Just a hunch,' Geronimo said. 'After that, if you and me are still here, I'll move the nitro off the timer and hand them over.'

'I need a place to put 'em,' Dumane said, looking around. 'Where they won't move.'

'Up on the altar,' Geronimo said. 'Might be a chalice. Should be wide enough to hold the bottles.'

'I ever tell you I hate bombs?' Commander Dumane said, crawling out from under the organ. 'Only took the damn job 'cause they told me it was a temporary transfer. Ten fuckin' years later, I'm still here, waitin' for some out-of-work psycho's erector set to blow me to pieces.'

'I ever tell you I love bombs?' Geronimo said, more to himself than to Dumane. 'Nothin' but me and the device. You can never beat a bomb. You just stop it. Till the next time.'

Geronimo put the pliers on the first part of the blue wires, waited a second, and then clipped them apart.

Dumane was next to him, hands wrapped around a chalice, eyes on the bomb.

'Two sets of reds, two blues, and two whites,' Dumane said. 'The guy's a regular George M. fuckin' Cohan.'

'Blues are dead,' Geronimo said. 'Gonna clip the white next.'

'Another hunch?'

'It's all I got to go on, Commander,' Geronimo said. 'Unless you got a thing for red.'

'Your call, G,' Dumane said.

Geronimo rested the pliers on a long strand of white wire. His hand was steady, eyes were calm. All the tension was internal, buried inside nerve endings, heart beating at such a furious pace he could feel it pounding against his vest.

He snapped the white wire and held his breath.

'It's the red,' Geronimo said. 'That's the main hookup. Once I give you all the nitro, take it to the truck. I'll meet you outside.'

'There you go, tryin' to get rid of me again.'

Geronimo turned to look at his commander, less than three minutes left on the timer, and smiled. 'I'm trusting you with the hard part,' he said. 'I don't like nitro. Makes me nervous.'

'I'll try not to trip down the steps,' Dumane said.

'Ready?' Geronimo asked, setting the pliers down on his chest and reaching for the first bottle of nitro.

'No.' Dumane removed the lid from the chalice and gripped its base with his left hand. 'But don't let that stop you.'

Geronimo's hands were steady as he lifted the first thimble-size bottle of nitro from its sleeve with two index fingers. He handed the bottle to Dumane without looking at him, his eyes never veering from the device, afraid to turn away. Dumane took the bottle with one hand, slowly rested it inside the chalice, and readied for the next.

Geronimo lifted the second nitro bottle, had it halfway removed, and then stopped. There was a thin copper wire attached to the base of the bottle, the other end connected to a sixty-second timer that started ticking down as soon as he touched the bottle.

'Shit!' Geronimo said, nearly dropping the bottle in his anger. 'Smartass little fuck!'

'Please God tell me I'm the one did something wrong,' Dumane breathed.

'The whole bomb's a setup. Everything's here, on this nitro bottle. The rest is all bullshit. Only one fuse, one bottle, and all the dynamite.'

'How much time?'

'Just enough to get lucky.' Geronimo held the bottle between his two index fingers, watching the clock tick down to forty-five seconds.

'Cut the wire,' Dumane said. 'It's your only move.'

'It's the move I'm *supposed* to make,' Geronimo said. 'Every move's been the one I'm *supposed* to make.'

'What ain't you supposed to do?' Dumane asked. 'Or maybe I don't wanna know this part.'

The clock was down to thirty seconds.

Geronimo could feel his pulse pounding against the sides of his wrists, sweat running down his forehead, into his eyes, stinging his vision. He took a slow breath and swallowed hard, throat dry as stone. He eased two more fingers around the center of the nitro bottle, tightened his grip, and then waited for the timer to tick down to ten seconds.

'You sure about this, G?' Dumane asked, gritting his teeth as he held the chalice tight and steady.

Geronimo pulled the nitro bottle from its slot. The short tug snapped both the nitro and the sticks of dynamite linked to it from the cord.

No sound came out of the dark and empty church.

The timer stopped at six seconds.

'Call in the cavalry, Commander,' Geronimo said, resting the back of his wet head against cold marble. 'We're done here.'

'Now, that's a funny request,' Dumane said, inching his

way slowly from under the organ. 'You being an Indian and all.'

'Redskin humor,' Geronimo said. 'Works all the time.' He placed the nitro bottle back in its slot, unsnapped his vest, and folded his hands across his chest. His fingers felt for the medallion and squeezed it through the cold wetness of his shirt. He closed his eyes and said a silent prayer of thanks to his God for helping him save the house of another.

He had visited his mother's people out in Arizona many times. They kept to their ways, ways he tried to learn.

Geronimo sat with legs crossed inside the large tent, facing the old man in the buckskin jacket. There was a full fire flaring between them, heat casting both faces in its auburn glow. The old man smoked tobacco from a thin wooden pipe and drank coffee out of a cracked black cup. Outside, heavy flakes of snow fell to the hard ground.

'Do you wish to smoke?' the man asked in a voice as lived in as an old sweater.

'I'm okay with just the coffee,' Geronimo said, the flames dancing like lit matches in his eyes.

'Your face is a tired one,' the old man observed, the base of the pipe wedged in between his gums, eyes staring at some unknown distant point. 'You are much too young a man to feel as old as me.'

'My mother thinks it's the work,' Geronimo told him. 'Each day can be my last.'

'That is true of all men,' the old man said. 'No matter the job. Only with yours, the fear cannot be hidden.'

Geronimo sipped from a cup of coffee and nodded. 'That's what I like about it,' he said. 'I like knowing that any day could be my last. I *like* facing the fear.'

'Have you ever surrendered to it?' the old man asked as he tossed the remains of his coffee into the fire, causing flames to spit higher. 'Allowed the fear to win?'

'No,' Geronimo said.

'Fear waits for us all,' the old man said. 'And when your day comes, you will know the heart of your strength.'

'I'm not afraid of a bomb killing me,' Geronimo said.

'What then?' the old man asked.

'I'm afraid of a bomb *not* killing me,' Geronimo said. 'It's my only fear.'

'A warrior is meant to die in battle,' the old man said, nodding in agreement. 'Not left behind for other men to pity.'

'I see some of the guys who used to work Bomb Squad,' Geronimo said. 'They come around once in a while, looking lost and empty. Legs missing, arms gone, eyes blown out. Acting as if they want to go on with their lives. But in their hearts they curse that bomb for not taking them when it went.'

'Then pray, Delgaldo,' the old man said. 'Pray for death.'

Geronimo was stuck in traffic near the Williamsburg Bridge and a half hour late for an appointment with his mother's doctor when he heard the call over his police scanner. The radio was calling the Brooklyn Bomb Squad to an abandoned warehouse in the Flatbush section to scan a suspicious device on the third floor. Geronimo looked at the clock on the dashboard and at the clogged cars in front of him. The morning papers were tossed on the seat across from him, each folded open to the sports section. Geronimo loved basketball nearly as much as he loved taking down bombs. In between stop-and-go traffic moves, he clocked the scores from the previous night's playoffs.

It was a sunny April morning in 1980, and Geronimo was only a few hours into his first Saturday off in three months.

The female voice over the scanner called the bomb unit for a second time, confirming the device and requesting backup patrol to seal off the area. Geronimo looked at the rows of cars ahead of him, snarled in four roads to nowhere, and slapped a red cherry cop light on the roof of his Chevy Impala.

He was on the scene in ten minutes.

He got out of the car, flipped his shield over the collar of a light tan sweater, and nodded to two officers holding back a row of onlookers.

'What's the word?' he asked.

'Bomb guys just went in,' one cop, the younger of the two, said. 'Must be serious shit. They came in three trucks.'

'Only way we know what goes down is when the guys walk out of the building,' the other cop, older, more seasoned, said. 'Or if we hear a blast.'

'You in on this?' the young cop asked.

'No,' Geronimo said, shaking his head and eyeballing the crowd. 'Just waiting for rush hour to thin.'

'Bar be a better place to wait,' the older cop said.

'I don't drink,' Geronimo said, walking past a police barricade and into the gathered crowd.

He checked the eyes and body language of the bystanders. Bombers plant devices for two reasons. They like the rush of the blast, relishing the fact that it was their handiwork that caused panic and destruction. The other reason is more basic.

They crave attention.

Geronimo had seen the statistics. More than three-quarters of bombers are cop buffs who make regular calls into the hot lines set up after a blast. Twenty-seven percent of all potential bomb suspects in the New York City area have, at one time in their lives, taken the police exam.

And 65 percent stay on the scene.

The bomber waits quietly among the crowd, wanting to see if the bomb unit can beat him at what he does best. If there is a blast, the bomber is among the first to volunteer his help. If the device is defeated, he's there to lead the cheers.

Geronimo, hands buried inside front pockets of his

71

faded jeans, walked through this throng, trying to find the guilty lurking among the curious.

It didn't take long.

The man was young and well dressed, gray slacks tailored, brown loafers buffed, blue button-down shirt visible under a navy blazer. His brown hair was combed straight back and gelled, the clear complexion of his freshly shaven face shining in the glow of the morning sun. He resembled what he wanted those around him to think he was: a young executive derailed on his way to work.

But the eyes betrayed him.

Geronimo kept his distance, half hidden by a trio of schoolgirls lugging large L. L. Bean backpacks on their shoulders. He saw the man's eyes scan the empty warehouse, knowing which window to peer at and which door the bomb unit needed to enter. There was a bomber's hunger to those eyes, a sense of anticipation, a confidence that maybe on this day the police would be a poor match for his expertise.

They were eyes waiting for blood.

Geronimo stepped around the three girls and edged closer to the wooden barricade. With his back to the bomber, he glanced at the ground, checking only the motion of the stranger's shadow. He heard a lighter click behind him and watched a thin stream of tobacco smoke as it filtered past. Geronimo turned his head toward the man, and the two exchanged looks.

The man saw the badge dangling around Geronimo's neck.

Geronimo saw the man's right hand bunched up in the folds of his jacket pocket, cigarette gritted between teeth, sly smile across his face.

A cool breeze brushed past the cop. His body relaxed, the way it did instinctively when he was left in a room alone with a device. He took his hands from his pockets and moved closer to the suspect.

They were surrounded by two dozen people – old women on their way to the deli, workers on morning

72

break, mothers taking toddlers out for a stroll. All attention was focused on the building and the commotion in front of it. The children gleefully watched the squad cars parked at odd angles, bright red lights twirling. The duty cops, backs turned to the crowd, talked about logged overtime, unconcerned about the gawking bodies.

'Hello, Bomb Man,' the man in the jacket said to Geronimo. 'I thought you'd be in on this.'

'You know me?' Geronimo asked.

'I know what you do,' the man said, still holding the grin. 'And you know what I do.'

'How much time?' Geronimo asked.

'Five minutes.' The man directed his eyes toward the building. 'Not one of my better works. They should be able to dismantle without much effort. Even without you.'

'Gonna be the last one you plant,' Geronimo said. 'Should have given it your best.'

'I'm not finished yet,' the man said.

Geronimo reached behind his sweater, pulled out a .45 Colt, and aimed it at the man. He spread his legs apart and cocked the trigger.

'Hands high,' Geronimo said, ignoring the cries of the people around him. 'Where I can see 'em.'

'Anything you say, Bomb Man,' the man said.

He raised his free hand first and then slowly took the other out of the jacket pocket. Geronimo looked at the hand and raised the scope of the Colt a half inch higher, toward the center of the man's head.

The man's fingers were wrapped around an unpinned grenade.

'I drop this and we all die,' the man said gleefully and in a voice loud enough to be heard by the people around him.

'You're dead before it touches ground,' Geronimo said.

'I hope so,' the man said.

A woman screamed.

73

Two men knocked over the wooden barricade, trying to get out of the way.

A young woman in a sweat suit pulled her baby from the stroller and stood there, shivering with fear, inches from the man and the grenade.

Two cops were up behind Geronimo, guns drawn, aimed at the man.

'They say you're the best, Bomb Man,' the man said. 'You think that's true?'

'Let the people go,' Geronimo said. 'Then we'll talk.'

'There isn't a bomb you can't beat,' the man said. 'That's what I've read.'

'Let them go,' Geronimo said. 'Make it you and me. That's the only way for you to find out.'

'If they go, you'll shoot me,' the man said. 'And I still won't have my answer.'

'I'm gonna shoot you no matter what,' Geronimo said. 'But I promise you'll have an answer before you die. If you let them go.'

'I want it now,' the man said. 'I want to see for myself if you're as good as they say.'

Geronimo knew the man was without fear. In the madness of his dark world, that feeling had been stripped away. More than the grenade in his hand, it was the lack of fear that gave the man the advantage.

With a smile, the man made his move.

He tossed the grenade toward the woman clutching her child.

Geronimo moved as he fired. Three quick 250-grain bullets flying at 860 feet per second landed in the man's forehead and chest.

He was dead before his head hit concrete.

The grenade bounced off the screaming woman and fell to the ground.

Geronimo, in full leap, landed on top of it, one hand holding the metal tight, the other slapped against the medallion hanging around his chest.

A second later, the grenade exploded across his body.

For Delgaldo 'Geronimo' Lopez, the dream he feared the most had come true.

He lost to a bomb and he lived.

5
Pins

Jimmy Ryan sat in the back seat of an idling black Ford van and watched the woman in the red patent-leather pumps cross Madison Avenue against the light. Her tight black skirt stopped at mid-thigh; her black blouse was covered by a red Lagerfeld jacket, double-breasted and snug. Her thick hair, black and curled, fell across her shoulders, swinging past a set of pearl earrings that dangled near her neck. She strolled with confidence and her figure matched her style.

Augie Calise, the young detective behind the wheel, muttered, 'I'm fallin' in love. Just sittin' here and lookin' at her, I'm fallin' in love.'

Andy Fitz, the detective sitting on the passenger side, slowly shook his head. 'You're married, shmoe.'

'Your point?' Calise asked, still looking at the woman as she sauntered through the entrance of a doorman building.

Ryan snapped open an attache case on his lap. Inside was a Sony SRS-P3 recorder, its high-frequency tape spooling from one end of the machine to the other. He turned the volume to high, sat back, and listened to the clicking sounds the woman's heels made as she walked across the lobby toward the elevator bank.

'Great sound,' Fitz said. 'It's like we're right next to her.'

'I'd feel better if we *were* right next to her,' Calise said.

76

'These guys smell a mistake, they're gonna take everything but her teeth.'

'They won't know she's wired,' Ryan said. 'Unless they strip her naked.'

'I'd do that even if I *didn't* think she was wired,' Calise said.

'Where'd you lay the wire?' Fitz wanted to know.

'Inside her right bra cup,' Ryan told him. 'They'll never find it.'

'Her bra cup?' Calise turned his head, staring at Ryan with awe. 'How the hell did you get it in there?'

'Secrets of the trade,' Ryan said, smiling. 'If I told you, Andy here would have to pump two into the back of your ears.'

Calise refused to smile back. 'Least you could do is let me take the wire out.'

'Sorry, Augie,' Ryan said, snapping a cord into a set of earphones and resting them around his neck. 'I'm the only one who can touch her. My hands've got a priority one clearance.'

'Who the hell gave you that?' Calise asked, checking the traffic in front of the building.

'I was born with it,' Jimmy Ryan said.

Jimmy Ryan was orphaned at birth, abandoned in an upstate New York hospital by frightened teenage parents. His childhood memories revolved around a series of loveless foster homes inhabited by faceless adults, too anonymous to call parents, too familiar to call strangers. He grew up quiet and alone, confiding in no one, reluctant to form bonds, knowing they could soon be severed by the sudden shrill ring of a telephone.

The calls always came at night.

They would soon be followed by the mad rush to pack secondhand clothes into a worn valise and the false warmth of hurried good-byes. The car rides to each new family were always silent. Jimmy would sit in the back, scrunched down in his seat, eyes peering out at the passing landscape, feeling empty and lost.

He never stayed with any one family for more than a year. His plight was similar to thousands of other unwanted youngsters his age, all pawns in a statewide bureaucracy shuffle that revolved around cash payments. Children locked inside the state's foster care system were peddled off to applicant families who agreed to take them into their homes for a maximum twelve-month period. In return, they would receive average monthly checks of $78 per child, money meant to cover food and clothing expenses. More often than not, the checks helped cover gambling habits and drink binges. At any time, either the child, foster parent, or a system representative could rescind the deal, trucking the orphan off to still another foreign place to call home.

In one eight-month period, between fourth and fifth grades, Jimmy was moved three separate times, each new set of parents welcoming him to his new home and then just as eagerly seeing him off only a few weeks later.

Jimmy's way of life didn't leave much room for hobbies. There were no baseball card collections to hoard or comic books hidden on dusty shelves to be read in the dead of night. There weren't any kittens to hold or fish tanks to tend. Though Jimmy loved to read, he owned few books of his own. Anything to make packing easier.

Jimmy did have one passion, and he fell back on it to help get him through those early dark years. With a magical talent for anything electrical, he welcomed the secondhand toys his array of foster parents would send his way. Plug-in remote-control robots that had smashed into too many walls, chewed-up tape recorders, acid-stained transistor radios. They all found their way into Jimmy Ryan's hands.

Slowly and with great care, Jimmy would take a gadget apart, reconfigure the wiring, and emerge with something virtually new. If he had the time and the tools, he would even add a few fresh dimensions to his re-creation.

In his empty hours, Jimmy pored through the electronics magazines he found in local libraries and carted out as many books on the subject as he had time to read. He absorbed all the knowledge available, stored it and shared it with no one. Then, when that knowledge would do him the most good, Jimmy Ryan would figure a way to put it to use.

Ryan planted his first bug when he was twelve.

He was living with a plumber, George Richards, who had a short-fuse temper and a wife with a flirtatious eye. They both drank heavily and often took the frustrations of a night's drunkenness out on the boy. The wife, Elaine, began her assaults with an angry voice and ended them with an even louder flurry of slaps, leaving Jimmy with a series of welts and bruises hidden under his shirts and sweaters. Afterward, she scolded him into silence and backed the warnings with hard hits across already reddened flesh.

Jimmy Ryan never uttered a word.

Instead, he laid a wire inside the main bedroom of the Richards' two-storey stucco house in Peekskill, New York. The wire was wrapped around a wooden board under the queen-size mattress. It connected to a remote mini-recorder taped under a bureau next to the bed. On those tapes, Jimmy listened and learned about the couple he was told to call Mom and Dad.

He heard about their mounting debts and backed-up loans. He laughed as George boasted about customers he double-billed and how Elaine had her doctor file false medical claims in return for half the insurance check. But the best tapes of all, and the ones that would extract the sweetest justice, involved Elaine and her lover, Carl, a real estate attorney who also happened to be her brother-in-law. They shared two passionate afternoons a week, finishing their lovemaking just before Jimmy got home from school. All of it, from moans of pleasure to rants against George, was picked up by Jimmy's spool of tape.

On the night he was sent away, packed valise in his left hand, Jimmy stood before George and Elaine.

'We're sorry it didn't work out,' Elaine told him, already on her third gin and tonic.

Jimmy nodded, checking the inside pocket of his tattered hunting jacket, making sure the dozen tapes were safely tucked away.

'Gonna miss having you here,' George said, holding a longneck bottle of beer.

'I have a gift for you,' Jimmy told George. 'To thank you for what you did for me.'

'You kiddin'?' George rested a hand on the boy's shoulder. 'You got me a gift?' He turned to Elaine, hitting her with a scornful gaze, then looked back at Jimmy with a smile.

Jimmy reached into his pocket and took out the set of tapes, neatly wrapped in flowered tissue paper and held together with a ribbon.

'Want me to open it now?' George asked, taking the package and holding it in both hands.

'Maybe you should wait,' Jimmy said, looking over at Elaine. 'Until you're by yourself.'

'Thank you,' George said, nodding his head. 'I'll never forget you doin' this.'

Jimmy buttoned his coat and picked up his valise. 'I know,' he said.

He walked past George and Elaine for the last time, toward the front door, a waiting car, and another set of parents.

The woman in the red pumps knocked on the door to Room 1211, silver bracelet jangling against her wrist.

'It's like she's knockin' on the front hood of the car,' Calise said. 'It's so damn clear.'

'Narcotics have their guys in place?' Jimmy asked, head down, fingers adjusting a series of sound dials.

'They got four in the next suite,' Fitz said. 'And three

more in a stairwell down the hall. She gets jammed up, should take less than a minute to get to her.'

'Unless they're asleep,' Calise said. 'Which is always fuckin' possible with those dimrods.'

The door handle snapped open and a man's voice warmly greeted the woman. He spoke in a thick Spanish accent.

'She's in,' Jimmy said, sitting straight up and flipping a red switch on to full volume.

'How long you givin' her?' Fitz said.

'All she needs,' Jimmy said. 'These guys are top line. They're gonna play her first. Make sure she's legit before they close the deal.'

'What about her?' Calise asked. 'How good is she?'

'I'll let you know in about half an hour,' Jimmy said, putting the earphones back over his head.

At seventeen, Jimmy Ryan did a two-year tour of duty with another foster family of sorts, the US Army. While stationed in Germany, the dark-haired, coal-eyed Ryan was allowed to fuel his passion by working as an electronic surveillance trainee. The army brass was impressed with his ability to handle their most sophisticated equipment and asked him to stay on for an additional four years, promising him tours of Mexico and the Middle East. Ryan, bored and unimpressed with the military regimen and tired of spending weeks without being able to cast his electric gaze on a beautiful woman, took a pass and signed out.

He was in New York City, taking a two-week seminar on wiretapping at the John Jay College for Criminal Justice, when he spotted a civil service flyer posted on a hall bulletin board. He ripped it down and signed up to take the New York Police Department exam. Six months later, working as a clerk for a small electronics firm on Queens Boulevard, Ryan got the letter that paved his way to becoming a cop.

He spent a dull sixteen months in uniform and then was

transferred to the Manhattan Drug Task Force, working undercover, doing what he had prepared all his life to do – lay down wires, plant devices, and listen to the secrets of others. The assignment also freed Ryan from the uneasy potential for gunplay, the area of police work he cared for the least. He was a listener, content to skirt the perimeters of other people's worlds, but never eager to enter any one of them.

There were more than enough guys on the squad who had become cops looking to play cowboy, feeding off the nerve rush of the split-second shoot-out. Jimmy Ryan, rugged and catalogue handsome, with a head of thick curly hair and a John Garfield smile, liked living on the outside, doing his police work from a safe distance. He carried only the one gun, the .38 Special, and had never fired it in the line of duty.

With the money he'd saved from the army, plus his heavy overtime earnings as a cop, Ryan bought his first home, a single-family wood frame on Staten Island, six miles from lower Manhattan. It was the first place he could ever call his own, and he stocked it with books, electronic equipment, stereos, radios – all the toys of a childhood he was never allowed to have.

He worked constantly; his expertise was sought out by every undercover operation team leader throughout the five boroughs. Ryan linked his affinity for computers to his electrical magic show and turned the tedious routine of police surveillance into a state-of-the-art experience. He could tap on anyone, from mob bosses to drug rollers to politicians bagging payoffs. He could lay a wire anywhere, from a car bumper to the hull of a yacht, the sound always clear, the reams of information the tapes generated almost always enough to put away the voice. He was the best bug the NYPD ever had.

The respect the other cops showed him was comforting to Jimmy Ryan. It was his first taste of family.

The cops on the job called him Pins.

Ryan loved bowling and was captain of the Manhattan Task Force team. Every Thursday and Sunday night, he could be found pounding lanes at alleys throughout New York, competing against other squads from around the city. He was the police league's MVP three years running, holding a steady 201 average and walking off with an armful of trophies.

As much as he loved what he was doing, he had his life beyond the police force planned out.

He would open a small electronics store within walking distance of his home and think about doing six-month tours as a professional bowler. Neither job would be done for the money, but for the pleasure.

They were simple dreams.

Ryan had spent a childhood locked away in silent places where faces and names blended together. It taught him not to stray far from the cold glare of reality and to trust only what he found comfort in, what he knew would never betray him. The cold, sterile world of electronic surveillance was all Jimmy Ryan ever counted on. The shiny brown lanes of smoke-filled bowling alleys were his sanctuary.

And like his home and the police department, the rare places he could call his own.

The man with the heavy Spanish accent sounded agitated.

'You were supposed to bring the cash yourself,' he told the woman in the red pumps.

'It couldn't be worked out,' the woman answered coolly, traces of a southern accent hidden by a dozen New York winters. 'So I had a friend arrange it. He should be here in a few minutes.'

'We didn't ask your friend to bring the money,' the man said. 'We asked *you*.'

'I've known him all my life,' she said, still cool. 'I trust him. So can you.'

'I trust no one,' he said. 'It is what's kept me alive.'

'Sad way to live,' the woman said.

'In my business, it's the only way to live,' the man said. 'Trust ends with a bullet.'

'He's on to her, Pins,' Calise said. 'You can hear it in his voice.'

'I'll go in,' Jimmy said.

'*You*?' Fitz scoffed. 'Since when do *you* go in?'

'You guys handle the equipment and I'll go up.'

'As *what*?' Calise said, turning to face Jimmy.

'Hotel's got computerized phone lines,' Jimmy said. 'It'll take me about two minutes to find the basement and short-circuit the phones in the suite. Then I go up, knock on the door, and ask to check the phones.'

'Dressed in a bowling jacket with your name on the chest and jeans,' Fitz said. 'What'd you do last night, take a bowling ball to the head?'

'We need the kilos and we need him,' Jimmy said, resting the attache case on the seat next to him and opening the car's rear door. 'And we need time to get both. This buys it for us.'

'What about the machine?' Calise said. 'You're the only one knows how to run the fuckin' thing.'

'It'll run itself,' Jimmy said, looking at the two cops. 'All you gotta do is listen. And be there if I need you.'

'Have I ever let you down?' Calise asked.

'Yes,' Jimmy said.

'When?'

'Every time I've needed you,' Jimmy said, stepping out of the car.

'Maybe today I'll fuck up and you'll get lucky,' Calise said.

'I'm counting on it,' Jimmy Ryan breathed.

He slammed the car door behind him, zippered the front of his black bowling jacket, and raced across the street toward the entrance of the luxury high rise.

The eighteen large packets of cocaine were piled in two neat rows on top of a glass coffee table. The woman in red sat on a couch, lit cigarette in her right hand, bemused look on her face, watching the man with the accent unzip the black duffel and saw his brown eyes gleam when he flipped it over, emptying a dozen thick pads of cash over the kilos.

There were three other men in the room.

Two sat at the bar, elbows stretched out, facing the group around the coffee table. The third man stood with his back to the bedroom door, hands hidden behind the folds of a white silk jacket, heavy lids covering albino blues.

'Before you go, there is something I would like you to do for me,' the man said. 'A small favor.'

'Do I have a choice?' the woman asked.

'No,' the man said.

'Then just tell me what it is,' she sighed.

'Take off your clothes,' the man with the accent said.

Pins was at the door, poised to knock.

Calise and Fitz were out of the van and into the high rise as soon as they heard the man order the undercover to strip. The narcs in the stairwell held their position, lead man with one hand gripped around the doorknob. The three detectives in the suite next door snapped on their vests and clicked their .44 semiautomatics into readiness.

The albino opened the door on the second knock.

'Who the fuck are you?' he said, staring down at the much shorter Pins.

'Telephone repair,' Pins said, catching a glimpse of the undercover's face behind the albino's left shoulder. 'Your lines are down.'

'We didn't call nobody,' the albino said, large hand on the edge of the door, ready to slam it shut. 'Go play with somebody else's phones.'

Pins had his gun in the albino's chest before he had a chance to breathe. 'You don't understand,' Pins said, his gun hand visibly shaking. 'I take my job very seriously. Now let me in.'

85

The albino took two steps back, hands at his sides, palms out. 'Two phones. Bedroom and out here.'

'There's three, putz,' Pins said, walking into the suite, looking at the woman in the red pumps, stripped down to her bra. 'You forgot about the one in the bathroom.'

'You walk in here, you don't walk out,' the albino said. 'I make sure of that.'

'Hey, fixing phones is a risky business,' Pins said, backing the albino against a wall. 'But the benefits can't be beat.'

The Spanish guy, Ramon, tossed the duffel bag back on top of the coffee table and turned to the man with the accent for a signal. The man put an arm around the woman in the red pumps and held her close to his side, rubbing against the lines of sweat running down her back. The albino slid an open blade down the side of his sleeve and cupped it in his palm.

They held position as the cops flowed into the suite.

Calise and Fitz were in the doorway, short of breath and guns drawn. The three narcs from the stairwell were in vests and shotguns, crouched down behind them. The four detectives from the adjacent suite had poured out and were braced two apiece on both sides of the hall.

'Looks like a lot of people want to use your phone,' Pins said, turning his head slightly toward the cops covering the room.

The albino saw the opening and took it.

He wrapped his fingers around the knife handle and swung it. The blade slashed open the sleeve of Jimmy's bowling jacket, drawing blood and knocking him to the ground.

Calise turned into the room, stepped over Jimmy, and fired four .38-caliber rounds deep into the albino's chest. The force slammed him against the wall, knife rattling to the floor. He slid down the side of the pink stucco wall, staining it with streaks of red.

'I hope that's not your bowling arm,' Calise said to Pins, looking down at him between his legs.

Then before Pins could say 'You're all heart,' the bullet came out of Ramon's .41 Remington Magnum and traveled into Calise's brain at a speed of 1,300 feet per second. Calise fell into a heap, the smile on his face frozen in death, crashing down on top of Ryan.

Ryan felt the breath ease out of Calise's body, his friend's blood pouring down the side of his face and onto his bowling jacket. Pins looked beyond Calise and over at the narcs by the door, hearing them curse and then empty their chambers into Ramon's white suit. He lifted his head and watched the dealer flip across the room, knocking over a chair and landing on top of a dinette table near the bar.

The man with the accent held his place next to the woman in the red pumps, his right arm still wrapped around her waist, his left hand holding a .32 short Colt to her head. The narcs and the detectives pointed guns and rifles at him.

'I walk out with her,' the man said. 'Or I die with her.'

The man with the accent tightened his grip around the handle of the gun and swallowed hard. The cops around him held their aim. Pins stayed still, blood still pouring down on him from Calise's wound.

Pins looked over at the woman in the red pumps. She ran a hand slowly up her leg, lifting the skirt until it showed the top of her stockings. Tucked inside the sheer frill was a white-barreled .22 Remington Jet. The man with the accent was sweating. Wavering. He jiggled the gun nervously, moving it from the woman's head to flash it menacingly at the cops lined up before him, then back to the woman. When he flashed his gun around the room a second time, the woman moved. She pulled out her gun, put it to the man's head, and fired off two rounds.

He fell to her feet, dead.

The woman tossed the gun to the floor, bent down, picked up her jacket and blouse, and walked out the open door, well aware of her fellow cops' stares.

Pins didn't move from the carpeted floor, now darkened

by his friend's blood. He put his arms around the dead cop, still too afraid to let him go, waiting for the hard faces with the body bags to come take him away.

The building was on the Upper West Side, in the high seventies, pre-war, seven storeys high, with an Otis elevator creaking up and down. Surveillance photos taken by an undercover unit scouting the area led them to believe that a three-bedroom unit on the sixth floor was being used to launder drug dollars. The apartment was always empty between nine A.M. and noon every day; the young couple renting it for $3,000 a month worked out at the Jack Lalanne on Broadway during that time. The undercovers needed Pins to drop a bug near the bed and a video camera somewhere close to the bureau.

It was less than an hour's work.

Pins pressed the two dozen black buzzers dotting the entry wall, waiting for some frazzled tenant to ring him in.

He moved to the elevator, watched the thick black door slowly close, and leaned on the button that had the number six on it. Pins was dressed in jeans and a thick blue baseball jacket, topped by a Yankee cap. In his left hand he held a thin leather briefcase. He popped two slices of red hot cinnamon gum in his mouth and got out of the elevator when it stopped at the sixth floor. He pulled a folded sheet from his back pocket to double-check the apartment number. He found it scrawled in black ink across the top of the wire sheet, 6F, and moved on down the hall.

It took less than thirty seconds for Pins to pick the lock and enter the apartment.

He moved down a long corridor, a large living room and two bedrooms to his left, a bathroom facing straight ahead. There was little in the way of furniture. A scrawny black cat hissed at him from behind a radiator pipe.

At the end of the corridor Pins turned right and walked into the master bedroom. The walls were painted dark blue, photographers' flashlights stood in each corner, and a Sony twenty-five-inch color TV rested on the bureau. In the middle: a king-size four-poster.

Pins tossed his case on the bed, zipped it open, and started to work. He laid a bug inside the thin pole of one of the lights, running it from the bottom up, past the wires and into the main fuse connector.

He grabbed a Minicam out of the briefcase and walked to the back of the television, planning to rest it alongside the main tube.

It was then he heard the footsteps coming down the hall.

They were heavy, a man's step rather than a woman's, wooden slats creaking with each imprint. Pins rested the back of the TV on the floor and moved toward the bed, looking for the radio that would link him with backup.

He had his back to the door.

A young man, thin brown hair disheveled, vacant look in his eyes, stood at the edge of the bedroom entrance. His entire body shook with anger.

'I knew I'd find you here,' he said.

Pins turned around, radio in his hand, and faced the man.

'You live here?' Pins asked.

'I'm Sheila's husband,' the man said. 'And you're standing in my bedroom.'

'I don't know anybody named Sheila,' Pins said, pressing down on the black transmitter button.

'You *should* know her,' the man said. 'You've been fucking her for almost a year now.'

'There's a mistake here,' Pins said, his voice steady. He stayed focused on the man's eyes, looking to talk his way out of this strange situation.

'I love her,' the man said. 'Can you understand that, you bastard? I love her.'

'Listen to me,' Pins said quietly. 'I'm a cop. I'm gonna take out my shield and show you. Okay?'

The man lifted his right arm and pointed it straight at Pins. There was a .22 caliber clutched in his hand.

89

'You're not gonna show me anything,' the man said, clicking back the trigger. 'And you're not gonna see Sheila ever again.'

'You don't know what you're doin'.' Pins was surprised at how level his voice was. He wasn't even yelling. 'I'm not the guy. I'm a cop.'

One look at the man and Pins knew he had moved beyond reason to reside in madness.

In a lifetime constructed around caution, Jimmy Ryan had made a mistake. He had misread the scrawled handwriting on the wire sheet. He had walked through the wrong door, 6F instead of 6E, and there he stood, inches from a jealous husband's rage, accused of having an affair with a woman he had never met.

The first bullet hit Pins in the right shoulder. The second shattered bone above the right elbow. The final two hit him in the chest and sent him to the ground, pain rushing through his body like a river.

The young man hovered over him, two more shells left in the chamber.

'You'll never see her again,' he said to Jimmy Ryan.

'It's sure startin' to look that way,' Pins said.

He heard the undercovers before he saw them, guns drawn, ready to fire. He looked up at the young man and watched him drop the gun back down to his side. He saw two undercovers rush over, yank the man's arms back, cuff him, and pull him away. Through it all, the man kept his eyes on Pins, a small smirk etched across his face.

A third undercover, Gennaro, ran over, leaned down, and lifted Pins's head, holding it in the crook of his right arm.

'We got an ambulance comin',' Gennaro told him.

'Think I need it?' Pins wanted to know, looking down at the blood flowing out of his bowling arm.

'Who's the shooter?' Gennaro asked.

'Just a kid,' Pins said.

Pins looked away from Gennaro. He turned to the

90

photo lamp in the corner. He tried to take a deep breath and smiled.

The small bugging device he planted in the neck of the lamp had picked up everything he said and did during his final moments as a cop.

It was the last bug Jimmy Ryan would plant as a member of the New York City Police Department.

6
Rev. Jim

Bobby Scarponi was a drug addict and an alcoholic.

He was twelve when he had his first taste of scotch; two weeks later he lit his first joint. Besides his ability to consume large quantities of any illegal substance, Scarponi was known for his chronic truancy and violent streak. He stole bikes and toys from his South Jamaica neighbors to help feed his expensive habits. His parents couldn't exert any control over the boy, finding it easier to ignore, as much as they could, the whispers that followed their troubled son.

Bobby never dealt drugs, but was a steady customer for a number of local dealers. If he got in too deep financially and couldn't make the payoff from what he could steal, he could bank on a discreet parental bailout. As a result, he was stripping the Scarponis of their security, slapping away at their pride, and digging into their future, which for them embodied nothing more ambitious than a two-bedroom Laguna Beach condo built around Albert Scarponi's construction foreman's pension.

Despite his problems and frequent run-ins with the police, Bobby Scarponi was a well-liked kid. In the pattern of the users and abusers he associated with, Scarponi learned early in his addiction to be a performer, to adjust his demeanor, hide the track, clear the eyes, and pretend to be normal. He had an easy way, blending natural charm with rugged features that managed to withstand the ravages of the drugs he ingested.

By the time he reached sixteen, Bobby had been in and out of four rehab clinics and undergone three years of ineffective counseling. He had worked his way up the pharmaceutical ladder from pot to glue to crystal meth to acid to cocaine. Then, on a cloudy April afternoon in 1966, Bobby put a thin needle to a fat vein and felt the hot rush of heroin for the first time.

He was now traveling on a narrow strip of road that often led its passengers to a head-on with death.

Bobby Scarponi was no exception.

Bobby sat next to his mother, Beatrice, on a park bench across from the empty playground. It was cold and late, deep into a Monday night. His mother turned up the collar of her brown parka against the chill wind, shoved her hands deep inside the front pockets, and stared down at the withered grass by her feet. She was a short woman, slender, with a thick head of prematurely graying hair and sorrowful dark eyes. She spoke with a slight trace of an accent, remnants of her years growing up in the Italian seaside village of Panza.

'I never lied to your father, Roberto,' she said. 'Tonight was the first time.'

'Relax, Mom,' Bobby said. 'It's gonna be over soon. We pay them the money and then we go home.'

'It's never over, *figlio*,' Beatrice said. 'As long as you buy what they sell.'

'Mom, please,' Bobby said, zipping up his green army jacket. 'No lectures, okay? It's bad enough we gotta sit in the cold and pay these dirtbags off.'

'You took your father's heart,' Beatrice said, looking at her son, a hand on his right leg, which was jiggling nervously from the cold and the need for a fix. 'You kill him a little bit each day. Every time you put that stuff inside your arms.'

'It's my life, Mom,' Bobby said, throwing a glance up and down the street, concern etched on his face.

'It's our life,' Beatrice said. 'And it's a wrong life right now.'

'I'm gonna quit,' Bobby said, turning to look at his mother, seeing the tears welling in her eyes. 'I promise you. I don't like this any more than you do.'

'You know, I was sixteen when I first met your father,' she said. 'I looked and I fell in love. I love him even more now. And I can't let him die and leave behind a junkie for a son. I can't live with that shame.'

'What about me?' Bobby asked, sadness wrapped around the question. 'You still love me?'

'I'm here, no?' Beatrice said. 'To give strangers money your father works in a hole to earn.'

'I'll pay you back,' Bobby said. 'I swear it.'

'Don't pay me with money,' Beatrice said.

'What, then?'

'Walk away from this life for good,' she said. 'From the drugs and these bums who sell them to you.'

'I said I was gonna quit,' Bobby said. 'This'll be my last payoff.'

'If you can't do that,' Beatrice said, cupping his chin, 'then take enough to kill yourself.'

'You want me to die?' Bobby said slowly. 'That's what you're tellin' me you want?'

'You're dead now, Roberto,' Beatrice said. 'You walk and talk, eat and drink, but inside you're dead. So, make it simple. For everybody. Stop what you're doing or let me have a grave to pray over.'

The dealer came up out of the shadows to stand by Bobby's left, a long, dark raincoat buttoned to his neck. The thin brim of a gray fedora shielded his eyes and hid his face; his hands were covered by thick black gloves. He was in his mid-twenties, long blond hair rubber-banded into a ponytail.

'Hey, Ray,' Bobby said in a startled tone, standing when he saw the dealer. 'I didn't hear you coming.'

'You got my money?' Ray asked, his tired voice sprinkled with venom.

94

'This is my mom,' Bobby said, pointing down toward Beatrice, who stayed in her seat, staring at the dealer with contempt.

'I don't give a fuck who she is,' Ray said. 'You got my money?'

'Most of it,' Bobby said, looking over Ray's shoulders, spotting the car waiting by a fire hydrant, smoke filtering out of the exhaust.

'I didn't ask for *most* of it,' Ray said. 'I want *all* of it. *Now.*'

'I brought five hundred,' Beatrice said to the dealer in the strongest voice she could muster. 'It is all we have left.'

'You're a thousand short,' Ray said.

'I'll have the rest in about a week,' Bobby told him.

'How you gonna do that, High School?' Ray said. 'Mama already gave you everything she's got, and she's all you know that's got money.'

'It's my problem,' Bobby said. 'I'll figure it out.'

Ray jumped off his stance and pounced on Bobby. His two gloved hands grabbed hold of the front of the zippered army jacket, lifting Bobby several inches off his feet.

'It ain't just *your* problem,' Ray said. 'It's *my* problem now. And I gotta solve it.'

He let Bobby go, pushing him back toward his mother, who sat rigid in fear, her hands locked across her face. Ray walked past the boy, stopping in front of Beatrice. He crouched down, his eyes meeting hers, two hands on her knees, and smiled.

'You tellin' the truth?' he asked her. 'Five hundred's all you got left?'

Beatrice nodded, too frightened to speak.

Ray took a hand off her knee and put it in his pocket. He leaned closer to Beatrice as the hand came out holding a black Indian-point switchblade. He pressed on a thin button at the bottom edge of the handle, releasing a seven-inch knife, sharp enough to cut through wood.

'I want all my money, Bobby,' Ray said, his eyes still on

Beatrice, his face close enough for her to smell his drink-stained breath. 'So I'm gonna ask you again. You got it for me?'

'Give me one more day.' Bobby moved two steps closer, trying not to sound as panicked as he felt. 'I'll get you the rest tomorrow. I swear it.'

'When tomorrow?' Ray ran the edge of the blade up the front of Beatrice's coat.

'I'll meet you here,' Bobby said. 'Same time.'

'You think your little junkie's tellin' me the truth?' Ray asked Beatrice.

'My son is a junkie,' Beatrice said, putting a hand on Ray's raincoat, bunching a small corner into a ball. 'But you are much worse. You live off junkies. And that makes you nothing but an animal.'

'This is between us, Ray,' Bobby said. 'Keep her out of this. Please.'

'You're the one that brought her,' Ray said.

'Take your blood money.' Beatrice pulled out the envelope with the five hundred dollars from her coat pocket, then shoved it against Ray's chest. 'And go.'

Ray took the envelope with his free hand, stood up, put it in his pocket, and turned to look at Bobby.

'Forget the rest of the money,' Ray told him. 'After tonight we're even, you and me. You want any fresh shit, you hustle it someplace else. Anyplace but me. Deal?'

'Deal,' Bobby said, nodding his head. 'Thanks, Ray. I appreciate it.'

Ray smiled at Bobby, turned back to Beatrice, grabbed her hair, and pulled it back with a hard snap. Bobby leapt to his feet but Ray easily knocked him away with his knife hand.

He brought the blade back to Beatrice's throat, his eyes gleaming, a relaxed smile on his face. He ran the blade against her neck, one long cut from the edge of the left ear across to the bottom of her right jaw. He watched the blood gush out in thick rolls and held on to her hair until

96

he saw the life float from her body. He watched Beatrice slump down the side of the park bench.

Ray Monte cleaned the sides of the knife against his victim's coat, snapped it closed, and walked off into the night.

'My pleasure,' Ray said to Bobby, leaving the young boy with his dying mother.

Bobby cradled Beatrice in his arms, letting her blood flow over him. He didn't cry, didn't speak, just held her close, head against her heart, rocking slowly back and forth. He hadn't touched her in years and couldn't remember the last time he told her he loved her. And yet he knew she would forgive him anything, even her own death.

He put his head down against the side of hers, his lips close to her ears and whispered the words to '*Partira*', the Italian ballad she had sung him to sleep with when he was a little boy.

They stayed that way until the dawn broke and the police arrived.

Bobby Scarponi buried his drug habit alongside his mother. He stayed clear of the streets and worked hard in school. He fought off the night-time urges when he hungered for a needle bubbling with heroin, for an escape from the life around him.

He lived with his father in a silent house. Albert Scarponi said goodbye to the only woman he ever loved, then turned his back on his only child. They shared a home but never spoke, the older man living quietly with his grief and anger, unable to forgive Bobby for leading his mother into the path of a dealer's knife. Albert's hatred was further fueled by his son's refusal to identify his mother's killer.

Ray Monte had walked free.

'Don't get any ideas about doing this on your own, Bobby,' one of the detectives told him. 'He'll kill you just like he did your mom.'

'The dealer didn't kill my wife,' Albert said, looking up at the detective. 'He only held the knife. She was brought there by her son. Her own blood.'

'You get a change of heart,' the other detective told Bobby, placing a card in the napkin holder in the center of the table, 'give us a call. Day or night.'

The two detectives left through the back door of the wood-shingled house, leaving Albert and Bobby Scarponi behind, alone in their two separate worlds.

From then on, Bobby Scarponi kept track of Ray Monte.

He would see him occasionally walking the streets of his Queens neighborhood, drinking coffee and pushing drugs, never far from a new car with a running engine. Bobby finished a two-year army tour while Ray sat out the calendar in a Comstock cell, doing three to five on an assault charge. They were discharged two weeks apart.

Ray Monte returned to the streets, ready to move back into the prime arena of the drug trade. He teamed up with an Irish crew working out of Forest Hills and set up shop on 168th Street in Jamaica, handling heroin and cocaine for the posses wresting control of the drug action from the old-time Italians. He took a cut from all the pot and illegal prescription sales generated in the area, and contracted out members of his outfit for hits on anyone who objected.

And he never carried a gun. Only a knife.

Bobby Scarponi sat across the desk from a detective with a long scar across his face, its edges brushing the lid of his right eye. The detective lit a cigarette and sat back in a creaky wooden swivel chair.

'Why you telling me all this now?' the detective, Sal Albano, asked. 'Why didn't you say anything before?'

'I wanted to see if I could make it through the Academy,' Bobby said. 'If I didn't, nobody needed to know.'

'How long've you been off the shit?'

98

'Eight years this March,' Bobby said. 'Shot three speed-balls on my sixteenth birthday. Two nights later, my mom got killed.'

'You ain't the first cop that ever took a hit on the hard stuff,' Albano said. 'Shit, these days, I think half the fuckin' guys in uniform are buzzed out of their skulls.'

'So I don't get booted?' Bobby asked.

'You're the best pure cop I ever trained,' Albano said, 'and I've been doing this long enough to know good when I see it. You stay clean, you've got no beef with me.'

'I asked to be put in a precinct in my old neighbor-hood,' Bobby said, sitting back in his chair, muscular frame relaxed, the once-dead eyes now clear and lucid. 'Any chance of that?'

'I'll make some calls,' Albano said. 'Shouldn't be a problem. But don't get used to it. Guy like you ain't gonna be in uniform long. An old friend of mine in Brooklyn needs a good young cop to work decoy. Told him about you. Expect a call in about six months.'

'I won't need that long to do what I have to do,' Bobby said, standing and reaching over to shake Albano's hand.

'Which is what?' Albano asked.

'Look up an old friend,' said Bobby Scarponi of the New York City Police Department.

The heavy April rain pounded the squad car as it circled the empty South Jamaica streets, fog lights on, wipers slapping aside thick streams of water. Bobby Scarponi kicked up the sound on the police radio and turned the window defogger knob down. He was starting his fourth month as a street cop and had already made a dent in cleaning up his old neighborhood. He had nailed four mid-level drug dealers and had taken down an armed felon hiding in a public school science lab. He reintro-duced himself to the local merchants, many of whom remembered him as the drug-crazed teen who shoplifted from their stores. Now he was there to protect them.

The street kids, aware of Scarponi's past, called him Rev. Jim, after the brain-frazzled character portrayed on the hit television series *Taxi*. The name made its way into the halls of Bobby's precinct and stuck. Scarponi didn't mind. It helped give him a street ID, a name they would remember, a key first step toward being a cop they would turn to for help.

The passing years had failed to soften the frost between Bobby and his father. They still shared a roof, but nothing more. Not even the first sight of Bobby in a policeman's uniform could shake loose his father's hate.

Bobby Scarponi understood.

He had resigned himself to his culpability in his mother's death, fighting daily to control the emotions boiling beneath his calm exterior. He knew those emotions would eventually need to be set free to exact their toll. Only then, perhaps, could he work toward building a peace with the man whose house he occupied but whose love he long ago lost.

Bobby Scarponi also knew that when the day came for him to open that emotional cage, the beast it unleashed would be aimed at Ray Monte.

Bobby pulled the squad car directly behind the parked Mercedes and shoved the gear stick into park, letting the motor idle. He put on a pair of thin black gloves and grabbed a brown nightstick, twisting the cord around his knuckles.

There were four men around the Mercedes, all dressed in long gray coats and brown fedoras, brims folded down to catch the rain. They separated when they saw Bobby approach, smiles on their faces but menace in their eyes.

Ray Monte stood in the middle, right leg up against a rear hubcap, thin cigar in his mouth.

'You know the world's a fucked-up place,' Ray said, 'when they go and give a junkie a gun and a badge.'

Bobby walked closer, taking small steps, measuring the

men, knowing they were all armed and backed up by a small crew drinking in the dimly lit bar behind him.

'Rain like this must cut into business,' Bobby said, his eyes on Ray.

'A junkie ain't no weatherman,' Ray said. 'All he cares about is the fix. Shouldn't have to be tellin' you that.'

'I remember,' Bobby said.

'You here to pick up the payoffs?' the chubby man to Ray's left asked, laughing through the question. 'They always send the new guys for the pickups. Breaks them in good that way.'

'You got it goin' pretty good, Ray,' Bobby said. 'I figure six blocks in the one-sixties, all kickin' in to you.'

'I eat,' Ray said, shrugging his shoulders, cigar smoke filtering up past the lid of his fedora.

'What happens if you go down?' Bobby asked. 'Who moves in on your take?'

'That's somethin' I wouldn't know or care about. Seein' as I ain't goin' any fuckin' place.'

'I figure Uncle Angie.' Water dripped down from the peak of Bobby's policeman's hat. 'He'll give your corners to one of the Jamaican gangs. Walk away from it with a bigger cut than he's getting from you.'

'By the time that happens, I'll have enough money to buy Florida,' Ray said, taking the cigar from his mouth and tossing it over his shoulder into a puddle. 'And you'll still be walkin' in the rain, bustin' joint-rollers.'

'You still carry that blade?' Bobby asked, moving in closer to Ray, watching the three men by his side stiffen.

'Always,' Ray said. 'You wanna see it?'

'I saw it once,' Bobby said. 'It's enough to hold me.'

'When your mother died, she didn't make a sound,' Ray said. 'She just went. Think you'll go the same?'

'You did her alone,' Bobby said. 'Didn't need anybody else. Now you got three. Maybe all that money makes you scared.'

Ray Monte smiled and looked over at his men. 'Go dry

off inside and get a drink,' he told them. 'Pour me one too. I won't be long.'

Bobby and Ray stared at one another, waiting as the three men brushed past, heading for the dark warmth of the old bar.

'You gonna draw down on me, Officer Bob?' Ray asked. 'I don't have a gun.'

'She wasn't carrying anything,' Bobby said, the rain coming down in heavier doses.

'She had her son to protect her.' Ray's voice was cold, heavy with hate. 'Except he didn't do nothin' but watch her bleed.'

'I've watched her die every day since then,' Bobby said, the blade of a knife slipping down the side of his police jacket. 'And every night.'

Ray Monte pulled the switchblade from his pants pocket and snapped it open. It was a sound that Bobby had heard again and again over the years. They circled each other warily, then lunged at the same time.

The knife went in chest deep, past muscle and bone, through vein and artery. Two hands reached for it, holding it tight, burying it deeper into flesh. The two men stared at each other, the rain around them mixing with the thick flow of blood, one set of eyes welled with sadness and tears, the other losing their grasp on life. The two leaned against the rear door of the Mercedes, wet bodies clinging together, low gurgles coming from the throat of the dying man.

'You didn't make any noise either,' Bobby Scarponi said to Ray Monte, letting his body go, watching it slide down the side of the Mercedes and crumple to the curb, head against a Firestone all-weather tire.

Bobby walked to his squad car, got in, put it in gear, and drove off, heading back to the station house.

His tour of duty done.

Three months after Ray Monte's death, Bobby Scarponi was transferred out of uniform and assigned to the

Brooklyn Decoy Unit. At twenty-five, he was the youngest member of a team that roamed the borough posing as potential criminal targets. Bobby, who loved acting, took to the detail as easily as he once took to drugs. More important, he cherished the risk involved.

For the cop they called Rev. Jim, it was just another way to get high.

In no time, he mastered the disguises of the job – from the drunken Wall Street executive asleep at a subway stop to the tattered rummy sleeping one off on a heat grate to the unruly drug addict hustling street corners for throwaway change. He was the best performer on the street, pushing his talents to dangerous limits as he lulled his suspects into action.

It was as a member of the Decoy Unit that Bobby Scarponi found himself leaning against a railing in Brooklyn Heights, looking out across the still river at the diamond glimmer of the Manhattan night. His hair was caked, clothes torn and soiled, black plastic garbage bags wrapped around his feet. He took a fast swig from an iced-tea-filled pint of Four Roses and turned to look at the two young girls on the park bench behind him, both drinking from cups of hot chocolate. The elder of the two, running about sixteen, held a cigarette between the fingers of a gloved hand. They giggled as they talked.

He moved a few steps down, dragging his feet, one hand on the rail, eyes catching a glimpse of his target, hidden behind a tree, a quick jump from the girls on the bench.

'We got company,' Bobby Scarponi said into the top button of his torn coat. A wire transmitter was attached to a band clipped to his waist. 'About five feet from the marks.'

The two backups were in a black Plymouth hidden behind a Parks Department shack a quarter of a mile away, guns on their laps, empty coffee containers strewn about their feet.

'You sure it's him?' the one behind the wheel, T. J. Turner, asked. 'Might just be a bum takin' a piss.'

'Bums piss *in* their pants,' Bobby whispered into his coat. 'It's part of what makes them bums.'

'You would know, Rev. Jim,' Tommy Mackens said from the passenger seat. 'Never met a decoy liked to wear pissed-in clothes as much as you.'

'It's not what you wear,' Rev. Jim said, 'but how you wear it.'

'Be careful with this guy,' T. J. told him. 'He's into the pain more than the takeoff.'

'He found two soft ones tonight,' Rev. Jim said. 'Not gonna get much of a fight out of these kids.'

'Hates bums too,' Tommy said, laughing. 'Might come beat the shit out of you.'

'I'll be ready,' Bobby Scarponi said.

He moved away from the railing, staggering his walk, singing 'Bye Bye Blackbird' in a soft voice marked by a drunken tilt. He kept his eyes away from the girls, ignoring their chatter, his ears tuned only to the rustle of leaves and the rush of feet.

He was twenty yards from the two girls when the man behind the tree made his move, rushing out to stand in front of the girls, their voices silenced by the sight of a gun. He was tall and solid, a wall of muscle packed under a black set of sweats. He had a ski mask over his face and gloves to hide his fingerprints.

'Don't hurt us,' one of the girls begged. Her thin face was hidden by thick curls of brown hair.

'Kind of hurt I got, you might like,' the man answered, his voice hard and low. 'You both stand up slow and get behind that tree.'

The girls were shaking too hard to move, tears running down their faces, gloved hands gripping the sides of the bench. The man stepped closer and stroked the barrel of the gun against the side of one girl's temple, nudging the blond hair tucked beneath the flap of her pink wool hat. She didn't turn her face.

104

'I can put it inside any kind of trim,' the man said with a small boy's giggle. 'Dead or alive, don't mean shit. Now, you two gonna walk or be dragged?'

' "Here I go singing low, Bye bye blackbird." Everybody!' Bobby was up behind them now, his voice loud, the pint of Four Roses held high, a big smile on his face.

The man turned to Bobby, gun in hand, eyes lit with anger.

'Take your shit down the road, bum,' he said.

The man raised the .38 Special, placing it inches from Bobby's chest, and tightened his grip around the trigger.

Bobby was close enough now. He slapped the gun away with his left hand and smashed the pint of Four Roses on the side of the man's head. As the glass broke against bone, the ski mask was drenched in iced tea.

But the blow only dazed the larger man.

As he hurled his body on top of Bobby, both falling to the ground, he landed two solid punches to Bobby's temple and one to his lip.

'Gonna kill you, bum,' the man said, wrapping a large gloved hand around Bobby's throat and pressing down hard. 'Gonna fuckin' kill you.'

'I keep tellin' you,' Bobby managed to say, his words garbled. 'I ain't no bum.'

The two girls sat frozen in place, staring at the struggle in front of them. T. J. and Tommy started the Plymouth and roared out from behind the park station, rear tires kicking up dust and leaves, the red cherry on top of the unmarked car twirling.

Bobby turned his head slightly to the right and spotted the .38 Special on the ground, inches from his hand. His legs were wrapped tight around the man's waist. Bobby landed two quick punches to the man's face, both with little effect. He was having trouble breathing, lungs searing with pain, his throat clutching. The glare of T. J.'s headlights illuminated the man's large frame. His weight sat like a boulder on Bobby's chest.

Bobby closed his eyes, took a short breath through his

nose, and stretched the fingers of his right hand, tearing the back of his coat as it scraped across the black concrete. But he reached the .38.

T. J. and Tommy were out of the Plymouth, their guns drawn.

'Let him go,' T. J. said in a relaxed voice. 'Don't even think.'

'You can't stop me,' the man said, eyes glowing as he pressed down tighter on Bobby's throat.

'I can,' Bobby said in a raspy whisper.

He had the gun barrel inside the man's mouth.

The man looked at Bobby, whose gaze was focused and determined.

It was the look Ray Monte had seen before he died.

It was the look of a man ready to kill.

The man slowly released his grip on Bobby's throat, holding his hands out to his sides. T. J. and Tommy came up next to him, cocked guns aimed at his head. Tommy snapped a cuff around one of the man's thick wrists and clamped it shut. He swung the arm down to the man's back, took the other hand, and locked it in cuffs.

'Okay, Rev.,' T. J. said, still holding the gun on the man. 'Take the jammer outta his mouth.'

'This piece of shit,' Bobby said between coughs, gun rocking in and out against the man's teeth. 'You see what he did to me?'

'He almost killed you,' Tommy said in a soothing tone. 'But he didn't. Now let him go so we can drop him off at the station, take the girls' statements, and then go grab us a bite.'

'And if there's time,' T. J. said, a firm grip on the back of the cuffed man's jacket, 'we'll come back here and see if we can find somebody else who might wanna kill you.'

'Forget killing me,' Bobby said, his voice cracking with anger. 'The fucking bastard pissed all over me!'

Bobby sat on the living room couch, nursing a Dr. Pepper, TV tuned to a late fall Giants-Eagles football game, the

106

sound muted. Ronnie Earl and the Broadcasters were playing on the corner stereo, halfway through a rendition of 'Drown in My Own Tears'. Outside, heavy snow blanketed the streets.

Albert Scarponi walked into the room and sat on the far end of the couch, a large tumbler of red wine mixed with water and ice in his right hand. He was wearing a white sweatshirt and black jeans, his feet covered by fur-lined moccasins. He had a three-day gray stubble across his face, and his left hand was slightly swollen, a winter bout of rheumatism starting early.

They sat, as they usually did, in silence, absorbed by the game and the music.

Albert looked away from the screen and stared at his son, as if noticing him for the first time.

'Tomorrow's the memorial,' Albert said, watching Harry Carson wrap an arm around the Eagles quarterback. 'If you want, we can go together. No sense us taking two cars. Not in this weather.'

The sound of his father's voice startled Bobby. He had grown comfortable with the wall of silence that surrounded them, not quite sure how to react to the sudden cracks conversation brought.

'You sure?' Bobby asked, lifting his legs from the coffee table, eyes on his father.

His father turned his head from the television, strong hands stretched across the tops of his legs. 'I think it's time for us to go together.'

'I usually stop off and pick up some flowers first,' Bobby said.

'Pink roses,' Albert said, nodding.

'I'm sorry, Pop,' Bobby said. 'I'm sorry I took her away from you.'

Albert stared at his son, tears flowing from the corners of his eyes. 'All these years I blamed you for what happened,' he said. 'Now I think, maybe it needed to happen for things to right themselves. Maybe she put herself there thinkin' it was the only way to get her son back.'

'The man that killed Mama,' Bobby said. 'He's dead.'

'I know,' Albert said.

'I killed him,' Bobby said.

'I know that too,' Albert said. 'I don't know how your mother would have felt about you doing somethin' like that.'

'How do you feel about it?'

'I'm proud of you, Bobby,' Albert said, speaking his son's name for the first time since his wife's death.

The cardboard boxes were torn and piled high in a corner, up against the step wall of the tenement, mounds of dirty snow and torn plastic garbage bags lodged near their edges. A cold wind, whipping off corners and side streets, blew across their flaps.

Bobby Scarponi sat shivering under the mound of boxes, his back crunched against cold bricks. He had his hands wrapped around a coffee thermos and his legs were folded to his chest. He was wearing black jeans, two pull-overs, and a thick blue windbreaker. A Red Sox baseball cap rested backward on his head. A hand radio sat by his side.

'You see anything yet?' From the warmth of a parked car around the corner, Detective Tony Clifton's voice came crackling over the radio.

'Just my life flashing before my eyes,' Bobby muttered into the box, stretching out his legs and resting the warm thermos between them. 'It's early still. These guys never come out till the soap operas are done.'

'Caddy still parked down front?' Clifton asked.

'Empty and with the windows down.' Bobby stared across the deserted street at the late-model pea-green Cadillac with the Florida plates. 'Been there all day.'

'That car sticks out like a set of tits,' Clifton said. 'You'd think these guys would show some sense.'

'It ain't a Mensa reunion, Tony,' Bobby said into the radio. 'It's a drug deal. Unless your stool gave us the wrong feed time.'

'My guy's never been wrong,' Clifton said. 'Just sit tight, Rev., and let the deal go down.'

'Must be warm where you are,' Bobby said, rubbing his hands across the tops of his legs.

'Like Miami in July,' Clifton said.

'Can't wait till I'm old and slow like you, Tony. Then I can sit in a ratty car, breathing in hot, shitty air, while a real cop does all the work.'

'Tell you what, Rev. Jim,' Clifton said. 'If it gets any colder, I'll stop over at the liquor store and pick up some more boxes. Come around and toss 'em on your pile.'

'I got only two words for you, Tony,' Bobby said, his lower lip shaking. 'Carbon monoxide.' Then his eyes shifted across the street. 'We got movement,' he said into the radio.

Three men stood in a narrow doorway, hands inside their coat pockets, eyes scanning the silent street. The pea-green Cadillac was parked directly in front of them. The man in the middle, short and bald with a thick black mustache, stepped out of the shadows, moved to the car, opened the passenger door, and got in. He put a cigar with a plastic tip in his mouth and lit it.

Bobby kneeled down on a box, watching.

'Any civilians out with them?' Clifton asked.

'I wouldn't worry too much,' Bobby said. 'Everybody in this neighborhood's a phone call away from an indictment.'

'Let's keep it clear,' Clifton said. 'Just in case.'

'Money man's already in the car,' Bobby reported.

'His connect can't be too far away,' Clifton said. 'Dealers hate being out in the cold.'

'Tell me something I don't know,' Bobby whispered to himself, resting the radio by his leg.

A tan Buick ragtop, lightning bolts painted on its doors, pulled up behind the Cadillac and cut its engine. Five men sat squeezed inside, windows rolled up, breath and smoke clouding the interior.

'Elvis is in the building,' Bobby said into the radio,

moving his .38 Special out of its holster and into his right hand.

'Sit tight, Rev.,' Clifton said. 'And let it happen. Won't be long.'

The two men in coats stepped out from the litter of the doorway and walked toward the parked cars. The one on the left, head down against the cold, dug a key from his pocket and opened the trunk of the Cadillac. The one on the right, unbuttoned coat flapping in the wind, stood next to the trunk of the Buick, his hand reaching out to lift it up when the driver popped it from the inside.

Bobby pushed aside one of the box lids, watching as the two men each pulled out identical leather briefcases, walked toward one another, and made the transfer.

'Houston, we have liftoff,' Bobby said into the radio. 'Come and get 'em.'

'Hold on to your boxes, Rev.,' Clifton said, slamming a red cherry light on top of his unmarked sedan and jamming the car into gear. 'We're just a phone call away.'

'Try not to hit any innocent bystanders before you get here,' Bobby said, turning the baseball cap brim forward.

'Too late,' Clifton said with a laugh, tossing the radio onto the dashboard.

Bobby Scarponi didn't see the two teenagers.

Blanketed in the seclusion of his cardboard complex, his only focus was on the two cars, the drug deal, and the bust about to happen. He didn't see the boys carry the red canisters of gasoline down from the corner Mobil station, lids off, their brains pan-fried with an angel dust and glue omelette, looking to torch the cardboard shanty and the bum who lived inside. They moved quiet as cats, first dousing the edges and then the sides of the tenement wall.

One lit a match and the other leaned over the side of the shaky banister and poured gasoline into the small opening Rev. Jim had cleared for a view.

Then they both laughed.

Bobby knew his career was over the second he tasted

the gas and smelled the fumes, his body locked in place, a steady calm engulfing him. He watched the match float down past his shoulder and then felt the sudden rush of heat and saw the blue and yellow of the flames.

He jumped out of his inferno, clothes burning, body torched. He was all smoke and light as he rolled onto the sidewalk, leaving shreds of melted skin and burning fabric in his wake.

He heard the sound of sirens, a steady round of gunshots and shouts coming at him from all directions.

Then Bobby Scarponi stopped his roll, his charred head hanging over a cracked curb, his partner kneeling beside him, holding a gun on his lap and crying in anger to the heavens.

Rev. Jim heard and saw none of it.

He was once again living inside a dark world.

BOOK TWO

I love war and responsibility and excitement. Peace is going to be hell on me.

– General George S. Patton

7
February 21, 1982

Holding a felt hat with both hands, the man walked through the double wood front doors of Nunzio's. He squinted, his eyes adjusting to the candlelit room. He stood next to the bar, scanned the empty stools, and turned to the ten small tables lined in rows of five to his left. He looked past the young couple sharing a cold antipasto platter and the three middle-aged women shoulder-hunched over large glasses of red wine.

The face he was looking for belonged to the man at the last table, whose back was to the wall. Framed pictures of Rocky Marciano, Jersey Joe Walcott, and Carmen Basilio hung just above his head. Steam from a large bowl of lentils and sausage filtered past a set of intense eyes, right hand holding a glass half-filled with San Pellegrino.

The man at the table lifted his left hand to wave him over.

'You look like you could use something to drink, Carlo,' Boomer Frontieri said.

Carlo Santori rested his hat on the counter separating table from window, took off his overcoat, and folded it over the back of a wooden chair. Boomer signaled a waiter with two fingers and a pouring gesture, and the waiter appeared immediately with a bottle of Chianti.

'What's the favor?' Boomer asked, very quietly.

'Jenny's gone,' Carlo said, his voice cracking, words bursting out, hands gripping the table edge for support.

Boomer put his soup spoon down and took a deep

115

breath, feeling the tinge of pain from the piece of metal still embedded inside a partial lung. Then he stretched out and rubbed the side of his right leg, the one with the scars from three surgeries.

'Tell me what "gone" means,' he said.

'We went away, me and Annie, for the weekend,' Carlo told him, eyes welling up. 'Down the shore. We left Jenny and Tony alone at the house. I didn't think about anything going wrong. I mean, Jesus, we were only a phone call away. One call, Boomer, that's all.'

'What *did* go wrong?' Boomer asked. A cop's edge still colored the question and his eyes never left his friend's face.

'They took a bus into the city,' Carlo said, forcing the words out. He struggled now to lift a glass of wine to his lips. 'Tony's idea. You know the routine. Check out the city, have a little fun. Not have parents on your back all the time.'

'How far'd they get?' Boomer sipped the Pellegrino, ignoring the wine.

'Port Authority,' Carlo said. 'Tony went in to use a bathroom. Told Jenny not to move from her spot. When he got out, she was gone.'

'How long ago?'

'Three days,' Carlo said, biting his lower lip. 'Tony raced all over the terminal lookin' for her. When he gave up, he called me. I could barely make him out. Kept screamin' into the phone, "Daddy, I lost her. I lost her."'

'Who called the cops?' Boomer asked, finishing off the water. 'You or Tony?'

'He did,' Carlo said. 'By the time we got back, Tony was already over at the midtown precinct. We took him home, sat by the phone, and waited. We were still waiting when Annie told me to call you.'

'Who's on it?'

'Maloney's the lead guy,' Carlo said. 'Somebody you know?'

Boomer shook his head. 'But I've been away awhile.'

116

Carlo drained his glass of wine and sat in silence, his eyes lost in the distance. He looked over at Boomer, his face flushed. 'Tell me she's not dead, Boomer,' he managed to say. 'Please, I beg you. Tell me my baby's not dead.'

'I can't tell you what I don't know,' Boomer said, reaching a hand across the table and gripping Carlo's forearm. 'I'd only be guessing.'

'Take the guess,' Carlo said, tears sliding down his face.

'You don't have the kind of money that screams ransom.' Boomer tightened his grip around Carlo. 'And Jenny's not the runaway type. Not from what I remember.'

'Which leaves us what?' Carlo wiped his eyes with the back of a sweater sleeve. 'The truth, Boomer. I want bullshit, I can get it from any other cop.'

'Raped and left for dead.' Boomer's eyes were like hot magnets burning through Carlo's skin. 'Or waiting to be sold to a flesh buyer.'

Carlo didn't flinch. He almost looked thankful. 'I want you to find out which it is,' he said quietly. 'I don't want to find out from some fuckin' stranger.'

'I'm a retired cop with half a lung and a limp,' Boomer said, releasing his grip. 'And I've been off the job closing in on two years. There's not much I can do except put out a few calls, make sure there's the right kind of follow-up.'

'She's just another name to them,' Carlo said, his sadness bolstered by defiance. 'But she's a face to you. I've known you all my life, Boomer. I don't think you'll be happy just making a few phone calls.'

Carlo stood, reached for his hat and coat, and looked down at Boomer. 'I'll be home with Annie,' he said. 'She's counting on you too.'

'You're betting on an old horse, Carlo.' Boomer sighed. 'That's not a smart thing to do.'

'I'm betting on a friend,' Carlo said. Then he turned

117

and left Nunzio's, tables now filled with cold and hungry customers.

Boomer looked away, staring out at the windy streets of a frigid winter night. He rubbed at his leg again, the pain always sharper when the temperature dipped below thirty. He thought back to that day in the hospital bed, his small room at Metropolitan shrouded in darkness. The chief of detectives standing above him, smile on his face, a gold shield and a small medal clutched in his hands. 'It's over, Boomer,' the chief whispered. 'You can rest now.'

Resting was all he'd been doing these last two years. There were no more doors for him to kick in, no more junkies to roust, no more dealers to take down. And he missed all of it. The stakeouts, the dives into dark rooms, the split-second walk between life and death. They were now only memories.

Boomer was forty but had enough scars and twisted bones to add another ten years to his body. Carlo had walked in and asked him to go back into a game he might not be able to play anymore. A game he shouldn't be playing. The smart move would be to call his friend and tell him the truth, admit that he was too beat up, in too much pain to do the job he needed done. That he was now a runner who could barely walk.

Admit to his friend, and to himself, that he just wasn't a cop anymore.

Boomer wasn't afraid to die. But he was afraid to fail. He had come to terms with being crippled and tossed from a job he loved. He could never come to terms with being a failure.

He looked up at a night sky filled with rumbling gray clouds and watched the snowflakes start to fall.

Davis 'Dead-Eye' Winthrop stood behind the glass doors and watched the man from apartment 17B double-park a pea-green Jeep in front of the building. He saw him run from the driver's side, slip and dodge his way through slush and ice, then wait as Dead-Eye held the door open.

118

The man was in his early twenties, dressed more for a safari hunt than life on the Upper East Side. He handed Dead-Eye the keys to the Jeep.

'There are a few boxes in the back,' he said in a voice that dripped with privilege. 'Get them out for me, would you? I'll be waiting upstairs.'

'I can't leave the door,' Dead-Eye said futilely, watching the man disappear around a wall and toward the elevators.

He lifted the collar of the brown doorman's coat, pushed down his hat, and pulled on a pair of brown gloves. Dead-Eye opened the door and stepped into the cold air. He stared inside the back of the Jeep, crammed with six heavily taped packing boxes. Car horns blared as he swung the trunk lid past his face and reached for the nearest box.

No one cared anymore about who he used to be; they knew him only for what he was. It had taken eight months for Dead-Eye's wounds to heal after the elevator shoot-out. Doctors were forced to remove half his stomach and a kidney. There would always be a numbness in his throat, from a bullet fragment that had shredded pieces of his vocal cords. He had caught two shots to his right hip, which made running painful and walking a chore. The muscles on his right arm would never be the same.

Dead-Eye was no longer a cop, the disability check sent to his home twice a month a constant reminder of that. His only action now was opening and closing doors and reminding old ladies to button their coats against the winter weather. He never talked about being a doorman, not to anyone, he just did it. He handed out packages and dry cleaning to smiling faces who didn't need to know his name, buzzed in delivery men dropping off take-out Chinese and pizza boxes and complained about the Knicks and Yankees to the UPS and FedEx drivers on his route. Then he went home to his family and tried to forget it all.

He managed to get the first box to the door, straining for breath, the muscles in his back tight against his coat.

Dead-Eye went for physical therapy three times a week, fighting to keep his body in one piece. He still worked out, ignoring the pain it caused, and he ate what little he could hold in what was left of his stomach. He was a cripple, but a damn stubborn one.

It took him a full hour to get the boxes up to the front door of 17B. He was sweating and his breath came out in a wheeze as he pressed the buzzer. The man opened the door holding a glass of white wine.

'I thought you forgot about me,' he said. He pointed to the den. 'Put them in there. Gently, please.'

Dead-Eye did as he was told, refusing to let the man see his struggle, closing his eyes to the pain. He put the last box in the den and walked out the door, tipping the lip of his cap to the man.

'Wait,' the man said.

Dead-Eye turned and watched the man reach a hand into his pocket. He pulled out a thick roll of bills, peeled off a dollar, and handed it to Dead-Eye. 'This is for your troubles.'

The man closed the door. Dead-Eye stood there, sweat running down his face, his right arm trembling, his stomach cramped with pain, holding a dollar bill in a gloved hand.

He crumpled the bill, tossed it on the mat in front of the door, and walked into the elevator for the ride back down. To finish off his shift.

Boomer slid his Cadillac into an open spot next to a fire hydrant, shifted the gear to park, and let the engine idle. The windshield wipers were still on low, slowly clearing away heavy streaks of rain. He put five slices of Wrigley's spearmint gum into his mouth and watched the man walk toward him, his head down against the rain, collar of a brown leather jacket turned up to brace the wind. The sounds of Ry Cooder's rendition of 'Little Sister' filled the car's interior.

The man was less than ten feet from the car when

Boomer leaned across the front and flipped open the passenger side door. He smiled when the man drew a .44 semiautomatic from the sleeve of his leather jacket and aimed it at the steering wheel.

'Thought you'd lost your touch,' Boomer said, watching the man shove the gun back up his sleeve and slide into the car, slamming the door shut.

'Lucky for you I'm in a good mood,' Dead-Eye said, lowering his collar with one hand, rainwater dripping on the brown interior. 'Spotted you at the corner. Could have taken you out before the light turned green.'

Boomer looked over at his ex-partner and smiled. The two had remained friendly in the years since their retirement, each helping the other through the dark days of therapy and inactivity.

Dead-Eye's father had lost his battle with cancer less than six months after his son was shot in the elevator. They spent those months together, the father dying, the son often wishing he were dying too. The two men talked, cried, sometimes laughed, tightening their already strong bond. It was during those precious months that Dead-Eye's father learned how much being a cop meant to his son.

Now, Dead-Eye at least had a job to fill his idle time. Boomer's plate was empty. He refused to take any of the standard ex-cop details, passing on offers to work security, tend bar, bodyguard the rich, or turn private investigator and chase deadbeats for short money. For Boomer it was either be a cop or have nothing, and right now he was standing up against a blank wall.

'You didn't bring me any coffee,' Boomer said to Dead-Eye. 'I had my heart set on a black.'

'The only black you gonna see in this car is me,' Dead-Eye said. 'Besides which, I don't drink that shit anymore.'

'Suppose you don't have any smokes either.'

'Cigarette's just the thing for a guy with one kidney and a scarred lung,' Dead-Eye said. 'Got a mint. Would that do you?'

'I'll stick with the gum.' Boomer shifted the Caddy into drive and pulled away from the hydrant.

'Where we going?' Dead-Eye asked, popping the mint into his mouth.

Boomer ignored the question and stopped at a red light. 'You working door detail tonight?'

'Start in two hours,' Dead-Eye said.

'Can you call in sick?'

'Depends.'

'On what?'

'On what you need,' Dead-Eye said.

Boomer put his right hand into his jacket pocket, pulled out a photo of Jennifer Santori, and handed it to Dead-Eye.

'She's twelve years old and I need to find her,' Boomer said.

'Snatched?' Dead-Eye asked, staring down at the smiling girl.

'Three days ago,' Boomer said. 'Over at Port Authority. Cops working it got nothing. Father's an old friend. Called me to see what I could do, and I called you.'

'Pull over by that phone booth on the next corner,' Dead-Eye said. 'Next to the deli.'

Boomer eased the car between a dented Chevy Caprice and a VW with Met and Yankee stickers covering the front and back fenders. Dead-Eye searched his pockets for loose change, found it, and opened the passenger door.

'While you're out there,' Boomer said, 'would you get me a coffee?'

'Fuck no,' Dead-Eye said, and slammed the door behind him.

Boomer and Dead-Eye worked the city streets for two full days and nights. They walked into old haunts looking to scare up some familiar faces, only to end up staring at blank eyes. They drove past familiar corners and saw new players in control, players who didn't even bother to give the two ex-cops a second look. Two years away from the action is a lifetime in the underbelly, and the names Boomer and Dead-Eye dredged from their memory banks were now either dead or doing hard time upstate. They felt old and rusty and were in constant pain. But the more they came up empty, the more determined they grew.

They were in the final hour of their second day when they spotted the reed-thin pimp in the black leather raincoat and purple felt hat. He smiled when he saw the two ex-cops walk up to his Times Square station. The rain had let up, replaced by a soft mist.

'Didn't know you two had any taste for the deuce,' the pimp said, his smile exposing a long bottom row of silver teeth.

'Cleve, that tinfoil look you got is gonna catch on,' Dead-Eye said, patting the pimp on the shoulder and pointing to his mouth. 'Let 'em laugh much as they want. You stick with it.'

'Be hostile, bitches,' Cleve said. 'I'm still happy to see your asses.'

'We're lookin' for a girl,' Boomer said, reaching his hand into his jacket pocket.

Cleve held his smile. 'Don't know what your action is, Boom-Man, but I'm sure I got the muff to cover it.'

'A *missing* girl, asswipe,' Boomer said, jabbing Jenny's photo against the lip of Cleve's leather flaps. 'Dropped out five days ago off a Jersey bus.'

'I don't buy runaways, Boom,' Cleve said. 'My birds fly pro. Any trim I break in, I marry.'

'She's not a runaway,' Dead-Eye said. 'She's lifted.'

'To sell or snuff?' Cleve asked, eyes searching the street beyond the ex-cops' shoulders, making sure his ladies were walking their beat.

'You play the market,' Boomer said. 'Not us.'

'Street ain't the same as you left it,' Cleve said, shaking his head, voice almost nostalgic. 'This crack shit that's movin' got everybody flyin' in crazy ways.'

'Save it for Mike Wallace,' Dead-Eye said. 'All we wanna hear is you spit up some names.'

'Don't have to give you shit, Super Fly.' The smile was back on Cleve's face. 'You can't arrest me. Your badges been stamped out.'

'I never shot a pimp on the job,' Boomer said, looking away from Cleve and checking the two hookers in hot pants and fake fur standing by a pink Lincoln, shivering in their six-inch heels. 'How about you, Dead-Eye?'

'Fleshed one once in the shoulder,' Dead-Eye said. 'Up in Spanish Harlem. He ran off down the avenue, screaming like an old woman.'

'There's a hundred wacks, easy, out here movin' kids,' Cleve said. 'I ain't no fuckin' yellow pages. Can't know them all.'

Boomer looked away from the hookers and stepped in closer to Cleve, lips inches from the pimp's left ear. 'Be a pal,' Boomer whispered, 'and give us your three best names.'

'I only go by their street names,' Cleve said, eyes moving from Boomer to Dead-Eye.

'We'll take what you can give,' Dead-Eye said.

'I'd peek at a lowball PR calls himself Crow,' Cleve said, toning down his voice. 'Works the terminal, lifting boys for the chicken hawks, sometimes takes a chippie home for himself.'

'You're riding a wave, Cleve,' Boomer said. 'Don't stop it now.'

'There's this white dude rides around the deuce in out-of-state wheels,' Cleve said, lifting the front flap of his coat and pulling out a filter-tip Kool. 'Nasty piece of business. Got more tattoos than skin. Couldn't miss him if you were blind and tied to a tree.'

'We get the idea,' Dead-Eye said.

'He deals in runaways,' Cleve said, putting a lit match to the cigarette, talking as he puffed. 'Hangs on to them for a week or so, chillin' his bones, then sells 'em off to an outside shipper.'

'Nice set of friends,' Boomer said. 'I should shoot you just for knowin' 'em.'

'We only walk on the same streets, Boom,' Cleve said. 'I don't ever chop wood with shit like that. I aim my end simple and clean. Keeps my pockets filled with cash, my dick covered with pussy, and my soft ass outta jail.'

'You should have your own talk show,' Boomer said. 'Now, get back on track, Romeo. Give us up another name.'

'There's a brother calls himself X,' Cleve said, tossing the half-smoked Kool out toward the curb. 'You know, like Malcolm X?'

'Minus the religion,' Dead-Eye said.

'He's as close to Malcolm as me to the Pope,' Cleve said. 'This fucker's out there, pulls in runaways and sells them over to some uptown crew that takes 'em, fucks 'em till they're knocked up, then deals them *and* the baby. Like a two for one.'

'Jesus Christ,' Dead-Eye muttered.

'He work the area steady?' Boomer asked.

'I see him enough to make me nervous,' Cleve said. 'He don't always sell what he picks up.'

'Why's that?' Dead-Eye asked.

'Sometimes the goods are too damaged,' Cleve said. 'Buyers take a pass, if you read what I mean. He ain't happy just gettin' his rocks soft. He's into the pain.'

'He have a regular spot?' Boomer said. 'A hang place.'

'I hear he scores his dope off a dealer works the Eighth Avenue end of the Port,' Cleve said. 'That'd be where I would gaze. But then, I ain't no shot-up super cop like you two.'

'Appreciate the info, Cleve,' Boomer said. 'You ever end up doin' a stretch, we promise to visit.'

'Bring you and your prison chick some home cookin',' Dead-Eye said.

'Like being in the can ain't bad enough,' Cleve said, silver teeth gleaming under the glow of the overhead streetlight.

'Just one more thing,' Boomer said, nodding over toward Dead-Eye.

'I gave up the three.' Cleve was annoyed. 'That's all I can do for free.'

'This one won't cost,' Boomer said, smiling. 'It's just a favor, Cleve.'

'What you need?' Cleve started to slow-step it toward the parked car and the waiting hookers. 'But make it quick.'

'The name of your dentist,' Boomer said.

Boomer placed the sharp end of a pocket knife in the dealer's ear. He had his left hand wrapped around the man's throat, force-lifting him inches from the floor. The dealer was thin and bug-eyed with long, greasy black hair covering half his face.

They were inside an empty Port Authority men's room, Dead-Eye leaning his back against the front door. The dealer's glassy eyes veered from Boomer to Dead-Eye, trying to place the faces of the men who had yanked him without warning from the street and dragged him into the first open door they found.

'I *know* you guys ain't dealers,' he said. 'And I don't *think* you're cops.'

'We're priests,' Dead-Eye said.

'And we're willing to save your fucking soul,' Boomer said, lifting the dealer higher up against the side of the grimy wall. 'So the only thinkin' for you right now should be about how can I make these guys happy.'

'Take my works,' the dealer said, fear kicking his voice into a higher gear. 'Got enough for ten, maybe twelve, easy, on the street.'

'You sell smack to a low-end run chaser calls himself X,' Dead-Eye said, pointing a finger toward the knife inside the dealer's ear. 'Give us his name, unless you want to spend the rest of your life reading lips.'

'You guys lookin' for chicks, no problem, I can help you out,' the dealer said. 'X is the best. He can find a fresh piece of fur in the desert.'

Boomer slid the edge of the knife across the side of the

126

dealer's ear, bringing a thin row of blood drops flowing down his neck. 'You guys ain't fuckin' priests,' the dealer muttered.

Boomer squeezed his hand tighter against the man's throat, muffling the sounds of pain, causing his eyes to bulge. 'The name is all I wanna hear from you,' Boomer said. 'We understand each other?'

The dealer nodded and Boomer lightened his grip. 'Malcolm Juniper,' the dealer said. 'We did a spin together up at Attica.'

'Where's he sleep?' Dead-Eye asked, popping four Maalox tablets into his mouth.

'Here and there,' the dealer said. 'No place steady. He's only been loose a few weeks.'

'Where's he sleeping tonight?' Boomer asked, wiping the knife blade on the sleeve of the dealer's torn velvet jacket. Then he took a handkerchief from his pants pocket and handed it to the dealer. 'Clean that blood off your ear,' he told him. '*After* you answer the question.'

'He's been stayin' at a park-and-lock on Thirty-ninth Street,' he said, putting the handkerchief next to his ear. 'Put down enough for a four-day stay.'

'When?' Dead-Eye asked.

'Yesterday,' the dealer said. 'Day before, maybe.'

'Don't be wrong,' Boomer said.

He turned away from the dealer and walked toward Dead-Eye and the exit door, slipping the closed knife into his back pocket.

'You think I'm gonna need stitches for this cut?' the dealer asked, jabbing the blood-soaked handkerchief against his wound. 'It feels pretty deep.'

'We ain't doctors either,' Dead-Eye said as he closed the door behind him.

Malcolm Juniper was twenty-seven years old and four weeks removed from a three-year spin at Attica prison on a rape and molestation conviction when he had spotted the teary-eyed girl from across the street. He smiled, took a hit off a joint, and turned the engine over on his cherry-red Chrysler Imperial. Ramming the gear stick into drive, he angled his way across the busy intersection, his glassy eyes barely aware of the traffic, smelling his prey.

'You look like you could use some help, sugar,' were Malcolm's first words to Jennifer Santori. He was leaning across the front seat, talking through an open window.

'I'm okay,' she managed to say. Jennifer stared at his scarred and chapped lips and the fingers of one hand that gripped the steering wheel.

'You okay, you wouldn't be standing out in the rain,' Malcolm said with a laugh. 'Be somewhere safe. Warm. Be with family.'

'I am with family,' Jennifer said.

'All I see is you,' Malcolm said.

'My brother,' Jennifer said, turning away to look past the car, down the distant streets. 'I'm here with my brother. He had to use a bathroom. Told me to wait for him here.'

Jennifer was lying. She was lost and looked it. It was so stupid of her not to wait for Anthony outside the bathroom door as he had asked. But he had taken such a long time, like he always did at home, and she just couldn't wait anymore. Not with all those people rushing past, some looking at her and smiling, others staring with empty eyes, dirty clothes held together by rope and cloth. Then there was the horrible smell, strong as a punch, of dried urine sprayed across walls and stuck to the floor. Jennifer clasped a gloved hand to her mouth and swallowed the urge to vomit.

She needed to get out. Just for a few minutes.

She rode an escalator up toward fresh air, which she welcomed with a deep breath. The ride was slow and creaky, and the guttural shouts of eager newsboys hawking morning papers filtered down toward her. She stepped carefully off the escalator, turned left, and was soon washed into a swarm of people moving with concerted speed to a variety of destinations. There was a smile on her face, and her curiosity overwhelmed, for the briefest moment, her fear of the unknown.

She was walking the streets of a city she had always heard about and seen perhaps ten times in her life. It was the city her brother talked about with a sense of wonder. The same city her father faced daily with dread and unease and her mother reserved for special occasions. She was in it alone, at pace with the people who called it home, in step with the hungry and the moneyed, the desperate and the dreamers.

She had crossed three streets before the warmth of adventure was replaced by cold awareness. She turned and tried to make her way back. It took a few moments, two wrong turns, and a quick run against a flashing light before she knew the truth.

The dream weekend she and her brother had planned had turned a dark corner.

And on that corner lurked Malcolm Juniper.

'Be better for you to wait in a dry place,' Malcolm said to her, reaching across to the passenger side door.

The light facing Jennifer turned from red to green, but she didn't move. 'He must have stopped to get something to eat,' she said.

'Well, I don't see him anyplace here,' Malcolm said. 'C'mon, sugar,' he added, throwing open the passenger door, 'least let me take you round the block – he's probably just on the other side.'

Jennifer hesitated before stepping into the car, too frightened to recall her father's constant litany of caution. She slammed the car door shut.

Malcolm Juniper walked out of the deli entrance and spotted Boomer and Dead-Eye coming toward him from across the street. Even from a distance, the two men, one favoring his right leg, the other breathing through his mouth, smelled like cop. Malcolm gripped the large paper bag filled with a six-pack of Colt .45 malt and turned the corner, trying to hold on to his calm, knowing the two men would be fast on him. Even if they grabbed him, they didn't have much. He wasn't armed, had clocked in regular with his parole officer, and had applied for work at three fast-food outfits. The very model of a parolee and the last man any cop could finger for a street kidnapping.

But Malcolm Juniper was a career criminal who had spent the better part of his adult years behind the cold bars of a lockup. His ex-con's survival instinct told him that the two men tracking him had no interest in probable cause or Miranda rights. These two looked serious, so they either wanted a snitch out, which would put Malcolm in street trouble, or they knew about the girl, which could land him behind bars until coffin time. Either way, Malcolm Juniper wasn't going in. Not on this day.

He crossed against the light, moving up to Fortieth and Eighth. The street was filled with early-morning stiffs heading out of the terminal and into work. Side streets were clogged with traffic, Jersey plates trying to squeeze into twelve-buck-a-day garage slots. The two men had drawn closer, walking less than twenty feet behind him, the white guy sure to be the first one to make the move, the brother not looking to be one to jump and tear on the street. But then, the worst beatings Malcolm Juniper ever took were from black badges and, if anything, the one stalking him looked fit to hand out the punishment.

Malcolm was straight enough to know not to outfight them, and he wasn't in the mood to deal with their shake-down shit, and he sure as sin wasn't going to be dragged to the house to be fingered on something he didn't do. It left him only one viable option, and he took it as soon as he crossed Forty-first and turned right, heading down Ninth Avenue toward less congested streets.

Malcolm tossed the bag filled with the Colts over his shoulder and started to run, heading for the rummy shacks down by the West Side Highway.

'Rabbit's on the go, Boom,' Dead-Eye shouted, starting to take chase.

'Let's try and keep him alive,' Boomer said, running alongside. 'For a change.'

'You're talking like a civilian now,' Dead-Eye said, ignoring the pain in his chest as he ran.

'He's makin' for the highway,' Boomer said, wincing from the pressure the hard concrete was putting on his bad leg. 'We gotta cut him off by the time he gets to Tenth.'

'If *we* make it to Tenth,' Dead-Eye said, starting to slow his pace, the burn in his chest growing with every deep breath.

'We're makin' him look like Jesse Owens,' Boomer said, the frustration in his voice spiking as high as the pain.

'With us chasin', *everybody's* Jesse Owens,' Dead-Eye said, wiping a hand across his forehead, brushing away cold drops of sweat.

They stopped next to a cab stand, both gasping for air, bent over, hands to knees, faces twisted in pain, Malcolm Juniper long gone from their sights.

Dead-Eye took a step back and leaned his aching body against a taxi. 'What are we doin'?' he said angrily. 'We're finished, man. This shit ain't for us anymore. We're done, you and me, and we got the papers to prove it.'

'It's just a little rust,' Boomer wheezed, walking in small circles, willing the pain in his chest and leg to flee from him as fast as Malcolm had. 'We've just gotta get our timing back.'

'We got all the timing we need,' Dead-Eye said, his voice wistful. 'Me for being a doorman and you for lifting a pasta fork.'

'You can't walk away from this,' Boomer said, grabbing Dead-Eye's jacket. 'It's all you know. And it's all I got.'

'I'm sorry about your friend's kid,' Dead-Eye said, slowly easing Boomer's hand away. 'And I wanted to help. But she don't need me. She needs a *cop* to help her. A *real* cop. Not some guy trying to remember what it was to be one.'

Dead-Eye patted Boomer's arm, braced his jacket

131

against the cold, and headed toward Eighth Avenue. Boomer stood and watched him, his breath still coming hard, the pain fading, tears rolling down the side of his nose. He walked over toward the front steps of a tenement, ignoring the stares of the cabdrivers on break. There were three garbage cans lined in front of the basement apartment. He flipped the lid off the nearest packed can, picked it up, lifted it to chest level, and heaved it into the street. He stared at the bags of waste as they weaved into the wind, loose strips of greasy foil and paper towels slapping against the sides of parked cars. He saw the dented can rumble down the sharp incline and come banging to a stop next to a no parking sign.

Boomer Frontieri looked over at the drivers, who stared back at him in silence. He took a deep breath and walked away, hands inside his pockets, leg still burning from the run, moving slowly down the quiet street, nothing ahead of him but time.

8

Malcolm Juniper stood in a dark corner of the one-room apartment and stared over at Jennifer Santori. The girl's face was tear-lined and bruised; her bare arms were extended, wrists locked in a set of cuffs attached to the top of a radiator pipe. She was naked from the waist up, thin legs bunched against the side of her hips, her frail body shivering in the cold emptiness of the room.

'You must be somebody special,' Malcolm said, eyes glaring down at the unformed breasts, 'cops be chasin' me way they did.'

Jennifer looked at the man she once believed would help her find her brother and tried to form the words to beg for her release. She forced her eyes to wipe away the blurry images and bring Malcolm Juniper into a clear focus. Her throat burned and her damaged body ached and she wanted more than anything to be back in the safe womb of the New Jersey home she so often used to think of as a dull prison.

It seemed like months since he had driven her around the Port Authority area for the better part of an hour, a concerned look etched across his brow, playing the role of Good Samaritan. He parked and ran out to buy her a Pepsi and a hot dog from an all-night stand, returning with the food, a smile, and a sincere reassurance that her brother would be found.

Jennifer grew tired, eyelids itching and burning from lack of sleep. Long bus rides tended to make her groggy, and that, coupled with the anxiety over losing Anthony, made it all the easier for her to ease into the backseat of the car, as Malcolm suggested, and curl up to nap while he continued his search, looking for a boy he had no intention of finding.

She woke up with his mouth over her lips. He forced himself on her for the better part of three hours, slapping her face and arms, running lit matches down the sides of her thighs and across her breasts during his restful moments. He poured cheap whiskey down her throat, laughing with glee when she coughed up the foul taste. He lit a crack pipe and forced the smoke of the cooked cocaine into her lungs, holding her head back, pushing her down deep into the rear cushion of the car.

They were parked in an abandoned lot near the Fourteenth Street meat market, the windows rolled up and steamed with breath and smoke, an overhead streetlight casting the car in its cloudy glow. He cuffed her hand to one door handle and her foot to another and forced a handkerchief into her mouth while he went out for cigarettes. He came back a short time later with another man, stoop-shouldered, haggard, and crazed, and let him have at her for the price of a Big Mac and a large Coke.

She blacked out during the final rape, letting the pain, the drugs, and the drink whisk her away on a blanket of dreams.

When she woke, she was handcuffed to a radiator, head pounding. She opened her eyes slowly, the room revealing itself in an array of shadows as streams of light flashed in from the streets outside. Her legs felt weighed down and her arms were cold and numb, dangling from the pipe above her head. She had trouble breathing, the insides of her lungs and nostrils scorched from their cocaine and whiskey diet.

Malcolm Juniper stood above her, wearing only a pair of brown socks, a crazed smile on his face, crack pipe in his right hand, kitchen knife dangling from his left.

'We're low,' Malcolm said, running the crack pipe past

her eyes. 'More's on the way. Junior's gettin' over a fresh load that'll turn your eyes. Won't be long.'

Jennifer stared up at him, biting down on her lower lip, her teeth breaking through the cracked and sore exterior, droplets of blood forming on the edges.

'Are you going to kill me?' she asked.

The words pressed themselves out slowly, each one enclosed in layers of pain and embarrassment. She wanted so much to cry, to shout out for help, but couldn't muster the strength required. Instead, she took in another long, painful breath and asked him again, 'Are you going to kill me?'

Malcolm Juniper crouched down and rested the crack pipe on the floor between them. He brought the sharp end of the knife up across the side of Jennifer's neck and pressed it tight against her skin. He reached up and rubbed her arms with his free hand.

'Killin' you be like burnin' money,' Malcolm said in as soothing a voice as he could muster. 'You worth way too much. I'm gonna make me a killin' all right. But it ain't the kind you be thinkin'.'

'I just want to go home,' Jennifer said to him, the rush of his acid breath warm on her cheeks. 'I won't say anything about this. Or about you. I'll just say I got lost.'

'You gonna be goin' home, baby,' Malcolm said, still in his seductive voice. 'Be a different home, is all. But that's down the road a ways. Right now you and me got to be thinkin' about Junior and how we need to make him a happy man.'

'Why are you doing this to me?' Jennifer wailed, more with confusion than with anger.

'You pay the good price for good smoke,' Malcolm said, looking past Jennifer, eyes and mind adrift on their own. 'And nobody's got better smoke than Junior. It's worth it. Whatever the price, it's gonna be worth it.'

'Why? Tell me why?' Jennifer begged in the soundless room, her upper body trembling from the sharp wind creeping through the cracked walls.

135

'Junior ain't normal like you and me,' Malcolm said, easing the knife away from Jennifer's throat. 'He don't give a five-cent fuck about money. So you can't just up and pay him out for the smoke. Cares even less about pussy, so there ain't no sense askin' him to a slow dance with you.'

Jennifer closed her mouth and eyes, rushing breath through her nose, choking back a violent need to vomit.

'Junior's religious,' Malcolm said, standing now, brushing the knife against the sides of Jennifer's arms. 'Fucker walks around prayin' all the time. He's into that voodoo shit, where you kill a cat or a dog, drink the blood, burn the bodies. But he always keeps somethin' for himself. Bone, tooth, nail, eyes. Hangs them on a gold chain around his neck. Keeps away what looks to do him in.'

Jennifer coughed up a mouthful of thick bile and spat it out on the floor, inches from the crack pipe resting on its side. Malcolm ignored it, running the knife slowly between the fingers of the girl's hands.

'So I'm thinkin' you and me, we gotta give Junior a little present,' Malcolm said. 'Somethin' he's gonna wanna have hangin' around that chain. You know what that present's gonna be, don't you, baby?'

Jennifer's eyes widened, the sudden rush of fear forcing her back to push against the wall and her hands to clench into tight fists. Malcolm whistled Otis Redding's 'Sittin' by the Dock of the Bay' as he undid the fingers of Jennifer's left hand. She kicked her legs at his side and tried to get close enough to bite, but he shouldered her head away and pried loose the index finger.

'Don't fight me, baby,' he said in a vacant voice. 'It's only a gift.'

Boomer stood halfway down the alley, back resting against a Jimi Hendrix poster, eating a cold slice of anchovy pizza and holding a cup of hot black coffee. He was wearing an unzipped black leather jacket, crisp jeans, work boots, and a blue Yankee cap. He had a .22 in the front pocket of the leather and a .44 semiautomatic tucked in the back of the jeans. He chewed the pizza, sipped the coffee, and studied the early-morning Harlem street, filled with blue collars on their way to union jobs, and on-the-nods half hanging near tenement doorways, dreaming of the next place to score.

Boomer took a final bite of the pizza, dropped the crust into the coffee container, and tossed them both into an open garbage can.

He took a deep breath and walked out of the alley.

He hadn't slept all night, sitting straight up in a lounge chair in his silent apartment, staring out into the cold air of an open window. For the first time in memory, Boomer Frontieri was a frightened man. He had adjusted to living with the pain of his disability, soaking the throbbing aches in his leg and chest not with pills doctors prescribed but with daily doses of the homemade red wine Nunzio had stored in his basement. It was the vague discontent that ate away at Boomer and ground his insides into thick masses of bubbly tension. He felt adrift and helpless.

Boomer wasn't expecting much when he retired from the job, and he wasn't disappointed. There were no official notices, no members of the top brass walking up to shake his hand and thank him for all the long hours he put in and for all the years he spent crouched in danger, waiting to give or take a bullet. He had made more than eight thousand arrests in his career with a conviction rate that needled out at 94 percent, and that didn't even get him so much as a nod from the file clerk behind the mesh cage who took his retirement papers, stamped them, and turned back to her coffee and soap opera.

Common sense told him that the girl was either dead or long gone from the area. But the cop inside shoved common sense aside and let the power and ego of the shield take charge. If she was alive, and if she was to be found, then Boomer Frontieri was the only cop, disabled or not, who could bring her home. He believed it with all the strength left in a body that had so recently betrayed him during that futile chase down a Manhattan side street.

It was why he had stayed up all night and why he was back there now, coming out of an alley off a Harlem corner, heading for a brownstone brothel run by a 350-pound madam with a glass eye.

If Boomer Frontieri's ride as a cop was going to come to an end, he wasn't going to let it be with him leaning against the side of a yellow cab, clutching at the cold air for breath, a circle of foreign drivers mingling around him, as indifferent to his plight as the pencil stubs down at One Police Plaza. After all the years and busts and chases and gunfights, Boomer needed to stamp a better ending to it all.

The ending required him to find Jennifer Santori. And maybe, if luck traveled down the same path, he would die in the triumph.

Boomer crossed the intersection, ignoring the light and walking against oncoming clusters of gypsy cabs on the prowl for downtown passengers, and headed toward the well-kept brownstone. He had his hands in his jeans pockets and his head down from the wind, lost in a whirl of thought. He heard the footsteps of the man coming up behind him, and saw the shape of the large shadow start to overtake his own.

He stopped walking and turned.

'Don't tell me,' Boomer said. 'You could have taken me out anytime you wanted.'

'Back in the alley,' Dead-Eye agreed. 'Head shot right into the garbage can.'

'I thought you were too old and shot up for this shit,' Boomer said, looking over at him. 'Or am I going deaf too?'

'I *am* too old and shot up,' Dead-Eye said. 'And so are you.'

'But you're here,' Boomer said.

'You and me broke every case we ever worked on,'

138

Dead-Eye said. 'They took us off the job because we were *wounded*. Not because we couldn't solve cases.'

'I'm goin' up to see Bel,' Boomer said, nodding toward the brownstone. 'You want in?'

'Just to talk?' Dead-Eye said, stepping up alongside Boomer. 'Anything more, I'll wait for you here.'

'I *never* need to do anything with Bel that doesn't involve talk,' Boomer said, walking up the brownstone steps. 'When that day comes, then I'll *want* you to take me out.'

'You wake up next to Bel,' Dead-Eye said, 'and it'll be my pleasure.'

Bel stirred a large cup of black coffee with a thick wooden spoon, her glass eye gleaming under the glare of the dining room chandelier. Boomer and Dead-Eye sat across from her, squeezed in together on a red velvet love seat. The five-room railroad apartment was well furnished and clean, its windows covered by red satin drapes, the wood floors hidden beneath thick shag carpets. Ornate lights with low-watt bulbs shaded by starched white handkerchiefs hung from every ceiling. A blanket of incense filtered through the halls, blending easily with varied scents of perfume and lingering marijuana smoke.

Bel sat on an overstuffed lounge chair, arms and hips resting against a variety of soft fluffed pillows. She was a large woman with an easy manner, round folds of black skin barely hidden by a sheer nightgown and a flowered purple robe. Her fingernails were long, each painted a different shade. Her chubby, unlined face was free of makeup, and her large feet were curled comfortably beneath her robe.

She flicked a gold-plated lighter and lit the end of a filter-tipped Lord cigarette. As she took in a deep drag, smoke curled up in small clouds in front of her damaged right eye. She kept stirring her coffee and smiled at the two former detectives.

'You boys looking for some security work?' Bel asked

in a voice treacherous as an ocean wave. 'Help me protect my girls against bad company?'

'We're not here for work, Bel,' Boomer said. 'We're looking for a girl.'

'Used to throw them at you for free back when you were badges,' Bel said, holding up her cup with a large paw of a hand, fat hiding any traces of knuckles, smile still on her face. 'You weren't interested then. Maybe now that you're both older, a piece of the triangle isn't as easy to come by.'

'We don't want one of yours,' Dead-Eye said. 'No offense.'

'None taken, sweetskin,' Bel said, swallowing down two large gulps of coffee. 'But just so you understand, I don't feed off another table. You want somebody else's girl, you got to go talk to somebody else.'

Boomer stood, took the picture of Jennifer Santori out of the front pocket of his leather jacket, and placed it on the circular table next to Bel's ashtray. He returned to his place next to Dead-Eye.

'She was lifted out of the Port Authority six days ago,' Dead-Eye said. 'We caught a bead on the lifter, a street rodent calls himself X. Real name's Malcolm and he deals in young trade, selling runaways and lost girls on the market.'

'Sounds like you know as much about this Malcolm as I could tell you,' Bel said. 'Besides, you know my trade is clean. I deal only in pros. I don't buy fresh meat.'

'We need you to tell us who does, Bel,' Boomer said. 'We've been off the loop the last few years.'

Bel picked up Jennifer's picture and studied it with her one good eye.

'Pretty girl,' Bel said. 'Twelve, maybe thirteen. And she's white. People be willing to pay extra for that.'

'Those are the people we want to meet,' Boomer said.

'The sort of business you're hunting has never been lacking for a crowd,' Bel said, placing the picture back against the ashtray, a fresh cigarette in her mouth. 'It's like selling a car. Once you sign over the papers, you pocket the money and never see the car again. It's the same with flesh. Except there's more money and no papers to sign.'

'If you were Malcolm, who'd you be lookin' to sell the girl to?' Dead-Eye asked.

'If I was Malcolm, honey, I'd swallow rat poison.' A look of disdain creased the rolls around Bel's face.

'Let's go one better, then,' Boomer said. 'Who's the last guy you'd like to see one of your girls end up with?'

Bel stared across the table at Boomer and Dead-Eye, the cigarette dangling from a corner of her lower lip, the glass eye locked on them in a dead gaze. She took in a deep breath, lungs filling with smoke, and rested the back of her large neck against the side of one of the soft pillows.

'Walt Billings,' she said. 'They call him Junior on the outside. He's a white guy with a rich daddy and a pretty sick sense of what passes for jewelry.'

'How sick?' Dead-Eye asked.

Bel lowered her voice to a near whisper. 'He collects body parts. Hangs them around his neck, wrists, ankles. God only knows where else. When Junior feels the need to add to his collection, he trades a lifter some dope for a girl. Usually a girl the cops have given up for dead. If that child in that picture ends up with Junior, you both pray for her to die.'

'Where's he shop?' Boomer asked, standing again, lifting the collar on his jacket and slipping a hand into his front jeans pocket.

'Manhattan mostly,' Bel said, finishing off the last of her coffee. 'Steers himself clear of the outside boroughs. I'm surprised you two never ran into him all those years you were out busting heads with the sinners.'

'If we'd run into him, we wouldn't be talkin' about him now,' Dead-Eye said, nodding his head toward Bel and walking over to the double-latched front door.

'Thanks for the news, Bel,' Boomer said. 'Anything I can throw your way?'

'Label it as a favor for an old friend,' Bel said, pursing her thick lips and tossing a kiss at Boomer. 'Tell you what, though. If I hear that Junior somehow landed faceup in a pine box, I wouldn't be short of smiles.'

'I just love it when I can make a woman smile,' Boomer said.

Malcolm and Junior both ordered large papaya drinks, leaning forward against the counter of a Times Square food stand, watching a thin black teen with a shaved head reach for two paper cups.

'Squeeze it out right, little man,' Malcolm said to the teen. 'I'm lookin' to drink juice, not foam.'

The teen looked blankly back at Malcolm and nodded.

'How come you didn't bring the girl down?' Junior asked. 'You know I hate payin' for what I haven't seen.' He was tall and solid, his body pumped by a personal trainer three mornings a week in a chic downtown gym. He was in his early twenties and had a handsome, unlined face topped by a mane of thick, blond, designer-cut hair, gelled straight back. He wore only expensive imported clothes bought and paid for by an indulgent mother he saw less than five times a year.

'Can't risk it out here,' Malcolm said with a flashy smile. 'But I did bring you a taste.'

Junior's eyes widened as Malcolm slipped a hand into a side pocket and came out holding a thick roll of toilet paper. He handed the wad to Junior.

'What's in it?' Junior said, his voice filled with Christmas morning excitement.

'A gift,' Malcolm said. 'Just to show my heart's in the right place.'

Junior carefully unrolled the toilet paper, turning his back on Malcolm and the teen. He covered it back up and put it inside his shirt pocket. 'Thank you,' he said, turning back to Malcolm. 'I really do thank you.'

'No sweat,' Malcolm said.

Junior took his cup of papaya from the teen. 'How

142

much you want for this fine little one?' he asked, taking a long drink, ignoring the thin line of orange foam it left across his upper lip.

'A week's worth,' Malcolm said. 'I need off the street for a few days. Get lost inside of some good shit, but I don't wanna end up dead doin' it. That's why I come to see Junior. You always deal me the best.'

'A week's expensive, Malcolm,' Junior said, shaking his head and finishing off his drink. 'I don't know what you think I am, but I'm not here to be taken.'

'I *know* what you are.' Malcolm stared back at Junior, holding his half-empty cup at chest level.

Junior's eyes turned to rocks and the muscles around his jaw clenched. 'What is that?' he said, his voice cold, his body taut. 'What do you think I am, Malcolm?'

Malcolm was quick to sense the abrupt change in Junior's body temperature, and he had heard enough street talk about his flash temper to know that he could easily be left for dead with a half-finished papaya cup in his hand.

'You a businessman, Junior,' Malcolm said, showing off his sweetest smile. 'That's what you are. A businessman. One of the smartest around.'

Junior tossed his empty cup into a trash bin to his left. The tension in his body eased, his shoulders relaxed, and a soft look returned to his eyes. 'Okay, then,' Junior said. 'Let's you and me do us some business.'

'What time?'

Junior flicked his wrist and checked his Rolex. 'Anytime after seven,' he said over his shoulder as he walked slowly toward the stairs that would take him out of the Times Square station and into the street. 'And clean her up before you bring her over.'

'I'll scrub the soap on her myself, Junior,' Malcolm said, smiling at the teen and pocketing the change that was left behind. 'Bring her by clean and fresh as a newborn baby.'

Boomer shoved his shield into the doorman's face and put an index finger to his shaky lips.

'Billings,' Boomer said. 'Floor and number.'

'Sixteen A,' the doorman said, sweat starting to form around the edges of his cap. 'But he's not there. He's out.'

'Got a key?' Boomer asked.

'Super has all the keys,' the doorman said. 'He lives around the corner, first apartment after the mailboxes.'

'Go tell him you need the key to 16A,' Boomer said. 'Tell him the tenant locked himself out, you'll have it back to him in a few minutes.'

'What if he doesn't believe me?' the doorman asked.

'Then you tell him there's a crazy cop out here with a gun just burnin' to put a hole in his chest,' Dead-Eye said.

'Go ahead, kid,' Boomer told the still-shaking doorman, putting his shield back in his pocket. 'Convince him. We'll watch the desk while you're gone. My friend here's in the business.'

Boomer and Dead-Eye stood behind a circular mahogany desk, staring down at a series of camera banks covering the building and elevators from all angles and a three-unit computerized phone system.

'Most of the doorman buildings have setups like this?' Boomer asked, clicking the cameras on at different locations.

Dead-Eye nodded. 'The ones with money do. This system's pretty new. Can't be more than a year old. Guy working the desk controls the elevator. You tell him the floor, he hits the button from here.'

'So you can get off only at the floor he presses,' Boomer said.

'Cuts down on break-ins,' Dead-Eye said. 'And you can clock who went to what floor at what time.'

'It work both ways?' Boomer asked. 'Up and down?'

'Just coming in. When you leave the apartment is still your business. It's when you enter that everybody knows.'

'What the guy at the desk doesn't know, these cameras do,' Boomer said, running a hand across the monitors. 'Every corner's covered.'

'It's like that in the building I work,' Dead-Eye said. 'I can tell you who throws out his trash and when they do it.'

'Anything happens up there with Junior,' Boomer said. 'We make sure it happens *inside* the apartment. Last thing we want is our mugs on these camera reels.'

'They'll catch us going in,' Dead-Eye said.

'Then we make our play out on the street,' Boomer said, looking up and seeing the doorman walk toward them. 'Or at a safer drop. For the record, we're here just to talk to the man.'

'You talk,' Dead-Eye said. 'I'll listen.'

'Don't matter if you talk or not,' Boomer said, slapping Dead-Eye on the back and smiling. 'We get pinched, you're the one's going to be put away.'

'How you figure?'

'White guy always walks,' Boomer said. 'Black guy takes the fall.'

'You sound exactly like my father,' Dead-Eye said as he shut down the cameras that covered the perimeter and hallways on the sixteenth floor.

'And mine,' Boomer said.

They walked out from behind the counter, nodded at the doorman, took the set of keys from his hand, and headed for the open elevator door.

They stood in the center of the two-bedroom apartment overlooking the Manhattan skyline, surrounded by a blend of leather and chrome furniture, six-figure paintings, sculptures resting on antique surfaces, and religious artifacts, all of which highlighted human and animal sacrifice.

'We don't need to take a poll to figure out how fucked up Junior is,' Boomer said.

'A goat head on the wall is always a giveaway,' Dead-

Eye pointed out. 'And you can't afford to miss the view over by the fireplace.'

Boomer turned and stared at a circular pattern of various animal parts nailed to the wall above the center fireplace, dried blood lining the sides like thin streak prints. Below them was a round oak-wood table covered by an assortment of candles of different sizes.

'A lot of what's up there's only a few days old,' Boomer said, taking a few steps closer, eyes studying the wall. 'This guy likes his kill fresh.' At that moment Junior's key jangled in the latch.

If Junior was surprised to see them, he didn't show it.

He took the key from the lock, slid it back into his pocket, and closed the door softly behind him. He had a lit cigarette cupped in his right hand, and tossed his Bill Blass lamb's-wool coat onto the back of a dining room chair. He was wearing cuffed tan slacks, brown loafers with tassels, a button-down cream-colored Calvin Klein shirt, and a brown Hickey-Freeman jacket. Everything about Junior smelled of money and upbringing.

'You two look too stupid to be burglars,' Junior said, smiling and sitting down in a leather recliner. 'So I figure you must be cops. Am I right?'

Boomer walked over to Junior and stared down at him for several seconds before he slapped him across the face with the back of his hand, the hard crack echoing through the room. A red finger welt covered Junior's face from the side of his head to his jawline.

'I have a few questions I need to ask,' Boomer said in a calm voice, feeling the cop gears clicking back in. 'And I want the answers I'm expecting.'

'And if I decide to tell you shit?' Junior said, his arrogance only slightly tempered. 'What then, assholes?'

Boomer reared back and landed another slap across the same side of the face, only this one was harder. A thin line of blood formed on Junior's lower lip.

'I ask the questions,' Boomer said. 'You're here only to give the answers.'

Junior wiped the blood from his mouth with the back of his hand. He looked past Boomer and over to Dead-Eye. 'And what's the nigger here to do?' Junior asked with a smirk. 'Take notes?'

This time Boomer punched him flush to the forehead, sending Junior's head snapping against the back of the recliner, a large red blotch forming in the center of his head, just above his nose, which was now flowing blood down to his mouth.

'Be polite,' Boomer said. 'It counts toward your final grade.'

'You two have no idea who you're playing with,' Junior said, trying to sound tough, blood running past his chin and down onto his shirt collar. 'None at all. If my father knew any of this, he would have the both of you in jail before dark.'

'Pop ever been up here?' Dead-Eye asked. 'Check out your collection? Or he just pays out whenever psycho son gets jammed up?'

'You're gonna be a dot on the sidewalk outside before your father even knows where the fuck you are,' Boomer said. 'So save the my-daddy's-rich routine for people who scare easy. Now, I wanna know names and places and I'm gonna get them from you. If I don't, I start putting *your* body parts up there on the wall. Nod if you're starting to understand.'

Junior nodded, blood streaming down the front of his shirt, his arrogance giving way to uneasiness.

Boomer snapped open the top two buttons of Junior's shirt, exposing a gold chain around his neck. Boomer's fingers slowly began to scan the items hanging down from it. They were dried animal parts mostly – teeth, nails, stretched skin.

Boomer stopped when he saw the finger.

It was human and the cut was fresh, pink polish still gleaming on the nail. The flesh around the finger was unlined, free of scars and the bruises of age. It belonged to someone young, and the lack of calluses confirmed to Boomer that that someone was a girl.

A hard look filled Boomer's eyes and Junior was quick to catch it. Fear started to creep into his voice.

'I don't know where that came from,' Junior said. 'I swear to you. It was a gift.'

'Hey, Dead-Eye,' Boomer said, his eyes not moving away from Junior.

'Yeah, Boom?' Disgust etched across the angles of Dead-Eye's face.

'I think I just came up with plan B,' Boomer said.

Malcolm put a light to the top end of the sheer plastic pipe and closed his eyes, letting the thin vapors of smoke fill his lungs and jolt his brain. His lips curled into a smile as he rested the hot pipe on his lap and looked across at the man with the long scar running down the right side of his face. The man sat with his legs crossed, staring out onto the empty side street.

They were in the back of a new four-door Cadillac that had plush leather seats and a well-stocked bar. A driver in a dark blue suit sat up front, keeping the engine on idle and the car warm.

'I never smoked rock was this clean,' Malcolm said, the smile on his face growing wider, his words coming out slow and slurred.

The man turned from the window and looked at Malcolm, eyes hidden by a pair of dark, wraparound ski shades. 'You supply what I need, Malcolm,' the man said, his lips barely moving as he spoke, 'and you'll die with a clean pipe in your hand.'

'A man can't ask for more,' Malcolm said with a nervous laugh.

'A man like you shouldn't,' the man said.

He had jumped out in front of Malcolm by the Eighth Avenue side of the Lincoln Tunnel entrance. A smart man in a smart suit, standing by a new car, wanting to talk

148

over a little business. He said he got Malcolm's name from Smiley Glimmer and was waiting there, ready to offer him all the free smoke he could handle. All Malcolm had to do in return was sit back in the car, get high, and listen.

Malcolm was in a hurry, rushing to get back to his room. He planned to wash down the taste of the girl with a week's supply of smoke Junior was going to dish as payoff. But the promise of a taste of rock, a taste that cost more than Malcolm would see in a year, was too strong for him to pass up. Besides, taking a couple of slides off the pipe would put him in a better mood, make him enjoy the girl even more before he handed her over to Junior.

The driver never spoke and the man only in short sentences. The man put a hand into his coat pocket and handed Malcolm two more cocaine rocks.

'These are for later,' the man said. 'Help you get to sleep the right way.'

'What's your market?' Malcolm asked, shoving the rocks into his shirt pocket.

'Girls,' the man said, lifting the crack pipe back to Malcolm's lips and lighting it with a flick of a gold butane. 'The younger the better.'

'Only kind I know to deal in,' Malcolm said, drawing in a deep breath. The smoke turned the soft skin behind his eyes a cloudy shade of gray.

'And there's one other thing,' the man said, smiling for the first time.

'What's that gonna be?' Malcolm asked.

'Babies,' the man said.

'Babies?' Malcolm held the pipe inches away from his mouth. 'What kind of babies?'

'The kind that cry till you rock them,' the man said, turning his attention back to the street. 'The ones that make men smile and women want to hold.'

'These babies for you?' Malcolm asked, still confused by the request.

149

The man turned back and looked at Malcolm. He removed the shades, dark eyes cutting a sharp path past the crack smoke and Malcolm's dulled senses. He reached a hand into his shirt pocket and slid out a black business card.

'For my boss,' the man said. He handed the card to Malcolm, who stared down at it, glassy eyes unable to read the name and Arizona address stenciled across the front in white letters.

'Keep it,' the man told Malcolm. 'And remember the name. When you have something, you call that number and someone will find you.'

'How much?' Malcolm asked, slipping the card into his jeans.

'Ten thousand for a baby,' the man said, putting the shades back on. 'Five thousand for a girl who can give us one. Twenty for both.'

'I always liked babies,' Malcolm said, nodding, a wide smile on his face. 'Now I like 'em even more.'

'They can help make you rich,' the man said. 'If you're smart.'

'I'm a doper,' Malcolm said, 'not a dummy.'

'The card in your pocket will decide that.' The man now leaned over and placed a Polaroid snapshot between the fingers of Malcolm's right hand. Malcolm brought the picture to eye level, squinting, trying to focus.

The photo was of a male body, charred beyond recognition, washed ashore on a desolate strand of beach.

'What's this?' Malcolm asked.

'It's not a what,' the man said. 'It's a who. He lost the card and let someone else see the name. That forced me to come get him. It took a long time to find him and it took him a long time to die.'

'What's on that card stays with me,' Malcolm said, seeing the photo in his hand with a clear eye. 'Bet your life on it.'

'I'll do one better, Malcolm,' the man said. 'I'm going to bet yours.'

*

Junior moved slowly down the street, sandwiched between Boomer and Dead-Eye, two blocks away from where they had parked the car. Cold blasts of air hit against his sweat-stained clothes, causing him to shiver and bury his hands deeper into his pockets.

'I told you the address,' Junior said, turning his head from the wind. 'Why do you still need me?'

'In case you lied to me,' Boomer said. 'I don't wanna have to go all the way back uptown just to kill you.'

'You aren't fooling anybody,' Junior said. 'You're gonna kill me no matter what.'

'Don't know about him,' Dead-Eye said. 'But I'm sure leaning that way.'

'Work with me on this one,' Boomer said. 'You come up with us and finger old pal Malcolm. He takes a ride in a patrol car and kills a few months down at Rikers. He's got nothing but time to tell all the brothers that you were the one stooled him out.'

'That's not right,' Junior said, shifting his head from Boomer to Dead-Eye. 'You said all I had to do was point out the building and give you the apartment number. You didn't say anything about me going up. You promised.' His voice degenerated into a whine.

'Here's a lesson for you, Junior,' Boomer said, gripping his arm to prevent a bolt. 'Never believe what a cop tells you.'

'Your daddy's got enough money to buy himself a judge or maybe pay off a family too scared to know better,' Dead-Eye said. 'But not enough money's been made can keep a street stool alive.'

'Like walking around with a loaded gun to your head,' Boomer agreed. 'Sooner or later, the trigger's gonna click.'

'You don't have to do this.' Junior's voice had risen to full-throttle panic. 'And who says I have to show you the right building. I could keep you two walking all fucking night if I wanted.'

151

'We better get there before my leg starts to ache,' Dead-Eye said. 'My mood turns ugly when that happens.'

Junior came crashing and flailing through Malcolm's wooden front door, crying out in pain as he landed on his hands and knees, his right hand coming to rest only inches from the handle of a bloody knife on the floor. Boomer and Dead-Eye stood in the entryway behind him, arms out straight, guns cocked and drawn, aimed at Malcolm's head.

'Move away from the girl,' Boomer told Malcolm, looking down at the still body. 'I want you with your back to the wall and your hands out flat.'

Malcolm let go of Jennifer's hair, took two steps back, and pressed his body against the wall. He was breathing through his mouth, his body tense and coated with a foul-smelling sweat.

Boomer, sliding the gun back into his hip holster, walked over to his friend's daughter. He crouched down and held her battered face, wiped away strands of hair and brushed off lines of blood and mucus. He slid his hand down to her neck and felt for a pulse. It was beating at a low rate, just enough to keep her alive.

'She needs a doctor fast.' Boomer cradled Jennifer's head with both hands. Fighting both the impulse to cry and the desire to kill, he turned to Malcolm. 'Where are the keys to the cuffs? And I don't wanna hear anything more outta you than the fuckin' answer.'

Malcolm kept his eyes square on the barrel of Dead-Eye's gun. 'Front pocket of my jeans.'

Boomer rested Jennifer's head against the wall and took four quick steps over to Malcolm's jeans, which were crumpled in the center of the room. He picked them up and took out a tiny set of silver keys. Along with the keys, Boomer pulled out a business card, black with white lettering. He pocketed the card and walked back to Jennifer. It was then that he noticed the missing finger.

Malcolm ran a dry tongue over an even drier set of lips.

Sweat dripped down the small of his back and he couldn't stop the right side of his face from twitching.

Boomer uncuffed Jennifer, brought her arm down gently to her side. He pulled a handkerchief from his back pocket and wrapped it around the top of her hand. As the girl let out a soft whimper of pain, he held Jennifer in his arms and lifted her up.

'It got a little crazy,' Malcolm said. 'That happens sometimes.'

Boomer had seen a lot in the years since he first pinned on his shield and he knew about the ugliness that filtered down the streets of his beat: men who killed the women they loved over the last hit on a pipe; dealers who sold poison to junkies, caring little that they would die within seconds of the rush; hitters who murdered strangers for cash and walked off into the night without care or concern; radicals so filled with hate they butchered the innocent in honor of some indefinite principle. All those he had seen and, over the years, had slowly come to understand.

But what he had seen over the past several days was a new form of evil. The man he stood across from and the other on his knees behind him were alien creatures to Boomer, each so willing to drop into the depths of an inhumanity he found terrifying.

There had been many criminals who'd crossed paths with Boomer whom he'd found pleasure in arresting. There were a handful he had killed because of the situation and the moment. But there had never been anyone he had wanted to kill for the pure emotional need to eliminate them.

Not until he crossed paths with Junior and Malcolm.

'I'm taking the girl,' Boomer said quietly. 'The police'll be here soon and take you and your friend away.' He took two steps back, and for a moment closed his eyes.

'Learn to pray, Malcolm,' Boomer said. 'Pray for a long prison sentence and for me to die the day before you get out.'

153

'Maybe,' Malcolm said, 'I don't have to pray so hard as you think.'

Boomer looked into Malcolm's eyes, saw the confidence suddenly show itself. He held his ground, gripping Jennifer's slight body closer to him, burying her head deeper into his chest, sensing what was about to happen.

One shot brought it to an end.

It came out of Dead-Eye's .44 and flew past the center of Junior's brain.

A low, guttural moan came from deep inside Junior's body. Thick, dark gushes of blood sprayed across Malcolm's face and over the back of Boomer's head and neck. Boomer turned to see Junior fall face first, the hole in his head large enough to shine a spotlight through, the knife held loose in the curve of his right hand. Behind them, Dead-Eye stood in a crouch position, his legs spread, right arm extended, smoke filtering off the barrel of his gun.

'You're not supposed to shoot a suspect in the back,' Boomer said. 'Or is that one of the classes you missed?'

'He wasn't a suspect,' Dead-Eye said, holstering his gun and walking toward Boomer, ignoring the body on the floor. 'And I didn't shoot him in the back. I shot him in the head.'

'Give the uniforms your statement,' Boomer said. 'I'll call in from the hospital to back it up. Then we'll take it all from there.'

'I'll tell 'em what I saw,' Malcolm said, his upper body starting to shiver. 'Swear to God, tell 'em everything. Unless you let me go. Now.'

'Look down at that big hole in Junior's head,' Dead-Eye said to Malcolm, turning his back on him long enough to close the door behind Boomer and the little girl in his arms. 'Then remember I've still got five more bullets in my gun.'

Dead-Eye rested his back against a far wall, his legs stretched out, arms folded across his chest. In the distance, he heard police sirens drawing closer.

'I don't see you puttin' down a brother,' Malcolm said. 'You don't look the type to kill your own blood.'

Dead-Eye pushed himself away from the wall, the siren wails growing louder, and headed straight for Malcolm. He pulled the gun from his holster, cocked it, and jammed it right under the naked man's chin.

'We don't have the same blood,' Dead-Eye said, barely moving his lips, shoving the gun in harder against the fleshy part of Malcolm's jaw. 'And, believe me, I would kill any brother who was scum like you. Even my own.'

He pulled the gun away, stepped over Junior's body, and walked to the apartment doorway. He opened the door, leaned his shoulders against the cracked hinges, rested his head on the wood, and stared up at a bare bulb hanging from a ceiling wire.

9

Boomer sat at his usual corner table at Nunzio's, hovering over a large bowl of penne with pesto. Across from him, Dead-Eye quietly cut into a thick char-broiled veal chop. Nunzio Goldman watched as they both ate, his back to a closed window, a large glass of red wine in front of him.

Nunzio knew his two friends had been through an ordeal these past few days. He could read it in their faces. Reading people was one of the things that came as second nature to Nunzio Goldman. He had spent his life on both sides of the law and managed to avoid any problems from either end. The good cops, like Boomer and Dead-Eye, trusted him. They knew that bets came in steady over his phone and that the sporting spreads for the Upper West Side were set behind his bar, but that kind of action didn't interest them. Boomer's mother bet a dollar on a number every day of her life, even hit one on a few occasions. Dead-Eye's father had had ten dollars riding every week on his beloved Giants during football season, with or without points. It didn't make it right, it just didn't make it a crime, not in their eyes. Not when off-track betting in New York State was legal, enticing people as easily as any street hustler to lay down money they could ill afford to lose. To Boomer and Dead-Eye's way of thinking, they were all bookies.

Dirty cops periodically tried to shake Nunzio down and were always sent away empty-handed. Nunzio made it his business to get as much information on them as could be dug up. If they were too dirty for his hands, he passed the folders on to the right people. If they were just looking to do some light skimming, he told the cops what he knew about their business and threw down a simple choice – either disappear from his line of vision or prepare to deal with Internal Affairs.

In Nunzio's world there was no black and white, only shades of gray, and he lived with ease within that cloudy area. He was a criminal who hated drugs and all that their sale embodied, but was comfortable in the company of hired killers who contracted out murders as easily as he sliced off strips of prosciutto. He ran an honest restaurant, treating customers with respect and serving only the finest foods he could afford. At the same time, he and his accountant devoted hours to cooking the books, keeping two sets of ledgers, reporting only the false set to the Internal Revenue Service. In the midst of a complicated universe, Nunzio Goldman kept his life and his ways as simple as he could manage.

'What kind of fallout did you guys get from taking out Junior?' Nunzio asked Boomer and Dead-Eye.

'His father says he's gonna sue the department.' Boomer paused, filling his mouth with pasta. 'He's put a team of six-figure lawyers on the case.'

'He know you were in on it?' Nunzio asked.

'He knows what he was told,' Dead-Eye said. 'Two retired detectives heard a rumor about a young girl being held against her will in an abandoned building.'

'When we went in, Junior panicked and came after me with a knife,' Boomer added. 'And Dead-Eye iced him.'

'That's not gonna be enough for Pop,' Nunzio said. 'He's gonna want the ones buried his son.'

'They can take my pension if they want it,' Boomer said, breaking off a hunk of bread from a basket. 'I don't give a fuck. Nothing can take back what they did to that kid.'

'Pop's gonna use his money to talk for him against the two of you. I'll use mine to talk against him. End of

157

the day, we'll see whose money talks louder.' Nunzio sipped his wine.

'How's Jennifer?'

Boomer put down his fork, took a sip from a glass of mineral water, and looked over at Nunzio, sadness easing its way across his face. 'The doctors, with all their fucking diplomas, told her parents that kids can rebound out of these kinds of things.'

'She say anything?' Nunzio said. 'Can she talk at all?'

'I was carryin' her down the street to my car.' Boomer's voice betrayed the weight of his emotions. 'I still couldn't get over the shape she was in. So much blood, so many bruises, you had to look to find skin. I was cursin' to myself, sick about the whole fuckin' business. Then she opens one eye, looks at me, and says "thank you".' Boomer put his head down and picked up his fork.

'I'm only sorry I didn't leave Malcolm's body on top of Junior's,' Dead-Eye said. 'Cancel out both their checking accounts.'

'What happens to him now?' Nunzio asked.

'Malcolm?' Dead-Eye said. 'He's looking at a hard ten. Even with a soft judge and a kind wacko report.'

'Doesn't seem like it's enough,' Nunzio said.

'It's never enough,' Boomer said. 'No matter what they end up with, it's never enough.'

'The family needs anything,' Nunzio said, finishing off his wine and getting up from the table, 'let 'em know I'll do all I can.'

They watched the restaurant owner walk toward the bar, giving quick greetings to diners along the way.

'How much juice does Nunzio really have?' Dead-Eye asked, leaning back in his chair.

'About as much as he needs,' Boomer said.

He paused for a moment and then reached inside the pocket of his blue button-down J. Crew shirt. He pulled out the card he had taken from Malcolm's jeans and slid it across the table.

'Lucia Carney,' Dead-Eye said, reading the name printed on it. 'Should that mean something to me?'

'She's got four names.' Boomer picked up the card and placed it back in his shirt pocket. 'Been married three times. All three husbands ended up dead.'

'Everything comes in threes,' Dead-Eye said. 'Good things and bad.'

'She works out of Arizona,' Boomer said. 'Runs a day care center. One of those drop-off-at-seven, pick-up-at-six places. Takes in about fifteen, maybe twenty thousand a year.'

'Any kids of her own?' Dead-Eye said.

'Can't have any,' Boomer said. 'She had a botched abortion when she was twenty. Messed up her insides. She was either living with or spending quality time with a drug runner down south. Beyond that, her early background's sketchy.'

'I'm ready for another Pepsi,' Dead-Eye said. 'You set with your water?'

'Get yourself two and a large bottle of Pellegrino for the table,' Boomer said, pushing his chair back and walking off toward the men's room. 'I'll pick it up from there when everybody else gets here.'

'Who's everybody else?' Dead-Eye asked, wondering where Boomer was taking all this, why he had devoted so much time to digging into the life of a three-time widow who spent her days watching other people's kids.

'Don't worry,' Boomer said, stopping between two empty tables. 'You'll like 'em. They're a bunch of cripples. Like you and me.'

Boomer Frontieri had stopped being a cop physically but not emotionally. His every action, every movement, every glance smelled of cop. He would regularly pass on tips he picked up from old street stools to the beat units and was one of the few retired cops brazen enough to make citizen's arrests. Once, not long after he'd been pensioned off, he spotted two teens mugging an elderly woman on

Sixty-sixth Street, over near Central Park. He cornered the two, confiscated their pocket knives, and yanked them face forward against a black stone wall. He needed to keep them in place while he phoned for two uniforms. After helping the woman to her feet and resting her against a parked car, he stopped a young student heading home from a nearby private school.

'What's your name?' he said to the startled boy.

'Joshua,' the kid said.

Boomer pulled the service revolver from his hip holster and handed it to Joshua. 'Make sure they don't move,' was all he said, pointing to the two teens over by the wall.

'What if they do?' Joshua said, holding the gun toward the pair, both hands shaking.

'Then shoot 'em,' Boomer said, limping off to the corner phone booth to call the local precinct.

The rescue of Jennifer Santori had brought Boomer back to life. He was angered and repulsed by all that he had witnessed, but it also made him feel like a cop again. His mind was back on red alert, and the adrenaline rush was nearly strong enough to drown out the pain of his wounds. The eventual capture was worth the risk of being hit with a fatal bullet. He knew now that was all he had to keep him going.

The risk.

After finding her card in Malcolm's pocket, Boomer spent three full days gathering information on Lucia Carney. His first meeting was with DEA Special Agent Tony Malazante, a head banger from his days working buys and busts in Alphabet City. Over two cups of coffee in a downtown diner, Malazante told him about a new brand of cocaine that was just hitting the streets. The dealers called it crack, the junkies called it heaven, and the narcs called it their biggest problem since the Golden Triangle glory days of heroin. New York got its first taste in late 1981. Since then, arrests had multiplied and demand for the drug quadrupled.

'What's the difference between that and regular blow?' Boomer asked.

'The hits are cheaper,' Malazante said. 'Five bucks gets you high for five minutes. Don't need a lot of cash to stay on the wire all day. You can pick it up stealing petty.'

'Who's in on it?'

'Everybody so far but the Italians,' Malazante said, sipping from a large cup of mocha. 'The demand's so high that a street dealer can set up shop on a Monday and have a full crew of twenty working for him by Friday.'

'Where's it coming from?' Boomer wanted to know, holding Lucia's card in his right hand.

'Same place all this shit comes from,' Malazante said. 'South America. Southeast Asia. And it's landing heavy on the streets. The rock comes in and the cash goes out, usually on the same day.'

'That's where Lucia comes in,' Boomer said. 'How big a hitter is she?'

'She started out small-time.' Malazante leaned his large frame against the back of a torn plastic booth. 'Now I'd say she's in the top three, easy. She's got a big outfit that's well run and, I guess you could say, unique.'

'What's unique about it?'

Malazante finished the rest of his coffee and leaned closer to his friend. 'I can help you with this, Boomer,' he said. 'But only up to a point. I don't know what you're thinking and I don't want to know. You and me didn't talk about this and I didn't leave this folder behind on my seat. If anybody asks, we met, had coffee, and talked about my kids.'

'You don't have any kids,' Boomer said.

'Then we didn't talk,' Malazante said, squeezing his girth out of the booth.

An old girlfriend from the FBI gave Boomer the statistics he needed about crack and a confidential printout on Lucia Carney. She promised to help in the future as well, in return for anonymity and the occasional dinner at Nunzio's. He spent a day working the computers at One

161

Police Plaza, cross-referencing Lucia's name with known cartel bosses and seven-figure dealers. In between, Boomer ate a quiet office lunch with Deputy Chief Ken Wolfson, a bright, personable man who collected rare comic books and was known on the streets as a cop who liked to see jobs done with as few questions asked as possible. He agreed to be Boomer's inside man so long as his involvement was that of a silent partner. Boomer would assume all the risks. Wolfson's cops would get the credit for any busts. Once that was agreed upon, the deputy chief opened a file drawer and laid out all the NYPD background information on Lucia Carney.

A connection from the Bureau of Alcohol, Tobacco and Firearms then gave Boomer a stat sheet filled with her known lift-and-drop locations. A neighborhood friend now working for a Secret Service unit in Maryland gave him a detailed report on her money-laundering capabilities and how the fast cash was washed overnight between one flight and the next.

In seventy-two hours, using the sources available to him, Boomer Frontieri knew as much about Lucia Carney as any cop in the country. He studied up on crack and read assorted medical documents detailing its instant addiction. He learned about mules and smurfs and the women who carried drugs and cash for Lucia and the men who killed at her whim. The more he read, heard and learned, the more determined Boomer Frontieri grew. His anger wasn't fueled by the fact that she was a drug queen. He had heard about other such women working the distribution end of the drug business.

It wasn't even the amount of money involved, even though it totaled out to a numbing multibillion-dollar-a-year network.

It was the way she did it.

Dr. Carolyn Bartlett sat on a gray folding chair, her legs crossed, blond hair combed back into a tight bun. The room was filtered with shadows, lit only by a fluorescent

162

bulb attached to the center of the wall, just above the roll-away bed. She read over the contents of a yellow folder which was clutched in her hands, crammed with the detailed notes and observations she had made over the previous four days.

Dr. Bartlett, though only thirty-six, was in charge of the hospital's rape and trauma psychiatric unit. In her four years at the hospital, she had seen all the horror imaginable.

Until the afternoon they wheeled in Jennifer Santori.

The sight of the young girl, the condition of her body, the sunken look on the face of the man who had brought her in, made Bartlett, for the first time, truly question what it was she did and what, if any, difference it made.

She closed the folder, resting it on the ground next to her Cuban-heeled black Ferragamo shoes, and ran her hands across the starched white sheets of the bed. She took a deep breath and touched the soft hand of the young girl asleep beneath those sheets.

She studied the silent, bandaged face. The girl's rest was disturbed only by the occasional twitch and moan. There were three IV pouches draining off into her right arm and bandages covering a multitude of wounds. Her left hand was in a cast that brushed up to her elbow, an empty space where the index finger should have been.

Dr. Bartlett leaned closer and touched each of the wounds with a gentle hand. She had clear blue eyes, a taut athlete's body, and a face that had not begun to betray her years. She had seen a great deal of abuse in her four years at Metro, but never anything close to this. It had taken nurses and interns two full days to wash off the caked blood and three days for Bartlett to get the child to give her anything more than a nod.

She had paid a visit to the suspect. She always made a point of doing that, even though some doctors in the department frowned on the idea. But it was important to her, allowing a rare glimpse into the other side of the room, in an invariably futile attempt to understand why such men – and they were always men – did what they did to their victims.

She didn't get much out of Malcolm Juniper, about as much as she got out of any of them. He smiled, asked for some coffee, even asked her how Jennifer was doing. She turned her back on him when he asked for her phone number, leaving him with a smile on his face and a look in his eyes that told her all she really needed to know. She walked out of the holding room thinking about her father, Richie Bartlett, a twenty-year veteran of the NYPD who had killed two men in the line of duty and who died working three jobs so his dream of a daughter with a medical degree could become a reality. She wondered how long Malcolm Juniper would have survived in a locked room with Richie Bartlett.

Dr. Bartlett sat back in her chair, her eyes locked on Jennifer's face. It was early for the dreams and nightmares to begin, but she knew they would soon be there for the girl who had seen so much darkness in such a short period of time. She knew that the girl's parents would turn to her for answers, for pleas to bring the nightmares to a halt, but all her years of training, all the books and files and reports, now boiled down to one horrible fact: She couldn't make those nightmares stop. They would be a part of Jennifer Santori for the rest of her days.

Helping Jennifer cope with the night visions was the best Dr. Bartlett could do. In truth, it was the only hope she could offer.

There was a bigger problem facing Dr. Bartlett, one she had wrestled with since she was first handed the file folder less than three days before. She knew that the police, the district attorney's office, every prosecutor assigned to her case, would need Jennifer's testimony, demand it, in order to secure a prison space for Malcolm Juniper. Without Jennifer Santori in the courtroom, there would be no conviction. There wouldn't even be a case. But having Jennifer testify would mean reliving the nightmare. It would mean sitting next to a judge and, worse, across

164

from Malcolm Juniper, telling all in attendance what had been done to her, in full detail, with as many follow-up questions as the defense team could muster. Questions meant to rattle a teenager and release the shackles from a man without remorse.

Dr. Bartlett stood and leaned closer to Jennifer. She stroked her hair, careful not to touch the thick bandages surrounding it, gently brushing back the loose strands. She wondered what she could ever do to make the pretty girl smile again.

Dr. Bartlett leaned down, kissed Jennifer twice on the cheek, squeezed her undamaged hand, and walked out of the room.

Her head was down.

Her decision had been made.

10

They sat crowded around a table in a rear room off the main bar. Boomer held the head, his back against a wood-paneled wall, just below a framed photo of Nino Benvenuti and Emile Griffith slugging it out for the middleweight title. Dead-Eye sat to Boomer's left, a large wine glass filled with ice and Pepsi in his hand, a puzzled look on his face.

There were four others gathered around the table, three men and an attractive woman in tight jeans, white crew neck, and soft leather jacket. Dead-Eye knew that they were all cops. They had the look and the attitude, each coming into the room with a swagger, greeting Boomer with only a handshake and a cautious nod.

If they were all cripples, like Boomer said, then they managed to hide their handicaps successfully. You couldn't tell much by looking at them, except for the guy hanging loose in the far corner, a young, dark-haired man in a hooded sweatshirt that couldn't hide the reddened, burnt skin around his neck, hands, and along the right side of his face.

Dead-Eye also had the guy across from him figured, more or less. He was tall and muscular, sitting with his hands spread flat across the tablecloth, a large glass of skim milk in front of him, a bowl of ice cubes off to the side. The others had asked for beer, wine, or booze. Generally, only two kinds of cops order milk in a restaurant: those trying to stay on the wagon – and this guy didn't look shaky enough to be walking down that street – and those who'd been shot in the gut. Dead-Eye was even willing to bet that a pat-down of the quiet guy in the bombardier jacket would shake out several packets of Maalox and a half-empty bottle of Zantac.

There was little in the way of small talk. Everyone waited for Boomer to open the conversation. But Boomer just sat there, sizing up each cop. The glasses were close to empty and the chunky guy in the bowling jacket was already on his third cigarette, when Nunzio came in with a fresh tray. He rested it in the center of the table, closed the door behind him, and sat on a corner stool.

'The place is closed, Boom,' Nunzio said. 'I just checked the last couple out.'

'You got any pretzels to go with this?' the guy in the bowling jacket, Jimmy 'Pins' Ryan, asked, lifting a long-neck Bud from the tray and taking a swig.

'We'll eat later,' Boomer said. 'After we talk.'

'Talk about what?' Delgaldo 'Geronimo' Lopez, the man nursing the glass of milk, said.

'A lot of things, Geronimo. We're going to start it off with a story about a lady. After that, if you're still interested, I'll tell you one about us.'

'Did Boomer just call you Geronimo?' the guy in the scruffy sweatshirt, Bobby 'Rev. Jim' Scarponi, asked. 'I mean, like the Indian?'

'You bothered by it or just curious?' Geronimo looked at Rev. Jim with a hard set of eyes.

'Neither one, Chief,' the Rev. said. 'And I mean that with respect.'

'Just so we're all on the same page and nobody steps on the wrong foot,' Boomer began, 'know this. Everybody in this room was once a cop. Each top of the line, best in the department. I'm including myself in there. And now we're all disabled, all of us collecting tax-free checks every two weeks. Everybody except for Nunzio over in the corner.'

'And he is what?' the woman, Mary 'Mrs. Columbo' Silvestri, asked.

167

'A friend,' Boomer said. 'And we're gonna need us one of those.'

'Does that mean the drinks are on the house?' Rev. Jim asked.

'He said I was a friend,' Nunzio told him. 'Not an idiot.'

'You really know how to warm up a room,' Mrs. Columbo said to Rev. Jim.

'I give it my best.' The Rev. winked. 'That's all you can ask.'

'You need us for something, Boomer,' Geronimo said. 'And it's not to sit here and drink with you. So, let's hear it.'

'I just finished something with Dead-Eye,' Boomer said. 'It started out as a favor for a friend. It ended up taking us to a whole other place.'

'I heard about it,' Mrs. Columbo said. 'A kid got grabbed off the streets. You caught the lifter and somehow his partner managed to walk into your gun.'

'The lifter had a business card in his pocket,' Boomer went on. 'With a woman's name on it. Lucia Carney is what it says on the card, and that's what she likes to be called. At least this week.'

'What's her angle?' Rev. Jim asked.

'I told you guys on the phone about her day care center,' Boomer said. 'That covers her, money-wise, with the IRS.'

'So what's her second job?' Geronimo said.

'She moves cocaine into the country,' Boomer said. 'Cocaine and crack. And then she moves the cash payments out. Guy I know in D.C. tells me she's got herself a crew of at least four hundred spread out across the country. Half of them are smurfs, all of them women. The other half work as muscle.'

'What the hell's a smurf?' Nunzio asked.

'Drug and cash couriers,' Rev. Jim muttered.

'She calls her smurfs the Babysitters' Club,' Boomer said.

168

'Like the children's books,' Mrs. Columbo said. 'I just bought a couple of them for my niece.'

'Right,' Boomer said. 'The ladies she uses are all neat and clean. No record, no arrests, no history of drug usage.'

'How do they work the transport?' Dead-Eye asked.

Boomer took a deep breath before he answered, scanning the faces in the room one more time.

He knew he was going to go after Lucia Carney. That decision was made the minute he ran her aliases through the DEA's BCCI computer. What he didn't know was whether he could get the people in the room to go along with him. He had chosen each of them very carefully, using his instinct but also assessing their individual backgrounds. They were all adrenaline junkies whose daily rush had been taken away long before they were ready to give up the high. Now they were all drifting, living from paycheck to paycheck, working second jobs they couldn't care less about, feeling closer to dead than alive.

They faced a dark future, one crammed with regrets, memories, and could-have-beens.

Boomer knew it.

He was betting they would too.

'Dead babies,' Boomer finally said when every face in the room was still enough to focus only on his answer. And his answer got everyone's attention.

'How?' Dead-Eye asked quietly.

'She finds a baby any way she can,' Boomer said. 'After our experience with Malcolm and Junior, we know there's no shortage of scum out there willing to lift a kid.'

'The dealers work the runaways,' Rev. Jim said. 'Always have. Turn 'em on to the junk, then throw 'em to the streets to earn what they spend on smack. Some of the girls get pregnant, they carry through and sell the kid. But that market's not big enough to supply a whole team of mules.'

'This crack shit's changed all the rules,' Boomer said, standing and resting his hands on the table. 'And Lucia's got every space covered. She's got the runaways, but instead of having 'em turn tricks, she has her crew get them pregnant and hand the babies over to her.'

'Probably buys whatever else she needs on the black market,' Mrs. Columbo said. 'You could move five, maybe ten thousand babies a year that way.'

'At the least,' Boomer said. 'And when all else fails, she lifts them. Home invasions, backseat of a car, front end of a stroller. Anywhere, anyplace, Lucia's crew will make the grab.'

'How much she moving?' Geronimo asked. 'Cash wise.'

'The feds put a rough estimate on it of at least two hundred and fifty million,' Boomer said.

'A year?' Pins asked.

'A month,' Boomer said.

There was a respectful silence before Dead-Eye asked, 'What about the babies? How's she work that angle?'

'She keeps the kids until they're about six, seven months old. Then they kill them.'

'I don't know if I want to hear this part,' Mrs. Columbo said, downing her scotch and wishing she had another.

'Didn't warm my insides either,' Boomer said. 'But it's what's out there and what's gotta be stopped.'

'They use the dead babies as mules,' Rev. Jim said. 'Cut 'em open, empty them out, fill them with cocaine for the flight up, and cash for the flight down.'

'You knew about this?' Pins asked, putting down his empty bottle of beer.

'I've heard rumors,' Rev. Jim said. 'Never knew if they were legit.'

'They're legit all right,' Boomer said. 'You get on a plane sitting next to a woman holding a sleeping baby in her arms, you don't even think twice.'

'Probably smile and tell her what a beautiful baby she has,' Dead-Eye said. 'Don't even notice that the baby slept through the entire flight.'

'I grew up with hard people,' Nunzio said. 'Tough people. Some were criminals, ran numbers, owned brothels, couple shot a guy or two. But I don't know any who would turn this way.'

'Where are the feds on this?' Mrs. Columbo asked.

'They're on it,' Boomer said. 'As best they can be. But you can't convict what you can't nail down. And it's not the mules they want. It's Lucia.'

'What do we know about her?' Dead-Eye asked. 'Besides her little habits of killing babies and burying husbands.'

'I've got private access to whatever they have,' Boomer said. 'And through them, the locals too. Files, surveillance, taps. What I get, I'll pass on to each of you. It's not a lot, but it should be more than enough to get us started.'

'Started on what, Boomer?' Geronimo asked. The muscles in his face were rigid.

'On bringing Lucia and her little crew of babysitters down.'

There was another silence in the room. Then Mrs. Columbo gave out with a mirthless laugh.

'There are cops out there for this,' she said. '*Real* cops. Not ones like us.'

'The real cops can't do it,' Boomer said.

'Why not?' Geronimo asked.

'Because they're the law and they have to follow it,' Boomer said. 'We don't.'

'Which makes us criminals,' Pins said. 'Not cops.'

'This is a major crew you're talking about,' Rev. Jim chimed in. 'They've got the money and the muscle. We can't keep up with that. At least I know I can't.'

'I can understand some of you being nervous,' Boomer said.

'I'm not nervous, Boomer,' Mrs. Columbo said. 'I'm scared. We probably all are. You were right about what you said before. We were the best in the business. But now we're not. I wake up in pain and go to bed the same way. Just like everybody else in this room. That's no shape to be in when you're chasing down a prime-time queen.'

'Six cops, crippled or not, up against a crew of four

hundred are pretty steep odds to begin with,' Dead-Eye said, wishing for the first time in his life that he smoked.

'You're forgetting someone, Dead-Eye,' Nunzio said.

Dead-Eye looked over at him. 'Sorry. Six and a half against four hundred.'

'That's better.' Nunzio nodded, pleased.

'Look, I admit I didn't always go by the book when I was on the job,' Geronimo now said. 'But this is about more than bending the rules. This is about breaking the law. That's one line I never thought of crossing.'

'I'll give you the strongest reason I can think of,' Boomer said. 'And it's got nothin' to do with Lucia.'

'Fuck the suspense, Boomer,' Mrs. Columbo said. 'Just tell us.'

'It'll make us feel alive again.' It was Dead-Eye who gave the answer, with a nod toward Boomer. 'Make us feel like we used to feel before they took it all away. That's a feeling worth getting back. Even if it kills us. Is that what you were going to say, Boomer?'

'Something like that,' Boomer said.

They all sat quietly and digested what they had heard. Each one weighed the task Boomer had laid out before them. It was warm in the room and throats were dry. Pins took off his bowling jacket and tossed it behind his chair. Geronimo leaned back and stretched. Mrs. Columbo kept her eyes on Boomer, both happy and angry that he had called her in. Rev. Jim ran a hand along his scarred neck and kept his head down. Dead-Eye stared into his empty glass.

'Nunzio, do I have to kill somebody to get another drink?' Rev. Jim said, breaking the silence.

'Only on Sundays.' Nunzio stood up, opened the door, and headed for the bar.

'You decided already?' Dead-Eye asked Boomer.

'I don't have family like some of you,' Boomer said. 'I don't have a job I might grow to care about. I've only got the shield. For me, it's an easier decision.'

'A shield doesn't cover breaking the law,' Pins said.

'I'm still doing what I swore to do,' Boomer responded. 'Bring the fight to the bad. I'm just doing it a different way, that's all.'

'It's a way that can get you killed in a heartbeat,' Rev. Jim said.

'Then I exit on my terms. And that's a contract I can follow and not look back on. Now all I'm looking for are a few other signatures.'

'And you're recruiting from among the wounded,' Dead-Eye said.

Boomer nodded. 'That's because they're the most dangerous.'

11

The brand-new pink stucco house was large, well lit, and heavily guarded. Motion spots rested behind the dozens of bushes, trees, and large fruit plants that dotted the half acre of property. Two all-terrain vehicles were parked and locked behind thick garage doors and a black Mercedes sat in the circular driveway, shaded by an overhanging palm tree.

The house had been sculpted in the flatbed manner that was so popular with the thousands of fresh faces migrating each year into the rocky terrain of Sedona, Arizona, and its surrounding regions. It had been designed and built on spec by a local company, then sold to a man named Garrison Cross, who paid in full, in cash, and had never once set foot inside. The furnishings had all been ordered through catalogues and department stores, shipped to a Phoenix warehouse, and paid for COD. The wildflowers that circled the exterior had been ordered from a greenery in Scottsdale, prepaid, and shipped, then planted in the middle of the night.

Inside, the rooms were large and spread out, the center hall, living room, and dining room dominating the wood-paneled first floor. A thick oak staircase led to the three bedrooms on the second. There were skylights and gas fireplaces in every room except the kitchen. Wall-clipped surveillance cameras recorded each move, from every possible angle. Two purebred German shepherds walked the rooms with complete freedom. Outside, the morning air

174

was fresh and brisk, with a cool breeze coming down from the cliffs. Less than a mile from the house, tourists, fresh off a fast-food breakfast, were already lined up in front of the Red Rock Jeep Tours waiting area, eager to bounce their way through well-charted terrain.

All the activity was in the kitchen, a large, airy space with bay windows, overhead fans, and a three-screen video display terminal bolted into the granite countertop to the left of the oversized microwave. Two middle-aged women in housecoats and slippers padded quietly across the thick tile floor, carrying cellophane-sealed two-kilo bags of cocaine. They were taking the bags from a large satchel on the kitchen table, then resting them in neat piles next to the sink. Three men in well-tailored suits stood at different ends of the kitchen, eyes hidden by dark shades, arms folded across their chests, silently counting off the piles.

The women were two bags away from emptying the satchel when Lucia Carney walked into the kitchen.

The three men dropped their arms to their sides when they saw her. She stared and smiled at each of them as she passed, the thick aroma of her Chanel perfume filling the air. Her dark hair was combed straight back, hanging down long over the shoulders of a black Karl Lagerfeld dress. She wore four-inch heels and her skirt was slit high on both sides, revealing ample portions of well-sculpted legs. The nails on her fingers and toes were painted dark red, her skin was tanned and unlined, and her brown eyes, while seductive and enticing, conveyed a distant and frightening chill.

Lucia was thirty-eight years old but looked much younger. She maintained her spectacular figure with punishing daily two-hour workouts. She took great pleasure in knowing that men both desired and feared her equally. It was what had helped keep her alive in what was a very dangerous occupation. But for Lucia Carney, surviving was always the priority.

She was born in a clinic in Houston, Texas, the third

child of migrant workers with little in the way of money and even less in the way of hope. At seven she was sent to Galveston to live with an aunt and her bedridden husband. They lived in a wood frame house with off-and-on running water and a bathroom hooked up next to the shed. Her aunt, a once-beautiful woman eaten away by hard times, worked as a waitress in a local diner during the day. At night she turned tricks in her bedroom while her husband sat in the kitchen propped next to a hand-cranked turntable, listening to Hank Williams and Patsy Cline.

Lucia was a poor student and found herself skipping more classes than she attended. By the time she was ten, she was helping her aunt serve customers in the diner, handing over the tips but eating as many of the cherry pies as she wanted. Her aunt noticed the way in which the weary men who frequented the diner fawned over the girl and how Lucia was quick to flirt back.

A month past her twelfth birthday, Lucia was moved out of the diner and sent to work in the shed next to the house. There, in the shadow of a twenty-five-watt bulb, sitting on a wooden bench rich with splinters, her back against the creaky shed wall, she gave oral sex to any man who paid her aunt the five-dollar fee. She always wore the same blue-flowered print dress her mother had sent her from Houston for Christmas, white socks trimmed with lace, and black buckled shoes shined daily with spit and water. She always kept her eyes closed and her hands wrapped tightly around the sharp edges of the bench. Tight enough to draw blood.

Lucia left her aunt behind when she was fourteen, traveling with the money she had earned running bets for her uncle and the extra cash given her by grateful customers. She also left behind the blue print dress and the black shoes.

Too many stops and too many wrong men later, she found herself living and partnered with an angel dust and coke dealer in a two-room apartment in Lexington, Kentucky. The gangly, brown-haired young man with the funny smile and the tattoo of Casper the Friendly Ghost floating down the center of his back was the first man in her life she didn't charge for sex. His name was Otis Fraimer, but she always called him Jerry and he never seemed to mind. She knew it wouldn't last, knew they were only one knock on the door or one bad buy away from a jail sentence or a bullet, but she felt comfortable with him. And she never did expect Jerry to die, to end up slumped over the steering wheel of a burning car, two shots through his heart and his throat slashed.

She left herself little time to mourn.

Not when Jerry's rival and the man responsible for his death, a fifty-year-old former gunnery sergeant with a severed leg and an engaging smile, offered to bring her in as a full partner. Harry Corain was intent on expanding his drug business, looking to move beyond the low-end money of downstate Kentucky and head into the fertile terrain of nearby Ohio, where the cities of Cincinnati and Columbus were more than eager to offer a demand equal to his supplies. Lucia, who was by then seventeen and tired of being poor, made the move and, in no short order, reorganized Harry's runners into small teams of movers and packers, insisting on a crew that was free of users and abusers. She left the muscle end of the business to Harry and his younger brother, Terry, a draft dodger as quick with a knife as he was slow with a word.

Lucia handled all the cash and coke transactions.

She gained the loyalty of the mules and sellers by cutting them in on a small percentage of the action, this despite strong protests from the Corain brothers. She hired a cancer-riddled career booster from Canton named Delroy Rumson to teach her all he knew about laundering money and reinvesting clean cash into safe, insured, and tax-free municipal bonds. In return for the knowledge she picked up during his six-month cram course, Lucia promised to keep up the $800-a-month home-care payments for Delroy's retarded daughter, Dorothy, after he died.

It was the first of many promises she didn't keep.

Lucia married Harry Corain on April 18, 1964. It was her twentieth birthday, and a week after the wedding she told him she was pregnant with his child, even though she had no intention of keeping either husband or baby. She was simply buying herself more time and using whatever pull Harry had among other midwestern drug runners to build on what she was already raking in.

Two months into the pregnancy, Lucia drove over the Kentucky state line into Cincinnati during the early-morning hours of a soft summer day and had an abortion performed in the basement office of a ramshackle two-story house half a mile off Ezzard Charles Boulevard. Dr. Ranyon B. Travis had long ago lost his medical license to drink, drugs, and bribery, and now found himself earning a living disposing of the unwanted for a three-hundred-dollar-cash-up-front fee. Travis had a modest reputation among the dopers and hookers working the riverfront strip and could be counted on to keep his business quiet, if for no other reason than that the years of booze and drug binges had made it impossible to remember.

Travis had been up all night with an underage co-ed and had already gone through half a pint of gin and two grams of coke when Lucia walked into the foyer leading down to the basement steps. He dressed quickly, splashed water on his face, swallowed two five-hundred-milligram Benzedrine tablets, and prepped Lucia for her abortion. Five minutes into the procedure, she felt a sharp, stinging burn in her pelvic region and immediately knew that the doctor with the shaky hands and shady past had butchered her beyond remedy.

She walked out of the house, leaving three crinkled hundred-dollar bills on the doctor's desk, blood still running down her legs, not answering Travis's apologetic pleas. Her mind forced her body to stride forward and ignore the growing pain that had replaced the curled fetus. Lucia had learned at the earliest age not to cry at the hurt life threw down a person's path, and she did not shed any

178

tears on this night. Instead, she found solace in thoughts of revenge.

Harry found her sprawled face down in the backyard of their house and rushed her to a nearby clinic that excelled at asking few questions. A three-day stay was all it took to heal the external wounds, stop the hemorrhaging, reduce the fever, and quell the infection.

Lucia smiled and kept her focus on the half-empty IV dripping into her arm as she listened to the soft words of a concerned intern tell her she could never have children. She was warmed by the knowledge that at that moment Dr. Ranyon B. Travis, who once headed the OBGYN wing of a northern Chicago hospital, was hanging from a back alley wall, two thick tire chains wrapped around his hands, his mouth sealed, and his eyes stapled open, being stomach-gutted by the sharp end of Terry's bowie knife. The pain was so intense Dr. Travis chewed off his tongue in the minutes before he died.

Lucia was spending a long weekend in New Orleans in the summer of 1966, looking once again to expand her drug operations, when she met Carlo Porfino sitting by himself at the back table of her friend Anna Cortese's blues bar. She joined him for a drink and then for the night. By mid-afternoon the next day, Lucia had found her second husband and a fast route out of Kentucky.

Carlo Porfino had affiliations with both the New Orleans and Chicago mobs and was moving heavy quantities of everything imaginable. He was the opposite of Harry in all respects and was not shy about flashing the cash to show Lucia a good time. He also learned quickly in their relationship that she was more than a bar pickup. She had a knack for the drug business, combining a natural ability to make people want to work for her with a ruthlessness that was often necessary in the powder game.

While eager to expand into new territories, Lucia was reluctant to give up what she had built back in Kentucky and Ohio. She turned Carlo's initial indifference into enthusiasm when she told him about the $100,000 a month Harry and Terry were taking in without having totally exploited the burgeoning market. She and Carlo cut a deal. Lucia would get 25 percent of all the Midwest action, plus an additional 10 percent of his southern end, in return for overseeing the operations from her new base in New Orleans. It was a deal a woman like Lucia would never pass up.

She and Carlo were married on the afternoon of July 27, 1967, in a small chapel overlooking a pre-Civil War cemetery. On that same day, Kentucky police found Harry Corain's electrocuted body floating facedown in a cast-iron tub, his left arm amputated at the shoulder and hanging loose off the side. He was less than ten feet from his baby brother, Terry, who had taken three Magnum hits to the head, his bowie knife still clutched in his right hand.

Lucia was twenty-three years old and well on her way toward stashing away her first million. She had laid the foundation for a national drug network that in fifteen years and one more husband would blossom into an empire that reached into forty-six states and eight foreign countries. By the time she was standing in the large, airy kitchen in Sedona, Arizona, Lucia Carney was feeding four hundred million a year into the coffers of the international drug cartels and organized crime families that relied on her for safe delivery of their cocaine and guaranteed transfer of funds.

She was their cocaine queen, a beautiful woman with a luscious smile and a cold heart. They called her the Dragon, since she had a tattoo of a small black one breathing flames stenciled over her right shoulder blade, a birthday gift years earlier from Carlo, who had a larger one anchored across his chest. She had grown to like Carlo. They had fun together and he always treated her with respect. He had helped link her up with all his organized crime connections and introduced her to the heads of the South American outfits. He taught her how to wash the coke and still keep it pure. And he was a master on

180

profit skimming, careful to leave behind a trail that always led to a greedier drug dealer.

Lucia often missed Carlo and sometimes regretted that she had had him killed. But he was getting in the way of her business, and Lucia would allow no one to do that.

Especially not a husband.

She got the idea for using babies one night while watching a Johnson & Johnson TV commercial. In the high-end drug circles in which Lucia traveled, babies were easy to get, easy to transport, and even easier to dispose of. By the mid-1970s, the black market was a bull market for newborns; this back-door, middle-of-the-night, cash-on-receipt business was a multimillion-dollar-a-year operation.

Within six months of watching the commercial, Lucia had made her mark on the baby industry. She opened clinics in eight states, each of them catering to unwed-and-pregnant teenagers on the low end of the income scale. The girls were all looking for good homes for their babies, some cash in their pockets, and the news of their pregnancies to be broadcast to no one. Lucia used third parties to hire only those whose medical credentials were beyond reproach. Once born, the babies were sent to safe homes, where they were fed and nurtured for six months. Then they were picked up by one of Lucia's soldiers, dropped off at a drug transfer center, usually a newly bought condo on quiet resort property, and killed.

At no time did the horror of her actions ever bother Lucia. For her, the infants were nothing more than a tool, a safe and inexpensive means of transport, allowing her to move large quantities of drugs and cash free and unde-tected. If what she did made her enemies in the drug trade fear her even more, then that was a dividend.

Over time, as the demand for baby transports began to far outstrip her dependable supply, Lucia began to send her troops out to the streets. There she found hundreds of willing partners unafraid to deal in the hot item of the moment. They kept tabs on runaways and drifters, prime candidates to get pregnant and either abandon or sell their children. They tracked birth records at hospitals located in low-income areas, where record-keeping tended to be as shoddy as the security, helping to make any newborn a perfect target. They secured welfare rolls, scanning the lists for mothers who had a drug problem or record and more than three children. Lucia's emissaries then offered them a better deal than what the state allowed.

The cartel leaders were so pleased with this grisly but safe method of operations that they offered up, free of charge, babies born to their strings of prostitutes. A number of other gangs willingly sold Lucia the women with whom they had grown tired, from old girlfriends to older wives, and, in some cases, their own daughters.

All done in the name of profit.

And at the expense of the innocent.

12

They had eaten their grilled salmon dinner in silence. Nunzio was the only one who got up during the meal, scurrying back and forth from the kitchen to the table with a large bowl of salad or a fresh bottle of wine. By the time the fruit and coffee were served, most of the cops had absorbed what Boomer had told them. They sat at the large table in the middle of the empty restaurant, the shades drawn down, only three of the overhead lights turned on, lost in their own internal struggle.

Geronimo fingered the medallion around his neck, the one his mother had placed there years earlier to ward off harm. He wondered if the others in the group felt as empty as he did. His days were blanks, working a steady shift at a job he cared little about. His nights were horrors, cold sweats mixing with wasted prayer and cries in the dark, wishing he had not lived through the grenade blast that had left him a whole man on the outside and half of one on the inside.

He had not gone near a device since that day. His retirement papers were put through for him while he was still in a hospital bed, about to endure the sixth of what eventually would grow to fourteen surgical procedures, all fruitless attempts to piece together abdominal muscles and lower intestinal tracts. The daily physical therapy he endured was as constant as the pain he forced himself to ignore. The pills he was prescribed sat in rows on three shelves of a medicine cabinet in a one-bedroom apartment in Ozone Park. Geronimo was surviving on antacids and willpower.

He worked for Unger Electronics on the Lower East Side, reporting to an overweight man with a bad back named Carl Ungerwood. It was a family-owned operation that survived mainly because of the popularity of its computer repair department, which was where Geronimo toiled. That was as close to a set of wires as he was willing to get since the blast. He still kept a cache of dynamite in a closet off the main hall of his apartment, more for the memory of who he used to be than for use.

Carl Ungerwood had a thirty-second temper that was mostly set off by problems with an ex-wife who was suing him for a piece of the business. He often directed his tirades at Geronimo, hurling insults and venom at a man the city had often decorated as a hero. Geronimo sat in silence during those moments, his eyes dark and distant. He saw the abuse as further punishment for what he had lost to the man with the grenade. That the pay from Unger Electronics was steady didn't matter as much to Geronimo as the fact that the work was as far removed from the New York Police Department as he could hope to get.

Unlike Boomer, Geronimo didn't miss being a cop. But he did miss the thrill of taking down a device. He would set time limits for himself when he worked on the computers, doing mental countdowns as he repaired burned-out modems and replaced weak transmission wires. But it just wasn't the same. There was no sense of mystery to a computer, not like with a device, where someone as good as Geronimo could will it, control it, thrive on its energy, or die in the clutches of its power. Alone with a device, Geronimo's life and his possible death took on spiritual weight. It was better than the slow death he was living through now, hunched on a stool in the back room of a dusty electronics store.

Geronimo couldn't speak for the others, but he sensed that their decision about whether or not they would join

184

Boomer in his battle with Lucia was a matter of choice. Not so for him. For a warrior like Geronimo, it was a matter of destiny.

'It's getting late,' Boomer said, taking a quick glance at his watch, 'and it's been a long night, so I'll keep the rest of this short. All I ask is for you to think about what I'm going to say. Think on it hard. And then let me know. Either way, I'll walk away with no problem about your decision.'

'How soon do you need our answers?' Mrs. Columbo asked.

'It doesn't have to be an overnight deal,' Boomer said. 'Come to it when you're ready. But come to it soon.'

Mrs. Columbo missed working homicide. Missed it desperately. At best, she was indifferent to her new job – selling insurance from a bland cubicle in a downtown office building. When she was a cop, she always used to pick up a phone after the first ring, waiting for the voice on the other end to tell her that a body had been found and a killer needed to be caught. Now she often let it ring four or five times, knowing it would only be someone asking about the new rates on their car insurance or looking for a two-week extension on a payment. She had stopped reading mysteries and watching them on television. She no longer followed the crime stories in the papers and on the news. Mrs. Columbo was afraid to do anything that would remind her of how much she loved the puzzle of a case.

She knew she should have been a happy woman. There was a husband at home who loved her and cared about her and a son to watch grow. There were PTA meetings to attend and Little League games to monitor. School plays needed to be put on and cake sale funds had to be raised. And while Mrs. Columbo packaged all these activities into parts of her day, she did it without any emotion. It was the same way she approached her physical therapy sessions, handling the difficult exercises with a cold

185

efficiency, hoping that the feeling would soon return to her lower back and ease the sharp pains running down her legs.

Every Sunday, on a rotating basis, Mrs. Columbo and her family had dinner with relatives. The packed dining rooms all looked and sounded the same to her, whether at her sister-in-law's Mineola ranch in Nassau County or her brother-in-law's Bergen County Tudor. The talk always revolved around family, bills, old squabbles, sports, and retirement. The language of middle-class life. She listened and participated, but her words were empty. Maybe it was because none of the talk was ever about an unidentified male found floating by the edge of the river late into the night. No one at any of the tables cared about what to look for at a crime scene, or how to read a suspect's walk and tell who was the one with the killer's heart.

Mrs. Columbo hated not being a cop. Every pained breath she took reminded her of that. Now Boomer was sitting across from her and offering a chance to be one again. She sipped her coffee and wondered if maybe the wounds she suffered had done more than just scar her body. She worried that they had also stripped away her skill.

'You still haven't told us what you want us to do,' Pins said, washing down his fifth beer of the long night.

'I want us to go after Lucia,' Boomer said. 'The people at this table up against whatever she's got.'

'Six disabled cops and a waiter making a move against an army of drug smackers who like killing cops a lot more than they like selling junk.' Rev. Jim leaned across the table, a hand on Boomer's forearm. 'I'm not one to give advice, but maybe you should give your idea a little more thought.'

Rev. Jim sat back and kept his gaze on Boomer. He still couldn't understand why he was chosen to be at this meeting. Sure, he had once been a great decoy cop and

186

loved working with different disguises and accents, but that was long before the fire burned the skin from his body. He wanted so much to be a part of what Boomer was putting together, but Rev. Jim knew he had nothing left but a smart mouth and an old gun, and that wasn't going to get anybody at the table very far. And it wasn't just the burns, it was the weakened muscles, the charred lungs, the left eye that constantly teared. These other cops didn't know what he needed to do just to get through one day. He gauze-wrapped his body in winter to keep the cold air from touching the raw skin, otherwise it would feel like dry ice on flesh. He wore long-sleeved shirts in the summer to keep away the rays of the sun and the cutting pain that they would bring. Boomer was asking him to be a cop again when there were some mornings he wasn't sure if he could even be a man.

Rev. Jim still needed three more skin-graft operations and many months of physical therapy. Even then there would be no promise of relief. On some nights, long past final call, lying in an empty bed, inside a cold apartment, Rev. Jim would stare up at the ceiling and wonder why he was even alive at all. It would be so easy on those nights to open his desk drawer, take out his .38, and swallow a bullet. Instead, he would reach for the cardboard box he kept under the bed. He would open its flaps and empty its contents on the sweat-stained sheets: his graduation photo from the Police Academy; a replica of his shield; a handful of colored ribbons; three folded citations for bravery; and the knife he had used to kill the dealer who murdered his mother. It wasn't much, but it was enough to keep him alive.

Rev. Jim kept his eyes on Boomer. He realized why the call had been made. Boomer knew he still wanted to be a cop. Still wanted to be a man. Scars and all.

'We're not walking into this blind,' Boomer said.

'That's the one thing we're missing,' Pins said. 'A blind guy.'

187

'We've all got the connections,' Boomer said. 'Federal and local are covered solid. We can pull files, run taps, have computer access. And on the other end Nunzio will hook us into the old wise guys. They hand us what the feds can't. Everything we need is a phone call away.'

'Why is everybody going to be so eager to help us?' Mrs. Columbo asked.

'They want Lucia to go down as bad as we do,' Boomer said. 'But they have to go by the book. Our book was taken away. In their own way, the real cops are just as disabled as we are. Maybe more.'

'What if we don't get killed?' Dead-Eye asked. 'What if we just get caught?'

'Jail time ain't a sweet time for a cop,' Rev. Jim said, taking a match from his mouth and putting it back in his shirt pocket.

'We keep a book,' Boomer said. 'Fill it with the names of everyone who helps us – from a cop who drops a dime on a guy to an ADA making a few copies of a confidential file.'

'We get pinched, we show the district attorney the book,' Dead-Eye said.

'We show him a *copy* of the book,' Boomer said. 'Tell him there are at least six others floating around. That should give him something to worry about.'

'It's like Allstate,' Nunzio said. 'An insurance policy.'

Everyone either laughed or smiled at Nunzio's crack.

Except for Pins.

He held his worried look. Pins didn't think he belonged here, just like he didn't belong in many of the places he'd been in his life. He knew why he was asked. That end was easy to figure. The group would need somebody good with a wire, and it wouldn't have taken Boomer long, after asking around, to end up looking his way. But this was a hard group, used to heavy action, not afraid to empty a clip inside a crowded room. And that just wasn't a road Pins traveled down.

The only thing he shared with the cops who sat around

188

the table was a damaged body. He might not have been in as much pain as some of the others, but the confident man who had walked into the wrong apartment less than two years before was long gone. In his place was someone with several vital organs that had been shredded by three bullets. That someone had mended slowly, working his lung capacity to the point where he could once again take deep breaths with only minimal amounts of pain. His right arm was numb from the elbow down, and he suffered from constant migraines, popping as many as five Butal-bital tablets a day to ease the pressure. Pins collected his disability pension, paid off the mortgage on his Staten Island home, and invested in a bowling alley. Three after-noons a week, he let the neighborhood kids in free to bowl as many games as they wanted. All he asked in return was for them to clean up after they were done and to put the balls and shoes back in place. Pins enjoyed having the kids around. It gave him a sense of family, which he craved. He wanted so much to fit in, to be part of a group. It was what he had on the job. It was what he had with the kids on the lanes. And he realized it was what Boomer was offering him from across the table.

For a man like Pins, belonging was all that mattered. Mixed with that desire, however, was a deeply hidden fear, one Pins thought he would never have to face again. It was the fear of the gun.

Like the other members of the group, Pins never worried about dying. But he didn't want to have to survive another wounding, didn't think he could walk through that pain and come out of it one more time. He also didn't know if he could complete the one act that seemed second nature to the other cops in the room – Pins didn't know if he could kill a man. His risk was always in laying down the plant, his action was in the wire, his trigger was turning on the tape. That was where he excelled. With this group, it was a talent that just might not be enough.

*

189

'When do we go?' Geronimo asked, scanning the faces of the others, trying to detect their levels of interest.

'I start Monday morning,' Boomer said. 'I'll be working out of Nunzio's basement. We'll keep everything we need down there. Anybody else who shows up that day starts with me.'

'This crew of ours,' Rev. Jim said. 'You gonna give it a name?'

'The Crips would be good,' Pins tossed in. 'But that LA gang beat us to the punch.'

'I haven't thought of one,' Boomer said. 'Is it important?'

'Eventually, Lucia's gonna wanna know who we are,' Rev. Jim said. 'Who it is fucking up her business. Be nice if we could tell her. Let her know who she's at war with.'

'Apaches,' Geronimo said in somber tones. 'We should call ourselves the Apaches.'

'Just because you've got a little Indian blood in you?' Dead-Eye asked. 'I've got African blood all through me. Don't hear me layin' any of that *Roots* shit on the rest of you.'

'In this case, we all have Indian blood,' Geronimo said, turning from one face to the other. 'In Apache tradition, when a warrior was wounded in battle, he was left behind by the tribe. Left to fend and care for himself. He had become too much of a burden to the tribe. That's us, Dead-Eye. That's all of us.'

'Do we get shirts and hats to go with the name?' Rev. Jim asked. 'You know, with our logo?'

'What about Nunzio?' Pins asked. 'What do we make him?'

'A scout,' Mrs. Columbo said, leaning her head against Nunzio's shoulder.

'Okay, we've got a name,' Boomer said, standing, reaching behind him for his jacket. 'And by Monday after-noon, based on who's here with me, I'll know if we've got a team.'

They all stood, picked up their coats and hats, shook

190

hands, and headed for the door, moving quietly, minds already drifting toward a decision.

Geronimo and Boomer waited for Nunzio, watching as he closed up the restaurant.

'That on the level?' Boomer said.

'What?' Geronimo asked.

'About the Apaches. And leaving their wounded behind.'

'How the hell should I know?' Geronimo said, smiling for the first time all night.

Boomer smiled back as he put on his jacket. 'Well, as of tonight it's a fact.'

'Sure it is,' Geronimo said, following Boomer and Nunzio out the door. 'First Custer, then Wounded Knee, and now the Apaches.'

13

Bobby Scarponi, shirtless, a hand towel draped around his neck, stared into the mirror. The exposed bulb just above the hanging glass cast the small bathroom in a series of shadowy contrasts. He ran a hand along the red scars covering the upper part of his chest and running into his neck and cheek. They were hard and crusty to the touch, a constant reminder of the flames that had changed the course of his life.

Rev. Jim lived in Queens, a one-bedroom apartment on the second floor of a private home owned by a carpenter and his wife who seemed to be foolishly too young for him. It was the kind of apartment usually reserved for a young man starting out. It was not meant as a final stop.

Rev. Jim walked out of the bathroom, passed the small kitchen, and stopped by the open window near his bed, thin white drapes flapping in the wind. He stared down at the quiet street below, filled with parked cars and lit by the glow from a series of houses similar to the one in which he lived. It was how he spent most of his nights, his mind crowded with visions of his mother dying by his side, flames and heat surrounding his body, his mouth too seared for him to scream.

He was afraid of lying down to sleep. It only brought the visions to life, causing him to wake up bathed in sweat and tears, having ripped and torn at his sheets and skin. So he rarely slept. Rarely rested. Rarely escaped the hell that was his past, present, and future.

Rev. Jim had often thought of suicide, but knew if he was ever really going to go that route, it would have happened after his mother's death. Rev. Jim was not the kind of man to go out with a note, a bag over his head, and a rope around his neck. He was a fighter and needed to find a better way out.

Boomer's plan seemed just the route he sought.

He turned from the window, went over to the refrigerator, pulled out a cold can of Budweiser, popped it open, and took two long slurps. He leaned his back against a cold wall and reached for the phone, dialing a familiar number with his free hand. He let it ring eight times before he hung up. His father had always been a sound sleeper; age had only made that sleep deeper.

Rev. Jim finished the beer, tossed the empty into a silver trash can near the window, and reached for the phone again. The voice on the other end responded on the third ring. He heard Boomer grumble a hello and waited. He took a deep breath, eyes searching past the houses across the way, gripping the receiver hard enough to crush it.

'I'm in,' he finally said. Boomer stayed silent on the other end. 'Good night.'

Rev. Jim hung up the phone, walked slowly back toward the open window, and waited for the morning sun to arrive and bring with it a small sense of relief.

The mule stepped out of the cab and looked up at the four-story Manhattan brownstone, the infant cradled in her arms. She walked slowly up the front steps as the cab sped off into the New York night. She heard the dead bolt on the front door click open as an icy blast of winter air snapped against the edges of her skirt. A large man in a red silk shirt and black leather pants stood braced next to the door. He nodded a greeting as she went past.

'Which way?' the mule asked, her eyes catching a glimpse of the .44 semiautomatic holstered and exposed under his sleeve.

'Take the hall steps,' the man said, locking the door

and turning his bulk toward the mule. 'The second door on your left.'

'Everybody there?' She moved toward the center hall, her heels clacking on the slick hardwood floor.

'Everybody that needs to be,' the man said, disappearing around a corner, heading into a games room with a full bar and pool table.

The mule took the steps in a rush, gripping the baby with both hands, eager to get on with her task. She turned a sharp corner at the head of the stairwell and nudged open the second door in the hall. She walked in and rested the still baby on a large wood table, next to six hefty stacks of hundred-dollar bills, each wrapped with thin strips of white twine. Four men, sitting in hard-backed chairs spaced throughout the oak-paneled, book-lined room, stood and joined her by the table.

'How much time do you have?' Paolo, the smallest of the men, asked, offering a cigarette from a half-empty pack of Marlboros.

'Flight to Atlanta leaves in two hours,' the mule said, refusing the cigarette. 'I make the exchange at the airport and catch a connecting to LA.'

Paolo turned from the mule and nodded at the three men huddling around the cash. 'We'll wait for you downstairs.'

'How long?' one of the three asked.

'Thirty minutes at the most,' Paolo said, leading the mule by the arm, walking her out of the room and shutting the door softly.

Joe Silvestri threw one pillow against the bedroom wall. Another clipped the shuttered windows and fell against a bureau lamp, knocking it harmlessly to its side. 'Is this what you been doin' all this fuckin' time?' he shouted. His anger was directed at his wife, Mary, who sat under a pile of blankets, her flannel nightgown buttoned to the collar. 'Cookin' up crazy schemes on disability night?'

'Stop yelling, please,' Mary said. She kept a tight rein

on her reaction and her emotions under control. 'You're going to wake up Frankie.'

'Almost losin' your life wasn't enough for you?' Joe continued to shout, stomping around the small bedroom in bare feet and red Jockey shorts. 'Almost leaving him without a mother wasn't enough to make you wanna turn your back for good? And almost leaving me, not that you give a shit, should at least be worth a little something after all these years.'

'All of that *is* important.' Mary kept her eyes on her husband, understanding his need to vent, trying not to let her words cut deeper into the frustration he harbored over never having the kind of wife he so much wanted. 'Don't think for a minute that it isn't.'

'If you do this, Mary, you gotta know it's over between you and me,' Joe said, stopping at the edge of the bed. 'I've lived through a lot with you, but I won't live with this. You lookin' to get yourself buried, get somebody else to help you do it.'

'Look at me, Joe,' Mary said, trying not to make her words sound like a plea for help. 'I've got scars up and down my body. I can't even look at myself in the shower without crying. I work at a job I hate when I'm there and hate thinking about when I'm not.'

'Not many people get shot selling insurance policies.' Joe spit the words out and sat on the side of the bed away from his wife. 'And they like you there. You're doing good work for good people.'

'It's not what I want,' Mary said softly. 'And it's not what I need.'

'Going out on a suicide job, that's what you want? And getting yourself killed and breaking the law while you're at it, that's what you need?'

'I'm dead now, Joe,' Mary said, pushing back the covers and sliding across the bed to sit next to him. 'You have to be able to see that. To know that. I'm never going to be the kind of wife you want. Especially not the way I am now.'

195

'You don't need to tell me.' Joe stared down at the violet carpet. 'I learned that a long time ago.'

'I need to try and get back to being the kind of cop I was,' Mary said. 'For no other reason than to feel alive again.'

'What about us?' Joe asked, turning to face her. 'What about me and Frankie? And what about me and you?'

'I love you both very much,' Mary said. 'But I love you both for what you are and who you are. That's all I'm asking from you in return. After all these years, you've got to know I'm not someone who keeps house. And I sure as hell am not someone who sells insurance.'

'And you're not someone who can cook worth a shit either.' Joe shook his head and forced a smile, putting an arm around his wife's shoulders.

'I'm a cop, Joe.' Mary rested her head on his chest. 'Like it or not, you fell in love with a cop.'

'And I'm still in love with one,' Joe said. 'No matter what you might think.'

'Then let me do this,' Mary said in a whisper. 'Please.'

'You want my okay for you to go out and get yourself killed.' Joe sighed. 'That's an awful lot to ask from *anybody*. Let alone your husband.'

'The only person I'd ever ask *is* my husband,' Mary said. 'I'm asking you to let me go out and feel what it's like to be alive again.'

'Who tells Frankie?' Joe asked after a long silence.

'We will,' Mary said with a slow smile. 'You and me. In the morning, while you're making us all pancakes.'

'Looks like I'm back to doing the cooking now too,' Joe said.

'And it looks like I'm back to being a cop,' Mary said, leaning against her pillow, holding Joe's hand and bringing him along.

'Don't die on me, Mary,' Joe said. 'That's all I'll ask from you.'

'That's a big step over what you used to ask,' Mary said, a full smile spread across her face now.

196

'What was that?' Joe said, slipping under the blankets alongside his wife.

'Not to burn the eggs,' Mary said.

In the shadows of the quiet room, they held each other tight, kissed, and slid farther under the blankets, finding warmth and comfort with each touch.

The mule spotted Erica standing with her back to a news stand, a small cardboard sign printed with the word STEVENS across it. She walked over, gave the woman a quick smile and a nod, and handed her the baby boy.

'Your plane's at the next terminal,' Erica said. 'Two stops on the tram.' She was dressed in a black pants suit, the jacket with too much shoulder padding. A thin shawl rested around her neck. She wore open-heeled slides and favored her right leg when she walked. She carried the baby in the crook of her left arm, more like a sack than an infant.

'Anything you want me to tell Leo?' Erica asked.

'That I need a vacation,' the mule said without a trace of a smile. 'They've run me ragged these last three weeks. I can barely stand up.'

'We're in the middle of a gold rush,' Erica said. 'There's too much money to make to let up now.'

The tram pulled into the stop area and a prerecorded voice alerted passengers as to their destination. The mule stepped aboard, grabbed a handrail, and looked at Erica, giving her a tired smile.

'I'll be back Tuesday,' she said.

The mule turned her back as the doors closed, leaving behind two late-arriving passengers.

Erica stayed on the platform and watched her go, holding the baby and, inside it, the $125,000 in cash.

Geronimo sat on a damp block of wood on the deserted beach, listening to a series of ocean waves batter the soft sands of the shoreline. His legs were crossed and his arms folded; his head was tilted up toward the star-packed sky.

A rush of cold wind blew through the back of his dark blue sweater and sent thick strands of his hair slapping across the front of his face.

This small strip of land had become Geronimo's favorite spot, a private beach nestled quietly away from the large clapboard homes of Ocean Parkway, down a side ramp from the Brooklyn/Queens Expressway. It was his refuge, a place to come, hole up and clear his head, re-energized by fresh salt air and marsh breezes. A place where he could feel safe and disconnected from the pressures of his life.

Geronimo was slow to recover from the multiple wounds he had suffered from the grenade. On a Brooklyn street, surrounded by caked blood, streams of smoke, and frightened screams, he had left behind a shattered stomach, chunks of his liver and kidney, and all of his small intestine. The months of rehab were painful and frustrating, and a man with less inner strength would have found it easy to quit. But Geronimo had actually thrived under the weight of such a battle, especially one so personal, and he made it his business to come out of it as whole a person as possible.

Barely able to digest even soft foods and cool liquids, he had to learn how to eat all over again. The early surgeries to piece his stomach back together were ineffective and painful. Still Geronimo would not give in, mixing weekly visits to an army of specialists with nightly sessions with a Native American mystic whose form of medicine knew no age.

Geronimo believed in the healing ways of the past and the recuperative powers of long-dormant ghosts. That was one of many reasons he spent so much time sitting in his private corner of beach, alone in darkness, lost in the shadow of the stars.

He took to his healing by walking in small steps and casting his will to the whim of past warriors, gaining from the study of their lives the strength he currently lacked and the force of spirit he had nearly abandoned after his disability.

When he wasn't being probed by technicians or losing himself to the fog of the mystic, he stayed by himself and prayed to the gods of his mother. His prayers were more than pleas for renewed health. They were soulful cries that he be made one again and be allowed to die as he was meant to die, as he was destined to die.

As a warrior.

Down deep in his heart he knew it was an impossible request. His future looked to be as numb and dull as the emptiness he felt in the pit of his stomach. It would be a mournful life devoid of action and confrontation.

He missed those tense moments with the instrument, the precious rare seconds when he was alone, only a slight twitch of the hand away from instant death. Those hours spent in front of a bomb, time slipping before him with each tick of the clock, were the hours Geronimo felt fully alive and in total control. It was the period during which he felt most united with the spirit of his ancestors. And he would give anything to experience that feeling again. That was what he prayed for.

It was a desperate prayer from a lonely man.

It was not until his dinner with Boomer, in a restaurant whose food he couldn't eat, that Geronimo realized his desperate prayer might be answered.

Lucia held out her empty glass and stared across the ocean as a young waiter nervously poured from a stainless-steel pitcher filled with perfectly chilled martini. She was stretched out on a blue lounge chair on the sun-drenched front deck of the *Maraboo*, a sixty-five-foot yacht her fourth husband, Gerald Carney, had bought for her as a wedding present. A black two-piece bathing suit revealed skin tanned the color of toast. Light beads of sweat dotted her thin arms, shapely legs, and flat, muscular stomach.

The boat was anchored three miles off the Bermuda coast and carried a full working crew of seven – one waiter, one chef, a nanny, and four armed bodyguards. The nanny was there to care for Gerald Carney's eight-year-old daughter from a previous marriage. The girl, Alicia, sat on a white beach towel and played to Lucia's left, dressed in a polka dot swimsuit and surrounded by a gaudy array of Barbie dolls.

Gerald Carney sat across from his wife, legs crossed, white sailor shirt hanging over a plump stomach. Carney was sixty-one years old, a retired investment banker born to money and bred to silence. He met Lucia in the spring of 1980 when she came to his Manhattan office seeking advice on how best to shelter her cash flow. He knew her business was drugs and had heard rumors about the hand she played in disposing of her previous husbands. But Gerald Carney had dealt with all breeds in his four decades of investing, laundering, and skimming money. His nefarious clients had made him a very wealthy man.

Carney and Lucia were quick to move their financial conversation from his office to a nearby bar and then, within weeks, to the bedroom of his Park Avenue penthouse apartment. They married on the same rainy afternoon that Carney's divorce from an East Side socialite was finalized. They chose to keep separate residences, Lucia more comfortable working out of her central bases of Miami and Sedona, while Carney kept to his Manhattan–Los Angeles axis. He asked few questions about her business and she asked none about his. But she grew to trust him in all matters financial. In less than a year's time, Lucia saw her hidden stash of five million dollars nearly double. Her new husband never met any of her associates and she was quick to shun the role of hostess on those rare occasions when they were in the same town. Theirs was a business partnership that made room for occasional moments of passion.

It was the kind of marriage Lucia had always dreamed about.

A fairy tale come true.

The Cross Bay Lanes were shut down for the night, outside lights dimmed, front doors bolted. Inside, the large Bud sign above the bar cast a green glow across the lanes, all of them dark except for one. A corner jukebox sent out a haunting Ry Cooder instrumental.

Pins Ryan stood crouched above the black bowling ball cupped in his hands. His feet were planted firm and balanced. He took three steps forward, arched the ball behind him, and brought it down in one smooth motion with his left hand. His front foot curved as the ball slammed against the hardwood and buzzed toward the pins, scattering eight of them, leaving behind only the three and four. Pins walked slowly back to the scoring table, took a swig from a bottle of Amstel, and then stood still, enjoying the quiet darkness of his alley.

He had bought a share of the place three months after the shooting, going in as full partner with two retired firemen from Ozone Park. The income from the alley, coupled with his disability pension, made Pins more than comfortable and afforded him the stable environment he had always sought. Besides, he could bowl seven days and nights a week without digging into his pocket.

He had neither a wife nor a family, but since so much of his life had been spent in solitary circumstances, this lack of intimate ties no longer seemed important. He had plenty of friends, most of them bowling buddies. And unlike many of the other disabled cops Pins came across from time to time, he didn't miss the job. On certain occasions, when a special call came in, Pins still laid down some plants for the department, pleased to note his wounds hadn't cost him his skills.

He removed the ball from its base, took his position, and blew out the two standing pins to record a spare. After penciling in his score for the opening frame, he took in a deep breath, relishing the stale smells of the old alley, looking around at the rows of shiny balls glistening in the light off the Bud sign. Behind him, racks of old bowling shoes, each colored uglier than the next, hung in straight rows of twelve across, based on size and use. He loved being in the alley, especially when it was dark and empty, a dozen lanes all to himself.

The alley was his home, a place for him to get away, roll as many games as it took for him to erase from his mind the places he'd been and the faces he wanted to forget.

But being a cop was where he was most needed.

If Pins could no longer fill that large void as a member of the department, he could easily do so as one of the Apaches. He could be their safety net, planting bugs in hidden places. A piece of his life's puzzle that had been missing for years could now be fitted back into its proper place.

Three games, one beer, and two cups of coffee later, Pins had decided to join up with Boomer's team of crippled cops. He would lay down the taps and wires to help the Apaches reel in Lucia Carney. He would ignore his fear of the gun and hide behind the shield of the electronic bug.

Those three games were the best Pins had bowled since he was invalided out of the force. The best since he'd started to use his left, rather than his right arm to bowl.

Boomer sat across from a gray metal desk stacked high with books, files, and newspapers, hands jammed inside his jacket pockets, gnawing on a thick wad of spearmint gum. He watched as Dr. Carolyn Bartlett reached down into her briefcase and pulled out a worn manila folder with Jennifer Santori's name written across the front in black felt-tip. She placed it on top of a six-deep pile of similar-looking folders, opened it, gave the cover sheet a quick read, then sat back in her tattered black swivel chair. She looked over at Boomer through tired eyes, her face shrouded by tension.

'I appreciate your stopping by,' she said, her voice echoing the exhaustion in her eyes.

'I was already in the neighborhood,' Boomer said casually, resisting the temptation to blow a bubble with his gum. 'I'm going to meet Jenny's folks over by the court-house. Watch that bastard get arraigned.'

'I know,' Dr. Bartlett said. 'They told me.'

'When did you talk to them?' Boomer sat up in his chair, his police radar kicking into alert.

'I called them late last night,' she said, pointing a mani-cured finger toward the brown couch and coffee table next to Boomer. 'I don't usually drink, Mr. Frontieri. But I needed one just to be able to make that phone call.'

'Call me Boomer.' He pulled his hands from his jacket pockets and looked over at the two empty coffee con-tainers, wine glass, and half-empty bottle of warm Chardonnay scattered around the end table. The couch cushions were crumpled and there was a thin brown blanket rolled up in one corner. 'It must have been a tough call. Looks like you spent the night here too.'

'I need your help with this,' Carolyn said. 'If you go against me, it will only make it rougher for everyone.'

'I don't know what this is, but I'm not going to like it, am I?'

'No,' she said, shaking her head, her eyes meeting his. 'You're going to hate what's being done and you're going to hate me for doing it. But I'm willing to risk all that if I come out of it having saved a little girl's life.'

'You need a drink before you tell me too?' Boomer asked.

'I've asked that the district attorney's office drop all charges against Malcolm Juniper,' she said in as firm a voice as she could muster.

'Your reason?' Boomer said, staying tight, keeping control of his temper.

'In order to convict, they'll need to put Jennifer on the witness stand,' Carolyn said. 'I can't allow that to happen.'

'Why not?'

'As it is, it's going to take years of therapy to get Jennifer to the point where what happened will fade to a distance she can live with. If I let her take the stand, let his lawyers have a shot at her, force her to relive every minor detail,

203

I can almost guarantee you she'll be nothing more than a vegetable for the rest of her life. I can't live with that. And I'm hoping you can't either.'

Boomer stayed outwardly calm but his hands bunched into fists and his eyes betrayed the anger burning inside. 'What about Malcolm? Without Jenny taking the stand, he'll go out on the streets and do the same thing all over again. To some other girl. You ready to live with that, Doc?'

'I've lived with it every day I've been in this damn job,' Carolyn said, her frustration rising to the surface. 'I've had to help piece back together too many Jennys. And I've had to sit and watch as too many Malcolms walked out of court free men.'

'What is it you want from me?' Boomer asked her.

'Talk to the family,' Carolyn said. 'Convince them it's the right thing to do for their child. If they want me to continue to help her, then this has to be the way.'

Boomer took a deep breath and ran a hand across his face. The image of Jennifer hanging from a pipe, seconds from death, her body a beaten and bloody mess, raced through his mind.

'In all my years on the job, I was pretty lucky,' Boomer said quietly. 'I usually got to see only the bad guys. And I went after them like no one ever has because I always knew that behind the face of a bad guy there was one of an innocent victim. So when I brought that bad guy in, it was my own way of helping out the victim.'

'You're still helping out the victim,' Carolyn said with sympathy. 'More than you will ever know.'

'We're helping out Malcolm too,' Boomer said. 'More than you'll ever know.'

'Would you rather I put Jenny on the stand?' Carolyn asked him. 'Would you rather torture her more, all for the sake of a conviction?'

Boomer lowered his head and his voice, staring down at thin, frayed strands of industrial carpet. 'No,' he said in a near whisper. 'I don't want that kid to be hurt any more.'

'Then talk to her parents,' Carolyn said. 'You can say things to them in a way that I can't.'

'Jenny's father came to me because he knew something I didn't,' Boomer said.

'What?'

'He knew that I'd bring in Malcolm and save his kid.'

'And you did bring him in,' Carolyn said. 'You and your partner did save her life. Don't let that get lost in all of this.'

'Maybe so,' Boomer said, standing up and zippering his jacket. 'But we did make one mistake. One very big mistake.'

'Which was?' Carolyn also stood. She reached out her hand and placed it in his.

'We brought him in alive,' Boomer said.

He shook Carolyn Bartlett's hand, turned, and walked slowly out of her office.

Dead-Eye banked a shot against the backboard, took a step back, and watched as the ball fell through the net. He let his son, Eddie, race for the bouncing ball, grab it with both hands, and toss it back to him.

'Your shot,' Dead-Eye told him. Both of them were smiling. 'Make it count.'

Eddie, one month past his third birthday, bounced the ball twice against the concrete court, then stumbled, scraping his hands and falling down to his knees.

'What happened to you?' Dead-Eye asked, lifting him to his feet and dusting off his hands.

'I fell,' Eddie said, brushing off the fall with a sad face and a shrug.

'Game's over anyway,' Dead-Eye said, reaching down to give his son a quick hug. 'I guess you know what that means?'

'Winner buys ice cream.' The smile rushed back to Eddie's face.

'I don't remember who won,' Dead-Eye said. 'Do you?'

'I didn't score, Daddy,' Eddie giggled. 'You did.'

'Looks like it's me buyin' again.' Dead-Eye feigned a sigh, lifting his son in the cradle of one arm, bouncing the basketball with his free hand and walking out of the fenced-in playground and toward the ice cream truck parked at the next corner.

They sat with their backs against the black wall of a handball court, their legs stretched out, faces up to the sun, each working over a double-swirl vanilla ice-cream cone. Eddie was getting as much on his chin and cheeks as he was in his mouth, occasionally dabbing at his face with a wadded-up ball of napkins. The grounds around them were quiet and empty except for two winos sleeping the night off on a set of park benches to their right.

'Is Mama mad?' Eddie asked, his gaze focused on the melting ice cream in his hands.

'Yes,' Dead-Eye said. 'She's very mad at me.'

'Why?'

'She doesn't want me to do something,' Dead-Eye said.

'Why?'

Dead-Eye looked down at his son, washed in ice cream, his innocent face crammed with a natural sweetness, his eyes blazing with curiosity. He reached over, picked him up, and wiped the ice cream from his face. He then sat Eddie between his legs, resting the boy's head against his chest.

'What kind of work does Daddy do?' Dead-Eye asked him, leaning down and kissing the top of his son's head.

'You let people into buildings,' Eddie said, looking up at him. 'Right?'

'I'm a doorman,' Dead-Eye said. 'That's right.'

'Before that you were a policeman. Mama said you were famous.'

'I wasn't famous,' Dead-Eye said. 'I was good. There's a difference.'

'Mama says you don't like opening doors.' Then Eddie asked, 'That why she's mad at you?'

206

'Being a doorman is a good job,' Dead-Eye said, looking out over the park, past the swings and slides, the backed-up traffic moving into Manhattan. 'It's just not the right job for me.'

'Mama says you wanna be a policeman again.'

'And that's why she's mad,' Dead-Eye said. 'She's afraid I'll get shot up all over again.'

Eddie jumped from his father's lap and turned to face him.

'I don't want you to die, Daddy.' There was a lilt of fear in his voice.

Dead-Eye laid his two hands on the sides of his son's face and stared at him for several moments, willing the fear from the boy's body.

'I want you to be proud of me,' Dead-Eye said. 'Same way that I'm so proud of you. When you grow up, I want you to go out and do what's in your heart to do. What you feel you have to do more than anything else. You'll find what that is, maybe early, maybe late, but you'll find it. Same way I found what I had to do. Then I got shot and I lost it.'

'Mama said you and Uncle Boomer are both crazy,' Eddie said.

'She's right about that,' Dead-Eye said, smiling at his son. 'We are crazy. But it's a good crazy, Eddie. The kind you need to have around every once in a while.'

'Are the bad people crazy?'

'Bad people are always crazy,' Dead-Eye said. 'That's why they do what they do. And sometimes it takes crazy guys like me and Uncle Boomer to go out there and stop them.'

'Are you going to be a policeman again?' Eddie asked.

'I never really stopped,' Dead-Eye said, resting his son back against his chest. 'But I won't do this until I know you're okay with it. Until I know you're backing me up. All good cops need a backup. So that's what I'm asking you to be.'

'Do I get a badge?' Eddie asked, lifting his head.

'Even better,' Dead-Eye said, reaching a hand inside the front pocket of his windbreaker and coming out with a replica of a detective's gold shield closed inside a leather flap. 'I made you a copy of my badge. That makes you my partner.'

'Uncle Boomer's your partner,' Eddie said, taking the badge from his father, his eyes opened wide in amazement.

'Uncle Boomer's my friend,' Dead-Eye said. 'And you don't have as many bad habits. So what's it gonna be? Are you with me? You gonna cover my back?'

'Yes, Daddy,' Eddie said, wrapping both arms around his father's neck, holding him tight, the shield dangling loose from his right hand.

Dead-Eye hugged his son close, his face nestled into the boy's shoulder.

They sat there, still and quiet in the chilly winter morning, their backs against a spray-painted wall, surrounded by barren trees, still swings, sleeping drunks, and congested traffic.

The courtroom was drab and silent. Court officers stood, arms folded, their backs to the few spectators in attendance. Judge Geraldine Waldstein, a thin woman with thick dark hair and sharp features, glared down at the defendant. Malcolm Juniper sat on a wooden chair wearing his only suit, a gray sharkskin, with a white button-down shirt and a thin black tie. Malcolm's lawyer, Jerry Spieglman, sat next to him, eyes gazing at an open folder.

Boomer sat in the third row, directly behind Jennifer's parents, Carlo and Anne. Dead-Eye had decided to wait outside. Like most cops, he felt uncomfortable in a courtroom. It was one of the few traits those inside the law shared with those outside. Boomer kept his eyes on the back of Malcolm's head, but his mind was in another place. He saw himself in uniform again, a rookie walking a Harlem beat with his mentor, Iron Mike Tragatti. Day after day, Tragatti, using his nightstick as a pointer, would hammer home the one lesson he insisted young Boomer learn.

'You see these people?' Iron Mike would say, pointing out the Harlem merchants opening their stores, preparing to serve their customers. 'They are the ones we're here to protect. They are the good. The bad are the ones who take from them. And they are the ones we put away. The courts call it justice. The people here call it safety. You and me call it our job. It's as simple as that.'

For two decades, Boomer Frontieri believed every one of those words. Believed them because they used to be true. But they weren't true anymore. Not on a day when he had to sit in a barren courtroom and stare helplessly at a mother and father, holding hands and crying as they listened to a new set of words, this time spoken by a judge with two children of her own.

Words that would set their daughter's tormentor free.

Judge Waldstein kept it simple and direct. Her shouts and frustration had been vented behind closed doors.

'You've got *nothing* else?' she had asked Kevin Gilbert, the assistant district attorney assigned to the case.

'Not without the girl, your honor,' Gilbert admitted. 'Erase her and I've got a room with two retired cops who shouldn't have been there in the first place, staring at one dead man and one naked one.'

'You have Dr. Bartlett's testimony,' Waldstein said. 'And you have photos of the crime scene.'

'It's all too cold and clinical,' Gilbert said. 'I need the jury to see Jennifer. It's the only way I can get a guilty.'

'Then we're wasting our breath,' Jerry Spieglman said. 'It's time to set the innocent free.'

'*I'll* decide when it's time, Counselor,' Judge Waldstein hissed.

In the courtroom, Judge Waldstein kept her anger masked behind a calm veneer. Her eyes were moist and strained as she uttered the phrase that shattered everyone else's serenity.

'Case dismissed,' Judge Waldstein said sadly.

Malcolm Juniper slammed an open hand on the scarred wooden table and clapped. Jerry Spieglman closed the folder and shoved it inside a soiled backpack.

Anne Santori bowed her head and sobbed quietly into the palms of her hands.

Carlo Santori turned and looked at Boomer Frontieri. It was the look of a defeated man.

Boomer took a deep breath, stood, and turned his back on the scales of justice, vowing never to enter a courtroom again.

Malcolm Juniper, a bounce to his gait, took the cracked concrete steps coming out of the Manhattan Criminal Court Building two at a time. He stopped short as soon as he spotted Boomer and Dead-Eye waiting for him on the sidewalk below, their backs warmed by a winter sun.

Malcolm's smile widened and he began to take the steps at a slower pace. He pulled a cigarette from his jacket pocket, turned his back to Boomer, Dead-Eye, and the wind, and lit up, using a cheap plastic lighter. He crunched the cigarette between his teeth, smoke leaking out one corner of his mouth, and barely disguised his glee from the ex-cops who had gone to such lengths to have him arrested.

'Scopin' out more innocent men?' Malcolm asked. 'Or you just come to apologize?'

'The judge and the DA cut you loose,' Boomer said, looking directly at Malcolm. 'Not me.'

'I ain't free but two minutes and you shot-up losers start hasslin' me.' Malcolm acted indignant, tossing the cigarette to the ground, inches from Dead-Eye's brown boot. 'My man Jerry here ain't gonna sit for that kinda shit.' Malcolm turned his head, looking over at the lawyer with a thick head of hair and a face layered with red pimples, whiteheads, and acne scars. 'That right, Jerry?'

Jerry Spieglman stepped forward, less confident than Malcolm about confronting Boomer and Dead-Eye. He was a low-tier lawyer building a practice from the bottom-feeder end of the pool. 'There's no need to further hassle my client,' Jerry said in a voice as light as his frame. 'He's been cleared by a court of law.'

'They got shit that can help that,' Dead-Eye said, pointing a finger at Jerry's scarred face. 'You let that get any worse, lepers are gonna start takin' a step back.'

'The only reason we're not pressing charges against the two of you is that my client wants this put behind him,' Jerry went on, trying to sound tough but not getting anywhere close. 'However, if you continue, you will force our hand.'

'Lemme pass it to you soft,' Malcolm added, full of swagger and dare. 'You breathe near me and you gonna be the ones in cuffs. That clear enough, Five-O? Or maybe all them bullets you two swallowed fucked up your hearing too.'

'Besides, you two guys are in enough trouble as it is,' Jerry said, taking his confidence cue from Malcolm, convinced now that he was in no physical danger. 'You don't need more. Certainly not from us.'

'How do you figure?' Boomer asked, curious. 'Us being the ones in trouble, I mean.'

'You're being named in the civil suit,' Jerry announced matter-of-factly. 'Along with the police department, the Santori family, and the city of New York. Malcolm was arrested for no just reason. Someone has to pay for that.'

'You're suing?' Dead-Eye asked, incredulous. '*You're* suing?'

'That's right, you crippled, mother-fuckin' losers.' Malcolm lit another cigarette. 'I don't wanna see you fuckers behind bars. Ain't nothin' in there for me. I want you out on them streets, workin' job after job and handin' that hard-earned green over to me. That's gonna eat you up, kill you quicker than any gun I could buy.'

Jerry stood between Boomer and Malcolm, nervously shifting his brown backpack from one hand to the other. Boomer took two steps toward him and put a hand on his shoulder.

211

'I want a word with your client,' Boomer said, squeezing the fingers of his hand tight across the top of Jerry's jacket. 'I want that word alone. And I know you're not going to have a problem with that. Am I right?'

'It's a reasonable request,' Jerry said, casting a quick glance at Malcolm. 'Not even you would be crazy enough to try something in passing view of the public.'

'All I see around me are skanks and ambulance chasers,' Dead-Eye said, glancing at the faces rushing by. 'We ain't exactly talking Vatican City.'

'I'll be over by the mailbox if you need my help,' Jerry told Malcolm. He lowered his head and slowly walked away.

'I needed your help *inside*, Jerry,' Malcolm said, inching closer to Boomer, taking a drag on the cigarette and letting the smoke flow toward the cop's face. 'Not out here. Not up against these limpin' fools. I got their shit down nasty.'

Boomer ignored the smoke and moved close enough to Malcolm to smell the nicotine and stale coffee on his breath and spot the marijuana seeds dotting his lower teeth.

'The court can give you all my money,' Boomer said in a low voice edged with violence. 'They can give you every dime I've got. And you can spend it any way that you want. Gamble it, sniff it, screw it. That doesn't mean shit to me. You walk your way, I walk mine, and we both live out our lives. But you even think about touching that girl again or taking one fucking thing from her family after all this and I will kill you in a way you never even knew existed.'

Malcolm's eyes widened in mock incredulity. 'I just hear a threat from the mouth of a cripple?'

'No,' Boomer said, standing as still as stone. 'It's no threat. It's a promise.'

*

Nunzio poured Boomer and Dead-Eye refills of their amaretto on the rocks, then held the bottle perched against his knees.

'*He's* suing,' Dead-Eye said. 'That motherfucker is suing the city!'

'And the city'll cut a sweet deal with him for sure,' Nunzio said, sadly shaking his head. 'They'll make sure it's kept under a tight wrap, but they want him out of everybody's picture. The best way to do that is to cut him a check and tell him to take a walk.'

'I never had a guy look at me the way Jenny's father did today.' Boomer gripped his glass with his right hand. 'It was all there on his face. Everything that kid suffered was right there, looking back at me.'

'You did your job,' Nunzio said. 'You both did. But there were other hands in this. You got no control over that. You can live with it or you can forget it. Either way, you gotta make it pass.'

Boomer said nothing, just stood and walked toward the bar, the lines on his weary face staring back at him in the large mirror hanging above the wide assortment of liquor bottles.

'He won and we lost,' Dead-Eye said. 'And when he gets that fat check, we lose all over again. Every fucking day he's alive, he wins all over again.'

'Guys like Malcolm don't live all that long,' Nunzio said solemnly. 'Things happen to people like him. Bad things. It don't take much. A call to the right ear is all you need.'

Both Dead-Eye and Boomer stayed still and silent after Nunzio's words. Boomer met Nunzio's eyes in the mirror, watched his face, empty of emotion, understanding the subtle weight of his words. He saw Dead-Eye look away from the window, his eyes catching Boomer's, his head giving a slow nod of approval.

Boomer turned from the bar and walked toward Nunzio, sitting on the edge of a stool. He stopped halfway between the bar and his two friends, picked up a hard-backed wooden chair, swung it over his head, and tossed it with a full force against the mirror above the bar. It landed in the center of the glass and shattered it, pieces large and small crashing to the wood floor and across the countertop.

'I'll pay you for that, Nunz,' Boomer said, his hands by his sides, his head hanging low.

'It's my treat, Boom,' Nunzio said, unfazed. 'I'll just take out for the chair.'

Boomer lifted his head and glanced over at Nunzio, his eyes welled with tears, his face flushed red.

'I have to go,' Nunzio said. 'You two stay as long as you want. Wreck the place if it puts smiles on your faces.'

'Where are you going?' Boomer asked, staring at the old man through wet eyes.

'To make a call,' Nunzio said. 'To find the right ear.'

It was a move both Boomer and Dead-Eye wanted to make but couldn't, and Nunzio knew that. They could never order a hit, pick up a phone, whisper a man's name and have him done away with. Even someone as despicable as Malcolm Juniper. They were tough cops but not cold-blooded ones. That's why they needed Nunzio as part of their team. He had made such calls before. He had grown up in the shadows of his father's world, a place where a nod of the head or the flicker of a light signaled the end of a life. Nunzio knew that the ones at the other end of the bullet were rarely innocents whose lives should or could be spared. He had learned at a young age that every time a call went out, it touched someone who was meant to die.

Nunzio stopped at the corner of Ninety-sixth Street and Amsterdam Avenue. He stood in front of a pay phone, the receiver in his right hand, dropped change into the coin slot, and pressed down on seven numbers.

He waited for the three rings and a pickup.

'Yes,' the voice on the other end said.

'Malcolm Juniper,' Nunzio said. 'Tonight.'

He hung up the phone and crossed the street against

214

passing traffic, heading for a corner news stand to buy a late-afternoon paper. The cold air felt clean and fresh against his face, and he whistled a show tune as he walked, the phone call now nothing but a memory.

Malcolm Juniper stumbled as he twisted his hand through his pants pocket, looking for the key to the midtown hotel room he had rented for the night.

The room was Jerry's treat, his gift for the sweet victory of the day. He even threw Malcolm three crisp hundred-dollar bills, an advance against their upcoming payday. Jerry told him the city was ready to settle, offering a tax-free six-figure sum if they just agreed to walk away, keep quiet, and forget about any lawsuits. Malcolm was all for the big check, but he wanted more. He wanted the police to hassle Boomer and Dead-Eye, maybe mess with their pensions, come down hard and teach the two cripples a lesson.

Teach them not to touch a player like Malcolm Juniper.

Malcolm had scored enough crack in three hours on the street to float his brain for a solid week. He had ordered up an Asian hooker to be sent to his room in less than an hour, pointedly asking the madam for somebody small, thin, and willing to handle rough action.

Malcolm was hungry for a party.

He dug out the key and with an unsteady hand slid it into the slot. He opened the door to the dark single-bed room and stepped inside, his right hand sliding up and down the wall, searching for a light. He kept the door open with the edge of his foot, allowing the light to filter in from the hall.

He stood on shaky legs, staring into the dark void of a hotel room, took in a deep breath, and gave out a short laugh. The warmth of the crack cocaine that flowed briskly through his body, combined with the sweet smell of the flowered room, had emptied him of all tension, all anger. He had made his score. He was a happy man who was only short weeks away from being a rich one.

Life was going to be good.

The man stepped out of the hallway shadows and stood behind Malcolm Juniper, moving with gentle motions. He was dressed all in black, from the brim of the fedora that hid his forehead and eyes to the desert boots that silenced his walk. He stood behind Malcolm and scanned the hall from left to right, a dark specter on a mission that would tolerate no interruption.

The man pressed the cold metal of a silencer against the nape of Malcolm's neck, feeling Malcolm's body arch and stiffen. He placed a gloved hand on the center of his back and eased him farther into the room. No words were exchanged, no emotions spent, as each man quietly understood the purpose of the visit.

There would be no party for Malcolm Juniper.

Nothing to celebrate. No hooker to stroke and torment through the long night. No big check to cash. No more innocent blood to shed.

Malcolm's journey was at an end.

The man in black closed the door behind him and locked it. The click of the cylinder caused Malcolm's eyes to flutter.

It was now only a matter of time.

BOOK THREE

Beat the drums of tragedy for me,
Beat the drums of tragedy and death.
And let the choir sing a stormy song
To drown the rattle of my dying breath.

Beat the drums of tragedy for me,
And let the white violins whir thin and
slow,
But blow one blaring trumpet note of sun
To go with me
       to the darkness
            where I go.

– Langston Hughes, 'Fantasy in Purple'

14
April 17, 1982

Outside the four-room second-floor apartment, the narrow Queens street was silent and still, leaves on the trees still damp from a late-afternoon shower. Cars were parked tightly on both sides, alarms armed, tires turned in curbside. All were empty except for two, which were parked directly in front of the building.

A middle-aged man sat upright in the lead car, a black four-door Buick LeSabre, smoking a thin cigar, windows rolled up tight. Periodically, the man checked both his watch and the safety on a .9-millimeter jammed inside the spine of the passenger seat. He was nervous and edgy, concerned that the people at work in the apartment above were leaving him little margin for error. He had chewed the lip of his cigar down to the quick, the smoke from its tip engulfing him in small circles. He was new to the country and even newer to a line of work that could easily end with a bullet to the head or a long prison sentence in a state with a name he couldn't pronounce.

The money made it worth the risk.

Three hundred in cash to drive a mule to the airport, another two hundred to gas the car and wait in the parking lot for the next pickup, and a final three hundred to wrap up the round trip. Eight hundred cash in less than four hours, three nights a week. Tack that on to the thousand-dollar salary he pulled in working for a private car service on Long Island, and Gregor Stavlav, less than three months in the States and a wanted man in his native

Greece, found himself smack in the middle of an American dream.

The car parked behind Gregor was dented, rusty, and dirty. He had given it a quick glance in his rearview mirror, then shrugged it off. It was the kind of car a student working his way through school, or a small-timer years past any chance at a score, might own. It was not the kind of car a man with money would be seen in, let alone call his own.

And it was definitely not a cop car.

That much Gregor, who prided himself on his knowledge of cars and the people who drove them, knew.

He would bet his life on it.

Rev. Jim loved his seven-year-old AMC Gremlin, loved the way it handled, even liked the way it looked. He took pride in the polished full-leather interior he had custom made at discount by a friend in Washington Heights and wasn't all that concerned by the ruined condition of the outer body. It was, for him, the perfect car.

He was stretched out across the front seat, head on the door rest, the heels of his construction boots flat against the passenger side jam, two .38 Police Specials crisscrossed on his chest. He slipped a cassette of Clifton Chenier and the Zodiac Ramblers into the tape deck and listened, at uncharacteristically low volume, as they stomped their way through 'The Things I Did for You'. Rev. Jim closed his eyes and took several deep breaths.

He wasn't sure if he was ready for what the Apaches had planned. This would be his first bout of heavy action since the fire that had disabled him, and while he could taste the fear, the adrenaline flow he always felt still hadn't kicked in. He knew the other members of the team were out there, positioned in the dark, ready to pounce, each of them probably running through the same emotional checks he was clicking off in his mind. He knew it was every cop's natural instinct to hesitate before going into a bust, but for reasons he couldn't quite pin down he seemed suddenly uncomfortable with those feelings.

Rev. Jim had always loved the rush that came with being a decoy, walking in blind, never knowing when or if the hit would come or if the assigned backup would really be there. It was all part of the play, risk being as important as the takedown. Rather than fear it, he had always welcomed it. Except for now.

Lying down next to the steering wheel of his beat-up Gremlin, Rev. Jim wondered if it was too late for him to be a cop again. Wondered if he had lost too much of what he needed.

He checked the red digital light on his wristwatch.

8:56 P.M.

In less than four minutes he would have his answer.

Boomer and Dead-Eye sat on opposite ends of the fire escape, backs to the wall, separated by the streaks of light pouring out from the kitchen. Both wore thin black leather jackets, thick black sweaters, and black racer gloves. Boomer had a .38 revolver in his right hand and another pushed into the back of his jeans. Dead-Eye had two .44 semiautomatics, both snug inside their shoulder holsters.

Boomer glanced into the kitchen and saw Carney's men talking in animated tones. Boomer knew the layout of the apartment and the backgrounds on the men inside from the sealed packet he had received earlier that morning from One Police Plaza. The two ring-leaders were called Albert and Freddie. There was a baby in a backroom. It was due to be shipped out that evening. If everything in the narcotics report held accurate, this would be the first hard slap by the Apaches against Lucia Carney.

'Two minutes more.' Dead-Eye checked his watch, then rested his head against the red brick wall, his eyes closed.

'Let's hope Geronimo hasn't lost the touch,' Boomer said. 'Otherwise we're in for a tough stretch.'

'Ain't Geronimo I'm worried about,' Dead-Eye said, still with his eyes closed.

221

'Who, then?' Boomer asked.

'Me,' Dead-Eye said.

Geronimo was on his knees, a short wire in his hand, a thick ball of plastique stuck to the door lock leading into the apartment. Mrs. Columbo and Pins were against the wall on either side of him, guns drawn, eyes on the stairwell and the other apartment doors.

'You going to make this?' Mrs. Columbo asked, looking down, watching Geronimo circle the coil wire into the plastique.

'It's easier taking them apart, that's for sure,' Geronimo said, his voice as calm as his manner.

'How long's that fuse gotta burn for?' Pins asked.

'Ten seconds.' Geronimo pulled a lighter from his jacket pocket and looked up at Pins. 'If I did it right.'

'What if you didn't do it right?' Pins said with just a bit of an edge. 'And it doesn't blow?'

'Then we knock,' Geronimo said, 'and hope they let us in.'

The front door blew out and exploded into six large chunks, taking out parts of the wall on both sides. Plaster, shards of tile, and blasts of dust whirled past the small foyer and out into the kitchen. The shudder of the bomb shook the apartment to its foundation and sent the men by the kitchen sink scrambling for cover.

Sprawled on the floor against cracked walls and toppled tables, the men were still quick enough to recover, drawing and cocking double-action revolvers, holding them out, arms extended.

Boomer and Dead-Eye both flinched when they heard the blast. But they held their position on the fire escape, waiting the agreed-upon ninety seconds for the dust to clear and for Geronimo, Pins, and Mrs. Columbo to stake out a solid post. The glass above them had cracked from

222

the explosion, but they could still see into the kitchen to watch the men regroup.

'You feeling young yet?' Boomer asked Dead-Eye, who was pulling his guns from their holsters.

'Young enough to be in love,' Dead-Eye told him.

Boomer lifted the kitchen window to waist level with the heel of one hand, letting out gusts of white smoke. He crouched down, pointing his gun into the open window. 'Then it's time to show them we're back.'

'And find out if anybody gives a shit,' Dead-Eye said, following him in.

Rev. Jim heard the rumble of the explosion and sat up, waiting for Gregor to bolt from his car. He had both his guns aimed at the back of the man's head, expecting him to jump out and hit the stairs to the house at full pace. Instead, Gregor held his place, cigar still stuck in the corner of his mouth, the interior of his car awash in smoke.

If the explosion didn't faze him, the quick clips of the four shots that came from Albert's gun made Gregor sit bolt upright behind the steering wheel. He rolled his window down, stuck his head out, and looked up at the apartment. His neck was glazed with sweat, his mouth was dry, yet he let the gun on the passenger seat rest there untouched. This was not part of the deal. He hadn't left Greece to be buried in America.

Gregor pulled his head back into the car, tossed the cigar on the sidewalk, rolled up the window, turned the ignition over, and pulled out of his parking spot. Rev. Jim smiled as he watched him speed off into the Queens night. Then he hopped out of the Gremlin, guns in hand, heading for the door of the apartment building. Rev. Jim turned and glanced down the street, the red taillights of Gregor's car still in his line of sight. He wondered if maybe the frightened driver with the hunger for American dollars just didn't have the right idea after all.

At least, this one night, he wasn't going to die.

*

Boomer came rolling out of the window and clicked off two rounds, hitting Freddie in the right shoulder and chest, sending him sprawling back to the floor. Dead-Eye, fast behind Boomer, jumped out of a crouched postion right behind Albert, jamming the barrels of both guns on the sides of his neck.

Geronimo and Mrs. Columbo fired eight rounds at the two men by the sink, three of the bullets clipping kitchen cabinets and lodging inside thick wall beams. Five bullets found their mark and sent the men sprawling to the ground.

Rev. Jim stood in the doorway, legs spread, two guns aimed into the apartment, looking for any movement. He exchanged a quick glance with Pins, who still held his position behind the end table, his gun by his side.

'Take the drugs,' Albert said in a calm voice, seemingly unfazed by the shooting and the massacred bodies around him. 'Take whatever you want.'

'You heard the man,' Boomer said, nodding to the four Apaches by the door. 'Take the drugs.'

Mrs. Columbo and Geronimo immediately holstered their guns as they walked toward the sink and the thick piles of cocaine. They took out Swiss Army knives, stepped around the bodies lying faceup on the ground, and sliced the cellophane packs down the center. Then they dumped the kilos into the sink, turned on the faucets, and let cold water take the powder down the drain.

'That's more than two hundred thousand you're throwin' away,' Albert said. He sounded more distressed over the disposal of the cocaine than over the loss of the lives around him.

'What's the time?' Boomer asked.

'We got three minutes till the cops show,' Pins said, the gun in his hand now replaced by a police scanner that allowed him to pick up all monitored calls. 'Maybe a few seconds less.'

224

Boomer walked over to stand across from Albert. 'The baby in there?' Boomer asked, looking at the bedroom.

Albert nodded. Mrs. Columbo went into it.

'Who the hell *are* you?' Albert asked, his eyes focused now on Boomer.

'I got the baby and its clothes,' Mrs. Columbo said, coming back from the bedroom holding an infant and an armful of small blue pajamas, diapers, a T-shirt the size of a handkerchief, and tissue-thin white lace socks.

'One minute,' Pins said. 'We better motor-out now. You can't count on them being right on time.'

'Put him under your jacket,' he told her. 'You can dress him in the car.'

Dead-Eye pulled the guns from Albert's ears and holstered them. Boomer took one last look around the apartment, then nodded to the others. They left through the open window, Geronimo first, followed by Pins, Mrs. Columbo, the baby, and Rev. Jim. Dead-Eye stood with one leg on the fire escape and the other on the kitchen linoleum.

'He lives?' Dead-Eye asked Boomer, nodding toward Albert.

'He lives,' Boomer said with a smile, still looking at Albert. 'Just long enough to tell Lucia what happened.'

For the first time all night, Albert's eyes betrayed him. Hearing Lucia's name washed away the cold façade of the career criminal. Now there was only fear.

'She's going to love to hear how you stood there and watched two strangers flush two hundred thou of her drugs down a kitchen sink,' Boomer said, walking away from Albert and putting a leg out through the open window. 'I can't figure if she'll have you shot or beaten to death. But, then again, you know her better than I do.'

Boomer climbed out the window, but as he started to close it he leaned his head in. 'The cops sure as shit aren't gonna believe your story either,' Boomer said to Albert. 'Whatever that story is gonna be. You have a good night now.'

225

Boomer closed the window behind him and disappeared into the darkness, leaving Albert standing in an apartment filled only with the dead. He listened as police sirens wailed in the distance. His future was now as clear to him as the bodies that lay sprawled by his side.

Lucia put the receiver back in its cradle and stared down at the phone for several minutes. The midday Arizona sun filtered through the open screen doors, the gleam off the swimming pool casting her face in its warm glow. Her hair was wet and pulled back tight; gold clips held two curled-up buns in place. She stood in the center of her living room, tanned and glistening with sweat, the straps of her two-piece designer bathing suit hanging loose from her shoulders, a calm woman at peace with herself and her surroundings.

Only her eyes and her shallow breathing betrayed the rage within.

Lucia ran a manicured hand over the smooth surface of the phone as if caressing the arm of a lover. She then reached down with both hands, lifted the phone off the polished wood coffee table, and with four violent tugs yanked it free from its wall socket. She spun around and threw the phone across the room, past the open screen doors. With a splash it landed in the shallow end of her forty-foot swimming pool.

The noise brought in her two bodyguards, who'd been sunning themselves by the edge of the deck.

'Get us on a plane,' she told them, her voice eerily quiet. 'The next one out.'

'Out where?' asked the bodyguard with the trim black goatee and a tattoo of Lucia's face on his right forearm.

'New York.' Lucia stood, legs apart, hands folded on her hips, staring out at the pool. 'I want to be there by tonight.'

'We takin' cargo?' the other bodyguard asked. He was as burly and muscular as the first, with a sharp razor cut and a long, ragged scar running down his hairless chest.

226

'No.' Lucia turned her gaze toward him. 'No cargo. But arrange to have some of your tools shipped ahead. We may have to fix a few items.'

The two bodyguards nodded and left the room to tend to their tasks. Lucia paced about in bare feet, sun still beaming off her face, forcing herself to regain focus. The raid on the drug den in Queens was the first move ever attempted against her crew, and its wake left much more than a bitter taste. It left behind questions. And in the drug business, questions were as dangerous as a loaded weapon.

The team that made the hit on the apartment were pros. No prints had been left behind. The shell casings came out of the barrels of street guns. They had their timing down, from the bomb latched to the door to the precision shooting. These weren't the actions of either low-level dealers looking to ice a big score or a renegade outfit tied into an existing crew. Albert would have picked up on those. He had been in the drug trade long enough to have done business with everybody working the streets, from first-rate groups to bottom-tier wannabes.

Lucia lit a cigarette and walked out onto the sun-bleached deck, blowing a stream of smoke into the hot desert air. She sat down and placed her feet in the crystal-blue chlorinated water, calmer now than she had been since Albert called her with the news. She lifted her face to the sun and played the heist over in her mind as it was relayed to her.

Other than walking out with the baby, the thieves hadn't stolen anything. They had washed two hundred thousand in cocaine down a sink without even a second's hesitation. So it wasn't money or drugs that piqued their interest. And they certainly didn't need to shoot their way into a Queens apartment to steal a baby she had paid a hooker $600 for three months earlier.

No, there was a professional logic to the attack.

That meant it was personal.

Whoever it was, they were coming after Lucia and they

weren't being coy. They wanted her to know. Maybe they were backed by somebody bigger or maybe they were lone wolves out looking for a name to match the bravado. Or maybe it went even deeper.

Maybe someone Lucia had touched, a young girl perhaps, or the relative of a child, now wanted to touch her back.

It didn't really matter to her. She would do all that she could to find them and erase them from sight. Lucia Carney was sitting on the crest of a six-hundred-million-dollar mountaintop and had come too far over too many long nights to let anybody throw her off.

The group that shot up the safe house had come out gunning for a battle.

Lucia was going to give them a war.

She tossed the cigarette into the clean pool, looked down at her reflection, and smiled, once again a happy woman.

The smell of death was in the air.

15

Boomer leaned the back of his chair against the wall and watched Mrs. Columbo feed the baby a bottle of warm formula. The other Apaches sat around a table in the main dining room at Nunzio's, nursing their drinks and replaying the actions of the night over in their minds.

'You look good with a baby in your arms,' Boomer said, smiling.

'It's been a long time since I held one this close.'

She thought back to when Frankie was the same age as the baby she held, Joe following the two of them everywhere they went, armed with a smile and a camera. It was a happy time for all three, filled only with warm feelings. She wished they could someday get back to that.

Boomer held his smile and stared at Mrs. Columbo and the baby, thinking only about what might have been.

'You make the call to social services yet?' Geronimo asked.

'We don't need social services yet.' Boomer answered the question without looking away from Mrs. Columbo, the baby serene and content in her arms.

'You sure as shit got a full plate planned out for us, Boomer,' Rev. Jim said. 'We break a drug ring *and* we babysit. You can't find a squad like us anywhere.'

'We look like a couple to you guys?' Boomer walked over to Mrs. Columbo and put his arm around her.

'A couple of what?' Pins asked, finishing off a glass of tap beer.

'I'd buy into it,' Dead-Eye said, understanding without being told what Boomer was really asking. 'Married since high school, two other kids grown and out of the house, money a little short, and then, the last thing you need, a surprise baby.'

'Is that what you doormen do with all your days?' Rev. Jim asked him. 'Watch soaps?'

'I work nights,' Dead-Eye said. 'And I listen to the radio.'

'Me and the wife here got ourselves a kid we can't afford,' Boomer said, walking slowly around the table. 'We're way low on cash and there's no way we can keep him. But we wanna make sure our baby has a good home to grow up in and good people to raise him. So where do we go for something like that? Who we gonna turn to?'

'I'll take Lucia for forty, Alex,' Rev. Jim said.

'Holy shit,' Pins said. 'You guys *are* fuckin' crazy.'

'Maybe,' Boomer said, stopping at the table between Geronimo and Pins. 'But I don't see it any other way.'

Mrs. Columbo instinctively held the baby tighter to her body. 'Are you really going to sell him back to Lucia?' she asked.

'Only way to get our foot in her door,' Dead-Eye said.

'There's a lot of layers between her and the sale,' Geronimo pointed out. 'It's not like walking into J. C. Penney's and finding her behind the counter. Lucia's never near the buy and always far away from the kill.'

'We take it one step at a time,' Boomer said. 'We start at the bottom of her outfit and work our way up.'

'Where the hell's the bottom?' Pins asked. 'It's not like this crew takes out ads.'

'You find a guy named Saldo,' Nunzio said, opening a manila folder and sliding out a half dozen head shots of a man with thick dark hair and a long scar running down the right side of his face. 'He's the guy who fed Malcolm the lady's business card. He's her main New York line into the baby market. Pays top dollar and asks very few questions.'

'What is it you *do*, exactly, Nunzio?' Rev. Jim asked, looking over at the older man with a trace of admiration.

'I listen,' Nunzio said.

'Pins, we'll get you an address and a plate number by early tomorrow morning,' Boomer said.

'I'll have him wired before lunch,' Pins said. 'You want him bodied too?'

'How the hell can you body-wire him?' Boomer asked. 'You're not gonna be anywhere close to the guy.'

'I don't have to be.' The confidence in his own abilities overcame Pins's shyness. 'I don't even have to meet the man.'

'What are ya gonna do?' Rev. Jim asked. 'Mail him the wire and ask him to put it on himself?'

'He gets his clothes cleaned somewhere,' Pins said. 'As soon as I have his address, I'll figure out where. I'll plant the bugs there *before* he puts on his clothes.'

Boomer glanced over at Dead-Eye, who looked back at him and smiled. 'My hunch is the guy works out of the East Side. We'll have the layout soon enough. I want the building covered in case of trouble.'

'If there's a super or a guy at the door, I can talk my way into having them let me do the windows,' Rev. Jim said. 'I'll look scruffy enough so they won't notice.'

'That shouldn't be too hard,' Nunzio added.

'Go in on a day there's a garbage pickup,' Geronimo said. 'Around the time they're working that street.'

'Why?' Boomer asked.

'I got a friend in Sanitation,' Geronimo told him. 'He'll let me work on the truck crew. This way I'm visible but nobody notices me. There's trouble, I'll be there.'

'That covers the ground and the outside of the building,' Boomer said. 'That leaves the roof for you, Dead-Eye. Your gut tells you something's not right, don't even hesitate.'

'What about me?' Mrs. Columbo asked. 'What am I doing while all this is going on?'

'Nothing,' Boomer said with a smile. 'You're my wife and no wife of mine's gonna have a job.'

Mrs. Columbo looked down at the baby, lifted him to eye level, and kissed his flushed red cheek. 'Your father's an asshole,' she cooed as she placed him on her shoulder and patted his back. Seconds later, the baby let out a loud burp.

'That's what he thinks of you,' Mrs. Columbo said with a laugh.

Lucia sat at the head of the eight-foot dining table, a yellow folder spread open beneath her elbows. A crystal ashtray and wine goblet were off to her left, a 1980 Merlot in one, a filter-tipped cigarette smoldering on the edge of the other. She stared across the length of the bare table at the private investigator sitting nervously at the far end. He had on a cheap coffee-colored suit, worn at the cuffs, a brown shirt in need of a wash, and a poorly knotted cream tie. He was thin and balding, the top of his head coated with beads of sweat, his small fingers softly drumming on the top of the table. Three of Lucia's men stood silently behind him, hidden by the shadows of the drawn brocade drapes that kept out the afternoon sunshine. There was a large glass of ice water in front of the man. It sat untouched.

'You're charging me two hundred and fifty dollars an hour plus expenses, Mr. Singleton,' Lucia said in a level-toned voice. 'I expect you to have something to show for it.'

'It's all there in the file,' Trace Singleton said. 'You can see for yourself.'

'I don't want to see for myself,' Lucia said in harsher tones. 'I want you to tell me.'

'That ambush on your apartment was pulled off by a group of cops,' Singleton said, wiping a thin line of sweat off his upper lip. 'Working on their own.'

'How do you know they were cops?' Lucia asked, taking a puff from her cigarette.

'That part's confidential,' Singleton said, smirking. 'That's one of the reasons I'm so good at what I do. You gotta trust me on it.'

'And if I don't trust you on it?' Lucia asked. 'What happens then?'

'Then I guess you and me can't do business anymore,' he said, glancing behind him at the three large men who never seemed to move.

Lucia pushed back her chair and walked down the length of the table, the fingers of her right hand skimming the dark wood surface. She walked past Singleton and over to one of her men. She looked up at him and smiled, slowly running a hand up the front of his blue silk shirt and down to his side, stopping when she found the handle of the .9-millimeter Luger. She pulled the gun from the man's hip and rested it against her stomach, her back still turned to Singleton.

'Were you telling me the truth?' Lucia asked, her eyes cold and steady, looking at her man, her question aimed at Singleton.

'About what?' Singleton turned slightly in his chair, one arm braced against the curve of the antique wood.

'That everything I need to know is in the file?'

'Everything's there,' Singleton said, his arrogance tempered by the oppressive heat in the room. 'Like I always say, you bring me in, you bring in the best.'

'You were also right about something else,' Lucia said, turning away from the man in the silk shirt.

'You get to know me better, you'll find out I'm right about most things.' Singleton was full of swagger now, squinting over at Lucia. The dim light in the room kept the gun in her hand hidden from his line of vision. 'Now, which thing in particular were you talkin' about?'

Lucia raised the gun and aimed it at Singleton. 'You and I can't do business any more.'

Lucia's index finger put pressure on the Luger's quick trigger and clicked off two rounds, both of which landed in Singleton's forehead, cracking open the back of his

233

head, sending blood and bone fragments splashing against the flocked red wallpaper. Singleton's upper body slumped against the back of the chair, resting there as if he were fast asleep.

Lucia handed the Luger back to the man in the blue shirt. He took it by the handle and shoved it into his hip holster.

'Have someone clean up the room,' Lucia told the three men. She walked back to the head of the table and picked up the folder. 'I've got some reading to do.'

'Where is your husband now, Mrs. Connors?' the well-dressed man behind the desk asked Mrs. Columbo, flashing a toothy smile.

'He's trying to find a parking spot.' Mrs. Columbo shifted one leg over the other. Boomer had made her wear a tight miniskirt and she was showing more than enough thigh to interest the man behind the desk. 'That's no easy thing in this neighborhood.'

'How did you find out about our agency?' the man asked, still with the smile, his eyes scanning Mrs. Columbo and the baby braced against her right arm.

'My friend Carmella,' Mrs. Columbo said. 'She told me you guys helped her out about six, maybe seven months ago. You found a good home for her baby and paid her off in cash. No questions. Is that part true?'

'Which part?' the man asked.

'About the questions,' Mrs. Columbo said. 'When Richie comes in here, if you start asking him a bunch of, you know, personal shit, excuse my French, he's gonna get nasty and walk out.'

'That wouldn't be smart,' the man said. 'He'd be leaving the way he walked in, with no money and a baby he doesn't want.'

'That's where you're wrong,' Mrs. Columbo said. 'I'm sorry, I don't know your name.'

'Edward.'

'You see, Eddie,' Mrs. Columbo said, 'my husband

234

wants the baby. I don't. I went through enough with the two I had and I don't need to raise more. What I need is to find me work, something that pays good and brings it in steady.'

'What kind of work?'

'Doesn't matter,' Mrs. Columbo said, looking around the barren room. 'Years ago, before I hooked up with Richie, I did it all, didn't care what it was. 'Course, I was a little better-looking back then, but I'm still willin' to do it all, whatever it is, so long as the money's there at the end. Maybe I shouldn't be telling you all this. But Carmella said – '

Edward interrupted her, his arms spread out in front of him, the smile on his face locked in place. 'Does your husband know about any of this?'

'Are you kiddin' me?' Mrs. Columbo said. 'Wait till you meet him. I mean, I love the guy and all, but my Richie's lucky if he can find his ass with two hands. There are guys just made that way. I'm sure you met some workin' this job.'

'A few,' Edward Glistner said, leaning back in his chair, resting his hands on top of his head.

'Then you know what I'm talkin' about,' Mrs. Columbo said, running a finger under the folds of the baby's chin.

'I might have a job for you,' Edward said, turning his head slightly at the sounds of empty garbage cans being tossed by the sanitation workers outside. 'If you really are as interested as you seem.'

'Let's hear it.' Mrs. Columbo looked over Edward's shoulder to catch a glimpse of Boomer crossing the street. 'Make it quick. Before Richie comes inside.'

'You don't want him to know?' Edward asked.

'Not till I know,' Mrs. Columbo said. 'Then, depending on what it is, we'll see if he can handle it.'

'It's everything you say you're looking for,' Edward said, checking the time on the wall clock. 'Steady hours and a pretty good salary.'

'What do I have to do?' Mrs. Columbo asked.

'Come back tomorrow,' Edward said. 'Without Richie. We'll work out the details then.'

'How about a hint?' Mrs. Columbo asked, throwing Edward her most alluring smile.

'Do you like to fly?' Edward asked, smiling back at her, then standing to greet Boomer as he walked into the room.

Pins waited outside Harry Saben's Cleaners, watching as the blonde in the skintight leggings dropped off three of Saldo's jackets and two of his slacks. He saw Harry, old and hunched from too many years behind a counter, fill out the work slip, his eyes more on the blonde's cleavage than on the cut of Saldo's clothes. The blonde took the slip, gave Harry a smile, and walked out of the store, heading east.

'Good morning,' Pins said to Harry, closing the glass door behind him.

'How may I help you?' Harry asked, traces of a childhood spent speaking Russian still in his voice.

'It's really about how I can help you,' Pins said. He reached into the side pocket of his windbreaker and flipped his detective's shield.

'You a cop?' Harry asked, squinting down at the badge through thick glasses.

'I'm investigating a ring that's ripping off designer labels,' Pins said. 'I'm sure someone as experienced as yourself in the business knows the routine. Take a second-hand jacket, tag a designer label on it, sell it on the street for three times the price.'

'I've heard of people doing things like that,' Harry said, nodding his head.

'Then you know there's a lot of money in it,' Pins said.

'I imagine,' Harry said. 'But what can I do?'

Pins leaned closer to Harry and lowered his voice. 'Can the department trust you?'

'Yes,' Harry said, lowering his voice right back. 'I'm

very pro-police. I'd like to see a couple of thousand more of you out there.'

Pins nodded. 'All right,' he said. 'I'm going to take a chance.'

'It's not a chance,' Harry said. 'Believe me, I'll go to my grave with what you tell me.'

'The blonde that was just here,' Pins said. 'I'm sure you noticed her.'

'Even at my age.'

'She's part of the ring,' Pins explained. 'These clothes she left, they're not designer clothes. They come out of some sweatshop in the Bronx.'

Harry reached down and felt Saldo's black Armani jacket. 'It looks so real,' he said. 'It even feels the way it should. The label's in it and everything.'

'I can get you a case of labels by this afternoon.' Pins reached over and grabbed Saldo's clothes. 'That's the easiest part.'

'Are you going to take those with you?' Harry asked with some concern.

'Don't worry,' Pins asked. 'I'll have them back to you by this afternoon, cleaned and pressed. When did you tell her they'd be ready?'

'Six tonight,' Harry said.

'Perfect.' Pins jammed the clothes under one arm and reached out a hand to Harry. 'I appreciate all your help.'

'It's been my pleasure,' Harry said, smiling and shaking Pins's hand.

'I'll see you in a few hours,' Pins said, heading for the door. 'Is there anything the department can do for you?'

'Is the place you're having those cleaned a good one?' Harry asked, walking around the counter.

'It's a special cleaner,' Pins said. 'Like running your clothes through a car wash.'

'Then there *is* something you can do,' Harry said. 'A small favor.'

'What?' Pins asked.

'I need to get a stain out of Mrs. Babcock's black

cocktail dress. I've put it through the wash three times and it's still there. I don't know what the hell she spilled on it, but I just can't get it to come out. Maybe your place can give it a shot?'

Pins smiled at Harry. 'Get the dress,' he said. 'I'll bring it back to you like new.'

'You're the best,' Harry said, rushing to the back of the store for the dress.

'I hope so,' Pins muttered.

Geronimo was lifting a large cardboard Zenith television carton filled with wires and a rusty old air conditioner when he spotted the doubleparked car. The black, late-model Lincoln was inched alongside a Toyota Corolla and a blue Renault, engine running, tinted windows up.

Geronimo tossed the box into the back of the sanitation truck and shifted the crush gear, his eyes on the Lincoln. The lead man shifted the truck and moved it slowly up to the next hill of garbage. Geronimo walked in the shadows of the truck, his head down, his mouth inches from the collar of his work jacket.

'That double-parked car doesn't look right to me,' Geronimo whispered into the tiny microphone wired inside his collar. 'You picking up anything from inside?'

'Saldo's in the backseat.' Geronimo heard the crisp sound of Pins's crackling words come through his ear mike. The thin wires from the audio devices ran down his neck and into a small box taped to the center of his back. 'He's got two shooters with him, both in the front. All three carrying heavy.'

Pins was parked on the north corner, dressed in the brown uniform of a Department of Transportation officer, behind the wheel of a battered tow truck.

'Shooters always carry heavy,' Rev. Jim's voice said through the mikes. 'Why should these two be any different?' He was on his third set of windows, turning slightly to drop a squeegee into a bucket of water and pick up a hand towel.

'Well, these two are out gunning for us,' Pins said. 'Somebody's tipped them. They know we're sending a plant into the building. They just don't know when or who.'

'Do Boomer and Mrs. Columbo know?' Dead-Eye asked, crouched against the iron door leading from the roof to the top floor of the brownstone.

'Their mikes are turned off,' Pins said. 'It's too risky otherwise.'

'It's your play, Dead-Eye,' Geronimo said. 'We'll walk it any way you want.'

'Just make it fast,' Rev. Jim said. 'I'm runnin' outta water and windows.'

'Pins, can you hear me?' Dead-Eye asked.

'Got you,' Pins answered.

'Back up into the block and tow that car out of there,' Dead-Eye told him. 'Geronimo?'

'I'm here,' Geronimo said, dragging a thick bag of garbage from the curb.

'Back-up Pins,' Dead-Eye said. 'Let's try and do this clean. We don't need a gunfight on the street. Rev. Jim?'

'Talk to me.'

'Get in here without too much noise,' Dead-Eye said. 'Just in case I get jammed up.'

'What about Boomer and Mrs. Columbo?' Pins asked.

'They've got a job to do,' Dead-Eye said, 'and so do we.'

'And Saldo?' Geronimo asked. 'How do we play him?'

'Let him take the ride with the tow truck,' Dead-Eye said. 'There's a better chance he'll run his mouth sitting in the car. Pins will let us know if he says anything we need to hear.'

'Can Saldo's wire pick me up when I get close?' Geronimo asked.

'Don't worry,' Pins said. 'As soon as you touch the car, I'll turn it off.'

'Anything else?' Rev. Jim asked.

'Yeah,' Dead-Eye said. 'Stay alive.'

239

Pins slammed the truck gears into reverse and backed the hook end close to the bumper of the Lincoln. The driver's side window rolled down and an overweight man in wraparound sunglasses stuck his head out.

'What's up, asshole?' he said in a Spanish accent, watching Pins lift a large wooden slab and place it under the front tires of the Lincoln.

'You're double-parked,' Pins said. 'That's illegal.'

'I'm in the car,' the driver said. 'I can move it.'

'You should have thought of that before,' Pins said. 'Once the wood's down, the job's a done deal.'

'What the fuck are you talking about?' the driver said, his face red with anger. 'You don't have to tow anybody anywhere. I'll move the fuckin' car.'

'The wood's down,' Pins said. 'You can't move it once the wood's down.'

'Fuck you *and* the wood,' the driver said.

The middle of the garbage truck stopped right next to the Lincoln. Geronimo approached from the passenger end, his hands down by his sides, one holding a .44 semiautomatic, a silencer attached to the muzzle. He gave two hard knuckle taps on the passenger window. The window buzzed halfway down, letting out miniclouds of smoke, most of it wrapped around the face of a man in light-colored clothing.

'We break a garbage law now too?' the man asked with mild irritation.

The man behind the wheel punched the dashboard repeatedly, his anger at full throttle. He had pockmarked cheeks and hair the color of straw hanging down the sides of his face. 'I hate this fuckin' city,' he shouted. 'Take a look at who's giving us shit. A fuckin' tow-truck driver and a garbage man.'

'Do you know you have to pass a test to get this job?' Geronimo said.

'I don't give a fuck!' the driver screamed.

Geronimo leaned his head into the car, looking beyond

240

the two men in the front, staring into the darkness of the backseat, where Saldo sat quietly through the commotion.

'You're all going to take a ride to the pound,' Geronimo said to Saldo. 'Believe me, you'll like it. You can roll down your windows and take in the water view. It's a better place for you to be than here. Have I painted a clear enough picture?'

Saldo nodded, his eyes and manner indifferent.

'You're no fuckin' garbage man,' the driver said.

Geronimo shrugged. 'I couldn't pass the test.'

'What are you then?' the man in the front asked.

'He's a cop,' Saldo said. 'They're both cops.'

'Cops?' the man behind the wheel said. 'The tow-truck driver too?'

'A lot of us have to work two jobs,' Geronimo said.

'Say the word,' the driver said, looking into the rearview at Saldo. 'We'll take these fuckers out right here and now.'

Geronimo lifted his hand and showed them the .44. 'Let's not be stupid,' he said to Saldo. 'They make a move on me and I move on you and we both know it's not worth it. So stick to the plan and enjoy the ride.'

Saldo stared into Geronimo's dark eyes, feeling the front end of the car start to tilt upward.

'We stay with the car,' he said to the two men in the front.

'It's been nice talking to you,' Geronimo told him.

'I hope we get to do it again,' Saldo said. 'Soon.'

Geronimo backed away from the car, the two men in the front staring angrily at Pins as he lifted the car into tow position.

'Kill the engine, please,' Pins said to them.

'I'd like to fuckin' kill you first,' the driver said.

'Hey, I'm nervous as it is,' Pins said with an innocent smile. 'I've never towed a car before. I would hate to lose you guys on the highway.'

The thick wooden door to the four-storey brownstone swung halfway open, the brass knob held by a large man

241

in charcoal-gray slacks and red suspenders draped over a black shirt. His eyes narrowed as he watched the commotion around the Lincoln. He moved his free hand to the small of his back, fingers wrapping themselves around the handle of a .32 short Colt. He saw the DOT man chain the car and lift it. The two men in the front were exchanging angry gestures while Saldo's shadow sat motionless in the back. He eased the Colt out of its holster and released the safety.

'I'm done,' Rev. Jim said, jumping down from one of the window ledges to the front of the door well, blocking the man's view. 'Now for the fun part. Getting paid.'

'Outta my fuckin' eyes,' the man hissed at Rev. Jim, the gun held against the side of his right leg.

'You ain't anything special to look at either,' Rev. Jim said with a smile, holding his work pail, half filled with water, in his left hand. 'You hand me the thirty bucks for the job and I'll turn invisible.'

The man looked at Rev. Jim and lifted the gun in his hand to chest level. 'Get the fuck outta here,' the man told him. 'Now.'

Rev. Jim held the smile on his face. 'They're only windows,' he said, turning his back on the man with the gun, still blocking his view with his body. He then swung the pail high above his shoulder and crashed it down against the side of the man's head. The man fell backward into the entryway, out cold, his gun falling to the floor. Rev. Jim stepped into the building and quickly dragged the man into the hall, locking the door behind them.

'We're in,' Rev. Jim said into his mike.

'Who the hell's *we*?' Dead-Eye asked.

'Just a friend I bumped into,' Rev. Jim said.

Dead-Eye stood with his back to the flowered paper of the hall wall, his two guns crisscrossed over his chest. He listened as the three men in the room to his right griped about the long hours they were forced to work in return for low pay and small chance for advancement. Dead-Eye took two steps to the side and braced both his feet against the doorway entry, guns now held out at waist level. The men looked up and chose not to move.

'If you're looking for money, you're on the wrong floor,' the one with a thick dark beard and shaved head announced.

'I heard,' Dead-Eye said.

'This is an adoption agency,' said the biggest of the three, a tall, middle-aged man dressed in a long-sleeved olive shirt and tan slacks. You come here for babies, not for bucks.'

'I came for your guns,' Dead-Eye said, walking into the room. 'Pull 'em out slow and slide them on the floor over to me, butt end first.'

'We'll find you, man,' the last of the three, young, with a bushy mustache and slight lisp, threatened. 'We'll hunt you down and burn you.'

'I lead a really boring life,' Dead-Eye said. 'Sounds like you'd bring a little spark to it. Now the guns.'

The men lifted their weapons from their holsters, bent their legs, and slid the guns over. The revolvers scraped against the hardwood floors, coming to rest near Dead-Eye's boots.

'That's only three,' Dead-Eye said.

'How many of us do you see?' the one with the beard asked.

'I see pros,' Dead-Eye said. 'Guys paid salaries to kill on orders. Those guys carry more than one.'

'Maybe we ain't as good as you think, spook,' the one with the lisp said. 'Maybe we're just startin' out. Not as smart as we should be.' Dead-Eye wasn't listening.

He was looking at the eyes of the third man, the one in the dark designer suit and black button-down shirt. The eyes that told him everything he needed to know.

There was someone standing behind him, ready to do some damage.

243

*

Boomer held the baby with both hands and watched him as he cooed and smiled. Mrs. Columbo rummaged through a large fake leather handbag open on her lap, looking for a tissue. With one hand she dabbed at her eyes and blew her nose. Her other hand stayed in the purse, holding her .38 caliber.

'I really hate to give up on the little guy,' Boomer said. 'It's tough knowing I'll never see him again.'

Edward responded in the most professional of tones. 'He'll be living in a good home. That I can assure you.'

Boomer looked down at the baby, then across at Edward. 'You're sure about that, right?'

'Our lists are made up of the best people in need of a baby.' Edward was growing impatient with Boomer's unending stream of questions. 'This child will go to private schools, travel to Europe, and live a life that wouldn't be open to him living with you and your wife.'

'Listen to the man, honey,' Mrs. Columbo urged Boomer. 'He's making sense here.'

'All right,' Boomer said, handing the baby back to Mrs. Columbo. 'I guess you got yourself a deal,' he said, pushing his chair back and standing.

'What's our next step?' Mrs. Columbo asked.

'It's very simple, really,' Edward said, his voice calm and in control. 'You hand me the baby and I hand you some money and we all walk away.'

'How much?' Mrs. Columbo asked.

'I usually pay six hundred,' Edward said. 'But you've caught me on a soft day. I'll make it a thousand.'

'A thousand dollars?' Mrs. Columbo said, wide smile on her face. 'Richie, did you hear? He's giving us a thousand.'

'That's great, honey,' Boomer said, looking out the window over Edward's shoulder, seeing the Lincoln being towed away.

'That's more than we made all of last month,' Mrs. Columbo said. 'I can't thank you enough, Eddie.'

Edward opened the central drawer of his desk, pulled

244

out an envelope, and counted out ten one-hundred-dollar bills. He handed them to Boomer, who folded them and shoved them into the front pockets of his jeans.

'I left the diapers and clothes in the trunk of my car,' Boomer said. 'Want me to and get them?'

'That won't be at all necessary,' Edward said. 'We're fully stocked.'

'Then there's nothing left to do but leave,' Boomer said. He leaned down and kissed the baby curled in Mrs. Columbo's arms. 'I'll wait outside,' he said to her, keeping his head down and walking toward the door. 'Don't take too long.'

'Won't be more than a minute,' Mrs. Columbo said.

She waited for the door to close before she stood and handed the baby over to Edward. He reached for him and held him face forward on his lap.

'You're not going to forget me, now, are you?' she asked Edward.

Edward shook his head no. 'I'll call as soon as there's a slot for you.'

'Can you make it quick?' Mrs. Columbo asked. 'I'm real eager to get started. We really need the money.'

'I just gave your husband a thousand dollars,' Edward said.

'You kidding me?' Mrs. Columbo said. 'With the bills we got, I'm lucky that'll last us through the weekend.'

Edward stared at her, smiled, and nodded. 'Do you mind working nights?' he asked.

'You're holding the only thing that kept me home,' Mrs. Columbo said, pointing to the baby in Edward's arms.

'Take the baby for a moment,' Edward said, holding out the child. 'I need to look up something on the computer.'

Mrs. Columbo took the baby and stood over Edward's shoulder. He clicked on the IBM at the side of his desk and watched it chart down a list of names and destinations. He hit a few buttons, leaned back in his chair, and smiled. 'Have you ever been to Maine?' he asked.

'No,' Mrs. Columbo said. 'But I always wanted to go there.'

'You'll be going tomorrow,' he said. 'I've just logged you in. Someone will call you and tell you what time to be at the airport. You'll be met there by a woman. She'll tell you what to do.'

'I don't know how I'll ever thank you,' Mrs. Columbo said in a seductive manner, handing Edward back the baby.

Edward picked up on it, gazing at her legs and holding the smile. 'I'm sure between the two of us, we'll come up with something interesting,' he said.

'I know we will,' Mrs. Columbo said. She leaned down and kissed the baby good-bye, resting one hand on Edward's shoulder.

'We'll speak again soon,' Edward said.

'I'll be by my phone,' Mrs. Columbo said, opening the door leading to the foyer. 'Waiting.'

Dead-Eye saw the shadow behind him lift a hand holding a gun. He rolled over on the hardwood floor and came up on his knees, surprised to see that it was a woman standing there, one of the mules from the other room. He had his gun aimed at her chest but didn't fire. Instead, he watched Rev. Jim come up behind her, grab her around the neck, and pull the gun out of her hand.

Dead-Eye turned and whirled back to the three men behind him, getting to them before they had a chance to pull out their stash guns.

'Everything cool?' he said to Rev. Jim.

'Like ice,' Rev. Jim answered, shoving the mule into the room. 'But what do we do with the Three Stooges?'

'Have the mule help you find some rope,' Dead-Eye said. 'We'll tie and gag the whole bunch and go out through the roof exit.'

'Boomer's already on the street,' Rev. Jim said. 'Mrs. Columbo's the only one still in.'

'She'll be out soon,' Dead-Eye said. 'And so will we.'

'Which means I'm the only one who got screwed,' Rev. Jim said.

'How you figure that?' Dead-Eye asked.

'I cleaned all their windows,' Rev. Jim said. 'And never got to see a nickel.'

'People always take advantage of the handicapped,' Dead-Eye said. 'Get used to it.'

Boomer and Mrs. Columbo walked with their arms linked toward the car parked at the corner.

'We can't leave that prick in there with that baby for too long,' Mrs. Columbo said, hatred in her voice.

'Pins put in a call downtown while you were still up there showing off your legs,' Boomer said. 'Edward's going to be taken down in about half an hour.'

'You should have an undercover team on sight until the others show,' Mrs. Columbo said.

'The two guys in suits across the street,' Boomer said. 'They'll make sure nobody runs in or out.'

'Good work,' she said.

'I try,' Boomer said.

'I'm on their list,' Mrs. Columbo said. 'I leave for Maine tomorrow night. A woman's supposed to meet me at the airport.'

'We'll have somebody meet her first,' Boomer said.

'I told you my plan would work, Boomer,' Mrs. Columbo said, beaming. 'Admit it. You wouldn't have thought of this. You probably would have just gone in there and shot up the place.'

'I'm limited in what I can do,' Boomer said, reaching for his car keys. 'And I don't think Eddie would have been as interested in *my* legs.'

Lucia stood in the center of the airport hangar, her back to the black Learjet. She was surrounded by eleven armed men. They were all young and brazen and were led by a tall man with a shaved head that gleamed under the glare of the hangar lights.

His name was Wilber Graves.

A thin, long-haired assistant in jeans, black polo shirt, and black pumps handed each of the men manila packets filled with background information on the Apaches – photos, home addresses, dates of birth. The men took the folders and kept their eyes focused on Lucia, dressed seductively in a black knit halter top, thigh-high skirt, and open-toed black pumps.

'There are seven names in the folder,' she said, her eyes moving from face to face with mannered ease. 'They are to be handled.'

'How soon?' Wilber asked, standing behind Lucia, his voice a deep baritone revealing his British boarding school education. Graves was born to a life of luxury and had the habits to prove it. But at a young age he had trained his full attention on doing what he liked to do best – kill.

'As soon as you find out what they know about us.' She answered without turning to look at him.

'Are you suspending operations until we finish the job?' Wilber asked.

'No,' Lucia said. 'All cargo still moves.'

'Don't let these people worry you,' Wilber said in a voice filled with confidence.

'I don't let *anything* worry me,' Lucia said, stepping closer to Wilber, watching as his blue eyes scanned the length of her body. 'I let other people worry. People like you, Wilber.'

'I won't disappoint you,' he said.

'That's good to know,' Lucia said.

Lucia walked away, her thin heels clicking against the thick cement floor. Wilber and his team watched her go, waiting for the Learjet to be fueled and take them toward their date with the Apaches.

16

Mrs. Columbo smiled over at her husband, Joe, as she piled an armful of clothes into a tan overnight bag. He was resting on the bed, hands behind his head, a paperback novel open across his chest.

'How's the book?' Mrs. Columbo asked.

'You haven't read it, have you?' Joe asked. 'You know how I hate it when you tell me how things end.'

'No,' she said, laughing. 'I haven't read it.'

'It's pretty good,' he told her. 'In fact, I think with this one, even you would have a hard time guessing the ending.'

'What's the plot?' she asked, folding her clothes neatly into the bag.

'People are found dead at a big research hospital,' Joe said, sitting up in the bed. 'No one can figure it. They come in for a simple operation. They come out a corpse.'

'It's probably somebody who works for the hospital,' Mrs. Columbo said with a shrug. 'What kind of research do they do?'

'Mary, I'm begging you,' Joe clasped his hands together. 'Let me have just this one book. Let me get to the end and not know.'

'What kind of research?' she said, sitting on the edge of the bed.

'Cancer,' Joe said, resigned to his fate.

'The head administrator,' Mrs. Columbo said. 'Tell me about him.'

'Straightforward and honest,' Joe said. 'Cares about the hospital and the people who work there. You're off base if you think it's him.'

'Was the administrator a surgeon before he quit to run the hospital?' Mrs. Columbo asked.

'I suppose,' Joe said. 'I have to go back and double-check.'

'That's your man,' Mrs. Columbo said, standing and walking over toward a bureau. '*And* your killer.'

Joe stared at his wife, trying to fight the temptation to pick up the book. He closed his eyes, took a deep breath, and went to the last chapter.

'I'm gonna grab a shower,' Mrs. Columbo said. 'Let me know how it turns out.'

She came out ten minutes later wearing a white terry-cloth robe and combing her wet hair straight back. Joe was leaning against a wall on the far side of the bedroom.

'So?' she said.

'I'm giving up mysteries,' Joe said. 'That's my last one. From now on, it's romance novels for me.'

'Like *those* endings are hard to guess,' Mrs. Columbo said.

'Remember when I took you to see *Chinatown*?' Joe asked. 'Halfway through, you knew John Huston was her husband, her brother, her uncle, whatever the hell he was to her. You *knew.*'

'Honey, it's my *job* to know,' Mrs. Columbo said, walking over and stroking his face. 'Remember?'

'It *was* your job, Mary,' Joe said quietly.

'Oh, Joe, let's not have this conversation again, please. I've got too much on my mind right now. If it's still bothering you, we'll talk about it when I get back.'

'We were going to take Frankie up to Maine the year you got wounded,' Joe said almost wistfully. 'We'd made the reservations and everything. Now here you are, going up all by yourself.'

Mrs. Columbo stood frozen in her place. Her eyes

narrowing in on her husband. 'Joe,' she said slowly, 'who told you I was going to Maine?'

'I don't know,' Joe was suddenly flustered. 'You must have mentioned it earlier.'

'Who told you, Joe?' Mrs. Columbo held both her place and her gaze. 'Who told you about Maine?'

'Does it matter?' he asked.

Mrs. Columbo's upper body shook slightly, her face was flushed, and her eyes were lit by rage. 'It matters a great deal. Do you know what flight I'm on too?'

'I want it to stop, Mary,' Joe said, ignoring the question. 'It's too dangerous. You're going to end up getting yourself killed.'

Mrs. Columbo sat on the edge of the bed. She was trying to think like a homicide detective, but the emotional rush was too strong. 'Do you know what you did, Joe?' Mrs. Columbo asked. 'Do you have any idea?'

Joe came over to her side and knelt down before her. 'I was trying to save the woman I love,' he said. 'That's all I did.'

Mrs. Columbo reached down and held his face with her hands. 'But you didn't,' she whispered. 'You put us all at risk.'

'No one's at risk if you stop it now.'

She shook her head.

'There's too many out there against you,' he said. 'You can't beat them.'

'Who did you go see?' Mrs. Columbo asked. There were tears in her eyes now. 'Who told you about us?'

'Deputy Inspector Lavetti,' Joe said after a long silence. 'He was a big help to me after you got wounded. Somebody for me to talk to now and then.'

'And you told him about me and the Apaches.' It wasn't a question. It was the quiet, firm statement of a homicide detective.

'I thought he was somebody I could trust.' Joe now wiped at his own tears.

'He's a dirty cop, Joe.' Mrs. Columbo reached down

to hold her husband in her arms. 'There's no way for you to have known that. But he went out and did what any dirty cop does. He called the people who pay him and told them who we were.'

'I didn't go see Lavetti because I wanted you caught.' Joe buried his head in his wife's robe. 'I went because I was scared I was going to lose you.'

'You were never in any danger of losing me, Joe,' Mary said quietly. 'I put my years in with you and I did it for only one reason. The only reason worth doing it – I loved you.'

'And do you *still* love me?' Joe asked. He stared into his wife's eyes, searching for the answer before he heard it.

'You have to deal with what you did,' Mrs. Columbo answered. 'And what you did was lay a death warrant on the whole team. You have to stand for that.'

'That's the cop answer,' Joe said. 'I'm looking for the wife answer.'

'It's the same answer,' Mrs. Columbo said.

Boomer sat behind the wheel of the dark Buick, window down to let in the moist spring air, looking across at Mrs. Columbo's house. Though he was never much of a smoker, he wished he had a cigarette. He settled for two slices of Wrigley's doublemint instead, chewing each piece slowly, rolling the foil into a ball and dropping it into the empty ash tin.

Boomer was a fastidious man who liked to do things in orderly fashion. He was one of the few action cops whose paperwork was always properly filled out and submitted within hours of an arrest. He hated surprises and he despised mistakes, and now here he was, sitting in the middle of both.

Boomer looked up when he heard the front door slam and saw Mrs. Columbo race down the steps, an overnight bag in her hand. She stepped around the front of the car, opened the passenger-side door, and slid in. Boomer kicked over the engine and pulled out of the spot.

They didn't say a word until they reached the Midtown Tunnel tolls.

'It was Joe,' Mrs. Columbo said.

'What was Joe?' Boomer asked.

'He's the one you're going to be looking for.' Mrs. Columbo tried hard not to burst into tears. 'He went to see Deputy Inspector Lavetti and told him about us.'

'He say why he did it?' Boomer asked softly.

'Because he loves me,' Mrs. Columbo said, turning her face to the passing traffic.

Boomer shifted the car away from the toll lines and pulled it over to the side of the road, inches from a red brick wall. He looked over at the cars heading into the city, his mind filled with too many unanswered questions and little time to get them resolved. He now had an enemy in the one place he never thought he needed to worry about – inside NYPD headquarters. He spit the gum out the open window and ran a hand across his tired eyes, for the first time starting to wonder if forming the Apaches was a risk worth taking. In their short time together, Boomer realized how vulnerable the unit was – prone to error, open to the unsuspecting nature of clandestine work – their individual strengths as active cops weakened by their wounds and the passage of time.

'He's not like us, Boomer,' Mrs. Columbo said. 'He's got more heart than brains.'

'How much do they know?' is all he asked.

'They know I'm going to Maine.'

Her face was sad and tired, the lights from the toll booths highlighting the fine features and running mascara. Boomer had always had warm feelings toward Mrs. Columbo. More than warm, if he was honest with himself. He admired the woman almost as much as he did the cop. There was always a relaxed ease to their friendship, with mild hints of sexual attraction.

'No,' Boomer told her. 'They know you *were* going to Maine.'

'You can't call this off,' she said, grabbing his arm and holding it tight.

'It's too dangerous. They'll be there waiting.'

'We've spent our lives going into places where people have been waiting,' Mrs. Columbo said. 'Why should Maine be different?'

'Because they'll be waiting for you.' He turned to her, wanting so much to put his arms around her and protect her. But he didn't. He just held the look and let it speak for him.

For all his bluster, Boomer Frontieri had a tough time connecting with women. Maybe it was his background. Maybe it was shyness or, worse, fear. Or maybe he just didn't want to make a mistake. Whatever the reason, he could never share his emotions with any woman he cared about. It had left him alone, without a wife, kids, or semblance of a real life. It was an emptiness that pained him even more than his wounds. For Boomer Frontieri there wasn't any choice. He *had* to continue his private war with Lucia Carney. It was all that kept him alive.

Mrs. Columbo put out her hands and held Boomer's face in them. 'Then *you* be there, Boomer,' she said in a soft voice. 'And make sure nothing happens to me.'

He said nothing for a long time. Then all he asked was 'You got another plan worked up?'

'Don't I always?' she said.

They sat around the table at Nunzio's, their food growing cold as they listened to Mrs. Columbo tell them about her husband's betrayal and Deputy Inspector Lavetti's deception. No one moved and no one other than Mrs. Columbo spoke. She laid it out for them like a cop, sparing no details or facts in the telling.

As they listened they all realized what it was they were hearing. The Apaches were into more than a fight. They were in a war with an enemy eager to take them on. And now their names and faces were known.

'Any of you want to walk from the table, this is the

254

time,' Boomer said after several moments of silence. 'The truth is, if we had any brains at all, we would *all* walk away. Face the truth and deal with it.'

'What is the truth?' Rev. Jim asked.

'That we are what we *know* we are,' Boomer said. 'Which is a big difference from what we *think* we are.'

'We've always known that truth, Boomer,' Geronimo said. 'We said yes to this knowing we were only half of what we used to be. Nothing's changed. Our destiny remains the same.'

'Nobody in here is eager to die,' Pins added. 'I know I'm not. But we always knew they would figure out who we were sooner or later. We've just got to make sure we're better prepared than they are.'

'They know who Mrs. Columbo is and what plane she's on,' Dead-Eye said. 'What they don't know is what she's going to be doing. Way I see it, we still hold the surprise card.'

'We can put it off,' Boomer said, impressed with the unity of the group. 'Give everybody a chance to think about it some more.'

'I've done all the thinking I need to do,' Rev. Jim said. 'It's time to go to the dance.'

'Let's just figure out a way to get Mrs. Columbo in and out of there,' Dead-Eye said. '*Alive.*'

'The same holds for you, Nunz,' Boomer said. 'Lucia's got your name too. You want to walk, now's a good time.'

'I'm where I want to be,' Nunzio said. 'In my restaurant.'

Boomer stared at each of them, looking for a dent in their resolve. He came away empty.

'Okay, then,' Boomer said with a smile. 'What the hell. Let's hear Mrs. Columbo's plan.'

'How about I make some coffee first,' Rev. Jim said, getting ready to stand.

'I'll make the coffee,' Nunzio said, putting a hand on Rev. Jim's shoulder. 'My stomach still remembers your last batch. It was strong enough to kill.'

'Maybe you should make that a part of your plan,' Dead-Eye said to Mrs. Columbo.

Dead-Eye soaked in the hot water of the ceramic tub, soap bubbles covering everything but his head. The heat from the water warmed his tired body. He had his head against the tile wall. A wet hand towel had been folded and slapped over his eyes.

Eddie crept quietly into the bathroom, removed the towel from his dad's eyes, and used it to stroke the sides of his face. Dead-Eye looked over at him and smiled, always amazed at how closely the boy he loved so much resembled his own father.

The boy reached a small hand into the water and came out with a palm full of bubbles, wetting the sleeve of his Snoopy zip-up pajamas.

'I'm using your bubble bath,' Dead-Eye said. 'That okay with you?'

'You can get some in your eyes and it won't burn,' Eddie said. 'But don't get any in your mouth. Okay?'

'I won't,' Dead-Eye said with a smile.

Eddie walked the length of the tub, dragging his hand through the water, making motor sounds with his lips. When he turned and came back up toward his father, his pajamas were wet to the length of the sleeve, four fingers cupped across the front of his face to hide the giggles.

'Take your jays off and come on in with me,' Dead-Eye said, sliding the zipper down to the edge of Eddie's right thigh.

Dead-Eye waited until his son stripped off all his clothes and then grabbed him around the chest as he moved feet first into the tub. Eddie eased himself gently into the water and rested his head against his father's chest, breathing quietly, watching as the bubbles floated off to his side.

'Do you miss Grandpa?' Eddie said after several slow moments.

'Very much,' Dead-Eye said, running a hand through

his son's hair. 'He was my best friend. Even though he wasn't always the easiest guy in the world to talk things over with.'

'Like when you told him about being a policeman?' Eddie asked.

'That was *not* the best of days to talk to Grandpa,' Dead-Eye said. 'He was pretty upset.'

'He told me you were a great policeman,' Eddie said, gazing up at his dad. 'But he didn't know why you wanted to be a great policeman.'

'That's the Grandpa we all loved,' Dead-Eye said.

'Would Grandpa be happy you were a great doorman?' Eddie asked, squeezing water out of a closed fist.

'I guess,' Dead-Eye said, leaning his head back against the tiles and closing his eyes. 'I think he'd have been happy with anything I did so long as it was honest work.'

'Would Grandpa be happy you're an Apache?' Eddie said, still playing with the water.

Dead-Eye lifted his head and opened his eyes, looking down at his son. 'How do you know about that?' he asked.

'I heard you and Mommy talking,' Eddie said. 'I was in my room. Sleeping.'

'Try sleeping with your eyes closed next time,' Dead-Eye said. 'You won't hear as much.'

'So?' Eddie said.

'So what?'

'Would Grandpa be happy?' Eddie sat up and looked at his father. 'About you being an Apache?'

'Yes,' Dead-Eye said, running a hand down his son's back. 'I think he would have been happy.'

'I'm happy too,' Eddie said, turning his attention once again to the now-lukewarm water to play with what was left of the bubbles. 'Now there's just Mommy left to make happy.'

'Let's take it one war at a time,' Dead-Eye said.

'Which one first?' Eddie asked.

'The one I can win,' Dead-Eye said.

Rev. Jim sat on the park bench, his legs stretched out, hands inside his pants pockets. It was dark and the buzzing streetlamp above offered little light. He pulled a hand from his pocket and ran it alongside the bench, feeling the chipped wood, the names carved in it, the rusty screws holding it in place. It was where his mother had sat on the night she died, waiting to pay off a drug dealer with borrowed money. He hadn't been back there since that night. Rev. Jim wanted very much to cry and shout out his mother's name. But too much had been ripped out of him over the years. He had no tears left to shed. Instead, he sat in the silent darkness and kept his hand over the wood of the place where a woman he loved once sat.

Pins watched the eight-year-old boy grab a bowling ball from its slot, crouch into position, and throw a hard spin down the center of the lane. Pins smiled as the ball curved its way to a strike.

'All right!' Andrew said, pumping a fist in the air. 'I'm going to beat you tonight, Pins. I just know it.'

'We'll see,' Pins said with a smile. He stood up, took a high-five from the boy as he walked past him, then reached for his ball.

There were many boys who made use of the open afternoons at the alley, but none more so than Andrew. The boy didn't talk much, reluctant to bring up a home life that revolved around drugs, beatings, and shouts in the night. Besides, Pins knew all he needed to know without asking. Andrew was there to bowl and to forget. So was Pins.

Pins reared back and tossed a strike down lane six. 'Still think you're going to beat me?' he asked Andrew.

'I *know* it,' Andrew said.

'Want to bet on it?'

Andrew cast his eyes down to the shiny floor. 'I can't bet you,' he said in a low voice. 'Got no money.'

'It's not a money bet,' Pins said.

'What kind, then?'

'I'm going to be gone for a while,' Pins said. 'I need somebody to look after the alley for me. Make sure things don't get out of hand. Interested so far?'

Andrew's face was lit with a smile. 'Yeah,' he said. 'You know it.'

'Now, *if* you win,' Pins said, '*if* you beat me, I'll pay you to look after the place. But if you don't, then you work the place for free.'

'That's a sucker bet,' Andrew said, strutting to the floor and reaching for a ball.

'Only for the loser,' Pins said, sitting back down and smiling up at the happy boy.

He and Andrew bowled late into the warm night. Outside, the happy shouts of Andrew's first victory over Pins could be heard echoing down the emptiness of deserted streets.

Geronimo sat in the steam room, a white towel draped around his waist, the medallion his mother gave him hanging around his neck. He let the steam wash over him, the sweat flowing down his body like a waterfall, his eyes closed. It was a ritual cleansing for Geronimo, a warrior about to go off and do battle. He knew his time had come, his destiny near enough for him to touch, and it brought a smile to his face. It was the way it was meant to be. He no longer needed to fear being found crunched over a broken computer terminal surrounded by dust and a blank wall, his heart filled with a sad weight. Instead, Geronimo would meet up with the device that waited for him. A device that would challenge his spirit and bring life back to his soul.

Geronimo removed the medallion from around his neck and rested it on the wooden slab by his side. He no longer needed its protection. His way had been found.

17

Mrs. Columbo walked toward the black van, a bundled latex-covered doll held close to her chest. The van was parked off the side of a hill, hidden by a thick cover of trees, ten miles north of Camden, Maine. Four armed men stood around the rear doors, polished shoes scuffing against the sandy ground. Two others sat in the front seat, windows rolled down, their necks leaning on headrests. A black Cadillac was parked at an angle next to the van, its four doors open to the late-night breeze, the three men inside checking and cleaning the clips on their semiautomatics.

The outskirts of resort towns were the favored exchange spots for Lucia's crew. Dealers and mules could come in and out, do business openly, and not garner any attention. The towns were accustomed to large numbers of visitors traveling, staying for only days or even hours before heading back home. It was easy to blend in.

It was even easier, as Lucia quickly discovered, to buy inexpensive condos on resort properties and utilize them as work bases and show places for prospective clients. Brokers especially were warm to investors who closed deals with cash. Lucia Carney owned seven such condos, all purchased in someone else's name, each located at a five-star resort situated within a long drive or a short flight to a central drug distribution city. In such places a mule and her team could blend in with soccer moms, golf-crazed dads, and scrambling toddlers, and just as easily disappear from view.

It was, without question, a perfect setup.

Mrs. Columbo's heels chipped against the corners of the tiny pebbles beneath her feet, kicking up small pockets of dust. She stared up at the van and could see the packets of cocaine, stacked high in the rear, all nearly glowing in the reflected glare of the Cadillac's lights. She walked slowly, hemmed in on one side by a short, gray-haired man holding a revolver, and on the other by a sour woman who had met her at the Portland airport, identifying herself only as Angela.

They had made the drive from Portland to the outskirts of Camden in less than an hour, riding in silence, Mrs. Columbo alone in the backseat of a Mercedes 450SL, occasionally looking down at the doll in her arms that luckily no one had yet asked to see.

She and Boomer had made it through LaGuardia with the help of two friends, former cops now working for the FBI, who waited for them by the checkpoint, flashed their shields, unfolded a few sheets of doctored documents, and ushered them through separately, bypassing the X-ray detectors which would have been sure to spot the cargo in Mrs. Columbo's arms and the guns in Boomer's satchel.

She and Boomer sat three rows apart on the small plane and avoided eye contact throughout the flight. The passenger seated to her right, a square-shouldered woman dressed in head-to-toe L. L. Bean, had asked to peek at her sleeping baby.

'I don't think that would be a good idea,' Mrs. Columbo told her, the harsh tone of her voice and the cold snap to her eyes backing the woman away. 'She's a light sleeper.'

Mrs. Columbo spent the rest of the flight with her head back and her eyes closed, running through all that had happened over the past few weeks. She had done a zero to sixty, going from an ex-cop with a sour disposition to a key member of an illegal unit bent on the takedown

261

of a cocaine queen. In the process, Mrs. Columbo found herself on the verge of a messy divorce, marked as a target by an on-the-pad cop, and now jammed inside a too-tight seat holding a prop baby stuffed with eight sticks of dynamite timed to kick in less than three hours.

It was exactly where she felt she belonged.

Boomer was first off the plane, rushing past the handful of people waiting at the arrival gate, their eager faces searching for friends and relatives. He stopped briefly in front of Mrs. Columbo's grim-looking party, brushing against the short man's tan leather jacket, eyes connecting for the briefest of moments before he made his way to the car rental booth.

'Your plane was late,' Angela said in tones as sharp as the cut of her skirt.

'If you've got a beef,' Mrs. Columbo said, shielding the baby from Angela's line of vision, 'the pilot should be coming out in a couple of minutes. Give his ear a bend.'

Angela's lips curled into what for her could have passed as either a smile or a sneer. As she whirled away, it was clear that she expected Mrs. Columbo and the silent man in the tan leather to follow close on her floppy heels, which they did.

'She a real bitch or just acting the part?' Mrs. Columbo asked her escort.

'Believe me, my wife is for real,' the quiet little man said in a voice befitting his size. 'It would be foolish for *anyone* to think otherwise.'

'I guess you'd be the one to know,' Mrs. Columbo said, and she shook her head as the man now walked at a faster pace, trying to catch up to Angela.

Geronimo and Pins were a quarter of a mile up from the black van, hidden by clumps of trees and a circle of large rocks. Pins had his back to the movement down below, legs folded under him, headphones on, picking up the conversation coming to him from the wire he had run down the prop baby's back. Geronimo put down his small binoculars and checked his watch.

'They smell anything yet?' he asked Pins.

'Not anything that I can pick up,' Pins said. 'But these guys make their moves with looks, not words.'

'Boomer and Dead-Eye should be here in about three minutes,' Geronimo said.

'And how long before that doll blows?' Pins asked.

'Six minutes,' Geronimo said, lifting two bolt-action rifles and recoil pads from a large black case by his sneakers. He handed one of the rifles to Pins. 'Worry about the ones by the van,' he said. 'I'll take the team in the car. That leaves Boomer with the two around Mrs. Columbo.'

'That car looks parked too close to the van,' Pins said. 'What if the dyno blows them both?'

'It shouldn't,' Geronimo said. 'Not if Mrs. Columbo centers the doll under the van the way I showed her. Besides, on top of that, I left thirty seconds for Rev. Jim to move the car away.'

'Next time don't be so generous,' Pins said, checking the nightscope at the center of his rifle. 'You'll only spoil him.'

Geronimo looked up at Pins and nodded. 'Thought I'd throw him a break,' he said. 'Just this once.'

'Kindness is weakness,' Pins said, resting the front of the rifle between branches of a tree, an open box of .375 H&H Magnum shells by his feet, headphones resting low on his neck.

'So's missing your target,' Geronimo said, lifting the rifle and taking aim from behind the large shadow of a boulder.

'I still don't like our end of the plan,' Dead-Eye said, sitting on the edge of a rock, four locked and loaded semiautomatic handguns spread out around him.

'If we go down to shoot it out, one of us is sure to buy it,' Boomer said, pacing around the dirt, rocks, and twigs.

263

'Pins and Geronimo can clip only so many off the back ridge. Rev. Jim's gotta get to the car and Mrs. Columbo's got enough to worry about with a fuckin' bomb in her arms.'

'I don't think Pins has ever pulled the trigger on a rifle,' Dead-Eye said. 'Which makes the odds very good that if he clips anybody, it's gonna be me.'

Boomer leaned against the rock and stared at Dead-Eye. They were a thirty-second run from the black van. They could see Mrs. Columbo and the heavy guns surrounding her, and they could feel the others hiding, their guns prepped, ready to take aim and clean out the Apache team.

'How many more than we can see do you think are out there?' Boomer asked, chewing on a thin twig.

'Hard to tell,' Dead-Eye said. 'But if they came looking for a total wipeout, I'd say about six more guns. Six more very good guns.'

'They're gonna expect us to shoot,' Boomer said. 'They're gonna be lookin' for us to come down with full loads.'

'Wouldn't you?' Dead-Eye said.

Boomer nodded and then smiled over at Dead-Eye. 'We got a minute thirty, then,' Boomer said, 'to go down and do what they would never expect.'

'Which is what?' Dead-Eye asked, sliding off the rock and reaching for his guns.

'Ask them to surrender,' Boomer said.

The man in the sunglasses walked slowly toward Mrs. Columbo. She had both hands wrapped around the prop baby, one of them hidden beneath the sheets of a thin cover blanket, fingers holding a .38 Special.

'I need the kid,' the man said in a slow-motion delivery.

When Mrs. Columbo didn't move, he walked closer and held out his left hand. 'I need the baby *now*,' he said.

Angela and the man in the tan leather jacket both

turned and looked at Mrs. Columbo, their eyes filled with a mixture of anger and suspicion.

'What's your problem?' Angela asked. 'Get on with it. Give the baby over to Carl.'

'I was expecting to get paid *before* making the handoff.' Mrs Columbo was surprised at how calm she was able to sound.

'And you can expect to be killed if you don't make it now,' the man in the tan leather said.

Mrs. Columbo looked down at the prop baby in her arms. 'Goodbye, sweet thing,' she said in soothing tones, a warm smile stretched across her face. She looked up at the man in the shades and then over at Angela and her husband. 'You get attached,' she said to them. 'You wouldn't understand. It's a mom thing.'

Mrs. Columbo kept her smile as she twirled around Angela and tossed the prop baby under the center of the black van, turned, and pointed her gun right in the woman's face. 'All of you,' Mrs. Columbo yelled without moving her head, her eyes focused on Angela's stunned gaze, 'listen to me! You got about a minute before that van blows and kills us all. We can shoot it out or we can get out. I'm gonna let the lady here make the call.'

Angela moved her eyes away from Mrs. Columbo and the muzzle of her gun long enough to see Boomer and Dead-Eye coming down the side of a sloping hill, guns at their sides. Rev. Jim had slipped out from behind a bush and was already near the Cadillac, a .38 Special cocked and pointed her way.

'You were ready to kill a few seconds ago,' Mrs. Columbo said to her in a low voice. 'Now are you ready to die?'

'What do you want?' Angela asked, the words lacking the edge they once carried.

'Let the van blow,' Mrs. Columbo said. 'And let us leave with the car and the money that's in the trunk. You and your people can scatter.'

'And if we don't?' her husband asked.

'Then what the bomb won't kill,' Mrs. Columbo said, 'the guns behind you and above you will. And you still lose the drugs and the cash. But I'm sure Lucia will appreciate the effort.'

'Forty-five seconds!' Boomer shouted from behind them, his gun pointed at no one in particular. 'This ain't somethin' that needs a lot of thought.'

'You will die too,' the man in the leather jacket shouted back at Boomer. 'Along with all of us.'

'There's one big difference,' Boomer said to him. 'I don't give a shit.'

Angela looked over at Mrs. Columbo one final time. 'What about you?' Angela asked her. 'Do *you* give a shit?'

Mrs. Columbo smiled and edged the barrel of the gun closer to Angela's cheek. 'What do you think?' she said.

Angela lifted her arms slowly above her head. It was all the men around her needed to drop their weapons and run from the van.

'Let's get in that car,' Boomer yelled, following Dead-Eye to the Cadillac, Rev. Jim already behind the wheel.

'She will find you,' Angela shouted out after Mrs. Columbo, watching as she removed the gun from her face and ran to join the others. 'She will find all of you.'

'That's what we're counting on,' Mrs. Columbo shouted back.

She was in the backseat of the Lincoln, her window rolled down, Dead-Eye next to her, Boomer and Rev. Jim in the front, dust from the back tires kicking up white puffs of sand clouds all around them. Angela and the rest of Lucia's crew were scattered up hills and down side paths, leaving an array of guns in their wake.

Geronimo and Pins stared down at it all, nestled safely on a rock on the ridge above.

'Now,' Geronino whispered to himself.

He didn't flinch as the loud explosion split the black van and rocketed it skyward, sending dust, metal, debris, and cocaine filtering through the air. Red, orange, and yellow flames were reflected in Geronimo's eyes, the heat of the blast and the strength of the strong steam air washing over him in one swooping wave of destruction. He smiled down at the site in complete admiration. Respectful of its force.

Lucia Carney stood in the bedroom of her Sedona condo, staring out at the fourteen-hole putting green, the light of a full moon filtering in through the shuttered glass. The thick white lace drapes were drawn to the edge of the porch windows and the blinds were slanted up. She wore a silk bathrobe slit down the sides, open in the front, and smoked a cigarette. She was deep in thought and didn't hear her husband, Gerald, walk into the room. He crept up behind her, drunk from an evening out with investment cronies, and wrapped his right arm around her waist, softly rubbing her naked flesh.

'Miss me?' he muttered into her ear.

'No,' Lucia said, her eyes still on the putting green, her mind several thousand miles away, picturing a lost shipment of cocaine and cash.

It wasn't enough for those bastard Apaches to blow six hundred thousand dollars worth of her untapped coke to the wind. They had to heap on an additional insult by driving off in one of her new cars, which was holding two hundred and fifty thousand in hundreds in the trunk. A sum that, she had discovered only hours earlier, had been donated in her name to child abuse centers in three states.

Gerald began to nuzzle the side of her neck, his hands lifting and groping the bathrobe in the clumsy manner of a man who should have stopped three drinks into the night.

'Go to bed, Gerry,' Lucia said, unmoved by her husband's actions.

'That's the plan,' he said, his head resting on the edge of her shoulder. 'You and me.'

Lucia pulled away from her husband and her view of the putting green, jamming the end of her cigarette into

267

an ashtray on top of a marble end table. Gerald stripped off his blue jacket and undid his matching tie, smiling at his wife, his body juiced by the sight of her bare skin visible under the sheer robe.

He blocked her path as she tried to move past him, his right hand caressing her breasts. 'Whatever you want,' he said to her, a broad smile on his face, fingers pulling at her nipples. 'That's what we'll do.'

Lucia stared at Gerald, wondering why she had stayed with him as long as she had. By now she already had more money than he did and had learned as much about investing as he was ever going to be able to teach. On top of which, she had all his contacts and could just as easily go directly to them to further expand her portfolio.

'Get naked,' she finally said to him. 'And turn down the lights. I'll be out in a minute.'

The loud shot from the Magnum brought two of her bodyguards storming through the bedroom door. They stopped, guns drawn, when they saw Lucia.

She turned to look at them, blood dripping down the sides of her face, the hot gun in her right hand. She slid off the bed and walked toward the two speechless men, handing one the gun.

'I'm going to take a shower and get dressed,' Lucia said in even tones. 'Have someone get rid of Gerald and then get us a private jet to New York.'

18

Pins sat across the bar from Nunzio, nursing a sweating glass of tap beer. It was early on a Saturday afternoon, two days after the Camden raid, and the place was quiet except for Ella Fitzgerald coming over the jukebox riffing her way through 'My Last Affair'.

'Freshen that for you?' Nunzio asked, polishing his side of the bar with a white cloth.

'No, thanks. It's still a little early. I'll stick to the one.'

Nunzio stared over at Pins and spotted a look on his face that shouldn't have been there. It wasn't so much fear or even concern that was etched across his strong features. It was more the weight of regret, the look of someone who found himself in the middle of a battle he had no business being in. Nunzio always thought Pins was the least comfortable member of the Apache team. The others were harder, tougher, more at ease with the action. Pins, Nunzio knew, was different. He still had too much heart.

In his specialty, Pins hadn't seen as many bodies as the others, was less aware of the ugly side of the street. He liked the team and enjoyed their company, coming to life when they were all gathered around a table, swapping war tales and stupid jokes. He went along with their plans and could be counted on to carry out his role, but, unlike the others, Pins wasn't driven by a need for revenge. He was the only cop, Nunzio felt, who, if given the choice, would take back his commitment and retreat to the quiet sanctity of his bowling alley.

'Okay if I ask you somethin'?' Pins said, pushing aside his glass of beer.

'Doesn't look like you're here to drink,' Nunzio said, 'and we're not open for lunch. So I figured it was talk you wanted.'

'The way things are going,' Pins said in soft tones, 'it doesn't seem like it's going to end good for any of us. You included.'

'Everything's gone your way so far,' Nunzio assured him. 'You've done some damage, caused the lady a few headaches, and, most important, you got her attention.'

'That's right,' Pins said. 'Those are all the reasons I'm worried.'

'Well, you're not wrong there,' Nunzio said. 'I'll give you that.'

'There's a weak link in every team,' Pins went on. 'I've been around long enough to know that. I don't want to be the weak link here.'

'You've held your end,' Nunzio told him. 'It wasn't your talkin' that got the lady sniffin' in our direction.'

'It just seems to come easier to the others,' Pins said, his words backed by Ella now singing 'Good Morning Heartache'. 'The action, I mean. It's like they're waitin' for it. Me, I'm always kinda hopin' we just take her down, cuff her, and hand her over to the feds.'

'You wanna walk?' Nunzio asked, spreading his hands across the bar. 'Might not be too late. Word can spread that you're out just as fast as it spread that you were in.'

'Maybe I *will* have another beer.'

Pins slid his glass toward Nunzio, who tapped out a refill with a foamy head and reached under the bar for a wooden bowl filled with pretzels.

'They're scared too, you know,' Nunzio said. 'We all are. And there's good reason to be. Not all of us are gonna make it outta this one alive.'

'I know that,' Pins said. 'Except with them, you can't

270

read it on their faces. With me, you pretty much can. I think that's the difference. It's a look that's easy to spot – by a cop or a shooter.'

'They're one up on you, Pins,' Nunzio said. 'They've been around the action so long, they learned how to hide the look. But that don't mean it ain't there.'

'What's your story?' Pins asked, finishing his beer. 'Why are you in this? You got a good life here, solid business, steady. You don't need to be in the middle of a war.'

Nunzio stared at Pins for several moments, then turned and reached for a bottle of Seagram's and two shot glasses. 'Knowin' my story ain't gonna be any help to you,' he said, topping off both glasses.

'You don't have to tell me, you don't want to,' Pins said. 'I was just curious.'

Nunzio swallowed his drink in a gulp, wiping his lips with a folded paper napkin. 'I got a daughter. Sandy,' he said, his voice calm, his body tense. 'You may have seen her around the times you been in here. She waits on tables the nights I'm short help.'

'I talked to her once,' Pins said. 'Seems like a nice lady.'

'She's a good kid,' Nunzio said. 'Her whole life, she never gave me any trouble. Married a good guy too. His name was Frank. Irish kid from a hardworking family. He worked two jobs and was going to classes over at Fordham at night. They were crazy in love with each other. Were gonna have a big family and be together forever.'

'But they aren't,' Pins said.

'Lots of times forever ain't that long a stretch,' Nunzio said. 'In Sandy's case it was only three years.'

Pins rested his hand on top of the older man's. 'You can stop there. I think I know the rest.'

'I don't think you do,' Nunzio said. 'They had a baby. A doll of a girl named Theresa. She was only three months old and she already had my heart.'

Pins grabbed for the bottle of Seagram's next to Nunzio's elbow and poured out two more drinks. He moved one glass closer to Nunzio.

271

'August 6, 1972. It was a hot day and hotter night.' Nunzio held the shot glass, not drinking. 'Nobody could sleep, least of all a baby about to break with her first tooth. Sandy and Frank took her out for a walk. It wasn't just the air they needed. With him workin' and studyin' most of the time, they didn't have all that much time to spend with each other. A walk's a good way to catch up.'

Pins could hear Nunzio's voice straining to stay firm.

'They were only ten minutes into the walk,' Nunzio said. 'It was a clear night and they were holding hands, the baby asleep in the carriage. And then, in a little less than five minutes, everybody's world got a lot smaller.'

'They were mugged?' Pins said, hoping the answer was that easy.

'Two guys were standin' in front of them before they even knew it,' Nunzio said. 'They forced them over into some tree cover. They beat Frankie, beat him bad, lookin' to leave him for dead. And they did things to Sandy I don't need to tell you about.'

'What about the baby?' Pins asked, his mouth dry, one hand bunched into a fist.

'Theresa?' Nunzio said. He blinked his eyes twice. He would not let tears fall down the front of his face. 'They took her right outta her carriage.'

'Jesus Christ!' Pins said. 'I'm sorry, Nunzio. I'm so sorry.'

'It changed everything, that night,' Nunzio said. 'Took years to put Sandy back together, bring her to a place where she could come close to leadin' a normal life. And Frankie . . . he never came out of it. Stuck around for a few months and then one morning got up, got dressed, and got out.'

'Where to?'

'Don't know,' Nunzio said. 'Don't need to know. We all handle our wars in different ways. He's handling his the only way he can.'

'They ever get Theresa back?'

'No,' Nunzio said. 'All my wise-guy contacts. All my cop friends. We all came up empty.'

'I don't know what to say.'

'Nothin' to say,' Nunzio said. 'Years go by, you bury it, but you never forget it. And then Boomer comes in here and tells me about Lucia. Now, I know Lucia had nothin' at all to do with takin' my little Theresa away from us. But you know what?'

'Tell me,' Pins said.

'She might as well have been the one,' Nunzio said. 'That's why I'm in. It's why we're all in. To get a taste of even. In our way of lookin' at things, it's as good as you can hope for. You can't ever get back what you lost, so you make somebody pay for it.'

Pins stared at Nunzio, his eyes moist.

'I'm just like the rest of the crew,' Nunzio said. 'And so are you, Pins. Our hearts been carved out by different people in different ways. It's only the taste of gettin' even that keeps us all going forward.'

They sat across from each other, sun filtering in through the large front windows, the silence between them welcome and relaxing.

'I'm going over to the bowling alley,' Pins said. 'Roll a few games. Helps clear my head. Wouldn't mind having company if you're interested.'

'You as good as they say you are?' Nunzio asked, the hardness back in his face and voice.

'Probably better,' Pins said, smiling.

'What will you spot me?' Nunzio asked.

'I'll give you twenty,' Pins said. 'We play three games, that's a sixty spot. Highest total wins.'

'How much we playin' for?'

'I don't want your money, Nunzio,' Pins said.

'You ain't gettin' my money,' Nunzio said, walking out from behind the bar. 'Now, how much?'

'Ten bucks a game,' Pins said. 'Twenty if you sweep the three.'

'Deal,' Nunzio said, rolling down his sleeves and putting on a black leather jacket.

'You ain't a ringer, are you?' Pins said, walking behind Nunzio toward the front door.

'You'll know in a couple of hours.' Nunzio shrugged his shoulders and walked out, leaving Pins to lock the door.

Boomer and Dr. Carolyn Bartlett walked quietly side by side down the south end of Thirty-sixth Street between Park and Madison. It was late on a warm Tuesday night, a cloudless spring night, a mild wind brushing against their backs. Boomer glanced over at her unlined face lit by an overhead streetlight, struck by the simplicity of her beauty and still surprised she had accepted his dinner invitation. He was attracted to Bartlett from the first and admired her for the stance she had taken in defense of Jennifer Santori. He wished he had said something to her about it back then. But, as usual, Boomer let anger stand in his way.

He had driven down to pick her up in front of her office building and taken her over the Fifty-ninth Street Bridge to a favorite Long Island City hangout, where they had feasted on southern Italian specialties prepared to heavenly perfection by the proprietor and his wife. During the course of the three-hour meal, they talked, laughed, easily broke down the barriers thrown between them by their work. They even joined Vincent, a retired cop from Naples, in an off-key rendition of 'Amore Mio'. Boomer introduced Carolyn to Fernet Branca, an after-dinner digestive with the smoothness of lighter fluid, and he watched with mild wonder as she shot back the drink in one gulp and was able to name three of the herbs used in its making.

They drove back into Manhattan in comfortable silence and she seemed amenable when he suggested that they park the car and walk for a bit. He curbed up next to a

274

fire hydrant, tossed an NYPD permit across the dash, and walked over to hold her door open.

'Are you still allowed to have one of those?' she asked, pointing to the permit.

'No,' Boomer said.

'Do you follow the rules on *anything?*' Carolyn asked.

'No.'

Carolyn slid a hand under his arm and moved herself closer to his side. 'I'm glad you called.'

'I owed you,' Boomer said. 'I ran a little rough on you about Jenny. Wrote you off as another bleeding heart. I should have known better.'

'Is that an apology?' she asked.

'It's as close as I get to one,' Boomer said. His eyes locked on Carolyn. 'But don't go getting used to it.'

'I won't.'

'You know, I talked to Jenny's dad the other night,' Boomer said. 'He told me she's starting to come around and that you've been a big help to her and the family. I appreciate that.'

'Is that the only reason you asked me out?' Carolyn said, stopping in front of her brownstone.

'No, that wasn't the reason,' Boomer said, turning to face her. 'That was just a damn good excuse.'

'What other reason, then, would you have to ask me out, Detective?' Carolyn asked, running a soft hand against the hard features of Boomer's face.

'Would you buy it if I said I didn't want to eat alone?' Boomer asked.

'No,' Carolyn said.

'How about if I told you I wanted free medical advice?' Boomer said. 'Would that one work?'

'No,' Carolyn said.

'How about if I told you I've thought about you every day since we met?' Boomer said, leaning closer to Carolyn. 'And that I picked up the phone a dozen times to call you but didn't because I'd've bet money you'd say no. Would you believe any of that?'

275

'There's a good chance on that one,' Carolyn said.

Boomer leaned closer and kissed her, holding Carolyn tightly in his arms, her hair brushing against his face. Her lips were soft and her breath was as warm as the light wind coming up off the East River. He held on to her for as long as he could, engulfed by the peaceful night and the passion of her kiss. They stood under the streetlight, the pains and fears of their jobs shoved aside for this brief moment.

'Now you know my real reason,' Boomer whispered, sliding his face alongside Carolyn's, his strong arms still holding her slight frame.

'And now you know why I said yes,' Carolyn whispered in his ear.

'I haven't felt like this in a long time,' Boomer said, forgetting what lay ahead, concerned only with the present. 'A *very* long time.'

Carolyn lifted her head to look at Boomer, cupping her hands around his face. 'Come up with me,' she said. 'But there's something you should know before you do.'

'You're married,' Boomer said. 'And your husband's asleep on the couch with a gun in his hand.'

'Besides that,' she said, laughing and leading him up the brownstone steps.

'You don't have any Fernet Branca,' Boomer said, following her.

'And I *never will* either,' Carolyn said, reaching into her shoulder bag for the key to the front door.

'That's as good as my guesses get,' Boomer said, standing behind her, arms around her waist.

She shoved the key in the latch, opened the door, and turned around to face Boomer. 'I'm afraid for you,' Carolyn said, losing the smile. 'I don't want anything to happen to you.'

'I don't want anything to happen to me either,' Boomer said, holding the door open with one hand.

'I'm pretty sure I'm going to fall in love with you,

276

Boomer. And it would be very nice if you were around long enough to see it happen.'

'I'll be around as long as you want me to be,' Boomer promised. 'You've got nothing to be afraid of.'

The smile returned to Carolyn's face as she wrapped her arms around him. They stepped into the foyer, let the door shut quietly behind them, and moved up the stairs toward Carolyn's second-floor apartment.

The peaceful spring night was theirs to call their own.

The black Lexus was parked across the street. Wilber Graves sat behind the wheel, smoking a Cuban cigar, a grin on his face as he watched Boomer and Carolyn walk up the brownstone steps.

'Our friend has himself a woman,' Wilber said to a young man seated on the passenger side of the car.

'Do you want me to deal with it now?' the young man asked.

Wilber looked over at him and spread his smile. 'You have no sense of romance, Derek,' Wilber said. 'Let the lovers have their night. Let them have something to remember. This way, when we reach for them and let them feel our touch, the pain will be that much harder to forget.'

'How soon, then?' the young man said.

Wilber took a long drag from his cigar, filling the front of the car with smoke. He took half of it back in his lungs with a deep breath. 'The cop will have his way tonight,' Wilber said. 'And come the morning, we will have ours.'

19

Dead-Eye was on his third turn around the Central Park reservoir, building up his lung capacity, trying to get back reasonably close to the pace he'd kept in the years before the elevator shoot-out. He was taking long strides, heavy beads of sweat soaking through his blue NYPD running gear, the center of his chest burning with a pain he willed himself to ignore. His legs stabbed at him with sharp bolts, his back muscles twitched in spasms, his stomach churned out its acid.

And still Dead-Eye ran.

The shooting had altered Dead-Eye's life in so many ways, but the physical changes were the hardest. His diet now consisted mainly of fruits, fresh-cut vegetables, and fish. He attacked his local gym three mornings a week, lifting and pulling for three hours at a heavy clip. The longer his workouts went, the more intense his pain grew. And despite stern warnings from a concerned battery of doctors, Dead-Eye made it a point to hit the track.

Four mornings a week, four miles at a time.

It couldn't make him whole again, nothing could do that, but it helped keep him sane. When he ran, regardless of weather or time of day, Dead-Eye always brought himself back to younger years when he raced along the Brooklyn piers next to his father. He was never able to beat him, but he always managed to finish the course, no matter how tired. During their daily runs, Dead-Eye's father had imparted to his son the two rules he held

278

absolute: Give everything you do an honest effort and never give up or give in.

It was the only way Dead-Eye knew how to live. Even with a body that was scarred and ravaged.

He was coming around a hard curve now, trees and brush to his right, the clear waters of the reservoir to his left. He checked the stopwatch in his hand. Forty minutes and two more miles to go. He picked up his pace, looking to finish in thirty-five.

The two men came at him from behind, and he never had a chance. They jumped out from a thick row of bushes, slammed Dead-Eye up against the chain-link fence, two guns drawn, both held against his chest.

The man on his left was decked out in a dark designer jogging suit. The other one had on a black leather jacket over a thin black turtle-neck and a pair of tailored blue jeans. Dead-Eye waited for them to talk, his breathing still heavy from his run.

'Your little bullshit game is over as of today,' the man in the jogging suit said. 'You walk away from it now and we'll forget all about the crap you pulled.'

'You go back to your friends and tell them that,' the one in the turtle-neck said, a touch of a lisp to his words. 'Tell 'em this is their last fuckin' chance to leave the table alive.'

'Give me a nod so I know you understand what we're tellin' you,' the jogging suit said.

Dead-Eye stared at the two of them and slowly nodded his head, beads of sweat falling onto the dark dirt by his feet.

The man in the turtle-neck reached a hand into the side pocket of his leather jacket and brought out a color Polaroid. He held the photo close to Dead-Eye's face.

'This is your boy, am I right, cop?' the man asked.

Dead-Eye didn't move. But his eyes flashed anger. There was a large X drawn in felt-tip crossing over his son's face. They had gone beyond touching a cop. They were touching family. He knew now there could never be

279

any turning back. Lucia and the Apaches were alike in only one respect. They were both in this fight to win. And Dead-Eye realized, looking at Eddie's picture, that the only winners were going to be those who were left alive when the fight was over.

The man in the sweat suit snapped open a black switch-blade and watched as his partner slid Eddie's photo over its sharp point. He smiled at Dead-Eye, flashing the photo and the knife.

'This might hurt a little,' he said.

He stuck the knife and the photo into Dead-Eye's right arm.

Dead-Eye's knees buckled and his arms shook. The knife wound awoke every sharp pierce his body had ever felt, from bullet to blade. His lungs screamed for mercy and he swallowed back a mouthful of bile. He gave in to the pain, wanting nothing so much as to fall to the ground and rest his head on the dirt track. Wanting so much for it to stop.

But Dead-Eye didn't fall. He looked out through a blurred vision knowing he now had the one thing he needed to get even. He had the faces of the two men etched across his eyes.

'You go back to your friends,' the man in the jacket said. 'Tell 'em about our little meeting. Find out how serious they are about dying.'

'And it ain't just them that goes down,' the other man said. 'It's everybody attached. Sons, daughters, wives, hus-bands, even your fuckin' pets.'

The man in the sweat suit pulled the knife blade out of Dead-Eye's arm and held it out for him to look at. 'Take the picture,' he said, smiling. 'Keep it for his scrapbook or his coffin. I'll leave it to you to decide.'

He watched the men cross over a steep ridge, walking in slow strides, their backs to the sun, guns holstered at their sides. Dead-Eye waited until they disappeared from sight, then he bent down and picked up his son's photo. He held it in both hands, blood from the stab wound running down his arm, across his fingers, and dripping onto the picture. He leaned the weight of his back against the fence, his face up, his eyes closed, reveling now in the sharp pain he felt. He stayed there for close to an hour, listening as clusters of other runners came charging past, puffing their way through a morning drill. He was sweating, willing the pain to come on stronger, knowing he would need the strength of that pain to fuel his anger further and carry him through to the end of his task.

With his arm still leaking blood, Dead-Eye wiped the flow of sweat from his face and checked the timer on his stopwatch. He then shifted his feet and picked up where he had left off. Dead-Eye continued down the reservoir path and finished his run, holding his son's photo crumpled in his right hand.

The pain his only comfort.

Geronimo and Rev. Jim stood against the railing and watched the field of eight horses canter by. The sixth race at Belmont Park was about to start. With racing programs folded open in their hands and small pencils hooked over their ears, they were trying to decide which horse to wager on.

'Number three just took a shit,' Rev. Jim said, scanning the program for the horse's name. 'That's always a good sign.'

'You can't go by that,' Geronimo said. 'They're horses. All they *do* is shit.'

'Catapult,' Rev. Jim said, circling the name on the program. 'Even his name sounds fast. And he's down at six to one. I'd say he's good for a win, place, and show. You want in, or what?'

'You have to have a sense for the horse,' Geronimo said, staring out at the rest of the field. 'You need to know how far he'll go for the win. If his heart has the courage it needs.'

'We're not askin' for him to *fly*, Geronimo. This ain't a

281

spiritual thing workin' here. We just want him to go a mile around a fast track, win by a nose, and pay for our lunch.'

'He won't win unless he *wants* to win,' Geronimo said. 'No matter what *we* want.'

Rev. Jim rested the program against his thigh and looked over at Geronimo. 'Just between you and me,' he said, 'are you really serious about this Indian shit you talk or are you just fuckin' with everybody's head?'

'I would be dead without that Indian *shit*,' Geronimo said. 'It's all I had to hold on to all those months in the hospital. There was no hope. There was only dread. If anyone knows that feeling better than me, it's you.'

'I couldn't talk for months after the fire,' Rev. Jim told him. 'If I could have talked, I would have asked for somebody to put a bullet in my head. There's a lotta ways a guy could go out and buy it. Having your skin burn away ain't the best of 'em.'

'I wanted to leave,' Geronimo said. 'Take my pension and head for the Southwest, bury myself in the culture.'

'Why didn't you?' Rev. Jim asked.

'The people I have there see me as this brave cop,' Geronimo said. 'To them I am invincible. A warrior who can't be felled. I couldn't go back to them in the shape I was in.'

'That why you joined up with Boomer?' Rev. Jim asked. 'To go out on your own terms?'

'We choose our way of life,' Geronimo said. 'I want to be able to choose the way I die. I don't mind going down against a device, but not the way it happened to me. Not with a grenade tossed into an open crowd. I always pictured being alone with a bomb and letting my destiny decide.'

'You might get your wish,' Rev. Jim said. 'From the looks of it, there ain't gonna be a shortage of fireworks.'

'I'll be ready,' Geronimo said.

Rev. Jim pulled out a crushed pack of Marlboros, shook one loose, and put it to his lips. He searched his pockets for matches and came up empty. 'You wouldn't have a light?' he asked.

Geronimo unzipped his flak jacket and reached for a lighter in the front pocket of a checkered hunting shirt. Rev. Jim looked over at the inside flaps of the jacket, each slot packed with sticks of dynamite. 'You care to explain that?' he asked in astonishment.

'Ever since I became an Apache,' Geronimo said, smiling, 'they're my American Express card. I never leave home without 'em.'

'You know why you're part of this team?' Rev. Jim asked, turning his attention back to the track. 'You're just as crazy as the rest of us. That's why you must have been a great cop. You gotta be crazy to be a great cop.'

'Are we crazy enough to beat back Lucia Carney?' Geronimo asked.

'She's probably thinking we are,' Rev. Jim said. 'She's got to figure by now we're not in this for the money. And there ain't anybody around gonna pin any medals on us if we *do* bring her to a crash. So what's our end? She don't know. And that should give us a little bit of a lead.'

'If she only knew the real reason,' Geronimo said. 'That we're just walking dead men looking for one last battle. To bring peace to our souls.'

'There you go with that Indian shit again,' Rev. Jim said.

Geronimo smiled, looking at the pack of horses race past him toward the finish line. 'That Indian shit just saved you a few bucks.'

'How you figure?' Rev. Jim asked, craning his neck to see how the horses finished.

'You're looking in the wrong direction,' Geronimo said. 'There's Catapult over there, bringing up the rear. Like I said, he just didn't have the spirit of a warrior.'

'Havin' a shitty jockey on his back didn't help any either,' Rev. Jim said.

They walked away from the rail and eased their way up toward the bleachers. They sat next to one another, spending the rest of the afternoon under the sun of a fast track, winning and losing money, laughing and eating the kind of food neither was supposed to consume. Enjoying a brief day of calm.

Boomer stared at the crushed photo of Eddie. The blood on it was caked and the felt-tip mark smeared. The rest of the Apaches sat around the circular table, Nunzio pacing behind them.

'He's your kid, Dead-Eye.' Boomer's voice was soft with concern. 'These are crazy fucks we're moving on, and killing kids doesn't seem to upset them all that much. So I'll let you call the play.'

'Eddie and Grace are taken care of,' Dead-Eye said in a calm, even tone. 'Now let's worry about us. Lucia sent me a message. Sent us all one, really. I think we should send one back.'

Boomer looked around the table, studying each Apache in turn. That felt-tip X scrawled across little Eddie's photo might as well have been drawn on every one of them. It was a call-out, a street move, a push by a criminal to force a cop to take a step back. Most cops would fade away. A few would stand their ground. But the ones Boomer chose as Apaches knew only one way. To move forward and attack.

'One hour, then,' Boomer said, standing and moving away from the table. 'Tenth Street and Avenue A. Nunzio'll lay out the plan. I'll see you there.'

'Where are *you* going?' Mrs. Columbo asked.

'To pick up a wrecking ball,' Boomer said, closing the front door of the restaurant behind him.

Boomer and Mrs. Columbo sat in the front seat of a yellow multigear Caterpillar rig. A half-ton wrecking ball hung from an iron hook, swaying lazily in front of them. Both wore white hard hats and heavy construction gloves as the machine slowly inched its way through late-morning traffic. Boomer had eased the dozer out of a Lower East

Side construction site whose foreman owed Nunzio a few hard favors, grinding gears as he moved the rig past crumbling tenements.

'Are you sure about this?' Mrs. Columbo asked, feeling out of place sitting so high above the traffic.

'You mean letting you ride shotgun? It's a risk, but worth a roll.'

'Not that, dorko,' Mrs. Columbo said. 'I was thinking more about your little idea of demolishing a building in downtown Manhattan in broad daylight.'

'It's as good as any other idea I've had,' Boomer said.

'That sure helps ease my mind,' Mrs. Columbo muttered.

'Besides, it gives you and me a few minutes to talk.' Boomer cranked the shaft back into neutral, looking up past three cars at a red light.

'About what?'

'Your husband.'

'He's off limits, Boom.'

'He made a wrong move going to Lavetti,' Boomer said. 'But he did it for the right reasons. He was worried about you, so he reached out for somebody he thought would help.'

'He could have talked to *me*.' Mrs. Columbo turned away to watch a small boy bounce a Spauldeen against a red brick wall.

'Well, you ain't all that easy to talk to sometimes,' Boomer said. 'Like most cops.'

'I can talk to you,' Mrs. Columbo said, still looking at the boy and the ball, her voice distant and quiet.

'I'm a cop *and* your friend,' Boomer said. 'That gives me a leg up on a husband.'

'You're saying I should go back with him?'

'You've got a life with him, Mary. And a son.'

'It's not much of a life,' Mrs. Columbo said. 'And I'll always have my son.'

'Just think about it,' Boomer said. The light turned

green and he moved the rig forward. 'That's all I'm saying.'

'It could have been me and you, you know.' Mrs. Columbo still wasn't looking at him. 'It wouldn't have taken much. To tell you the truth, I'm kind of surprised it never was.'

'I am, too.' Boomer glanced over at her. 'But you know, sometimes the could-have-been leaves you with a better feeling. We would have had ourselves a few good months, maybe even a couple of years. But we wouldn't have made it past that.'

'Thank you, Ann Landers,' Mrs. Columbo said.

'You and me, we know each other more than fifteen years now and we can still talk to each other like this. But if we were married, we probably wouldn't even be *looking* at each other. And both of us packin' guns. I'm telling you, it could've gotten ugly.'

'Real fast,' Mrs. Columbo said with a laugh.

'Plus, you're a better shot,' Boomer said.

'Most wives are,' Mrs. Columbo said. 'Cop or not.'

'That's why I'm still single.' Boomer signaled to make a left turn.

'So, you gonna tell me about her?' Mrs. Columbo asked. 'Or do I have to get all my info secondhand?'

Boomer nearly rammed the ball end of the dozer against the back of a Dodge Dart. 'Remind me to pistol-whip Nunzio next time I see him.'

'He couldn't help himself,' she said. 'I squeezed it out of him. I *was* a homicide detective, remember?'

'I went out on a date,' Boomer said. 'Not a hit.'

'And . . .'

'*And* I had a great time. *And* I'm gonna see her again. *And* that's all I'm gonna say for now.'

'Why?' Mrs. Columbo said. 'You turning shy on me all of a sudden?'

'No,' Boomer said. 'I'm anything but shy.'

'Then why won't you tell me about her?' Mrs. Columbo asked, grabbing on to Boomer's right arm.

'Because we're here,' Boomer said.

Geronimo ran up to the driver's side and jumped onto the side panel runner.

'Rev. Jim and Pins in place?' Boomer asked.

'They're on each end of the avenue, rerouting traffic,' Geronimo said. 'And they're not all that happy about it.'

'Why?' Mrs. Columbo said. 'They've got the easiest job. Next to mine.'

'They're back in uniform.' Boomer laughed. 'I got two sets of blues from a friend down at the Chinatown precinct.' As Mrs. Columbo covered her mouth with her right hand, joining Boomer and Geronimo in the laugh, Boomer asked, 'Building empty?'

'I went with Dead-Eye and checked through every floor,' Geronimo told him. 'Nothing in there except for a couple of attack dogs that we cleared out and enough cocaine to make every junkie in the city smile for a week.'

'Why no guards?' Mrs. Columbo wanted to know.

'She doesn't need any,' Boomer explained. He turned the dozer so the wrecking ball faced the front of the building, the street now empty of all traffic. 'Any dealer or junkie even thinking of making a move on her would be too scared to touch the place. Even with nobody there, that building is more secure than Fort Knox.'

'Until now,' Mrs. Columbo said.

'You bet your sweet little ass until now.' And with that, Boomer shifted the gears on the rig forward.

Geronimo grabbed on to a yellow pole alongside the large front wheel, signaling Dead-Eye away from the front entrance with his free hand. Dead-Eye smiled and nodded, walking closer to the dozer, waving Boomer forward.

'Aim for the center of the building,' Dead-Eye yelled, his hands cupped around his mouth. 'That way you're sure to knock something down.'

'Listen to him,' Boomer muttered, moving the rig at full throttle. 'All of a sudden he's Fred Flintstone.'

Boomer brought the rig to a halt as soon as it jumped

287

the curb. He rammed the gears into park, then began to shift and pull the wrecking ball crank toward the boarded-up first-floor window.

'I guess it would be a waste of time asking if you've ever run a machine like this before,' Mrs. Columbo said, watching the ball sway from side to side.

'Total.' Smiling, Boomer eased the shaft forward and watched in awe as the ball crashed against the pre-war façade of the building.

The first loud hit brought brick, wood, and dust particles tumbling to the ground. Geronimo and Dead-Eye stood on opposite ends of the building, gold shields hanging from leather straps around their necks, huge grins on their faces, holding back small clusters of passers-by.

Boomer turned in his seat and looked over at Mrs. Columbo. 'You wanna give it a shot?' he asked. 'Unless you think you're not strong enough.'

'Move it over, old man,' Mrs. Columbo said, standing in her seat, waiting for Boomer to slide down from the rig.

'Try not to kill anybody,' Boomer told her.

Mrs. Columbo cranked the gear forward, moving the wrecking ball away from Boomer and toward the left side of the building. 'Clear the decks,' she shouted as the ball hit with a louder crash than the first blow, breaking through to the gut of the tenement, dismantling its center foundation and bringing two floors down with an enormous thud.

'Here we are, demolishing a fucking building during lunch hour,' Boomer shouted over to Dead-Eye. 'And what don't we see *anywhere*? A cop.'

'It must be true, then.' Dead-Eye said. 'They're never around when you really need them.'

'Not even a brown shirt to write up a violation,' Boomer said, scanning up and down the avenue. 'I mean, shit, we've gotta be breaking some traffic law here.'

'It doesn't matter.' Dead-Eye shrugged. 'We've never

paid for a ticket in our lives.' After a pause he asked, 'Who filled you in on the building?'

'It's on the DEA scanner sheet,' Boomer said. 'And it matched up with the information I got from our guy downtown.'

'Everybody knows the places, but nobody makes a move,' Dead-Eye said.

'That all changed today,' Boomer said.

They watched Mrs. Columbo maneuver the wrecking ball against the building for the last time. It teetered on the verge of a total collapse, then it all fell in one massive heap, caving inward. A cloud of dust flowed out to the street, and sounds of distant horns and sirens could be heard.

Dead-Eye walked through the debris, stepping over crushed rock, splintered wood, darkened packets of cocaine, and a nest of dead rats. He stood over a small mound of red bricks and put a hand inside his jacket pocket, coming out with the crumpled, marked-up photo of his son. He leaned over and placed the picture under a cracked edge of one of the red bricks, then stood up, turned, and walked toward his fellow Apaches.

'That's just in case Lucia has any trouble figuring out who blew up her stash,' Dead-Eye said.

Carolyn Bartlett let the hot water run over her body, still tired after an arduous day of coaxing information out of reluctant patients. She had taken on her daily run with relish and looked forward to her post-shower addictions – a low-cal dinner, reading through several chapters of a historical romance, Bach on the stereo and, sometime within the next hour, hearing Boomer's voice coming over the phone by her bed.

She had been reluctant to get emotionally involved with someone so closely linked to one of her patients, especially a man such as Boomer Frontieri. By falling for Boomer, who openly worked outside the boundaries of the law to get what he felt was justice, Carolyn also shattered a promise she had long ago made to herself: Never date a cop, retired or not. But here she was, in less time than it took to fill out a case file, as involved with Boomer as anyone could expect to get.

Carolyn turned the water off, slid the shower curtain open, and reached for the thick white towel folded on the marble sink. She wrapped it around her body and notched it in place. She picked up the silver hairbrush her grandmother had given her on her sixth birthday and ran it through her long wet hair. She wiped a hand across the steam-drenched medicine cabinet mirror and checked her face. The stress of her work had yet to add wrinkles to her skin, but Carolyn knew those days would soon be close at hand. She smiled, remembering Boomer leaning over her and telling her she had the soft, pure face of an angel. She hoped he would always feel that way.

She walked into the living room, slid a tape of Bach into her stereo system before heading into the kitchen to check out which Lean Cuisine Special she should feast on. She slipped a chicken and broccoli on a bed of white rice into her small oven and set the cooking timer. She was padding back, in bare feet, toward the refrigerator to pour herself a glass from a half-empty bottle of Orvietto Classico, when she saw the shadow against the living room wall.

Then Bach went silent.

Carolyn could see the telephone from where she was standing, the red message light flashing on the answering machine, and figured it to be her only move. Her mind racing, her thought processes marred by fear, she ran blindly from the kitchen toward the phone. She made it as far as the end table. A dark-gloved hand grabbed her by the hair and pulled her back. She felt hot breath on her neck and grizzled skin scratching against her face.

'He's not at home,' Wilber Graves said to her. 'He's out. With his friends.'

'What do you want?' Carolyn asked, trying to keep a calm voice and a level breathing pattern.

'I want everything the cop calls his own,' Wilber said. '*Everything*.'

A few moments later Carolyn stood in front of the telephone, the towel stripped from her body and thrown to the floor. She was fully naked, her hands bound tightly behind her with chicken wire, the tip of a Spanish-made red-handled switchblade pressed against the side of her neck. Wilber rubbed Carolyn's body with his free hand, moving gloved fingers in a slow motion up against her firm breasts, down the contours of her stomach, over the front of her thighs. Occasionally, he slipped a finger inside her vagina.

'You won't believe this,' he said to her. 'But I really wish I didn't have to kill you.'

'Why are you waiting?' Carolyn asked. Her eyes stared straight ahead, trying to will herself to another place, a safer one, where men didn't kill on whim or orders and where a woman could listen to Bach, read a book, and wait for someone she loved to call and tell her so. She could smell the Lean Cuisine dinner burning in the oven, too many minutes past done.

It almost made her want to smile.

The phone rang at seven minutes past eleven.

The first ring jolted her, the tip of Wilber's knife edging in deeper, cutting into the side of her skin, drawing blood. Wilber removed his hand from Carolyn's waist, picked up the phone, and placed it against her ear. He let her hear Boomer's voice on the other end. Wilber smiled at her as he moved the phone away and cradled it on the side of his neck.

'Hello, Detective,' Wilber said into the receiver.

'Where's Carolyn?' he heard Boomer say.

'She's snug and warm right here in my arms,' Wilber said. 'I have to tell you, you have excellent taste in women. That's surprising in a police officer.'

'Anything happens to her . . .'

'Something *is* going to happen to her, Detective,'

Wilber said. 'We were just waiting for you to call before it does.'

'Let her go!' Boomer's shout could be heard well beyond the range of the receiver.

'I will,' Wilber said. 'I promise you that. But first, would you like to hear her say good-bye?'

Wilber pressed the receiver against Carolyn's ear.

'Speak to him,' he told her.

Carolyn closed her eyes and took a deep breath, the knife pressing against her neck. 'I love you, Boomer,' she said.

She never felt the cut. Her head turned light, the room spun around her in slow circles, the front of her body went warm with blood. Her legs weakened and sent her to the floor, a slight moan coming from her lips as her head touched down on the wooden planks.

Wilber hovered over her and watched her die, calmly ignoring Boomer's frantic shouts into his end of the phone.

'My name is Wilber Graves,' he said into the phone once Carolyn had taken her final breath. 'I've just killed a woman who loved you, and it was my pleasure. Good-bye, Detective.'

Wilber placed the phone back on its cradle, took one more look down at Carolyn, and closed the knife. He turned the stereo back on to Bach, went into the kitchen, and turned off the oven before he walked out of the apartment.

His work for the night at an end.

Boomer went to the wake, where the coffin was sealed, and to the funeral, held under the angry rain of a late-spring day.

He had been fast on the crime scene, arriving within minutes of the precinct sector car. The two young officers hovering around the apartment had been decent enough to cover her naked body with a white sheet stripped from her bed, a sheet he and Carolyn had slept under together.

Boomer pulled it back and stared down at the woman he had grown to know so well in such a short time. Her lips and nails were already starting to pale, her clear skin taking on the waxy color of the dead. The open wound still gurgled blood. Her eyes were closed, her mouth curved in a twisted smile. Boomer crouched down and leaned over to kiss Carolyn's still-warm lips. He reached for the edge of the white sheet and slowly lifted it past her face. He zippered his jacket, stood, nodded to the two officers, and left before the meat truck arrived.

At her funeral, Boomer stood out, a stranger among family, sitting in the back row of a candlelit church, listening to the faces who had shared decades with her talk about their memories. He only half listened, his eyes staring down the curved arms of the aisles at the closed oak coffin air-locking the body of a woman who had died for no reason.

Boomer pictured Carolyn's easy smile and allowed his mind to drift off, to conjure up images of the life they might have had together. These images – places they would visit, dinners they would share – were fleeting.

The time for romance was over.

Other images took hold.

Boomer had never met Wilber Graves, but he knew him well. Hard-edged and soulless, a gun for hire whose thrills were fed watching a human being bleed a life away. He would soon meet up with Wilber Graves and it would end as it was destined to end, with one man standing above the other.

He and the Apaches had started the war. Lucia and her crew were now making their move. People would die. Most were deserving, some might be innocent. To win, the Apaches could no longer see themselves as ex-cops out to right a wrong. They had to dig deeper, search harder, strip away their layers of weakness and humanity, and face their foes on an equal footing.

Boomer knelt in the pew, head buried in his hands, and

prayed to the God in the room to give him the strength he needed.

To destroy his enemies.

The enemies who erased Carolyn Bartlett from the center of his life.

Boomer dropped two red roses in Carolyn's open grave, then stared blankly as four workmen guided the coffin down into the open pit. The heavy rain washed over his head and down the sides of his neck, but he stayed until there was no one left by the graveside. He didn't exchange any words with Carolyn's family, nor did he offer words of sympathy to the assembled women dressed in short black dresses and veils that hid reddened eyes. Boomer could think of nothing to say that would help ease their painful burden.

So he stood there quietly, head bowed, hands folded under dark and ominous clouds, letting an angry rain lash away at the guilt he carried in the caverns of his heart.

Behind him, hidden under the heavy leaves of an old tree, Nunzio and the rest of the Apaches stood in silence.

The Apaches were sitting in the back room of Nunzio's, waiting out the rain. There was an amplified energy to the room, the sense that the next hours would determine everyone's fate.

They were all there except for Pins. His tardiness was out of character. He was usually the first to arrive. Maybe he had decided to roll a few extra games before the action kicked in.

Boomer had yellow surveillance folders spread out in front of him, an illegal gift from a friend in the Washington office of the Secret Service. He had been hunting Lucia Carney for the past eight months on a money-laundering scheme.

Boomer, hands on his chin, not looking up, said, 'Nunz, throw Pins another ring. This ain't a day to call in sick.'

'I just tried him,' Nunzio said. 'If he's at the alley, he's not pickin' up.'

'Anybody hear from him today?' Boomer asked, scanning the faces around him.

'I talked to him last night,' Rev. Jim said. 'He knew we were meeting and he knew what time.'

'It's not like him,' Mrs. Columbo said, sipping a decaf espresso. 'He's not the kind to blow off a meeting.'

A young waiter in a white jacket and thin black tie peeked into the small, crowded room. 'Excuse me,' he said, 'I don't mean to bother.'

'Whatta ya got, Freddie?' Nunzio asked.

'A phone call,' Freddie said. 'Just came in. The guy didn't stay on all that long.'

'What'd he want?' Nunzio said.

'Told me to ask if any of the guys were up for a night of bowling,' Freddie said.

'He give a name?' Boomer asked in a cold voice.

'Wilber Graves,' Freddie said.

Boomer and the Apaches stood in the center of lane six, shrouded in darkness. The only light in the alley was a heavy-watt spotlight shooting down from the back of the bar, beamed on the bowling cage. Pins was tied to the cage, thick cord rope binding his arms and upper body to the iron mesh. His face was swollen, one eye puffy and closed, blood trickled out of his mouth and nose. He was on his knees, his feet tied by wire, his head held up by a rope around his neck tied to a thin steel beam. Strapped to Pins's chest were a dozen thick sticks of dynamite, a timer in the center clicking down from an hour's limit. Six different-colored explosive wires were entwined around his chest, legs, and arms.

The entire bowling cage was wired and set, three separate devices timed at various intervals.

Boomer and Geronimo walked over to Pins. Mrs. Columbo and Rev. Jim stood behind them. Dead-Eye was searching the rest of the alley, two guns drawn.

'I didn't see them,' Pins said, talking through swollen

lips. 'They came up from behind. There were three of them. I guess I screwed up.'

'You didn't screw up anything,' Boomer said, taking a wad of tissues from Mrs. Columbo and wiping blood off Pins's face. 'You just breathe easy and leave the rest to us.'

Geronimo stripped off his jacket and sweater, tossing them in an empty lane. He took a knife from his back pocket, got on his knees, and started to run the blade along the wire lines.

'What do you see?' Boomer asked, sweat starting to flow down the small of his back.

'Six numbers,' Geronimo said. 'Each attached to different wires. Two strings of wires are dummies. The chest timer is coded to blow in eight minutes, but that could be a decoy. And there's two separate sticks up above, latched to the rope around his neck.'

'Can you break this?' Boomer asked.

'I need somebody to go to the car and get my kit outta the trunk,' Geronimo said.

'I'll do it,' Rev. Jim said, waiting as Boomer tossed him the keys.

'After that I figure you should all get the hell outta here,' Geronimo said, 'and leave me to my work.'

'Can you break this?' Boomer asked again. 'I want an answer, Geronimo.'

Geronimo stood up, turned, and faced Boomer. 'Probably not,' he said. 'But I've got a better chance than any of you.'

Rev. Jim came running back in with a heavy black satchel and handed it to Geronimo. Mrs. Columbo stood off to the side, eyes closed. Dead-Eye came up behind her, his guns holstered. He stared down at Pins, his face flush with anger.

Boomer stooped down and leaned toward his friend. 'I'm sorry I got you involved in this, kid,' he said softly.

Pins managed a smile around the blood. 'Not me,' he

said. 'You guys made me feel what it was like all over again.'

'Like what was like?' Rev. Jim asked.

'Being alive,' Pins said.

And then there was silence. Until Pins tried to speak again.

'The guy that did this...' he said, swallowing a mouthful of blood, straining to get the words out.

'Wilber Graves,' Boomer said. 'I know the name.'

'What you don't know is, I wired him.'

It took a moment to register. The Apaches stared at Pins in amazement. He managed a nod, and forced a smile. The look in his eyes acknowledged their awe and accepted it gratefully.

'While they were workin' me over,' Pins said, 'I dropped a line in his jacket pocket. You can hear him on the scanner.'

There was silence again.

It was broken by Geronimo.

'Sooner everybody leaves, sooner I can get started,' he said. 'I don't have all that much time.'

Boomer stroked the sides of Pins's face, his fingers red with the young man's blood. The two exchanged a long look, then Boomer stood and left, followed by the other Apaches, each of whom saluted Pins with a closed fist to their hearts.

Geronimo jumped to his feet and tapped Boomer on the shoulder. 'If I don't crack the device, I'd like you to do me a favor.'

'I don't wanna lose two of you,' Boomer said.

'The favor,' Geronimo said. 'Will you do it?'

'Name it.'

'Blow that bitch away,' Geronimo said.

Sweat ran down the sides of Geronimo's arms and face. He was inching along on his knees, working slowly beside Pins, scanning wires, operating as much with gut as he was with knowledge.

'I'm gonna give the blue wires a snap,' Geronimo said.

'What's that gonna do?' Pins asked.

'If we're lucky, not a thing,' Geronimo said. 'And it'll leave us one less device to worry about.'

'What if we ain't so lucky?' Pins said.

'We won't know it,' Geronimo told him.

Geronimo took a deep breath, squeezed the tip of his hand pliers over the blue wire, and snapped it apart. Beads of sweat mixed with blood flowed down Pins's face as he gave Geronimo a knowing nod. 'I woulda guessed red myself,' he said.

'It's a good thing you're the one that's wired and not me.' Geronimo wiped at his eyes with the sleeve of his blue Bomb Squad T-shirt.

'How much time left?' Pins asked.

'Why? Gotta be somewhere special?'

'They designed this bomb just for you,' Pins told him. 'They said you were the best, but not even you could crack what they laid in here.'

'You were always the quiet one,' Geronimo said. 'Wrap a little dyno around you and suddenly I can't shut you up.'

'I don't need you to die with me,' Pins said. 'I can do this alone. I've done everything else that way, don't see why dying should be any different.'

'They shoulda taped your mouth shut too.' Geronimo was on his back, next to Pins, ready to snap down on a green wire. 'Would've made my job easier.'

'Boomer, Dead-Eye, the others, they need your help, Geronimo,' Pins said. 'A lot more than I do.'

Geronimo snapped off the green wire, shoved the clipper in his waistband, crawled back several inches farther, and started to remove the wire from Pins's feet. He tossed the wire behind him and inched his way back to the front of the cage.

'Just so you know and it registers,' Geronimo said, wiping the sweat from Pins's forehead with the front of his shirt. 'There are two things in this life I've never walked away from. A device and a friend.'

'Then you're gonna die in here,' Pins said. 'With this friend and with this device.'

'I wouldn't have it any other way,' Geronimo said. 'Now, that timer is telling me we got ourselves a little less than three minutes. I could snap off a few more wires and hope we stay lucky, or, if you want, I can just kick back and we shoot the shit. Your call, Pins.'

'We never did get a chance to talk all that much,' Pins said.

'White or red,' Geronimo said. 'Pick one.'

'I still like red,' Pins breathed.

'Devices love creatures of habit,' Geronimo said with a smile. Then he pulled the clipper and snapped off the white wires. 'File that for the next time.'

'How many of those wires we got left?' Pins asked.

'Hard to figure. They laid on a lot of 'em. Crisscrossed 'em all on top of it. Most are dummies, only one is lit. So we got that, plus the dyno hooked to the rope around your neck, which can go off of any wire. Best I can do is try to get to the central coil and snap it down, but it would be more a guess than anything else.'

'Bottom-line it for me, Geronimo,' Pins said. 'Where we goin' with this?'

Geronimo laid the clipper down on the shiny floor of the bowling lane. He took off his shirt, wiped the sweat off his body, and sat down. He folded his legs and rested his arms on top of them. He turned and looked over at Pins, drenched in blood and sweat, his legs lifeless from having held one position for such a long time. He took several long, slow, deep breaths.

'The device wins, Pins,' Geronimo finally said. 'We can't beat it.'

'Yeah, we can,' Pins said.

'I'm listening,' Geronimo told him.

'Don't wait for it,' Pins said. 'Let it blow on your terms.

You're the best at this. So let the best decide when the fucker goes up.'

Geronimo smiled at Pins as his right hand reached for the clippers. 'Pick your color,' Geronimo said.

'I'm a stubborn little bastard. I'm gonna stick with the red.'

'Red it is,' Geronimo said.

He stood on his knees, one hand grasping Pins's shoulder and the other holding the pliers wrapped around a thin red wire.

'I hope you're not wrong,' Geronimo said. The smile on his face faded. Then it came back. Pins met it with a smile of his own.

'Bet on this one,' Pins said.

Geronimo snapped down on the red wire and waited for the flash. Once again willing a device to his terms.

The four Apaches were jolted in their seats by the loud explosion. They were in Boomer's car, at the far end of the parking lot.

They watched the bowling alley implode. Shards of glass and thick debris flying in all directions. The ceiling caved in, smoke and dust filtered through the air.

Mrs. Columbo gave out a low moan. Rev. Jim was crying and swearing in a rage of emotion. Dead-Eye balled his hands into fists, rubbing them against his legs. Boomer was a mask of stone, the flames reflecting off the darkness of his deep-set eyes. He felt inside his leather jacket, his hand gripping the sticks of dynamite Geronimo had given him. He pulled his hand away and turned the ignition on the car, shoved the gear into drive, and pulled out of the lot.

'Where we going, Boom?' Dead-Eye asked.

'To finish it.'

'We know where?' Rev. Jim wanted to know, glancing back at the smoke billowing from the bowling alley.

'We will,' Boomer said, looking through the rearview.

'Pins wired Wilber. We'll pick him up on the scanner on our way to Nunzio's.'

'That where we going now?' Mrs. Columbo asked. Her voice was stoic, almost mechanical.

'That's our first stop,' Boomer said.

'And the second?' Dead-Eye asked.

'To pick up a friend.' Boomer lowered his foot to the gas pedal, pushing the speedometer past seventy.

'Anybody we know?' Dead-Eye asked.

'Deputy Inspector Lavetti,' Boomer said, throwing Mrs. Columbo a quick look over his shoulder and rolling his window up, the night chill too bitter against his face.

'At least it's somebody we can trust,' Rev. Jim said, slouching in his seat and closing his eyes to the sounds of the night.

20

They stood in the center of Nunzio's cramped basement, surrounded by red wooden wine barrels and thick crates marked with a government seal. Several of the crates had been eased open with the flat end of a crowbar. An iron door leading to steps and street level was locked and barred. A series of bare bulbs hung overhead.

'Everything you need, you can find inside the crates,' Nunzio said, approaching one and resting a tray loaded with five cups of coffee on it.

'Where did all this stuff come from?' Dead-Eye shook his head in awe. He took a cup from the tray and walked from one crate to the next, his eyes fixed on the astonishing cache of Ingram submachine-guns, semiautomatics, grenades, launchers, timers, bullets, vests, knives, and liquid explosives.

'You're not my *only* friends,' Nunzio said.

'We need one other thing from you,' Boomer said. He passed on the coffee, instead filling a plastic cup with wine from one of the barrels.

'Tell me,' Nunzio said.

'A private plane. With a pilot you trust. We're going to need to move all the equipment out of state and my airport connection can't help me walk in with this heavy a load.'

'You want him for the round trip?' Nunzio asked.

Boomer took a look at the Apaches before he answered.

302

'Yes,' he said. 'We'll be comin' back. One way or the other.'

'Where to?'

'Arizona,' Boomer said. 'Small town, about thirty miles outside Sedona. I'd like to be in the air in about two hours. We picked up Wilber yappin' away over Pins's wire. In between the laugh and the brag, he talked about taking his crew back to Lucia's compound.'

'They want to fight you on their turf,' Nunzio said. 'Why not wait and take 'em out on your own ground.'

'We just lost two good cops on our own ground,' Mrs. Columbo said.

'You don't even know the layout,' Nunzio said. 'How many guns she's got, what you're up against. You gonna do it, do it right, Boomer. Don't turn it into a suicide ride.'

'This *is* the right way,' Boomer said. 'It's the way it's supposed to be. Us against them.'

'From the phones on that plane we can reach out to all our federal contacts,' Rev. Jim said. 'Ask 'em to tell us what they know about her spread.'

'And then we tell 'em we're going in,' Boomer said. 'Ask them to follow us out a few hours later.'

'How you so sure they're gonna go along with somethin' this crazy?' Nunzio asked.

'They don't have a choice,' Boomer said. 'They're not gonna blow us out of the sky and they're not gonna rat us out. Besides, half the guys we deal with would kill for the chance to be with us.'

'Lucia's expectin' you to go after her,' Nunzio said. 'That should be worth a thought.'

'I think it's time we met,' Boomer said. 'After all we've been through together.'

Deputy Inspector Mark Lavetti stood under the awning of a doorman building on Madison Avenue, fixing the collar on his brown tweed jacket. He was a handsome man in his early forties, his lean figure topped by a thick

303

head of curly dark hair. He had been a member of the New York City Police Department for twenty-one years and had never recorded a major arrest. He was a test cop, making his steady climb up the ranks by cracking open books in schools rather than cracking heads out on the streets.

He was born with a taste for the sweet life and from his first weeks at the Police Academy was quick to smoke out a pad and knew how best to squeeze his way in on the action. He took his first envelope while still wearing the grays of a trainee, fifty a week to fill a local dealer in on which probie cops were eager to score free joints and lines, no questions asked. In return, the dealer sold their names to the turf leader of their precinct.

By the time he stood under the awning of the building on Madison Avenue, Mark Lavetti was pulling down twenty-five thousand in cash a month, feeding info to major dealers in the five boroughs. He never went near the money himself, instead using a rotating team of relatives as a pickup posse, letting them move the cash from sealed locker to selected bank and mutual fund accounts.

Lavetti was a master at covering the money trail.

His three-bedroom co-op was in his mother's name. The sporty Corvette he drove when not on duty was owned tire and gearshift by a sister in Mineola. He had a summer home in Woodstock mortgaged to an uncle living in a nursing home. His yearly vacations came courtesy of a cousin who ran a tourist agency.

Despite the rumors floating out of various precincts, the top brass saw Mark Lavetti exactly as he wanted to be seen – a clean cop riding the fast track.

His biggest score had also been his easiest.

Mark Lavetti was on the phone seconds after Joseph Silvestri walked out of his One Police Plaza office. He listened to the sad man tell him about his wife's involvement with a band of disabled cops, assured him all would be kept confidential, then set up a meeting with a main feeder to Lucia Carney's drug business. Outside Gate D

304

at Shea Stadium, Lavetti handed over the six names of the Apaches to a man he knew would want them dead. In return, he accepted a manila envelope crammed with $100,000 in cash.

And he never gave the matter another thought.

Lavetti walked at a brisk pace down Madison, wondering whether to detour over to Lincoln Center to pick up a pair of opera tickets for himself and his new girlfriend, a model who was easily impressed by such things, or wait until after dinner and then drive past. His car was parked at the corner of Sixty-second Street, next to a hydrant, an official NYPD tag in the front window. As he got closer, he noticed a dark blue sedan double-parked close to his car, blocking his exit, the driver nowhere in sight.

He took the keys from the front pocket of his slacks, ready to call in the car and have a truck come tow it, angry he hadn't just parked in the building garage as usual.

'Where you off to tonight, Inspector?' Boomer asked, coming out of the shadows of a shuttered dry cleaners, standing behind Lavetti, both hands in his jacket pockets.

'Who the fuck are you?' Lavetti asked.

'I'm surprised you don't recognize me,' Boomer said. 'I'm an Apache.'

'What the fuck's that supposed to mean?' Lavetti asked. But a shift in his tone betrayed his disquiet.

'You put a price on me.' Boomer stepped closer, holding the urge to pull the trigger on the gun inside his jacket. 'And on my friends. Somebody started to collect. Two of them died today.'

'Are you crazy!' Lavetti said. 'Do you know who you're talking to? I'm a cop. A deputy inspector!'

'The two who died were *cops*,' Boomer said. 'You're just a punk with a badge. But tonight you're in for a treat. I'm going to give you a chance to *die* like a cop.'

'I'm not going anywhere with you,' Lavetti said, starting to turn and run.

'Then you'll die right here.' Boomer pulled the gun

from his pocket and pressed it to Lavetti's temple. 'On the street, like the piece of shit you are. Either way, I don't give a fuck. It's your decision.'

'Where are we going?' was all Lavetti could manage to say.

Boomer turned Lavetti around and cuffed him as he pushed him toward the back seat of the dark blue sedan. 'To visit an old friend of yours. And I bet she's gonna be real happy to see you.'

'I could have you killed,' Lavetti said, glaring at Boomer from the backseat. 'One call, that's all it'll take.'

'A lot of guys have made that one call, Lavetti,' Boomer said, kicking over the engine and peeling out of his space. 'I'm still here. And they're all dead.'

Boomer and Dead-Eye were crouched down, hidden by shrubs and darkness, staring across a golf pond at the heavily guarded three-storey house.

'I count at least eight in front,' Boomer whispered. 'Figure the same number in back. And double that for the ground crew.'

Rev. Jim and Mrs. Columbo were stretched out farther up the ridge, Lavetti shoved facedown alongside.

Except for Lavetti, they all wore bullet-resistant vests under their black shirts. On the plane ride over, the four of them had jammed a full arsenal of semis around their hips and waists, loaded up on grenades and ammo, and listened while Boomer laid out what sounded like nothing less than an invasion.

'You really think any of this is going to work?' Rev. Jim asked at one point.

'Are you kidding?' Boomer said. 'It'll be a fuckin' miracle if it even comes *close* to working.'

'I'm glad to hear you say that,' Dead-Eye said. 'I was starting to worry.'

'With our luck,' Mrs. Columbo said, jabbing a thumb toward Lavetti, 'he'll be the only one to make it out alive.'

306

'Don't bet on that,' Boomer said, staring over at Lavetti, who had stayed silent through the entire flight.

'Run that Greek fire deal by me one more time,' Rev. Jim said.

'I'm new at this myself, so bear with me,' Boomer said, holding up a white five-foot plastic tube. 'But the way Geronimo told it, you air-gun the nitro through the tube and it shoots out above the water, a lot like a torpedo out of a sub. It bounces off the water and right into the house.'

'It leaves behind a flame trail,' Dead-Eye said. 'So you can use it as light too.'

'An air gun and nitro,' Rev. Jim said. 'What could go wrong with that?'

Boomer had alerted his federal sources from the air and bargained himself an hour's worth of attack time. 'Don't worry, Tony,' he said to a voice at the other end of the phone. 'As it is, you're giving us about thirty minutes more than we need. We'll try and leave you nothing to clean up.'

Before Tony clicked off the line he said, 'I don't know which is better, if we find you dead or alive.'

'If you find us,' Boomer said, 'I'd count on dead.'

Lucia Carney drank from a glass of white wine, looking out into the darkness. Wilber Graves stood next to her, a smug smile on his face. She was dressed in a black pants suit, her hair hanging down around her shoulders, a .45 silver-handled semiautomatic lodged against the base of her spine.

'They're here,' Lucia said. 'Hiding in the shrubs somewhere.'

'They won't get far,' Wilber said. 'Or even close. They'll be dead before they reach the house.'

'A shame,' Lucia said. 'I was hoping to at least meet them. To fly all this way and go to all this trouble, just to end up dead on a golf course.'

'There are six men on every floor inside the house,' Wilber told her. 'Just in case.'

'And where will you be?' Lucia asked.

'Where I belong,' Wilber said. 'Next to you.'

Lucia finished her drink and smiled. 'Time will decide where you belong, Wilber,' she said as she walked past him without looking up.

'We hold to the plan for as long as we can,' Boomer said, looking past Dead-Eye toward Rev. Jim and Mrs. Columbo. 'If we make it out, we regroup here and head back to the landing strip.'

'Don't I at least get a gun?' Lavetti asked, still stretched out on the ground.

'Know how to use one?' Rev. Jim asked.

'Of course I do,' Lavetti exclaimed.

'Then the answer's no,' Mrs. Columbo said. 'We may be crazy, but we ain't stupid.'

'Don't think of yourself as an Apache,' Dead-Eye told him. 'Think of yourself as a bulletproof vest we don't have to wear.'

'It's like havin' my very own shield,' Rev. Jim said. He snapped one cuff around Lavetti's wrist, closing the other end on his own. 'Wonder how many bullets he takes before I tire of draggin' him around.'

'Enough to kill him, I hope,' was Mrs. Columbo's answer.

'We ready to do this?' Boomer asked, standing and zipping his jacket.

'No,' Dead-Eye said. 'But if it means getting out of this heat, I'll give it a shot.'

'Dead-Eye and I will walk down the front path like we're invited to a party,' Boomer said. 'Soon as you can, Rev. Jim, get that Greek fire going across the pond.'

'It'll either be flames or me shootin' past that water,' Rev. Jim said.

Boomer turned to Mrs. Columbo. 'Mary, you get as

close as you can and launch those rockets just like we showed you on the plane.'

'Don't worry,' she said. 'If I can drive a wrecking ball down a Manhattan street, I can sure as shit shoot a rocket against the side of a house.'

'We all meet inside,' Boomer said. 'First one to Lucia takes home the prize.'

'We're all going to be killed,' Lavetti said, panic firmly set in. 'She's in there waiting. They're *all* in there waiting. If you turn back now, I can work something out. Have her back off. It's your only way out.'

Boomer stepped over to Lavetti and slapped him hard across the face. 'As soon as the shooting starts, uncuff yourself from him,' Boomer said to Rev. Jim. 'He'll be surrounded by his friends.'

'See you at the fair.' Rev. Jim began dragging Lavetti with him toward the golf pond.

Boomer watched them go, then turned to Mrs. Columbo. He touched her cheek and smiled. 'You sure you're gonna be okay?' he asked.

'You worried because I'm the only woman on the team?' Mrs. Columbo asked.

'I'm worried because you're the only woman I care about left alive,' Boomer said softly.

'You really know the right time for romance,' she answered with a smile. She lifted her launcher and rocket pack and headed off in search of a shooting site.

'That just leaves the two of us,' Dead-Eye pointed out.

'You're a smart man.' Boomer placed a hand on his friend's shoulder. 'How the hell d'you end up with a guy like me?'

'Born under a dark cloud,' Dead-Eye told him. 'And there's nothing I can do to change it.'

'Let's go make some noise, then.' They began to walk down the well-lit path, knowing there were eyes on their every step. They turned a slight curve and saw the house, a quarter of a mile ahead.

309

'They're not gonna let us get much closer,' Boomer said.

'I wouldn't have let us get this far.'

'Maybe we got it all wrong,' Boomer said. 'Maybe they don't want us dead.'

'That's what Custer thought. Up until that first arrow.'

'Why are you waiting?' Lucia asked Wilber, anger in her voice and eyes.

'Can you see them yet?' Wilber asked. 'I thought you wanted to see them.'

'Enough with your stupid little games, Wilber,' Lucia said. 'I want to see them *dead*.'

'They *are* dead,' Wilber said. 'They just haven't been told yet.'

'Well then, have the men let them know,' Lucia said. '*Now*.'

Wilber opened the windows to the terrace, stepped outside, and gave the signal.

Rev. Jim eased the nitro ball into the air gun, then placed the front tip of the gun inside the opening of the five-foot plastic tube. He and Lavetti were crouched at the edge of the golf pond, directly across from the rear of the house.

'You have any idea what you're doing?' Lavetti asked, desperate.

'Not a clue.' Rev. Jim moved both hands slowly, dragging Lavetti's cuffed wrist along.

'It won't work,' Lavetti said. 'I can tell from your face even *you* know it won't work.'

'You're a very negative guy.' Rev. Jim looked him over. 'Maybe yoga would help.'

Mrs. Columbo dropped the rocket into the launcher pad, her hands, face, and back drenched with sweat. She twisted the base shield to her right and pressed the red button, turning from the launcher. She waited with eyes shut for a blast that never arrived.

'Dammit, Mary,' she muttered to herself. 'Don't screw up. Not here. Not now.'

She peeked over the lid of the launcher and shook her head.

'What a dope,' she said, still mumbling, realizing she had put the rocket in backward.

She struggled to pull it out, turned it around, and then placed it back inside the cylinder.

'Please, God,' she whispered, her eyes closed. 'Please make it work.'

A stream of bullets rained down on Boomer and Dead-Eye, pelting the path at their feet.

It was the signal they wanted.

Boomer turned right, Dead-Eye left, each with a grenade in hand, tossing them out into the dark night. After six grenades had blown patches of grass and pieces of men into the air, they each unzipped their jackets and wrapped their hands around the handle of an M-60 machine-gun. They stood back to back, pumping bullets in all directions, Boomer leading the way to the house.

They saw the Greek fire before they heard it.

A large ball of flame raced across the rear pond, up onto the back lawn, flush into the house, blowing out windows and walls. Three other blasts followed in quick succession, causing equal amounts of damage.

Mrs. Columbo's missiles found their mark as well.

The first one overshot the main house and blew up the garage. The next two took out five men and half the second floor.

Boomer and Dead-Eye reloaded, kept firing as bullets whistled past. Only one found them, clipping Boomer on his right elbow.

Dead-Eye was running the M-60 like a concert baton, leaving in his wake the moans and thuds of the wounded and dying. Boomer cleared the front of the path, stopping

311

his cascade of bullets long enough only to throw out a few more grenades.

Missiles and nitro blasts lit the sky.

'I guess they know we're here,' Boomer shouted.

'Think they're ready to surrender yet?' Dead-Eye asked, spraying two more face down into the grass.

'When we get inside, we'll ask,' Boomer said, lighting a stick of dynamite and tossing it toward the front door.

Rev. Jim uncuffed Lavetti, picked him up, and started to run with him toward the house. But Lavetti broke free and drew ahead.

'Wilber!' Lavetti began to shout. 'Don't shoot! It's me! Mark Lavetti. Don't shoot!'

Rev. Jim headed off in the opposite direction, around the left side of the pond, running toward the gaping hole in the first floor caused by one of his fireballs, using an Uzi submachine-gun to further light the way. He turned to take a look at Lavetti, frantically waving his arms and calling out Wilber's name.

'Hope he finds you,' Rev. Jim said.

Mrs. Columbo, free of the weight of the rocket launchers and heavy packs, walked quickly down an unguarded rock road and soon found herself by the rear of the house. She smiled as she stepped inside. Wait till Boomer hears about this, she thought. He'll never believe it.

The door blew open and Boomer and Dead-Eye jumped through a circle of fire, guns still spraying bullets in all directions.

'Here's where we split,' Boomer said, standing and shooting in the main entry. 'I'll take the second floor.'

'That leaves the third for me.'

'Call if you need me,' Boomer shouted, running up the front hall steps.

'Other way around, friend,' Dead-Eye said, racing through the kitchen and taking the back staircase.

312

Wilber Graves moved through fire and smoke, stepping over dead bodies, looked out incredulously at Lavetti, standing near the golf pond, shouting his name.

Wilber lifted the machine pistol in his hand, aimed it at the corrupt cop, and waited until he was close enough for their eyes to meet.

'Wilber,' Lavetti yelled, blinded by smoke and flames. 'That you? That you, Wilber?'

'It's me,' Wilber said.

He then calmly pumped three bullets into Mark Lavetti's chest.

The first two found flesh and bone.

The third shattered the bottle of nitro Rev. Jim had slipped inside the pocket of Lavetti's black windbreaker.

The explosion sent Wilber flying onto his back and killed anyone on the back grass who wasn't already dead.

Rev. Jim saw the blast from the second-floor balcony. He shook his head and turned away.

'Some friends you found yourself, Lavetti,' he said.

Mrs. Columbo walked along the wall leading to the second-floor den. Gunfire erupted throughout the house and thick plumes of smoke filtered down the halls, tearing her eyes. She had a .38 Special in her right hand, held down against her thigh. There were scattered bodies and debris everywhere.

She stepped over a black-suited shooter, face down in his own blood, and turned a curved corner, bumping into a tall man with deep lacerations on his face and arms.

'You must be the one they call Mrs. Columbo,' Wilber Graves said.

Mrs. Columbo went to lift her gun, but his hand was faster. Graves reached out to hold it in place with a powerful grip. She heard the snap of a switchblade and watched as he moved closer, the fear of the knife stalking her once again, paralyzing her.

She saw the blade come up but could do nothing.

She waited but the knife came no closer. Wilber Graves

313

had noticed her vest, knew the knife in his hand wouldn't penetrate. Mrs. Columbo smiled.

'I'm not making it easy for you, am I?' she said.

'I prefer you didn't,' Wilber said, smiling back.

Mrs. Columbo lifted a knee to Wilber's groin and brought the bone of her elbow flush against his nose, breaking it and blinding him with his own blood. He let go of her hand and fell to his knees. She lifted her gun hand and rested the pistol against the top of his head.

'Pull the trigger,' Wilber whispered.

Mrs. Columbo made the error every cop dreads.

She hesitated.

She flashed back to the night she was attacked, her body ravaged by a madman's angry knife. She could see the blade swish up and down and felt the pain each time it cracked through skin. She was meant to die that night on that street.

Instead, it would be another man, holding another knife, who would decide the ending to her life.

Wilber Graves shoved the blade of the knife into her knee and twisted it. Mrs. Columbo let out a low groan and dropped the gun. Her left leg went numb and she felt dizzy, holding on to the wall for support. Wilber lifted his right hand and slid her down next to him. He pulled the knife out of her leg, reached behind her to undo the vest. Mrs. Columbo looked at the ceiling, her eyes barely able to focus, her upper body cold, the side of her leg warmed by the flow of blood.

'I'll miss you, Mrs. Columbo,' Wilber told her.

'Wish I could say the same,' Mrs. Columbo said.

Wilber lifted the edge of her vest and rammed the knife deep into the center of her stomach, sliding it up until he bumped against the muscle of the chest cavity. He left it lodged there, too deeply imbedded to remove. Mrs. Columbo looked at him through glassy eyes, a sharp rush of pain mingled with a soothing numbness. She turned her head to the wall, closed her eyes, and thought about her son.

No one could harm her anymore.

Boomer was the one who found her.

He fell to his knees, slipping on her blood. He lifted her head and cradled it. She was still breathing, if barely, tongue licking at her lips. She opened one eye and did her best to smile.

'It took this to get you to hold me,' she whispered.

Boomer didn't speak. Couldn't speak.

'I told you I could handle the rockets,' she said.

He nodded.

'You proud of me?' she asked.

'Yes,' he said slowly. 'Very proud.'

'Means a lot,' Mrs. Columbo said.

'I love you, Mary,' Boomer said. But those were words she never heard. Mrs. Columbo had already leaned her head back against Boomer's arms and closed her eyes for the last time.

Boomer took off his windbreaker and covered her. He reached over, picked up her .38 Special, and jammed it inside the front of his pants. He undid the Velcro of his vest, and tossed it over his shoulder.

Then Boomer stood and walked away from one more fallen Apache.

Dead-Eye was cornered, bullets coming at him from four sides, ripping through the closet door he stood behind. He was low on ammo and couldn't lift his right arm, which had taken two hits from a .44 caliber. There were six shooters closing in, two working pump-action shot-guns. He had enough ammo and one good hand left to take out at least two. He took a deep breath and decided to make a rush at the gunmen.

If Dead-Eye was going to go down, it wasn't going to be hiding behind an empty second-floor coat closet.

He jumped from the door, left hand out, gun held at an angle, firing off as many clips as it carried. He hit one of the shotguns in the chest, sending him over a railing.

He swirled and took out a suit rushing from behind, and then took a hit himself in the right leg, bringing him down to one knee.

The four moved in closer, prepared to end a battle and a life. Dead-Eye looked at them and grunted.

'Wouldn't have any bullets you could spare?' he asked.

'Just two,' the shotgun shouted back. 'Both of them going into your fucking head.'

'Thanks anyway,' Dead-Eye said.

Rev. Jim came up the back steps, two .44 semis criss-crossed in his hands. He pumped three rounds into the back of the shotgun, sending him face down next to Dead-Eye. The other three sprang for cover.

Dead-Eye grabbed the shotgun, pulled the trigger, and took out part of a wall and one shooter. Rev. Jim walked past, dropped a handgun in his lap, and chased the other two down a corner hall, smoke and flames coming out the barrels of his guns. The last two bullets in the chambers left the men down and dead.

'I don't want to hurt your feelings,' Rev. Jim said, standing over Dead-Eye. 'But you don't look so good.'

'It's the heat,' Dead-Eye said. 'I *hate* the heat.'

'Can you walk?'

'Not far,' Dead-Eye said.

'Can you shoot?' Rev. Jim asked.

'Just with my left hand,' Dead-Eye said. 'Right one's gone. At least for today.'

'Your one hand is still better than my two,' Rev. Jim said.

'You loaded?' Dead-Eye asked.

'Got enough rounds left where we won't embarrass ourselves.'

'You'll move faster without me,' Dead-Eye said. 'Just leave me a gun and go.'

'Nobody gets rid of me that easy.' Rev. Jim put a loaded semi in Dead-Eye's left hand, a .38 in his waistband, and a .44 bulldog in his right.

'I told you my right arm's no good,' Dead-Eye said, forcing himself to his feet. 'Can't feel it.'

'Your trigger finger numb?' Rev. Jim asked, tossing Dead-Eye's left arm around his shoulders and holding his waist with his right hand.

'No,' Dead-Eye said.

'Then why waste it?' Rev. Jim asked.

Dead-Eye and Rev. Jim made their way slowly down the hall, arms linked together, four guns in their hands, spraying bullets in all directions, leaving a line of blood behind them as their trail.

Boomer stood in the doorway of the second-floor master bedroom, watching Lucia Carney rummage through the center drawer of a bureau, her back to him.

'Nice place you had here,' he said.

She turned. From her demeanor, they might have been at a formal dance instead of the middle of a firestorm. 'You must be Boomer,' she said. 'Please come in.'

'I *am* in.' Boomer held Mrs. Columbo's .38 in his hand.

'I expected to see a larger man.' Lucia stepped away from the bureau.

'Firemen are tall,' Boomer said. 'Cops are short. That's how you can tell us apart.'

'You've cost me considerable amounts of time and money, Boomer.'

'And you've cost me four friends. Somehow it doesn't even out.'

'I learned very early on that there's a price for everything in life,' Lucia said. 'And everyone I've met has one. I just haven't figured out yours yet.'

'That's an easy one,' he said. 'You.'

'What?' She moved closer to him.

'*You're* my price,' Boomer told her. 'When you go down, I'll walk away.'

'Your type's not the kind to kill a woman,' Lucia said. 'Even a woman like me.'

Boomer stared into Lucia's eyes and knew there was

317

someone else in the room. He managed to turn just as Wilber's knife was about to shear his back. It flew past the front part of his right shoulder, but its force knocked him up against a wall and sent the gun he held to the floor.

'I've killed your friends,' Wilber taunted, his broken nose giving a deep nasal sound to his voice. 'And now you will feel the same pain they did.'

Boomer waited until Wilber stepped closer, then rushed him, landing against his chest, both men falling to the floor. Boomer held back the knife hand and landed three solid lefts to the side of Wilber's face.

Wilber Graves had firmly pressed a button that should not have been touched. There was an out-of-control rage to Boomer now, fed by the images of Pins, Geronimo, and Mrs. Columbo. He threw punches in a mad fury, breaking his hand against the hard bones of Wilber's jaw and temple.

Boomer beat Wilber until he could no longer lift his arms. He fell over him, exhausted, lifted his head, short of breath, to look up at Lucia, who still stood above him.

He didn't see the knife.

Wilber held it with four fingers and lifted it high above his head, barely able to see out of the slits of his eyes. He dropped the knife deep into the center of Boomer's back.

Boomer let out a sharp yell, and fell face forward. He peered back at Wilber, who was watching, waiting for the cop to die.

Boomer spread his hand out, reaching for the fallen .38. He wrapped his fingers around it, turned at an angle toward Wilber. The killer's face was a mask of red, his eyes vacant and distant as he struggled to his feet.

Boomer inched up to his knees, the pain in his back sharp, and clicked the trigger on Mrs. Columbo's gun. 'This is from Mary,' Boomer said to Wilber Graves. He fired one shot into Wilber's stomach and watched him crumple to the floor. 'And this is from Carolyn.' The

318

second bullet went into Wilber's head. The assassin curled into a heap, then never moved again.

Boomer slowly, painfully, lifted himself against the side of the wall, leaving smears of blood in his wake. He walked with stilted, pained steps over toward Lucia, watching her reach behind the small of her back for the gun she had wedged there.

'I've never run into anyone like you,' Lucia said, pointing it at him.

'You would have, sooner or later.' He inched closer to Lucia, walking on legs he couldn't feel. 'There's always going to be somebody like me out to stop somebody like you.'

'And how do people like you do that?' Lucia said.

'Any way we can.'

Before she could move or respond, Boomer took a deep, pain-filled breath and made a leap for her. Her gun exploded, but Boomer never even felt the bullet ripping into his chest. They both fell to the floor, his blood dripping over her designer clothes. He looked into her eyes, saw the flash of anger, the touch of madness that had made her drug runners tremble. But he wasn't a drug runner.

He was a cop.

Boomer closed a fist and landed two sharp blows against the side of Lucia's face, knocking her out cold. He then pulled a cigarette lighter from the front pocket of his blood-soaked jeans and clicked it open, staring at the blue flame. He reached behind him and pulled a roll of dynamite from the back of his jeans.

It was Geronimo's roll.

He lit the forty-five-second fuse and shoved the dynamite down the front of Lucia's blouse.

Boomer crawled away from her on hands and knees, the pain so real it had a taste. He glanced at Wilber's prone body for a final time, and closed the door behind him with his foot.

He made it halfway down the hall when the dynamite

319

blast took out the entire room and sent him flying toward a corner stairwell.

'The bitch is history, Geronimo,' Boomer mumbled, resting his head against a marble step.

The three Apaches were all on the second floor.

Dead-Eye had his head down, leaning against a wall, weakened by his wound. Rev. Jim sat against a banister, his clothes caked, a bullet rendering his right leg useless. Boomer was spread facedown on the tile floor in a pool of blood, Wilber's knife in his back.

They were surrounded by smoke, flames, and the dead. They could hear the sounds of sirens and fire engine horns closing in.

'Hey, Boomer,' Rev. Jim said.

'What?' Boomer said without lifting his head.

'I don't wanna upset you or anything, but there's a knife stickin' out of your back.'

'I needed a place to hang my hat,' Boomer told him.

'Good thinkin',' Rev. Jim said.

As they waited in silence for the rescue squads to come and clean up, Dead-Eye turned to his right. One of the wounded shooters was crawling for his gun.

The shooter looked at Dead-Eye, his hand around the pistol handle. 'Hey, nigger,' the shooter said, straining to lift the gun. 'Don't you ever miss?'

Dead-Eye curled the .44 he held in his left hand and squeezed off one round, hitting the shooter in the center of his forehead, dropping him dead.

'No,' Dead-Eye said, leaning his head back against the wall.

'Ask a stupid question . . .' Rev. Jim said.

The laughter of the wounded Apaches echoed through the shell of the burning house and floated out across the ruins of a fallen drug-empire.

The ones they said could never be whole again had achieved victory.

Epilogue

Every man has his own destiny. The only
imperative is to follow it, to accept it,
no matter where it leads.

– Henry Miller, 'The Wisdom of the Heart'

January 1983

Boomer sat at the head of the small table, sipping a cup of tea, watching Dead-Eye and Rev. Jim go deep into a game of chess.

'Is that as boring to play as it is to watch?' Boomer asked.

'Yes,' Rev. Jim said.

'So why play it?' Boomer said.

'We don't have any checkers,' Dead-Eye said.

The physical healing was almost complete.

Boomer and Dead-Eye had spent a month in an Arizona hospital. Rev. Jim was set loose after two weeks, during which he managed to fall hard for one of the night nurses. They each had to endure painful daily physical therapy sessions, which by now were a given in their lives.

As expected, there had been no legal complications from the attack on Lucia's compound. The feds were more than eager to grab credit for the takedown of Lucia Carney and her crew. The Apaches watched the press conference on a TV in Boomer's hospital room.

'If they could only bust as good as they bullshit,' Rev. Jim said, turning off the set, 'there'd be no crime.'

They never did get to the private plane that waited for them three miles east of the compound. Instead, they drove out of Arizona in a rented convertible. Along the way they stopped to visit with Geronimo's Native American adviser. The old man listened with bright eyes as they told him how Geronimo had died a brave warrior, unafraid and proud.

'We'll miss him,' Boomer told the old man. 'He was a good friend.'

'There's no need,' the man said in a voice filled with strength. 'His spirit lives and travels alongside you. And alongside those who will follow you.'

'The only things following us these days are flies,' Rev. Jim said.

The old man smiled and nodded. 'No one chooses their road,' he said. 'Especially the brave.'

When he got back to New York, Boomer headed straight for Mrs. Columbo's house. He sat at the small kitchen table across from her husband and son. He pulled her shield from his pocket and handed it to young Frank.

'She'd want you to keep this for her,' Boomer said to the boy.

Frank held the badge and stared at it. 'It's all she cared about,' he said, his voice choking. 'Being a cop.'

'You're wrong about that,' Boomer said. 'She cared about you. A lot.'

'Did you love her?' Frank asked, looking up from his mother's shield.

'Yes,' Boomer said, looking right back.

'Did she love you?'

'Yes,' Boomer said. 'But not in the way you're thinking. Not in the way she loved your father.'

'What way, then?' Frank asked.

'She loved me for what I *did*,' Boomer said. 'She loved your dad for who he *was*. There's a big difference.'

'I don't see it,' Frank said.

'You don't have to see it now,' Boomer said, standing. 'But one day you will. And I hope I'm around when you do.'

They had returned to the predictable boredom of their everyday lives.

Dead-Eye was back on doorman duty, working a

building on East Sixty-fifth Street. In his free time he played catch with Eddie and took long drives with his wife.

Rev. Jim went into construction, taking charge of the crew Nunzio had hired to rebuild Pins's bowling alley. The old man thought he could turn it into an afternoon retreat for the neighborhood kids.

Boomer busied himself with daytime stops at movies, museums, and libraries. His nights, as always, were spent at Nunzio's.

Dead-Eye moved a knight against one of Rev. Jim's rooks, swiping it from the board.

'That's it?' Boomer said. 'Fifteen minutes you stare and wait and that's what you do?'

'Couldn't get to his queen,' Dead-Eye explained.

'People in comas have more laughs,' Boomer muttered.

Nunzio walked over, dragging a chair, holding a cup of coffee.

'There's a call for you,' he told Boomer, sitting down to watch the game. 'Before you take it, tell me who's ahead here. I don't want to break into their concentration.'

'If you get an answer,' Boomer said, 'I'll buy dinner for the table.'

'I'm winning,' Dead-Eye said.

'I'll have the steak special,' Rev. Jim added.

Boomer pushed his chair back and headed for the phone by the bar.

'Who is it?' he asked Nunzio.

'Wouldn't say.'

'Why not?'

Nunzio shrugged. 'Maybe he's shy.'

Boomer came back to the table in less than five minutes. There was a glow to his face and in his eyes. Dead-Eye, Rev. Jim, and Nunzio all stared over at him.

'You gonna tell us?' Dead-Eye asked. 'Or do we play another game?'

'How much longer till you finish this one?' Boomer asked.

'We can stop anytime,' Rev. Jim said. 'If we've got a good reason.'

'Wanna take a ride with me?' Boomer asked.

'Where to?' Dead-Eye said.

'See a guy who's in a little trouble,' Boomer said. 'He thinks maybe we can help.'

Boomer looked at his three friends, and, as the smiles formed on their faces, he nodded.

'I ain't ever gonna get that doorman's pension,' Dead-Eye said, pushing the chessboard aside.

'Maybe they'll let you keep the suit,' Rev. Jim said, reaching for his cap. 'It looks good on you.'

Nunzio sat at the table and watched the Apaches walk out of his restaurant into the frigid afternoon of a winter's day. He watched them leave to be what they had always been.

Cops.